D0578209

2,001 amazing Cleaning secrets

by Jeff Bredenberg

Reader's Digest

The Reader's Digest Association, Inc.
Pleasantville, New York • Montreal

2,001 Amazing Cleaning Secrets

PROJECT EDITOR
Don Earnest

PROJECT DESIGNER
Michele Laseau

PRODUCTION TECHNOLOGY MANAGER
Douglas A. Croll

MANUFACTURING MANAGER
John L. Cassidy

CONTRIBUTING COPY EDITOR
Susan C. Ball

CONTRIBUTING INDEXER
Nan Badgett

HUMOR ILLUSTRATIONS
© Tom Klare

HOW-TO ILLUSTRATIONS
© Bryon Thompson

Reader's Digest Home and Health Books

EDITOR IN CHIEF AND PUBLISHING DIRECTOR
Neil Wertheimer

MANAGING EDITOR
Suzanne G. Beason

ART DIRECTOR
Michele Laseau

MARKETING DIRECTOR
Dawn Nelson

VICE PRESIDENT AND GENERAL MANAGER
Keira Krausz

The Reader's Digest Association, Inc.

PRESIDENT, NORTH AMERICA,
   AND GLOBAL EDITOR-IN-CHIEF
Eric W. Schrier

Copyright ©2004 by The Reader's Digest Association, Inc.
Copyright ©2004 by The Reader's Digest Association (Canada) Ltd.
Copyright ©2004 by The Reader's Digest Association Far East Ltd.
Philippine Copyright ©2004 by The Reader's Digest Association
   Far East Ltd.
All rights reserved. Unauthorized reproduction, in any manner, is
   prohibited.
Reader's Digest is a registered trademark of The Reader's Digest
   Association, Inc.

Library of Congress Cataloging-in-Publication Data

Bredenberg, Jeff.
   2,001 amazing cleaning secrets : faster, easier, better ways to clean
your home and everything in it / Jeff Bredenberg.— 1st ed.
      p. cm.
Includes index.
   ISBN 0-7621-0489-9 (Hardcover)
   ISBN 0-7621-0603-4 (Paperback)
   1. House cleaning. I. Title.
   TX324.B74 2004
   648'.5—dc22

                                              2003021043

Address any comments about *2,001 Amazing Cleaning Secrets* to:
Managing Editor
Reader's Digest Home and Health Books
Reader's Digest Road
Pleasantville, NY 10570-7000

To order additional copies of *2,001 Amazing Cleaning Secrets*,
call 1-800-846-2100.

For more Reader's Digest products and information, visit our website at

Printed in the United States of America.

   3 5 7 9 10 8 6 4   (hb)

   1 3 5 7 9 10 8 6 4 2 (pb)

   US 4513/G

A word before you rush off to clean the house...

For years I put up with filmy looking drinking glasses. It's not that I'm slovenly or dim-witted, but like most people, I'm a creature of habit. The glasses came out of the dishwasher with a hard-water deposit that seemed etched into the surface. No amount of scrubbing or dish detergent could remove it. But it seemed a shame to throw out a set of perfectly good drinking glasses. It was much simpler to just keep using them—and to quit inviting guests to dinner.

Then one day as I was cruising through my local wholesale club, I spied a five-liter jug of distilled white vinegar, enough to take a bath in. And something clicked. This stuff is acetic acid, a powerful and versatile cleaner that can attack—among a zillion other things—hard-water deposits. While it might seem absurd to try to clean a cabinetful of glasses with a dinky regular bottle of vinegar, this tanker truckload of it had serious potential. And the cost: pocket change.

When I hauled the vat-o-vinegar into the kitchen, my wife rolled her eyes—the same look I get when I start spritzing around the house, testing some new recipe for home-brewed cleaner. But her skepticism soon turned to delight. I filled a large plastic bowl with vinegar and dunked our glasses into it two or three at a time. When I removed them after a few minutes, they looked off-the-shelf new.

Now, I *know* that I wasn't breaking any new ground. If I had really given it a thought, I could have worked out this solution long ago. But it took stumbling across a cheap source of bulk vinegar to spark my imagination, and a small corner of my life has been changed forever.

My hope is that, as you read this book, you'll have 2,001 similar revelations. My co-writers and I have interviewed hundreds of experts and sifted through wheelbarrow loads of research to turn this into the ultimate household-cleaning book. You'll be astounded at how easy it is to clean every single thing you own using only readily available tools and materials. We even arm you with a surprisingly simple step-by-step "ZAP" system for thoroughly cleaning your entire house in the least amount of time. With this advice in hand, your surroundings will sparkle, your possessions will last longer, your family will be healthier, and you'll save tons of money.

Perhaps best of all, your loved ones will shower you with praise. Witness the words of one of the little guys I share my home with:
"Yey, the glasses are all sparkly again!"

Jeff Bredenberg

contents

Part One

The Easiest Path to a
Clean Home

Chapter 1

Clean Thinking

We know a man with a serious cleaning habit. When he wakes up for his morning jog the stars are still out. He runs two blocks in the dark down to a school's athletic field, where he logs a couple of miles before sunrise. On his first few laps around the track, however, he does an unusual thing: He tosses the students' litter—water bottles, soft drink cans, potato chip bags—into trash barrels. He plucks forgotten sweatshirts out of the dewy grass and hangs them on the benches to dry. He doesn't expect anyone to pin a medal on him. At best, he figures, some coach might scratch his or her head, wondering who the Fairy Godmother of the Running Track is.

Our litter-lugging friend's one moment of "recognition" came when he snatched a jacket out of the grass and headed off to hang it on a bench. *Another* runner popped out of the darkness, exclaiming, "That's my jacket!"

There are two morals to our story: First, you'll find cleaning is most effective and least bothersome when it's done as a regular part of your everyday life. Second, if you do anything to the point of obsession—even cleaning—you're going to end up in trouble.

His moment of embarrassment aside, our friend's heart was in the right place. Too many people see cleaning as an odious chore that can't be avoided (but is all too easy to put off). We're here to convince you of the opposite: That if you have a positive attitude about cleaning and its benefits, cleaning becomes something that is much easier to accomplish.

Take a thoughtful, even laid-back approach to cleaning. This book covers the full spectrum of topics related to cleaning—from smart routines and the right gear to handling unexpected messes and cleaning specific items. But underlying it all is one key idea: The more savvy you are about cleaning—the more you know about it and the more organized you are about it—the less effort, time, and money you will have to spend actually doing it.

Later, in Chapter Six, you'll find a fail-safe, tried-and-true system for cleaning your house. ZAP (zoned attack plan) is a truly time-saving strategy for weekly housecleaning. It is a super-efficient plan that eliminates double work and switchbacks and lets you get your house spick-and-span with the least effort. ZAP knocks hours off your cleaning time. And, yes, it makes house-cleaning almost fun. But first let's take a broader view of cleaning.

The Three Kinds of Cleaning

In a moment, we'll get into the details of what we call "clean thinking": the mindset that works best for easier, faster, more effective cleaning. But to understand "clean thinking," it's important to understand the categories of cleaning. There are three:

Immediate cleaning prevents small, easy-to-clean-up messes from becoming big, tough messes. Let's say that after cooking dinner, your stovetop has a few spatters of grease on it. You could leave it—it's scarcely noticeable. But if you take a minute to wipe the stove with a sponge or cloth every time you use it, the job will take only seconds, the stove will be restored to pristine condition, and you'll be preventing what could eventually become a multilayered buildup requiring hours of remedial attention.

In the immediate cleaning mode, you clean up messes right away. Otherwise, messes accumulate, stains and grime set in, and your family learns that a dirty house is acceptable.

Maintenance cleaning is done regularly, but not necessarily often. This kind of cleaning can be put on a schedule. For example, you could decide to clean the shower once a week (perhaps even set the day) and wash the curtains twice a year. Maintenance cleaning can be organized in a written plan. Or it can be simple habits, like always cleaning the kitchen immediately after dinner is done.

Remedial cleaning covers cleaning after long periods of neglect, such as tackling the refrigerator after a year's growth of drips and spills accumulate on the bottom shelf. That kind of remedial cleaning is preventable. You can avoid it by taking immediate steps or following maintenance routines. Remedial cleaning also includes what you do after a disaster, major or minor, such as a flood or a pet accident on the carpet.

The big danger is that remedial cleaning can easily become abusive cleaning. That happens when a mild cleaner fails to budge the dirt, so stronger and more abrasive cleaners and tools are called into service. Abusive cleaning often does more damage than the original dirt did.

simple SOLUTIONS

Contain and Maintain >

Cleaning tasks fall into three categories. Here are some examples.

Immediate
• Toweling off the shower stall after each use.
• Having family members remove their shoes at the door.
• Washing dishes immediately after using them.

Maintenance
• Spraying the shower stall with soap scum remover once a week.
• Vacuuming all the dirt that family members track inside each week.
• Making sure all dishes, glasses, and cooking gear are cleaned up each night before bedtime.

Remedial
• Spending hours scrubbing away a year's worth of soap scum and mildew.
• Vacuuming whenever the neighbors make jokes about your herd of dust bunnies.
• Wasting your Sunday scrubbing hardened food from the week's dishes and pots so you have something to cook with.

Planning for a Clean Life

At its essence, the "clean thinking" philosophy is to clean things immediately or on a regular maintenance schedule, so that you almost never have to do any remedial cleaning. Here are some of the easiest ways to achieve this.

Always focus on the benefits of cleaning. There are many.
- A feeling of being in control instead of out of control
- Renewed pride in your environment
- A healthier, safer home
- More and better time with your family
- A more active social life
- Reduced stress

If you hate cleaning and organizing, why not try to change your attitude? Look for the beauty and value in those activities. That's the advice of Bruce Van Horn, who writes and teaches about living more simply. Yogis have long taught the value of doing simple chores such as cleaning, Van Horn says. Yogis describe the benefits of "karma yoga," or being in a meditative state of awareness as you clean or garden: It is calming, focusing, and centering. The idea is to let go of your mental clutter—the bills that need paying, your dispute with your boss—and focus on the job at hand. Be in the moment.

Barry Izsak, owner of Arranging It All, a consulting firm in Austin, Texas, finds similar results without the yoga. Izsak says cleaning helps him be more serene. "When I'm under a lot of stress, doing something mundane and methodical is therapeutic and calming," he explains. "It's a back-to-basics kind of feeling."

Treat cleanliness as a value that your whole household shares. If you are always the sole cleaner of the home, then what are you teaching everyone else? That they can be messy, and someone else will take care of it. Instead, make it a familywide job to keep your home clean. And make them proud of it.

Part of this means giving children cleaning chores beginning at an early age. When they're very young, they'll enjoy it because they're working with you. Later they may come to see the chores as onerous, but if they've been properly trained, they'll do them anyway. Explaining how to train children to do chores is simple; the actual training process is less so. But it comes down to this: Insist that the children do what you've asked them to do: no excuses from them, no idle threats from you. One day they'll thank you for the training and discipline.

Build cleaning routines and procedures into your everyday life. This may be the single most important thing for achieving the spick-and-span home of your dreams. It means making your bed every morning (and teaching your kids to do it too). It's always wiping your feet at the door; putting dishes directly into the dishwasher; having a mail-sorting routine that puts bills, catalogs, coupons, and correspondence immediately into their right place. With routines like this, you can keep the time spent housecleaning to a minimum.

Have strategies for keeping your home both clean and neat. Neat means counters are clear, coats are hung up, clutter is under control. Clean means the floors aren't muddy, the corners aren't cobwebby, the doors aren't smudgy. While the two often go hand in hand, it is possible to have a messy home that's clean, or a neat home that's dirty. Neatening and cleaning need not happen together. But it's certainly easier and faster to clean a neat room that is neat.

Understand the special cleaning requirements of the things you own. What materials are your carpets, furniture, appliances, curtains, and clothes made of? The more you know about materials, the better you'll be able to clean them. When you make purchasing decisions, take into consideration how the items should be cleaned.

Don't despair at messes, but rather, see the order and cleanliness that can emerge from them. Visualizing the result in advance is one powerful tool for clean thinking. "Before-and-after pictures are very motivating," says organizing pioneer Harriet Schechter, owner of MiracleOrganizing.com and author of *Let Go of Clutter.* But when you're still in the "before" stage, you have no "after" picture to inspire you. By visualizing, you can make one.

Pick a spot in the house that bothers you because it's dirty or disorganized. Conjure up an image of order or cleanliness. You might even draw a picture, Schechter suggests, or write a description.

Take visualization a step further and create a small clutter-free area, just to see how it feels. Pick a desk or table that bothers you and put all the stuff on it into a box. For the moment, don't worry about sorting it. After the table or desk is clear, dust it, wash it if it needs it, and just savor the feeling: clean and orderly!

expert advice

How Little Squirts Learn to Clean >

Regina Leeds, an organizing expert based in Los Angeles and the author of *The Zen of Organizing,* tells of a client who has seven children. The children have been raised to pick up after themselves, clean their belongings, do laundry, and clean house.

How does the mother do it? When a child is about 18 months old, she puts a rag and a spray bottle in the tyke's little hands and teaches him or her how to clean something a child can easily reach and appreciate—say, a toy truck. As her children grow, their cleaning reach is extended until eventually they know how to clean the whole house. By the time they are 18, they know how to take care of themselves.

Chapter 2

10 Golden Rules of Cleaning

Yes, your primary goal in cleaning is to remove dirt. But at what cost? Surely you don't want to injure yourself. Surely you don't want to damage the very thing you're trying to clean. And surely you want to get it done as quickly and with as little effort as possible. Stick to these ten rules, and you're golden.

① Clean It Up Sooner Rather Than Later

Spills and stains are generally much easier to clean up when you attack them right away. When you treat that tomato sauce splatter on your dress shirt without delay, for instance, it offers little resistance. If you wait until the next day, you'll be sporting a permanent-looking red polka dot that you'll expend a lot more cleaning solution and time getting out. Similarly, clothing or carpet stains are easiest to remove when they're fresh. The longer you wait, the more chance the stain has to set.

The rare exception to this rule: Mud tracked onto your carpet is easiest to clean when you've let it dry first. Wait until it's bone dry and crumbly; then just vacuum it up.

② Clean from the Top Down

Don't fight gravity when you clean. You'll lose. Working from high to low almost always works better in cleaning situations.

When you're cleaning the entire house, start on the top floor and work your way down to avoid tracking through rooms you have already cleaned.

When you're cleaning a room, first remove the cobwebs from the ceiling and upper molding. Then dust the ceiling fan and light fixtures, followed by window frames and wall hangings. Moving downward, conquer the furniture, baseboards, and floors. This ensures that any dust shaken loose from on high does not settle on something you've already cleaned below. You don't want to dust the room twice, do you?

Similarly, when you clean windows and mirrors, start up high and work your way down, because your cleaner obeys gravity. This saves you elbow grease and time.

The rare exception to this rule is wall washing. If you start at the top when you're washing a wall in your home, dirty water will drip onto the lower areas you haven't cleaned yet, making streaks that will be tough to remove.

Think Dry, Then Wet

When you're cleaning a room, start with the cleaning jobs that require dry methods (dusting, sweeping, and vacuuming, for instance). Then move on to wet methods (using an all-purpose cleaner and glass cleaner, mopping, and the like). This way, there will be less dirt floating around in the room to cling to wet surfaces.

Start with the Least Harmful Approach ❹

Use your gentlest cleaning methods first and move up to more aggressive techniques only if necessary. And know your materials well enough so that you will stop your cleaning efforts before you do damage. Better to suffer along with a small spot on your stovetop, for instance, than to ruin the surface with steel wool.

Let Time Do the Work for You ❺

A little time management trick will make your cleaning easier and faster. When you plot out your approach to a cleaning task, remember to spray on your cleaning chemicals first and then find another little job to do while the cleaner does its dirty work. If you're cleaning in the kitchen, for instance, spray your cleaner on the counters and appliances, then occupy yourself with removing old food from the refrigerator while the cleaner soaks in. When you come back to wipe clean, there will be little or no scrubbing to do.

Carry Your Supplies with You ❻

Carry your core cleaning products with you. This will save you from making multiple trips around the house looking for the right tools and cleaners. Pick up one of these accessories at a home improvement store or hardware store:

- A cleaning caddy—a plastic or rubber carrier with a handle and compartments for holding your gear
- A sturdy, large plastic bucket with a good handle
- A rolling supply cart
- An apron with roomy pockets

Put all of your cleaning supplies into the receptacle you've chosen, including clean rags, paper towels, and a trash bag for emptying all of those wastebaskets, and cart it with you from room to room. If your house has more than one floor, keep a fully stocked caddy on each level.

Don't weigh your carrier down with specialty products that are needed for only one job around the house. Store toilet bowl cleaner, for instance, under the bathroom sink.

When in Doubt, Make a Stealth Test

Before you use a new cleaning technique or product, test the method on an inconspicuous area of the object you're cleaning. This rule also applies when you first clean an object that is delicate and might be damaged by a cleaning compound. Testing will show you whether the object is colorfast and whether the cleaning method is likely to do damage.

Don't Deluge Easily Damaged Items

When you clean an item that could be harmed by a liquid cleaning product (electronics, computer screens, framed artwork, or framed photographs, for example), first spray the cleaner on your cleaning cloth and then wipe. Don't spray cleaner directly on the object you're cleaning. Cleaner dripping into your electronics could do them damage, and cleaner dripping into a frame and soaking the matting could harm your artwork.

Read the Directions

Yes, you've heard this before. But the makers of all of those wonderful furnishings in your home do know best how to clean them. And the makers of your cleaning products know best how to use them. So when at all possible, follow the manufacturer's

TEN GOLDEN RULES OF CLEANING

directions when cleaning anything. This goes for everything from toasters to silk blouses and down comforters to miniblinds. File the directions and cleaning tips that come with any new appliance, rug, or other household item. Don't remove those care labels that come on clothes, linens, and other potentially washable objects.

Protect Thyself

Last but not least, take care of yourself. Many cleaning products contain acid, bleach, abrasives, and other ingredients that can damage your eyes, skin, nose, and even your lungs. So make sure your cleaning kit includes a pair of rubber gloves and protective safety glasses. If it's not too steamy, wear old long pants or sweats and an old long-sleeved shirt to cover your arms in case of spatters from cleaning products. Cover your hair with a kerchief or baseball cap.

To protect your nails, dab a line of petroleum jelly underneath your nails to keep out dirt. Dot more on your cuticles to keep them from drying out, roughening, and splitting from exposure to cleaning chemicals.

Don't let your cleaning products get mixed together. Some combinations—chlorine bleach and ammonia, for instance—will produce poisonous gases.

When you're using cleaning chemicals, make sure the room you're in is properly ventilated.

Chapter 3

Stopping Dirt at the Door

What's the *best* kind of dirt? Dirt that you never allow into your house in the first place. That's dirt in its proper place—dirt you don't have to clean up. As we all know from the "ounce of prevention" saying, it's easier to head off a problem than to fix it after the damage is done. So learn to stop dirt in its tracks.

Wrestle Dirt to the Mat

Actually, what you want to do is stop the dirt in *your* tracks—specifically, on the soles of your shoes. Use doormats at every entrance to your home, inside and out. Remember: Most of the grime in your home comes from the outside, the bulk of it hitchhiking in unnoticed on people's feet.

Choosing the right doormats will measurably curb the time you spend cleaning and chasing down dirt, says Sarah Smock, marketing director of Merry Maids Inc., a housecleaning business with franchises across the United States. The heavy-duty mats that retail stores, supermarkets, and hospitals use to keep dirt at bay are a terrific choice here. Typically called walk-off mats, they can be purchased in janitorial supply shops and home improvement stores. The name tells the tale here: They're called "walk-off" mats because people coming into the house walk across them, giving the dirt on their shoes the brush-off. Mats for outside your door are usually made of rubber- or vinyl-backed synthetic turf. (Astroturf is one popular brand.) Inside, walk-off mat choices come in nylon or olefin with either vinyl or rubber backing. The indoor variety is available in several dark, dirt-defying colors to coordinate with your décor, says Merry Maids' Smock. A walk-off mat should be long enough so that both of a person's feet walk across it before entering the house, and the width no wider than the door itself. The mat should never impede the door's movement, either.

Floor mats are also a good idea near such high-traffic or spill-prone spots as the kitchen sink, the refrigerator, the tub, and the toilet, says Mary Ellen Rymanski, who has cleaned houses in

Philadelphia suburbs for more than 20 years. "Cleanups are much easier when all you have to do is clean a mat instead of the floor," she advises. "Think of all the stuff that gets dripped on the floor in front of the sink or the fridge, for instance."

Doormats need minimal maintenance. Just haul them outside occasionally and give them a good shake and also give them a once-over with the *vacuum cleaner* now and then.

When mats are really grimy, *hose* them down and scrub them with a *squirt of dishwashing liquid* in *warm water*. Rinse and allow them to thoroughly air-dry. Another method: Try a *wet/dry vacuum* or *upholstery shampoo* to freshen them. Make sure your mats are completely dry before you put them back on the floor. Moisture caught underneath the mats could damage your floors. When your mats get threadbare, replace them—worn mats don't do their job as well as new ones.

To reduce the dirt entering your house, limit the number of entrances that are used. This way, you'll cut down on the places where people and pets can track dirt in. And if most people enter your house through a mudroom with an easy-wipe floor, a ton of grime will never make it to first base in your abode.

An even better idea: Make your house a shoeless zone for everyone. Encourage family members, guests, and friends to shed their shoes just inside the entrance. Provide a decorative basket or some other receptacle where people can stash their shoes. Keep some fresh "house" slippers on hand for guests—slippers that never set foot outside, so they'll be clean as can be.

Design Away Grime

It's not every day that you get to buy new furniture or redecorate the kitchen or bathroom. But when you do, choose your surfaces wisely.

Easy-care decorating choices abound. For instance, there are a number of no-wax, no-refinish floors to choose from. For countertops in the kitchen or bathroom, you'll find that solid surfaces—those that have few or no seams, don't have indentations, and are impervious to spills and marks—are remarkably easy to keep clean.

Over time, many drapes, curtains, and other window coverings become magnets for dust and cobwebs. Instead of dust-catching materials, choose fabrics treated with a stain-and-dust-resistant finish, or treat the fabric yourself with a product such as Scotchgard fabric protector, following package instructions.

To kidproof a child's bedroom, a playroom, or the kitchen, use Benjamin Moore's AquaPearl paint (available at paint stores) on the walls. It may cost a tad more than other well-known brands, but the pigment will stand up much better to scrubbing, says Deborah Wiener, a Silver Spring, Maryland, interior designer who is known for her "real life" solutions. The paint was designed for use in hospitals, restaurants, and schools, so marker and crayon wipe right off of it.

Have you made a mess of a family room wall by taping and tacking children's artwork to it? You can have a full-wall gallery in your home without the eyesore. Just cover the wall in a *magnetic paint* (available in paint stores) and use magnets to post the work of your budding Michelangelos.

Patterns and designs camouflage dirt and grime, whereas solid colors hide little. And don't forget your pets when you redecorate. If you have a black Labrador retriever or another dark-haired breed, for instance, light-colored surfaces may not be the wisest choice.

If concrete or mortar joints haven't been sealed, they can slough off bits of sand and concrete dust onto surrounding surfaces. To keep this grime at bay, use *sealers* such as Drylok Masonry Treatment and Drylok Concrete Protector, available at hardware stores and home improvement stores.

Cook Up Some Preventive Measures

When you have cooked a meal, your kitchen should not look like the food fight scene from *Animal House.*

To keep airborne grease and such away from counters, turn on the exhaust fan when you're cooking on the stovetop.

To cut down on jumping tomato sauce and other messes, use big pots and pans, with their lids. When you deep-fry, sauté, or otherwise cook foods that spit, line kitchen counters around your stove with *newspapers or paper grocery bags*, cut open to extend them. (Always keep these papers away from any heat source.)

For oven splatters from a pie or casserole bubbling over, sprinkle the stains with *salt* to keep the smoke down and to make your eventual cleanup job much easier.

To protect the fabric in kitchen chairs, which is always under assault, especially from kids dribbling oatmeal and ice cream, have the fabric laminated for easy wiping. If you have removable cushions on your chairs, have just one side laminated. The easy-wipe side is for everyday use, and the other side is for special occasions. To find someone to laminate fabric for you, consult a fabric store or go through an interior designer.

Clear the Air

Your air circulation system is another happily labor-free way to keep dirt out of your home. Think about it: If you have ductwork for heating and cooling, sooner or later every molecule of air in your house must pass through this system.

Keep a nice, clean filter in there snagging the dust out of the air. Replace the filter at least twice a year to prevent that airborne grime from wafting all over the house. Switch filters as often as once a month if the filter collects lots of dust during the heating and cooling seasons.

If your ducts are clogged with dust and debris, or if you can see mold building up in there, call in a professional duct cleaner, who will clear everything out with a high-powered vacuum. (See "Choosing an Air Duct Cleaning Service," on page 374.) Your ducts may get particularly grimy if you've done work that throws around a lot of dust (say, wood floor refinishing or remodeling), if your furnace malfunctions and throws soot around willy-nilly, or if you frequently use a fireplace or wood stove.

Make sure your windows and doors seal tightly. Some utility companies will inspect your home without charge to determine whether you have any cracks where heat or air-conditioning could be seeping out—which means that dirt could be creeping in through the same cracks.

Keep Tools Sharp—Well, Clean Anyway

Worn-out cleaning tools—sponges, mops, squeegees, and such—are a waste of time. They make you work harder to get the job done. Dirty cleaning tools are worse, because they're downright counterproductive, smearing grime and germs all over the things you're trying to clean. Here's the lowdown on upkeep:

- Pitch cleaning tools when they look chewed-up and tired.
- Regularly launder cleaning rags in your washing machine, using **detergent**, **hot water**, and **1/2 cup of white vinegar** or a **scoop of oxygen-boosting additive**, such as OxiClean, to freshen their scent.
- Wash cellulose sponges—those sometimes nasty repositories of germs and offending odors—in the **washing machine** or in the top rack of your **dishwasher**.
- Replace the **bag** in your **vacuum cleaner** at least once a month—more often if you have pets that shed. Vacuum bags need air inside to suck properly, so be sure to change them when they are two-thirds full. Keep those vacuum brushes clean, too.

Try a Closed-Door Policy

Dirt just likes to travel. It's happiest when it can roam freely all over your home, hiding in those nooks and crannies where it's the most labor-intensive to find and remove.

So stop dirt at the borders. That is, habitually keep your doors, drawers, cabinets, closets, and other barriers closed. This will keep dirt out in the open, where vacuum cleaners and cleaning cloths will be able to deal with it more readily.

If you're working on a messy, dust-producing project in the house, keep the doors to the room you're working in closed. Better yet, hang **protective plastic** across the door and any air vents to confine the dust to one room.

Periodically wash screens and other dirt-trapping window coverings (plantation shutters, miniblinds, and the like) to keep dirt subdued. Remember that dirt loves company and acts as a magnet for more.

Smart Pet Tricks

Keeping your dogs and cats clean will reduce the amount of dirt they can bring into your house. These preventive maintenance tips will help:
- Station a **clean rag** by the door that your pet uses so that muddy, wet paws and claws can be wiped off before your beloved animal makes unsightly tracks through the house.
- Once a week, take your dog outside and give its fur a good going-over with the type of **brush** recommended for its coat.

Do this well away from the house, so that the tufts won't tumble inside.

- The miracle way to lift pet hair from furniture and other surfaces? Wipe with a **damp sponge or cloth**, and the hair will gather in clumps. An alternative: Use one of those special **rubber brushes** with nubs on it that is intended for grooming cats (available at pet stores).

- Nothing beats your **vacuum cleaner** or a powerful **handheld vacuum** for pulling pet hair out of your rugs and carpets.

Chapter 4

Clearing Out Clutter

Who was it who boldly decreed: "Let there be clutter!" Pandora, perhaps? In the Greek myth, she opened a box the gods had given her and unleashed all manner of ills upon the world.

Or perhaps we inherited a hoarding instinct from our primitive ancestors, who saved and stored whatever they could because they had so little. And what little they had was subject to attack by the elements, predators, and marauders.

In modern times, the hoarding gene is about as useful as the eat-till-you're-stuffed gene—and has similar effects.

Whatever the cause, there's clutter, clutter everywhere. "Clutter happens to all of us," says Barbara Hemphill, who has 25 years of professional organizing experience and is coauthor of the book *Love It or Lose It: Living Clutter-Free Forever.* "The question really is: How quickly can we recover from clutter?" she says.

You've probably heard the saying "Don't put it down—put it away." If following that advice solves your clutter problem, you're lucky. The greater problem comes if there is no "away." To put a spin on another old saying, if there is no place for everything, how can everything be in its place?

What Is Clutter?

There is no single definition of clutter, because one person's clutter is another's delight. But people who help others declutter their surroundings agree on a few principles.

Here are some basic ideas about clutter:
- Clutter is anything that bothers you because it is disorganized or chaotic.
- Clutter consists of things you don't love or don't use—unfinished projects and too many objects in too small a space.
- Clutter makes you feel overwhelmed, smothered, not in control of your space, victimized, scattered, or unfulfilled.
- Clutter may be a symptom of a lack of clarity about who you are and what your life is about.

- Clutter is like the static on a radio. It's a distraction and an interference.
- Clutter is stressful.

The first step in getting rid of clutter is, according to professional organizer Harriet Schechter: Make the decision either to accept clutter and quit complaining about it—or to do something about it.

The benefits of removing clutter include these:
- You will find that cleaning up is easier.
- Your desk/table/room/house will *look* cleaner.
- You'll have more time for things that are important to you.
- You'll feel better.

Steps for Confronting Clutter

Although looking at clutter typically makes people feel paralyzed and overwhelmed, the process of getting rid of it is actually quite simple, according to organizing expert Regina Leeds.

Organizing your home, office, files, desk, or anything else boils down to three steps.
1. Eliminate the things you don't need, want, use, or love.
2. Categorize what remains by grouping similar things together.
3. Organize the categories by having—here's that old chestnut again—a place for everything and everything in its place.

Whatever system of organization you come up with should fulfill three requirements, Leeds says. The system should be
1. Beautiful, in the sense that it makes you happy to look at it and work in it
2. Functional, because such beauty without function is meaningless
3. Easy for the user to maintain

Analyze Your Clutter Clusters

Once you've decided to do something about clutter, begin by analyzing your clutter clusters. Make a list of them. If you have trouble doing that off the top of your head, then go room to room and make a written note of any clutter you encounter. Then group the items into categories.

Paper is a major clutter category. If you have clutter, some of it is almost certainly paper. What is your specific pattern of creating

simple SOLUTIONS

Throw a Decluttering Party >

If you want some outside help but don't want to hire a professional organizer, enlist a friend to become a "clutter buddy," says organizing expert Harriet Schechter. Make a date every week or so: One of you takes two or three boxes of clutter to the other's house. Go through your clutter together, and use triage and a timer to move quickly through the items. Allot, say, 30 minutes to each box. After two or three hours, celebrate over dinner.

A trusted friend makes the best clutter buddy, Schechter says, because spouses and family members are more likely to be judgmental. The idea is to create a festive atmosphere in which to help each other "see what's absurd" in the mess. And it's important to laugh with, not at, each other.

paper clutter—unread newspapers and magazines, old mail, unorganized clippings, children's school papers, old love letters, notes, or lists? All of the above?

Clothing is another common clutter factor. Is your problem that clothes aren't organized, or is it that you're chronically unable to get rid of things that no longer fit, are out of style, are worn out, or are never worn for some reason?

After those two categories, clutter patterns look like the many tributaries of a mighty river—they're all over the map. Some common kinds are clutter related to home office space, pets, books, videos and CDs, electronics, hobbies, children's toys, and kitchen utensils.

Before you begin your clutter attack, recognize that the feeling of being overwhelmed goes with the territory, and don't let it stop you. Break the job into small parts, because each tiny part that you conquer will lift your spirits.

To pick a starting point, find the area that bothers you the most. If it's a large area, like the basement, pick one tiny part—let's say a bureau you've stored there. Now pick one tiny part of that—a single drawer.

Or maybe your most irritating area is the kitchen table, where you can hardly find space to eat because of all the papers and other stuff. Pick a pile from one corner of the table.

Medics' Secret: Triage

Go to work on your chosen area using a triage system. The term comes from a system of priorities used in an emergency room or at a disaster scene to sort patients according to how urgently they need care. In other words, it's a system of categorizing and setting priorities.

A triage system for dealing with clutter includes categories for
● Discarding
● Keeping
● Taking action

When applying a triage system, your discard pile may include items to be trashed, donated, sold, or recycled. Items to keep may be papers to file, clothing to hang up, or sports equipment to put away. Things to take action on might include bills to pay, school papers to sign, library books or videos to return, or purchases to exchange. Triage can be applied to any kind of clutter or potential clutter, including incoming mail, piles of paper, and boxes of stuff stored in the attic.

Make your judgments quickly. As you perform triage, don't linger over items. Be ruthless. Depending on how old your pile is, you've managed without some items for weeks, months, or years. So you can probably do without them forever.

If you have things you are going to keep and store away—for instance, children's clothing that will be handed down to younger kids in a few years—sort and label them well. For example, have separate boxes for "1–2 years," "3–4 years," and so on. Don't mix everything together and create a future nightmare when you want to find something.

If you have a lot of sentimental memorabilia, ask yourself whether there is some other way to keep it. Instead of saving your daughter's science project, for example, take a photo of her with the project and throw the project away. Keep photo albums and scrapbooks up to date, well labeled, and accessible.

Turn Off the Tap

Even before you have completed a household organization plan, start taking steps to reduce incoming clutter. Think of your clutter as an overflowing bathtub. Before you mop up the water on the floor and bail out the tub, you turn off the spigot.

For less clutter in your life, here are some steps to consider:
- Focus more on doing and being in your life, not having.
- Whenever you're tempted to buy something, decide whether your buying impulse falls into the "worthwhile" or "future clutter" category. Like the right marriage partner, the worthwhile items will be just as worthwhile if you wait.
- Buy cloth shopping bags and use them to cut down on bags you bring home.
- Stop subscriptions to magazines that you somehow never get around to reading.
- Instead of buying things that you'll use just once or rarely ever, rent them.

Chapter 5

Laundry—Loads of Advice

Thanks to automatic machines that do all the washing and drying for you, laundry day has changed drastically over the past century. Instead of boiling wash water in a big black kettle, scrubbing clothes against a corrugated washboard, squeezing the water out with a hand-cranked wringer, and hanging the clothes on a line to dry, today you simply toss the clothes and a measured amount of detergent into a machine and flip a switch, then toss them into a dryer and flip another switch. Bingo: clean, fresh-smelling clothes.

Doing the laundry used to be a muscle job—the dirtier the clothes, the harder you scrubbed. But as machines, fibers, and fabrics have evolved over the years, so have laundry products and techniques. Today, laundering is mostly a mental exercise, a matter of deciphering the hieroglyphics of care label symbols, keeping up with the latest new-and-improved laundry products, recognizing the differences between fabric types, and understanding the chemistry behind stain-removal techniques.

Everyone has clothes to clean. Not everyone cleans them as well as they could. They wing it or get by on the bare minimum. This chapter will help you do a better, more thorough job on your laundry. You'll be more knowledgeable, more confident, and more efficient. Your clothes will be cleaner, brighter, fresher, and longer lasting.

Sorting: Color and Beyond

Sorting clothes is easy, right? Darks go in one pile, and whites in another. That's a good start, but if you really want to do it right—and keep your clothes looking their best—also sort by similar construction and soil level.

Sorting by color. Separate whites from colors and light colors from dark colors. When in doubt, read care labels. If the label in a particular garment says to wash separately, that means the dye colors will run. Even tiny amounts of dye can transfer to other fabrics, making the clothes look discolored and dingy.

Sorting by soil. Separate heavily soiled or greasy items from lightly soiled ones. Lightly soiled clothes will pick up the extra soil and grease, making whites look gray or yellow and colors look dull.

Sorting by construction and material. Separate out clothes that are loosely knit or woven and clothes that have delicate trimmings or unfinished seams that can fray. Wash those on a shorter cycle that features more gentle agitation. Also separate lint producers—such as fleece sweat suits, chenille items, new terry cloth towels, and flannel pajamas—from lint attractors, such as corduroys, synthetic blends, and dark things.

First, Some Prep Work

While laundry prep work is not as extensive (and tiresome) as, say, painting prep work, it is important for getting the cleanest clothes. And you know what they say about an ounce of prevention. A few routine steps before starting—like removing crayons from your child's pocket—can prevent a laundry disaster.

- *Empty pockets.* Remove lipstick, lip balm, paper (especially tissues), candy, nails, and, yes, crayons—plus anything else squirreled away in pants and jackets. Keep a small brush handy to brush dirt and lint out of cuffs.
- *Close zippers and Velcro.* This prevents snags and keeps your Velcro from getting matted (and losing its staying power) with lint and thread.
- *Bag your hose.* Put panty hose and items with long ties in a mesh bag to keep them from snagging and tearing.

Stain Strategies

It's always best to try to remove stains when they are fresh. But sometimes stains sneak in under the radar screen. These you need to address before washing. If you let them pass through a washing cycle (or the dryer), the stains may become permanent. If you treat them beforehand with the right stain-removal solution, however, you stand a good chance of removing the stains for good. Here are a few general tips for pretreating clothes with certain stains. For more detailed techniques for removing stains, see *Stains* on page 338.

Soak protein stains in cold water. These include egg, milk, feces, urine, blood, and the like. Soak for half an hour. Run the stain under *cold water*, gently rubbing the fabric together with your hands to loosen the stain. Avoid warm or hot water, which can cook the proteins, setting the stain permanently.

Pretreat oil and grease stains with *liquid laundry detergent or pre-treatment spray*. Apply the detergent or spray, such as Shout or Spray 'n Wash, directly to the stain.

Soak tannin stains (coffee, tea, soft drinks, fruit jelly) for a half hour in a solution of *1 teaspoon of liquid detergent* (preferably one containing enzymes) per *1/2 gallon warm water*. Do not use soap or a soap-based product. Soap can make the tannin stain harder to remove.

After washing, check to see whether the stain is gone. If it isn't, do not dry. Try again to remove the stain and then repeat washing.

The Main Event: Washing

The invention of the automatic washing machine was to household cleaning what the advent of the gas-powered mower was to lawn care—revolutionary. The automatic washing machine accomplishes what once took hours of skin-scalding, backbreaking work. And the machine does it better, getting clothes cleaner and treating them more gently. Today, machines, especially the new generation of front-loaders, are more efficient than ever.

Most people pick up their laundering skills in bits and pieces. The following is a more thorough lesson in washing, with a few tips that just might surprise you.

Evenly distribute clothes in the washer. The spin cycle relies on a balanced load. Never wrap sheets or long garments around the agitator post. That can tear fabric and jam the machine. The best loads are ones that mix small and large items—for instance, sheets mixed with hand towels and socks.

Don't overload the washer. The wash cycle depends on clothes rubbing together to remove the soil. If the washer is too full, the clothes will not have enough space to rub together. Powdered detergent may not have room to adequately dissolve, and you may end up with clumps of powdered detergent stuck on your clothes. Moreover, there must be enough free-flowing water to carry away the soil removed from the clothes. Check your washer's manual for the recommended maximum load.

Pick the right setting. Most clothes, of course, do fine with the normal or regular setting. Use the gentle or delicate setting (typically shorter agitation and spinning cycles) for lingerie, loose knits, washable woolens, and rayon fabrics. The permanent press setting usually has normal agitation but includes a cool-down rinse to reduce wrinkling.

Choose the right water temperature. The hot cycle draws directly from your household hot water supply. Warm is a 50/50 or 40/60 hot and cold water mix. Cold draws directly from the cold water line. Each of these can vary greatly depending on the distance of your water heater from your washing machine and on the season. (Incoming cold water, for instance, can range from near freezing in winter to 80° F in summer.) When using the hot or warm cycle, run a hot-water tap in a nearby utility or bathroom sink until the hot water fills the pipes. This way you will cut down on the amount of cold water that inadvertently mixes in with the hot in the washer. Use the following as a general guide:

- *Hot (120° F):* Use for whites and colorfast fabrics and heavily soiled clothes (such as underclothes and cloth diapers). The hot water is needed to kill bacteria. When starting a hot-water load, make sure your water heater has had a chance to replenish its hot-water supply after being exhausted by family showers and dishwashing.
- *Warm (105° F):* Use for noncolorfast fabrics, moderately soiled loads, synthetics, wrinkle-free fabrics, knits, silks, and woolens.

Generation Next: Front-Loading Washers

Front-loading washers are not exactly new. And they haven't exactly caused a laundry equipment revolution. Most people still use top-loading models with a central agitating post. But attitudes are changing.

Although more expensive, the new models have many advantages. They're more efficient, in some cases using only a third of the amount of water standard washers use. That not only saves water, but

it also saves the power needed to heat it. Front-loaders clean as well, if not better, than top-loaders. And the tumbling action is gentler on clothes.

However, there are disadvantages as well. Front-loading washers call for different kinds of detergents—ones that are low foaming—to prevent excess suds that can impede the tumbling (soil-removing) action of the clothes. In addition, there is less water to rinse the detergent away. If

you have purchased one of these new front-loading washers, make sure that you use a detergent specially suited for it or that you use less of your regular detergent. If you have trouble finding the proper detergent, contact the manufacturer of the machine. Or contact the maker of your favorite brand of laundry detergent to see whether the company can tell you how much of its standard detergent to use.

● *Cold (85° F):* Use for dark or bright colors that you know will bleed and for lightly soiled loads. Powdered detergent will not dissolve well in cold temperatures, so use liquid detergent with cold water.

Use the right detergent for the job. Use general-purpose detergents for most wash loads. Use light-duty detergents for washing lightly soiled and delicate fabrics. Liquid detergents work better in cold water and on oily stains. Powders are especially good for removing ground-in dirt and clay.

Add the right amount of detergent. This sounds like a no-brainer. You just scoop up the powder (or fill the cap with liquid) and toss it in, right? Yes, but you may need to vary the amount of detergent you use. The main cause of clothes coming out yellow, gray, and dingy is not using enough detergent.

The standard measure of most detergents is based on a 5- to 7-pound load of clothes, moderately soiled, cleaned in an average water volume (17 gallons in a top-loading machine) in moderately hard water (3.6 to 7.0 grains per gallon). If you have a larger load, heavy soil, or harder water, you will need to use more detergent. Check your owner's manual for recommendations about detergent usage specific to your machine.

Soften your water. If you have hard water, meaning there is excess calcium, magnesium, and other minerals present in your water, you will have a laundry handicap. These minerals react with soaps, reducing their effectiveness and forming a sticky curd that is hard to remove from fabrics. In addition, detergents that contain silicate or carbonate builders can react with the minerals to leave insoluble deposits on your clothes. If your clothes come out of the wash looking gray and dingy and feeling rough, you may have a hard-water problem. (Other symptoms of hard water are rings around your bathtub, white residue around faucets and drains, and soaps and shampoos that don't seem to lather well.) Contact your water utility, your county Cooperative Extension Service, or a water treatment specialist for advice on testing your water's mineral content.

To soften hard water (often a problem for homeowners who use well water as opposed to municipal water), you can install a water-softening system to solve the problem. Water softeners are available at home improvement stores, such as Home Depot, and through water-treatment companies, such as Culligan. For a temporary solution, add a water-softening product, available at grocery stores, directly to the wash or rinse cycle.

Laundry Extras

Along with detergents, the list of laundry products designed for more specific uses is growing: all-fabric bleaches, softeners, and boosters, for instance. At least one century-old product—bluing—is making a comeback, too. Here's a look at some laundry extras.

Bleaches come in two varieties:
- Chlorine bleach (sometimes labeled as sodium hypochlorite)
- All-fabric bleach (containing sodium perborate, hydrogen peroxide, or some other chlorine substitute)

Chlorine bleach is the most effective whitener and sanitizer, but we all know how strong chlorine bleach is. It can fade or alter the color of fabrics and can weaken fibers.

As a general rule, never pour full-strength liquid chlorine bleach directly into a washer load. Always dilute it or dispense it through a machine's bleach dispenser, following the instructions found on the bleach container. Don't soak cottons in a bleach solution for more than 15 minutes. (If the stain remains after 15 minutes, that means it's not going to go away.) Don't use chlorine bleach on silk, wool, spandex, polyurethane foam, rubber, or anything with rubber or spandex elastic.

All-fabric bleaches are not as harsh and may be safe for colors. At the same time, they are not as powerful or fast-acting as a chlorine bleach.

Enzyme presoaks are good for loosening and removing stains, especially protein stains (milk, egg, urine, and feces), before the wash cycle. When added to the wash cycle, they act like boosters to improve the washing.

Prewash stain removers are often spray products containing some combination of concentrated detergents, alcohol, mineral spirits, or enzymes. These are especially good for removing oily or greasy stains from synthetic fibers.

Bluing is an old-fashioned product that is actually used to make whites whiter. It's not a bleach (so it's environmentally friendly). In effect, bluing is just that—blue dye. When white fabric is new, it contains blue coloring (invisible to the naked eye) that makes the white brighter. After repeated washings, the blue coloring is removed, leaving whites with a yellowish tint. By adding bluing to your wash, you replace the microscopic blue pigment, and your whites look new again. (See The Laundry Blues box on the next page for a bit of the history of bluing.)

The *Laundry Blues*

A century ago, everyone who did laundry knew about bluing. It was how you got whites really white. But, alas, thanks to the washing machine, modern detergents, and bleaches, bluing was nearly forgotten—until recently. Today, some environmentally conscious consumers are rediscovering bluing, which they consider an ecologically sound alternative to bleach.

Here's how bluing works. Instead of removing dirt or bleaching it white, bluing, known as an optical whitener, adds the slightest hint of blue to your whites, making them look brighter and whiter. Most white clothes start out with added blue tints, but those tints fade after repeated washings, sometimes making whites look yellow and dingy. Bluing,

which is basically a fine blue iron powder in a water suspension, is a safe and easy way to add back the blues. (Nevertheless, as with other laundry products, it shouldn't be swallowed and should be kept out of the reach of children.)

Brad Norman, who owns the company that makes Mrs. Stewart's Bluing, which has been around since the 1880s, says that he hears from consumers who use his bluing on their white animals to make them whiter. "People showing horses treat their manes and tails," he says. "I got a call from the owner of a Samoyed, a white dog breed, who was getting ready for a show. She used a little too much and ended up with a blue dog." One guy, he says, intentionally used too much before entering

a parade with his ox. He was going as Paul Bunyan, whose ox, Babe, was blue.

"Everybody in the 1920s and '30s knew about bluing, and they knew how to use it," says Norman. In the old days, special bluing tubs were set up beside the rinse tub. Today, you dilute a few drops of bluing with water and either add it to the wash cycle or to the final rinse cycle. "These days, we kind of have to retrain people," he says. "A lot of people think that if a little is good, a lot is better." With bluing, that's just not true.

Bluing is an old-fashioned bargain, too: A single bottle of the highly concentrated stuff, which costs only a few dollars, can last a year or more.

Detergent boosters, as the name suggests, help detergents do their job by increasing stain- and soil-removal action, altering the pH of water, and brightening clothes.

Water softeners and conditioners are quick fixes for hard water. Added directly to the wash or rinse cycle of your machine, both of these products soften the water, making the detergent work more effectively.

Fabric softeners come in liquid that you add to the final rinse cycle of your wash load or in sheets that you add to the dryer. These products make fabrics softer and fluffier, reduce static cling and wrinkling, and make ironing easier. Beware, though: If overused, fabric softeners can reduce the absorbency of towels and cloth diapers. Dryer sheets, if overused, can leave oily looking splotches on medium-colored items.

Starches, fabric finishes, and sizings, either used in the final rinse or after drying, stiffen fabrics, making them look crisp and fresh. They tend to make ironing easier and fabric less susceptible to soil and stains.

Now Take Them for a Spin

Like the washing machine, the automatic dryer has made life much easier for modern families. Dryers mean dry clothes in winter, on rainy days, and in crowded cities, where even if you could stretch a line between buildings, the smog from factories and automobile traffic would leave your clothes sooty. And as with washing machines, there are tricks in using dryers that can help you dry clothes without wrinkling or damaging them.

Check clothes for stains before drying. If you overlook a stain that the washer failed to remove, you could set it permanently by drying it. If you find a stain, treat the stain and rewash.

Shake damp pieces before drying. This loosens them and helps them dry faster and more completely. Pull out anything that you want to line dry.

Don't overload the dryer. A dryer needs airflow to do its work. Clothes that are bunched up in a dryer will take longer to dry and will wrinkle more easily.

Don't underload the dryer. Believe it or not, a nearly empty dryer does not work as well as one that is fuller (but not too full). The tumbling effect is reduced in dryers with small loads, and that prolongs the drying period. If you must dry a small load, find a few towels that are already clean and dry and of a color similar to the wet clothes, and toss them into the dryer to improve the process.

Use the right setting. Most dryers have automatic settings:
● Regular, for loads made up mostly of all-cotton fabrics
● Permanent press, for synthetics
● Cool or low, for lingerie, hand-washables, washable woolens, and heat-sensitive items marked "tumble dry–low"
The permanent press cycle typically features a cool-down period after the drying is completed to reduce wrinkling.

Avoid overdrying. Leaving clothes in the dryer too long causes shrinkage, static buildup, and wrinkling. Overdrying actually sets wrinkles, making them hard to remove.

To reduce wrinkling, remove items from the dryer as soon as they are dry. And don't let them lie in a heap in the basket. Hang them up or fold them as soon as possible. Remove permanent press items while they are damp and hang them on a rustproof hanger. Close buttons and snaps, straighten creases, and brush out any wrinkles.

Clean the lint filter after each use. Not only does this improve airflow, which makes the dryer work better, but it also reduces the chance of a dryer fire.

Use a mesh bag for drying nylon hosiery. It will protect those delicate items.

For items that call for flat drying, such as sweaters, squeeze out excess water (but don't wring, or you may cause wrinkling). Roll the garment in a clean, dry towel to absorb water. Then shape and lay out flat on a dry towel or drying rack.

Pressing Issues

The goal for most people is to do as little ironing as possible. On the other hand, most people like the results that ironing gives them—crisp, unwrinkled shirts and slacks with respectable creases. How else to explain the explosion of permanent press and no-iron fabrics?

Sometimes you have to iron, however, and when you do, you want to be effective. Here's how, plus a tip or two for making the job easier:

Wash and dry your clothes correctly. Follow the previous advice for reducing wrinkles before your clothes get near the ironing board. Chief among that advice: Don't overload your dryer and don't overdry your clothes. Sometimes all you need to do is smooth a garment with your hands and fold it or hang it and put it away. Dry things well, and you will cut your ironing time down considerably.

Try touch-up ironing. Instead of giving a garment the full going-over, you might just have to run your iron quickly over collars and cuffs.

Read care labels. They will instruct you in the best technique for ironing a particular garment.

Keep your equipment handy. Don't pile boxes in front of your ironing board or leave your iron in a tangle of cords on the closet floor. The setup hassles will discourage you from ironing the next time. And the next time. And the next.

Keep your ironing board and iron clean. Otherwise, you might stain clothes the next time you iron them.

Sort items by ironing temperature. Start with low-temp fabrics, such as silks and synthetics, and move on to high-temp items, such as cottons and linens.

Iron clothes while they are still damp. This makes the job easier, since wrinkles are not as set in the fabric. When you've finished ironing, hang your garments immediately to help them stay fresh and pressed.

To keep wrinkling to a minimum, start ironing with small areas, such as cuffs, collars, and sleeves, and then work your way to the larger areas. Iron lengthwise on fabric; this will help prevent the fabric from stretching.

Never iron stains. The heat will set the stains permanently.

No Stain, No Pain: The Miracle of Nanotechnology

Picture the scene: You're at a dinner party having a great time when a stray elbow bumps your glass of merlot and wine splashes into your lap. You don't panic. You don't cry. There's no need for club soda, no soaking and blotting and more soaking and blotting. You simply wipe the spill off your clothes with a paper towel and ask for a refill. No, you're not wearing some racy new rubber suit. You're wearing stain-resistant clothing made possible through nanotechnology.

Scientists are using nanotechnology—the manipulation of materials on an atomic or molecular scale—to treat certain natural and synthetic textiles so they are stain-, wrin-

kle-, and waterproof. One way is by coating a fabric's fibers with microscopic liquid-repelling nanowhiskers (billions of atoms in structures that look like hairs or whiskers). Each whisker measures 10 nanometers long. (*Nano-* means "billionth," so a nanometer equals one billionth of a meter.) How small is that? Well, a single grain of sand measures 100,000 nanometers across.

The application of nanotechnology to textiles works better than the more familiar method of stainproofing fabrics—coating them with a special layer of fabric protector such as Scotchgard. Such treatments wear off and make fabric stiff, even shiny. Fibers that have

been altered molecularly don't change. Neither does the feel of the fabric. You can't even tell there's a stain-resistant treatment on it. That is, until a spill hits it. Then, because the nanowhiskers create a barrier of air around the fabric fibers, the spill simply beads up and rolls off or waits patiently to be removed.

Developed by a company called Nano-Tex, which licenses its techniques to manufacturers, nanotech textile products are already on the market, under brand names such as Lee, Gap, Eddie Bauer, and Land's End. The next breakthrough from Nano-Tex? Clothes that don't absorb odors. Smells like a good idea.

Fabric Finesse

Not all fabrics are alike, and not all fabrics can be cleaned alike. Although you should always check the care label in a particular garment, here are some specific tips for cleaning some of the most common fabrics:

Acetate. Used often in linings because it does not pill or suffer from static cling, acetate is also made into dresses, suits, and sportswear. Most acetates are dry-clean only, but some are washable. For the washable variety, you typically hand-wash in warm water with mild suds. (Don't soak colored items.) Do not wring the item dry. Instead, lay it flat to dry. While it's still damp, press it inside out with a cool iron. If you are finishing the right side, use a pressing cloth. When removing stains from acetate, never use acetone or a nail polish remover that contains acetone. The acetone will dissolve the fibers.

Acrylic. Known for its ability to wick moisture away from the body, acrylic is a popular material for socks, as well as other clothing items. Garments made from acrylic can be washed or dry-cleaned. Generally, you should machine-wash, using a warm-water setting. Add a fabric softener during the final rinse. Acrylics are heat-sensitive, so tumble dry at a low temperature. To avoid wrinkling, remove from the dryer as soon as dry. When hand-washing is required, as with delicate items, use warm water and a mild detergent. Rinse and gently squeeze out the water, smooth out the garment, and dry on a rustproof hanger. Lay sweaters and knits flat to dry. For ironing, use a moderately warm iron.

Alpaca. Made from the fine, soft hair of the alpaca, a cousin of the llama, alpaca is gaining in popularity in this country as a substitute for wool. Nearly all alpaca can be dry-cleaned, and some can be gently washed. Woven items should be dry-cleaned, whereas knitted garments, such as sweaters, should be washed by hand in cool water with a mild, undyed soap or shampoo. Don't twist or wring. Lay it out flat to dry, pressing with a dry towel to remove excess water. Touch up with a cool iron as needed.

Cashmere. A fine wool made from the undercoat of the cashmere goat, cashmere is as soft as it is expensive. Most cashmere can be dry-cleaned, and some can be gently washed. Most woven cashmere requires dry-cleaning to retain its shape. But knitted cashmere, such as sweaters, can—and should—be hand-washed. Careful washing helps them retain their luster and loft. Use a natural, undyed soap and cool water. Move the sweater around in the cool water for a few minutes. Rinse repeatedly—until the rinse water is clear. Lay out the sweater to dry, pressing it with a dry towel to remove excess water. If you need to touch it up with an iron, do so carefully, using a pressing cloth.

Cotton. By far, cotton is the most widely used fiber found in today's clothes closets. Since not even boiling hurts the fibers, cotton can be machine-washed in high temperatures using any good detergent. You can use chlorine bleach safely on cotton whites (but never soak for more than 15 minutes, since the bleach will break down the fibers) and all-fabric bleach on dyed cottons. Cotton is an absorbent fiber and requires lots of drying time. Because it wrinkles easily, it often requires pressing. Use a hot steam iron.

Linen. Linen is made from flax, one of the oldest textile fibers. (It dates back to at least 5,000 B.C.!) Today, you can wash some varieties of linen, but others should be dry-cleaned. Sometimes it's up to you. Linen has a natural pectin that keeps it stiff and crisp. Washing removes the pectin, making is softer. If you prefer crisp linen, then have your linen dry-cleaned. Otherwise, machine-wash it in warm water and tumble dry. It tends to wrinkle and often requires pressing. Use a steam iron on medium or high heat.

Nylon. The second-most common synthetic after polyester, and the strongest fiber available, nylon is relatively easy to care for. It can be machine-washed in warm water. To reduce static cling, add a dryer sheet to the dryer and remove clothes from the dryer as soon as they have finished drying. If you need to iron nylon, use a warm iron.

Polyester. Strong, durable, shrink- and wrinkle-resistant, polyester is a miracle fiber, the most common of the synthetic fibers. It does tend to take on oily stains easily, however. In general, polyester is easy to clean, which helps account for its popularity. Most polyester items can be washed or dry-cleaned. Wash in warm water and tumble dry at a low temperature setting. To prevent pilling and snagging, turn knits inside out. To reduce static cling, use a dryer sheet and remove garments as soon as they have dried. When ironing, use a moderately warm iron.

Ramie. A vegetable fiber similar to flax, ramie comes from the stem of a shrub that originated in Asia. The fibers are strong (but they have low twisting and bending strength), do not shrink, and have a lustrous appearance. Much like linen, ramie can be machine-washed in warm water and tumbled dry or dry-cleaned.

It tends to wrinkle and often requires pressing. Use a steam iron on medium or high heat.

Rayon. Developed in 1910, rayon was the first synthetic fiber. Originally, most rayon was dry-clean only, but there are more and more washable rayons on the market. Check the care label for any rayon garment you're unsure of. Dry-clean-only rayon that gets wet (even in the rain) can bleed dyes, shrink, and grow stiff. Washable rayon is typically hand-wash only. (Since it loses up to 50 percent of its strength when wet, rayon can be destroyed easily by the agitating action of most washers.) Wash in lukewarm or cool suds, squeezing the suds through the fabric, and rinse. Never wring or twist rayon. Shake out or smooth the garment and hang it on a rustproof hanger to dry. Lay sweaters flat to dry. While the garment is still damp, iron inside out on low heat. For finishing on the right side, use a pressing cloth.

Silk. Made from protein fiber produced by the silkworm (the finest silk fiber is produced by worms that eat mulberry leaves), this ancient material connotes fabulous wealth and exotic locales. It is expensive and must be treated accordingly. Most silk is dry-clean only, since laundry detergents can harm silk. If the care label says that hand-washing is OK, use a mild soap and lukewarm water. Never use bleach with silk. When ironing, iron inside out on low heat.

Spandex. Developed in the late 1950s, spandex is lightweight, durable, and known for being flexible. That's why it turns up in bathing suits, panty hose, and tights. (Lycra is simply a brand name of spandex.) You can machine- or hand-wash spandex. Don't use chlorine bleach, however. Either let drip dry or put in a dryer on a low setting. When ironing spandex, use a low temperature setting and iron in swift strokes, never letting the iron linger in one spot.

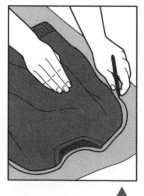

▲

Wool. A natural fiber that comes from sheep, wool has been around for thousands of years. It is known for its warmth and ability to shed wrinkles. There are many types of wool and different ways to care for it. Generally speaking, you should dry-clean wool. Do it at least once a season or when needed. You can also hand-wash wool. Since wool loses its shape when wet, when washing a wool sweater, first lay the sweater out on a piece of clean paper (wrapping paper works well) and trace the shape ◀. You'll use this for laying the sweater out while drying. Use warm water and a mild detergent that contains no bleach. Don't soak. Rinse well. To dry, roll the sweater in a clean towel and squeeze

Tag Tips

Since the adoption of the Federal Trade Commission's Care Labeling Rule in 1972, sewn-in care labels have been required in all clothing sold in the United States. The labels give instructions for the best way to care for a garment, including how to properly clean, dry, and iron and what techniques and products to avoid. The original ruling said that the labels should include written instructions in English.

In 1997, the FTC amended the ruling to allow symbols to be substituted for words. However, the symbols can be baffling. Here's a handy explanation of them.

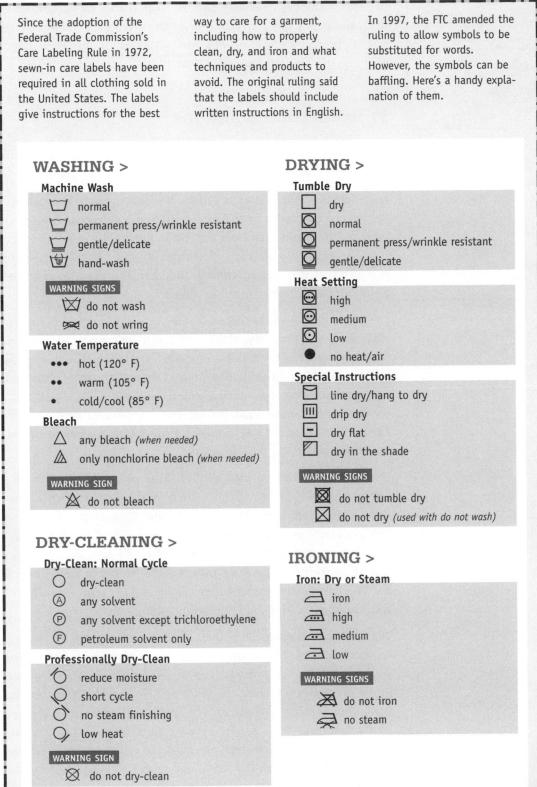

WASHING >

Machine Wash
- normal
- permanent press/wrinkle resistant
- gentle/delicate
- hand-wash

WARNING SIGNS
- do not wash
- do not wring

Water Temperature
- ••• hot (120° F)
- •• warm (105° F)
- • cold/cool (85° F)

Bleach
- any bleach *(when needed)*
- only nonchlorine bleach *(when needed)*

WARNING SIGN
- do not bleach

DRY-CLEANING >

Dry-Clean: Normal Cycle
- dry-clean
- any solvent
- any solvent except trichloroethylene
- petroleum solvent only

Professionally Dry-Clean
- reduce moisture
- short cycle
- no steam finishing
- low heat

WARNING SIGN
- do not dry-clean

DRYING >

Tumble Dry
- dry
- normal
- permanent press/wrinkle resistant
- gentle/delicate

Heat Setting
- high
- medium
- low
- no heat/air

Special Instructions
- line dry/hang to dry
- drip dry
- dry flat
- dry in the shade

WARNING SIGNS
- do not tumble dry
- do not dry *(used with do not wash)*

IRONING >

Iron: Dry or Steam
- iron
- high
- medium
- low

WARNING SIGNS
- do not iron
- no steam

out excess water ◀. Put a piece of plastic (an old dry-cleaning bag, for instance) over the pattern you made, to prevent dyes from the paper from bleeding onto the sweater. Pat the sweater out to fit the shape. Smooth out wrinkles. If the item needs pressing, use light steam and a press cloth.

Problems and Solutions

Sometimes clothes just don't turn out right. Here are some common problems and the likely solutions to the problems.

Your clothes come out gray or yellow. You may need to increase the amount of detergent in the next load, use a **detergent booster**, or increase the temperature of the wash water. However, the gray could be from dye that has bled from darks to lights, suggesting you need to sort better. **Bluing** added to the wash load sometimes corrects graying in white fabrics.

You notice detergent residue on clothes. Your powdered detergent isn't dissolving properly. Make sure the loads aren't too full. Use **liquid detergent** with cold-water cycles. Try letting the washer fill with water, adding the detergent, and then adding the clothes. If the problem is caused by hard water, try using a water-softening product in the next load. To remove hard-water residue from clothes, soak them in a solution of **1 cup white vinegar** per **1 gallon warm water**. Rinse and rewash.

There's a lot of lint on your clothes. You probably need to sort better. Separate lint producers, such as fleece sweat suits, chenille items, new terry cloth towels, and flannel pajamas, from lint attractors, such as corduroys, synthetic blends, and dark fabric. To remove the lint, use a **lint roller** or pat with the sticky side of **masking or packing tape**. Check to make sure pockets are empty of tissues and other paper before you wash. Make sure the washer and dryer lint filters are clean.

You have a problem with pilling. This is most common among synthetic fabrics. Try turning synthetic clothing inside out before washing. (Pilling is caused by abrasion of fibers, and this cuts down on abrasion during the wash and dry cycles.) You can also wash your synthetics together in a gentler, shorter cycle. Using a liquid detergent will help. To remove pills, snip them off with a **battery-powered pill remover** (available at sewing stores and discount retailers) or pull the fabric tight over a curved surface and carefully shave the pills off with a **safety razor**.

Chapter 6

The ZAP Cleaning System

ZAP! Your Weekly Housecleaning Is Done, Top to Bottom

Professional housekeepers say you need two things to do a speedy but thorough job of cleaning your home:

1. Focus: For the three hours or so that you're going to spend cleaning your home from top to bottom, commit to stripping the distractions out of your life. No dawdling over the magazines you should be stuffing into the recycling bin. No watching Oprah when you should be plucking the wilted lettuce out of the fridge's vegetable drawer.

2. Organization: In other words, you need a plan for cleaning your house—to establish a pattern, to lock into a rhythm. That's when you reach your maximum efficiency.

Well, bless our baking soda, do we have a system for you! The Zoned Attack Plan (ZAP)—so named because you concentrate on one portion of your house at a time—is the ultimate can't-miss time-saving strategy for weekly housecleaning.

Don't Waste a Moment

Before we get to the specifics of how to ZAP your home, let's establish some time-saving ground rules.

- *Clean from left to right and top to bottom* in each room. A systematic, clockwise approach to a room eliminates a lot of retracing of steps. And a top to bottom system lets gravity work for you and avoids duplication of effort. You don't want the dust from your window ledges falling on a freshly polished table, for instance.
- *Keep cleaning supplies together and close at hand* to make every movement count. Interrupting the bathroom cleaning to track down window cleaner slows your momentum.
- *Deal with the clutter in your home separately*. Decluttering can be extremely time consuming, and if you combine it with

cleaning, you'll be seriously slowed down. This approach assumes you'll lay down the law with other family members: No clothes strewn about the bedroom, for instance; no dishes left in the sink; and no newspapers blanketing the den floor.

- ● **Move furniture toward the center** of the room when it's time to dust. This way, the dust from the molding, sills, and such will settle to the floor, where it's easy to vacuum up. Once you've vacuumed the perimeter of the room, you can push furniture back into place and vacuum the rest of the room.

- ● **Set a deadline** for completing your cleaning. Knowing up front how much time you'll spend cleaning can make the list of chores less daunting.

- ● **Learn to multitask**. If you absolutely *must* answer the telephone while you're cleaning, use this chat time to do some low-concentration tasks, such as cleaning windows, polishing a table, or loading the dishwasher. Get a cordless phone and a headset (important for your neck) and work while you talk.

- ● **Don't turn on the TV**. You'll waste time waiting to find out how Marvin is going to break the news to Samantha. Instead, entertain yourself with upbeat music to keep energized.

- ● **Use both hands** while cleaning. Dust or wipe furniture surfaces with one hand while lifting objects with the other. Scrub

Maid to Order

We all need a break from housecleaning once in a while. When you're ready for some professional help—either for yourself or as a gift to a beleaguered loved one—following these guidelines will ensure a trouble-free experience:

- • Decide whether you want to hire a cleaning service or a single housekeeper. Cleaning services typically dispatch teams of two to four, who complete the work more quickly. Solo cleaners will often take on tasks that the services avoid, such as washing laundry, doing the dishes, and picking up clutter.
- • Ask for references from cur-

rent and former clients. Call those people and find out what they liked and disliked about the arrangement.

- • Ask the company whether they conduct background checks on their employees and what type of insurance they carry to cover damage or theft.
- • Before you hire anyone, nail down precisely what they'll clean, how long they'll be in your home, and whether they'll bring their own cleaning tools or use yours. (They typically clean when you're not around, so you won't be there to supervise.)
- • If there are items you don't want cleaning people to

touch, such as the frame of an original oil painting or a family heirloom, discuss those issues in advance.

If you live in a small town, expect to pay $15 to $20 per hour for an individual cleaning person. In larger cities, the rate runs $25 to $35 per hour. Cleaning services typically charge $20 to $30 per hour per cleaning person. Expect to pay more for the first cleaning, because workers are usually making up for months or years of housecleaning neglect and will need to spend significantly more time than they will on subsequent visits.

THE **ZAP** CLEANING SYSTEM

counters with a cloth in each hand. Squirt spray cleaner with one hand and wipe the surface with the other.

● **Pull an old, clean cotton tube sock over your dusting hand** and lift objects with the other hand as you clean. If you have arthritis or problems with your hand dexterity, it's helpful to wear a rubber glove on the hand you use for lifting objects.

● **Spray a lint-free towel with window cleaner** and keep it handy for cabinets or tables with glass inlays.

● **Collect pet hair from chairs and couches** using rubber gloves and a circular motion—assuming you have pets that shed. Toss the rolled-up hair on the floor and suction it up when you vacuum the floor later.

● **Place items from another level in a plastic bin near the stairs** and take them with you the next time you *have* to make a trip to that level. If you live in a multistory house, you'll save yourself frequent trips if you do this whenever you spot something that is on the wrong level.

How Often Should I ...?

If we told you to polish your silver each and every week, you'd roll your eyes and give up, right? We checked with experts who have both feet solidly planted in the real world. Here's how often you should perform cleaning tasks that are not part of the weekly ZAP routine.

Every day:
• Put things away when you finish using them.
• Wash dishes, wipe kitchen counters, clean up stove spills, and empty trash as needed.
• Squeegee showers after use to prevent mineral deposits and mildew.
• Wipe sinks.
• Make beds and straighten rooms.

Twice a week:
• Dust-mop hardwood floors to prevent scratching from dirt.

• Put away clutter.
• Vacuum if you live in a dusty region or have children and pets that track in lots of dirt. Otherwise, weekly vacuuming should suffice.

Once a month:
• Wipe or vacuum baseboards and blinds.
• Sweep the garage, patio, and walkways.
• Vacuum upholstered furniture with the brush attachment.
• Clean ceiling fixtures in one room per month (rotate).
• Wash throw rugs.
• Dust ceiling fans.

Every three months:
• Polish wood furniture.
• Remove cobwebs from ceiling corners, stairwells, and such.
• Change or clean furnace and air-conditioner filters (less frequently in low-use seasons).
• Clean the oven (monthly if

grunge builds up quickly).

Every six months:
• Wash windows inside and out. Do this quarterly for windows near work spaces (the kitchen sink or a desk, for instance).
• Declutter storage areas in the basement, attic, and garage.
• Vacuum, flip, and rotate mattresses.
• Polish silver.
• Air out pillows.

Once a year:
• Move heavy furniture to clean behind and underneath.
• Vacuum rug pads and the backs of area rugs.
• Clean drapes and carpets.
• Turn area rugs 180 degrees to even out wear.
• Wash walls.
• Clean chandeliers.

- **Get a 25-foot extension cord for your vacuum** so that you won't waste time plugging it in again in every room.
- **If it's truly not dirty, don't clean it.** There's no point in wasting time on a guest room or living room that's rarely used. Give it a light dusting and forget it.

Assemble Your Arsenal

An effective cleaning system starts with good tools and products. The high-efficiency ZAP system requires that you use a **plastic or rubber cleaning caddy** with dividers, stocked with everything you'll need as you make your rounds. (Alternatives: A **large plastic bucket**, a **rolling supply cart**, or an **apron with large pockets**.) Arrange items in the caddy so that it's well balanced. Avoid specialized items that accomplish only one job, such as soap scum cleaner or special counter spray. If you must have such cleaners, store them near the place that you're most likely to need them. You don't want to wear yourself out lugging around an overloaded caddy.

Fill your caddy with these:
- *A glass cleaner*
- *A general-purpose cleaner*, such as Formula 409, Fantastik, or Bio-OX (a concentrated orange oil–based cleaner with hydrogen peroxide)
- *A heavy-duty degreasing cleaner* (Top Job or Mr. Clean, for instance)
- *A powdered scouring cleanser* (such as Bar Keepers Friend or Comet)
- *Wood polish*

You'll also need a few extra tools. Some of these items may not be mentioned in the weekly ZAP routine described next, but you will need them for some cleaning jobs you'll be doing:
- *A lamb's wool duster*
- *A nylon scrub pad*
- *A stiff-bristled toothbrush* for scrubbing around faucets
- *A 1 1/2-inch, soft-bristled paintbrush* for dusting lampshades and removing cobwebs
- *A toilet bowl brush*
- *Rubber gloves*
- *Clean cotton rags*
- *A large trash bag*
- *A plastic squeegee* for bathrooms

- *Safety glasses* to protect your eyes from splattering cleaner or airborne dirt
- A *plastic bin* for collecting items that belong on other levels or in other parts of the house

Check your tools regularly to make sure they are up to the task. A crumbling sponge mop or worn-out broom causes you extra work. A vacuum cleaner with a broken guard will damage baseboards and furniture.

For a multilevel house, keep a completely stocked cleaning caddy on each floor. Also keep basic tools, such as a broom, dustpan, and mop, on every level. This will save you a lot of running up and down stairs to get the tools that you need and, truth be known, it will keep you from putting off certain cleaning tasks until another day.

Divide and Conquer

ZAP is a systematic cleaning plan for getting your home spotless, top to bottom, every week. It divides your home into four zones. Using easy-to-follow steps, you completely clean each zone before moving on to the next. ZAP is designed to eliminate duplication of effort, extra trips around the house, and counter-productive moves like wiping dust onto a floor that you just vacuumed. Here are the four zones:

Zone 1
Bedrooms, bathrooms, and hallways

Zone 2
Kitchen, informal dining area, and den or family room

Zone 3
Formal living room and formal dining room

Zone 4
Laundry room and other miscellaneous spaces

"A lot of people have no idea how to clean," says Mary Findley, one of the cleaning specialists who helped with the development of this system. (See Expert Advice sidebar.) "A step-by-step process will help people realize what to do. The ZAP system doesn't leave any doubt in your mind. It's how the professionals work. You've got the whole process."

You're psyched. You're equipped. You're armed with the best speed-cleaning techniques. Now put it all into action with the ultimate step-by-step plan for weekly housecleaning. We'll start where you will make the biggest impact, the high-traffic Zone 1 areas—bedrooms, bathrooms, and hallways. This plan assumes you have a two-story house. If you don't, you're going to have to move. Ha-ha. OK, you can adapt the plan to fit your home.

1. Go into each bedroom, strip the sheets off the beds, and toss them into the hallway. Go into each bathroom and toss the towels, washcloths, tub mats, and bath mats into the hallway, too. Gather all of these washable items in a laundry basket and dump them in the laundry room. Start a wash load with the tub mats, bath mats, and a couple of towels.

2. Get the cleaning caddy you keep on the second floor. Go into the upstairs bathroom and start spreading around the cleaning chemicals. Spray bowl cleaner (stored under the sink) inside the toilet bowl. Spray all-purpose cleaner on the toilet rim, toilet seat, countertop, and sink. Sprinkle your bathtub cleaner in the tub.

3. Empty the trash basket into your plastic bag.

4. Now use a little elbow grease. Spray a clean rag with window cleaner and clean the mirror. Scrub the inside of your toilet bowl with the toilet bowl brush. Wipe down the counter, sink, toilet exterior, and toilet rim. Scrub the tub with a nylon scrubber sponge. Rinse the tub. Spray all-purpose cleaner on the shower walls and wipe them down. (Note: This prevents mixing two cleaners in the tub, which you want to avoid.)

5. Mop the floor, backing out of the room.

6. Go into one of the upstairs bedrooms and empty the trash basket into your plastic bag.

7. Move any light furniture or other obstructions toward the center of the room, away from the walls.

8. Dust the entire room, starting at the entryway and moving from left to right (clockwise). Using your lamb's wool duster, take one wall at a time, working from top to bottom, including valances, window frames, wall hangings, and furniture.

9. Now vacuum around the entire perimeter of the bedroom. (See why you moved the furniture?) Return the furniture to

its original position. Starting at the far corner of the room, vacuum the rest of the room, backing out the door.

10. Go into the other upstairs bedrooms and repeat steps 6 through 9.

11. Give the upstairs hallway a quick dusting, moving left to right, top to bottom, one wall at a time.

12. Put away the upstairs cleaning caddy. Vacuum the upstairs hallway, backing toward the stairs. Take the trash bag with you and back down the stairs, vacuuming the stairs as you go.

13. For the first-floor bathroom, repeat steps 2 through 5 (except use your first-floor cleaning caddy).

14. For first-floor bedrooms, repeat steps 6 through 9.

15. Dust and vacuum the downstairs hallway.

16. Go to the laundry room and unload the washer. Put everything but the rubber tub mats into the dryer. Load the washer with dirty sheets and towels. Hang the tub mats somewhere (a clothes rack, for instance) to drip dry.

Kitchen, Dining Area, and Family Room Zone 2

Nice work—you already have some of the biggest cleaning jobs behind you. Next we tackle three other high-traffic spots: your kitchen, your casual dining area, and the family room.

1. Get your first-floor cleaning caddy. Go into the kitchen and pull out a microwave-safe bowl. Pour in 2 cups of water, put the bowl of water in the microwave, and cook on high for 3 to 5 minutes.

2. While the microwave is running, go around the kitchen and dust all surfaces, left to right, top to bottom. Spray an all-purpose cleaner on the stovetop (make sure it's cool first), the oven door, the refrigerator, and the counters.

3. Take a clean cloth and move from left to right around the kitchen, wiping down the counters and appliances. While you're at the stove, wipe any food spills from the burner grates (gas stove) or coils (electric). Move any countertop appliances and wipe under them as you go. When you get to the microwave, make sure the water has cooled for at least a minute. Dump the water out and wipe down the steamed interior of the microwave.

4. Pick one section of cabinets to clean each time you clean the kitchen. Spray that section with all-purpose spray and wipe.

THE **ZAP** CLEANING SYSTEM

5. Toss out any old food in the refrigerator and pick one shelf or drawer to clean. Spray it with glass cleaner (for light cleaning) or get the Lysol from under the kitchen sink (for heavier cleaning or disinfecting).

6. Sprinkle the sink with scouring powder and scrub it with a nylon pad. Rinse.

7. Mop the floor.

8. Go to your casual dining area. (If you have an eat-in kitchen, take care of the table and chairs in step 3.) Dust your way around the room, left to right, top to bottom. Dust the light fixture. Pull the chairs away from the table. Wipe up any spills or crumbs from the table and chairs. Mop or vacuum under the table and move the chairs back. Clean the rest of the floor.

9. Go to your family room. Move any light furniture into the center of the room. Move around the room dusting—from left to right, top to bottom, one section of wall at a time. Dust the valances, window frames, wall hangings, furniture, and electronic devices.

10. Now vacuum the perimeter of the family room. Return the furniture to its original position. Vacuum the rest of the room.

11. Go to the laundry room. Take the towels, washcloths, and bath mats out of the dryer and set them on a counter. (Don't bother folding.) Take the sheets and towels out of the washer and put them in the dryer. Load any remaining sheets and towels in the washer.

Zone 3 Formal Living and Dining Rooms

Take a deep breath, take a swig of water, and pat yourself on the back. You're almost done—and you've left the easiest for last!

1. Go into your formal living room. Move any light furniture (lamps, end tables, and such) into the center of the room.

2. You know the drill by now. Dust the room, moving from left to right, one wall at a time. Dust from top to bottom, including valances, window frames, wall hangings, and furniture.

3. Vacuum the perimeter of the living room. Return the furniture to its original position.

4. Lift the seat cushions out of the sofa and love seat and then vacuum underneath with the brush attachment. Vacuum the center of the floor.

5. Go to the dining room and repeat steps 1 through 3.

6. Dust the dining room table and the chairs around the table.

7. Pull the chairs away from the table and vacuum under the table. Return the chairs to their original positions and vacuum the rest of the room.

Laundry Room and Miscellaneous Spaces Zone 4

Time to polish off the last couple of rooms of the house and then wrap up the loose ends.

1. Go to the laundry room, remove the sheets and towels from the dryer, and add them to the unfolded pile on the counter. Move the last of the laundry from the washer to the dryer.

2. Empty the laundry room's trash basket into your plastic bag.

3. Since this is not a high-traffic area, a quick dusting will do. Move around the room left to right, top to bottom, dusting the shelves, appliance tops, and sink. Wipe up any detergent spills on the appliances with a damp rag.

4. Mop the floor.

5. Continue the pattern of dusting and then vacuuming or mopping in the other miscellaneous spaces of your home— foyer, sunroom, enclosed porch, utility room, office.

6. Put your vacuum cleaner and cleaning caddy away (assuring the little dears they can come out to play again in a week).

7. Take your plastic bag full of trash out to the garbage can.

8. While you're outside, take your welcome mats out onto the lawn and shake them out.

9. Take your dirty cleaning cloths to the laundry room and toss them in the washer.

10. Once all of the sheets, towels, and such are dry, spread out one of the sheets from an upstairs bedroom and put all of the other laundry on top of it, along with the tub mats that were drip-drying. Pull the corners of the sheet together to make a sack. Haul it all to the first-floor bedrooms and put the sheets back on the beds. (This is why you didn't bother folding.) Return the towels, washcloths, bath mat, and tub mat to their places in the first-floor bathroom. Then carry the remaining laundry upstairs and repeat.

11. Take a bow. Or take a nap—your choice.

Asphalt
Burns
Candlesticks
Dust
Enamel
Grease
Houseplants
Irons
Knives
Lamp shades
Mildew
Needlework
Odors
Pet equipment
Quilts
Smoke Roofing
Tar
Umbrellas
Vases
Water stains
Zippers

Part Two

Encyclopedia of

Everyday Cleaning

a

Air

We use air every minute of every day—and it's *free*. The problem is, heat and air-conditioning don't come free, so we spend much of the year with our homes hermetically sealed to save money. But trapped in there with us are dust mites, airborne chemicals, cooking fumes, and, with some of us, cigarette smoke, carbon monoxide from fireplaces and wood stoves, pet dander, and other pollutants and irritants.

Some simple air-cleaning solutions cost nothing.
- Good ventilation will do more than anything else to freshen the air in your home. When you get up in the morning, open a window in each room of the house for five minutes no matter what the temperature is outside.
- Smooth surfaces—tile or hardwood floors, for instance—will keep the air cleaner, too, because allergens love to collect in upholstery, curtains, and carpets.
- Using baking soda or vinegar to absorb odors may reduce smells, but they aren't really doing much to clean the air. The same is true of aerosol spray air fresheners, which pump more chemicals into your environment.

Clean your furnace filter regularly. Forced-air heating and cooling systems are major contributors to indoor air pollution. They blow air all around your house through a system of ducts, spreading dust, mites, and mold. At least a couple of times a year, change the furnace air filter that stands between the furnace blower and your home's ductwork. Also consider getting small vent filters that fit over the vents in each room. Avoid sleeping directly in the path of furnace vents, unless you *prefer* that those blown particles settle in your lungs rather than on your dresser. If dust has built

For Super *Sneeze Control*

For more serious allergen control, consider buying an air filter unit—especially if allergens are a medical problem and less expensive approaches haven't solved it. There are several technologies to choose from, but for general removal of particles from the air, you'll probably have the most success with a HEPA filter (that's high efficiency particulate air filter, for you trivia buffs). Most HEPA filters are small units, much like a dehumidifier, that sit in your room and trap microscopic particles by drawing air through fine disposable filters and returning the air to the room. The filters are so efficient that they're often used in hospitals and industrial "clean rooms." You can also get a HEPA filter for a central heating and cooling system, but that kind is very expensive.

up inside the ducts, call a professional duct-cleaning service to vacuum them out.

Control the humidity in your home. Heating systems can create extremely dry air, which can be corrected with a humidifier or by placing bowls of water near your heat source. Ideal humidity for your home is about 40 to 50 percent. Let the air get much damper than that and you encourage mold growth. If you use a humidifier, remember to clean it frequently to prevent mold from growing in it. You might think houseplants would do great things for your home's air, since they gobble up carbon dioxide and expel oxygen. But you might be better off flexing your green thumb outdoors—those moist pots of soil are splendid breeding grounds for mold.

To control allergens in the air around you, you have to go to the source of the problem.

● To control pet dander and mites, wash your pets frequently—every two weeks if someone in your home has allergies.

● To keep smoke to a minimum, limit the number of fires you have in the fireplace and, if you or another member of your household simply must have a cigarette, smoke it outside.

● To keep dust mites under wraps, put a plastic mattress cover over that mattress where you spend a third of your life, and put a mattress pad over the plastic. (Otherwise, the plastic will collect your perspiration.)

See also ***Fireplaces, Furnaces,*** *and* ***Humidifiers***.

Air Conditioners

Being cool will cost less if you clean your air conditioners properly. Whether you have central air-conditioning or window units, dirt and debris can restrict airflow through the filter and around the cooling elements, forcing the unit to work harder and use more electricity than necessary to do its job.

Cleaning a central air conditioner's filter is the most important thing you can do to keep it functioning well. The filter, which snatches dust and other gunk from the air that's being distributed around your house, is usually indoors and is shared with your furnace. You'll find it next to the furnace, at the beginning of your air duct system under a grate or cover. (See illustration in ***Furnace***.) Pull the filter out once a month and check it. If it's covered with dirt, which can happen in just a month during times of heavy use, the filter needs replacing or cleaning. If your system uses a ***disposable filter***, just slide a new one into place. (Look for arrows on the filter indicating the direction of airflow.) If you have a reusable aluminum or plastic filter, take it outside and use a ***garden hose*** to wash it. Then prop it upright and let it *dry thoroughly* before sliding it back into place.

▲

Cleaning a central air's outdoor unit—that large R2D2-shaped thing in your yard—should be done once a year at the beginning of the season. Do it more often if you live near a dirt road or other source of dust and grime. First turn the unit off. (Use the circuit breaker or the electrical disconnect on the unit—not the thermostat.) The electrical parts of your unit should be well sealed against the weather, but check anyway that no parts are exposed. (Call a technician if they are.) Then take off the grille and panel on top of the outdoor unit. The grille and top panel are usually attached by hexagonal cap nuts that can be removed easily with an ***adjustable wrench***. Also remove any guard covering the coil that's wrapped around the unit. The guard is usually held by screws or bolts at the bottom. Then tie ***plastic garbage bags*** around the fan motor and any other exposed electrical parts. Gently brush dirt from the outer fins and coil with a ***stiff-bristled brush***. Using your ***garden hose***, spray from inside the unit ◀ to wash away grass clippings, twigs, and dirt on the coil. Hose away any fire ants, too. These insects like to set up housekeeping around the warmth of condenser units. They can block airflow

For a Smooth-Running *Air Conditioner*

- Before restarting a central air conditioner in the spring or after a long shutdown, restore power to the unit for 24 hours. This produces the heat needed to separate the oil from the refrigerant so that the compressor can run more smoothly.
- Before restarting any air conditioner after a brief interruption, turn off the thermostat for at least five minutes to lessen strain on the compressor.

- To avoid damaging the compressor on an air conditioner, don't operate the unit when it's below 60° F outside.
- Lubricate the fan motor yearly if the motor has oil ports. (The ports usually have metal or rubber caps and are found on older units.) Use nondetergent, lightweight SAE 20 oil; add no more than ten drops per port to an outdoor central unit, five drops for a window unit.

- Prune vegetation away from an outdoor unit by 2 feet on each side and above. When mowing, spray grass clippings away from the unit. And in the fall, keep the fan grille free of leaves.
- Keep potential obstructions, such as curtains, furniture, and houseplants, 2 feet away from a window unit. Outside, trim shrubs that block the unit's coils or the airflow to them.

and damage your unit's electronics. Don't use cleaning chemicals, brushes, or a power hose on your condenser unit, because they can damage the delicate aluminum fins.

Cleaning a window unit's filter regularly during the cooling season is just as important as it is for a central system. A window unit usually has a plastic filter that slides out of the front of the unit at the top, side, or bottom. On some models, you have to open the front panel to lift out the filter ▶. To clean the filter, hold it under *running water* in the sink or spray it with the *garden hose*. Make sure it's *absolutely dry* before you replace it.

Cleaning a small window air conditioner should be done once a year at the end of the season. Turn off your unit, unplug it, and remove it from the window. Take it outside and use a *screwdriver* to take the cover off the unit to clean the interior coils. Inside you'll find two coils, the evaporator coil (positioned inside the house, near the controls) and the condenser coil. Your *vacuum cleaner* can take care of light dirt and dust. Your *garden hose* will take care of heavier dirt, but this can be a little tricky, because you don't want to get the inner electrical parts wet. Place a wood block or brick under the unit to elevate the side with electrical components so the water will drip away from the electrical housing. Then hose the coils down gently. Make sure all parts are dry before you put the air conditioner's cover back on. Clean the plastic and metal exterior of your unit with a damp cleaning cloth. As with a central air unit, don't use cleaning chemicals, brushes, or a power hose on your room unit. After cleaning, store the unit for the winter or reinstall it, putting a plastic cover over the exterior.

Cleaning a large window unit—which has an interior chassis that slides into a securely mounted cabinet—can usually be done without completely removing the chassis from the cabinet. First, unplug the unit and remove the front panel. Then pull the chassis forward out of the cabinet and place a *solid support*, like an old table or a sawhorse, under the front edge. You should be able to reach most of the interior parts with the chassis only partly outside the cabinet. Use a *vacuum* with a *crevice attachment* to clean the coils.

Alabaster

As early as the 5th century B.C., thin slices of translucent alabaster were used as windowpanes in the Middle East. But

After Bob Eaton finishes cleaning an alabaster light fixture, he adds a touch that gives it a soft glow, removes surface scratches, and provides a protective coating. The secret is petroleum jelly. Eaton, of Metropolitan Lighting Co. in New York City, puts a soft cloth or chamois over his fingers, dips into the petroleum jelly, and gently rubs it into the alabaster with circular motions.

today, you're more likely to find this delicate, porous stone used for vases, urns, bowls, and figurines. Translucent varieties are used to diffuse light in light fixtures.

The safest way to clean alabaster is just to wipe the object clean with a dry, pure *cotton cloth*, because the stone is easy to damage. Don't soak an alabaster object in water, don't use any other cleaning chemicals, and don't use any abrasive materials.

If a piece needs more cleaning, squirt some *mild dishwashing liquid* into *water*, dip a *sponge* into the soapy water, and squeeze. (You don't want the sponge dripping.) Sponge the water on and rub gently. Rinse the sponge with fresh water and gently wipe the object again. Dry with a *cotton cloth*. If the alabaster is from a light fixture, let it dry at room temperature for two hours before returning it to duty. Otherwise, the heat could cause the damp alabaster to expand and crack.

Aluminum

Much of the aluminum that enters your life these days is extremely easy to care for.

Cleaning aluminum window and door frames is not a real problem. They are sold with a tough coating—white, primarily, but sometimes bronze or brown. An *all-purpose cleaner*, such as Formula 409, will spiff them up nicely. But why not take care of two cleaning chores at once? Clean your windows with Windex or another *glass cleaner*, then wipe down the aluminum with the same stuff.

Clean aluminum siding once a year. Left to its own devices, your home's aluminum siding will degrade over time, developing a chalky feel on the surface and eventually breaking out in tiny dark spots that can't be removed. To prevent this, clean the siding with trisodium phosphate (also called TSP), available in hardware stores, or with an item you're more likely to already have in stock—an ordinary laundry detergent, such as Tide. Mix the *trisodium phosphate* with *warm water*, following the package directions. Be sure to wear *rubber gloves* and *protective goggles*. If you're using laundry detergent, mix *1/4 cup of bleach-free powdered laundry detergent* in a *bucket* with *2 gallons of warm water*. Rub the cleaning solution on with a *sponge* and rinse it off with a *garden hose*.

If your aluminum siding has dark streaks, they were probably caused by pollution, and there's a good chance that the streaks may not respond to TSP or laundry detergent. In that case, you can return some vigor to that tired-looking aluminum with a liquid abrasive, such as Vim Liquid Abrasive Cream. But use it very carefully, because it's an abrasive, even though a mild one. Dampen a cleaning cloth with a little water, dab on some of the cream, and rub it into the cloth. Then rub the cloth just on the streaks, very lightly. Rinse immediately with a garden hose.

Cleaning older bare aluminum, the kind sold with a mill finish, presents more of a challenge. It may have started out shiny, but it tends to oxidize from years of exposure to the air, turning it a darker gray and giving it a rough feel. To clean this old-time aluminum, apply some **WD-40**. (Spray it on or apply it with a *cleaning rag*.) Then go over the aluminum with *fine steel wool (00)*. Move the steel wool back and forth (not in circles), and don't rub so hard that it scratches. When you're finished, wipe the oil off with a *clean rag*. Test this method on an inconspicuous area first. This technique will make your aluminum lighter and brighter, but the effects of oxidation can't be totally erased. If you're still not happy with the appearance of your aluminum, consider giving it new life with a coating of latex paint. (Oil-based paint won't stand up to the expansion and contraction that aluminum goes through outdoors.)

Antique Clothing

Cleaning antique clothing is an exercise in avoiding modern conveniences, which are generally too harsh for fragile fabrics. This is easy-does-it handwork.

The safest way to clean fragile garments is to give them a sponge bath. But before you start, fix any tears in the fabric—otherwise the stress of cleaning will make matters worse. Then mix a *squirt of mild detergent* (such as Ivory dishwashing liquid) in *1 gallon of water* and dab the solution on gently with a *sponge*. Rinse by sponging on clean water. Try not to get the garment sopping wet.

To remove browning or stubborn stains that don't respond to a sponge bath, treat them to a long soak. Pick up a container of

WATCH OUT

Don't take antique clothing to a regular dry cleaner. The chemicals dry cleaners use are too harsh, and their pressing techniques stress the fabric too much. If you really need professional help, find a dry cleaner that specializes in old fabrics.

a gentle *sodium perborate–based whitener*—Nancy's Vintage Soak is the most common brand—at a linen shop, an antique store, or on the Internet (at www.vintagesoak.com). Mix *2 or 3 tablespoons of whitener* in *1 gallon of warm water*. Place the garment and the solution in a *plastic tub* and let it sit—don't agitate—for one to three days. Then rinse with *fresh water* until the rinse water comes clean. If your tap water is hard, use *distilled water* for rinsing instead so that minerals won't discolor the fabric.

Drying an antique garment is a delicate operation. Never wring antique fabric. Lay it flat to dry if at all possible. Be careful when moving a wet garment, especially lace or other fragile fabrics. Just the weight of the water can tear the fibers. To move the garment, lay it on a *bed sheet* and carry the sheet.

Storing a fragile garment also requires special care. Don't starch an antique garment before storing it. Starch attracts insects and stresses the fabric along folds. If possible, store the garment spread out flat. If space doesn't permit flat storage, roll it up. Rolling the garment around an object isn't necessary, but if you use wood or a cardboard tube, beware—they could brown the fabric. Protect the cloth from any such material (wood drawers and cardboard boxes, for example) with *sheets of acid-free tissue* (available at quilt shops). Don't store your garment in a plastic bag—it needs to breathe.

Antique Furniture

When cleaning antiques, less is better. Some of the cleaning methods you'd readily use on everyday furniture can ruin the look and reduce the value of an antique.

The safest approach to cleaning antiques is to limit it to simple dusting once every week or two. Wipe your antiques down with a *soft*, *dry*, *nonabrasive cloth* or *chamois*. Avoid furniture polishes—they will just leave a film that will attract more dirt, and polishing can damage the finish.

A more aggressive cleaning method might be considered if you're willing to risk it. But first make sure that the finish isn't too fragile (breaking down, separating, or in the case of veneer, lifting). If the finish is in good health, wipe it down with a *slightly damp cloth* and follow up immediately with a *dry cloth*. (Never saturate an antique with water—that would ruin even a stable finish.) If you need stronger cleaning power, mix *1 tablespoon of mild*

RULES
OF THE GAME

When cleaning antique clothing >

1. Avoid regular dry cleaners.

2. Mend any rips before you clean.

3. Don't use your washer and dryer.

4. Sponge clean.

5. Never wring dry. Dry flat—not hung.

6. Don't store ironed or starched.

dishwashing detergent in *1 gallon of water*. Dip your cloth in the solution, wring it out, and wipe the furniture down quickly. Follow up right away with a dry cloth. (Test this method first on an inconspicuous spot to make sure the finish holds up OK.)

Waxing antique furniture is something you should do no more often than every three years—and, again, only if the finish is stable. A *dark paste wax* (available at hardware stores) is a good idea, because it won't leave a whitish residue in crevices, which lighter waxes tend to do. Apply a thin coating of the paste wax with a *soft cloth*. Follow up right away with a *clean cloth*, rubbing the wax off until it's dry. (Normally, you would let the wax dry before buffing, but this technique allows you to apply a thinner coat and is friendlier to the finish, because it does not require rubbing as hard.)

If an antique has a water stain—and the item is not very valuable—you can try waxing the mark. Start by using a *soft cloth* to apply a *paste furniture wax* to the stain itself to see how much the surface darkens. Work your way outward from the stain, attempting to create a match with the surrounding surface. If your antique is valuable, however, don't attempt to fix the stain yourself. Get help from a professional restorer.

Appliances

To find out how to clean most appliances, look under the name of the appliance itself. Here we offer some general instructions on keeping those endlessly multiplying small appliances spick-and-span.

To clean a small electrical appliance, first unplug it—and let it cool if it's been in use recently. Most small appliances can just be wiped down with a damp cloth. If it has food splatters on the outside, mix a solution of *warm water* and *dishwashing liquid* to dip your cleaning cloth in. Keep the water and suds away from the electronics of the appliance. Never put an appliance in water unless its instructions say it's OK to clean it that way. Some appliances have washable parts that should be removed from the electronic base to make cleaning easier and safer (can openers and slow cookers, for example).

See also **Coffee Grinders, Coffee Makers, Electric Grills, Food Processors, Irons, Microwave Ovens, Ovens, Range Hoods, Refrigerators and Freezers, Stoves, Toaster Ovens, Toasters, Trash Compactors, Waffle Irons,** and **Washers and Dryers**.

simple
SOLUTIONS

Protect Your Antiques >

• Don't store them in a dry room. A humidity level that's comfortable for your skin will be fine for furniture as well.

• Don't store them in a room with fluctuating humidity or temperatures. Both can cause cracking.

• Keep them out of direct sunlight.

• Don't place drinks on antique furniture. Wipe up any water immediately with a dry cloth.

• If a piece has gilding (gold leaf) anywhere, be extremely careful. A damp cleaning rag can wipe water-based gilding right off. Use a dry rag and a delicate touch to clean gilding.

Aquariums

With an aquarium, proper cleaning is a life-or-death issue for your finned friends, so take it seriously.

For a new aquarium, cleaning starts on Day 1. Clean all of your new gear—tank and accessories. Soap and detergent are no-no's. The residue will hurt the fish. For new equipment, just use plain old *warm or cold water*.

Check your aquarium's water once a week for its pH, nitrate, nitrite, and ammonia levels. Read up on the chemical tolerances of your particular fish species, so you will know when it's time for a change of water. (The folks who sold you all of that gear will be glad to ring up a *water chemical test kit* as well.) A number of variables affect how often you will need to change the water: how many fish you have, how big they are, the species, the size of the tank, your lighting, and the kind of filtration you're using. You don't really change *all* the water at once. Just change 10 to 25 percent of the water in your aquarium, and expect to do it about every two weeks.

To change the water, round up enough *buckets* to handle 10 to 25 percent of the water in your tank. (You can use the same bucket over and over, but you'll have to keep stopping the siphon while you dump it out.) Use a *siphon hose* to draw the water out. A clear hose is best, so you can see what you're sucking up.

Don't refill the aquarium with water straight out of the tap. Nearly all tap water has chlorine added, and that will hurt your fish. (Many pet shops will test a sample for you, or you can use a home water chemical test kit.) To remove the chlorine, either use a *dechlorinating product*, such as Stress Coat, or let the water sit in a basin for 24 hours before pouring it in, giving the chlorine time to dissipate naturally. In any case, make sure the new water is about the same temperature—within one or two degrees—as the water left in the aquarium.

To remove algae, use *algae scrub pads* (available at your aquarium store or pet store) and clean the inside walls of your aquarium whenever the fuzzy little green stuff becomes visible. If you don't like sloshing around in the water with your hands, try a *magnetic cleaning system*. One magnet, attached to a scrub pad, goes on the inside of the glass, and another magnet goes on the outside for dragging the scrub pad around. Remember, algae thrive on light, so the more light your aquarium gets the more algae you're going to have to clean up.

simple SOLUTIONS

Nature's Vacuum Cleaners >

Why not hire some live-in workers for your tank? The following species are happy to gobble up algae so you won't have to. Just make sure they're compatible with the other critters in your tank. You're inviting them to have dinner, not *be* dinner.

• **Freshwater**
Chinese algae eater *(Gyrinocheilus aymonieri)*
Plecostomus species
Snails (assorted species)

• **Saltwater**
Turbo snails *(Turbo fluctuosus)*
Scarlet reef hermit crabs *(Paguristes cadenati)*
Blue leg hermit crabs *(Clibanarius tricolor)*
Astrea snails *(Astrea tecta)*

Clean the filter in your tank once a week—or more often, depending on the feeding habits of your fish and how many fish you have. Most tanks have a mechanical filter, and models vary; follow the instructions that come with yours for removing, cleaning, and replacing the filter. A clean filter means better water, which means healthier fish.

Another filtering tool in your aquarium-cleaning arsenal is *carbon*. It gives your water that sparkling-clear look by removing the yellowish cast caused by food and waste. Carbon may already be a part of your mechanical filter. If not, you can buy a carbon holder or even make your own: Put the carbon (available at your aquarium store or pet store) into an old pair of *panty hose*, tie a tight knot to secure it, and cut away the excess fabric. Place your carbon filter where it will get good water flow in the tank.

To thoroughly clean an old tank—especially if some of your fish were diseased—remove any fish to another container and empty the tank. Then refill the tank with fresh water and add *2 teaspoons of bleach* for every *1 gallon of water*. Let it sit for at least 30 minutes. Empty the tank, rinse it well, and then refill. Now neutralize any bleach residue by adding *2 or 3 drops of sodium thiosulfate* (available at pet stores and hardware stores) per *1 gallon of water* and let that sit for another 30 minutes. If you can't get

An Underwater *Dirt Devil*

That gravel at the bottom of your aquarium isn't just for looks. It's also a biological filter that traps gunk in the water. Give it a gentle vacuuming each time you change your aquarium's water. (If you're thinking of firing up your wet-and-dry vacuum, go stand in the corner.)

You can buy special aquarium vacuums, but making your own is easy, say Michelle Gunn and Lori Watkins, experts at the North Carolina Aquarium on Roanoke Island. Attach a clear plastic siphon hose to the top of a small plastic soft drink bottle. (The hose needs to be large enough to fit tightly over the bottle.) Cut the bottom off the bottle. Then place the bottle on the bottom of the tank. When the siphon starts drawing water (you thought to bring a bucket, didn't you?), it will suck up the dirt, waste, and old food without disturbing the gravel. Move from one patch of gravel to the next, working your way across the aquarium floor.

Since you'll be using this technique at water-changing time, you'll have to stop when you've removed your target amount of water. It may take you two sessions to cover the entire aquarium floor. You can also install a special filter under the gravel, which will reduce the need for vacuuming.

sodium thiosulfate, pick up a dechlorinating product (see water-changing directions on page 60) at your aquarium store and follow the directions for neutralizing bleach. Empty the water once again and rinse. Now fill your aquarium with water that you have dechlorinated. Tell your fishy friends they can move in and unpack their bags.

Here are some preventive measures that can cut down on the time you have to spend cleaning your tank:

- The location of your aquarium has cleaning ramifications. If you put it in direct sunlight, you'll have a constant algae battle on your hands, not to mention problems with overheating (the same problems you'll have if you leave your aquarium lights on too much).
- The cleaning considerations are not very different for freshwater and saltwater fish. But if you're a beginner, start with freshwater fish. They're less sensitive to variations in the chemical levels in the water. Besides, tracking the salinity of a saltwater tank is yet another aquarium-management issue that could push a beginner over the edge.
- Don't give your water beasts too much food. Fish don't have refrigerators, so the leftovers float around, driving up the levels of harmful chemicals. Watch your fish at feeding time. When they begin to slow down their rate of eating, dinner's over; don't add more food.
- Inspect your fish every day to see whether they have any injuries, infections, or parasites. When you buy new fish, let them stay in a "guest room" for a month—a separate quarantine tank—so you can monitor them for any diseases that could wipe out the rest of your fish.

Artwork

With unframed paper-based artwork, such as prints, etchings, and drawings, it's best to approach cleaning with a healthy dose of forethought and prevention. Paper is easily damaged, and any medium applied to it has a much more tenuous bond than, say, oil on canvas. Prints, etchings, drawings, watercolors, and pastels just can't be cleaned. So do the wise thing and preserve these pieces of art under glass and framing. That way, you clean the exterior casing, not the artwork itself. And the value and longevity of your artwork increase.

To clean a framed work, take it off the wall and lay it flat. Remove dust by wiping all surfaces—front and back—with a *soft, dry*

cloth. Don't use a feather duster or a paper towel, which could scratch the glass or frame. To clean the glass, lightly moisten a **soft cleaning cloth** with **glass cleaner** and wipe the surface. Don't spray cleaner directly onto the glass. The cleaner could wick behind the glass and damage your artwork.

When cleaning paintings, there are more *don'ts* than *dos,* unfortunately. The good news is that dust doesn't tend to settle on paintings themselves, because they hang vertically. Don't attempt to dust a painting. Feathers from a feather duster or fibers from a cloth can snag on the paint surface and damage it. And leave that vacuum cleaner with its brush attachment in the closet as well. If you simply can't resist dusting a painting, wave a **feather duster** at it, making sure it doesn't actually touch the surface, and the resulting wind will do the job. Don't blow on your painting—there's inevitably some damaging saliva in human breath.

Dust will settle, of course, across the top of your painting's frame. But you still have limited options. The frames around valuable paintings often have delicate gilding—feather dusters and clothes are a no-no on an elaborate older frame. (If you have modern frames, they're OK.) But all is not lost. Remove any attachment from your **vacuum** hose and put a **soft flannel cloth** over the end, secured with a **rubber band**, to reduce the suction. Dislodge dust from the nooks and crannies of your delicate frame with a **soft watercolor brush** and use the covered hose to catch the airborne particles. Or use a **baby aspirator** as a gentle blowing tool to dislodge the dust.

If there's a smoker in your family, protect your paintings by covering them with glass. (You can wipe the glass, of course, with a cloth spritzed with cleaner.)

Cleaning sculptures is an exercise in the art of light-touch simplicity. Avoid the kind of harsh chemicals you get with commercial cleaners. And avoid soaps of any kind, since it's hard to know how they will affect various sculpting materials and finishes. Also resist the temptation to use feather dusters, as the feathers can get caught in crevices and break off a piece of the sculpture or damage veneer finishes. Clean plaster of Paris objects with a **cloth** lightly dampened in **distilled water**. For harder, more durable sculptures you can use plain **tap water**.

To dust a wood sculpture, spray a **dusting product**, such as Endust, onto a **soft cloth** (old T-shirts are great) and gently wipe the entire surface once a week, pulling dust out of crevices. You can use a **very slightly damp cloth** on your wood sculpture, too, but take care that no moisture is left behind to damage the wood. This is

OOPS!

The Incredible Shrinking Artifact >
Eileen Clancy tells the sad story of an engraving entrusted to an underqualified conservator. The caretaker, thinking the historic artifact was paper, immersed it in a water bath for cleaning. Routine testing, however, would have revealed that it was actually parchment—sheepskin—which should never come into contact with water. The piece shrank to half its size and hardened into a worthless lump.

The lesson, says Clancy, owner of Conservation of Paper, Parchment & Photograph, in Denver: Don't clean a valuable piece of art yourself. For a referral to a professional, call the American Institute for Conservation of Historic and Artistic Works at (202) 452-9545. Even then, make sure the conservator you're dealing with has experience in the type of object you want cleaned or repaired.

There's a folktale floating about that claims you can clean a painting by rubbing it with a cut potato or a slice of bread. The theory is that mild enzymes or acid in the potato will clean the artwork and that the bread will absorb dirt particles. Balderdash, says Simon Parks, owner of Simon Parks Art Conservation, in New York City. Smearing your dinner on a painting is just doing it damage. In his 30 years of experience, Parks has found that restorers spend most of their time fixing the cleaning mistakes of well-meaning amateurs. So keep your food in the pantry where it belongs.

not speed work. Proceed carefully, because some areas can be more delicate than others. Don't use silicone-based products, such as Pledge, which will soak into the wood and build up. If your sculpture is stained from longtime exposure to impurities from a fireplace or a heating system, take it to a professional conservator for advice.

You can also use the dusting method described for paintings: Cover your **vacuum** hose with **flannel**, secured with a **rubber band**. Then use a **soft watercolor brush** to whisk up the dust, and suck it up with the vacuum cleaner.

To wax a wood sculpture, first remove any buildup from furniture polish or furniture cleaning soap. As a test, dip a **cotton swab** in **mineral spirits** and dab it on an inconspicuous spot to see whether it damages the finish. If not, apply the mineral spirits to a **soft cloth**, such as an old T-shirt, and gently stroke the cloth over the sculpture. Be careful not to snag the cloth on any end grain of the wood, which could pull wood fibers free. Then apply your wax to another **soft**, **clean cloth** (again, a T-shirt) and gently rub it into the surface. **Carnauba wax** works well and comes in a variety of colors (clear for a white sculpture). **Briwax** is good, too. Or try brown **shoe polish**, which will match the color of the wood and help cover any scratches. Talk to a conservator before waxing stone, marble, plaster of Paris, or a painted surface.

Also see **Photographs**.

Asphalt

Sure, asphalt is tough stuff, but there are a surprising number of cleaning considerations where the rubber meets the road.

To clean your driveway or other asphalt surface, give it a good washing once a year. Remove leaves and dirt with a **broom or leaf blower**. Mix **1 scoop of laundry detergent** in a **bucket** with **1 gallon of water**. Splash some onto the driveway as needed for spot cleaning and scrub with a **push broom**. Then give it a good rinsing with a **garden hose**. (High-pressure hoses or steam washing could damage the asphalt.)

Clean gasoline and oil spills as quickly as possible. Asphalt is a petroleum-based material. This means a puddle of gasoline or oil could eat a hole in your driveway. Sop up a spill with **paper towels** and spray away any of the remainder with a **garden hose**. For a little more muscle, mix **laundry detergent** in **water** as described above, and work at the spot with a **stiff-bristled scrub brush**. And next time, take preventive measures: Lay down some cardboard, newspaper, or plastic when you add oil to your lawn mower.

To remove asphalt stains on clothing, pretreat the stain with an *enzyme stain removal product* from your laundry room and toss the article in the *washing machine.* You also can spray it with an *orange oil household cleaner*, which will dissolve the stain, but you will have to rinse the cleaner out of the garment before putting it into the washer. If you get asphalt on your shoes, spray them with *orange oil cleaner or WD-40* and scrape the asphalt off with *a paint scraper or putty knife.* (Make sure to rinse your shoes well before you go tromping around the house.)

To remove asphalt on your tools, again the *orange oil cleaner or WD-40* trick works. Spray it on, wait a few minutes, and wipe it off. *WD-40 lubricant* will do the job, too (as will turpentine, paint thinner, gasoline, or kerosene, but they're not recommended because they're highly flammable). Don't forget the damage that these products can do to asphalt—it stands to reason that you shouldn't be spilling any of these liquids onto your driveway.

To remove asphalt from your car, drop by an auto repair shop or auto supply store and pick up an *asphalt- or tar-removal product* designed for that purpose and follow the package directions.

Here are some asphalt maintenance tips that will keep your driveway looking better longer:

● Reseal your driveway with a commercial sealant every two or three years to protect it from the weather and to maintain its looks. If you reseal more often, you'll get too much buildup of the material, which will start to crack.

● Fill cracks in asphalt without a lot of delay. Eventually, your driveway will crack—that's just life on the streets. Use an *asphalt-patching product* (available at hardware and home improvement stores). This is not just a cosmetic consideration. Filling driveway cracks prevents weeds from growing in the holes, worsening the situation, and it deters erosion, which can undermine your driveway and cause more cracking.

RULES
OF THE GAME

To Pave the Way for a Happy Driveway >

1. Sorry, kids. When your car is standing still, don't turn the steering wheel back and forth. This can damage the asphalt—and your tires—especially on a hot day.

2. Don't place heavy or pointed objects on fresh or hot asphalt. Examples: the kickstand of a bicycle or motorcycle, chairs or tables, ladders, a car jack.

3. Gasoline and oil will damage asphalt, so wipe up spills quickly.

4. Use a sealant on your driveway every two or three years to protect it from the elements and maintain that spiffy black look.

Attics

Neglect your attic, and you could have a dust and mold factory hanging over your head. Give it a good cleaning once a year, and you'll not only remove a source of these irritants from your home, but you'll also have a valuable storage space that you won't dread going into now and then.

Mold in the attic is a sign that you have a moisture problem—maybe a leaky roof, maybe poor ventilation. To get rid of the mold, first cut off the source of moisture that's keeping it so happy. Get the leak fixed, or improve the airflow so that the attic stays dry. There should be soffit holes where the roof meets the floor and overhangs the walls of the house. Having a ridge vent system—a continuous vent along the peak of the roof—installed would make the airflow even better. Consider having one installed when you reroof.

When the leak or airflow problem has been fixed, it's time to clean up the mold. First, vacuum up what you can from the affected areas. Then, wearing a respirator, use a stiff brush to loosen any mold that remains, and vacuum again. Finally, paint over the affected areas with a mold-inhibiting paint. And go tell your friends you've broken the mold!

Before you start—especially if it's been several years since you even *went* into your attic—you should gear up to protect yourself. A ***disposable respirator*** is inexpensive and will protect your lungs from dust, spores, dander, and other nuisances. You may need an ***apron*** to protect your clothes, ***goggles*** to protect your eyes, and ***rubber gloves*** for your hands (latex gloves or something more heavy-duty, depending on the extent of the job). If your attic is already used for storage, make sure everything's organized before you attempt cleaning. This means storing small items in labeled boxes, grouping together boxes that contain like items, and opening up walkways so that you can get to any box in any part of the room.

To actually clean the attic, fire up the ***vacuum cleaner*** and start sucking up dust from the top down—ceiling, beams, walls, and floor. (Wearing the disposable respirator is a good idea in any event, but if you're going the dustpan-and-broom route, it's essential.) If your attic already has things stored in it, don't just clean around the boxes—clean under them, too. Once the major grime has been vanquished, you're ready to give the area a light once-over with a ***damp cleaning cloth*** dipped in a solution of ***water*** and ***mild dishwashing liquid***.

Awnings and Canopies

A grungy awning or canopy can mar your house's curb appeal, which is how real estate brokers refer to the impression your house makes on passersby. Even if you're not selling, curb appeal is important. And even if your canopy is not visible from the road, keeping it clean will help it last longer.

Cleaning acrylic awnings is usually a breeze because most have a soil- and stain-resistant finish. Where necessary, use a *stepladder* to reach the awnings. Spot-wash by applying a solution of *warm water* and *mild dishwashing liquid* with a *sponge*. Rinse thoroughly with *clean water* and air-dry. For stubborn stains, use a *fabric stain remover*, following the directions on the container. Again, rinse well and air-dry.

Mildew on an acrylic awning is usually found not on the fabric itself but on dirt, leaves, and other materials that are not removed from the fabric. Acrylic awnings themselves don't promote the growth of mildew. To remove mildew, mix *1 cup of bleach* with a *squirt of mild dishwashing liquid* in *1 gallon of warm water*. Apply to the entire area and allow it to soak in (but not to dry). Scrub with a *sponge*. Rinse thoroughly and air-dry. Don't use bleach on logos or prints on the awning.

Cleaning vinyl or fabric awnings is usually done with commercial cleaners that work best if you don't wet the awning before cleaning it. On a *stepladder*, if necessary, use a *garden sprayer* to apply *vinyl and fabric cleaner* (such as SkyClean 2 in 1 Vinyl Cleaner & Protectant) evenly in a saturating mist. Start from the bottom of the awning and work up. Before the cleaner dries, scrub the awning with a *sponge or soft- to medium-bristled brush*. (Brushes work best on fabric awnings.) Never use abrasive cleaners or scrubbers. Rinse by spraying with a *garden hose* until the runoff water is clear. You'll want to remove all the cleaner, because leftover cleaner will leave a chalky film once it dries. Don't use a pressure washer to clean your awning. It's ineffective and can cause permanent damage.

Mildew on a vinyl or fabric awning can be removed using a solution of *1 cup of bleach* per *1 gallon of warm water*. Before using the solution, however, test it by rubbing a solution-soaked *cotton swab* on a hidden section of awning to make sure it does not cause the colors to fade or run. Don't let the bleach solution dry on the awning. Rinse completely with water.

b

Baby Equipment

As any new parent can attest, that little bundle of joy is a big bundle of work. Babies require a lot of equipment, and equipment that is properly cleaned places fewer demands on their fledgling immune systems.

Yet it's important to find the right balance between cleanliness and germ phobia. Although careful cleaning is indeed necessary while a baby is building immunity during its first six months of life, it's not necessary to scrub down and sterilize everything in sight. But do be especially meticulous in cleaning any item that ends up in a baby's mouth—bottles, nipples, pacifiers, and utensils used to feed your baby.

Cleaning baby bottles is not as arduous as it used to be. Once upon a time, nervous new parents were told they had to sterilize their newborns' bottles by boiling them in water on the stove. That regimen has relaxed. As soon as Junior has downed his bottle, rinse it out under **running water** so that bacteria are less likely to develop and the bottle will come clean more readily. Wash the bottle and nipple in **hot water** with **dishwashing liquid**, taking special care to remove any caked-on milk in the interior corners and the underside of the nipple. (A **bottle brush** will help a lot.) Force soapy water through the hole in the nipple. Rinse thoroughly with **running water**. Position bottle and nipple in a **clean dish rack or on paper towels** to drain and air-dry.

An alternative: Put the separated bottles and nipples in the **dishwasher**, positioning the bottles upside down and the nipples pointing up so that water does not collect inside. Use **high heat** and the **drying cycle**.

The Hands That *Rock the Cradle*

When it comes to baby hygiene, the pediatrician's clarion call is simple and straightforward: "Wash your hands!"

"That is a very important factor in how disease spreads," says Dr. Marianne Neifert, a board-certified pediatrician and mother of five who's popularly known as Dr. Mom in her parenting books and magazine columns. "I always wash my hands before I handle a baby."

A newborn's immune system starts working on its own at about six weeks. Before that, the sum of a baby's immunity consists of whatever the mother supplied during pregnancy and through breast-feeding. To fend off bacteria, train the entire family to wash their hands before holding the baby, and don't be afraid to ask guests to do the same. Frequent hand washing with soap and water will stop the spread of most common germs. No special antibacterial products are required. And don't forget, Dr. Mom cautions, that hand washing is equally important before preparing a meal and after changing a diaper.

You can store the clean bottles in a cupboard. But in most households with babies, the bottles don't sit still long enough to gather dust.

To keep a changing table clean, place *a couple of clean paper towels* on it before each diaper change to protect the pad from germs. If the mess saturates the paper towels or extends beyond them, clean up with *detergent* or *liquid soap* and *water*. Rinse off the area with *water*, then pour a little *rubbing alcohol* on a *clean cloth* and wipe down the pad and table.

To clean a diaper pail, use a freshly prepared solution of *1/4 cup of bleach* to *1 gallon of water*. Wear *rubber gloves* and rinse well with *running water*. A diaper pail should be a tightly lidded can. Line it with a *plastic bag*. When it's full, tie the top tightly and haul it out to a garbage can.

To clean strollers and high chairs, sprinkle *baking soda* on a *damp paper towel or clean cloth* and wipe down the item, then rinse with *warm water*. (Baking soda is a mild alkali that can make dirt dissolve in water. It acts as a mild abrasive when not totally dissolved.) A sponge is a bad idea for washing the surfaces of baby equipment, because bacteria can become trapped in the sponge and spread to other surfaces the next time it's used.

To clean a crib, use *baking soda* (as described above) to wipe crib rails. Wash baby bed linens in a *washing machine*, using *hot water* to kill bacteria.

To clean baby toys, remember that a lot of plastic and rubber toys will stand up to the rigors of the *dishwasher*. Toss them in regularly to keep microbes or organic material on the toys to a minimum. Wash stuffed animals in a *washing machine*, using *hot water* to kill dust mites.

Backpacks

A little bag of tricks is all you'll need to keep your backpack looking good and staying strong.

Cleaning a book bag or keeping a nylon daypack looking presentable is an uncomplicated task. Just toss it into the *washing machine* on the *gentle cycle* with your regular *laundry detergent*.

Cleaning a hiking backpack is simple, too. But with its stiff frame, a hiking backpack obviously won't fit into a washing machine. Instead, use a *vacuum cleaner* to remove dirt from the zippers and

OOPS!

You Snooze, You Lose Groggy Parents >

This news may save you from a serious meltdown. Baby bottles that are used and cleaned scrupulously day in and day out need not be boiled on the stove, notes Dr. Mark Wiseman, chief of general pediatrics and community health at Children's National Medical Center in Washington, D.C. And a good thing that is. He tells the story of one patient who—weary from the late nights that new parents know so well—dozed off during a bottle-boiling session. The patient awoke to find that the plastic bottle had melted!

simple SOLUTIONS

Keep It Dry >

Whether a backpack is wet from rain or washing, mildew can destroy the fabric. Before you store it, leave it out in the sun or in a dry room until it's completely dry.

seams. Applying *water* will work too, but it's messier. The important thing is not to let the grit build up, because it will damage the zippers and weaken the seams. Always tend to the backpack soon after a hike. Remove the items inside. If there is a food spill or crusted mud, wipe it off with a *damp sponge* dipped in a *bowl of warm water* with a little *dishwashing liquid*. Remove stubborn stains with *spot remover* made for clothing. But there's no need to get carried away: Most hikers view a well-worn backpack as a badge of honor, proving they've walked the walk.

Banisters

A beautiful staircase and banister can be the centerpiece of a home's entrance, so don't let everyday grime diminish its wow factor. It's worth the extra effort to keep it shining.

Dust a painted banister with a *soft, water-dampened cloth*. If it's especially dirty, add a *couple of drops of mild dishwashing liquid* to *warm water*. Then wash and rinse a small section at a time, keeping the cloth well wrung out, and wipe with a *dry cloth*. Oil polish is best avoided on painted wood, since it can cause discoloration. Wax is rarely needed, but if you use it, choose a light-colored wax for light-colored paint.

Dust a wooden banister with a *soft cloth* and *furniture polish*. That'll restore moisture to the wood and keep the dust collected on the cloth from floating back onto the balusters (the posts or spindles that support the banister). When dust collects in the intricacies of the balusters, use a *cotton swab* to clean out the really tight spaces.

To make your own cleaner for banisters or any other woodwork: Mix equal parts of *white vinegar*, *pure turpentine*, and *boiled linseed oil* in a *jar*. Shake the solution well (or it will separate) and wipe it onto the wood with a *cloth*. Rub the cleaner in and be sure to wipe it off. (Otherwise, it will dry sticky.) Leave the cloth to dry outside to avoid the risk of spontaneous combustion.

Barbecue Grills

Outdoor cooking has never been hotter, but before you fire up the grill this year, make sure it's prepared for optimum performance. A clean machine makes for tastier, healthier meals.

To clean a grill, remove the grill grates and clean it inside and out with *2 parts hot water* to *1 part grease-cutting dishwashing liquid*. (With gas grills, you'll need to cover the gas receptacles with *aluminum foil* to prevent water from leaking inside.) Scrub with a *nylon brush* to prevent scratching, follow with a *hot water* rinse, and *towel* dry. Finally, apply *vegetable oil*, using a *clean cloth*, to the grill's outside surface. That'll keep the grill shining and lubricated against the elements.

To clean grates, several methods work well. First scrub them with *a wire brush* and the *hot water and dishwashing liquid* combo described above. If they're too encrusted for elbow grease alone, spray them with *oven cleaner* or coat with a mixture of *2 parts ammonia* and *1 part water*. Place the treated grates in a *garbage bag* lined with *paper towels*, tie the top closed, and stash the bag out of reach of pets and children for a couple of hours or even overnight—powerful chemicals are at work. Take care not to let the chemical cleaner touch any aluminum or painted surface on the grill. When you reopen the bag to remove the grates, point the opening away from your face to avoid inhaling the potent fumes. Thoroughly *hose* off the grates, wipe them down with *hot water* and *dishwashing liquid*, and rinse.

If you have a *self-cleaning oven*, cleanup couldn't be easier. Just put the grill grates in the oven and let the intense heat do the work for you.

When cleaning a gas grill, you need to take these additional cleaning and maintenance steps, suggested by the National Propane Gas Association—especially at the beginning of the grilling season:

The *Thrill* of the Grill

The wood-burning smoker is a favorite with serious grill hounds, and it's the weapon of choice of the Iowa Hawgeyes, who were the 1999 barbecue champions of the World Pork Expo in Des Moines, Iowa.

When competition is fierce, details count—and that includes the proper care and cleaning of the grill itself.

Mike Tucker, who heads the Hawgeyes, based in Ankeny, Iowa, sticks to "primitive methods" to clean the inside of his smoker. "Just build a hot fire in the cooker—hot enough to incinerate everything in there," he says. First, though, he removes the grill's thermometer, because when the inside heats to the required 300° F to 400° F, it can melt nonmetal parts.

His grate-cleaning method is simple, too. Tucker hauls them to the local do-it-yourself car wash and blasts them with a high-pressure hose. "That way, the mess is at the car wash and not at your house."

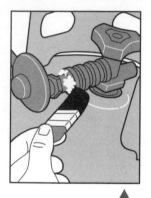

1. For starters, make sure the gas is turned off at the tank before cleaning.
2. Inspect the burners for cracks and corrosion, and if damaged, replace them.
3. Using a *pipe cleaner or nonmetallic bottle brush*, clean the grill's venturi tubes, which carry gas to the burners. These tubes make an excellent hiding spot for spiders, whose nests can block the flow of gas and cause an explosion.
4. Check for leaks in the connector hose. Brush the length of the hose with *soapy water* ◄ and turn on the gas. If you smell gas or see bubbles, turn off the gas, tighten the connections, and repeat the test. If the propane is still leaking—a potentially dangerous problem—you'll need a new hose.

To clean lava rocks, use a *stiff-bristled brush*, or remove the rocks and clean them with a *degreasing cleaner*. As cookouts continue through the summer, turn the lava rocks periodically to burn off the dripped grease.

To cut down on cleanup, burn off grease from the grates and rocks immediately after cooking. Leave the fire turned on for 10 to 15 minutes with the cover closed. Let the grill cool and then scrape away the residue with a *wire brush*. This job will be even easier if you coat the grates with a *nonstick cooking spray* just before you throw on the food.

Now, did you want that burger with or without cheese?

Baseboards

To clean wood baseboards covered with polyurethane or oil-based (gloss or semigloss) paint, remove scuff marks and dirt with a *sponge* and *a grease-cutting all-purpose dishwashing soap*. You can also use a *household spray cleaner*, such as Fantastik, but remember to spray the cleaner on a *cloth* rather than on the baseboard, to prevent streaking. For really tough stains, test an inconspicuous corner with *scouring powder* and a *plastic scrubbing pad*. If it doesn't affect the finish, you can apply the method to the entire baseboard. A general cleaning rule of thumb comes into play here: Use the least aggressive cleaner initially, then resort to more aggressive tactics as the scuffs dictate. Baseboards covered with stain or flat paint require the gentlest cleaning method (*water, dishwashing liquid*, and a *washcloth*).

To clean vinyl or rubber baseboards—more properly called cove molding—spray on a *wax stripper* and let it soak in for a few minutes to loosen old wax and grime. Scrub with a **nylon brush** and rinse. Then, to make the job easier next time, apply a coat of **floor finish**, such as Mop & Glo.

An ounce of prevention can save you a lot of work. Baseboards take a beating in most homes, especially while you're vacuuming carpets or mopping floors. So make sure the rubber bumper guard on your vacuum is fully attached and doing its job. If you use a squeegee mop, check for sharp metal edges that will scar baseboards. And if you use a strong cleaner on floors, quickly wipe away spills and splashes that could discolor baseboards.

Basements

Dealing with a dirty or flooded basement can be the most daunting task on a homeowner's cleaning list. It's hard work and potentially dangerous if mold and mildew are present. Short of calling in the professionals, there aren't many shortcuts.

To clean an unfinished basement, roll up your sleeves, strap on a **dust mask**, and get ready to give those **rubber gloves** a workout. Start by knocking down cobwebs with a **long-handled broom**, then thoroughly sweep the floor and brush away debris from the walls. In a **pail**, mix **hot water** and an **alkaline-based household detergent**, such as Spic and Span, according to label directions. If the walls need cleaning, wash them first, using a **strong-bristled floor brush with a long handle**. Always start at the bottom and work up to prevent streaking. While standing in one spot, wash

The Best-Cellar List

A popular home improvement project is finishing an unfinished basement. Professionals say that converting a cinderblock basement into a family room, office, or guest suite is about one-third the cost of building an addition. When you tackle the renovation yourself, the savings are even more substantial.

Whether you do the work or not, some simple precautions will "save hours and hours of cleanup in the end," says Fred Hightower, owner of Pro Team Construction in Roswell, Georgia.
• To keep dust and dirt from infiltrating the rest of the house, use plastic sheeting and duct tape to seal the stairway from the house to the basement.
• In a new bathroom, put masking tape around fixtures prior to installing drywall. Before grouting a tile floor, mask off the bathtub or shower.
• During construction, change the filters in your furnace and air-conditioning system weekly. Installing drywall and sanding generate a huge amount of dust, which can clog the unit. It's much cheaper to replace filters than to repair or replace a heating or cooling unit.

as much as you can reach, then rinse with **warm water**. Continue until the walls are finished.

Next, scrub the floors, again using hot water and household detergent. Because concrete is porous, strong odors, such as animal waste, can be hard to eradicate. If a strong scrubbing doesn't do the trick, you can seal the floor with a **concrete sealer**, which is stronger than wax. Follow the label directions and spread it on with a **mop**. Repeat the application for really tough odors. After cleaning, open any doors or windows to air out the room and help the drying process.

If mold or mildew is a problem, take an extra step after cleaning. Mop the walls and floors with a solution of **1/2 cup of chlorine bleach** to **2 gallons of water**, then rinse well. Keep in mind that the bleach will kill existing mildew, but the mildew will return unless the source of the moisture problem is addressed.

To clean a finished basement, use the same methods you would use in other rooms in the house. The procedures will vary depending on whether the walls are painted, paneled, or wallpapered and whether the floor is carpeted.

Baskets

Baskets have become a fixture in most homes, whether they're stored in the basement until Easter rolls around or displayed year-round. Either way, their woven construction makes them virtual dust magnets. A few simple cleaning rules can keep you basking in baskets.

To clean an unfinished wicker basket, a gentle **vacuum** is all that's required, since too much moisture will damage the basket. On fragile baskets, though, forego the vacuum cleaner—its suction may be too powerful. Instead, dust a fragile basket with a **damp cloth**.

To clean a varnished or painted basket, start with a gentle **vacuum**. Then use a **spray bottle** filled with **water** and **a tablespoon of vinegar**. The spray allows you to penetrate the small areas between the wickerwork. Wipe the basket dry with a **very soft cloth**, such as a baby diaper or baby washcloth, because they're less likely to get caught on rough edges. Use a **cotton swab** to get to the tight places. Air out the basket in the sun or a dry room, but keep it away from heat sources, which can warp the basket.

To clean most other baskets, use a **vacuum cleaner**, followed by a mild solution of **water** and a bit of **dishwashing liquid** on a **soft**

simple SOLUTIONS

New Life for an Old Basket >

To rescue a worn-looking basket, give it a coat of spray paint. First, check whether small pieces of broken wicker are sticking out. If so, use wire cutters to trim them. Then hang the basket on a metal clothes hanger, attach it to a tree, and spray-paint it. Let it hang there for several hours to dry.

cloth. Apply a **soft brush** if needed for problem spots. Avoid any cleaner with phosphates, which can eventually cause the basket to disintegrate.

Bathtubs

When it comes to spaces that soothe, it's hard to beat the bathtub. But be prepared to take the grit with the glory—maintaining a temple of clean takes regular care.

For everyday care, wipe down the tub after each use with **water** and a **cloth or sponge** to keep stubborn soap scum under control. Staying on top of the problem like this goes a long way, especially considering that most bathtubs today come with dire warnings about the danger of abrasive cleaners. And it's certainly true that if you scrub your way through the tub's protective finish, you'll soon have stains that are embedded in the tub's material—whether it be fiberglass, porcelain, or enamel.

To clean a porcelain tub, make your own simple rub-a-dub formula: Prepare a paste made of **borax** and **water**, dip a **soft scrubber sponge** in it, and scrub away. To polish stainless steel parts of fixtures, gently rub with **baking soda** on a **damp sponge**. Rinse well with **water**.

To remove rust stains, use an **orange oil–based cleaner**, such as Touch of Oranges. When the bathtub is dry, apply a small amount to a **soft scrubber sponge** and rub in a circular motion. The rust stains lift right off. Rinse with **water** and repeat if necessary.

To remove blue-green stains—caused by water with a high copper content—make up a paste: Combine equal amounts of **cream of tartar** and **baking soda** (usually a tablespoon of each is enough) and add some **lemon juice** drop by drop until you have a paste. Rub it into the stain with your **fingers or a soft cloth**. Leave it for half an hour and rinse well with **water**. Repeat if necessary.

Cleaning fiberglass tubs can be difficult because mild cleaners have little impact on a seriously soiled unit and abrasive cleaners applied with too much scrubbing pressure will quickly dull the finish. For everyday cleaning, spray on a **household cleaner** or **tub-and-tile cleaner** and wipe with a **nonabrasive sponge**. If it reaches the point that you have to bring out the big guns, use a **powdered cleaner**, such as Comet, and a **light-duty scrubbing sponge**. Be sure to rinse well with **water** so that the chemicals won't stay on the surface.

WATCH OUT

When using any new cleaning product that you're unsure about, always test it first on an inconspicuous area to see that it doesn't cause damage to the material you are cleaning. And don't mix bathroom cleaners, lest you create a toxic stew with noxious gases. Mixing chlorine bleach with ammonia is particularly dangerous. It's OK to use more than one type of cleaner as long as you rinse well between applications.

Now that you've finished your tub, you're ready to sit back and enjoy a little splendor in the bath.

Beadwork

The ancient craft of beading has taken on a new life in recent years, and the baubles are showing up on everything from vases to blue jeans to picture frames. Some beads are remarkably durable, others quite fragile. So when your beads need a little brightening, follow the doctor's credo: First, do no harm.

Beadwork on casual clothing has become a fashion staple and can be cleaned at home more readily than the fine beading on formalwear, which is best left to professionals. Beads used on jeans and casual wear are typically made of plastic and can usually be put in the *washer* with *mild detergent* on the gentle cycle. Still, it's important to double-check the manufacturer's cleaning instructions on the label.

Loose glass beads are the easiest to deal with. Wash them in a *bowl* of *warm water* and *mild dishwashing liquid*. If the beads are textured, use a *soft toothbrush* to loosen grime in crevices. Then rinse thoroughly with *water* and *towel* dry.

Strung beads are more vulnerable than loose beads, because the thread that holds them all together needs special consideration. Wash a beaded necklace or bracelet in the same solution of *warm water* and *mild dishwashing liquid* in a *bowl*, but don't let the beads soak. Rinse them with *water* immediately after cleaning, pat dry with a *towel*, and leave them lying flat—not hanging, which can stretch the thread—until the thread has had time to dry completely. Or use a *soft toothbrush* that has been dipped in a *bowl of dry baking soda* and brush the beads gently ◀. Then rub them with a *soft cloth*.

Vintage beads require even more caution. Instead of submerging them in soapy water, wipe them gently with a *damp cloth* dipped in a solution of *1 part vinegar* to *4 parts water* and air-dry.

Beams

Exposed beams look good and lend a spacious feel to any room—but it's beauty at a price. Mostly found in cathedral ceilings, beams tower above a conventional ceiling, and reaching those lofty heights is usually the biggest challenge.

simple SOLUTIONS

Glued-on Beads >

Glass beads on a vase or picture frame or ornament can be cleaned with glass cleaner, but remember to spray the cleaner on the cloth instead of directly on the item. Then wipe and air-dry. Harsh solvents can loosen the glue that keeps the beads in place.

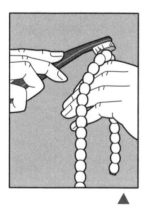

▲

To dust beams, get out your *vacuum cleaner* and its *extension wand*, snap on the *brush attachment*, and get ready for some Michelangelo–like neck stretches. Or you can attach a *lint roller replacement tube* to a *paint roller* and run it across the exposed surfaces. You may need a *stepladder* to reach the higher parts of a cathedral ceiling.

If the beams are really dusty and dirty, you'll need to wash them, which requires using an *extension ladder*. For wood covered with a urethane finish, mix a *mild detergent* with *water*, then wipe and rinse a small section at a time using *washcloths* or, for harder-to-reach areas, a *sponge mop*. Go easy with the water solution—you want to wipe the beams, not drown them. That's especially true when they're unfinished. For those beams, follow the same steps as for finished beams, but omit the detergent and clean only with *water*.

Bedspreads

Laundering a bedspread, particularly if it's large or lofty with batting, can be difficult to do at home. Most home washers and dryers just aren't big enough to accommodate them. So you might want to take your bedspread out for a little drive—to the neighborhood self-service laundry, where washers and dryers are bigger than most home varieties. Before washing a spread, check the care label to make sure it is washable. Pretreat heavily soiled areas with a *prewash product*, such as Shout. Set the *washer* on the highest water level, delicate agitation, and normal spin. Add *detergent* and partially fill the washer's tub with *warm water*. Stop

An Ounce of *Stain Prevention*

Whenever you buy a new bedspread or have one custom-made, keep track of fabric care instructions. Many bedspreads today are sewn from fabric coated with Teflon, Scotchgard, or other stain repellents. These coatings wear off with repeated washings or dry cleanings, says Gina Crill, postsales support specialist with 3M, maker of Scotchgard. Spreads can always be treated again to keep stains at bay. You'll need three cans of Scotchgard to re-treat a standard-size bedspread. (Use the water-based formula.) Some dry cleaners will treat bedspreads at a cost of $20 and up.

If your spread is custom-made, information about the fabric's stain-resistant treatment, if any, is often printed on the fabric edge itself or on the paper bolt the fabric comes on, says Beth Shupe, an in-home consultant with the Calico Corners store in Scottsdale, Arizona.

the washer, add the bedspread and push it down to submerge. Turn on the washer again, finish filling the drum with water, and complete the cycle.

To dry a spread, transfer the spread to the *dryer* and select the setting appropriate for its fabric type. Add a couple of *clean, dry towels*, and then give it the Billie Jean King treatment—toss in several *clean tennis balls* that will knock against the spread to keep its filling from clumping. Stop the dryer twice to make sure the spread isn't getting too hot. Shake it out once, too, to make sure batting doesn't jam in one corner.

To fluff up a candlewick bedspread—that durable, still-popular knotted or tufted kind your grandmother probably fancied—try this nifty approach. Wash as described above, then hang it on an *outside clothesline* in a stiff wind, with the knotted sides facing. The knots will perk up as they rub against one another. Another way to fluff it up: Once your candlewick spread is dry, spread it on a clean floor and sweep with a *pristine broom*.

Belts

If it's going to hold your pants up day in and day out, well, that's an item you want in fine working order. Dry-cleaning or machine-washing a belt is almost always a no-no. This is because fabric belts are usually backed with vinyl, cardboard, or plastic, which can stiffen, crack, or bleed when cleaning solvents are used. An all-fabric belt—one without these backings—can usually be dry-cleaned as long as the buckle isn't metal and the belt is sewn and not glued together. Check the edges of a belt to see how it was made. Grimy or perspiration-stained fabric belts can be spruced up at home, and so can those popular preppy striped men's woven belts. Leather belts are also easily spiffed up at home.

To clean a fabric or woven belt, cover your work area with a *towel* and spread out your belt. In a *bucket*, mix *1/2 cap of gentle fabric cleaner*, such as Woolite, with *1 quart of cool water*. Dampen a *cleaning cloth* with this solution and apply to a small part of the belt's edge to see whether it's colorfast. If the colors don't bleed, carefully dab at the belt, without rubbing, one section at a time. As the cleaning cloth gets dirty, rinse and moisten again with solution. Use *another cloth*, wrung out in water, to rinse and to blot. To dry, blot with a *dry towel* or use a *hair dryer* on the lowest setting. Another tactic: Spread the belt on a towel to air-dry.

If the buckle is metal and got wet in the cleaning process, buff with a *cloth*.

To protect a new leather belt and prolong its life, apply a *leather protector*, one that contains no wax or silicone, according to the package directions. (One brand, Apple Polish, is sold at luggage and shoe stores and at www.applepolishes.com.) Should your belt get dirty or stained, clean it with a *damp sponge or cloth* dabbed in *saddle soap*. Wipe off the excess and buff it to a shine with a *dry cloth*.

Bicycles

Whether your bicycle is a three-speed relic or an expensive mountain bike, keeping it clean makes for longer life, better performance, and an attractive ride. When you wash your bike, always remember to inspect the tires for wear and tear. Bent rims can create small pinches that grow over time if tires aren't properly inflated. So be sure to inflate your tires to recommended levels.

To make cleaning easier, consider buying a *bicycle work stand*. It will stabilize the bike as you wash it and let you take off the wheels if you want. Work stands sell at bike shops starting at about $30. Another alternative: Suspend your bike with *ropes* from a strong, *low-lying tree branch*. If you're concerned about the mess that caked-on mud might make beneath you, work over a *garbage can*. Leaning the bike against a wall is OK, in a pinch, but makes your work more cumbersome and your bike more likely to topple over.

Start cleaning a bike by knocking off any visible dirt with a *stiff-bristled brush*. Then use a *garden hose* on low pressure to rinse your bike. You want the water to trickle out, rather than spray with force, because water under pressure can force grime into the chain and other moving parts. For the same reason, never use a power washer or put your bike through a car wash.

Degrease the drive train next. The hardest bike parts to keep clean are always the chain and the other parts of the drive train—the pedals, derailleur, rear hub, and such—so tackle them first. Protect your hands with *work gloves*. Then apply a *degreaser*, such as Simple Green or WD-40, to a *soft cloth* and clean the chain, a few links at a time. Move the pedals forward to work on a new section of chain. Once you've cleaned the chain, carefully remove it from the chain ring (also called the chain wheel)—the metal wheel whose pointed teeth keep the chain in place. Using a *small screwdriver*, carefully remove any caked-on gunk caught between the teeth. Then slip a cloth between them, rubbing it back and forth as if you were flossing your teeth.

Now wash the entire bike. Use a *big sponge* and *1/4 cup of dishwashing detergent*, such as Joy, mixed in a *bucket* of *warm water*. Don't forget the seat and its underpinnings, handlebars, and handgrips, and be sure not to miss the brake levers and under the fork that connects the handlebars to the frame. Wash the wheel rims and tires. Gently soap the drive train to remove any residue from the degreaser. Rinse the bike completely with a *garden hose* and then ride it in the *work stand* to slough off excess water. *Towel* off the bike and ride it a few blocks to shake off more water. Then towel it off again completely.

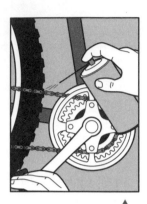

Lubricate the chain with more *WD-40* or an *aerosol lubricant*, such as Boeshield T-9, sold at many bike shops. Turn the crank backward as you spray ◀. Lubricant attracts dirt, so use it sparingly and wipe off the excess with a *soft cloth*.

Wax a clean bicycle for much the same reason that you polish a new pair of shoes. The wax protects the bike and deflects dirt, keeping your ride looking fine. This applies whether you ride through puddles in your neighborhood or wheel down a mountain at breakneck speed.

Bike waxes, available in paste and liquid form, are sold at any cycle shop. Following the instructions, apply *wax* with a *soft cloth*, being careful to hit the bike's various tubes, joints, and other hard-to-reach spots. Or try this easier approach: Spray your

When Your Mojo Isn't Working

Most cyclists don't discover that they've lost their mojo until they do the dirty work of cleaning their two-wheelers themselves or hand over the muddy mess to an expert, says Matt McPeak, an appropriately named bike mechanic who rides the Rockies when he's not cleaning and fixing bikes.

A mojo is a good-luck charm. Superstitious cyclists (there are a lot of 'em, it seems) wire mojos onto their bikes, usually underneath the seat, explains McPeak, a mechanic at the Bike Line Westminster shop outside Denver. A cyclist's mojo is usually a tiny plastic figure, such as a G.I. Joe, a toy dinosaur, or (McPeak's favorite) a pig's head with horns.

Sometimes the mojo falls off and gets lost during a ride or gets chewed to pieces when it falls into the derailleur. An avid cyclist who loses his or her mojo goes nuts, McPeak says, adding that the next time out, the cyclist has "the worst ride" ever.

Maybe a clean machine isn't all it's cracked up to be.

BICYCLES

bike with a common *furniture polish that contains wax*. (Behold and Bee's Wax Old World Formula Furniture Polish are two common types.)

Store your bike in a *dry place* to discourage rust. Never lay a bike on its right side; you could damage the freewheel, chain rings, and derailleurs or throw them out of alignment. Use a *rack* to transport your bike by car, rather than laying it in the back cargo area. After every ride, brush mud and debris off the tires. Wipe dirt and moisture off the frame, seat, handlebars, cranks, and pedals with a *soft cloth*. If the chain is wet, dry it and lubricate it lightly.

Binoculars and Telescopes

There's nothing like a close-up of a tufted dust bunny to spoil a bird-watching outing.

To keep binocular lenses clean, first blow gently on each lens, without spitting, to remove loose debris and dust. Or use a *lens cleaning pen*, which has a soft natural brush at one end and a cleaning tip on the other, to get into the crevices ▶. (Most camera stores carry lens pens, lens tissue, and cleaning fluid.)

Brush off the lens lightly with a *sheet of lens tissue*. With a *clean sheet of lens tissue*, sprayed lightly with *lens cleaning fluid*, wipe the lens with a circular motion. Gentleness is the key here, since rubbing too hard can remove the protective coating. With a *third sheet of lens tissue*, remove the remaining fluid. Repeat with the other lens. Never use your shirttail or facial tissue for this job because their fibers could scratch the coating. Also resist the temptation to use a commercial glass cleaner on your lenses. The ammonia in most glass cleaners will eat away the coating.

To clean the exterior of binoculars, dampen a *soft cloth* with *water* and wipe. Keep rubber eyecups and focus knobs lubricated with a *vinyl* or *rubber preservative,* such as Armor All.

When cleaning a telescope, less is always more. Telescope optics should be cleaned no more than two times a year because their reflective coatings are easily damaged. Carefully remove the mirror from the tube, then use a *camel hair brush*—sold at most camera stores—to remove surface dust and dirt. Dampen a *sheet of lens tissue* with *lens cleaning fluid* (or make your own cleaner using *3 parts isopropyl alcohol* to *2 parts distilled water*). Wipe the mirror, eyepiece, and lenses from the center to the outer edge, using minimal pressure. (Telescope optics are even more

OOPS!

Spit-Free Zone >

Amateur photographer Dave Szymanski was out snapping deer one day when he saw a man nearby spit on the lenses of his expensive Leica binoculars and then use his shirttail to dry them. Szymanski, regional manager for Cutler Camera, a store chain in Wilmington, Delaware, almost dropped his camera at the sight.

"I was horrified," he says. "I told the guy, as calmly as I could, that using his saliva and shirt could really mess up his binoculars."

delicate than binocular lenses and don't take kindly to being rubbed in circles.)

Should the optics collect dew outside, don't wipe them dry. Instead, let them air-dry, then clean with distilled water and lens tissue. (Distilled water leaves no spots.)

To protect your telescope, always use the dust caps. And keep your 'scope inside when not in use to prevent rusting. Most telescopes have an aluminum coating that can last 10 years if it's kept spick-and-span. Before you store a telescope, wipe the outside dry with a soft cleaning cloth.

Birdbaths, Bird Feeders, and Birdhouses

Just as our bathtubs, kitchens, and houses need constant attention to keep them clean, so do the identical spots we set up for our feathered friends. Keep birdbaths, feeders, and houses free of fungi, algae, and bacteria, and those birds will happily return for more. The key here is to team elbow grease with your favorite scrub brush and a tired toothbrush.

Clean a birdbath once a week during warm weather, the busy season for birds of a feather to flock together in the sun-warmed bath you provide. Remember that birdbaths with stale standing water can turn into fertile breeding grounds for mosquito larvae, so the dumping and cleaning of birdbaths is imperative.

First, use a **scrub brush with stiff bristles** and **warm water** to scrub out the birdbath. If the bath has a telltale ring from algae or other deposits or feels slimy to the touch, it's time to get aggressive. Mix a solution of **1 part bleach** to **10 parts water** in a **clean bucket** and use that to scrub the bath. Be sure to wear

Ring Around the Birdbath

Birds don't take kindly to the residue that soap can leave behind in a birdbath, feeder, or house, so reach for the bleach instead. "Bleach won't harm birds, as long as you use it in a weak concentration," explains Gary Slone, assistant director of the Wildlife Care Center at the Audubon Society of Portland, Oregon. "Bleach also breaks down quickly in the environment, so there's no danger there either." The only risk is that bleach can sometimes whiten a wooden bird feeder or house. So don't let either soak in a bleach solution. Instead, rinse thoroughly and swiftly, then dry.

And shy away from treating wooden birdhouses and feeders with any wood preservative containing petroleum distillates. The fumes they emit could harm birds.

BINOCULARS AND TELESCOPES

rubber gloves to protect your hands. (If you don't like the notion of using bleach, mix equal parts of **white vinegar** and **water** and scrub.) Rinse well with **fresh water** and air-dry.

Clean bird feeders every two weeks year-round. This is because birdseed and other bird food get damp and moldy in humid conditions, and the birds feeding at your trough could get sick. Take apart your wooden feeder, if you can. Dust off the pieces with a **wire brush**, then scrub with **warm water** and a **stiff-bristled scrub brush**. If the feeder is really funky, wear **rubber gloves** and mix **1 part bleach** to **10 parts water** in a **clean bucket**. Vigorously scrub inside and out. Rinse thoroughly and then dry. For plastic or metal feeders, brush them out, then rinse with **warm water** and dry with **a soft cloth**. Or let them dry in the sun.

Let's not forget the feeders for nature's little helicopters, hummingbirds. Flush out your feeder every few days during warm weather with **hot water** and replace the stale sugar-water solution inside with fresh stuff. Hummingbirds are susceptible to the diseases that can grow in moldy sugar water.

Clean a birdhouse during cold weather, when birds aren't feathering their nests inside. If the birdhouse has a removable side or top panel, take it off and dip the pieces into a solution of **1 part bleach** to **10 parts water**. Brandishing an **old toothbrush**, dig into the cracks and crevices—this is where feather mites, which feed on bird feathers, often lurk. You don't want these bugs infesting the next generation to take up residence in your birdhouse. To guard against mites, as well as fleas, flies, larvae, and lice, use a **1 percent rotenone powder** or **pyrethrin spray**. (Both are insecticides sold at hardware stores.)

Blankets

Are friends telling you not to wash your blankets? They're all wet! Most blankets, even some wools, can be washed at home. Be sure to check care label instructions before attempting any at-home washing, though. And make certain that your washer and dryer will hold the blanket comfortably. Otherwise, the blanket won't rinse or dry properly. If home equipment is too small, take your blanket to a self-service laundry with a commercial-size washer and dryer.

Before washing a wool blanket, check the label to make sure it is washable. If it isn't, have it dry-cleaned. If it is, measure the blanket and save the measurements for later. Pretreat any spots or stains with **stain remover**, following label directions. If the binding (the narrow fabric along the edges) is really grungy, use a **nylon-bristled scrub brush** to gently scrub it with **1/2 cup of liquid dishwashing detergent** or make a paste of equal parts **mild detergent granules** and **water** and apply it carefully. Gentleness is critical here because the binding could shred if it's old and worn.

To machine-wash a wool blanket, fill the **washer** with **cold water** and a **mild detergent** (Downy, Dreft, or Woolite), letting it agitate for a minute to dissolve the detergent. Add the blanket, distributing it around the agitator and wetting it thoroughly. Allow the blanket to soak for 15 minutes, then start the washer again and allow the washing cycle to complete. Spin the blanket one minute, then push the timer forward to the deep rinse cycle. Allow the washer to finish its cycle.

To hand-wash a wool blanket—if your blanket won't fit into a washer, or you just hanker for a messier alternative—fill the **bathtub** with **cold water** and add **1/4 cup of mild laundry detergent or 1 teaspoon of liquid dishwashing detergent**. Put the blanket in and press down to wash. To rinse, fill the tub several times with **fresh, cool water**. Squeeze out—but don't wring!—excess water by rolling up your sodden blanket in **two or three large white towels**.

To dry a wool blanket, you have several drying options:
● Use your **dryer** with the *No Heat* setting.
● Spread out **dry towels** atop a shady **picnic table**, flatten the blanket out on them, and stretch it to its original shape, using the measurements you saved.
● Hang the blanket over **two tightly strung clotheslines** that won't droop under the blanket's weight.

If you chose the second or third approaches, plump up the blanket afterward in the **dryer** on the *No Heat* setting.

To clean a nylon flock blanket—Vellux is the most common brand—put it in the **washer** in **warm water** and **laundry detergent**. Dry in the **dryer** on medium heat. Remove pronto. Never dry-clean a nylon flock blanket—never spot-clean it, for that matter. Cleaning solvents can eat away the two thin layers of polyurethane foam inside the velvety exterior. (Mothballs have the same effect, so never store nylon flock blankets anywhere near them.)

To clean a cotton or acrylic blanket, it's just fine to launder it. Wash the blanket in a **washer** with **cold water** as part of a normal load, being careful not to overload the drum. Dry a knitted cotton blanket in a **dryer** on low heat so it won't pill. For other cotton blankets, the regular setting is OK. Or you can hang a cotton blanket from a taut **clothesline** to dry. Tumble-dry an acrylic blanket on low heat.

Blinds

Blinds are like miniature dust-collecting shelves. Ignore them, and you'll have an entire dust library in no time. Don't worry— we'll pull a few strings to make the cleanup easy.

To dust your blinds, use the **brush attachment** on your **vacuum cleaner** and adjust the blinds to expose the flat surface. Then, from top to bottom and left to right, vacuum the entire surface. Reverse the slats and repeat. Other options:

- Use a **lamb's wool duster** to clean the slats.
- Rub an **old paintbrush** along each slat.
- Saturate a **cloth** with **rubbing alcohol** and wrap it around a **rubber spatula**, which you then stick between the open slats to dust.
- Wear an old pair of **thick absorbent cloth gloves** and wipe the slats by hand ▶.

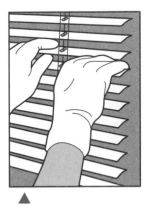

▲

Blinds made of natural materials can be damaged by water.

- Parchment, paper, or rice paper should not get wet at all. Clean them as you would nonwashable wallpaper—with **commercial cleaning putty** or an **art gum eraser**. Or find a **spot remover** that claims to work on the material at hand and test it on an inconspicuous area first.
- Wood and bamboo blinds should not be immersed in water. Wipe them down with a **damp rag** soaked in a solution of **liquid dishwashing detergent** and **water**. Then dry them quickly with a **fresh rag**.

Washing aluminum and vinyl blinds is fine, but don't use harsh cleaners or abrasives on them. And don't use any cleaner with ammonia on aluminum, because it will damage the finish. To clean aluminum or vinyl blinds, you have a couple of choices: You can wash them right where they're hanging, or you can treat them to a stint in the shower or tub.

- To wash blinds while they're on your windows, mix **2 ounces of trisodium phosphate** (a concentrated cleaner sold at hardware stores) in a **bucket** of **clean water**. Protect your eyes with **goggles** and put on **rubber gloves** and a **long-sleeved shirt**. Wipe down the blinds with a **soft rag** dipped in the mixture, then dry them with **another soft cloth**.

simple SOLUTIONS

Backyard Spritzer >

If your blinds are washable, why not spritz them off outside on a nice day? Spread an old shower curtain or piece of plastic on a level part of your driveway, open the blinds, and spray them with a garden hose. Then use either of the washing solutions mentioned here to clean the slats with gloved fingers. Rinse thoroughly. Dry with clean towels, or air-dry.

- To give blinds a bath, raise the blinds, unlock the brackets at the top, and remove them from the holder. Run enough **warm water** in the **tub** to cover the blinds and add **1 to 2 cups of powdered dishwasher detergent**. Protecting your hands with **rubber gloves**, place the blinds in the water and extend them. Dip the blinds several times to loosen grime. Then let them soak for five minutes. Use your gloved fingers to clean both sides of each slat. Drain the dirty water and either rinse the blinds in **another tubful of water** or give them a spritz in the **shower**. Spread out the blinds on a **clean towel** and blot with **another towel**. When the blinds are completely dry, spray them with an **antistatic aerosol spray**, such as Static Guard, or **wipe fabric softener** sheets on each slat. This keeps them from attracting dust, hair, bugs, and other yucky stuff.

Bloodstains

"Out, damned spot! Out, I say!" cried Lady Macbeth, fretting over imaginary blood on her hands. Real bloodstains are just as hard to get out, but don't despair! There are several effective methods—some of them quite surprising—that will do the job.

Keep in mind these three points when you have a bloodstain to clean up:
- Tackle a bloodstain as quickly as possible. The stain is much harder to remove as the blood dries.
- Always use **cold water** to flush a bloodstain, because any kind of warmth, be it from water or from a clothes dryer, could set the stain.
- Refrain from scrubbing too vigorously. Otherwise, you'll leach the stain into the clean fabric that surrounds it.

For blood spilled on clothing, first blot the stain with **cold water** on a **clean rag**. Don't rub. If the stain persists, mix a **few drops of liquid dishwashing detergent** with **1 cup of cold water** in a **bowl** and dab this on the stain, allowing it to set for at least 10 minutes. Rinse by blotting again with a **clean rag** wrung out in **cold water**. Use a **dry rag** to blot it dry. If the stain won't come out, add a **splash of ammonia** to the detergent mixture and try, try again.

Here are some other methods for removing bloodstains from garments:
- Hydrogen peroxide can work wonders on garment bloodstains, but only if the garment is white or otherwise colorfast. (Test the fabric first by dabbing peroxide on a cotton swab,

then on an inconspicuous area.) Spread out the stained area over a **sink** or **laundry tub** and pour **full-strength hydrogen peroxide** through the stain. Scrub gently with a **scrub brush** or an **old toothbrush**. Rinse with **cold water**.

- A tactic your grandmother probably used: Mix **1/2 teaspoon of table salt** with **1/2 cup of water**. Pour the water on the stain and allow it to dry. Rinse thoroughly with **fresh water**.

- Still another technique: Use **an oxygen alkaline stain remover**, such as OxiClean, on fabric that you know to be colorfast. Make a paste of 1 scoop of OxiClean to 1 cup of water. Scrub this into the stain, let it dry for two hours, and then rinse with cold water.

- In a pinch, and right after a bloodstain occurs, pour **club soda** through it or dab and blot carefully with a **clean rag**.

For bloodstains on washable upholstery, cover a fresh spot as soon as possible with a paste made from equal parts **cornstarch** and **cold water**. Rub gently and dry in the sun, where the blood should leach onto the cornstarch. **Brush** lightly. If this doesn't work, try the technique a second time. Or make a similar paste with **cornmeal** and **water** or **talcum powder** and **water** and follow the same procedure.

For bloodstains on carpeting, cover the stain with equal parts **meat tenderizer** and **cold water**. Let this sit for 30 minutes. Then **sponge** it off with **cold water**. Or sprinkle a carpet stain with **table salt**, then with **cold water**. Gently blot with a **clean cloth** and wipe with a **sponge**.

For bloodstains on cotton bedding as well as clothing, an unlikely but often effective method is to use shampoo. The key here, as always, is to attack the stain right away. Douse it with a **capful of**

Spit and *Polish*

When nothing else is handy, police officer Will James recommends using your own saliva to eradicate small bloodstains. For small stains, thoroughly wet a piece of string or thread in your mouth and use it to blot at the stain. For larger spots, saturate a cotton ball or the edge of a clean rag with your saliva and blot.

James is putting his knowledge about bloodstains to work. An eight-year veteran of the Lower Pottsgrove Township Police Department in suburban Philadelphia, James recently started J-Tech Bio-Recovery, a company that cleans up bloody crime and natural death scenes and other places where blood and bodily fluids spill.

Another of his tips: Use full-strength toothpaste—the white kind, not a colored gel—on bloodstains. Dab it on the stain and wipe up with cold water on a fresh rag.

shampoo (any kind will do), making certain the shampoo covers every bit of the stain. Rub the area until the shampoo is completely absorbed, then wet with **cold water**. Once those telltale bubbles appear, scrub vigorously with a **stiff-bristled nylon scrub brush**. Rinse the stain in **cold water**. If a ring remains, repeat.

Boats

Buoy your spirits by washing that dirty boat.

When washing a wooden boat, you have to be careful. Most are painted, and solvents or abrasives can eat through the paint. Use a mild, biodegradable detergent, such as Wisk or Meguiar's Boat/RV Gel Wash, available at marinas. Dissolve *1 cup of detergent* in a **bucket** of **water** and use a **large sponge** to clean your boat from stem to stern, preferably when it's out of the water. If dirt is particularly stubborn, use a **cleaning pad** with a bit of scratch to it, such as one of the gentler Scotch-Brite pads. (Look for the "light duty" label.) To keep bare teak boats sparkling, mix *1 part ammonia* to *10 parts water* in a **bucket**. Scrub with a **soft-bristled nylon brush**.

To wash a fiberglass boat, the tools of choice are good old soapy water—**mild, biodegradable detergent** in a **bucket** of **warm water**—and a **large sponge**. When attacking stubborn crud or greasy stains, avoid using solvents such as lacquer thinner or acetone, which could etch the tender fiberglass surface. Instead, use **mineral spirits** (paint thinner) on tough dirt, dabbed on a **soft cloth**. Thoroughly rinse the boat with **water**. Use **marine wax**, sold at marinas, as directed to rewax any spots where the wax has worn off. Always wax your boat with marine wax before you store it for cold weather.

To wash a polyethylene vessel—canoes, kayaks, and other small boats today are sometimes made of this durable yet pliable plastic—give it the standard mild-detergent-and-water treatment described above. If you have obstinate stains, apply a touch of **mineral spirits or acetone** on a **soft cloth**. If these don't work, and only as a last resort, use a smidgen of **lacquer thinner** on a **soft cloth** to remove a stain.

Wash your painted aluminum boat as you would a painted wooden one. (See instructions above.) If your vessel is unpainted, consider it almost indestructible. That means that you can use a strong solvent, such as **lacquer thinner or mineral spirits**, to remove hardened grit.

BLOODSTAINS

Books

For a cultured person such as yourself, the only kind of dirty books you'll ever be concerned with are the sort that are gathering dust on a forgotten shelf or get splashed with mud on the way home from school.

To clean books, it's best to just dust them, using a *vacuum cleaner* armed with its *soft brush attachment* ▶ or wielding a *feather duster*. Or dip a *clean rag* in *water*, wring it out, wipe the books, and then dry with *another rag*. If the cover of a book is smudged with fingerprints or smeared with food, use a *damp rag* to remove spots. If you need more cleaning power, mix *1/2 cup of mild detergent*, such as Dreft or Ivory Snow, in a *bucket* of *cool water* and test it on an inconspicuous spot. (Sometimes covers will come apart if you use too much soap and water, so it's best to test first.) For a cover that appears safe, wipe with a *rag* slightly dampened with the detergent solution, then dry with a *soft cloth*.

Can't stand that grimy paperback cover? Use a *soft eraser* to clean it up. But be careful: Too much pressure can rub off some colored inks.

A technique favored by booksellers: Use *Talas Clean-Cover Gel* on cloth or paper covers (available at http://talasonline.net). Follow the directions on the jar.

When cleaning leatherbound volumes, use restraint. Try wiping with a *clean cloth* first, or use the *vacuum* to remove visible dust. Fine booksellers sell leather cover cleaners, but be careful: Some conservationists no longer favor using products that contain neat's-foot oil, lanolin, or other oils that can permanently darken or stain the cover and give it a greasy feel. Another consideration is that leatherbound books treated with oil tend to mold when they're jammed in a bookcase.

expert advice

A Book Fan >

Book conservationist David Baldwin of West Chester, Pennsylvania, favors this technique for freshening a musty book: Set up an oscillating fan nearby and open the book so that its pages rustle as the fan sweeps over it. Once the book is dry to the touch, sprinkle the pages liberally with medicated baby powder. Use a soft brush to remove any excess.

Boots

Many boots come with a protective coating that keeps them shiny bright until they take that first step outdoors. But in most cases the coating will wear off, so that dirt and grime can work their way in, clogging the pores that allow the boot to breathe and dry and breaking down seams as well as the leather or fabric itself.

To dislodge dirt, first bang your boots together. Then wipe off surface grime and dust with a *damp cloth*, paying special attention to creases and wrinkles. Dive into those stubborn stitched areas with a **dry, stiff nylon brush or an old toothbrush**.

To clean a boot, close the zipper on the boot (if it has one). Wet the **nylon brush** and rub it on one side of a **bar of soap**. Then scrub down the zipper channel. Wipe it dry with a **soft cloth**. Then undo the zipper and, using a dry corner of the soap bar, rub down each side of the zipper to lubricate it for an easy slide. Wipe off the excess with a **soft, dry cloth**.

For a smooth finish, get rid of the old wax or factory coating. Using either **saddle soap or a fabric cleaner,** such as Woolite, and a **dry cloth**, rub the entire outside in small circles until stains disappear. Stuff the boots with **crumpled newspaper** and let them dry at room temperature. Ready for polish!

If you have salt stains on your boots, get rid of them fast—salt breaks down leather and fiber. Pick up a **calcium neutralizer product** from a shoe store or leather shop and follow the package directions to get rid of those wavy white lines. If it doesn't do the trick immediately, let it dry. Then spritz some **water** on the stains and reapply the **neutralizer**.

simple SOLUTIONS

Scuffs Aren't So Tough >

Here's how to give scuff marks the boot. They often come right off with a few swipes of a pencil eraser. For more stubborn scuffs, mix 1/5 cup ammonia with 1 cup water and 1 cup rubbing alcohol. Use a soft cloth to gently rub the solution into the scuff mark until it disappears.

Bottles

Cleaning the outside of an ordinary bottle is as simple as any other glass-cleaning task. The real challenge, of course, is removing gunk from the inside—unless you happen to have a Lilliputian cleaning crew.

To scrub the outside of a bottle, use **warm water** and **dishwashing liquid**. Mildly abrasive **dishwashing pads** are fine for use on modern glass. If the glass is pre-20th century, use **copper wool pads** (not just copper *colored* pads).

To remove hardened residue inside, let the bottle stand full of soapy water (**warm water** and **dishwashing liquid**) for several hours, until the residue softens and can be loosened by shaking or by use of a **bottle brush**. If dirt still remains inside the bottle, here are two ways to provide a little extra help:

● Pour a **thimbleful of uncooked rice or sand** into the bottle ◀, fill it again with **warm, soapy water**, and shake.
● Fill the bottle with **water** and drop in a **denture-cleaning tablet**.

A tough white crust can build up inside a bottle that has held water for a long time. You may be able to remove this by filling the bottle with a **cleaner designed for vanquishing mineral deposits**. Lime-A-Way is a good bet.

BOOTS

Another kind of white hazing is tougher to deal with—etching, caused by some elements of the glass leaching away after long exposure to liquid. A cure for etching is beyond the ability of the average Jane or Joe, unless you want to fork over hundreds of dollars for an exotic tumbler machine. Professional bottle cleaners (yes, they exist) will do the job for $10 or more per bottle. So think seriously about the value of that bottle.

See also **Baby Equipment** *(for baby bottles) and* **Decanters**.

Brass

Let's get down to brass tacks. There are two kinds of brass to consider—brass with a protective lacquer coating (most common) and raw brass. Raw brass is the bigger challenge to care for, since this copper-and-zinc alloy oxidizes when it is exposed to air, resulting in tarnish. Removing tarnish from raw brass requires some elbow grease.

To remove dirt from lacquered brass, mix *mild dishwashing liquid* (such as Dawn) with *warm water* and apply it with a *nonabrasive sponge or cloth*. Rinse with *fresh water* and dry thoroughly with a *soft cloth*. Buff with an *extremely soft cloth* (cloth diapers are recommended) or *chamois*. Avoid terry cloth and paper towels, because they will scratch the surface.

To remove tarnish from raw brass, take a tip from antique dealers and the military: Use a *metal polish* like Brasso, which contains cleaners to eliminate the tarnish, abrasives for polishing, and oil to protect the brass from the air. Follow the instructions on the package. Use only a thin layer of metal polish—more is not better.

simple SOLUTIONS

Getting a Sticker Off >
To remove a sticker from brass, don't attempt to scrape it off—this could damage the finish. Apply rubbing alcohol or Bestine Solvent and Thinner (available at art supply stores) to a cloth diaper. Wipe the solvent onto the sticker and let it sit for a few seconds. Then wipe the sticker and its gummy adhesive away. Buff with a clean diaper.

When Life Hands You Tarnish, *Use Lemons*

When a commercial brass cleaner isn't available for removing tarnish from raw brass, Michael Supranowitz gets dazzling results with a squeeze play. The owner of Handyman Services in New York City, Supranowitz slices a lemon in half, sprinkles the cut surface with salt, and then squeezes the lemon over the brass that needs cleaning. He wipes down the brass with one soft cloth and then buffs the brass with a second soft cloth. The technique works equally well with lacquered and raw brass.

An alternative: Make a paste of baking soda and water (or just use toothpaste, also a mild abrasive). Apply the paste to a soft cloth and then rub the brass. Wipe clean with a fresh cloth.

Once it's clean, rub unlacquered brass with a light coating of mineral oil, olive oil, or lemon oil to protect it from further tarnish. Lacquered brass doesn't need this protection.

To keep your unlacquered brass gleaming, you will need to polish it every few months.

To spiff up soot-grimed brass fireplace equipment, the aforementioned cleaning techniques may not be sufficient. If so, try rubbing the brass with **extra-fine steel wool (0000) or very fine emery cloth**. Careful, you're in abrasive territory now. Rub the metal in one direction only—not with a circular motion. Once the brass is clean, follow up with a commercial **brass polish**.

Brick

Exposed interior brick can be cleaned by simply putting the **brush attachment** on your **vacuum cleaner** and running it over the wall. The brush will loosen the dust and dirt, and the vacuum will suck it up.

On exterior brick that stays damp and shaded, mold, mildew, and algae are commonly a problem. To kill and remove the growth, mix **1 ounce of bleach** with **1 quart of water** in a **bucket**. If you find you need more strength, increase the bleach. Wearing **rubber gloves**, dip a **stiff-bristled brush (not metal)** in the solution and scrub the brick. To rinse, **hose** the brick down with fresh water.

simple SOLUTIONS

Cleaning Under Pressure >

A high-pressure hose can work magic in cleaning brick, but be careful—the pressure can damage both mortar and bricks, especially bricks with a sand finish. Use a low setting and keep the nozzle 2 feet from the wall. Aim for the brick, not the mortar.

For cleaning dingy brick, some masonry professionals swear by lye, an oven cleaner like Easy-Off, or a drain opener like Drano. These are extremely harsh substances, so wear **rubber gloves**, **long sleeves**, and **protective goggles**. Oven cleaner, which comes in an aerosol container, is easiest to work with. To use, spray on **full strength oven cleaner**. Lye and drain opener come in crystallized form. To use, pour **3 tablespoons of lye or drain opener crystals** into a **bucket** and add **1 gallon of water**. (This way you don't have to do any mixing.) Apply the solution with an old rag. Whichever cleaner you are using, let it sit for 15 minutes and follow up with a **scrub brush**. Apply the cleaner again if necessary and scrub once more. Rinse with water.

To brighten soot-stained brick, try this old masonry trick. Mix **20 ounces of a cola soft drink** (its acid adds cleaning muscle), **1/2 cup of a household cleaner** such as Spic and Span, and **1 gallon of water** in a **bucket**. **Sponge** the solution onto the sooty brick and let it sit for 15 minutes. Scrub with a **stiff-bristled brush** to loosen the soot. Rinse with a **clean sponge** and **fresh water**. (Outside, use a **hose**.) To make the solution more powerful, add more cola. An alternative: Buy a **commercial soot remover** from a store that sells fireplace gear, follow the product's directions, and save the cola to quench your thirst on a hot day.

Bridal Gowns

Unless your gown is wash-and-wear, never try to clean it yourself. Granted, a lot can happen between the alterations and the altar, and it usually happens when you're dressed and ready to walk down the aisle. But if you have an emergency kit for those last-minute accidents, a spill won't spoil your day.

To fix a last-minute stain, don't use spot cleaner on your gown. Just leave that can at home. If you're lucky, it might—might—remove the spot, but it also will damage the fabric. If you're going to use hair spray, apply it before you don the your dress. Nothing dulls beading like hair spray.

● If clumsy feet leave scuff marks along the bottom of the gown, make like a schoolmarm and mark over them with a *piece of white chalk*.

● Accidental spots or spills? *Talcum powder* will disguise them. Just sprinkle some talc on the spots and let it absorb the moisture. Barely noticeable.

● Whether a little dribble or a major spill has marred your gown, *club soda* is your best friend. It helps to treat any spills or spots immediately—they will only be more difficult later. Depending on the location of the stain, you might have to undress and dress all over again. Working from the inside out, use a *man's dry handkerchief* to blot up as much of the stain as possible. Be sure to dab, not rub. Then wet the handkerchief with the club soda and, again from the inside, dab, don't rub.

If the gown needs a final touch-up, press only on the inside of the gown. And don't use steam. If the fabric hasn't been prewashed, steam can create spotting or a color change. Place a *dry handkerchief* between the *iron* and the gown. (You don't want to use a towel, because terry cloth can leave lint.) Then press in a downward direction. Don't move the iron back and forth—it destroys fibers. Press one area, then move the cloth to another.

When the honeymoon is over, don't put off taking your gown to the *dry cleaner*. You might want to hand it down to someone or even sell it, and without the proper care, your once-priceless wedding gown will become yellow and useless to anyone else.

First, take off any easily removable trim and shoulder pads. Then search out those devilish spots that you so glibly ignored

expert advice

A Slick Way to Save the Day >

It's inevitable. Aunt Sally, who wears too much makeup, will make her way—rouged, lipsticked, and powdered—to your wedding gown. And she'll most likely smudge you with a kiss or a hug just before pictures are taken. With this little tip from Edwin Wudyka, owner of Huntington Cleaners outside Detroit, you'll be ready when Aunt Sally puts her head on your shoulder.

Dry cleaners use a formula they call "paint-oil-grease" because that's what it removes. But if there's no time for dry cleaning—the photographer is waiting—take a can of WD-40 ("Nothing else," warns Wudyka) and spray a very light mist of the lubricant on a cloth. Then dab—don't rub—with the cloth to remove the makeup stain.

while you were whooping it up at the reception. Dry cleaning usually removes the obvious—makeup, grass stains, food spills—but you may also have gotten some invisible spills (Champagne is a classic) that show up later. If you can remember where they are, give the dry cleaner a heads up. Otherwise, when your gown is preserved and stored, the Champagne stains will be, too.

When you store your gown, don't put it in plastic or expose it to sunlight. Instead, ask the dry cleaner to wrap your gown in *acid-free tissue* and store it in an *acid-free box*. This is the best way to slow the aging process.

Briefcases

To clean the inside, empty the briefcase and shake it over a trash can to get rid of broken pencil leads, scraps of paper, and the grit and grime that accumulate in offices, airports, and the trunks of cars. Vacuum out everything else, using a *hand vacuum cleaner or the crevice attachment of a regular vacuum cleaner*. Use a spritzer bottle of *water* to lightly spray the lining. Pour a little *laundry or dishwashing detergent* on a *small terry cloth towel* and rub lightly on any persistent stains. Immediately wipe the lining with a *dry cloth*. Don't close the case—let it air-dry.

To clean the outside, use a *liquid saddle soap* or put *a couple of drops of detergent* in a *small bowl of warm water*. Swirl to create some bubbles. Dip a *washcloth* in the water and quickly wipe down the briefcase. If your briefcase has a zipper, take a *dry bar of soap* and rub it down the zipper. It will clean and lubricate the zipper at the same time. Remove excess soap by wiping with a *dry washcloth*.

Brocade

Brocade isn't just a fabric. It's a combination of fabrics woven into a raised design. So when attempting to clean it, you must take into consideration the fabric contents of the weave. Brocade can be made of wool, cotton, silk, synthetic fiber, or any combination thereof. The cleaning depends on the fiber. But an on-the-spot remedy often does the trick.

Removing a stain from brocade is an inside job. First, remove as much of the stain as possible by lifting it off with a *dull-edged knife*, such as a dinner knife. Don't treat the remaining stain from the top, or you'll just work the stain into the fibers. Force the stain out from the back by placing the fabric, stain-side down, on an **absorbent terry cloth towel**. **Club soda** will help lift the stain. But if you don't have any, use **lukewarm tap water**. Pour a little on a **paper towel** and dab it on the stain, forcing it onto the terry cloth towel. Dab a spot, then move to another spot and dab again. Keep dabbing until the stain disappears.

Bronze

Artists with specialty paints can re-create the look of weathered bronze in a faux finish called verdigris, which is very popular and can be costly. But if you're patient, real bronze will do the job all by itself. With time, bronze creates its own protective patina—a pretty, earthy green color. But with the no-cost natural process, you still have to clean it, and you must be careful to remove all residue of water. Lingering moisture and even plain old grit can degrade bronze. If you lose a little of the patina during the cleaning process, don't worry—it will keep coming back like a, well, good penny.

To clean bronze, remember that, in essence, you're cleaning two different metals at once. An alloy, bronze is a combination of copper and any other metal except zinc. Like any decorative surface that is exposed to the environment, bronze can accumulate a layer of film or dust (or dusty film) that needs removing. First, wipe away any loose or surface dirt with a **soft cloth**, then go at it again with a **soft toothbrush** to get into crevices and ornamental work that are more difficult to reach.

Wipe Lightly and Carry a *Soft Cloth*

You can buy bronze with a factory-finish lacquer, which will protect it from changes in color as well as corrosion. Never apply a chemical cleanser to lacquered bronze. A weekly swipe with a damp cloth will keep it in good shape. Linda Cobb, the Queen of Clean and author of *How the Queen Cleans Anything*, recommends using a damp microfiber cloth, and she prefers the Act Natural brand. "It's like thousands of scrubbing fingers that remove dirt," she says. Best of all, you might not have to polish, because the microfiber cloth actually polishes as it cleans.

Lacquer, like luster, doesn't last forever. If it begins to crack or peel, Cobb recommends a fresh coat (a job for a professional metalworker). Otherwise, weather and dampness will creep in and corrode the bronze beneath. Regular dusting with a soft cloth is considered good maintenance. But don't rub too vigorously. Just wipe, especially if there are any decorative projections.

For a more thorough cleaning, carefully wash the bronze with a solution of *1 tablespoon salt* dissolved into *3 1/2 quarts of water*. For the toughest grime, dissolve *1 teaspoon of salt in 1 cup of white vinegar*, then add enough *flour* to make a paste. Let it sit on the bronze for 15 minutes to an hour. Rinse with clean, *warm water*. Be sure to *towel-dry* the piece thoroughly, because moisture and salt by themselves can degrade the bronze. Imagine the damage lingering salty water could do!

Burns

If your clothing has a burn mark, most professional cleaners will tell you that you're sunk; reweaving by a professional is your only option. That may be true. But what if you're going to meet your future in-laws for the first time and your spouse-to-be lands red-hot cigarette ash on your jacket? Here's an easy quick fix that will get you through dinner.

1. Lay the garment on a *table* with the lining facing up. With *scissors*, snip a couple of inches of lining loose at the seam. Snip only as much as is necessary to find the garment seam underneath. Then cut a small piece of the garment fabric, approximately the size of the burn, from the inside seam.

2. Locate the burn on the inside of the garment. Take a piece of *duct tape*, large enough to cover the burn amply, and apply the tape to the burn on the inside of the clothing. With a *needle and thread*, sew the lining back into place temporarily with long, loose stitches. Turn the garment over to see the burn from the outside.

3. Using your scissors, snip the small piece of garment seam fabric into the smallest pieces you can. You want the cut-up fabric to look as much like fibers as possible. Then press the "fibers" into the burn so that they adhere to the duct tape underneath ◄. It won't have the same seamless effect as reweaving, but you'll likely be the only one to know there's a burn.

For burns on upholstery, cross your fingers. If the burn didn't completely penetrate the fabric, you might be able to disguise the scorch mark. Wet a *paper towel* with *plain water* and dab it on the burn. Be careful not to rub or you'll damage the fibers further. Blot with a *dry paper towel*. If that doesn't take most of the charred spot out, put a drop of *mild liquid laundry detergent* on a *wet paper towel* and blot the spot. Follow up by blotting with first a *wet paper towel* to remove the detergent and then with a *dry paper towel* to absorb the char stain.

For more serious charring or burn holes, there's not much you can do beyond patching the fabric, which probably won't be pretty. Take the furniture to a restorer to discuss whether it would be cost-effective to re-cover the piece.

If your upholstery is fake leather, you may be able to fix burns with a **hole-patching kit**, available at hardware stores and auto supply stores. This repair will involve spreading a colored paste over the hole and letting it dry. Follow the package directions.

With burns on wood floors and furniture, there's a little more hope. If the burn isn't all the way through the wood, you might be able to remove enough of the burn to make it unnoticeable.

- If the burn is small, use a **cotton swab** to apply a little **turpentine** to it. If char remains, rub lightly with some **superfine steel wool (0000)**. If your handiwork leaves a small indentation in the surface, fill it in with **clear nail polish**. You might need to apply several layers of nail polish to build up the surface until it is level and smooth.
- If the burn is mostly just a scorch, you might find that a little bit of **rubbing alcohol** works a lot of magic. Put a little on a **soft cloth** and dab it on the scorch. It will dry quickly, but wipe away any residual moisture. Repeat the process until you are satisfied. If you don't have rubbing alcohol on hand, heavily sprinkle **dry baking soda** on a **wet sponge** and rub in small circular motions until the char disappears.
- If it's burned beyond a scorch but not too deeply into the surface, you might do a cosmetic fix using a thin paste of **cigarette ashes** mixed with a little **mineral oil**. With a soft cloth, gently rub in the direction of the grain. Do that twice and follow with coats of **clear nail polish** as described above.

Butcher Blocks

Ask a professional chef how to clean a butcher block that has a protective coating, and he or she will tell you to take it to the dump. Varnish or polyurethane should never be an ingredient in food preparation.

The first step in keeping an unvarnished butcher block like new is to season it when you first bring it home and regularly thereafter. To season a butcher block, warm a little **mineral oil** in a small **saucepan** on the **stove**. Don't let it get hot—warm will penetrate the wood nicely. Using a **soft cloth** dabbed into the oil, rub in the direction of the grain. Let the oil soak in for four or five hours, then wipe off any excess using a **soft, dry cloth**. Repeat the process. Seasoning your butcher block once a month sets the stage for a clean, sanitary work surface.

To clean a butcher block, don't *ever* use any household chemical cleaners. They could be harmful and, at the least, the residue will be distasteful on food. All you need to keep those prep surfaces sanitary is *1/2 tablespoon of chlorine household bleach* mixed with *2 quarts of water* in a *bucket*. Dip a *small scrub brush* in the chlorine water and scrub in hand-sized circles, taking care not to saturate the wood. When wood absorbs water, it swells. Then, when it dries out, the wood cracks, making a convenient trap for food, grime, and germs. So brush the butcher block clean and quickly wipe away water with a *hand towel*.

When bleach isn't in the pantry, here's another solution to getting the grime out of a butcher block without wetting the wood too much: Mix just enough *salt* into *lemon juice* to make a paste. Rub it, with a *cleaning cloth or sponge*, hard enough onto the wood to free those stuck-on or wedged-in food particles. Then rinse out the cloth or sponge and wipe the butcher block clean. The result won't be as germ-free clean as cleaning with bleach, but it's a good alternative.

If the surface is oily or sticky, even after a brisk scrub, you might need to get out the toolbox. Scrape up any buildup with a *putty knife*. Then gently attack the block with *superfine sandpaper*, beginning with a 60-grit. Graduate to finer grades of sandpaper—all the way to 220 grit—until you're satisfied. Then wipe clean with a *damp cloth or sponge*.

Finally, don't forget to season the block again. Some say linseed oil will do, but chefs prefer mineral oil, because it won't turn rancid.

Buttons

Before beginning, make sure you know what your buttons are made of. You don't want to put strong metal polish on buttons with a gold or silver finish. And you never want to use shoe polish on buttons—body heat could transfer the polish to the garment. If your buttons are covered with the same fabric as the garment, or if they're plastic, care for the buttons the way you would for the garment.

To clean leather buttons, remove them from the garment. While a wool sweater might make it through a machine wash, leather and some other natural button materials won't. *Saddle soap or a* *leather cleaning and conditioning solution with lanolin* (mink oil, for instance) will clean leather or leather-covered buttons beautifully. But don't wash it off. Let it dry and then buff it to a shine with a *soft cloth*.

To clean wooden buttons, remove them from the garment and use a *wood oil cleanser*, such as Murphy Oil Soap. Follow the directions on the container. The buttons will absorb most of the wood oil soap. Remove any residue with a *soft cloth*.

To clean bone or ivory buttons, remove them from the garment. Mix a small amount of *lemon juice* with enough *salt* to make a paste. Lightly brush it on with a *soft toothbrush* and then wipe them clean with a *damp cloth*.

To clean buttons made of horn, dampen a *soft cloth* with a small amount of *mineral oil* or *baby oil*. Rub to remove stains, then wipe with a *dry cloth*. Do *not* immerse horn in water.

To clean metal buttons, you can try the age-old remedy of *toothpaste*, but make sure it's natural, like Tom's, or one that doesn't have the chemicals that wear down surfaces. (Avoid anything that boasts "tartar control" or "whitening.") An alternative: Dissolve *1 teaspoon of noniodized salt* in *1 quart of water*. (Iodized salt can cause discoloration.) Dampen a *soft cloth* in the salt solution and polish the surface. Rinse well with *water*. Then polish with a *soft, dry cloth*.

C

Calculators

To clean a calculator, first disconnect any electrical cord and move it out of the way. Then thoroughly dust both sides with an *eye shadow brush*, being careful to brush away lint and accumulated dust or dirt. If your calculator is superfuzzy with lint, brush it off with a *soft, dry toothbrush.*

Keeping keys clean can be difficult. Because fingers transfer all kinds of gunk—such as newspaper ink and sticky sugar—the keys are like magnets for lint and dirt. To get rid of anything that doesn't belong, dip a *cotton swab* into a *small amount of rubbing alcohol*. Press the swab onto a *paper towel* to eliminate excess alcohol. (Who knows what kind of numbers your calculator will come up with if you have liquid seeping into the works.) Swab each key lightly. For the bigger surfaces, such as the back of the calculator, you can use a *cotton ball*, dipped in alcohol, to get rid of unsightly dirt.

Camcorders

simple SOLUTIONS

Clean Tapes Equal a Clean Machine >
As a precaution, keep your tapes dust free. Since it's better not to clean your camcorder at home, you can stretch the time between professional cleanings by storing your tapes in a box. When a tape sits out unsheathed, dust gets into the grooves. Then, when you load it in the camera, it introduces dust to the inside of the camera. A plastic case or a cardboard box helps keep tapes dust free.

Most camera professionals will tell you not to clean your own camcorder. There are too many integral little parts that are easily damaged. If you mess up while cleaning your camcorder, most camera repair shops will consider it "tamper damage," and they won't take responsibility for any subsequent problems. But there are times when it just makes good sense to take a dab at it—when your toddler splashes juice on it, for instance, or when you've brought home a little of the beach in your camera case.

Treat outdoor exposure to salt, moisture, or dirt as soon as you can. Reporters who cover extreme weather, such as hurricanes, know how quickly exposure to elements, especially to salt, erodes and rusts a camera and its workings. Although you don't want to go inside the camera to clean it, you can do what the reporters do: Dampen a *clean, soft cloth or towel* with *rubbing alcohol* and wipe the surfaces thoroughly. You don't want the cloth to be saturated—just damp enough to remove that fresh coat of goo or grime. Make sure that the dock where you load the cassette tape stays closed.

When cleaning a lens, it's best not to touch it or a viewfinder with anything other than *lens tissue*, available for little money anyplace that sells camera equipment. Household facial tissues frequently contain additives, such as lanolin, that you don't want on the lens. The only other acceptable alternative is to use a **soft, natural-bristled brush** (an artist's brush or a makeup brush). If you use the brush, make sure it's new. Even brushes that have been washed can contain residue that you don't want to transfer to your lens and viewfinder.

To clean the heads in a camcorder, go to the store where you bought your camcorder and pick up a **dry cleaning tape** that is compatible with your camera. Simply load the tape, press *Play,* and let it run for the recommended amount of time.

Cameos

The intricate carvings and grooves that make cameos so charming provide handy hiding places for grime that can dull their beauty. Cameos are made of coral, resin, certain stones, and, most commonly, certain seashells. Different colored layers provide the characteristic contrast between the relief carving and its background. These are delicate materials, and they need protection from dirt and dryness.

Cleaning a cameo is simple, no matter how complex the design. A dusting periodically with a **soft-bristled brush** will help keep particles from settling into crevices. The brushing may be followed by rinsing with **warm water** and drying with a **soft, lint-free cloth**.

Give a cameo a soapy bath about twice a year. Never use a harsh cleaner. Put **a few drops of mild dish detergent or a gentle wash detergent** such as Woolite into a **bowl** with about **2 cups of warm water**. Swish the cameo around, wet a **soft toothbrush**, and scrub—gently. Never let cameos soak, because soaking could damage the shell. After the soapy bath, rinse the cameo in **warm water** and dry it with a **soft cloth**.

Moisturize a cameo after its bath. A cameo that is too dry may become cracked or chipped. Use a fine oil, such as **olive oil, mineral oil, or baby oil**—or follow an old-fashioned practice of using **oil of wintergreen**, available in drugstores, to give your cameo a fresh and surprising scent. Use a **cotton swab** to apply a little oil to the surface. Let it sit overnight, then wipe off any oil you can still see with a **soft cloth**.

Store cameos in a **soft cloth or lined box** away from heat and light.

Cameras

Cameras are compact bundles of extremely delicate parts. Cleaning them without doing damage in the process is a daunting task. What you use to clean them is also somewhat controversial. If you want endless discussions of the pros and cons of every known camera cleaning product, you can find them on the Internet. Search under the name of your camera and the name of the product you're interested in.

To clean the lens, first examine it with a *magnifying glass*. Any kind of foreign material, including gunk you can't see with the naked eye, will mar your pictures and may damage your lens.

To get rid of dust or dirt on the lens, start with air. Photo shops sell a blower brush, which, as the name suggests, combines a brush with a blower. The blower on most of them is actually ineffective. Better is a *bulb syringe*, which you can get at any drugstore. Still more effective is a *can of compressed air*. Also know as "canned air," it's an aerosol can containing air under pressure and a nozzle extension. Some say canned air gives too big a blast, but it is widely used. One brand of canned air is Dust-Off, available for about $5 at stores that sell photo supplies, computers, or electronics.

If your lens is removable, check the back end occasionally and clean it in the same way as the front.

To remove persistent specks that don't respond to the air treatment, brush them away with a *blower brush or soft watercolor paintbrush.* You can also use a cleaning cloth. But you don't want to move specks around—that will only damage the lens or its coatings. So take care in choosing a cloth. The best is a *microfiber lens cleaning cloth*, which can also be used on the body of the camera and can be washed and reused. These cloths trap particles among their fibers rather than on the surface. One example is the Micro Optic Cleaner cloth, available for about $7 from photo shops. If you can't lay your hands on a lens cleaning cloth, go to plan B: *lens tissues*, also available at camera stores.

To remove fingerprints or really persistent specks, you may need to use lens cleaning fluid. There are many types on the market. Check your owner's manual for recommendations. If your camera has a plastic lens, make sure the lens cleaner is suitable for plastic as well as glass. Use a *few drops of lens cleaning fluid* on a *microfiber cloth*—never directly on the lens—and clean with a light, circular motion. Fingerprints should be cleaned

simple SOLUTIONS

Keep It Clicking >

Some precautions will help keep your camera clean and well functioning:

• Protect the lens with an ultraviolet filter (even if you remove it for picture taking) and lens cap. With many new cameras, you can't lose the lens cap because it just slides aside. But you still must remember to close it after use.

• Don't store a camera where it will be exposed to direct sunlight, high humidity, rapid changes in temperature (which may cause condensation), or temperature extremes.

• Wipe off the batteries and the contact points in the battery chambers before inserting new batteries to help prevent corrosion.

• Consult your owner's manual for hints about preventive maintenance and specific information about your camera.

immediately in this way. If left for a long time, fingerprints can actually etch themselves into the glass.

Fingerprints are finger food for glass mold, a type that doesn't need as much moisture as most other molds need. The mold will also feed on dust, and it can destroy the surface of a lens. Using your camera in the sunshine every so often will usually be enough to prevent glass mold. If you aren't going to be using your camera for a long time, take it out of the case. Camera cases can build up moisture and grow mold quite easily.

To clean inside the camera, use **compressed air** and a **soft watercolor brush** to banish dirt from the film chamber, followed by a gentle wiping with a **microfiber cloth.** Don't forget the inside of the lens cap and the inside of your camera bag.

When cleaning a digital camera, make sure it is unplugged before you start. One new product, a **lens pen**, combines a retractable brush on one end with a cleaning tip on the other. There are various models on the market at prices ranging from $5 to $15. They are especially recommended for digital cameras.

Keep It Simple, and Everything Will Click

Ed Romney has made a career of restoring really grungy cameras, sometimes using such things as diesel starting fluid as cleaning agents. He has helped foster a growing interest in antique cameras and their restoration. His advice to the average amateur photographer: Don't clean it— keep it clean.

Romney began his love affair with cameras in the 1930s, helping out in his father's photography studio. In 1969 he started his camera restoration business out of his home in Drayton, South Carolina. After cleaning and repairing thousands of old cameras, he now writes about that topic (and others) and sells his books from his website, www.edromney.com.

For maintenance, Romney subscribes to the basics of cleaning a camera, but that's about it. "It's a pity to do unnecessary things to a camera," Romney says. "More lenses are destroyed by cleaning than anything else. Overpolishing a lens is an awful thing to do."

He uses clean rags and a little Windex on lenses. He has no objections to special lens cleaning fluids or cleaning cloths, but he finds them unnecessary. "And there are so many, and the names keep changing," he says. "A lot of it is a little bit too cultish."

He likes treating leather parts with neat's-foot oil and uses a rag dabbed with silicone spray—"I use the cheapest"—on the body.

Romney is worried about the mold that can attack lenses and literally eat them. If you look at the lens with a magnifying glass and see "hairy things," it's got mold, he says. To kill it, he wipes the lens with a rag dipped in a 50-50 mixture of ammonia and hydrogen peroxide.

More cameras are thrown away because they are dirty than because they are broken, he maintains.

Can Openers

Poisoned by your can opener? Don't laugh; it can happen. When you consider the mixture of chicken soup, tuna fish, dog food, and other remains of the day (or week, or month) on the blades, a can opener's potential toxicity isn't surprising. The juices left on the blades have been shown to harbor the bacteria that cause food poisoning, skin infections, pneumonia, and other maladies. To avoid trouble, make it a habit to wash the blades after each use.

Cleaning a handheld can opener is a snap. Just wash it with the dishes, either by hand or in a *dishwasher*.

Cleaning an electric can opener is also simple, because most have blades or cutting assemblies designed to be removed and washed with the dishes. Older models may not have detachable blades. In that case, clean the cutting parts, being careful not to cut yourself, with a *cloth* dampened with *water* and a little *dishwashing detergent*. If you're dealing with accumulated black gunk, scrub it with an *old toothbrush*. Regular cleaning thereafter will keep the machine clean. To clean the machine's body, wipe it with a *damp cloth* with the unit unplugged. Never immerse an electric can opener in water.

Candlesticks and Candelabra

The easiest way to clean wax from candlesticks is to wipe the wax off while the drips are still warm and soft. But this may seem overly fastidious in the midst of a dinner party.

To remove hardened wax, try this general-purpose method: First, remove all you can with your fingers or with assistance from a *soft wooden stick*, such as a Popsicle stick. You can also use a hair dryer or *warm water* to soften the wax as you work. Never use a knife or other metal object. When you've removed all you can, clean the waxy residue with *mineral spirits*, available at hardware and paint stores (see Watch Out sidebar). Dab it onto a *soft cloth* and rub the waxy spots until they're gone. Then polish the candlesticks with *panty hose* and finish according to the directions for the material the candlesticks are made of. (See entries for *Copper*, *Brass*, *Silver*, and other materials.)

Don't put it in the fridge. One recommendation that's been around for years is to remove hardened wax by first putting candlesticks in the freezer. The cold will make the wax brittle and easier to remove by breaking it off. However, experts advise against this treatment because freezing could actually break your candlesticks. Some are made from two or more kinds of metal, which could expand and contract at different rates.

But the candles themselves are a different story. If you stash candles in cold storage for a couple of hours before using them, they'll burn more slowly and with less dripping. That'll mean less mess to clean up.

Caning

Used on antique and contemporary chairs, footstools, and other small furniture pieces, caning is made of woven bamboo or reeds. Historically, it was often intended to support cushions, which also helped protect it. Cushioning is still a good idea.

To clean caning, use the *brush attachment* of a *vacuum cleaner* regularly to suck out loose dirt, or dust it with a brush, such as a *paintbrush*. To wash dirtier caning, use a little *mild detergent* in *water* applied with a *sponge, cloth, or medium-stiff brush*. Rinse with *clear water* and dry with a *towel or soft cloth*. Don't use harsh detergents or cleaners.

To prevent stains on caning, clean up any spills promptly with a *wet cloth* or *soap and water*. A stain may be impossible to remove. If you do get a stain, your best bet is to follow the lead of many old-timers and paint the cane.

To fix a sagging cane seat, provided the material isn't broken, wet the seat thoroughly from underneath with a *sponge* ▶. The underside is more porous than the top and will absorb better. Then let the caning dry in the sun.

Carpeting

For routine carpet cleaning, carpet people say there are three things to consider: vacuum cleaner, vacuum cleaner, vacuum cleaner. Vacuuming removes about 85 percent of carpet dirt. To get down to the deep dirt, you need to periodically give your carpeting a more thorough cleaning than a vacuum cleaner can provide. How often depends on your lifestyle, but the recommended range is every six to 18 months.

Vacuuming your carpeting every day would be ideal. But we don't live like people in 1950s TV commercials, where women seemed to spend most of their days doing housework—in high heels, no

▲

less. Let's face it: Daily vacuuming is unrealistic for most households today. But do make it a point to vacuum carpeting at least once a week, even if it doesn't appear dirty. Heavily trafficked areas should be hit a little more often. And be sure to vacuum up promptly any obvious soiling before it gets ground in.

For vacuuming your carpet, the more powerful your machine is, the better. You can use either an **upright vacuum**, which was created with carpets in mind, or a **canister vacuum with a power nozzle**, which does almost as good a job as an upright. Both of these have a rotary brush, designed to loosen the dirt in carpets. Here are some tips:

- Set your vacuum cleaner for the pile level of the carpet—unless your vacuum automatically adjusts to the pile level.
- When you vacuum an area, use slow, even strokes and go back and forth several times, flipping the nap by going alternately

What's Your Carpet Made of?

How your carpeting responds to dirt and your efforts to eradicate it depends on the material—of the carpet and of the dirt. Unfortunately, most people have no clue about the materials their carpets are made of, unless the carpet is wool. Wool is the most expensive, and shoppers who choose wool want that material in particular. Shoppers choose other fibers mainly because of the appearance and price of the carpeting, not because of what they want from the fiber.

If you're serious about owning high-quality carpeting and keeping it clean, know your fibers and consider fiber when buying. There are two basic categories: natural and synthetic.

Synthetic fibers include nylon, olefin or polypropylene, acrylic, blends of those materials, and "pop-bottle carpet,"

made from recycled plastic bottles (polyethylene terephthalate [PET], if you really want to know).

- Nylon is the best of the synthetic materials. It is the toughest, and it resists soil and stains quite well. If the fibers get compressed by a heavy object sitting on them, they can be revived with steam.
- Olefin is cheaper and is also quite stain resistant. It is the only carpet material that can sometimes accept bleach. Its chief disadvantage: The fibers crush easily.
- Acrylic is also relatively inexpensive and resembles nylon in some ways. But it is not as strong and is unsuitable for high-traffic areas. And it is susceptible to pilling and fuzzing.
- Blends have characteristics of their components, but since

those components react differently to stains, removing stains may be more difficult.

- Recycled-bottle carpet resembles nylon and olefin and has similar stain-resistant properties.

Natural fibers include wool, sisal, hemp, jute, and seagrass.

- Wool is durable, naturally resistant to stains and dirt, and more expensive than synthetics.
- Sisal, hemp, jute, and seagrass are all made from plants, and they come in a wide variety of weaves and prices. Plant-based materials are more likely to be found in area rugs than in wall-to-wall carpeting. These carpets will not stand up to shampooing or steam cleaning. Use as little liquid as possible when treating stains.

against and with the grain. Finish with strokes that all go in the same direction.

- Vacuum under furniture as best you can with *extension attachments*. About twice a year, move the furniture and vacuum the area under it thoroughly.
- With a rug, it's a good idea to occasionally turn it over and vacuum the underside.
- If your vacuum cleaner won't suck up cat hairs, threads, or other fine items, use a *lint roller* or a piece of *doubled-over tape* to pick them up.
- New carpeting produces a lot of extra fluff. It's normal—nothing to worry about.

Professional steam cleaning is the ideal way of removing deep down dirt from your carpet. There are several types of professional carpet-cleaning methods, but the Cadillac of them all is *hot water extraction*, *or steam cleaning*, done using a *truck-mounted unit*.

If you call in the pros, make sure that's really what you're getting. There are plenty of glorified do-it-yourselfers pretending to be professionals. If you follow the suggestions in the "How to Choose a Pro" box on the following page, you won't get any surprises when they show up at the door. They'll swoop in with a big truck, get the job done fast, and be out of your way. The big truck's purpose isn't to impress you, but to hold powerful equipment. One piece is a heating unit that keeps the water very hot throughout the cleaning process. Another is a very powerful vacuum, which will suck up all the water that the cleaner puts down.

If you steam clean carpeting yourself, the results won't be as good as a professional job. But let's say you just don't want to spring for the professional job. Maybe your carpet is old and you're going to replace it in a couple of years, but in the meantime you want to perk it up with a do-it-yourself steam-cleaning job. In that case, the most economical solution is to rent the *most powerful steam-cleaning machine* you can find. At the same time, rent a *shop vacuum* that will suck up water as well as solids. Follow the directions on the cleaning machine, and change the water often. At the end, go over the carpeting with the shop vacuum and draw out as much additional water as you can. Get as much air circulation as possible in the room, and don't walk on the carpet until it's dry.

If using a rental unit persuades you that do-it-yourself cleaning is the way to go, and expense is no barrier, explore owning your

RULES
OF THE GAME

What Would Hippocrates Do? >
When confronted with a spill on your carpet, remember Hippocrates' famous commandment to physicians: First, do no harm.

If your first instinct is to grab a sponge and rub the spot, curb it. Rubbing will only grind the spill more deeply into the fibers.

While treatment of spills will vary with the carpet material and the substance spilled, here are a few principles that apply to all:

1. Scoop up any solids and use something absorbent to soak up any liquid that hasn't sunk in yet.
2. After you've absorbed everything you can, blot the spot with white towels or rags. Work from the outside in so you won't spread the stain.
3. When you've blotted up all you can, use water to dilute what remains, and continue to blot.
4. If that doesn't complete the job, proceed to a low-tech cleaner. If that doesn't work, call in the professionals. Many amateurs do harm by using harsh, ineffective cleaners.

own deep–cleaning unit. Home machines are about the size and shape of upright vacuum cleaners. While they aren't as powerful as the professional or rental cleaners, some of the newest home machines do an adequate job.

Three carpet-cleaning methods to avoid at all costs are listed below. You may be tempted to save money by trying one of them—either doing it yourself or hiring a professional. But if you do, be prepared to be disappointed:

- *Shampooing* uses a machine with a very aggressive brush and a cleaner mixed with water applied to the carpeting. The brush doesn't pick up any dirt. It swirls everything around to create a foam. The idea is to let that dry and vacuum up the crystals. It is not effective.

- *Spin bonnet cleaning* adapts floor-buffing techniques to carpets. A "bonnet," or round absorbent pad, is dipped into the cleaning solution and wrung out, then attached to a machine that spins it around. The bonnet is supposed to be removed and cleaned or changed when it is visibly dirty. But it cleans only the top of the carpeting. It grinds in dirt, creates soil and detergent buildup, and can damage the fibers and pile.

- *Dry cleaning* is touted as an alternative method that won't cause overwatering of carpets. It uses an absorbent granular material, which is laced with a solvent. It is distributed over the carpet and brushed in, left to absorb soil, and then vacuumed up. The

How to Choose *a Pro*

If you're going to the expense of hiring a professional to clean your carpets, make sure you get a good one. Here's how you can evaluate the professionals, according to the Carpet & FabriCare Institute of Mission Viejo, California:

• Be sure the cleaner uses the water-extraction or steam-cleaning method supported by a truck-based unit.

• Ask what training the cleaner has had. Cleaning carpets does take some.

• Choose a cleaner with a professional certification, such as the IICRC label (bestowed by the Institute of Inspection, Cleaning and Restoration Certification) or the Carpet and Rug Institute's Seal of Approval. Another good sign is membership in trade organizations.

• Expect the cleaner to inspect the job beforehand to look at the condition of your carpeting and the type of fiber it is made of.

• Ask for an estimate—in writing and itemized. (A good professional should provide it that way without being asked.) With a written estimate, you'll know what is covered, and you won't be surprised by extra charges. You can save money by doing a thorough vacuuming before the cleaner arrives and by moving the furniture yourself, but make sure the estimate reflects the tasks that you, rather than the professional, will be doing.

• Examine the guarantee and make sure it suits you.

• Ask for references, and check them out.

• Be sure the cleaner is insured.

CARPETING

trouble is, it isn't very effective, and the solvent evaporates in the air, polluting your home.

Removing spots on carpeting is something you have to expect to do yourself, because onto every carpet a little wine must fall. Or barbecue sauce. Or pet poop. You can't afford to call in the professional cleaners every time your boss dribbles her sloe gin fizz on your carpet. So it pays to learn how to mop up the little messes in between deep cleanings.

The techniques for attacking stains are as varied as the stains themselves. The approach you use depends in part on how much you value your carpet. If your carpet is old and beaten up, you can afford to be daring. If it's brand-new, of high quality, and carpeting you want to have for many years, be more cautious.

Here's a pyramid to help you decide which spot-removal technique to use. Choosing a spot-removing strategy is a bit like picking foods from the Food Guide Pyramid. On the food pyramid, you're supposed to eat a lot of the foods depicted at the bottom (fruits, vegetables, and grains) and eat the stuff at the top (fats, sweets, and oils) sparingly. On the Stain Removal Pyramid ▶ the broad bottom part includes that most gentle and universal of cleaning substances—water. The higher you go on this pyramid, the more extreme the treatment and the less of it you should use.

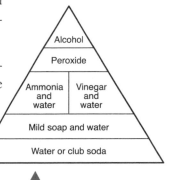

Before we examine each step in the pyramid, a few basics to remember: Stain removal usually requires tenacious blotting. (See the instructions in the box "What Would Hippocrates Do?") Be sure to blot, not rub. Before moving on from one step in the pyramid to the next, test the next solution on an inconspicuous area of carpet. Put a little of the treatment on the carpet, let it sit for about 10 minutes, and blot with a clean white rag. Inspect the rag for any dye from the carpet, and inspect the carpet for any damage from the cleaner. If either occurs, the solution isn't really a solution; it's another problem. In the case of wool, if it doesn't respond to water and the mild soap solution, you should call a professional.

OK, here are the techniques to try, in order, as we ascend the Stain Removal Pyramid. Remember to blot, not rub. Use these techniques only one at a time, and rinse well between steps.

1. After you've cleaned everything you can by blotting, dilute what remains with *water* and blot some more. You can also dilute spills with *plain club soda*. (No flavors, please!) The fizziness and salts it contains will sometimes help it work better than water, and it's just about as safe.

2. If after water and club soda treatment you still have a stain, here is a safe, simple, general-purpose spot cleaner to try: Mix **1 teaspoon of a mild dishwashing detergent** with **1 cup of warm water**. Blot it on the spot. Be sure to rinse thoroughly, because getting cleaning chemicals out is important, too.
3. Try a solution of **1 tablespoon of ammonia** and **1/2 cup of water** on old spots, blood, and chocolate.
4. Try a solution of **1/2 cup of white vinegar** and **1 cup of water** on mildew stains and spills with an odor, such as urine.
5. Try **full-strength 3 percent hydrogen peroxide** on tomato-based stains, red drinks, alcoholic drinks, fruit juice, grass stains, coffee, and chocolate.
6. Use **rubbing alcohol,** full strength, on oily stains, ballpoint pen ink, candle wax residue, and grass stains.

Special situations may call for special removal techniques:
- For oily spills, such as mayonnaise, salad dressing, and butter, try saturating the spot with **cornstarch**, a good absorbent. Allow it to dry, then **vacuum**.
- For candle wax dripped onto your carpet, use a **warm iron** over a **paper towel** to take up as much wax as possible. Then dab on **rubbing alcohol**. If there's still a stain, go to the general-purpose spot cleaner described above. (See step 2.)

For Spills, **Pick Up the Phone**

When you get a spill on your carpet and you're tempted to reach for one of those commercial spot-treatment products, try the phone instead. That's the advice of Mike Perras, executive director of the Carpet & FabriCare Institute.

"Those products are absolutely wonderful for the companies selling them," Perras says, "and absolutely terrible for the consumer using them."

About 90 percent of the time, when a professional carpet cleaner is called in to treat really bad spots, such spot-cleaning products have made them worse, according to Perras.

He advises carpet owners to blot up what they can from a spill, dilute the residue with water, and continue to blot. Beyond that, he advises seeking advice before using any kind of cleaner. If you know the kind of fiber your carpet is made of, so much the better.

For advice, you can call CFI, a nonprofit organization dedicated to training and education, at (800) 227-7389. CFI doesn't sell any products. It can recommend professional cleaners, but only in California, Arizona, and Nevada. However, it can recommend other nonprofit groups that serve other areas.

The information line for the Carpet and Rug Institute is another source of impartial advice. The number is (800) 882-8846.

You could also call a professional cleaner in your area. Professionals are usually happy to offer advice on spot cleaning.

CARPETING

- Pet "accidents" (we all know the little dears sometimes do it on purpose) produce odors as well as stains, and the problem is compounded when urine is not detected immediately. The longer it stays, the worse it gets. First, flush the spot with **water** and blot with an **old towel or rag**. Then use the general-purpose spot treatment. (See step 2.) Rinse that with the vinegar mixture. (See step 4.) Rinse again with water and blot. Finally, apply a **half-inch-thick layer of dry, clean white rags, towels, or paper towels**, weight them with a **heavy object**, and allow them to sit for several hours. If they're still damp when you remove them, repeat with a **fresh layer of absorbent materials** until they come up dry. (This is also a good formula for treating spilled beer.) The odor will not come out as long as any urine remains. Most commercial products sold to eliminate odor just mask the smell temporarily.

- If a carpet has a musty smell, baking soda will help. If you've been removing spots from the carpet, let the carpet dry out completely first. Then sprinkle **baking soda** over the entire carpet, let it sit for three to five hours, and **vacuum** it up.

- Not all substances can be removed from carpeting. Chlorine bleach, iodine, mustard, insecticides, and plant fertilizers, to name a few, are likely to create permanent stains. Many foods, beverages, medications, and cosmetics contain dye, and their spots also may be permanent. Sometimes a professional restorer can fix a permanently damaged area by spot-dyeing, reweaving, or retufting. Or a professional installer can replace a section of carpet using a scrap or a piece taken from an inconspicuous spot, such as your closet floor.

Cars

For most of us, cars are our second most expensive possession, our transportation to work and play. Cars reflect our personalities and our dreams. For many, a car is a friend and a companion—a very sensitive, you might even say thin-skinned, one at that. Modern car finishes are pretty delicate: Over the primer is a single layer of waterborne acrylic paint with pigment and then several layers of paint with no pigment, called clearcoat. While the clearcoat adds depth and brightness to the color, it adds no additional protection, so total coverage is often no more than 5 millimeters thick. That's not a lot between your metal and corrosive elements. So the idea is to maintain a clean surface and a solid protective layer of wax. Interior surfaces take

simple SOLUTIONS

Try Some Salt in Your Wine >
So you're celebrating your home renovation. Wouldn't you know it: Someone has spilled wine on that brand new beige carpeting. And it's *red* wine.

Don't cry. Instead, grab a box of salt. It's a great absorbent.

Spread it liberally on the wine so that it soaks up all the liquid. When all the salt is red, vacuum it up. Then apply some club soda and blot it. Follow up with more salt. Keep repeating this technique until the salt no longer turns red. This could take several days. If the spot becomes dry while there is still color in it, wet it with water or club soda before adding more salt. Then blot with a water-soaked towel, followed by a dry towel. Repeat as many times as necessary to remove the salt that the vacuum didn't pick up.

a beating from the elements as well, so they need regular TLC, too. The International Car Wash Association recommends washing your car every 10 days and waxing every six months. Beyond aesthetics, it's a way of protecting your investment and avoiding damage.

Choosing a car washing site is the first step. The weather has finally cleared. You're ready to hang out the "Open for Business" sign for your home car wash. You're tempted to soak up some rays as you scrub down the sedan. Looks good on TV, but the truth is, sunshine is a car washer's enemy. You get water spots more readily on the clearcoat. The heated metal dries soap into a film before you can rinse it off, and your wax crusts into hard-to-wipe streaks.

So park it under a shady tree? Careful there, too, since debris falling from the tree can cause other headaches. (Imagine a finger-nails-on-chalkboard squeak as you unwittingly scrub twig bits across the paint. Imagine a rain of yellow pollen.) You may also find yourself facing two mortal enemies of car finishes—bird droppings and tree sap. (Always wipe bird "calls" off as soon as possible. It may take a specialized solvent to remove tree sap.) Better choices are a **carport**, a **garage** with good ventilation and drainage, or a **shady area not directly under a tree**. Another alternative is a **coin-operated car wash bay**.

An ecological consideration: Don't park too near a storm drain. Your soapy water is untreated and will wash from the drain directly into local rivers, creeks, and streams.

Next, look at your watch. Do you have a good four hours to devote to the process? Good. Now take off your watch and any belt buckle or jewelry that might bang against the car and leave scratches where you just want shine. Time to round up your tools and supplies.

Selecting the right cleaner is important. Car experts of all stripes are emphatic on this point: Dishwashing soap is for dishes. Used on a car, it can do more harm than good. Its detergent can thin the vehicle's protective layer of wax or, if the finish is worn, it can actually scratch or further break down the paint. So instead of shiny-and-sparkly, you get dull-and-scratchy.

You'll find **nondetergent car cleaners** in mass merchandisers, discount clubs, and auto supply shops. Avoid those that promise a shine, because they are likely to contain silicone, which can streak your paint and result in glare off shiny interior surfaces. Mix the cleaner according to label instructions for the exterior and in a more dilute mix for interior surfaces (2 to 3 drops per gallon).

expert advice

Put Up with the Static Cling >

When you're washing your car-cleaning rags, don't use dryer sheets on them in the dryer, says Chuck Bennett, CEO of Zymol (manufacturer and distributor of car-care products) and author of *The Authoritative Guide to Automotive Detailing*. Dryer sheets contain silicone, which will leave streaks on your car.

Look for established brand names like Meguiar's, Mothers, Simonize, Turtle Wax, 3M, Greased Lightning, and Zymol.

Selecting cleaning rags is a matter of personal choice, but a near-universal favorite is a piece of ***100 percent cotton terry cloth towel***. Towels are superabsorbent and grow softer with use and age. They're especially great for drying. Be sure to grab a really old one—not, say, one of the new fluffy monogrammed guest towels. New towels contain unstable dyes and silicone for sizing, so you'll have filthy guest towels as well as color and silicone streaks on your car.

All-cotton cloth diapers, **T-shirts**, and ***shop rags*** are fine for interiors, but their weaves can be abrasive on your car's tender dermis. And be careful using sponges on the paint. Some, such as sea sponges, are notorious for hiding grit in their holes. Other options: ***disposable wash mitts filled with car soap, microfiber towels***, and **chamois cloths**. One word about chamois: It's clingy. Use it only to push water across the car, not to dry. Never drag it flat across the finish—it will drag away wax.

On rag-washing day, skip the fabric softener and dryer sheets. These products contain silicone, which causes streaking.

Using a garden hose for rinsing makes life a lot easier. If you don't have a hose at home, you can use the wand in a coin-operated car wash. Spray in a steady, medium flow, not a high-pressure blast, which can grind dirt granules into the paint. With a continuous, moderate stream, the water flows across the car's outer surface in sheets, gently washing away sand, salt, pollen, dirt, and other debris as well as soap. The wheels are the exception—there, a strong blast works well.

A rinsing rule of thumb: Spray in directions that water normally travels across or down the car, because that's the way the car is designed to slough off water. Otherwise, you may shoot water into body vents and other design features where water isn't meant to go.

Selecting a polish should be done with care. Made with fine abrasives, polishes are designed to lift light oxidation so you can see the true color of the paint better. As their name implies, they brighten the finish. Read labels. Find a polish that indicates that it's "safe for modern car finishes" or "safe on clearcoat." And always apply polish on a clean car with a cool surface.

Selecting a wax is easy because a number of good brands are widely available. Liquid waxes are easiest to use. With a paste wax, it's easy to transfer grit into the original container—putting your finish at risk. Not only does wax give the paint its glossy sheen

simple SOLUTIONS

Glass Cleaner Under Your Hood >
You can save a wad of money on glass cleaner by using alcohol-based windshield wiper fluid to spiff up your windows and mirrors. For summertime or indoor use, mix 10 ounces of alcohol-based wiper fluid with 20 ounces of water in a 32-ounce spray bottle. For use in freezing temperatures, mix half wiper fluid and half water.

and sharpen the color, but it also preserves the paint by helping it retain oils that reduce oxidation, the process that leads to the dreaded R-word, *rust*. It's also a layer between your paint and the world, a barrier to ultraviolet rays, pollutants, bird droppings, grime, bugs, tar, and tree sap. While the International Car Wash Association recommends waxing every six months to maintain a solid protective coat, you may need to do it more often—say, every three months—if the season or the region you live in exposes the car to harsh conditions such as a heavy bug season, high dust and heat, or salt. And if your ride is red, black, or white, consider waxing more often, since these colors are more susceptible to acid rain and UV rays.

A word of warning about spray-on, wipe-off detailer products that promise to help maintain that freshly waxed look between wax jobs: Many are alcohol-based, so they actually strip wax.

Use a bead test to find out whether you're still getting good protection from your wax, regardless of your timetable for waxing. Rinse the entire car with the hose and notice how the water droplets bead up around the car. If they are more than a half-inch across, or if the water stays on the surface in sheets, it's time to wax.

Clear the drain holes early in the car-washing process. Many people are astonished to learn that cars have drain holes that need occasional attention—the life of the car is at stake. The drain holes are located under each fender and quarter panel and at the bottom of each door panel ◀. These rubber eyelets let out rainwater and melting snow that leak down the outside of the fenders, panels, and windows. If the holes are plugged with debris, the moisture gets trapped inside the body and can cause the vehicle to rust from the inside. Clear the holes by running a *cotton swab* into and across the opening. Later, when you rinse the car, any buildup will drain out.

Start cleaning the car interior by running a *vacuum* over the seats and seat crevices (a *flat-tube attachment* helps here), then the floor mats and floor carpeting. (Here's where you get to collect on your habit of dropping change into tough-to-reach places.)

Cleaning floor mats is the next step after vacuuming. Take out the mats and *hose* them down. Fill a *bucket* with *water* and add *2 or 3 drops of nondetergent cleaner* per gallon. Dip in a *stiff-bristled brush* and scrub. If this is an early-spring cleaning, scrub well to evict winter hibernators like road salt. After scrubbing, rinse the mats with the hose until the runoff is clear. Vacuum them with a *wet/dry vac*, if you have one, or just set them aside to air-dry—but not in full sun, which could fade them.

Cleaning doorjambs is a smart first or second task. By starting with the parts of the door you don't see when the doors are closed, you don't risk getting cleaner and wax on already-clean surfaces, such as your seats and carpet. Open the door wide and thoroughly clean around the door opening and the edges with a *soapy rag*. Afterward, take *a dry exterior-use rag* and wipe the inner door and sills dry. Dry all the painted surfaces, then *polish* and *wax* them. (See Waxing on page 118.)

Cleaning carpets is key because the floor is the interior surface that takes the biggest beating between washings. Scrub the carpets with a *stiff-bristled brush* and *carpet/upholstery cleaner*. (A household brand is OK.) If you're using a *wet/dry vac*, don't be afraid to wet the carpet with a little *water* to loosen tough deposits of salt and dirt before you scrub it. Then sweep up the water, loosened salt, soil, and debris.

Cleaning seats is simple because they usually need only a quick once-over. You have your choice of using *upholstery cleaner* and a *soft-bristled brush, vinyl cleaner* and a *rag*, or *saddle soap* and a *dampened sponge*. To remove pet hair from upholstery, wrap *wide masking tape* around your hand and wipe with the tape. For leather seats, make sure your rag or sponge is only damp, because too much water will damage them. After cleaning the leather, apply a thin, even coat of protective *leather conditioner*, such as

How to Get Away Clean

There it is, in pale script on the dirt-encrusted door of your trunk: "Wash me." And you know it's time to obey. But before you grab the hose and begin, keep these rules in mind:

• Make it shady. During cleaning, the sun is not your car's friend. Park in shade—but not under a tree.

• Round up your supplies before you begin. You don't want to have to drive a soapy car to the auto supply store because you forgot something.

• Know your suds. Dishwashing soap is for dishes. Buy a non-detergent car cleaner.

• Bag a good rag. With cotton rags, make it soft, 100 percent cotton, clean and free of fabric softener or sizing. Old bath towels are a favorite.

• Rinse right. Resist the impulse to blast away dirt and grime. Hosing with a moderate stream and constant flow of water creates a sheeting action that gently washes away debris and cleanser without scratching.

• Don't be a drip. Letting your car drip dry leads to water spotting and soap film. Work in sections, washing, rinsing, and drying as you go.

Lexol. Don't overcondition. Leather needs to be able to absorb moisture from the air.

Cleaning door panels is tricky because their surfaces have lots of crevices and, usually, electrical switches. After first wiping the panel with a *soapy rag*, dampen (don't get it sopping wet) an *old toothbrush* and a *thin cloth* and use the toothbrush to clean out crevices. Wrap the cloth around a *plastic knife* to clean the electrical switches, repositioning the cloth as needed to keep soft fabric over the knife edge. The trick here: A damp cloth won't drip into switches and cause them to fail or short-circuit. (Use the same method for dials and switches on the dash.) Wipe dry.

Cleaning window interiors is important if you want to see out clearly—and you want to be sure other folks can clearly spot who's driving that shiny-clean car when you're done. Give the interior glass the treatment with a solution of *1 part white vinegar* to *8 parts water*, mixed in a *spray bottle*. Or use a *nonammonia glass cleaner*. (Ammonia-based household glass cleaners and foam glass cleaners can dry out neighboring plastic, rubber, and vinyl.) You may hear hot water recommended for cleaning glass. One danger is, when the air temperature is low, the hot liquid could cause cracking.

Newspaper is an old favorite glass-cleaning wipe, reputed to have a polishing effect. It may not be as effective as it used to be, though, as formulations used in printing newspapers have changed. If you do use newspapers, be careful to not leave smudges on nonglass parts of the car. For no-streak drying, a better choice is a *low-lint cloth.* (Old pillowcases are a good choice.) Finally, roll door windows down and clean the tops, where dirt and film tend to be thickest.

Cleaning the dashboard, steering column, center console, and other vinyl and plastic surfaces is the finishing touch for the interior. If they are dusty, first wipe them down with a household *dusting cloth.* A convenient new alternative is nonwoven *disposable dusting cloths*, such as the Swiffer brand. Use a *small, dry natural-bristle pastry brush* to dust hard-to-reach areas such as vents and dashboard corners.

Mix *1 part all-purpose household cleaner*, such as Simple Green, with *8 parts water* in *a spray bottle*. Spray and wipe with a *clean cloth*. Use a *damp cloth-covered plastic knife* on dash dials and switches. (See Cleaning door panels, above.) If there are any scratches on the clear plastic lenses on your dash, mask them by rubbing on *baby oil* or a *clear-plastic treatment* such as Meguiar's cleaner and polish, available at auto supply stores.

simple
SOLUTIONS

Car Window Winter Wonder >

One of the things you hate most about winter is scraping that layer of ice off your windshield when you're late for work. To wake up to a frost-free car windshield, coat it the night before with a solution consisting of 3 parts vinegar to 1 part water.

Dress the dash and other nonupholstered, nonglass surfaces to prevent cracking and fading. Use a **UV-blocking interior protectant**, preferably one that's silicone-free.

All dressed? Now, *that's* gorgeous!

Start cleaning the car's exterior by checking the finish and trim for bugs and tar, and apply **bug and tar remover** to loosen them, following the manufacturer's instructions. Washing will remove the oily residue that the petroleum-based bug and tar remover leaves behind.

Washing wheels and tires is one activity where it's OK to blast with water, since it takes force to dislodge stubborn road grime and send it packing. Use a **pressure nozzle** to **hose** out inside the wheel wells and give the tires a cleaning blast. Mix **nondetergent car cleaner** with **water** in a **bucket** according to the package directions. Then scrub the wheels with the solution, using a **stiff-bristled brush or a rag**. A **soft-bristled toothbrush** will let you get at places where the brush won't fit.

A cardinal rule: Once you've used rags, brushes, and car-wash solution on the wheels and tires, don't reuse these same dirty materials anywhere else on the car.

Washing the car body starts with using a **hose** to spray the car—working from the roof downward. (Dirt, as they say, flows downhill.) With the first rinse, water will flow through those newly unplugged drain holes and wash away any residue from inside the doors and body. Mix **nondetergent car cleaner** with **water** in a **bucket**. Apply the solution with a **car-wash mitt or a soft rag**. Go for a mitt that's all wool or a wool-polyester blend. One hundred percent polyester is just too rough on your paint. Never suds up the entire car and then rinse, because that gives the cleaner time to air-dry and leave a film. Work your way around, soaping, rinsing, and drying the metal and trim in sections no larger than what you can reach without moving your feet (about 3 feet by 2 feet). Work from the roof down, making sure your rag stays free of stones, tar, and debris. Never continue to use a mitt or rag that's fallen on the ground.

Try this old detailer's trick: Have **two buckets** of **car cleaner solution**, which can be used one of two ways. Either designate one for "rough" or especially dirt-prone surfaces and the other for "smooth," less debris-laden ones, or use one bucket for your first soap pass (the "dirty" bucket) and the other for a second soap pass (the "clean" bucket). Segregate your rags accordingly.

Wash and dry painted metal gently. There's no sense in thinning its protective wax layer or making it uneven by rubbing too

hard. A detailer's secret for gentle drying: Hold a *towel* at both ends and drape it over the wet surface. Drag it across the surface toward you. That way, you don't apply any potentially wax-stripping pressure, as you might when rubbing with the rag in your hand. Consider doing two rounds of drying as well, to make sure you've done a thorough job.

Cleaning the trim is the next step. Spray vinyl and plastic parts with an *all-purpose household cleaner solution* (see Cleaning the dashboard, page 116) or use a *nonsilicone vinyl cleaner* (matte finish) according to label directions. Clean chrome with *chrome cleaner* according to label instructions. Use *fresh water* to rinse completely under any moldings—debris and dirt can collect there, creating a layer that can trap condensation. Trapped moisture eventually spells rust. Reverse the air direction on your *vacuum* and use it to blow-dry door handles, mirror cavities, and window moldings. Otherwise, when you drive they'll splash water that will be memorialized as water spots on your finish.

Cleaning window exteriors is no different from cleaning their interiors. Just spritz and wipe the glass with a *vinegar solution* or *nonammonia cleaner*. (See Cleaning window interiors, page 116.) Use *low-lint cloths* for drying.

Once the car is clean, unless it's brand-new or you're sure the wax layer is holding up (see Use a bead test, page 114.), you may need to polish, wax, and buff it.

The big payoff is in sight, and it's shine, shine, shine.

Polishing removes surface paint that has oxidized. Use a *car polish* if your paint finish appears bright, not hazy, and follow label instructions. A visible haze on the paint indicates more oxidation damage than a polish can mend and means your baby needs a little professional help. Take the car to a detailer for the machine buffing and hand-rubbing, cleaning, and polishing it will take to remove that level of oxidation. When you wash and wax regularly, you minimize the need to polish—or eliminate it.

Waxing can be done with either a *liquid or paste wax*. Follow the label instructions to the letter. As noted earlier, it's easy to pick up grit with paste wax, so be careful how you handle that applicator. A favored method for applying and removing wax is to use long, straight strokes that follow the same pattern that air takes as it moves around the automobile. The reason? Straight strokes don't leave behind the swirls in the finish that circular motions can. And if, by chance, you scratch the car, straight scratches are easier to remove. However, always read and follow

simple SOLUTIONS

The Poop on Polish >

When birds foul your car, you can't wait around till next Saturday's washing to deal with the problem. It'll only get worse, and the splat may etch into the paint finish. Mist-and-wipe detailing products, available at automotive stores, make the job easy. Spray the mist on the car and wipe it off with a clean cloth—before it has time to bond to the finish. An added benefit: You won't have to wax as often. Disposable, pretreated wipes that store easily in the glove compartment are also available in automotive shops and many discount retailers.

label instructions for applying the product you're using. Again, work in sections. When your applicator or rag starts to drag as you pull it, flip it over or use a clean section. If the product instructions say to wait until the wax dries to a haze, do it—this gives the wax time to work and makes it easier to remove.

Keep wax away from plastic moldings and rubber seals and trim pieces, from which it'll be next to impossible to remove wax once it dries.

There's no need to scrub as you apply or buff wax. The idea is to leave a good coat of wax behind. It takes only 3 to 4 foot-pounds of pressure to be effective—that's about the weight of your hand and arm.

For buffing, use your *softest rags*. Do it in the same straight motions you used to wax. When your rag moves smoothly across the surface and the residue is gone—voila!—you're done.

Cassette Players

If your cassette player is losing its highs and lows, it's time to break the sound barrier. The audio problem may very well be caused by dust and grime combined with the oxide buildup that occurs when an audiotape moves through the player. You can improve the sound by cleaning the tape path.

Keep in mind that the cheaper the tape you're using, the more quickly the oxide will accumulate in your player. Clean the player after every 75 hours or so of use and at least twice that often if you're using poor-quality tapes.

To clean the tape path, you need to wipe over everything that the tape touches as it's played—the heads, tape guides, chrome pin, and black rubber roller. Saturate *three to four cotton swabs* with *isopropyl (rubbing) alcohol* and thoroughly swab each area ▶. The chrome heads should be wiped both vertically and horizontally. Keep cleaning until the final cotton swab comes away with no brown residue. Don't worry about black residue from the roller—that's from the rubber.

You can also buy *cassette cleaning tapes*, which generally don't clean as thoroughly as the cotton swab method but are a good alternative for tape players whose insides are hard to reach, like those in car stereos. Most cleaning tapes contain a diluted alcohol-based fluid. You just pop the tape into the cassette player and let it rotate for 10 to 15 seconds.

Now you're ready for some easy listening.

OOPS!

Scratch and Sniffle >

Here's a worst-case scenario: You're happily scrubbing down your chariot when—ouch!—you realize you just dragged a rag full of tiny particles across the finish, leaving tiny scratches. Your best weapons against this: plenty of water on the surface and care in using your rag. Some detailers lead with their free hand, feeling across the surface of the car before they drag their rag across it.

▲

To extend the life of cassettes, store them properly. Keep them out of extreme heat (that includes the backseat of your car in midsummer) and away from direct sunlight. Store them in their cases away from magnetic fields created by computers, televisions, and video equipment.

See also ***CD Players and CDs*** *and* ***DVD Players***.

CD Players and CDs

When your CDs start skipping or the disk won't spin, there's a good chance the player's laser lens needs a quick shine. A clean machine produces better sound, and a little regular maintenance could mean you won't miss a beat.

While a variety of mechanical failures can sideline your player, it's worth taking a few minutes to see if cleaning will solve the problem—especially when you factor in the high cost of professional repair.

Cleaning the laser lens is inexpensive and simple on top-loading players and portable units. Front-loading players and carousel units require removing the player's cover and finding the lens. Often there are too many mechanisms in the way, and extensive disassembling should be left to the pros. In those cases, you can attempt to clean the lens with a ***cleaning disc***, available for about $10 to $15 in many stores that sell CDs. The disc looks like a CD, but its shiny side has tiny brushes on it, and as the disc spins it brushes the lens. However, the lens has to be able to "see" before the disc can spin, so a really dusty laser lens often won't respond when a cleaning disc is inserted.

But if your player's laser is in plain view in a top-loading model, even the most inexperienced home mechanic can clean it. Before you begin, unplug the CD player. If it's battery-powered, make sure the unit is off. Then do the following:

1. Locate the laser lens, which is a round glass bubble about a quarter-inch in diameter. The slightest bit of dust can prevent the laser from "reading" the CD.
2. Dip a ***cotton swab*** in ***rubbing alcohol*** and squeeze out the excess into a ***paper towel*** so it doesn't drip.
3. Using a circular motion, gently rub the lens for 5 to 10 seconds. The lens will move a little, but that's OK.
4. Let it dry. Depending on how much alcohol was left on the lens, it will take 10 to 20 minutes to dry. The CD player won't turn until it has sufficiently dried out.

Cleaning your CDs from time to time is also important, not only so that they play without distortion but also to prevent dust on the CDs from clogging up the player's works. Using a *CD cleaning cloth or a soft cloth* moistened with a little *rubbing alcohol*, hold the CD by its outer edges in one hand while cleaning with the other. Wipe the CD from the center to the outer edge, as though you were wiping the spokes of a wheel from the hub to the rim.

Proper storage of your CDs will go a long way toward extending their playing time. Store them in their cases, and inspect them periodically for dust and fingerprints, which can cause a tracking error. Keep your player and CDs out of direct sunlight.

One last tip: If the player is brought directly from a cold location to a warm one, moisture may condense on the lens, which will prevent the unit from playing. If this happens, remove the CD and wait about an hour for the moisture to evaporate.

See also **Cassette Players** *and* **DVD Players**.

Ceilings

If you want to brighten your overhead view, take aim at that grubby ceiling. Ceilings attract airborne dirt, cigarette smoke, and grease. Cleaning them is a project that's tempting to put off, since ceilings are hard to reach and awkward to clean. But a few tricks of the trade can minimize the misery. Whenever possible, use long-handled tools instead of balancing on a ladder or step stool.

Dusting the ceiling is sometimes all that's needed, and to do that, all you need is a *long-handled duster*. An effective duster, especially for removing cobwebs, is the Dazzle Webster All-Purpose Duster by Sunshine, which is generally available in home improvement stores. The device, which has a 60-inch extension handle, captures and holds fine dust and dirt and eliminates cobwebs without smearing. A *long-handled lamb's wool duster* or a *vacuum with a brush attachment* also works well.

To clean a dirty ceiling, you have to do the job by hand. First, you'll need to do a little prep work. Put down *drop cloths or newspapers* to protect furniture, electronic equipment, and floors. Wear *safety goggles* or other eye protection, because you're likely to dislodge small particles you can't really see coming at you. You'll probably want to wear *rubber gloves* as well. You can use a

simple SOLUTIONS

Face Up to a Drippy Situation >

If you use liquid cleaners to clean your ceiling, there's a better than even chance that some of that liquid will come dribbling down your arm onto your clothes or into your face. The solution: Wear rubber gloves and fold the ends up into cuffs, so anything that drips from your hands stays in the glove.

sponge mop with an extender handle, but you'll have to be careful to apply even pressure and get an even distribution of the cleaning product so it won't streak. Or you can use a *dry foam rubber sponge*, which means hauling out a *stepladder*. Take care to follow basic safety rules, such as placing the ladder securely on a level surface to prevent tipping, and never standing on the top step.

For painted ceilings, whether they're covered with oil-base or latex paint, a general-purpose cleaner, such as Spic and Span or Mr. Clean, works well. Mix *2 to 3 ounces of general-purpose cleaner* in *1 gallon of water*, dip your sponge in the solution, wring out the excess, and wipe the dirty area. Rinsing is necessary only if the ceiling is heavily soiled, but whether or not you rinse, you'll need to wipe away the excess moisture with a *dry towel* to prevent bead marks.

A spray-on acoustical finish on a ceiling has a rough surface that is best cleaned using a *vacuum cleaner* with a *soft brush attachment*.

Ceiling Tiles

An easy remedy for dirty acoustical ceiling tiles can be found in your medicine cabinet: hydrogen peroxide, an environmentally friendly product that contains powerful oxidizing agents.

To clean vinyl-coated ceiling tiles, buy 3 percent hydrogen peroxide solution (rather than the special industrial-strength version), which is widely available in grocery and drugstores. And wear *goggles* to keep debris and the peroxide mist out of your eyes. Mix about *1 ounce of hydrogen peroxide* in *1 quart of water* and pour it into a *spray bottle*. Peroxide, a mild bleach, will whiten the tiles. Best of all, no rubbing is required—simply spray the mixture on the tiles, applying it evenly, and let it air-dry.

To clean noncoated ceiling tiles—which generally aren't washable—use a *dry sponge cleaner*, such as a Wonder Sponge. Dry sponges are made from natural rubber and are sometimes treated with mild detergents. When using a dry sponge, wipe the ceiling tiles with an even, sweeping motion.

Ceramics

When it comes time to polish up your most cherished feat of clay—or porcelain, or earthenware—observing caution is job number one. Handmade ceramics used only for display run the greatest risk of being damaged during handling. So use both hands when lifting, and support the item from its base.

Dusting a decorative ceramic item is required only occasionally. And *dusting mitts*, such as Pledge Grab-it Mitts and Swiffer Mitts, work well because they contain no cleaning solutions to produce a residue that could discolor your pottery. The mitts are made of textured cloth and work by trapping dust and dirt in the fibers. But if the object has a rough surface, like raku pottery does, use a *dry, soft cloth* for dusting. The tiny holes in textured mitts will snag on rough areas.

Cleaning a ceramic item depends on what kind of ceramic it is.
- Machine-made, functional ceramic bowls and other pieces that do regular kitchen duty can be cleaned in the *dishwasher*.
- Handmade ceramics should be cleaned by hand, using a *soft cloth*, *mild dishwashing liquid*, and *water*. Don't soak the item, which can lead to staining. Instead, dampen a cloth with soapy water, wipe away the dirt, rinse with a *clean, damp cloth*, and let the piece air-dry in a *drainer*. Drying with a cloth increases the chance that the object will slip through your fingers.

To protect decorative ceramics on display in your home, buy *museum wax* at a craft and art supply store. Place the wax under your pottery to hold it firmly in place. If someone bumps into the table where it's displayed—or your cat brushes up against it—it won't go tumbling. The wax can be easily removed, yet holds firmly enough that you have to twist the object to remove it.

Chandeliers

Any homeowner who's spent thousands of dollars on an elegant chandelier needs to know about keeping crystals clear. You can buy the finest crystal in the world, but if it gets dirty, it's indistinguishable from cheap crystal.

A chandelier should be cleaned whenever it looks dusty, milky, or cloudy. There are several methods to restore a chandelier's dazzle, depending on how dingy it has become. But if you maintain it regularly—say, a couple of times a year—you probably won't have to remove all the crystals and wash them by hand.

If a chandelier is not too dirty, set up a *stepladder* in one or two spots where you can easily reach the chandelier without stretching and use one of these two methods to clean the crystals:
- The simplest way is to lightly dampen a *chamois cloth* with a little *water* and wipe each crystal ▶ while it's still attached to

▲

expert advice

A Humpty Dumpty Dilemma >

Before you start removing dusty chandelier crystals for hand-washing, make absolutely sure you know how to put the chandelier back together again.

Either clean a small section at a time or track down the trimming diagram that came with the chandelier, suggests Eileen Schonbek Beer, creative director of Schonbek Worldwide Lighting in Plattsburgh, New York, a family-owned chandelier company. If the diagram is long lost, take a photo of the intact chandelier or do a drawing before disassembling.

the chandelier frame. To clean the chandelier frame itself, just wipe it thoroughly with a *dry cloth*.

- The two-glove method is also popular. Buy a *pair of white cotton gloves*, available in most home improvement stores, and dampen one glove with a *glass cleaner*, such as Windex. Spray the cleaner onto the glove—never directly onto the chandelier, since a spray cleaner will eventually work its way into any tiny nicks or scratches in the frame finish, which can cause corrosion and ruin the frame. Massage each crystal with the damp glove, then wipe it immediately with the dry glove.

If a chandelier is really dirty, you'll have to take down the crystals and wash them by hand—no dishwasher shortcuts. Start by climbing your *stepladder* and removing the bulbs and setting them aside. Then carefully remove the crystals. Run *warm water* in a *dishpan or sink* until it's about a quarter full. Add *1 capful of white vinegar* and *1 drop of dishwashing liquid*. The combination will remove any grease or residue on the glass but will minimize the suds created, which are hard to rinse off.

Place a *folded towel* in the bottom of the sink. Wipe each crystal with your hands, then individually rinse each one under *running water* and dry with a *soft cloth*. If you don't dry them you'll have water spots.

Finally, wipe the light bulbs with a *damp sponge*, dry them with a *cloth*, return them to their sockets—and enjoy the light show.

Chewing Gum

When chewed-up chewing gum winds up in your carpet, clothes, or hair, you've got a sticky situation that will only get worse. Gum hardens over time, making it increasingly difficult to remove. But prompt action and a few time-honored gum control techniques will get you unstuck.

Using ice cubes to freeze gum and make it easier to remove is a simple and popular trick for removing gum from carpets, upholstery, and washable clothing. Begin by scraping off as much of the gum as possible with a *dull nonserrated knife*. Then put *one or two ice cubes* in a *self-sealing sandwich bag* and rub the bag over the spot until the gum freezes. Using the knife, scrape away more gum. Repeat as needed to remove all the gum.

To remove gum from a carpet, heat combined with a little chemical action is effective—but be sure to test this method first in an inconspicuous area to make sure the material is colorfast. Start by heating the gum with a **blow-dryer** for a minute or two. With a **plastic sandwich bag** on your hand, lift off as much of the heated gum as possible. If the gum starts to harden, heat it again and lift off more gum until as much as possible is gone.

Then massage **1/2 teaspoon of deep-heating rub** evenly into the spot. Use an extra-strength deep-heating rub, such as Ultra Strength Bengay. Turn the blow-dryer on high and heat the area for 30 seconds. Then use **another plastic bag** to lift off the remaining residue. Finally, add **1 teaspoon of mild detergent** to **1 cup of water** and blot the spot with **paper towels or a cloth rag** to lift any stain. Stubborn stains can also be treated with **spot remover or dry-cleaning solvent**.

To remove gum from clothing, follow the procedure described above for carpets, except apply the deep-heating rub to the opposite side of the cloth. After 30 seconds of blow-drying, the gum should peel off. Then wash the garment as usual, whether by hand or in a **washing machine**.

You can also try this variant of the ice-cube treatment: Seal the garment in a **plastic bag** and place it in the **freezer**. After it's frozen, just scrape the spot with a **dull knife** to remove the gum, and launder as usual.

To get gum out of hair, try this: Work **peanut butter or oil** into the gummy spot for a minute to soften the gum. Gently pull out the gum with a **paper towel**, then **shampoo** and rinse the area.

simple SOLUTIONS

Chew on This >

Removing chewing gum from sidewalks and streets is a huge and costly burden for cities throughout the world. For removing gum on a massive scale, chemical solvents are the premier cleaning method.

But before you resort to chemical warfare for the wad of gum stuck on your walkway, try some nontoxic, high-velocity water. Attach a jet nozzle to your garden hose, the kind used for power spraying, put it on its most powerful setting, and fire away at the spot. The quicker you attack the chewing gum, the more easily it will come up.

Chimneys

Where there's fire, there's smoke—and when it's in your fireplace, you'll eventually have a chimney that needs a clean sweep. Sooty chimneys can lead to chimney fires, which occur when creosote, a highly combustible residue created by burning wood, ignites. The resulting flames burn many times hotter than the wood in your fireplace—hot enough to melt the mortar in the chimney—and the red-hot sparks that burst from the chimney could set your home on fire.

To prevent such disasters, have your chimney cleaned regularly by a professional chimney sweep. Cleaning chimneys is difficult, dangerous work that requires special brushes and equipment tailored to fit the precise measurements of your fireplace flue. However, you can and should clean out the ashes in your fireplace when they start piling up. Shovel the ashes into a metal container with a tight lid—never a paper bag—and store it away from any combustible materials (including a wooden deck) before final disposal.

The frequency of chimney cleaning will depend on how much you use your fireplace. At the least, an annual inspection is needed.

To inspect a chimney yourself, you need to be in good shape and not mind climbing on the roof. Using a *powerful flashlight* and a *straight ladder* to access the roof, check the chimney openings both from the hearth and from the roof. On the roof, you'll have to remove any spark arrester or weather cap before you start.

- Look for obvious obstructions like bird nests. This is important even if all you have is a gas-log fireplace. While gas burns more cleanly than wood, a gas fireplace must be inspected for proper venting to keep odorless, poisonous carbon monoxide out of your home.
- Check the extent of creosote buildup. The creosote will be black or brown and could vary from a dripping tarlike substance to a shiny hardened mass. The highest concentration of creosote usually occurs in the top one-third of the chimney.
- Look for indications that you've had a chimney fire. Chimney fires, which roar hot until the energy source is spent or extinguished, sometimes occur without anyone's realizing it. Such fires can weaken the mortar, crack the tile lining of the chimney, or cause the lining to collapse. Any of those factors mean that heat from subsequent fires could reach and ignite combustible parts of the house, such as the wooden framing. Signs of a chimney fire include puffy creosote with rainbow-colored streaks, warped metal on the damper or metal smoke chamber, cracked or missing flue tiles, creosote flakes or chunks on the roof, and cracks in the exterior masonry.
- Inspect the outside of your chimney to make sure there are no cracks that could allow water to seep in. Changes in temperature will cause water that leaks in to freeze and thaw, which can cause mortar to crumble.

To find a reputable chimney sweep in your area, check the Chimney Safety Institute of America's website (www.csia.org) for state-by-state listings. The institute certifies chimney sweeps and tests them on their knowledge of chimney and venting systems. Then call your local Better Business Bureau to make sure the sweep is in good standing, and find out whether the company carries business liability insurance in the event of accidents.

To cut down on creosote buildup, burn wood that's been dried for six months to a year. Freshly cut wood has a higher moisture content than seasoned wood, which results in a smokier fire.

Hardwoods such as oak, maple, elm, and ash burn more slowly and with a steadier flame than softwoods such as spruce and pine, which cause faster creosote buildup.

See also **Fireplaces** and **Fireplace Screens and Tools**.

China

The term *fine china* evokes images of fragile delicacy, but most china manufactured today is made to be functional as well as elegant. Companies know today's busy consumer wants utility as well as beauty. So most china made in the last 25 years is dishwasher safe and says so explicitly on the bottom of the piece.

A notable exception is dinnerware with a band made of a precious metal such as platinum or gold. The high heat of the dishwasher's drying cycle will cause the metal to soften. You should also avoid lemon-scented detergents, because they contain citrus, which can corrode the metal, whether you're washing by hand or machine. Hand-washing is also required for antique or hand-painted china. The force and heat of the dishwasher is too much for fragile pieces.

Washing china in the dishwasher does require a little extra attention. Load the pieces carefully so they won't bump into each other and chip. Make sure aluminum utensils and lightweight foil containers don't rub against dishes during the wash cycle, because that can create black or gray marks.

To hand-wash antique or hand-painted china, start by lining the bottom of the **sink** with a **rubber mat or towel**. Half-fill the sink with **warm water** and a **mild dishwashing liquid**. To prevent chipping, take care not to overload the sink with dishes. Remove rings and jewelry to prevent scratching the china and, for the same reason, wash flatware separately. Use a **soft cloth or sponge** for cleaning. Here are some more tips:

- Wash or soak the items as soon after eating as possible, to prevent the problem of dried-on food and staining. Acidic foods such as mayonnaise and eggs can damage the glaze if left on for long periods.
- To remove dried food, soak the china in a grease-cutting **dishwashing liquid**, then scrub gently with a **nylon scouring pad**. Never use a metal pad, and avoid steel wool and gritty cleansers as well.
- Be careful when placing the dishes in the **drainer** to prevent scratches and chips.

Wash china figurines and sculptures by hand using the *mildest soap*—Ivory, for instance. Hand-dry with a *soft cloth*. If the piece has a wooden base, don't let the wood get wet.

See also **Dishes**.

Chrome

Chrome is common, all right: Older car bumpers are plated with it, as are toasters, electric frying pans, appliance handles, shower-heads, metal shower frames, and faucets. Since chrome is usually plated onto another metal, be gentle when you clean it, or you can wear it right off. And don't get abrasive with chrome. Cleaners with "scratch" in them can indelibly mar the surface.

To clean chrome, remember never to wash removable chrome items from your kitchen in greasy dishwater, because the next time the items get hot during cooking, that grease is likely to burn on. Trying to remove burned-on grease is a thankless task.

1. To clean chrome, try **dishwashing liquid** in **warm water** first, applied with an **old toothbrush** to work into cracks and crevices. Then rinse with **water** and polish to a shine with a **soft cloth**.
2. If that doesn't do the trick, use **baking soda** sprinkled onto a **damp sponge or cloth**. Let the soda sit on the chrome for an hour, then rinse with **warm water** and dry with **another cloth**.
3. Or rub down chrome with **undiluted cider vinegar or white vinegar**—no need to rinse. **Ammonia** can also be used—but rinse it off with **water** and dry completely.

Here are some other tricks for cleaning chrome:
- Chrome range burner rings often get grimy and sticky. To shine them up, rub with a paste made from **vinegar** and **cream of tartar**.
- Did a plastic bread wrapper melt all over your chrome toaster or toaster oven? Dab a little **acetone or nail polish remover** on the melted mess, then buff with a **soft cloth**. Keep the remover far from plastic parts, because it could eat them.
- Rub a chrome surface with **half a lemon** dipped lightly in **salt**. (If you have no lemons, use **white vinegar** and **salt** on a **soft cloth**.) Rinse well with **water** and buff to brilliance with a **dry cloth or paper towel**.
- For chrome trim on faucets, kitchen appliances, and cars, apply **baby oil** with a **soft cloth** and polish to restore luster. If hard water has left deposits, use a **commercial cleaner**, such as Lime-A-Way.

- Spiff up chrome furniture bases with **cider vinegar or rubbing alcohol**.
- To rid chrome of rust spots, especially on car trim and bumpers, crumple **aluminum foil** into a wad and rub with gusto, shiny side exposed. This technique also works wonders on golf club shafts.

Clocks

When cleaning your clock, what you *don't* do is as important as what you do. The most important aspect of cleaning a mantelpiece, wall, grandfather, or other nice mechanical clock is maintaining the internal mechanism to prevent wear and tear. To take care of the inner workings, it's best to entrust your clock to an expert to have it cleaned and oiled. Clocks are too easy to damage going the do-it-yourself route. Service the mechanism every two to three years. Remember that time may be your worst enemy, but dirt in any timepiece comes in a close second.

Cleaning and oiling the inner workings of a clock are possible if you're exacting. The first step is to wipe the inner workings with a dry, soft cloth to get rid of the worst of the dust and grime. Then apply *special clock oil*, which you can obtain at clock shops but not at hardware stores. It typically comes with a penlike applicator. People often try using WD-40 first before they abandon the project and cart the clock to a professional. Don't do it! WD-40 is not a proper lubricant for clocks—it wears the mechanism out even faster, attracting dirt rather than repelling it. If you do clean and oil the clock yourself, use a *clamp* to hold

OOPS!

Springing into Action >
One occupational hazard to note before you embark on cleaning the insides of a mechanical clock: If you don't tightly clamp down the springs and other movable parts, they can go flying every which way. So says Roger Mackey, a clock repair and cleaning expert in Macfarlan, West Virginia. "I've seen clockworks go flying all over the room, chipping teeth and breaking stuff," recalls Mackey, who started cleaning and repairing clocks in 1968. His best counsel is to let the experts clean your clock, especially on the inside.

This Explanation Is *Just the Ticket*

An entry about cleaning clocks would not be complete without an exploration of the peculiar expression *clean your clock*, meaning "punch you" or "knock you out." How did the dainty task of dusting off a timepiece get equated with such an act of violence? Could it be that we've historically

associated human faces and clock faces, and smacking one or the other would surely jolt loose any cobwebs?

There are a few theories floating about, but *Cassell's Dictionary of Slang* gets the most specific: The term *clean the clock* is old United States railroad terminology. To stop

suddenly, the engineer would hit the air brakes, bringing the air gauge (or "clock") down to zero—or "clean." Cleaning a *person's* clock, then, meant bringing the person to a dead halt. All aboard with this explanation?

down springs and other movable parts. (See the Oops sidebar.) And don't put too much oil on the gears and the plate.

Cleaning the exterior of a clock, assuming it's a wooden clock, is done as you would do any other fine piece of furniture. Use a *furniture oil* to feed the wood. (Lemon oil works well and smells pleasant.) To dust a clock case, use a *dust remover*, such as Endust or Lemon Pledge, spritzed on a *soft cloth*, not on the clock itself.

Wipe the piece covering the face—be it glass, acrylic, or another clear plastic—with a *clean, soft cloth*. If you know the cover is glass, it's OK to use a *window cleaner*, such as Windex or Cinch, but never spray the cleaner directly on the clock. Spray it on the cloth and wipe ever so gently.

Coffee Grinders

Wake up and smell the coffee! Whatever you do when cleaning out that electric coffee grinder, don't take it swimming. Immersion in water can ruin a perfectly good grinder.

Clean a coffee grinder after every use. Lest this become an electrifying experience, always begin by unplugging the unit. Brush out the grinder with a *pastry brush, old toothbrush, or special coffee grounds brush*, sold at gourmet kitchen stores and some coffee shops. This doesn't have to be a grind—simply make sure you leave the stainless steel inside the grinder shiny, so that tomorrow's batch of beans won't be sullied by stale grounds from yesterday's pot. (The organic oils in coffee beans can get funky fast.) Wash the plastic lid with a *sponge* in *dishwashing liquid* and *warm water*; rinse and dry with a *soft cloth*.

Two more methods you can try:
1. Dampen a *paper towel* and swab the inside.
2. Run a small *handful of uncooked white rice* through the coffee grinder, especially if you use it for grinding anything other than coffee beans. Most coffee experts advise against using your machine for grinding dry spices, by the way, since the smells from grinding ingredients such as cinnamon sticks and dried basil are nearly impossible to get out.

Coffee Makers

Coffee makers often get corrupted with minerals and other impurities from the water you use to make that good cuppa Joe. The harder the water, the more deposits it will form on the inside of your coffee maker. To keep your coffee maker perking along, clean it at least once a month—if you use the maker every day—to rid it of this whitish scale, or every two months if you brew a pot less often. Failing to clean your coffee maker's inner workings will affect heating and brewing time and will adversely affect the taste and aroma of your coffee. Always check your owner's manual before embarking on any of the following cleaning methods. In general, no electric coffee maker should be immersed in water.

To clean an electric drip coffee maker—the most popular variety on the market today—you have your choice of three tried-and-true methods:

- Fill the water reservoir, half with *cold water* and half with *white vinegar*. Place a *clean paper filter* in the basket—minus the java, of course. Run the coffee maker through its entire cycle. Repeat the brewing cycle two more times, using *plain water* each time to flush out the remaining crud.
- Fill the reservoir with *water* and add *2 tablespoons of decalcifier* (such as CLR Calcium Lime Rust Remover, available at hardware stores) or *2 tablespoons of water softener pellets*. Turn on the coffee maker and run it once through the complete cycle, then a second time with *plain water*.
- Fill the reservoir with *hot water* and add a *denture tablet*. Run the machine through its complete brewing cycle, then run it once more using *plain water*.

Wash the coffee carafe in *hot water* with *dishwashing liquid* and rinse with *water*. Then remove any other removable parts and do the same. You can wash these pieces in the top rack of the *dishwasher*, but their colors may fade. If so, buff them with a *soft, dry cloth*.

To clean an electric percolator—the kind your mom and grandmother made famous—fill the pot with *water* and add *1/4 cup cream of tartar*. Run it through the complete percolating cycle, then wash well with *hot, soapy water*, rinse completely with *fresh water*, and let dry.

Coins

To coin a phrase, if you're thinking of cleaning a coin you suspect might be valuable: Don't! Cleaning coins at home is usually a lousy idea if you think they're worth something. On the other hand, if you don't cotton to the idea of grungy spare change dirtying your pocket, there's no reason not to wash it.

expert advice

Brew Your Own Cleaning Solution >

Starbucks coffee expert Chris Gimbl suggests brewing your own coffee maker cleaning solution. He uses lemon juice instead of white vinegar because the smell is more pleasant.

Fill the reservoir half full with water, then to the top with pulp-free lemon juice, advises Gimbl, a spokesperson at the company's Seattle, Washington, headquarters. (Use a ready-to-use lemon juice, such as ReaLemon, because squeezing your own takes too much time, not to mention requiring too many lemons! And straining out pulp and seeds "can be a real pain," Gimbl says.)

Run the coffee maker through its entire cycle. Discard the solution in the coffee pot, then run the brew cycle two or three more times with plain water until you don't smell lemon anymore. Wash all removable parts in hot, sudsy water, then rinse and dry.

Once you've cleaned your pocket change, bake coins in a low oven to dry them instead of allowing them to air-dry or laboriously hand-drying each and every one, advises Robert Wilson Hoge, curator of American coins and currency with the American Numismatic Society in New York City. "Because coins are made of metal, and metal can corrode after exposure to water, you want to avoid this when you clean coins," Hoge says. He suggests spreading washed and rinsed coins on a lipped cookie sheet, then drying them for 5 to 10 minutes in a 200° F oven.

To clean a valuable coin—or just one that you think could be valuable—take it to a professional coin dealer or conservator for a careful face-lift that will remove normal wear and tear. When a collectible coin is cleaned, its value can plummet unless the cleanup crew knows exactly what it's doing. A coin spruced up by an amateur develops an oddly dull, sometimes scoured look rather than bearing the blush of normal oxidation and handling.

To clean ordinary coins, give them a warm bath without the rubber ducky. Put the dirty coins in a *lidded jar*, add *warm water* and *1 or 2 drops of dishwashing liquid*, put the lid on, and gently shake. Then rinse with *running water* and pat dry with *paper towels or a clean rag*. Whatever you do, don't use lemon juice or anything else acidic. Never use abrasives either, as they'll scratch the surface.

To sanitize grimy coins—if you're worried about the spread of germs (and who isn't, these days?)—saturate a *cotton ball or cotton swab* with *rubbing alcohol* and wipe the coins. No need to rinse them, since the alcohol soon evaporates.

Another cleaning technique is to soak coins in olive oil. (Hold the balsamic vinegar, please!) Put the coins in a *lidded jar* filled with *olive oil* (not the expensive extra-virgin stuff—use a lesser supermarket brand instead). Change the oil when it gets funky and cloudy. The entire process can take anywhere from a few days to several months, depending on how mucked-up your coins are.

Combs

Combs come in many sizes and several materials these days. Most are fashioned from rubber, plastic, or bone, all durable materials that take kindly to a sound drubbing.

To clean any comb, first remove hair clinging to the teeth. Then try this nifty homemade version of Barbicide, the solution barbers and hairdressers use to sanitize their combs. (It also works for brushes; see Hairbrushes.) Mix in a bowl or covered jar *16 fluid ounces of warm water, 1/4 cup of household ammonia, and 1/4 teaspoon of liquid detergent or shampoo*. Stir or shake to combine. Submerge the comb in the liquid and soak for 10 minutes. Use a *small, stiff-bristled fingernail brush or old toothbrush* to loosen up hair oils and grime clinging to the teeth. To sanitize the comb further, rub the teeth with a *cotton ball* saturated with *rubbing alcohol*. Rinse the comb with *warm water* and allow it to air-dry before using.

To clean a baby's comb, swish it in a solution of *1 teaspoon baking soda* dissolved in a basin of *warm water*. Rinse with *fresh water* and air-dry.

To clean a fine-toothed metal comb used to rid a child's hair of lice and their nits, or eggs, you need to take extra care. Here are three solutions:

- Soak the comb in a solution of *1 part chlorine bleach* to *9 parts water* for 15 minutes, rinse, and air-dry. (If you don't dry it thoroughly, a metal comb will rust.)
- Soak the comb in *hot water* (at least 130° F) for 5 minutes.
- Seal the comb in a *plastic bag* for two weeks. (Gasping for air, those nasty nits and lice eventually suffocate.)

simple SOLUTIONS

Wipe Away That Grime! >
Here's how to add teeth to your comb-cleaning regimen: Give that dingy comb a quick touch-up by rubbing it with a disinfecting wipe. (Clorox Disinfecting Wipes is a popular brand.) Let the comb dry, then rinse and air-dry again.

Comforters

Typically, a comforter is quilted and reversible, covers the top of the bed, and drops 15 inches over the edge at the foot and sides. Comforters are usually filled with bonded polyester fill but sometimes have down inside.

Check the fabric care label first to make sure the comforter is washable. If it is, make sure it fits into your washer and dryer without cramming. They can be troublesome to launder at home because most home washers and dryers simply aren't big enough to swallow them. If the comforter is crowded in the washer, it won't get clean. (And when jammed into a too-small dryer, the comforter could scorch in some areas while remaining wet in others.) If your home equipment is too small, take it to a self-service laundry, where the equipment is more commodious. Or, if the care label dictates, have it dry-cleaned.

Before washing the comforter, use a *brush attachment* to *vacuum* the comforter, ridding it of excess dust. Be careful not to suck up any loose threads. (If your comforter has lots of loose ends, put *nylon netting*, available at fabric or bridal stores, over the brush end of your vacuum and secure it with a *strong rubber band*. A spent pair of *panty hose* also does the trick.)

To wash the comforter, first make sure the fabric is colorfast by rubbing a bit of *prewash stain remover*, such as Shout or Clorox Stain Out, in an inconspicuous spot. Pretreat stains and heavily soiled areas, working it into the fabric gently with a *soft nylon-bristled scrub brush*. Wash your comforter solo in your *washer* with *warm water* and *laundry detergent* on the *gentle cycle*.

To dry the comforter, selecting the right heat setting on your *dryer* for its fabric. Add *two clean, dry bath towels; a clean tennis shoe; or several pristine tennis balls* to the drum to knock against the filling and keep it from clumping. Stop the dryer at least once to make sure the comforter doesn't scorch inside. Also shake it out once, to be certain the filling doesn't clump in one corner.

*See also **Bedspreads**.*

Computers

Computers collect more than just dust, grimy fingerprints, crumbs, hair, fingernail clippings, and other unidentified miniature objects. We've heard reports that they have been home for cookies, Batman action figures, spider nests, and half a cheeseburger.

   A computer can be given a quick once-over with a vacuum or dust cloth as part of your regular cleaning procedure. But it's a good idea to give it a more thorough cleaning occasionally. Once every three months is sufficient, although you'll want to clean the screen every month or so. If you're leery, take it to a professional. If you opt for the at-home treatment, the first step is to make sure the computer is turned off and unplugged.

To clean the screen of a traditional tube monitor, dust it with a *clean cloth or a facial tissue.* To remove fingerprints, wipe with a *slightly damp cloth. Special towelettes,* sold at office supply stores, may be used on the screen, but they sometimes leave a soapy film. Try an *all-purpose cleaner* instead, such as Fantastik or Formula 409, sprayed on a *cloth* and then wiped on the screen. Avoid ammonia-based cleaners, because they sometimes leave unsightly streaks.

To clean a new flat screen monitor, you need to use special care. This also applies to the screen on a laptop. First unplug the power supply, then lightly dampen a *clean, soft, lint-free cloth* (no paper towels or facial tissues on these babies!) with *water* and *isopropyl alcohol* (not ethyl alcohol; see warning at left). Wipe the screen gently with a back-and-forth-motion, never in a circle. Wipe the display case gently with a *nonabrasive, soft, dry cloth* to pick up dust. And take these precautions to prolong the life of your flat screen: Never tap or touch the screen with your pen, finger, or other object. And don't slap sticky notes on your screen.

WATCH OUT

If you have a new flat LCD monitor—or a laptop—never use products containing acetone, ethyl alcohol, toluene, ethyl acid, ammonia, or methyl chloride to clean the screen. They can damage it.

COMFORTERS

To clean the keyboard, which is a magnet for all sorts of gunk, first turn it upside down over a ***wastebasket*** and give it a good shake. Most crumbs and dust will fall right out. Then ***vacuum*** it with your ***brush attachment.*** To clean the keys, rub them and the surrounding plastic with a ***cloth*** dampened with ***rubbing alcohol***. Or purchase a ***special keyboard cleaner-degreaser***, sold at electronics stores. Using a ***can of compressed air***, available at hardware stores, blast away hair, crumbs, and dust from between the keys. Rubbing keys with a ***fabric softener sheet*** will keep dust-attracting static at bay.

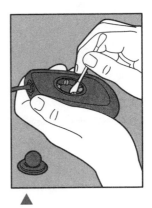

▲

To clean the mouse, unscrew the mouse-ball cover on the bottom and take out the ball. Wipe it down with ***denatured alcohol***, available at paint stores, on a ***soft cloth***. Remove any dust or fluff inside the mouse-ball socket with your finger. Then, with a ***cotton swab*** dipped in ***alcohol***, clean the three rollers the ball touches inside the socket ▶.

To clean inside the computer, you can also use ***compressed air***. To open an upright computer, unscrew one side of the case. One side is usually held by screws with knurled heads that you can turn by hand, but on some models you may need to use a ***screwdriver***. Don't touch anything inside that you don't have to. Keep your fingers away from cards, cords, and other parts. And be sure the compressed air wand is at least 4 inches from the machine. Blow air into the power supply box (that's where the power cord enters) and the fan at the back of the case. Then blast a bit of air into the CD and floppy disk drives. Before replacing the side, wipe it with a ***damp cloth***. Let it dry before putting it back on.

A Mouse *by Any Other Name ...*

People do all sorts of things near their computers. They eat over them, accidentally dump coffee and other drinks onto their keyboards, and sometimes jam four or five CDs at a time into the CD-ROM drive. And then, of course, there are the children who are fascinated by little holes and love to shove big things into small places with their tiny hands.

David Larrabee, senior technician with Second Source, a computer sales, service, and Internet company in West Chester, Pennsylvania, has seen it all. In his day, Larrabee has pulled keys, a peanut butter sandwich, and a soggy oatmeal cookie out of floppy disk drives.

Larrabee's favorite computer-cleaning story harks back to the day when a PC user brought in his machine to be cleaned, complaining of its stench. It turns out that residing in the place normally reserved for the modem was a dead mouse. "Mice love computers," Larrabee says with a laugh. "The machines exude heat, and mice find plenty of wires to munch on."

The moral of this story: Beware any odd smells emanating from your computer. It could be that a mouse—not the electronic kind, mind you—has set up shop inside.

To clean computer equipment exteriors, simply wipe the outside surfaces with an *all-purpose cleaner*, sprayed on a *soft cloth*. Dust can collect in ports where you attach cables. Use the *compressed air with wand* to blow the ports clean. Or give them a swipe with one end of a *cotton swab* dampened with *rubbing alcohol*. Use the other end of the cotton swab to dry them.

To clean the glass bed of your scanner, use *mild soap or an ordinary glass cleaner without ammonia*. (Ammonia cleaners, unless they're completely wiped off, leave a film that could make scanned documents look weirdly oily or speckled.) Spray the glass cleaner onto a *soft cloth* rather than squirting it on the glass itself. Another approach: Use *denatured alcohol*. If there's a metal ruler scale along the edge of the glass, avoid getting it wet. That goes for the glue holding it down, too. Never use paper towels on your scanner. Even the more expensive types can make fine scratches on optical surfaces. Use *soft, lint-free cloths* instead. An old cloth diaper or clean T-shirt is perfect.

See also **Printers.**

WATCH OUT

• Don't use ordinary household spray cleaners on your keyboard. If the liquid gets under the keys, it can damage the keyboard by shorting the contacts under the keys.

Concrete

Cement your understanding here about how to clean concrete. The essential first step? Determine what caused the grime or stain, if you can, and then act accordingly—and fast. The longer an untreated stain stays on concrete, the more likely it is to seep in to become part of the whole. Methods vary on how to clean concrete, but the fact is that cleaning up that garage floor, patio, walkway, driveway, or other concrete is an essential part of regular home maintenance.

Clean concrete at least once a year. Before you start, be sure to protect adjacent glass, metal, wood, plants, or other decorative materials with a *tarpaulin* or *old shower curtain*. Try one of the following methods listed in order of increasing wallop. Always test the method in an obscure spot to make sure it works. Never use a metallic brush on concrete, as metallic fibers can get trapped in the concrete, where they'll rust.

● If the concrete is old and crumbly, brush it—lightly—with a *soft brush*. If that doesn't do the trick, try *warm water* and *mild detergent*, adding *white vinegar* to the water if the soil and stains persist.

● Wet the concrete with *warm water* and let it absorb the water a bit. Then scrub with a *soft, nonmetallic brush*. Wash off the concrete with a *garden hose* fitted with a *high-pressure nozzle* and let it dry.

- If that isn't enough, add *1/4 cup of mild dishwashing detergent* to a *pail* of *warm water* and scrub again.
- Failing that, use a *stronger detergent*, mixed with *water* and *1/4 cup ammonia*, applied with a *stiff nylon brush*.
- For obstinate grime, mix *trisodium phosphate* (TSP), which you can buy at hardware stores, in a *pail* with *warm water*, according to the package instructions for heavy cleaning jobs. Scrub with a *rigid nylon brush*, then rinse with a *garden hose* and let air-dry.
- Another approach: Rent a *pressure-washing machine* to squirt off dirt that's not ground into the concrete. Set the pressure at *3,000 pounds per square inch* and use a *flat-fan nozzle*.

To remove serious stains, such as tire marks, grease, oil, and other stubborn materials, you're going to have to get aggressive. For fresh grease stains, first sprinkle *dry cement, kitty litter, or sand* on the spot, letting it sit an hour to absorb the gunky mess. Then sweep it up with a *broom* and *dustpan*. For more irksome grease spots, use a *commercial degreaser*, following label instructions.

Contact Lenses

Deciding which solutions to use for your contact lenses can be dizzying. The vision care aisle at drugstores and supermarkets is chockablock with products. To make sense of it all, first understand that there are two basic kinds of contacts today. Soft lenses are by far the more prevalent of the two, commanding about 85 percent of the market, with gas-permeable (GP) lenses being most of the remainder. (GP lenses are not to be confused with the old hard lenses, which currently account for less than 1 percent of total U.S. contact lens sales.)

Here are a few basic guidelines of sound contact lens care that you should follow regardless of whether you wear soft or gas-permeable lenses:

- Clean and disinfect your lenses once a day. Always use fresh solution to clean and store your lenses.
- Always wash and rinse your hands thoroughly before handling the lenses. Don't use perfumed soaps or scented hand cream— let alone make homemade salsa with jalapeno peppers—right before touching your contacts. Dry your hands with a clean, lint-free towel.

- Close the sink drain or at least cover it with a washcloth.
- Never use tap or bottled water as a substitute for the store-bought lens care system your eye care expert recommends. Water can bear a microorganism (Acanthamoeba) that can cause serious eye infections.
- Clean your accessories (lens case, cleaning/disinfecting containers, vials for enzymatic cleaners, and the like) after each use exactly as the directions advise. Typically, this involves cleaning, rinsing, and air-drying.
- Throw out your lenses once a month, or as often as is recommended, to reduce the chance of infection.

The cleaning program for the two major types of contact lenses is basically the same: Clean, rinse, disinfect. In times past, there were three different products for this. Today, cleaning, disinfecting, and rinsing solutions are usually all-in-one. Get into the habit of always handling your right lens first to avoid confusion. Here's how to proceed:

1. Remove the right lens and clean it by gently rubbing the lens in the palm of your hand with *a few drops of rinsing/disinfecting cleaner*. (Some newer solutions have a no-rub feature, useful for people who frequently rip their lenses while cleaning them.)
2. Rinse the lens to remove any leftover cleaner, cosmetics, and other substances. Be sure to rinse the lens for as long as package instructions direct.
3. Place the lens in your *lens holder* and fill it with your chosen *disinfecting solution*. This step kills microorganisms that may have a mind to breed on your lens.

Repeat the process with the left lens. Disinfecting time varies from product to product, but most directions urge you to soak lenses overnight.

Two other important points to keep in mind are these:
- Soft lenses pick up protein deposits more readily than GP types do. If your lenses start to feel grainy or your vision becomes clouded, chances are you need to use an *enzymatic cleaner* daily or weekly, according to package directions.
- Some people have allergic reactions to some contact lens solutions. About 10 percent of people, for instance, are allergic to thimerosal, a preservative sometimes used in saline lens solutions. Experiment to see what works for you.

Coolers

Ideally, you should clean your cooler after each use. The method for cleaning depends a lot on what you've had in it. Diet Cokes on ice? Easy. Just rinse it out with *water*.

To clean a large cooler more thoroughly, haul it into the backyard and *hose* it down. Pour a *couple of drops of dishwashing liquid* onto the wet cooler and scrub it, using a *clean rag, sponge, or scrub brush*. Then turn the cooler on its side, so water will drain out, and rinse with a *hose*. (You also can do this in the *bathtub*, where the *hot water* would help with tougher cleaning jobs. Just wash those teensy coolers in the *kitchen sink*.)

To sanitize a cooler—if you've been carrying raw meat in it, for example—mix *1 teaspoon of bleach* in *1 quart of water*. Apply the solution to the cooler with a *sponge or rag*, or pour it into *a spray bottle*, squirt it on, and wipe. Then rinse with *fresh water*. Once your cooler is clean, let it air-dry with the lid open before you store it.

To remove stubborn food stains, make a paste by mixing *baking soda* and *water* in a *bowl*. Dip a *clean rag or sponge* into the paste, rub the spot, and rinse. If that doesn't work, apply a *nonabrasive household cleaner*, such as Formula 409, Fantastik, or Soft Scrub, with a *rag*. Using an abrasive cleaner could scratch the interior of your cooler, giving dirt and bacteria a place to hide—and making your cleaning job harder.

To clean a soft-structure cooler, mix *mild dishwashing liquid* in *water* and wipe the cooler down inside and out with a *clean rag or sponge*. Rinse and air-dry. Don't machine-wash, and don't use bleach on this type of cooler.

Copper

Copper is a metal and, while it's harder than silver, it's still softer than either brass or bronze. For cleaning purposes, it comes in two flavors—lacquered and unlacquered—as well as many sizes and shapes. Lacquered copper, which is usually on decorative items, has a finish baked on at the factory. Unlacquered copper, found mostly on cookware, tarnishes easily but will brighten with elbow grease and the right techniques. Rarely will you see lacquered copper cookware or utensils. If you do, you should remove the finish before using them for eating or cooking.

To clean a decorative copper item with a lacquered finish, you only need to dust the piece with a **dust cloth** or **vacuum** as part of your regular cleaning process. If it's dirty, you might want to wipe it with a **damp cloth**. Lacquering on decorative pieces works OK until cracks appear in the finish. Then the piece must be stripped of its coating with **acetone or lacquer thinner**, applied full strength with a **cloth**. Or boil the item in **2 gallons of water** with **1 cup of washing soda**. (Arm & Hammer Super Washing Soda is one popular brand.) The lacquer should peel right off. Wash with **dishwashing detergent**, rinse with **running water**, and dry with a **soft cloth**.

If you want the piece lacquered again, have a professional metal finisher do it.

To clean copper cookware, you should first be aware of the don'ts. Never use any scratchy cleaning tool on copper. You run the risk of leaving marks. And bleach will seriously discolor copper if it stands for a few hours or more. Don't use oven cleaners or glass cleaners like Windex, either—they'll make quick work of your copper because they will corrode it.

If copper cookware is really in bad shape, remove corrosion before you polish. Several cool methods exist to do this.
- Sprinkle the piece with **salt** and a little **white vinegar**.
- Cut a **lemon** in half, dip it in **salt**, and rub.
- As long as the piece can stand the heat, boil it in a large **kettle** filled with **water, 1 cup of white vinegar,** and **1/2 cup of salt**.

Whatever method you use to clean your cookware, rinse with **fresh water**, dry well with a **dish towel**, and buff with a **soft cloth**. If you want more shine, apply a **commercial copper cleaner** according to label directions.

Here are two more tips to help you clean copper:
- Crevices—where the handle joins the pot, for instance—can be tough to clean. These spots are also magnets for paste polish buildup. Use a **cotton swab or horsehair brush** and **rubbing alcohol** to banish the gunk.
- Swab small copper items with **ketchup** applied to a **cotton cosmetic pad or cotton swab**. You'll be surprised by how quickly they gleam.

Cork

When it comes to cleaning a cork floor, walk softly: Be sparing with whatever liquid you use. Most cork floors are sealed with polyurethane to prevent them from lapping up spills and other

stains. Still, you don't want water or other liquids to penetrate the seams. Otherwise, the glue and floor itself could lift off the subflooring. Should this happen, you might pop a cork, because you would probably have to reglue the entire floor—an expensive proposition.

To clean a cork floor, sweep up loose dirt with a ***broom*** and ***dustpan*** first. Then apply a ***quick-drying, alcohol-based no-wax floor cleaner*** (such as Bruce) with a ***damp mop***. Dab a bit of cleaner on any sticky, persistent spots and then blot with a ***soft rag***. Never use acids like white vinegar on your cork floor, whether it's sealed or not.

Heavily trafficked areas—the foyer, walkway, and kitchen, for instance—should be coated with polyurethane every two to three years. Be sure a floor expert performs this task. Floors must first be scrubbed with a special pad to rough up old sealant.

To clean cork walls, which usually aren't sealed, rub them with a ***putty-style wallpaper cleaner or a dry foam-rubber sponge***, available at hardware and paint stores. Any spots may be carefully hand-sanded with ***superfine (0000) sandpaper*** to remove them. But hear this: Cork on walls is usually only 1/8 inch thick, so be careful not to turn your cork into an unsightly patchwork.

To clean a cork or cork-backed item, such as a coaster, a trivet, or a mat, wet it with ***cold water*** and scrub with a ***pumice stone or pad***. Rinse with ***water*** and air-dry in a cool, dry place.

simple
SOLUTIONS

Bread (and Tape) to the Rescue >

Ducks love stale bread, and you can make salad croutons with it, too. But there's yet another use: Tear off a hunk of that dried-out staff of life and scrub gently on stained cork. It cleans the cork without damaging it. An alternative: Try patting the grungy spot with tape.

Countertops

Keeping countertops pristine serves two purposes: Your kitchen looks nicely kept and, since countertops are where most food preparation takes place, they become less of a breeding ground for bacteria.

Countertops have come a long way since Formica, a plastic laminate, reigned supreme. Today, the most common type of countertop is a solid-surface synthetic. (Corian is one popular brand.) Other popular types are marble, granite, and engineered or synthetic stone. You would do well to read the manufacturer's directions for cleaning your kind of countertop.

General countertop maintenance calls for removing the stuff on top first, then cleaning up surface dirt and crumbs with a ***soft-bristled brush or handheld vacuum***. Wet a ***nylon-backed sponge*** with soapy water (***dishwashing liquid*** in ***warm water***) and use the soft side of the sponge to wash the counter, backsplash included.

Let soapy water sit on the surface a few minutes to soften any spots. Switch to the scrubbing side to remove any intransigent spots. Rinse with **warm water** and buff dry with **a clean, lint-free towel**. Or squirt with a **window cleaner** such as Windex, wipe clean with a **sponge**, rinse with **water,** and dry so that it doesn't look dull or streaky.

Plastic laminates, such as Formica, don't take kindly to anything scratchy. Instead, sop up spills immediately with a **sponge**, then use a **soapy sponge or all-purpose cleaner** such as Fantastik to wipe the counter clean. For obstinate stains, try one of these two approaches:

- Sprinkle with **baking soda** and rub with a **soft, damp cloth**. Then rinse and dry with **paper towels or a soft cloth**.
- Make a paste of **lemon juice** and **cream of tartar**, spread it on the stain, and let it sit for 15 minutes. Then rinse and dry.

Remember, the older they get, the more laminates need a gentle touch. They can chip, scratch, and lose their shine as they age.

Solid-surface synthetics, such as Corian, can withstand light abrasion. Wet a **scrub sponge**, such as a green Scotch-Brite pad, or sprinkle a **mildly abrasive cleaner**, such as Soft-Scrub (without bleach), on a **damp sponge** and apply with gentle pressure. Rinse with **water** on a sponge and dry with a **soft cloth**.

Regularly polishing solid surfaces is impractical for most people because counters are washed so often. But for special occasions, DuPont (the maker of Corian) recommends **Hope's Countertop Polish** because it imparts a nice gleam. For a high-gloss shine, use **white polishing compound**. (TurtleWax makes one common brand.) Both products are available at hardware and home improvement stores.

Stone countertops, usually made of marble or granite, are increasingly popular these days. Counter to popular belief, stone-faced countertops are rather delicate. Acid etches marble, and anything greasy stains granite. To clean marble and granite, start with the don'ts: Never use anything abrasive. Instead, wash with **a few drops of plain or antibacterial dishwashing liquid** on a **damp sponge**. Rinse the surface completely with **clean water** and dry with a **soft cloth**. Or buy a **cleaner formulated for stone** from your supplier.

Here are some more tips on maintaining your stone countertop:

- Blot up spills pronto with **paper towels**. Don't wipe—that only makes it worse. Flush the spot with **warm water** and **mild soap**, rinsing several times before drying with a **soft cloth**.

COUNTERTOPS

- Use *coasters, trivets*, or *place mats* under glassware and dishes to protect surfaces from scratching. Heat damages marble, so never set anything hot on it.
- Stone countertops are sometimes sealed with a penetrating commercial sealant. Make sure that wherever you prepare food, the sealant is nontoxic. *Salad oil* is an effective nontoxic and homespun coating for food preparation areas.

Engineered stone usually resembles granite but requires no sealant and little extra care. Wash with *soap* and *water*, an *all-purpose cleaner* such as Formula 409, or a *window cleaner* such as Cinch.

See also Granite and Marble.

Crayon Marks

Lavish on them all the pads of paper in the world, and still crayon-wielding youngsters will be mysteriously attracted to the walls of your home. Pint-sized artists are also known to leave their mark on clothing, furniture, carpet, and other flooring. And crayons can make a mess of the dryer where, forgotten in a pocket, they can melt and stain clothing.

To remove crayon from most smooth surfaces, be they painted walls, glass, metal, tile, marble, or porcelain, spray the marks with a *penetrating lubricant* (specifically, WD-40), then wipe with a *soft cloth*. The lubricant WD-40 is the weapon of choice when it comes to removing many crayon marks. It lifts off the stain by getting between the mark and the surface. Spray a little WD-40 first in an obscure spot to make sure it won't harm what you're cleaning. If that lubricant doesn't do the trick, dip a *sponge* into a solution of *dishwashing liquid* and *warm water* and wet the crayon mark, rubbing with a circular motion. Rinse with *warm water*, then air-dry.

To banish crayon from clothing, place the fabric on *paper towels*, then spray with *penetrating lubricant* (again, WD-40). Spray more of the lubricant on a *clean rag* and apply it to both sides of the stain. Allow the lubricant to sit for two minutes. Then, using your fingers, rub *1 or 2 drops of dishwashing liquid* into the stain on *each* side. Replace the *paper towels* as they absorb the crayon. Launder the clothing in the *washer* using the *hottest water* possible and the *heavy soil setting*.

Other approaches that you might try:
- Use a light touch on the stain with a *dry, soap-filled steel wool pad.*

- Or rub the stain gently with **baking soda** sprinkled on top of a **damp sponge**.
- In a pinch, dab the spot with **waterless hand cleaner** (commonly used in industrial or shop areas), then launder in a **washer**. Or pretreat the stain with **hair spray** before washing.

To remove crayon on upholstery and carpeting, scrape up as much crayon as you can with **a metal spoon or dull knife**. Then wet the mark with **WD-40** and let it stand five minutes. Apply elbow grease and a **stiff-bristled brush**, then wipe with **paper towels**. Spray again with WD-40. Dab **1 or 2 drops of dishwashing liquid** onto the stain and work it in with the brush. Then wipe with a **damp sponge**. If the stain persists, repeat. Or use a **solvent spot cleaner**, such as Energine Spot Remover, according to directions.

To remove crayon on floors, you use different methods depending on the type.
- On vinyl no-wax flooring, use **silver polish**. Rinse well with **water** and dry with a **paper towel**.
- On a wood floor, give a crayon mark the Ice Age treatment: Place an **ice-filled plastic bag** on the mark to make it brittle, then scrape with a **spoon or dull knife**. Or place a **clean rag** on the mark and heat it with an **iron** (no steam). The rag will soak up the melted wax.

Crystal

Let's make one thing crystal-clear: *Never* put crystal in the dishwasher. Crystal is too fragile and soft for the dual action of dishwasher and detergent, which can etch and dull its surface. To preserve the special sparkle of crystal, always hand-wash it—unless it has silver or gold gilt, in which case you should use warm water only, no soap.

To wash crystal, line the bottom of your **sink** with a **doubled-up towel or rubber mat**, fill the sink with **warm water**—not hot—and add **2 or 3 drops of dishwashing liquid**. Wash one item at a time. Grasp stemware by the bowl, not the stem, and wash gently. A bartender's trick is to pump the glass up and down in **warm water** to rinse. Dry upside down on **a lint-free cotton towel or vinyl dish rack**. Better yet, put clean **thick gloves or cotton socks** over your hands and dry the crystal immediately with an **old linen towel**. This way, you'll leave no fingerprints or watermarks.

CRAYON MARKS

To remove stains, try this three-pronged approach:

- First, mix a paste of **lemon juice** and **baking powder** (a finer grind than baking soda) and rub gently on the crystal with a **sponge**, then wash and dry. (Baking powder is about as abrasive as you can get with crystal without risking damage.)
- Tougher stains may be "riced": Put **2 teaspoons of uncooked rice** into the crystal piece, add **water,** and swirl. Repeat, if need be.
- For stubborn stains, fill the crystal receptacle with **warm water** and drop in a **denture tablet**.

Here are some more crystal-cleaning tricks worth considering:

- Try the conservator's way of cleaning crystal: Mix equal parts **ethanol** (otherwise known as grain alcohol or denatured alcohol) and **water.** Then add a **few drops of ammonia.** Apply the solution to the crystal with **cotton cosmetic pads** or those **lint-free pads** you use to clean a fax machine. Rinse and dry. (Don't try this on gilded crystal.)
- To dry a decanter or vase, use a **handheld blow-dryer** (cool setting). Otherwise, it can take three or four days to air-dry a decanter without the stopper.
- For extra shine, add **1/4 cup of borax, white vinegar, or lemon juice** to the rinse **water**.
- To wash the grooves of cut crystal, dip a **frayed toothbrush** into **vinegar, lemon juice, or soapy water** and scrub.

Curlers

When you curl your hair, the last thing you want to see when you gaze in the mirror are traces of grime in your hair left over from the curlers. Nor do you want to ruin your hair with harsh cleaning-chemical residue.

To wash curlers that are submersible in water—plain rollers, Velcro rollers, foam-coated wire sticks—fill your bathroom **sink** with **warm water**, mix in a **couple of teaspoons of shampoo or facial cleanser** to create suds, and let soak. As a general rule, if a cleaner is gentle enough for your face or hair, it is fine for your curlers. Use a **wide-toothed comb** to gently pull out any hair stuck in the curlers. Then wipe with a **rag** to remove caked-on film. Rinse with **fresh water** and either dry with a **clean towel** or air-dry.

For stubborn stains, such as hardened setting lotions or gels, mix up a solution of **1/4 cup warm water** and **1 tablespoon liquid fabric softener** in a **cup**. Gently scrub the solution in with a **vegetable brush**. Rinse with **water** and dry.

To clean electric curlers, which are not submersible, use a *rag or vegetable brush* and the *fabric softener solution*. Rinse by wiping the curlers with a damp rag and then dry.

Curling Irons

Cleaning curling irons can be tricky. You must remove the shellaclike crust of singed hair and hair spray that builds up over time. But here's the hitch: Because they are electrical appliances, you can't soak them in water. And you don't want to use toxic chemical cleaners, since they can leave chemical residue in your hair.

Luckily, we have a nontoxic recipe that works wonders.

Clean your curling iron if it starts to smoke when you use it. But rather than waiting until it smokes, it's better to clean it about once a month. When you clean, always make sure the appliance is completely cool.

First, try dipping a *cotton swab* in *rubbing alcohol* and applying it to the barrel of the curling iron. If that does not clean it completely, mix *1/4 cup warm water and 1 tablespoon liquid fabric softener* in a *cup*. Dip a swab into the solution and clean the remaining areas. The fabric softener should dissolve the baked-on gunk. For really stubborn patches, gently scrub with a *brass-wire brush*. When you are finished, wipe the curling iron clean with a *damp rag* and then dry it with *another rag*.

Follow the same instructions for heat rollers, crimping irons, and flat curling irons.

Curtains

Curtains are the unsung heroes of the home furnishings world. Day in and day out, they stand sentinel against the ravages of summer sun and winter drafts. And—most people don't know this—they form an integral part of the home's airflow system, filtering dust out of air that blows in and out of windows. You owe it to your curtains—not to mention your lungs—to keep them clean and dust free.

Dust your curtains once a month or so as part of a regular household dusting. There's no need to take them down. (Who has the time to do *that* every month?) Instead, dust them where they drape using your *vacuum cleaner with a dusting brush or an upholstery attachment*. Use an *extension tube* to reach the tops. If you don't have the right vacuum attachments, use that tried-and-true cleaning implement, the *feather duster*.

Clean your curtains about once a year. First, look for the manufacturer's cleaning recommendations, which should be on a tag sewn inside the hem. If there is no tag, try to decide what sort of treatment the fabric gets. Depending on the material, you will either machine-wash, hand-wash, or dry-clean the drapes.

If curtains can be machine-washed, put them in the *washer* on the *delicate cycle*. They may look sturdy and stable, but being continually exposed to the sun can weaken curtains by breaking down the fibers in the material. Consequently, the minute you wash them, they may begin to deteriorate. Likewise, be gentle when drying curtains in a machine. Use the *permanent press setting* on your *dryer*; it has a cool-down feature that will help prevent wrinkles. High heat can set wrinkles in the fabric, especially when the cycle ends abruptly, leaving the curtains in a ball. An alternative to tumbling curtains until they are dry is to remove them from the dryer and hang them while they are still damp. This will reduce wrinkling and may even help you avoid having to iron them. If your curtains are not very dirty, skip the washing altogether and freshen them by tumbling them in a dryer using no heat.

If curtains require dry cleaning, make sure that you find the best shop for the job. Most neighborhood dry cleaners don't have the special knowledge or equipment to handle curtains. Find one that does. Some cleaners will even measure your curtains beforehand and guarantee that they will come back the same length, which is important.

Cushions

Keeping cushions clean is more than a matter of appearance. Microorganisms called dust mites, which can trigger allergies, often lurk within a dirty couch's folds and fibers. Flop down after a hard day's work, and you may find yourself in a sneezing fit. By removing the dust regularly, you not only keep your cushions looking fresh (and keep the dust from staining them once it is ground in or moistened), but you also improve the quality of your home's air.

To remove dust—and the tiny critters inhabiting the dust—clean cushions about once a month using a *vacuum cleaner* with the appropriate attachments, such as an *upholstery brush* and a *crevice*

tool. To avoid sucking out the feathers, don't vacuum down-filled cushions that are not lined with downproof ticking. No vacuum cleaner attachments? Simple: Use a *soft-bristled brush* to gently brush away the dust.

To give a more thorough cleaning, or to remove stains, wash your cushions. As a general rule, don't remove the cushions from the upholstery cover. First, check the upholstery manufacturer's suggestions, usually tagged to upholstery fabric sold after 1970. This tag will tell you whether you should use a water-based shampoo, a dry-cleaning solvent, or neither of the two. Next, pick an inconspicuous spot on the cushion and pretest whatever cleaning technique is recommended. If there is shrinking or bleeding or running of colors, contact a professional cleaner. If not, proceed.

Even if shampoo is allowable, use as little moisture as possible. You do not want to wet the cushions' stuffing, because it dries very slowly and can make conditions even rosier for moisture-loving dust mites. The trick is to clean using suds only.

● The easiest solution is to use a *foaming commercial shampoo in an aerosol can*. Follow the directions on the can, which typically tell you to allow the foam to stand until dry and then *vacuum* it off.

● To make your own shampoo, mix *1/2 teaspoon liquid dish-washing soap* per *1 quart of warm water*. Make suds by squeezing a *sponge* in the solution. Scoop the suds off the top and apply them sparingly with a sponge to the cushion surface. Rub gently in the direction of the fabric's grain. Rather than letting them dry as you would a commercial shampoo, work on a small area at a time, lightly rinsing each area as you go with a *clean, damp sponge*. Again, avoid soaking the fabric. Be sure to remove all the suds, or the residue will cause the fabric to soil faster.

If the fabric calls for dry-cleaning only and you want to just clean a stain, you can do it yourself, using a *commercial dry-cleaning solvent* such as K2r or Carbona. Don't pour the solvent onto the stain. Instead, moisten a *clean white cloth* with the solvent and use the cloth to draw the stain out. Blot repeatedly—never rub. Rubbing can stretch or damage the texture of the fabric. Always use solvents sparingly and in a well-ventilated area. And don't use solvents on cushions filled with latex foam rubber padding, because the solvent can dissolve the padding. However, if you need to clean the entire surface of a cushion, have it professionally cleaned.

CUSHIONS

Cutting Boards

First, the bad news. Those dastardly meat- and poultry-borne microorganisms that linger on dirty cutting boards—*Salmonella, E. coli, Campylobacter*—can kill you. But before you panic and throw away all your cutting boards—or worse, swear off steak and chicken—here's the good news. Not only is death by microorganism extremely rare, but by properly cleaning your cutting board—a quick, simple task—you can kill 99.9 percent of the bad stuff and continue eating what you like without fear.

To wash a plastic cutting board, just run it through a *dishwasher*, and the hot water and sanitizing ingredients found in dishwasher detergent will kill harmful pathogens. Make sure you wash your cutting board as soon as possible after each use, especially after preparing meat or poultry products.

To wash a wooden cutting board, it's best not to use a dishwasher because the dishwashing process may warp or loosen the glue that holds together laminated wood. You're better off using a *scrub brush* to scrub the board by hand with *dishwashing liquid in hot water* each time you use it. The soap helps lift the meat debris that may harbor the pathogens, and the scrubbing action ruptures the cells of the microorganisms. Done thoroughly, hand scrubbing is as effective as machine-washing.

To sanitize a cutting board, a good thing to do occasionally, mix *1 teaspoon of bleach* in *1 quart of water* and apply it directly to the cutting surface with a *scrub brush*. Do not rinse. Instead, let the board air-dry to give the bleach a chance to do its thing. If you need the board sooner than that, let it stand for at least one minute, and then pat it dry with a *clean paper towel*.

expert advice

Cutting Board Common Sense >

"If possible, have two cutting boards," suggests Bessie Berry, manager of the USDA's Meat and Poultry Hotline. "Use one for meat and the other for raw foods, like vegetables and fruit. To keep them straight, use a nontoxic marker to label the handles or along the edge."

And, she says, don't get too attached to any one board. "If your cutting board has deep grooves from lots of cutting, you can't clean it as thoroughly. Throw it out and get a new one." It's a small price to pay for peace of mind.

Decanters

The dirty decanter is the cleaning world's brainteaser. The puzzle: to reach the cavernous space that lies beyond a decanter's narrow neck in order to scrub away stubborn stains such as lime deposits and red wine rings. And after you clean it, there's the challenge of drying it. If ever there was a need for a genie—armed with a miniature scrub brush and rags—this is it. But the puzzle can be solved. Here's how:

Begin with the outside, washing your decanter by hand. Never put a decanter in a dishwasher; the heat and vibration can easily break its delicate glass neck. If the decanter is an antique or made of fine crystal or cut glass, wash it in a *plastic basin* rather than in a hard sink to reduce the chances of breakage. Or line the bottom of your sink with a *rubber mat* or a *doubled-over towel*. Then just use a *sponge or soft-bristled brush, warm water*, and *mild dishwashing liquid* to wash the outer surface.

Cleaning the inside depends on how dirty or stained the decanter is. There are several approaches. The simplest is to fill it halfway with *soapy, warm water*, hold your hand over the top, and gently shake. Still stained? Swirl a mixture of *rock salt* and *vinegar* around inside the decanter. The salt will gently scour the surface while the vinegar helps remove stains, especially lime deposits. If rock salt and vinegar do not remove wine stains, try swishing a small amount of *warm water, baking soda*, and *rock salt* in the bottle.

Another approach: Put *water* in the decanter, drop in a *denture cleaner*, such as Efferdent, and let it stand overnight. No matter which method you use, rinse with clean, warm water.

▲

Dry your decanter completely, so that it does not fog up after you replace the stopper. Worse than being unsightly, that moisture could harbor dangerous microorganisms. Instead of drying your decanter by inverting it in your dish rack, which increases the chance of breakage *and* takes forever, try this trick: Drain most of the water out of the decanter by holding it upside down. To remove final moisture, wrap a *paper towel* around the handle of a long-handled *wooden spoon* so that the towel extends slightly beyond the end. Stick the towel-wrapped spoon into the decanter and let it rest on the bottom overnight ◀. By morning, the towel should have absorbed most of the condensation. If you can't wait until morning, gently blow warm air into the decanter with a *hair dryer*. Be careful, though: Too much heat can crack delicate glass.

Decks

Think of your deck as an outdoor room, one exposed to sun, wind, rain, and ice. To keep your deck looking its best, you need to clean it—not as regularly or meticulously as you do your indoor rooms, but well enough to maintain it for the long term. Even decks made of weather-resistant or pressure-treated lumber deteriorate unless they are cared for. And, contrary to popular belief, the pressure washer is not the best way to clean a wood deck. Before you reach for the nozzle, read on.

Sweep your deck regularly to keep it free of leaves and twigs. This is the most basic step you can take. Otherwise, the tannins from tree fallout will stain the wood surface, and the piles of decomposing organic matter will hold moisture, leading to mildew and rot. Use a *heavy-duty broom* to sweep your deck regularly, taking care to keep the gaps between boards clean. If leaves or twigs get stuck in the gaps, scrape them out with a *putty knife*. The more often you sweep, the easier it will be on you and the deck, especially if the leaves are dry.

To remove dirt and mildew and brighten the color of your deck, periodically (once a year or so) give it a more thorough cleaning. Start by mixing a solution of *1 cup of trisodium phosphate (TSP)*, a safe all-purpose cleaner and degreaser available at most hardware stores, with *1 gallon of warm water*. Using a *long-handled stiff-bristled brush* (a long handle is easier on your back and knees), scrub the deck with the TSP solution. Rinse by washing down the deck with a *hose*. The TSP runoff will not harm surrounding foliage. (Note: If you have a covered or partially covered deck that is not built to withstand rain, clean it as you would an indoor hardwood floor. Do not soak it with water.)

To remove stains and stubborn mildew, use a bleaching solution: *1 to 3 ounces of sodium percarbonate*, also known as oxygen bleach, per *gallon of warm water*. Unlike chlorine bleach, which can break down the lignin that holds the wood together and harm plants, oxygen bleach is relatively gentle and nontoxic. Simply apply it with a *mop or brush*. Don't scrub. Wait 15 or 20 minutes for it to soak in and then *hose* down the deck to remove the solution. If you use a *wood sealer*, such as Thompson's Water Seal, on your deck, you will need to reapply it after washing the deck with TSP and oxygen bleach, which strip away sealers along with dirt and mildew.

OOPS!

High Pressure, High Risk >

Pressure washers are dangerous, and here's proof. Homeowner Bill R. of Virginia rented a pressure washer to clean his deck. Like many people, he had never used one before, and the rental company gave him very little instruction—and no safety advice. When he accidentally passed the nozzle over his gloveless hand, the jet of water ripped through the soft skin on the back of his hand, damaging two tendons. It took 20 stitches to sew up the wound, and Bill had to spend the night in the hospital.

Don't use a pressure washer! Pressure washers are expensive, dangerous, and harmful to the wood you are cleaning. The extreme water pressure will break up the wood fibers—what you're trying to prevent—leaving the surface fuzzy, more susceptible to the weather, and in poor condition for refinishing with stains and sealers. Only use them as a last resort, and then be very careful. Use the lowest pressure setting available, between 800 psi (pounds per square inch) and 1,200 psi, and never use a pinpoint nozzle. Hold the nozzle at an angle at least a foot away from the deck's surface.

Dehumidifiers

Dehumidifiers are part of a home's airflow system. They cut down on moisture as well as the mold and microorganisms that thrive in moist environments. If you don't clean your dehumidifier, you may cancel out its beneficial health effects. And as with any electrical appliance, keeping your dehumidifier clean is important for its operating efficiency and longevity.

Cleaning a dehumidifier is easy. Periodically dust the outer cabinet with a *damp, oil-free cloth*, and clean the front grille and the coils under the grille using the *dusting attachment on a vacuum cleaner* ◀. Once a month—or more often if necessary, depending on use—scrub the drip pan and the inside of the water reservoir with a *sponge or soft cloth* and *mild dishwashing liquid* to discourage the growth of mold or mildew. At least once a season, remove the dust and lint from the cold coils inside the unit with a *soft-bristled brush*. Most dehumidifiers have an air filter in the front grille area. Replace or clean it at least once a season. The procedure is the same as it is for a window air conditioner.

See also Air Conditioners.

Dentures

Who hasn't seen those television commercials showing denture wearers enjoying coffee, blueberry pie, and other teeth-staining foods? The advertiser's message: Buy our denture cleaner and eat worry-free. Like many ads, those are misleading—but only slightly. While not as simple as dropping your choppers into a glass of cleaning solution, denture cleaning should require little more effort than brushing your original set of teeth.

Here are some precautions you should take to protect your dentures:

• Never use a brush with stiff, coarse bristles, which can damage the materials that make up dentures.

• Don't use gritty powdered cleansers or toothpastes, which can also cause damage.

• Don't clean dentures with bleach. It can whiten the pink part of the dentures and corrode the metal framework on partial dentures.

• Never use hot water to rinse your dentures. The heat could warp them.

• Never let your dentures dry out, which could also warp them or make them brittle.

As with real teeth, your dentures should be kept free of food particles, plaque, and stains so that your mouth can remain healthy and attractive. And removing plaque—that germ-harboring dentist's nemesis—from dentures requires the same regular brushing that real teeth need. The difference, of course, is that with dentures, you take them out to brush them.

Brush your dentures twice a day. Dentures are delicate and—we hardly need mention—expensive. They may break even if dropped a few inches. For that reason, brush them over a *folded towel or a bowl of water*. Go over them lightly with a recommended *denture brush or a soft nylon toothbrush*, using a *cleanser your dentist recommends*. For an economical alternative, use *mild hand soap or dishwashing liquid*. And remember: You can keep your dentures cleaner by also lightly brushing your gums, tongue, and the roof of your mouth. (But not with hand soap!)

Soak your dentures for at least 30 minutes a day in a dentist-approved *denture cleanser* (yes, like the ones advertised on TV, such as Efferdent). Soaking will remove stains and kill germs, reducing mouth infections and odor. For convenience and privacy while you're without your teeth, soak your dentures overnight or while you're showering. Then rinse off the cleanser by lightly brushing the dentures with the *soft-bristled brush* under *cold running water*.

OOPS!

Acci-Dental Washing > Attention, denture wearers! Do not try the following. According to dental educational consultant Margaret J. Fehrenbach, MS, who is a registered dental hygienist, a man she knows slipped a set of dentures into his pants pocket one day and forgot about them. When the pants went through the washer and dryer, so did the dentures. Funny thing was, after the spin cycles, the dentures, which had always bothered him, fit better and hurt no more.

Dish Drainers

Since your dish drainer is meant to hold clean dishes, a dirty dish drainer defeats the purpose. It is important to keep your drainer clean and free of mold and bacteria.

Wash your dish drainer periodically in *warm water* with *liquid dishwashing soap*, using a clean *sponge*. Do it separately, not while you're washing other dishes, since harmful bacteria can taint the dishes you are trying to clean. Use a **scrub brush** to remove stuck-on food and mold. Air-dry the drainer upside down on a **clean towel**.

Sanitize the dish drainer every few weeks by soaking it in a solution of **1/4 cup of bleach** per **1 gallon of warm water**.

Dishes

What's more Americana—more Norman Rockwell—than standing around the kitchen together after a homey dinner and washing dishes? Nowadays, that family ritual is more of a memory than a reality, thanks to dishwashers. And with the new generation of dishwashers sporting "gentle" settings and "air-dry" options, washing dishes by hand is heading for extinction. But dishwashers blast jets of hot water that can cause any ornamentation to fade. Anything with a metal decorative border is doomed. So if you really want to take the best care of your heirloom china, don't take any chances. Do it the way Grandma did—by hand.

To hand-wash delicate china—any china that's fragile, antique, or gold plated—get out the **rubber gloves** and the dishwashing liquid. And don't even think of using steel wool or anything else

Getting the Most from Your Dishwasher

Here are some dishwasher-use tips that will help you get your dishes (and pots and pans) cleaner and help conserve energy and water:
• Load dishes so that they are separated and face the center of the machine. Put glasses and cups between prongs, not over them.
• Don't position large dishes (or pots or pans) so that they block the spray arm, the spray tower, or the flow of water to the detergent dispenser.
• Use only dishwasher detergent in your machine—never soap, laundry detergent, or dishwashing liquid. Follow the label directions for the amount. Less is needed if your water is soft (or artificially softened), more if it's hard.
• Use a rinse agent to speed drying if your water is hard, but skip it if you have soft water.
• Run hot water at the kitchen sink until it feels hot before turning on the dishwasher.
• Don't bother to prerinse moderately soiled dishes. Just scrape off any food.
• Run the machine only when it's fully loaded and do it at night or during off-peak utility hours. During hot weather, running the machine at night will also save on cooling costs.
• Use the hold-and-rinse cycle only when you need to leave dishes overnight but want to avoid odors.
• If your dishes aren't very dirty, use the lightest washing cycle.
• Air-dry dishes when you don't need rapid drying. And don't warm plates in a dishwasher; use the oven instead.

Give Your China a *Face-Lift*

No matter how careful you are, delicate china is going to get its dings and smudges. Linda Cobb, Do It Yourself Network host and best-selling author (*Talking Dirty with the Queen of Clean*), says it's easy to rejuvenate china that's showing its age.

- To get rid of those hairline cracks that seem to come from nowhere, soak the china overnight in a large bowl of warm milk (no warmer than what you would feed a baby). Then gently hand-wash as usual. Those crazed lines will disappear.

- Where, oh, where did those mysterious black marks come from? Did we eat dirty food? Scuff a shoe on a plate? Likely neither. Black marks can be the result of a couple of things, such as cutlery in the hands of a zealous eater or contact with aluminum in the dishwasher. To get rid of the black marks, sprinkle a little baking soda on a damp cloth and rub the spot. Or try a little nongel toothpaste on a plastic scouring pad.

- To lift tea stains from cups, mix 2 tablespoons of chlorine bleach in a quart of water.

Soak the cup in the solution for no more than two minutes and rinse immediately.

- Hard water sometimes causes a film to develop on china. To remove it, fill a bowl with 1 1/2 cups of chlorine bleach and place it in the lower rack of the dishwasher. Load your china into the washer and run it up to the dry cycle, then shut it off. Empty the bowl, rinse it out, pour in 1 1/2 cups of white vinegar, and return it to the dishwasher. Turn the dishwasher back on and let it run through the rest of the cycle.

with texture. A sponge or a dishcloth will do everything you need. Before you even turn on the spigot, place a *towel* in the bottom of the sink. Then remove your rings or at least turn any jewels on them inward, toward the palm of your hand. This will cut down on chipping caused by jewelry while you wash. Also turn the faucet to the side to avoid clashes with delicate objects, such as your grandmother's gravy boat.

Fill the sink with *moderately hot water* and a healthy *squirt of mild dishwashing liquid*. It never hurts to add *2 tablespoons of white vinegar* to the water. (This boosts the power of inexpensive dishwashing liquid and makes even the best dish detergent work better.) Then slide the dishes in edgewise, which allows the temperature of the dish to equalize gradually. If very hot water hits a fragile dish too quickly, you're begging for cracks in the china. Once the dishes are stacked carefully in the sink, pour a little extra dishwashing liquid on a *sponge or dishcloth*. Then resist the urge to scrub. Instead, wash in small circular motions. It might take longer than a vigorous scrubbing, but it will protect your china. Put *1 tablespoon of white vinegar* in the final rinse, and you'll be able to see your smile in the reflection.

Before doing good china in a dishwasher, it's best to run a test. Buy the most inexpensive piece that's made in your pattern. Put it in the back of the dishwasher and forget about it for a month while you use the machine normally. At the end of the month, take a gander. If there's no change in its appearance, you'll know it's safe to use the dishwasher for your good china. If it's faded, well, you'll be buying more rubber gloves.

When storing good china, it's important to be gentle, too. Try to store your china so that it doesn't touch. A layer of pliable paper—*paper towel, paper plate, or napkin*—will keep pieces from scraping. Hang cups, if possible. And when dealing with tops—to tureens, sugar bowls, and teapots—turn the top upside down, so that the handle or other protruding part is protected inside the bottom piece.

Doghouses and Kennels

True enough, you don't have to change your pet's bedding as often as you change your sheets. But most of us wait way too long to freshen Fido's cozy corner. Once a month isn't too often.

Start cleaning a doghouse or kennel by tossing it like you would a teenager's bedroom. Get everything out. If you use straw, throw it away. If your doggie likes to curl up in blankets, pull 'em out and toss 'em in the *washer,* just as you would your own blankets. *Hose* down the house or kennel, inside and out. You might need to lift one end to drain all the water. Then get ready to scrub.

When washing a doghouse or kennel, don't use anything that you wouldn't want your pet to lap up. Chemical household cleaners will make a home sparkle. But dogs aren't as particular about the way their home looks as they are about the way it smells. A pine-scented habitat might smell sparkly clean to *you,* but your dog might disagree. Instead, use a *plastic-bristled brush* to apply an *organic cleaner,* such as Simple Green, or try one of these homemade solutions:

- Mix *4 tablespoons of lemon extract or lemon juice* with *1 gallon of water*.
- Mix *1 cup of vinegar* to *3 cups of water*.

Either of these environmentally friendly alternatives will get rid of all the must and dirt and will leave your hound's habitat clean and smelling good without a hint of chemicals.

Replacing the bedding is the last step. If your doggie likes straw, put in some *fresh straw* and sprinkle it with *baking soda* to make the freshness last longer. If your pet prefers blankets, let the washed blankets dry in the sun for extra freshness; then sprinkle some *baking soda* on them.

*See also **Pet Equipment**.*

DISHES

Dolls

A collector's doll may bear a hefty price tag, but a kid's beloved baby doll—no matter how bedraggled—is priceless for the memories it carries. And just the amount of handling a child's favorite doll gets makes it a magnet for dirt. Careful cleaning and maintenance are equally critical for saving a prized baby doll for future offspring or for maintaining the value of an expensive collector's item.

To wash a doll's clothing, begin by stripping the doll. Then make sure its clothes can be washed—do a test on an inconspicuous spot on the clothing. Using an *eyedropper*, put a drop of *liquid laundry detergent* where it won't easily be seen, such as on a seam or a hem. If you can't see it after it dries, you're in the clear. Toss the doll's clothing in a *lingerie bag* and put it in the *washer* with the *laundry detergent* in *cold water* on the delicate setting. Don't dry the clothes in the dryer, however. If the clothes shrink, you can't expect your doll to diet. If the weather is good, hang them to dry on an *outside clothesline* for a fresh smell. If the weather is bad, lay the pieces on a *towel* to dry.

To clean the doll itself, remember that a *damp cloth* will remove a lot of the grime a doll picks up in the sandbox, in the attic, or just from being loved. If the doll needs a bath, fill a sink with *warm water* and mix in *2 tablespoons lemon extract* (available in supermarkets). If the doll's body is all plastic or rubber, dunk the dolly, much as you would a real baby. You might even invite your child to give baby a scrub with a *washcloth* made soapy with a little *dishwashing liquid*. Saliva mixed with anything—dirt, oatmeal, sugar—can set like cement, so for the extra-tough dirt that comes with a lot o' lovin', a gentle scrub with *a soft toothbrush* is just the ticket. If you need a little extra cleaning power, dip the toothbrush in a solution of *1 tablespoon of hydrogen peroxide* and *2 cups of water*. Just make sure you rinse everything well before the next kiss.

To clean a collector's doll, also begin by stripping the doll. Never use a damp cloth on a porcelain collector's doll, because it might etch the paint. Instead, use a *dry, soft cloth* to remove surface dirt from the "flesh" surfaces. For detailed areas—around the eyes or fingers, for instance—use a *natural bristle artist's paintbrush* to remove trapped dirt and dust. This should be all you need to do, because, luckily, collectors' dolls don't tend to pick up serious stains. If the clothing is old or delicate, you can remove the musty smell that comes with age by hanging the clothes out in fresh air. If the clothing is not fragile, you might want to consider washing it using the method described for regular doll clothes—but be sure to do the eyedropper test first. For clothing stains that you don't want to wash, a *household spot remover* might get them out. Check the label for the best application procedure. Or you might try a solution of *2 teaspoons of lemon juice* mixed with *2 cups of water*. Dip an *absorbent cloth or a paper towel* into the solution and dab—don't rub—at the stain. It should lighten up right away.

Doormats

Yes, doormats are *supposed* to get dirty—it's their job. But at some point, your doormat will have absorbed all the dirt it can take. Then it simply becomes the bridge over which dirt travels into your house.

Knock out the dirt to start. Don't be timid. Grab two adjacent corners of the doormat and shake hard. The loosest dirt will leave willingly. Then drape the mat over a *post or a clothesline* and use a *baseball bat* to beat it like a piñata. After you've beaten out all the loose dirt, take a *wire brush* and dislodge the stubborn stuff. If there's any gooey gunk like wax or chewing gum still clinging to the mat, press an *ice cube* against the offending lump until it's brittle enough to scrape off with a *spoon*.

To remove serious stains on a doormat made of rubber or rope, use an *aerosol spot remover*, such as K2r. If you think it needs a more thorough cleaning, wash it in the *clothes washer* on a gentle cycle. For wooden doormats—or for troublesome doormat stains generally—mix *4 tablespoons of lemon extract* (available in supermarkets) *or lemon juice* with *1 gallon of water*. Use a *stiff plastic brush* to scrub with the solution until the stain goes away.

Doors

Doors collect dust and dirt just as walls do. So whatever you use on the walls is probably just right for doors as well. Few doors are as flat as walls, though, so you have to be equipped to attack those crevices to get them really clean.

To remove surface dirt, dust down the door with a *dry towel*. Then tie a *soft, old towel* over the bristle end of a *broom* and brush into

DOLLS

the angles and crevices where dust mounts up. If there's a lot of detail work on the door, use **a soft toothbrush** to get into the tightest corners.

Wash the door once you've cleaned off all the surface dust and dirt. If you have a stained wooden door, use **wood oil soap** and mix it with **water** according to the directions on the label. For painted doors, a couple of home brews will do the job effectively.

- Mix **1 gallon of warm water** with **1/2 cup ammonia, 1/4 cup white vinegar**, and **1/4 cup cleaning soda**. (You can find cleaning soda in the laundry section of the grocery store. Arm & Hammer Super Washing Soda is a good choice.)
- Mix **1 cup of ammonia** and **1 teaspoon of mild dishwashing liquid** in **1 gallon of warm water**.

Soak a **natural sponge** until it's completely pliable. Then squeeze out as much water as possible. You should wash from the bottom upward to avoid run marks. So beginning at the bottom of the door, scrub with the sponge in small circular motions. Rinse the sponge often and thoroughly to avoid putting dirt back on the door. If you keep a clean solution, you won't have to rinse.

To clean door hardware, the good news is that you don't have to remove it to clean it or the door. Leave the screwdriver in the toolbox and grab a box of **plastic wrap** (Saran Wrap, for instance). Place a layer on the door surface around the hardware you want to clean, securing the plastic with **masking tape**. If you're dealing with metal, such as a door knocker or kick plate or even a doorknob, a **metal cleaner**, such as Maas metal cleaner, will spiff up all types of metal, including brass. It has jeweler's rouge in it, so it's very gentle but does an excellent job. With glass or ceramic doorknobs, you don't need the plastic wrap. Just take a few swipes with a **rag** dampened with **rubbing alcohol**, which won't hurt the great cleaning job you've just done on the door.

Down

Washing down isn't brain surgery. In fact, you use only what you normally use to do laundry: your washer and some detergent. It's all in the technique. If your washing machine is large enough, put in as many down items as it will hold: jackets, vests, pillows, even sleeping bags—nothing is verboten.

Do a test first—if you want to be sure the item will come out looking at least as good as it went in. Mix **1/4 cup of water** with **2 tablespoons of powdered laundry detergent**. Put a few drops on

Down and Dirty >

Your down garment prob-
ably has a tag that says
you have to dry-clean it.
But if the tag just says
"Dry clean," you can get
away with gentle
machine-washing, says
Lucinda Ottusch, lead
home economist for the
Whirlpool Institute of
Fabric Science. If the tag
gets wordier—"Dry clean
only"—pay heed.
Whichever you decide,
stick with one method of
cleaning or the other,
warns Ottusch. Don't
alternate dry cleaning
with washing. Dry clean-
ing removes all the natu-
ral oils from the down,
which makes the feathers
brittle. If you then wash
the garment, the feath-
ers will break.

an inconspicuous spot of the fabric, such as on the lining, the
hem, or an inside seam. Don't rinse. Wait until it's dry. Then you
can see whether the dyes have been affected. It's the color of the
item that you need to worry about; the down itself will be fine.

To wash a down item, check that there are no holes in it before
you even turn on the water. That little place where you nicked
your jacket with your ski pole can flood your washer with feathers. When you're sure items are secure, add to an empty *washer*
the amount of *detergent* prescribed on the box; then fill the drum
halfway with water. (Cold water is best. Try warm water if the
outside of the garment really requires more cleaning muscle.
Never use hot.) Add and submerge the down items. They'll soak
up the water. Put *towels* on top of the down items to keep them
submerged. Then finish filling with water. Run the washer
through a cycle, using regular agitation. Stop the washer at least
once during the cycle to press air out of the down. This will keep
the items submerged. And use only the regular spin cycle. A
high-speed spin will send all the feathers down to one end of the
garment, unless it's quilted or baffled.

To dry a down item, it's fine to use a *dryer*, but be sure to do it at
the low temperature setting. Some people toss in their sneakers
or tennis balls to keep things fluffed. (If you do, make sure they're
perfectly clean.) But you don't have to use anything at all.
Instead, partway through the drying cycle, remove the down
item from the dryer and fluff it by hand. Then return it to the
dryer. If your machine has an automatic sensor to tell you when
drying is done, ignore it. Down can fool the sensor. The cover
may be dry, but the feathers inside may still contain moisture.

Drains

A preemptive strike on your drains—before you get a full-
fledged clog—will make life oh-so-much easier and cheaper.
When a drain becomes slow moving, you can prevent that loom-
ing call to the plumber by stopping the problem in its early
stages. The solution couldn't be simpler. It employs common
household items, and you don't even have to mix.

If you have a slow-moving drain, it means sludge is building up in
the pipe. When that happens, pour *1 cup of salt* into the drain,
followed by *1 cup of baking soda*. Then pour a *full kettle of boiling water* down the drain. The abrasive salt and baking soda will
break down the clog. If the problem is congealed grease, the clog

will loosen immediately. Don't turn on the tap for several hours, if possible. The longer that you can go without diluting your work, the better.

If hair is the problem, you'll need a stronger solution. This one will work: Dissolve *2 tablespoons of cleaning soda*, such as Arm & Hammer Super Washing Soda (find it with laundry products in the supermarket) in *1 quart of hot water* and pour it slowly down the drain. Let it work for 10 minutes; then run *hot water* until the drain seems clear.

If a disposer-equipped drain is slow, the drain trap and garbage disposer are probably gunked up with food particles. To cure the problem, first pull out the drain trap (that little basketlike thing that sits in the drain hole at the bottom of the sink). Hold it inside the *trash can* and tap it to loosen the food, paper bits, bloated dog food, and such. Replace the drain trap, twisting the knob to the closed position, and pour *3 inches of warm water* into the sink. Add *1 cup of baking soda*. Turn on the garbage disposer and let it run only a couple of seconds before you twist the drain trap knob to the open position. The water pressure will push any remaining food particles through the drain trap and give the garbage disposer a good scrubbing at the same time. Turn on the tap for *running water* and let the disposer run until you get that free-spinning "all clear" sound.

See also **Garbage Disposers**.

expert advice

Whip Up a Twister >

Before you get a clog that shuts down dinner party preparations, treat your drain to a little maintenance. Linda Cobb, best-selling author and Do It Yourself Network television host, says a monthly dose of the following homemade cleaner will ensure smooth sailing down the drain.

Pour 1/2 cup of baking soda right down the drain. Don't turn on the water yet. Instead, immediately follow the baking soda with 1/2 cup of white vinegar. "It will form a little white tornado," says Cobb, assuring that "this is a good thing." Wait 30 minutes. Then flush with cool water.

Drawers

We all have junk drawers—those receptacles for a thousand-odd objects that have no other obvious home. Do we ever just dump the whole messy menagerie into the trash? Of course not. There are treasures in there we'll need someday (if we can ever find them). But clean we must, if just to make sure nothing living has taken up residence within.

Sort through the contents of the drawer you want to clean first. Empty the drawer. Dump it. Everything, no matter how much it makes you cringe. Lay down some *old newspapers* before you start, and you'll save yourself the chore of vacuuming up all the grit, paper scraps, and bits of plastic that have broken off one gadget or another.

Separate the dumped contents into as many piles as you think necessary, beginning with "keep" and "toss" piles. You can sub-categorize, if you want. If you're like most people, you'll find a year's supply of pens. (Transfer the ones that still have ink to the mug or desk drawer where you store writing implements.) Eliminate everything you're not sure you'll need—that dried out highlighter is a good candidate.

To clean the drawer, you first need to check to see what your drawer is made of.

● For wood, use a little **wood oil soap**, mixed according to directions, or mix **1 quart of warm water** with **2 tablespoons of dishwashing detergent** in a **large bowl**.

● For laminated plastic, use **2 tablespoons of white vinegar** mixed with **1 quart of warm water**.

● For metal drawers, put some **baking soda** in a **small bowl** and add just enough **water** to make a paste.

Thoroughly soak a **sponge** and squeeze well, then wipe away at the drawer, inside and out. You can let the drawer air-dry, but if you're in a hurry to stow the junk again—only the must-keep stuff—dry it with a **paper towel**.

Dust

The average American house accumulates 40 pounds of dust a year. Dust varies from house to house and from location to location around the country. Generally speaking, that film that your kids love to write their names in is made up of particles of more than 5,000 different materials, including skin flakes, pet dander, pet hair, human hair, food bits, pollen grains, mold spores, insect parts, sawdust, and fiber.

Dust *Busters*

Here are some no-fuss tricks to try when you want to do some spot dusting:

• To clean stained or natural-finish woodwork, put a tea bag in hot water and let it cool. Then dampen your cleaning rag or sponge with the cooled tea and run it over the woodwork.

• To clean blinds, which can get filmy with dust, wipe the slats with a cloth dampened with vinegar, which sanitizes as it cleans. This is a good trick for chandeliers, too.

• To remove dust, lint, or hair from furniture or an item of clothing, wrap masking tape around your hand and then press your hand over the surface of the item. Unwanted fuzz, dust, or lint will stick to the masking tape.

• To get rid of all the dust trapped in a pleated lampshade, use a small, medium-bristled paintbrush. This works for figurines, too.

• To give freshly dusted furniture a pretty sheen, mix 1/2 teaspoon of light olive oil (not dark) in 1 quart of water. Apply with a clean rag.

Just pushing dust around is what many methods of dusting do. Feather dusters are great, for instance, for cleaning blinds—as long as you make sure to shake the duster outside frequently. A dry dust cloth just moves the dust or suspends it. Even a vacuum cleaner—unless it uses a HEPA (high efficiency particulate air) filter—redistributes a certain amount of the dust it's supposed to be snaring, but it's still the major weapon in the dust war.

Why do we dust? Aesthetics are a big reason, of course. But there are some health concerns related to dust. Dust can be a reservoir for contaminants. Lead and pesticides, for instance, are known to accumulate in household dust. In addition, there are a lot of elements in dust, such as mites, that can cause allergic reactions related to asthma.

To dust a room and cut down on the time dusting takes, *vacuum* everything first—furniture, walls, windowsills, upholstery, the coffee table, it doesn't matter. Vacuuming is key to dust removal, because it removes a lot of dust without creating a dust storm in the process. Follow up with *a damp cloth*, and your room should be dust-free for a while.

Naturally, you want to truly remove the dust, rather than kicking it up into the air. *Electrostatic cloths*, Grab-it Mitts, for example, hold the dust. A *damp washcloth or microfiber cloth* will also hang on to the dust. But if you use a washcloth instead of disposables, be sure you wash it after every use. When the damp cloth doesn't seem to be quite enough, mix *1 tablespoon of lemon extract* in *1 quart of water*. Use the solution to redampen the cloth, and you'll cut through the film.

DVD Players

The more mechanical parts your DVD player has, the more susceptible it is to accumulating dirt and dust. Portable models are even more susceptible, because they are moved from environment to environment. Dirty discs or lenses lead to mistracking, skipping, irregular speed, and lousy reproduction quality. When your player displays any of these symptoms regularly, it might be time to give it a good, careful going-over.

Cleaning the player's lens is the most important part of keeping the player running smoothly. But don't open anything that requires a screwdriver. Most warranties become void if you open

WATCH OUT

Never put a damaged or warped disc into the player. It can hit the laser arm, which requires perfect alignment to work properly. It's an ounce of prevention that counts.

Cleaning DVD Discs >

Keeping your discs clean is the first step in maintaining a DVD player, because discs can carry dirt into the player's interior. Always hold them by the edges. A shot of compressed air is the quickest way to rid discs of dust. If a disc needs more attention, wipe it with a soft, dry cloth, starting at the center of the disc and moving straight out to the edge like the spokes on a wheel. Don't use solvents or household cleaners on a disc. Always store a disc in its case to keep it dirt-free. Keep it out of direct sunlight and away from heat sources.

the casing. You're better off sending it off for service. Instead, just press the button to open the mechanical drawer where the DVD sits. Spray a *gentle blast of compressed air* inside the opening to force out any dust or lint. It's not a bad idea to spray the disc tray, too. Be careful to hold the can perfectly level. Otherwise, you might get a shot of the propellant in its liquid form, and you never want to have anything liquid near a DVD player. And don't hold the can any closer to the player than the distance recommended on the can. You control the intensity of the blast by adjusting the distance between the can and the player, and you don't want to damage the laser reader mounted on an arm inside. It's that arm that reads discs, the same way an old-fashioned record player needle reads vinyl.

Some manufacturers make *special lens-cleaning discs* that will keep the laser lens good as new. Just open the drawer that holds the DVDs and place the cleaning disc in the tray. When you close the tray and hit Play, the cleaning action begins. Some cleaning discs, such as Maxell's, use an angular brush made of ultrafine synthetic fibers containing copper. Such discs not only clean the DVD player's lens, but also dissipate static that will attract dust.

To clean a player's exterior, a simple wipe-down with a *soft, dry cloth* is usually all that's needed. If the cabinet is extremely dirty, mix some *dishwashing liquid* in *water* and get your *cleaning cloth* just barely damp before wiping it down. Avoid cleaning solvents (for example, alcohol), since they could damage the casing.

DVD PLAYERS

Elastic

You probably can count on one hand the items of clothing you own that don't have elastic. Whether it's underwear or socks, exercise gear or cruise wear, almost everything these days has at least a hint of elastic or an elastic derivative, such as spandex.

To keep your elastic clean and in good shape, launder frequently in a *washing machine*, using *warm water* (100° F is ideal, for you preciseniks). Whatever the item, if it touches your body, your body oils will get on it. Body oils can damage elastic, and cold water will never get the body oils out completely, meaning your elastic will break down over time. Regular *laundry detergent* is all you need if the water you use is nice and warm. If you must bleach, use only *nonchlorine bleach*. And if there's a particular stain you're worried about, let it sit for 15 minutes in an *enzyme presoak*, such as Biz.

To maintain the life of elastic, dry on a low setting and don't overdry. You don't want your stretchy stuff to become crunchy.

Electric Grills

Although the grills named after boxer George Foreman are the best known, there are several makes of countertop grills. When attempting to clean anything that has a cord or that begins with the word *electric,* make sure the unit is unplugged before you even turn on the water. Otherwise, a dirty grill could be the least of your worries. The grilling surface requires the most thorough cleaning, unless you don't mind dried bits of last week's chicken breasts on this week's T-bone. If you're cleaning the grill right after cooking on it, make sure the surfaces have cooled first. You don't want any barbecued sponges—or fingers. On the other hand, a grill is easiest to clean when it is still slightly warm, before food particles harden.

If the grilling surface is not removable, don't immerse the unit in water. (Some electric grills have parts that can be safely cleaned in the dishwasher.) Most electric grills are one-piece models that typically come with a nonstick finish and are meant for counter-top use. Many have a long plastic drip tray for catching grease, as well as a *plastic cleaning spatula* contoured to fit over the ribbed grilling surface. The spatula is handy for scraping charred food particles off the grilling surface and into the drip tray. Once you have dispensed with the larger bits of food, wipe the ribbed grilling surface with a *damp sponge or cloth*—not a wet one. To tackle especially sticky stuff, put a little *dishwashing detergent* on the sponge. Be sure to rinse the sponge frequently, since it will get grimy quickly. Follow the sponging step with a few swipes of a *damp cloth*—again not a wet one—to get rid of as much moisture as possible.

After disposing of the collected grease, wash the plastic drip tray with *dishwashing detergent* and a *wet sponge*. If the spatula has collected a thick layer of greasy, charred food, soak it for a few minutes in *warm water* with a *squirt of dishwashing detergent*, then wipe it clean with a *scrubber sponge*. Rinse the drip tray and spatula with *running water* and let them air-dry.

To clean the outside of an electric grill, first remove the grilling surface (if it's removable) and leave it out while you attack the other surfaces. A quick wipe of the exterior with a *damp sponge* will take care of most grease splatters. An alternative: Clean the outside casing with a *waterless hand cleaner*, such as Goop, by first eliminating surface dirt with *dry paper towels* and then applying a little of the hand cleaner to a *clean paper towel*, rubbing the exterior in small circular motions.

Let the cleaned grill air-dry or, if you need to accelerate the drying process, use a *hair dryer* on a low setting. Make sure the grill is perfectly dry before you plug it in again.

To clean a hibachi style electric grill—one that has a grilling rack like a conventional charcoal grill—unplug it, let it cool, and dismantle it according to your owner's manual. With the electrical elements set aside, wash the grilling rack, the lid, and the metal or ceramic basin in *warm water* with *a squirt of dishwashing liquid*. Scrub as needed with a *nylon cleaning pad*. Wipe any plastic parts with a *soft cloth* dipped in the water-and-detergent solution. Rinse with *fresh water*.

Do not immerse the electronic parts in water. If needed, wipe the heating element with a *soft cloth or soft brush*, taking care not to scratch the surface.

Electric Shavers

It's human nature. You haven't seen that teeny brush that came with your electric shaver since you opened the package on your birthday two years ago. Now your shaver is running like the Little Engine That Couldn't.

To keep your shaver in proper running order, brush it after each use to dislodge the whisker dust, dead skin, and other stuff that's clogging the works and damaging the blades. Many shavers have a removable head cover. Pop it off and brush the underside, avoiding the delicate screen. If you've lost the *tiny brush* that came with your shaver, use a *small toothbrush* (one that's retired from dental duties, please). Then remove the shaving head and gently brush the cutting mechanism itself ▶. A blast from a *can of compressed air* will also dislodge any embedded detritus that stands in the way of a smooth shave.

▲

If you use a shave stick—a compressed powder product that dries up perspiration and facial oils to create a smoother shave—the powder can gum up your electric shaver blades. To cure this, dip a *cotton swab* in *rubbing alcohol* and wipe the blades.

If your shaver requires more cleaning, it's time to go commercial. Some manufacturers of shaving goods sell an *aerosol spray cleaner and lubricant* for electric shavers. In general, you spray the cleaner on and run the shaver for several seconds. Follow the package directions.

To clean the exterior, unplug your shaver and wipe the surfaces with a *damp washcloth*. If anything insists on clinging to the outside, use a little *alcohol* to wipe it off.

Enamel

Imagine that instead of the glossy appliances and basins you use every day you had to make do with one or more rusting refrigerators, washing machines, stoves, ovens, grills, bathtubs, and sinks. That's what you'd have in a world without enamel. Enamel is a baked-on coating for metals that doesn't rust or react with acids or chemicals and is usually easy to clean. Enameled steel or enameled cast-iron cookware can be a little more of a challenge because of the heat-meets-food factor.

To clean enameled surfaces, such as appliance surfaces, dissolve *2 tablespoons of baking soda* in *1 quart of warm water*. Wipe the surfaces with a *cloth or sponge* dipped in the solution and rinse with *fresh water* on a *clean cloth or sponge*. To remove cooked-on deposits, see *Stoves*.

To clean enameled cookware, let the pot cool first. Never begin your cleanup by putting cold water into a hot pot (or vice versa). Wash in *hot water* with *dishwashing detergent*, rinse in running

simple SOLUTIONS

Burnt-On Food >

Even the best chefs face this problem. Cover the stuck-on food with baking soda and let the pan sit for several minutes while the soda absorbs the acids and oils. Then wash as usual. If the food still won't budge, add 1 quart of water and 2 teaspoons of baking soda to the pan, simmer for 15 minutes, and wash again.

water, and dry. Pots with metal or plastic handles may be washed in the *dishwasher*, but pots with wooden handles should not be. Never use an abrasive cleaner or metal scouring pad. A *plastic or nylon scourer* is fine.

To care for enameled cookware, remember:
- Keep the cooking heat on low or medium except when boiling water.
- Never subject an empty pot to high heat.
- Use nonscratchy wooden or plastic cooking tools.

Erasers

Thousands of schools have employed the time-honored way of seeing to it that felt chalkboard erasers are clean: letting the students do it. Old-fashioned slate blackboards are a rarity now, but felt erasers still work fine on most newer boards—white boards, green boards, and dry-erase boards—depending on what type of marker is used.

The simplest method for cleaning felt erasers works as well now as it did in times past. Go outside, hold an eraser in each hand, and clap them together, trying to keep the chalk dust from invading your clothes and lungs. If you can't assign the job to a student, enlist a *vacuum cleaner*, which works quite well.

Erasers made for dry-erase boards should be cleaned with *bar soap or dishwashing liquid* under *running water*. Let them air-dry.

To clean a rubber pencil eraser, rub an *emery board* or piece of *sandpaper* over it until the black part that makes those awful smudges is gone. This method will also help rejuvenate an eraser that has become hard and brittle. The newly exposed rubber will be clean and soft.

Exercise Equipment

For lots of people, cleaning gym equipment is as easy as removing the shirts hanging on the handlebars. But for those who actually use their stationary bikes, treadmills, or weight machines, the goal is to keep the equipment more than clutter free. You want it to remain sanitary and operating smoothly.

Wipe the perspiration off the equipment after you've finished using it, because the salt in your sweat is corrosive. This goes for all machines, especially those with metal parts. Wipe down control panels to keep moisture from seeping into them and ruining the sensitive electronics. To make it easier, keep a roll of **paper towels** handy in your workout room.

Every once in a while, wipe down the equipment with a **sponge or cloth** moistened with a bleach solution—*1 to 2 ounces of bleach* in *1 quart of water*. This will kill any lingering germs.

To clean a treadmill and keep it running properly, use your **vacuum cleaner** to clean under the machine every other week. Every three months, vacuum around the motor casing. Most people don't realize it, but dirt is the biggest killer of treadmill motors. Along those lines, here are two tips from a personal trainer:

● First, don't wear the same shoes on your treadmill that you wear outside. Instead, keep a fresh, indoors-only pair for treadmill training.

● Second, consider putting your treadmill on a rubber mat instead of directly on the floor or carpet. All that friction causes a buildup of static electricity, which will attract motor-clogging dust bunnies and carpet lint.

Follow both tips and you'll clean less and have a longer lasting treadmill.

To clean an elliptical machine—the gizmo that combines the exercise of climbing stairs with that of riding a bicycle—wipe it down with a **moist rag**. To keep an elliptical machine from squeaking and skipping, clean and lubricate the machine's rails and wheels. Follow the manufacturer's recommendations or wipe with a **cloth** moistened with **silicone spray**.

To clean a weight machine, treat it like a car. (It probably cost as much.) The painted metal parts are similar to your car's painted metal body. Once a year, use a **car cleaner** (available at auto supply stores), diluted according to the package directions, to clean the grime off the paint. Rinse with a **clean wet towel** and dry with a **dry towel**. Wax the machine with your favorite **car wax**, again following the package directions. This prevents scratches, reduces grime buildup, and brings out a warm shine.

Periodically, clean and lubricate the weight machine's guide rods to keep the weight stack from sticking. Clean the rods with a **dry paper towel**. Wipe them with a **cloth** moistened with a **silicone spray**. Don't overdo it, however, because too much lubrication can also make them stick together.

To keep up a stationary bike, the most important thing to do is to clean and lubricate the chain every three months or so. Clean

 **OOPS!**

Walking on Sunshine >
Boston-based personal trainer Jeff Rutfield, who recommends treating your home gym equipment as you would a car by washing and waxing it, knows someone who took his comparison too far.

"He used rubber and vinyl protectant Armor All on the belt of his treadmill," Rutfield said. It wasn't such a far-fetched thing to do, considering that the belt's rubber is similar to a tire's sidewall. And it worked—the belt was even shinier than when it was new.

However, Rutfield said, "The next time he used his treadmill, he went flying off." Armor All's one major drawback: It's slippery.

the chain by carefully holding a *dry rag* on it and slowly turning the pedals to run the chain through the rag a few times. Next, lubricate the chain with a *Teflon or silicone spray lubricant*, available at bicycle stores. To avoid splattering, don't jump on and pedal right away; let the lubricant dry, which should take only a few minutes.

Have your equipment professionally serviced every year or so if you use it with any regularity. Ask the people you bought the gear from to recommend a service technician.

OOPS!

Fanning the Flames >

At Hanscom Air Force Base in Massachusetts, a dirty fan started a fire in one of the base apartments.

Rental housing, such as that on the base, is especially likely to harbor dirty exhaust fans, because tenants come and go, and no one thinks about cleaning those fans.

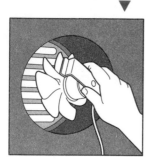

Exhaust Fans

Here's a test: Hold a *tissue* up to the grille where the air enters the exhaust fan in your bathroom, kitchen, basement, or attic. Turn on the switch. If the tissue stays tight against the grille, that's good. If the tissue flutters, that's bad. Your exhaust fan has become an exhausted fan. Dirt may be the problem. Attic and basement fans should be cleaned once a year; bathroom and kitchen fans, every six months.

To clean an exhaust fan:
1. Turn switch off. Unplug fan or disengage circuit breaker.
2. Remove the grille and wash it in *warm water* and *dishwashing soap*. Rinse and dry. A kitchen exhaust fan will also have a filter that needs washing.
3. On many models, you can remove the fan and motor by unscrewing the mounting bracket and unplugging the cord ▶.
4. Whether you remove them or not, *vacuum* the fan blades with the *nozzle attachment*. Then wipe them off with a *damp cloth*. Also vacuum and wipe the inside of the housing.
5. Clean the motor and other dusty parts with a *stiff paintbrush*.
6. If you notice bad wiring or if the fan doesn't work, call an electrician. Don't attempt to fix it yourself.

Wash the filter in a range hood exhaust fan every month or two. This filter, usually aluminum, is for catching cooking grease. Remove it and wash it in the *dishwasher* or in a solution of *hot water* and *dishwashing detergent*. Don't use ammonia, which will darken the metal. Rinse, dry, and reinstall the filter.

Range hood fans that recirculate the air, rather than venting it outside, have a charcoal filter that must be replaced about every six months.

EXERCISE EQUIPMENT

Eyeglasses and Sunglasses

In this age of stylish eyewear, it can no longer be said that "boys don't make passes at girls who wear glasses." Dirty glasses are another matter. Both men and women dislike gazing into the eyes of their beloved through bleary, dreary lenses.

For general cleaning of eyeglasses, wet cleaning is better than dry cleaning. Most of us have grabbed a tissue or pulled a handkerchief out of a pocket to wipe our glasses, but that can smear dirt around and scratch the lenses. Dirt particles are hard, whereas lenses are soft and getting softer. Almost all lenses today are plastic, and plastic lenses are especially susceptible to scratching.

For daily cleanings, pass the glasses under *running water* and dry them with a *tissue* or a clean *microfiber cleaning cloth* made especially for eyeglasses. The microfiber cloths are washable and can be purchased at drugstores or optical shops. Packaged single-use *towelettes* made for eyeglasses are also good cleaners and are convenient when you're on the move.

To remove oily smears from your glasses, pick up a specially formulated *lens cleaner* at a drugstore or mass merchandiser and follow the package instructions. These cleaners are ideal for all cleanings, so use them at least periodically if not every time you clean. Using water alone will not remove oils. Even mild dishwashing detergent can damage coatings over time, and harsher cleaners (including anything with ammonia) can damage them immediately. Lens cleaners may seem like an unnecessary expense, but they will help keep your lenses from getting cloudy and scratched, thus prolonging the life of your glasses. The best lens cleaners even leave behind a thin film, a kind of instant coating, which further brightens the lenses.

A wide variety of special lens coatings, including polarizing, tinted, transitions, mirror, ultraviolet protective, and antireflective, is available for eyeglasses. Regular lens cleaners are fine for all but the latter, which requires a special *antireflective cleaner*.

To clean the frames of your eyeglasses, mix a *few drops of mild dishwashing detergent* in *2 cups of water*. Dip a clean, soft *toothbrush* into the solution and gently scrub around the frame, the nosepiece, and the earpieces, avoiding the lenses as much as possible. Rinse under *running water* and dry with a clean *cloth*.

simple SOLUTIONS

Got a Screw Loose? >

Next to dirty lenses, the most annoying glasses problem is having a screw loose in the hinge.

If a screw comes loose repeatedly, you need something more than a screwdriver. A thread sealant will solve the problem. One kind is Permatex Medium Strength Threadlocker Blue, a sealant that's available in auto supply stores. Put a drop on the screw before screwing it in, and it will hold. A drop of clear nail polish will also work, although it may not last as long.

Fans

Remember the ceiling fans in the 1942 movie *Casablanca*, gently stirring a breeze at Rick's Café? How romantic would they have been with a blanket of gray fuzz atop each blade? Not only would dust buildup have been a turnoff for Humphrey Bogart and Ingrid Bergman, but it would have wreaked havoc on the efficiency of those ceiling fans as well. Although table fans, floor fans, and window fans lack the allure of ceiling fans, they also need to be cleaned.

For day-to-day cleaning, pull out a *lamb's wool duster* and a *stepladder or step stool* and give the blades of your ceiling fans a quick dusting. Other types of fans have grilles that protect the blades. Clean the grilles and other housing regularly using a *vacuum* with a *small brush attachment*.

Do a more thorough cleaning every month or two during times of heavy use. First, disengage the circuit breaker for a ceiling fan and unplug others. Remove the grilles. Then round up the usual suspects: a solution of *water* with a little *dishwashing detergent* and a *sponge or brush*. Dampen the sponge and wipe the blades. Rinse the sponge in *clear water* and wipe again. Then dry with a *clean cloth*. Be careful not to bend the blades, because that could upset their balance and make the fan wobble.

If the grilles have accumulated a lot of grime, it might be simplest to take them outside and wash them under a *hose*. Use a *stiff brush* to clean off stubborn crud.

Fiberglass

Fiberglass is commonly found around the home in bathtubs, shower stalls, sinks, fixtures, outdoor furniture, and window parts. Its smooth surface layer—that's what sparkles—is easily marred, so learn how to care for fiberglass while it's still bright. Sparkling fiberglass is easy to clean. Dull fiberglass is a chore to spiff up.

To clean fiberglass, always use *nonabrasive cleaners and scrubbers*. After each shower, rinse the shower walls with *water* and wipe them down with a *squeegee or chamois cloth* to avoid a buildup of water residue and soap scum. Once a week, wash with a little *mild dishwashing detergent* and *warm water*, applied with a *sponge*. Always rinse cleaners off with *clear water*.

To attack mold and mildew, mix *baking soda* with enough *water* to make a paste. Wet the fiberglass with *water*, dip a *sponge* in the

paste, and rub gently. Rinse with *clear water*. This also works for general cleaning.

To remove soap scum on your fiberglass, mix a solution of *1 part ammonia* to *4 parts water*. Or use a *cleaner containing phosphoric acid*. Rub on with a *sponge or clean rag* and rinse immediately and thoroughly with *clear water*.

Hard-water deposits can also be removed with *boat hull cleaners*. (Many boats are fiberglass, after all.) Look for such cleaners at hardware or boating stores and follow the package directions.

To remove glue, tar, or oil-based paint stains, put a little *acetone nail polish remover or paint thinner* on a *clean cloth* and lightly rub until the spot disappears. Then wash with *dishwashing detergent* and *water*. Finally, rinse with *clear water*.

To help preserve the finish of fiberglass, take another tip from sailors. A couple of times a year, use an *automotive white polishing compound* on any dull or scratchy areas. Then apply a light coat of *automotive white paste wax*. Buff with a *clean cloth*. The surface will be slippery, so use on walls only, not on floors. This treatment will also help protect outdoor furniture.

Filters

A common-sense rule: Anything designed to catch dirt should be cleaned often. Filters fit the description. There are all kinds of filters, but dirty ones don't work very well and will cost you money, because motors will use more energy to pass air or water through dirty filters than clean ones.

Cleaning air filters is usually a snap: You throw out the old one and install a new one. That's how it works with forced-air furnaces. You find the slot in your furnace housing where the air intake duct supplies air to the furnace and, once a month during the heating season (the cooling season, too, if you have central air), you pull out the filter and toss it in the trash. Then you install a *new filter*, making sure you match the direction of airflow with the indicator on the edge of the filter frame. At the very minimum, change a furnace filter twice a year.

Air-conditioner filters, which may be disposable or washable, also need monthly attention. If the filter is washable, remove it and *vacuum* up as much dust as you can. Then rinse it under *warm running water* ▶ or swirl it around in a solution of *1 tablespoon of baking soda* and *1 quart of water*. (Don't use soap.) Rinse and dry.

▲

Air cleaners may be tabletop, room, or whole-house models. The disposable fiberglass or washable metal mesh filters on whole-house systems should be changed or cleaned with **warm water** monthly when they're in use. Filters in which the air passes through a medium such as charcoal should be changed annually.

Room or tabletop models of air cleaners may use filters that must be changed every few months. Others use ionizing technology that gives dust particles a negative charge so they will stick to something with a positive charge. Follow the filter-cleaning instructions that come with your unit.

Home water-filtering systems often use activated carbon filters that collect gunk. The activated carbon usually comes in cartridges that need to be replaced when they no longer work. The tricky part is figuring out when they've quit doing their job. Sometimes you can tell by the taste of the water, if the filter is designed to remove chlorine, for example. Some filters come with lights or other indicators telling when it's time to change them.

You might want to make sure your filtering system has been certified to meet the standards set by the National Sanitation Foundation. Then you'll know that the manufacturer's guidelines for changing the filters have been tested and found adequate.

See also **Air, Air Conditioners,** *and* **Furnaces**.

Fireplaces

Ironically, fireplace cleaning duties are simpler during the wood-burning season and more of a project off-season.

During the fire-burning season, cleaning will usually consist merely of removing some of the ashes periodically. (The fireplace will actually work better with a couple of inches of ash remaining.) Many fireplaces have an ash pit, which is a receptacle underneath the area where you build a fire. If yours does, open it and push excess ashes into it. Or use an **ash shovel** to deposit the ashes in a **metal bucket with a tight-fitting lid**. Store the ashes outdoors in the tightly covered can for two days before final disposal, an important precaution because "dead" ashes containing live embers have started many a conflagration.

During the off-season, do a more thorough fireplace cleaning. Use a **rubber eraser** on any smoke streaks that have crept up the exterior of the fireplace. If your fireplace has warm-air circulators, clean the ducts with a **vacuum cleaner**.

A cozy fire is widely cherished, but the mess that goes with burning wood in a fireplace is much loathed. Many people have solved that paradox with a gas fireplace.

Gas is a clean fuel, and a properly working gas fireplace basically needs no cleaning on the part of the homeowner, says Mark Gulamerian, a technical support staffer at Hearth & Home (HearthandHome.net), a fireplace retailer based in Ledgewood, New Jersey. It should, however, get an annual cleaning and inspection by a professional to ensure that the venting, controls, and valves are working properly. The retailer who sold you the gas fireplace may do such servicing or can direct you to someone who does.

Don't ever burn anything except gas in the fireplace, and learn how your particular model operates. (There are four types.)

"Read the owner's manual—don't start the fire with it," Gulamerian says. If the fireplace is working properly, don't tempt fate by tampering with the log or its internal workings. However, if you smell gas or if excessive soot suddenly shows up on the log or the glass, that's a sign to call for servicing.

You may also want to clean up the black buildup of creosote, a highly combustible residue created by burning wood, on the inside of the firebox. (The firebox is the place where you build your fire. Some people like to use the firebox for displays of candles or flowers during the off-season.) Remove the screen, andirons, and grate, and sweep up all the ashes with a **broom** and **dustpan**. Use a **wire-bristled brush** for the first attack on the creosote. If you want the firebox to be cleaner, use **1/4 cup of washing soda** (available in grocery stores in the detergent section) in **1 gallon of water** and apply it with a **sponge**. Brush with a **stiff-fiber brush** and rinse with **clear water**. Wear **rubber gloves**, since washing soda is caustic.

The off-season is also the time to have the chimney cleaned. This is a job for a professional chimney sweep, who will check the flue for leaves, bird nests, cracks, and soot buildup.

See also **Brick, Chimneys,** and **Fireplace Screens and Tools** *below.*

Fireplace Screens and Tools

Your entire fireplace arrangement may dazzle you with charm in the evening, but in the harsh light of the next day, your equipment is likely to look rather battle weary.

Clean a fireplace screen with a **vacuum** as part of your regular cleaning routine in the room. A screen catches more than the sparks that want to go flying into the room. It also catches a lot of dust. Periodically, give it a more substantial cleaning with soap and water. If you pick a sunny day and work outside, the chore will be almost pleasant. Make a sudsy solution of **warm water** and a few squirts of **dishwashing liquid** and scrub the screen with a **stiff-bristled brush** dipped in the solution. Then rinse it off with the **garden hose**. If you're working inside, rinse with a **sponge** dipped in **clean water**. Allow the screen to dry thoroughly. If it has brass parts, clean them with a **brass polish**.

WATCH OUT

The cleaning of fireplace doors is a subject that's rife with conflicting advice. Your best bet is to check your owner's manual for its recommendations. These doors are usually made of safety glass, making them harder to break, but some also have heat-proof coatings that may be harmed by harsh cleaning materials.

Clean fireplace tools (shovels, pokers, tongs, and such), as well as andirons and grates, with the same brush and soapy solution. Use **extra-fine (000) steel wool** on rust or stubborn dirt. Dry the tools with a **soft cloth**. Give them a light coat of **mineral oil** with a **clean cloth**; then wipe them dry with **another cloth**.

If rust is a problem on your screen or tools, you can renew the finish with a coat of **high-temperature black spray paint**, sold in hardware stores.

Clean glass fireplace doors with a touch of caution. (See Watch Out.) But there is one certain guideline: Doors should be cleaned only when they're cool, never when they're hot. Common glass cleaners, such as Windex, don't work very well on black creosote deposits. A solution of ammonia and water will clean them up, but the solution also may strip your doors of their heatproof coating. Instead, try this:

1. Dip a **damp rag** in **ashes** from the fireplace and rub the glass with that. Then wipe dry with a **clean cloth**. Or dip a **cloth** in **white vinegar** and wash. Dry with **newspaper**.
2. If you're still seeking perfection, try rubbing with **automotive white polishing compound**. You can buy it in hardware stores or auto supply stores.
3. Try **Rutland Hearth & Grill Conditioning Glass Cleaner**, made especially for glass fireplace doors. Like most such specialty products, it's fairly expensive, but you may decide it's well worth it. The cleaner is available at hardware stores, home improvement centers, and chimney and fireplace shops.

See also **Brass**.

Fishing Rods

You fell for some nice fishing gear hook, line, and sinker. Now you want to keep it functioning and beautiful for years to come. The biggest enemies of your gear are sand and—especially—salt, which are abundant at many favorite fishing spots (unless you fish only fresh water). The trick is to consistently clean up after every outing you make. If you put equipment away while it is wet, slimy, and salty, its performance will suffer.

To clean your rod, mix *1 teaspoon of dishwashing liquid* in *1 quart of water*. Dip a *cleaning cloth* in the solution and wipe the rod. Rinse the soap off with *running water* and wipe it dry with a *clean cloth*.

If mud or other stuff has built up around the line guides, scrub them with an *old toothbrush* dipped in the soapy solution. Use the same treatment on dirt around the reel seat that can't be wiped off.

Don't shine your rod with oil, which can destroy the protective coating and eventually loosen the line guides and reel seat. Bamboo rods are an exception—polish them with a *cream-type furniture polish*.

To lubricate the joints of the ferrules (those metal connector sleeves) and keep them clean and smooth, dab a little *petroleum jelly* on one joint and slide the two pieces together and apart several times. Use a *cotton swab* to wipe off the petroleum jelly and dirt. If the ferrules have become rusted, you may be able to clean them with *fine steel wool (00) or sandpaper*, but you don't want to spoil the fit and wind up with a rod that flies apart when you're casting. It may be best to send the rod to a repair specialist.

Not Reel Simple

Reels are loaded with springs, screws, nuts, washers, bearings, gizmos, sprockets, shims, and shafts, most of them tiny. It is a real challenge to take a reel apart for cleaning and get it back in working order with nothing left over. You can avoid the job, or at least postpone it, by careful routine care, which simply means washing the reel after every outing. Use water or a teaspoon of dishwashing liquid in a quart of water. Scrub gently with a soft-bristled toothbrush. Also wash your tackle, including any lures that you used. Rinse everything well and dry with a clean cloth.

After every couple of outings, do a partial takedown of the reel, advises Chris Sox, consumer service technician at Shakespeare Fishing Tackle, in Columbia, South Carolina. Strip out the main drive gears and the pinion gear and soak them in a degreaser, such as mineral spirits, available at hardware and home improvement stores. Then wash them with warm water and dry well.

Periodically, a reel will need to be *really* taken apart, cleaned, and oiled. If you are determined to do the job yourself, make sure you have the internal diagram and parts list that came with the reel, and follow the directions. However, this is really a good job for a professional. Check with your local bait shop or send the reel away to a professional shop.

To clean the rod grips, use the *same cloth and soapy solution*. Cork demands careful handling, because rough treatment could cause pieces to break off. A very dirty or damaged cork grip is another candidate for a professional repair job. Allow cork grips to air-dry to avoid mildew.

Fishponds

One way to clean your manmade fishpond would be to turn the job over to a great blue heron. Herons eat lots of fish, and too many fish make a fishpond dirty. Fish urine, like that of other animals, contains toxic ammonia.

The best approach to the problem is to work with nature rather than against her. Even a small pond is a complex ecological system, and the right mix of two plant groups—submerged plants to oxygenate the water and floating plants to provide shade—will help control algae. The mix must be in the right proportions to work effectively. A good book on creating ponds will tell you how to do it.

Routine pond maintenance consists mostly of removing debris such as dead leaves from the water. Use a *long-handled swimming pool skimmer net*. Don't expect your pond to be Absolut-vodka clear. The water should be a pale green. Environmental balance takes a long time to establish, so don't be too quick to upset it by emptying and refilling the pond.

A major pond cleaning is called for when there is a lot of muck or too many fish in the water. The pond may have been over-stocked, or the fish may have multiplied. In either case, you may have to find new homes for some of your scaly friends. A rule of thumb is that each fish in a pond should have about a barrel of water. The best time—and many experts say the only time—to clean a pond is in early spring, when cool temperatures provide a less stressful environment for the fish and plants. Even so, always keep the fish and plants that you remove from the pond in the shade to avoid stressing them. Here's what to do:

1. Begin by removing the edge plants and then the floating ones, pot and all. Put them in the shade.
2. Use a *bucket* to draw water off the top (the cleanest part) of the pond. Place a *kiddie wading pool* in a shady spot and fill it with the water, which will be the right pH and temperature to hold the fish. Save as much of the rest of the pond water as you can in *extra containers*, unless it is really disgusting.

simple SOLUTIONS

A Cleaner Home for Your Fish >

To keep a pond cleaner, an aerator of some kind (any device, such as a fountain that mixes air into the water) will help, as will freshwater snails. And don't forget the blue heron.

3. Start removing the remaining water with a **pump** or **siphon**. As the water level drops, remove the submerged plants and put them in the kiddie pool, too.

4. When the pond has been half drained, remove the fish with a **net** and transfer them to the kiddie pool. Cover it with a **mesh screen**, in case you have any aspiring flying fish.

5. While there is still water at the bottom of the pond, clean the sides with a **soft-bristled scrub brush**. Continue to drain until the bottom layer of crud is in sight. Then stop pumping and remove the bottom debris with a **dustpan**.

6. Rinse the sides of the pool with a **hose** and then remove the pump and rinse that. Gently scrub the bottom.

7. Replace the plants before you begin refilling. Use a **water conditioner**, available at pet or aquarium stores, to neutralize chlorine in the new water. Return the water that you saved in the kiddie pool and other containers to the pond, and let the pond warm slightly before returning the fish.

Flags and Banners

You've probably seen a flag patriotically displayed alongside the words "These colors don't run." It's a ringing endorsement of bravery but an unreliable guarantee of laundry performance. Most flags have colors that, if each were the color of an individual item in your laundry hamper, you'd separate and wash in different loads. Banners, often with appliquéd designs and depicting seasonal or whimsical themes, also often use contrasting colors.

To keep the colors pure, first check the box or bag that your flag or banner came in—if you still have it—to see whether it has directions for cleaning. If directions aren't available, try to determine what kind of fabric the flag or banner is made of. Those of recent vintage are usually cotton, nylon, or polyester.

Washing a nylon or polyester flag or banner is usually safe. Put it in a **washing machine** on a **gentle cycle** in **warm water** with a **mild laundry detergent**. You can hang it out to dry on a **clothesline** or dry it on a **low setting** in the **dryer**.

Dry-cleaning a cotton flag or banner is usually necessary—especially if you value it highly—because it is likely to bleed if washed. A wool flag or banner should always be dry-cleaned. Some dry cleaners will clean flags free of charge, especially around patriotic holidays. If you want to take a chance, go ahead and launder a cotton flag or banner. If the colors run, you may

simple
SOLUTIONS

Keep It Flying Proudly >

To extend a flag's life, take it down when it rains, snows, or is very windy. If a flag does become wet, let it dry thoroughly before you fold or roll it. Otherwise, you're inviting mildew to take up residence.

WATCH OUT

Old flags with historical value should be treated with great care. Consult a professional conservator at a local museum.

be able to undo the damage with **Synthrapol**, a special soap made for removing excess dye, or **Carbona Color Run Remover**, whose name is pretty self-explanatory. Look for them at mass merchandisers, fabric stores, and arts and crafts supply stores.

Flatware

Your flatware should be so shiny that dinner guests could use a knife blade like a mirror to see themselves. They probably shouldn't, but they should be able to.

Rinse your flatware under **running water** immediately after eating. You may not want to actually wash the dishes if, say, you're entertaining, but rinsing will remove food that might cause pitting or staining. Be especially diligent about eggs, fruit juices, tomatoey foods, lemon, vinegar, salty foods (including butter), mustard, and salad dressings. Silver is most vulnerable, but stainless steel, despite its name, isn't completely immune to the threat of corrosion. You can also soak flatware in **warm water** in a **sink or dishpan**, but don't soak hollow-handled ware for long, lest it loosen the soldering.

Wash stainless steel flatware in the **dishwasher** normally, along with your dishes, but don't spill detergent directly on the pieces, because it could pit or spot them. However, your flatware will be shinier and more lustrous if you dry it by hand with a **soft dishcloth**.

If your stainless steel flatware has dulled over the years, you can brighten it by soaking it in **1 gallon of hot water** mixed with **1 teaspoon of ammonia**. Rinse with **clear hot water** and dry well with a **clean cloth**.

Wash silver flatware, both plate and sterling, by hand. Use **dishwashing liquid** in **hot water**. Rinse with **clear hot water** and dry immediately with a **soft dishcloth**. Don't use abrasive cleaners or scrubbers, such as steel wool. They will dull the finish.

The sulfur in eggs and egg products (such as mayonnaise) will cause silver to tarnish—instantly. So do pollutants in the air, but they work more slowly. Tarnish is not removed by regular washing. You'll have to use a **silver polish** on that.

Clean pewter flatware with **rubbing alcohol** on a **soft cloth**. Then follow up with the **hot, soapy water** treatment.

*For how to polish silver, see **Silver Jewelry** and **Silver Serving Pieces**. Also see **Pewter**.*

FLAGS AND BANNERS

Floors

Not all floors are created equal. Even among general categories such as wood, stone, or tile, there are vast differences between specific examples. Maple isn't pine, marble isn't granite, and quarry tile isn't glazed.

Still, all floors are subjected to dirt and wear, and some basic cleaning techniques apply universally. Check the Floor Cleaning Pyramid box on page 182 for general floor cleaning methods, and when you've exhausted those, try the recommendations under the following headings for specific floor types.

To clean wood floors, the bad news is that you really should get down on your hands and knees. That's right. And you can't swab water all over the floor—it must be used sparingly. So get ready to play Cinderella.

When damp mopping won't do, try one of these general-purpose cleaners:
- Mix *1/2 cup of cider vinegar* in *1 gallon of warm water*.
- Brew some tea using *2 tea bags* per *1 quart of water*. Don't use instant tea.

Dip a *soft cloth* or *sponge* in the solution, wring it out, and wipe the floor. Buff with a *soft, dry cloth*.

The object of caring diligently for wood floors—aside from keeping them looking good—is to avoid having to do a sanding job. It's a lot of work if you do it yourself. It's a lot of money if you hire it done. It's messy. And it removes from your floor not just the old finish but a layer of wood. Each time you sand, you're working your way toward the basement.

The Lowdown on *Wax Buildup*

Guess what? High-traffic areas will wear out their wax sooner than low-traffic areas. This means the road less traveled can get a nasty wax buildup. A telltale sign is a yellowed or discolored floor. Removing all the wax requires harsher cleaning than usual and should be done only when necessary and no more often than once a year.

Here are two recipes for a wax stripper:
- 1/2 cup of ammonia and 1 cup of laundry detergent in 1 gallon of warm water.
- 1/2 cup of washing soda (available at supermarkets in the detergent section) in 1 gallon of warm water.

In either case, apply some solution and scrub with a stiff brush, electric scrubber, or extra-fine steel wool (000) pads to loosen the old wax. Work on a small area at a time and mop up the solution after the wax has been softened. Repeat the process in other areas until the entire floor is stripped of wax. Rinse thoroughly with a solution of a gallon of water and a cup of vinegar. After drying completely, apply new wax.

Determining a wood floor's finish will help you determine how to care for it. If the floor was installed or last refinished before the mid 1960s, the finish is probably varnish or shellac. These finishes rest on top of the wood, are often waxed, and require a whole-floor sanding before a new finish can be applied. Later finishes may be polyurethane, which penetrates the wood, should not be waxed, and can be touched up by new urethane applied to just the worn places.

You can tell one from the other by scratching the surface with a *coin* in an inconspicuous place. If the finish flakes, it is probably shellac or varnish. If the finish does not flake, it is probably a polyurethane finish.

To check for wax, put a *couple of drops of water* on the floor. Wait 10 minutes and check to see whether white spots have appeared under the water. White spots mean the floor has been waxed. If there are no white spots, it hasn't.

The *Floor Cleaning* Pyramid

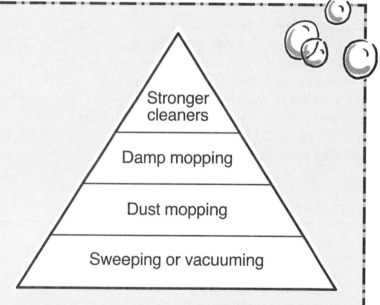

Remember the famous Food Guide Pyramid? You're supposed to choose a lot of the foods depicted at the bottom of the pyramid (fruits, vegetables, and grains) and eat the stuff at the top sparingly (sweets and oils). On the Floor Cleaning Pyramid, the broad bottom includes the cleaning methods that apply to all types of floors and that should be used most frequently. Frequency of use declines as you go up the pyramid, and the top is reserved for specialized cleaners for different flooring materials.

Here are other general guidelines for floor cleaning:
• Vacuum or sweep up loose dirt frequently.
• Chase dust bunnies with a dust mop.

• Wipe up any spills immediately.
• Clean with a damp mop or cloth (using plain water) weekly or more often. Change the water as soon as it gets cloudy.

• Go to stronger cleaners only when a damp mop doesn't do the job.
• Rinse thoroughly after using any kind of cleaner.

FLOORS

On varnished or shellacked floors, a *solvent-based liquid wax* for wood works well. It removes dirt and most of the old wax (preventing wax buildup) and leaves a thin coating of new wax. You can apply the cleaner with a *soft, dry cloth* attached to a *long-handled wax applicator*, but you would do a better job on your hands and knees. You can also use an *electric polisher*, changing *pads* frequently. In any case, you must buff afterward with a *clean cloth*. Never use water-based self-polishing wax on wood floors.

On urethane-finished floors, rub with a cloth containing a little *furniture oil* to give them more shine. (Read the label to make sure it doesn't contain any wax.) Be sure to use very little; too much oil will attract dirt—and turn the floor into a skating rink.

To clean stone flooring, try this low-tech method: Sprinkle damp *sawdust* over the floor, scrub with a *stiff brush*, and sweep up the sawdust with a *broom* and *dustpan*. Follow up with a *vacuum*.

Many kinds of stone flooring, especially marble, need a *neutral pH cleaner* (sold by businesses that sell and install stone flooring). A *mild dishwashing liquid* mixed with *water* will also work nicely. Consult the dealer who sold you the stone for recommendations for specific cleaners if more power is needed. There are also professionals who can refinish stone floors.

To clean ceramic tile floors, a quick pass with a *damp mop* is often all that is needed. Indeed, cleaning ceramic tile would be a breeze if tile were all you had to clean. It's that pesky grout between the tiles that's a problem.

When damp mopping alone isn't enough, mix one of these cleaning solutions:
- *1 capful of rubbing alcohol* in *1 gallon of water*
- *1 tablespoon of borax* and *2 tablespoons of ammonia* in *1 gallon of water*.

Apply the solution with a *mop or an electric cleaner-polisher*. Rinse well with *clear water* on your mop. A *commercial cleaner* such as Spic and Span or Mr. Clean will also do nicely.

If the grout needs special attention, mix *1/4 cup of vinegar* with *1 gallon of water* and scrub the grout with a *toothbrush or nylon scrub pad*. For heavy-duty treatment, scrub with a mixture of *1 cup of chlorine bleach* in *1/2 gallon of water* (wear *rubber gloves*). Let the solution stand for 20 minutes, mop the floor twice with *clean water* to rinse thoroughly, and wipe dry. To make future cleaning easier, seal the grout with a *silicone sealer*, which is available at home stores, hardware stores, or stores that specialize in tile.

WATCH OUT

Acids (such as vinegar) will etch marble, and strong alkaline solutions (such as washing soda or trisodium phosphate) will break down the surface and leave it rough.

What a cad! The heel had its way with your house and then left nasty, stubborn black marks on your floors.

Try rubbing heel marks with a pencil eraser first. If that doesn't work, rub a hardwood floor with a rag dabbed in a little mineral spirits. On vinyl flooring, smear a drop of baby oil over the mark, wait a few minutes, and wipe the mark away with a rag.

To clean vinyl flooring that just needs touching up, use a *damp mop*. If the soil requires something stronger than water, mix *1 cup of white vinegar* with *1 gallon of water* and apply with a *mop*. If that doesn't do the job, try *2 tablespoons of borax* in *1 gallon of warm water*. In either case, apply a small amount with your *mop*, then rinse thoroughly by mopping with *plain water*.

For more shine, apply a *thin coat of wax* to a dry, clean floor. The one-step wax-and-clean products don't work as well as a regular wax. A self-polishing wax (such as Johnson One Step No Buff Wax) is easy to apply, but it will build up over time. A solvent-based paste wax (such as Johnson Paste Wax) is more work and must be buffed but—wouldn't you know it—provides superior results.

No-wax vinyl has a polyurethane finish intended to keep a shine without waxing. It will stay shiny for a long time if it is kept clean, but eventually the finish will dull. Follow the manufacturer's directions for a *polish* or *sealer* to renew the shine.

If hair spray has built up on the no-wax floor in your bathroom, use shampoo to wash it off. (It works on hair, after all.) Mix a *squirt of shampoo* in *1 gallon of warm water*, mop, and rinse.

To clean laminate flooring, keep in mind that, like wood, it should not be mopped by slopping lots of water around on the floor. (Laminate is the manmade flooring that comes in tongue-and-groove planks that often simulate wood.) Don't use ammonia, solvents, abrasives, general-purpose cleaners, polishes, or waxes on laminate. Despite these restrictions, laminate is a breeze to clean.

Some manufacturers recommend their own special cleaner, which is usually fairly expensive. Here is a less expensive version that works just as well: *1 cup white vinegar*, *1 cup rubbing alcohol* (to make it dry faster), *1 cup water*, and *3 drops of dishwashing liquid*. Mix in a *spray bottle*, shake, spray it on the floor, and spread it with a *mop*. No rinsing is needed.

If your laminate gets scratched, you may be able to buy a *touch-up stick* from the manufacturer. In the event of severe damage, a professional installer may be able to replace a plank or two.

Flowerpots

A beautiful flower in a dirty pot is like a beautiful cake on a food-encrusted plate. They don't go together. You don't clean flowerpots solely for aesthetic reasons, however. Plants and their soil may contain viruses, bacteria, fungi, or pests, which can be passed along to the next pot occupant.

Clean your flowerpots using the same method, whether they're made of plastic, glazed or unglazed clay, ceramic, or other materials. Wash with *liquid dishwashing detergent* and *water*, as you would dishes. Scour with a *stiff brush* to remove algae and mineral deposits. Wash again with a solution of *10 parts water* to *1 part chlorine bleach*. Rinse with *fresh water* and let dry in the sunshine—a great sterilizer.

Here are some more tips on cleaning flowerpots:

- If you'd prefer to avoid scrubbing, soak the pots for about an hour in a solution of *2 parts water* to *1 part white vinegar*. The minerals and algae should wash right off.
- To avoid that crusty white buildup of mineral deposits around the top inner edge of the pot, take an *old candle* and rub it around the rim. That will seal the surface, making mineral buildup less likely.
- You might also heed the message of that white scaly stuff. It's trying to tell you that you're giving your plants too much fertilizer. Many indulgent plant parents do that, so consider cutting back. Get a good book on caring for houseplants and follow its advice.
- To keep dirt from spattering out of the flowerpot when it rains or when you water the plant, put a *layer of pebbles* on top of the dirt.

Flowers

Fresh flowers are among the cheeriest things on earth. There's not much to be done to improve on nature, other than brush off the stray piece of dirt with a *soft paintbrush* and coax them into lasting a long time.

Dusting artificial or dried flowers is something you need to do occasionally. The first line of defense is to blow off the dust. Use a *feather duster* or a *hair dryer* ▶ on its *lowest, coolest setting* for sturdy blooms. Use a *turkey baster* to squirt air on more fragile artificial or dried flowers.

▲

By the way, "silk" flowers is usually a misnomer today. Most fabric flowers are made of polyester or other blends.

For a more thorough cleaning, try this method, which is safe for both plastic and fabric flowers. (Some people say they've used it successfully on dried natural flowers, too, but proceed at your own risk.) Draw enough *water* into the *sink* (or *bathtub*, if necessary) so that the flowers can be submerged. Add a *squirt of*

Here are some ways to slow the passage of blooms to has-blooms:
• Cut off any leaves below water level.
• Wash the vase and change the water daily.

• Use a simple preservative in the water, such as 2 table-spoons of white vinegar and 2 teaspoons of sugar to a quart of water. (Sugar feeds the flowers, and vinegar inhibits the growth of unwant-

ed critters.) Or use 1 part tonic water to 2 parts water.
• Keep the flowers cool and out of direct sunlight.
• Cut off the ends periodically.

---

mild dishwashing soap and slosh it around to make suds. Then put the flowers in the water, holding them down to cover. Gently raise and lower them a couple of times. Drain the water and rinse the flowers with the *side sprayer* at the sink or under the *shower* in the tub. Let them air-dry thoroughly.

Here are some more flower-enhancing tricks that you might want to try for artificial or dried flowers:

● Use a *steam iron*, set on the *lowest setting*, to perk up those tired paper flowers.

● Dried natural flowers will last longer if they've been given several light coats of sealer from an aerosol spray can. You can use *hair spray* or a *clear lacquer or acrylic sealer* (available at hardware stores). The flowers can be resealed after cleaning.

● For a final act, you might gild your lilies when they're beyond cleaning. Spray artificial or dried flowers with *gold or silver spray paint* to use them for holiday or other decorations.

Foam Rubber

The nice thing about foam—whether it's the old rubber used from the 1940s to the 1960s or polyurethane, the preferred mate-rial since the '70s—is that it's porous. That means all you have to do to keep the foam that's in your cushions, pillows, or mattress-es fresh is to *vacuum* them. Spills are another story. They'll require a little more elbow grease.

To clean spills or marks on the foam's surface, first remove any covering (clean it separately); then use a *rag* dampened with *dish-washing detergent* and *water* and rub the surface. Never put soap and water directly on the foam, because it will absorb the liquid. Let the foam air-dry thoroughly before you put the cushion cover, sheet, or pillowcase back on.

Heavy spills that have seeped into the interior of the foam require special attention. Run *water*—only water—through the foam, then squeeze out as much water as you can. If you use soap or other cleaning agents, you'll just have to rinse those out, too, or risk creating a breeding ground for bacteria.

To clean a deep stain from a small cushion or pillow, place the foam in the *bathtub* or *sink* and run *water* over it. For larger cushions, use a *shower nozzle* or *garden hose*. Don't try this on a mattress, which can only be surface cleaned.

Even when you're dealing with a major stain, keep water to a minimum, because it will take 24 to 48 hours for the foam to dry. There's nothing you can do to speed the process, either. Above all, don't ever rest foam near a radiator or heat source or put small pieces in a dryer: The stuff is flammable.

No matter how good a job you do, some odors and stains—such as pet urine—may not come out if they seep into the interior of the foam rubber. You may just have to replace it.

Dirty Pillow? *Bag It*

To quickly and thoroughly clean a foam rubber pillow or cushion, all you need is a plastic bag and a vacuum cleaner, says Dan Lambert, president of Baxter Rubber in Fairfield, New Jersey.

Remove any attachment from the end of the vacuum cleaner's hose. Put the pillow in a plastic bag; then stick the end of the vacuum hose in the bag, twist the top of the bag closed, and hold it in place. Then turn on the vacuum. The foam will become condensed as the vacuum sucks the air and dirt out of the foam. When you turn the vacuum off, the foam will return to its original shape. This technique cleans both sides of the pillow at the same time.

Food

Clean food—and food that's safe to eat—starts with a clean you. Take it from the Centers for Disease Control and Prevention: The most important thing you can do to keep yourself healthy and prevent the spread of illness is to wash your hands frequently with *soap* and *water*. Traveling is no excuse for letting up on cleanliness. Take along *wipes* or *gel formulas* (no-water-needed cleaners such as Purell Instant Hand Sanitizer). Once you're squeaky clean, you're ready to prepare food.

To clean fruits and vegetables, you don't need anything special. If you're wondering about the fruit and vegetable washes you see in supermarkets, the U.S. Department of Agriculture says they're not necessary. Washing with *plain water* will do. Just be sure you don't skip any fruits and vegetables—even the organic ones. They all need to be washed.

While organic items may not have residual chemicals on them, they can have the same amount of dirt, dust, and mold spores.

Here are cleaning specifics for certain foods:
- For vegetables and fruits with a firm surface, such as potatoes, celery, and apples, use a ***vegetable brush*** to scrub the skin under ***running water***.
- For leaf vegetables and fruits with a soft skin, such as peaches, strawberries, and raspberries, rinse under ***running water*** only.
- Rinse mushrooms by holding them under ***running water*** or dunking them in a ***bowl of water***.
- To dry vegetables and fruits, use a clean ***towel*** or ***paper towel***. A ***lettuce spinner*** works for greens. If you're preparing vegetables to cook, you don't necessarily need to dry them.
- Cut away any bruised or damaged areas from fruits and vegetables with a ***sharp knife***. Immediately refrigerate any fresh-cut items.
- Rinse fish quickly in ***cold water*** to remove ice, slime, and any loose small scales you can't see.

And here are some don'ts:
- Don't use a brush on soft-skinned vegetables or fruits. You'll damage them.
- Don't use detergents or soap. The produce could absorb the residues, which you could ingest.
- Don't wash raw poultry, beef, pork, lamb, or veal before using. You may think you're helping to make the meat safe, but you're not. Cooking destroys surface bacteria at 160° F.
- Keep raw meat, fish, and poultry in containers. Never place them directly on counters or the refrigerator shelves. Never let the juices of raw meat drip onto other foods, and never use the same utensils on cooked foods that you have used for handling raw meat.
- Don't wash eggs before storing or using them. They're already washed during commercial egg processing. You'll just remove more of the "bloom," the natural coating on just-laid eggs that helps prevent bacteria from permeating the shell.

Food Graters

If you're a cook who likes the freshness of home-grated cheese, citrus rind, and hard spices, such as cardamom, nutmeg, and cinnamon, a grater is a must-have gadget in your kitchen. It's also a pesky tool to clean because some foods get trapped in the grates or leave a residue.

How to Truly Get the Grit >

Rinsing is not enough to get the grit out of lettuce or spinach leaves. The greens need a bath, says chef Greg Fatigati, a lecturing instructor with the Culinary Institute of America in New York. Fill a clean kitchen sink with enough cold water to cover the greens, and submerge them for 30 to 45 seconds. Swish the leaves around with your hand and then empty the water in the sink. Clean the sink to remove the sand and grit. Repeat the process. Keep washing, draining, and washing until you see no more sand and grit in the sink when you let the water out.

To keep a grater cleaner when you're grating citrus rind on the finest grate, wrap the grater in plastic. The *plastic wrap* adheres tightly to the form and shape of the grater, keeping the rind out of those nooks and crannies and allowing for easier collection of all the zest.

To clean the grater, soak it in warm to *hot, soapy water*. Use a *pan brush* with short bristles or even an unused *toothbrush* for the smaller grates. To protect the bristles of your brush, hold the grater upside down and brush with a bottom-to-top stroke (the opposite of the grating motion). You can put a grater in a *dishwasher*, as long as the grater isn't made of tin, which can quickly oxidize when it's not dried thoroughly.

To dry, place the grater on a *dish rack* or a *lint-free towel*.

Food Grinders

Safety first. Because a food grinder is often used to process raw meat, poultry, and seafood, proper cleaning is critical to preventing the transmission of harmful bacteria, such as *salmonella*. The best grinders disassemble completely, allowing you to clean each piece thoroughly.

To clean the grinding plates, first soak the parts in a soapy solution of *hot water* and *dishwashing liquid* to dislodge most of the food. You can finish the job in a *dishwasher* (always consult the manufacturer's instructions first), set on a *heavy cycle*.

If you're cleaning the parts by hand, one expert prefers a soak with a little salt (*1 tablespoon of salt* to *1/2 gallon of cold water*) for about 10 minutes to dislodge the food. Then you're ready to scrub the plates and blade with a *brush* in *hot, soapy water* to kill bacteria. To help get meat or other remnants out of the holes in the plates, poke *wooden kebab skewers* through the holes.

Lay the parts on a *cloth towel* and let them air-dry fully. Or you can place the parts in an *oven* at a temperature of 150° F for 10 to 15 minutes. If you put aluminum alloy blades in the dishwasher, they'll quickly start to rust when they sit and dry. Once the blades are dry, rub *vegetable or salad oil* lightly over them to protect them from rusting.

To clean a food grinder's motor unit, sanitize it with either a commercial *kitchen sanitizer*, such as Lysol, or a solution of *1 ounce of bleach* to *1 gallon of warm water*. Fill a *spray bottle* with the solution, spray it on the housing unit, and wipe it off.

Food Processors

Somewhere among the jungle of gadgets on your kitchen countertop there is probably a food processor. This piece of equipment is an enormous time-saver—it purees, minces, mixes, kneads, blends, and more. But much like a food grinder, the multitalented food processor requires a multifaceted approach when it comes to cleaning. That is, it should be cleaned part by part.

For general cleaning, use the *side sprayer* on your sink, with the water pressure on as high as possible to remove stuck food. For really tough cleaning jobs, use the outdoor *garden hose*—it'll have the same effect as a high-powered restaurant kitchen sprayer. Another time-saver: If your recipe doesn't require the use of the feed tube on top of your food processor, cover the bowl with a strong piece of *plastic wrap* before locking on the lid. This will prevent splattering on the lid and minimize cleaning.

To clean the power unit of your food processor, turn it off and unplug the unit. Wipe it with a *damp cloth*. Wipe off the safety motor drive cover and reinstall it on the unit, if necessary. Never use coarse or caustic cleaning products on the power unit or immerse it in water.

To clean the attachments, put them in the *dishwasher*—all except the blades. Since items can shift in the dishwasher, the blades could bend, be dulled, or be burned if they touch a heating element. Wash the blades in *hot, soapy water*, dry with a *cloth*, and store for future use. Some experts prefer to hand-wash the plastic bowl of a food processor in *hot, soapy water*. This protects the bowl from the harsher dishwasher detergent, which can make the plastic brittle and prone to breakage. On some models, the plastic bowl has a safety spring located where the bowl attaches to the food processor. It's difficult to get this spring thoroughly dry, so after you've given the bowl a quick wipe, let it air-dry before reassembling the processor. Otherwise, the spring may rust.

Fountains

Whether you're tending the 160 fountains in Kansas City, Missouri—known as the City of Fountains—or just the one on your patio, the same rule applies: Fountains have to be cleaned part by part.

Washing your fountain periodically with a solution of *1 part bleach* to *10 parts water* will help inhibit algae.

To prevent mineral deposits from forming on bowls, the motor shaft, or other parts of the pump (which could cause it to fail), always use *distilled water, rainwater*, or *dehumidified water* in the fountain. If your fountain is so big that using distilled water is not practical, treat the water with a *mineral deposit inhibitor*, such as Protec (a companion to Fountec), or another product recommended by your local fountain or garden store.

To remove mineral deposits—should they develop despite your best efforts—you'll first need to know what your fountain bowl is made of.

- Some materials, such as resins and copper, are soft and should be cleaned with a *cotton rag*.
- Slate can be cleaned with a *soft-bristled brush*—but don't use soap. Slate can be porous; if it absorbs soap, your fountain could turn into a bubble bath.
- Other fountain bowl materials can be cleaned with an *abrasive sponge* and *white vinegar* or a *mineral deposit cleaner*, such as CLR Calcium Lime Rust Remover, available at hardware stores and home improvement stores.

If your preventive maintenance is working, you may need to clean your fountain parts only once a year. If you're getting mineral deposits, you'll have to clean the parts more frequently—likewise if you're not using a water treatment product. In general, you should sterilize your fountain after you clean it and before you reassemble it by dipping all parts, including the pump, in the mild bleach solution mentioned above (*1 part bleach* to *10 parts water*).

To clean the fountainhead, you will need to know what it's made of:

- Most molded fountainheads are cast from a polyester resin mixed with fillers such as powdered marble. These materials are strong but scratch easily, so the best way to clean them is with *warm, soapy water* and a soft *sponge*. Before using *tile cleaners* or other acids on a cast resin fountainhead, check it by putting a few drops of the cleaner on the bottom of the fountainhead and scrubbing it a bit with a *toothbrush*.
- When cleaning concrete or natural stone, never use an acid cleaner. *Dishwashing detergent* or *bleach* mixed with *water*, plus a *scrub brush*, will work fine.
- Clean slate as described above for removing mineral deposits.

To clean a fountain pump, first check to see how well it's working. Most pumps have some sort of inlet strainers or screens to ensure that small pebbles and other debris don't get into the pump and jam or damage it. Watch the water flow in your

fountain. If you notice it's slowing down, clean the pump before it clogs entirely, overheats, and burns out. (Then you'll have to replace it.)

With indoor pumps and simple outdoor pumps, you can follow the instructions that came with the pump to learn how to take it apart and reassemble it. If your pump has an adjustable flow, note the setting when you remove the pump for cleaning, in case you inadvertently change it. Once you have the pump apart, clean it with **warm water**, **dishwashing detergent**, and an **old toothbrush**. Dip the parts in a **bleach solution** and reassemble it.

The more complex, industrial-type fountains are trickier to clean and should be entrusted to a professional.

Fountain Pens

Writing with a fountain pen is an indelible experience—the nib stroking across paper, the ink flowing smoothly. If you appreciate this fine art, you should learn how to keep your fountain pen in top working order. All fountain pens—whether they have a metal or gold nib—should be cleaned after four or five fillings or four or five cartridges.

To clean your fountain pen, flush the nib section by running it under plain **tap water** at room temperature. For ink deposits that may have stood in the pen for a long time, make one of the following four solutions. They'll help the water penetrate areas in the pen more quickly and thoroughly:

- **1 drop of dishwashing detergent** in **1 cup of water** at room temperature.
- A **couple of squirts of household cleaner**, such as Formula 409 cleaner, in **1 cup of water**.
- A few squirts (about a teaspoon) of a **bleach cleaner**, such as Clorox Clean-Up, in **6 ounces of water**.
- 1 cap of nonsudsy household ammonia in 1 cup of water.

To clean self-filling pens, the kind you dip into the ink, place your **cleaning solution** (see above) in a **glass** and draw it into the pen, just as you would to fill the pen with ink. Then place the nib in the water and let it all soak for two hours to two days, depending on how long the ink has been in the pen. To rinse, draw **fresh water** into the pen and empty it.

To clean a pen that's not heavily caked with ink, fill the pen with solution and empty it two or three times.

Cleaning ink-cartridge pens is a little trickier because there's no device on the pen to force the cleaning solution through the very fine internal channels of the nib. Squeeze an *empty ink cartridge* to force the air out, dip it into one of the *cleaning solutions* mentioned before, and release it, drawing the solution into the cartridge. Attach the cartridge to the nib section as if it were full of ink, and squeeze the cleaning solution out of the cartridge and through the nib. Repeat the procedure a couple of times.

More tips for cleaning fountain pens:

- India ink or waterproof inks aren't recommended for fountain pens. They should be used only with the type of pens that are dipped into an inkwell.
- Avoid letting hot water, alcohol, or acetone come in contact with your fountain pen, because they could damage certain parts of it.
- The barrel (the shaft that holds the ink) and cap of your pen can be washed in *cold water*. Use a *cotton swab* to clean the interior of these long, narrow cylinders.
- Dry each section of your pen before putting it back together. A cotton swab is useful for this task, because it can get into all parts of the pen.

Furnaces

Most homes today have forced-air furnaces. They work this way: A blower forces warm air through supply ducts and into rooms through registers or diffusers. A cold-air duct returns the air to the furnace, where it's filtered of dust and dirt particles, reheated, and recirculated. Don't worry. You, as a homeowner, aren't expected to maintain the entire furnace. Modern furnace technology is just too complicated—and getting more so. But there are some cleaning chores you can do to keep your furnace running efficiently and reduce service calls.

Cleaning or changing the filter is the number one maintenance job for the homeowner. Most service calls can be traced to dirty filters that affect the efficiency of the furnace. All filters should be checked once a month. (Tip: Why not check the filter every time you pay your utility bill?) Disposable filters typically need to be changed every month during the heating months. (Prices range from $1 to $20, and in this case you get what you pay for. Higher quality filters do a better job.) Cleanable filters will need to be cleaned every 60 to 90 days—either in a bathtub, sink, or laundry tub or outside. Hopefully, you already know where your furnace's filter is located and how to change it, but if you don't, it's either inside the blower compartment or in a slot on the cold-air return duct near the point where it joins the furnace. The filter just slides in and out ◀.

Electronic filters are cleanable. Follow the manufacturer's instructions. If you don't clean an electronic filter, which charges air particles, you could eventually cause damage to the heat exchanger.

If you have a cleanable filter and pre-filter, you can take two approaches. Turn off the furnace, remove the filter, and then
- spray the filter with *water*, followed by a *cleaning solution*, such as Formula 409 or Fantastik. Let the cleaner sit for a few minutes and thoroughly rinse. Use the *shower nozzle* if you're working in a bathtub or use a *garden hose* if you're working outside. Protect your bathtub from scratches with a *mat*.
- rinse the filter in *cool water*. Next, fill the bath halfway with *hot water* and a *mild detergent*, such as Dreft. Immerse the electronic filter grid and let it sit for half an hour. Hold the sides of the filter and lift it up and down and then swish it from side to side in the water. Empty the water and rinse the filter with *cool, clear water* from the *shower nozzle*.

Whichever cleaning method you choose, make sure cleanable filters are completely dry before reinstalling. Otherwise, you risk receiving an electrical shock or short-circuiting your furnace.

Clean the outer part of the furnace with a *damp cloth* to remove dust that could collect and get into the fan motor and furnace. Keep the area around your furnace free of flammable liquids and anything else that could catch fire. To keep your furnace in tip-top shape, have it inspected annually by a professional.

Furniture

Your wood furniture needs regular maintenance just as surely as your car does. Consider that dining room table you bought a few years ago. Wouldn't it be nice if, years down the road, your grandchildren prized it as an antique?

Figuring out what type of finish your furniture has is the first order of business. If your furniture has an oil finish, you should only dust and re-oil it. If it has the more common hard finish—such as varnish or lacquer—you have more options.

Oil finish or a hard finish? Here's how you tell the difference: Put a *few drops of boiled linseed oil* on the wood and rub it in with your finger. If the wood absorbs the oil, you have an oil finish. If the boiled linseed oil beads up, you have a hard varnished or lacquered finish.

To clean oiled furniture, dust with a *dry cloth*. Don't use a dust-attracting product on the cloth, and make sure the cloth is soft and free of buttons, zippers, and anything else that might scratch the wood. Then apply oil to the wood (*boiled linseed oil, tung oil*, or an *oil recommended by the furniture's manufacturer*). Rub the oil in with a *clean cloth*. Do this an average of once a month. So you've been neglectful? Re-oil your furniture every two weeks for a couple of months to allow it to catch up on missing oil.

To protect oiled furniture, never put cloth items or water on it. Cloth items will absorb the moisture from the oil and dry out your furniture. Unfortunately, oil offers the least protection of any finish—get any water on it and you're done—yet it requires the highest maintenance.

To clean varnished or lacquered furniture, dust first with a *soft rag* or *stick duster*. It's OK to add a little *dust-attracting product*, such as Endust, to the rag or duster but not straight onto the furniture. Let it dry before you dust. If necessary, you can clean hard-finished furniture with a *damp cloth* and *mild detergent*, such as Dawn. Now you're ready to polish.

To polish a hard finish, apply a *furniture polish*, such as Old English in an aerosol can. First, mist the surface of the furniture and use one area of a *rag* to spread the polish, wiping in a circular motion. Turn the rag over and wipe off the excess polish. Avoid polishes that consist mostly of silicone and paraffin wax, because both of these ingredients tend to build up and eventually soften or ruin a finish.

To clean varnished or lacquered kitchen furniture, you'll need to take a different approach, because it is exposed to grease and cooking oils. Use a *cloth* that has been barely dampened with *dishwashing detergent* and *water* to remove the oily substances. Follow up with a *cloth* dampened with *plain water* and then *polish*. For more cleaning power, use an *oil soap*, such as Murphy, diluted according to the package directions. (Test an inconspicuous spot first.) Polish your kitchen table at least three times a week. Every three months, clean it using the *mineral spirits* method described in the next paragraph.

To give a hard finish a thorough cleaning and remove built up wax, you'll need a few very soft rags. Old diapers that have been washed many times are splendid. Soak one *rag* with *mineral spirits*. Wipe your furniture thoroughly, flipping the rag frequently. Thoroughly go over all areas several times with the rag, and don't be afraid to apply more mineral spirits frequently. Now dry the surface completely with a *soft, dry rag*. Repeat this wiping and drying process at least three times using a *fresh rag* each time.

Once the furniture is clean, you can polish. Spray the *polish* on the wood and rub it in with a *rag*, going in a circular motion. Now use *another clean, soft rag*—or flip the polishing rag to a dry spot—and wipe with the grain of the wood to remove excess polish. Carved wood should be cleaned in the same way, regularly with polish and once a year with mineral spirits. The only difference is that you'll need a *soft toothbrush* to get into the intricate carved details.

If a finish has become sticky, this usually means it has failed—the result of too much polish buildup, exposure to oils over the years, or the finish's having degraded over time. Use *mineral spirits* and *superfine steel wool (0000)* to remove the old finish, rubbing with the grain of the wood. Wipe three or four times with a *rag* and fresh mineral spirits. When you're done, the furniture will have to be refinished. Talk to a professional or follow the package directions on the finishing product you choose. Don't do this to a valuable antique. Take it to a pro.

To clean painted wood furniture, dust it with a *water-dampened cloth*. If necessary, use a *mild, nonabrasive detergent* (such as dishwashing detergent) and *warm water*. Dip a *rag* into the cleaning solution and wring it nearly dry. Work on a small section of wood at a time. Rinse with *clear water*. Dry the surface with a *clean cloth* quickly before continuing.

Waxes and polishes are usually not needed on painted furniture, but if you do use a wax on a light-colored painted piece, use a *white*, *creamy type polish* to avoid discoloration. Never use oil, oil polishes, or oil-treated cloths on painted furniture.

A very old piece with its original finish should usually not be repainted or refinished, because you risk ruining its value.

To make your own furniture cleaner for removing old polish and dirt, put *1 quart of water* in a *pot* on the *stove*, add *2 tea bags*, and bring to a boil. Cool the solution to room temperature. Dip a *soft cloth* in the tea and wring the cloth until it's damp. Wipe the furniture, buff it dry with a *soft cloth*, and decide whether you should polish it.

FURNITURE

To make your own furniture polish, follow either of these formulas:
- Mix *1/3 cup of white vinegar* and *1 cup of olive oil.*
- Mix *3 drops of lemon extract* and *1 cup of mineral oil.*

You can substitute *baby oil* for the olive or mineral oil. Rub the polish into the surface with a *clean rag*, using circular motions.

Here are some more tips for dealing with special situations involving your wood furniture:
- Removing candle wax from furniture is risky because you can cause further damage. Use *ice* directly on the wax to get it as cold as possible and immediately wipe up excess water. Once the wax is very cold, try carefully inserting *a butter knife* under the wax to see whether it will pop off. If this method doesn't work, don't attempt anything else. Consult a professional.
- If you have a fresh paint stain on your furniture, remove latex paint with *water*; remove alkyd (oil-based) paint with *mineral spirits.* To remove a dry stain, saturate the spot in *boiled linseed oil*. After the paint softens, lift it off carefully with a *putty knife*. An alternative: Wipe with a *cloth* dampened in the boiled linseed oil. Remove residue by making a paste of *boiled linseed oil* and *rottenstone*, a polishing powder sold where you buy refinishing supplies. Rub the paste along the grain, and then wipe it dry and wax or polish it.
- If paper is stuck to your wood furniture, dampen the paper thoroughly with *salad oil*, wait five minutes, and rub along the grain with *superfine (0000) steel wool*. Wipe dry.

*See also **Antiques**, **Bronze**, **Chrome**, **Fiberglass**, **Glass**, **Marble**, **Upholstery***, *and **Wicker**.*

A Nutty Cure for Watermarks

Got a white water spot on the finish of your dining room table? Peanut butter can get you out of that jam. Rub creamy peanut butter into the finish with a soft rag, over and over in a circular motion, says furniture store owner Bruce Chadima. If scratches appear, reapply, following the grain. The oils and abrasion from the peanuts will have a renewing effect on the finish. Next, take a dry cloth and wipe well. If the area now appears shinier than the rest of the surface, apply to the spot a car wax with a mild cleaner in it, such as TurtleWax or Meguiar's. Then polish your furniture.

The peanut butter method works miracles, particularly with hazy-white water spots. Solid white water spots and the more severe black water spots probably require the attention of a professional restorer.

Furs

Traveling a Fur Piece? >

Marc Rubman, vice president at furs.com, offers these guidelines:
- Don't pin jewelry on it, and avoid sharp necklaces or bracelets. Use shoulder bags sparingly.
- Wear a scarf around your neck to protect the collar of your fur.
- Avoid insecticides, mothproofing, and other chemicals around your fur, including perfume and hair spray.
- Get into your car carefully. Don't sit on fur, or at least don't sit on the same spot consistently. When you exit your vehicle, shake out any crushed places.
- At a restaurant, if the coatroom looks overcrowded, keep your coat. Fold it on a chair at your table and cover with a napkin.
- On a plane, leave it on your lap or fold it loosely, lining out, and place it in an overhead bin on top of the luggage.

Exquisite to look at and soft to the touch, fur is also a work of art—one of the last completely handmade articles of clothing. If you have a fur coat, treat it with the respect it deserves. There is plenty you can do to preserve your fur's head-turning quality, but the actual cleaning is really the realm of professional furriers. If you try to clean—or even brush—your fur yourself, you most likely will damage it. The advice here applies whether your fur is the real thing or fake.

Have your fur cleaned regularly by a fur specialist, not a dry cleaner. Fur should be cleaned or serviced once a year, unless it has hardly been worn. In that case, have it cleaned at least every other year. Here is the only cleaning you can do yourself: To give your coat a light dusting, put the coat on a *hanger*, hold the neck of the hanger, and shake the coat.

When you put away your coat between uses, it needs to breathe. Never keep a fur coat bagged. It will eventually dry out. If you insist on some kind of covering, use a *cotton bag*, which allows for some breathing.

If your fur coat gets wet, let it dry on its own. Don't place it by a radiator or attempt to blow-dry it. The skin will burn, and it will get hard and stiff because the oils in the skin will be drying out too. Fur will easily stand up to snow or light rain, but if your fur gets totally soaked, take it to a professional furrier right away.

To store any type of fur coat, place it in a *cold storage* (45° F) unit with a constant humidity (50 percent). Once the first frost appears, fur coats can be taken out of storage. Retailers, department stores, or dry cleaners store fur coats, but they usually send the coats to wholesalers, which have large fur storage vaults. It's a good idea to research where your coat will be stored.

Games

Most game makers these days are savvy enough to know who their main customers are—kids—and to make their games as indestructible as possible. That means lots of easy-to-clean plastic parts and surfaces. When game boards are made out of paper, however, cleaning gets trickier.

To clean plastic or rubber game parts, wipe them off with a *sponge* or *cloth* dampened with a solution of *mild dishwashing liquid* and *warm water*. Rinse by wiping with a *clean, damp sponge or cloth*. Air-dry completely in a countertop *dish rack* or on a *towel* folded on your kitchen counter.

To clean paper-coated game boards, first try wiping with a *cloth* or *sponge* dampened only with *water* (wrung out as much as possible beforehand). You want to avoid soaking the paper, which could damage the board or cause it to buckle. If the game board's colors begin to bleed, stop. If you need more cleaning power, try wiping with the *soapy solution* mentioned above for plastic parts. Pat the board dry with a *clean white cloth*.

Garbage Cans

No matter how persuasive the advertisements on television, most brands of garbage bags leak at one time or another. And when they leak, nasty liquids find their way into your garbage can, attracting flies and giving off bad odors. Time to clean.

Clean your garbage can outside, where you can get down and dirty with it. Use a *garden hose* to flush out any residue. Fill the bottom of the can with a bleach solution (*4 to 8 ounces of chlorine bleach* per *1 gallon of water*). If you can use warm water, even better. Add a *squirt or two of dishwashing liquid*. Using a *toilet scrub brush*, clean the bottom and sides, sloshing the bleach-and-soap solution up the sides as you do. Empty and rinse with your hose. Air-dry outside.

To repel flies, ants, and other insects, sprinkle *borax* on the bottom of the can once it is dry.

Garbage Disposers

You don't need to use any manual labor to clean a garbage disposal unit. These small-but-feisty kitchen appliances have their

Protect Your Games >

• To remove dirt and leave your paper game board stiff and glossy, lightly spray it with laundry sizing. Wipe it up quickly with a damp cloth, then pat it dry with a dry cloth.
• Mist your clean game boards with a spray furniture polish, such as Pledge, and quickly wipe it off with a clean cloth. Wiping off sticky fingerprints will be a snap.

own built-in scrubbing action. To keep your unit smelling fresh and running properly, all you need to use are a few common household items.

To keep food waste from building up inside your disposer, keep these rules in mind:

- Grind only small amounts of food at a time.
- After you've finished grinding food, run a steady, rapid flow of **cold water** through the spinning garbage disposer for up to 30 seconds. Even if instinct tells you that hot water cleans better, stick to cold water. It solidifies fatty and greasy wastes so they will be chopped up and flushed down the drain.
- Don't pour oil or grease through the disposer.
- Don't grind large bones. (Small bones are OK and even help break up grease deposits.)
- Don't grind bulky, fibrous material, such as cornhusks.
- Never put corrosive lye or chemical drain cleaners into your disposal unit.

▲

To remove any fatty wastes that might build up inside the disposer, periodically grind a **handful of ice cubes** mixed with **1/2 cup of baking soda** ◀. Together the powder and cubes (which of course are cold) will safely scour the inside of the unit. To eliminate odors, grind **lemon peels** or **orange peels** every so often.

Garden Ornaments

To clean or not to clean: That is the question when it comes to garden ornaments. Just as one school of thought in the antiques world supports leaving original finishes intact (a look others consider grungy), some people feel that a little algae, plus a bird dropping or two, give an ivy-tucked concrete cherub a more natural look. We'll let you decide. But if the decision is to clean, here's what you can do:

To clean garden ornaments, realize that much of what you'll be cleaning is actually alive. Organic matter, such as algae, moss, mold, and mildew, all thrive on statuary, birdbaths, and the like—anywhere there is moisture and warmth. Add to that dust and dirt, dead organic matter, and those bird droppings, and you end up with quite a mess (or, excuse us, a lovely patina). You can kill the organic stuff and remove the rest with a simple, inexpensive solution of **4 to 8 ounces of bleach** to **1 gallon of water**, with a **squirt or two of dishwashing liquid** thrown in and worked into suds. Apply it with a **long-handled brush** and gently scrub until clean. Rinse with the *garden hose*. This works for nearly all of the popular lawn ornament materials, including concrete, stone, and polyester resins.

Because bleach can damage the plants in your garden, move the ornaments to the driveway for cleaning. For anything too large to move, use the cleaning agent sparingly and rinse with a *sponge* and *bucket* of *clean water* instead of the hose. Don't use chlorine to clean a pond that contains fish. If you clean a birdbath, be sure to flush out the cleaning solution completely.

To clean gazing globes (aka mirror balls), use a window-cleaning solution: Mix *1 cup of white vinegar* in *1 gallon of warm water* and add a *squirt of dishwashing liquid*. Apply it with a *spray bottle* or a *clean cloth*. Gently scrub until clean and either rinse with a *hose* or dry with a *dry towel* or *newspaper*. If the ball is stainless steel, wax it with *car wax* once a year to renew its shine and give it a protective coating. And wipe out scratches with an *automobile scratch remover*.

See also **Birdbaths, Bird Feeders, and Birdhouses**.

Glass

If money is no object, you'll do fine cleaning your windows with commercial glass cleaners. (But take care: They usually contain ammonia, which can damage the finish on painted wood and tends to leave streaks.) But if you count your pennies—and who doesn't?—keep reading and learn how to make your own mild but effective window-cleaning solution.

To make your own nontoxic glass cleaner, mix *1 cup of white vinegar* in *1 gallon of warm water* and add a *squirt of dishwashing liquid*. Apply it with a plastic *spray bottle*. (A *funnel* will make filling the bottle easier.) Scrub the windows clean with a *clean sponge* or *cloth*. For caked-on grime, scrub with a *soft, long-bristled brush*.

To avoid leaving lint traces, wipe the window with a *squeegee* (large windows) or polish with *newspaper* (smaller panes). Try to avoid washing windows when the sun is shining, because they will dry too quickly and streak. When cleaning glass tables or any other glass that lies flat, use newspaper instead of a squeegee.

Here are some more tips for cleaning glass:
- To remove hard-water mineral spots, use *straight vinegar*.
- For scratches in glass, rub a little *toothpaste* into the scratch and polish with a *soft cloth*.

RULES
OF THE GAME

If You DO Do Windows >
1. Start at the top and clean down.
2. Apply the solution with a spray bottle.
3. Lightly scrub with a sponge or cloth.
4. Wipe clean with a squeegee or polish with newspaper.
5. If you're cleaning with a squeegee, keep a rag in each pocket—one for wiping the squeegee, and the other for cleaning the corners of the glass.
6. If you're cleaning inside windows, lay a towel on the windowsill to catch drips.

- To peel off paint and stuck-on adhesives, scrape with a *razor blade*. Don't use a putty knife, however, because it's duller and can damage the glass.

See also **Windows**.

Body *Rub*

The earliest squeegees, dating to around 500 B.C., were cleaning tools, but they were not used for glass. Often fashioned out of gold or bronze, the spoonlike strigils, as the instruments were called, were used to scrape the oils and sweat from the skin of Greek athletes after exercising or competitions. The word *squeegee*, which wasn't coined until the mid-19th century, possibly derives from the Middle English word *squelen*, which is the root of the word *squeal*—the sound a rubber squeegee makes when it is drawn across a smooth surface.

Glassware

Anyone can clean a drinking glass. But to get rid of streaks, spots, and unappetizing rim stains—to make your stemware and highball glasses really sparkle—you've got to know how to dry them properly.

Clean glassware first when you're washing dishes by hand, since glasses are usually less dirty than pots, pans, plates, and utensils. (If you don't clean the glasses first, then change the dishwater before you get to them. Otherwise, you'll get the glasses dirtier than they were when you started.)

Use *dishwashing liquid* mixed with *hot water.* Wash with a *soft, clean sponge or dishrag*. Don't reach for the abrasive pot scrubber. That can scratch glass. Rinse with *even hotter water*—as hot as you can safely stand. Hot water not only helps cut grease, but it also beads up and steams off (the first step toward good drying). Avoid excessive suds, which make glasses harder to rinse and slippery to handle, increasing the chances of their breaking or chipping.

No matter how well you've cleaned glassware, if there is slow-drying water left on your glasses, chances are it will leave streaks or spots. Fogging causes some of the worst spotting. To avoid the "greenhouse effect"—when glasses placed upside down on their rims fog up inside—dry glasses upside down on a *drying rack*. If you don't have a rack, put them upright on a towel and make sure air can circulate inside the glass for rapid drying.

GLASS

To remove the lime buildup on glassware that occurs when you wash it in the dishwasher, use a **commercial rinse agent** (such as Jet-Dry) during the washing cycles. This helps water sheet off while the glass is drying inside the foggy washer. Or fill a **large plastic bowl** with **white vinegar** and give each glass a 15-minute bath. Then rinse with **running water** and air-dry.

To remove food-coloring stains left in glassware by the dyes in powdered soft drink mixes and other beverages, fill the glass with a solution of **2 tablespoons of household ammonia** in **1 quart of hot water**. Let it stand for 30 minutes and then rinse thoroughly with clean, **cool water.**

Hand-washing is best for fine glassware (even if you'd prefer to use your dishwasher). To avoid scratching the glasses, remove your rings, watches, and bracelets, especially those with diamonds. Swing the faucet head out of the way, so there will be no chance that you'll accidentally smack your great-grandmother's goblet against it. Using both hands, clean one piece at a time in **hot, soapy water**. Gently wash with a **soft cotton cloth or clean sponge**. For stubborn dirt, scrub gently with a **soft toothbrush**. Rinse twice, first in a **sink or dishpan** full of **tepid water** with a **capful of vinegar** mixed in and next under a gentle shower of **tepid water** from the **tap or side sprayer**.

To clean really fine glassware, here's a conservator's formula: Mix **equal parts ethanol** (ethyl alcohol, or grain alcohol) and **water** and then add a **few drops of ammonia**. Water and the ammonia do the cleaning, while the ethanol aids evaporation. Apply the solution with **cosmetic pads, cotton pads,** or the **lint-free pads** used for cleaning fax machines. Don't use this technique on glass with decorative gilt.

Gloves

Cleaning gloves can be tricky for a couple of reasons. First, in addition to stains and soil on the outside of gloves, you have to remove the dirt and oils left by your own skin on the inside of gloves. Second, gloves are complicated, full of cracks and crevices designed to conform to the shape of our hands. There is a trick, though, that almost makes cleaning gloves fun, assuming that they are washable.

To clean gloves, wash them while they are on your hands ▶, instead of awkwardly trying to flatten them out to scrub the palms and then clean in between each flaccid finger. This way

Glassware Hand Care >

1. Put a rubber pad or heavy folded towel in your sink (or use a plastic dishpan). In a divided sink, also put a towel over the ridge.

2. Wash in hot water and mild dishwashing liquid. Avoid too many suds. Rub stuck-on food gently with baking soda but never anything more abrasive.

3. Handle stemware by the bowl, not the stem.

4. Rinse glasses in a sink or pan of hot water.

5. Air-dry upside down on a dish rack. Or arrange the glasses upright on a towel. Never stand them upside down on a flat surface. This leads to fogging and spotting.

6. For that special dinner party, buff your dried glasses with a soft, white, lint-free cloth.

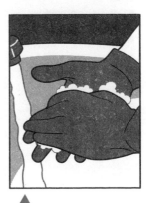

▲

you can position each glove exactly as you'd like it, while scrubbing with the other hand. (Even better: Have your mate clean the gloves that you're wearing, and vice versa. Whatever else you wear is up to you.) Mix up a mild, sudsy solution of **warm water** and a **drop or two of dishwashing liquid**. When you're finished washing, remove the gloves and rinse them in a **sink** full of **clean water**, emptying the sink and repeating until there is no more soap residue.

To dry gloves, roll them up in a **dry towel**. After unrolling them, blow them back into shape and lay them out flat on the towel at room temperature. Never squeeze or wring gloves and don't dry them using a heat source, such as a radiator or hair dryer. If you have to iron them, lay them between the folds of a **clean towel** and pass the **hot iron** over the top layer of the towel.

*See **Leather** or **Suede** if your gloves are made from either of those materials. To clean a baseball glove, see **Sports Equipment**.*

Gold Jewelry

WATCH OUT

• Avoid getting chlorine on gold at all costs. It will cause the gold to deteriorate over time. Remove gold jewelry when cleaning with chlorine bleach and even before entering chlorinated pools and hot tubs.
• Don't clean gold with toothpaste, even though some jewelers recommend it. Some toothpastes contain harsh abrasives, such as silica (found in quartz), which can dull a glossy gold finish.

The whole point of gold is to shine. While it does not tarnish like silver, gold will over time develop a dingy, oily film from lotions, powders, soaps, and the oils secreted by your skin. And gold that has been alloyed with other metals—copper, silver, or nickel—can tarnish and smudge. To revive your gold jewelry's luster, clean it regularly.

Here's the mildest method of cleaning gold—and also the easiest and most economical: Mix a **bowl** of suds using **warm water** and a little **dishwashing liquid**. Soak the gold jewelry briefly and then gently scrub crevices and design details using a **soft toothbrush** or **eyebrow brush**. Place the jewelry in a **wire strainer** and rinse under **warm running water**. Pat it dry with a **chamois cloth**. (Any **clean, white, soft cotton cloth** will do in a pinch.)

For a stronger cleaning solution, mix **equal parts cold water** and **ammonia** (and save the money you would have spent on a commercial jewelry cleaner). Soak the jewelry in the solution for 30 minutes. Again, gently scrub with the **toothbrush or eyebrow brush**. Rinse with **water**. Let the jewelry dry on a **soft towel**.

Having gold professionally cleaned is the safest and most effective—if also the most expensive—method. Take your jewelry to a jeweler and have it cleaned with an ultrasonic cleaning machine. They dip your jewelry in a container of liquid, send high-frequency vibrations through the liquid, and—*voilà!*—the dirt and grime drop off. Have several things cleaned at once, and you will save money on each piece. Or, if it's the same jeweler you bought the piece from, he or she might do it free of charge.

White Gold's *Shiny Little Secret*

If your white gold is beginning to yellow, that probably means it was rhodium-plated. Most white gold is.

Contrary to popular belief, there is no such metal as white gold. Rather, white gold is gold (naturally yellowish in color) alloyed with silvery metals, such as nickel, and usually plated with rhodium to brighten it even more. You probably won't see any worn plating on earrings and necklaces, but on white gold jewelry that gets physical abuse, such as rings and bracelets, you might notice yellow blotches on the surface. (Our gold-cleaning techniques will not remove the plating.) If so, simply have your jeweler replate the jewelry with rhodium.

Gore-Tex Fabric

Today, Gore-Tex is a household word. But this brand-name membrane, found in rain jackets and other outerwear, is just as miraculous as ever for its ability to be simultaneously waterproof and breathable. You'll improve both functions by keeping your Gore-Tex fabric clean. Gore-Tex is both washable and dry-cleanable, making cleaning it a snap (another reason to love the stuff).

To clean a Gore-Tex garment, follow the cleaning instructions on the label in that garment. Typically, the instructions will be to put the garment in a *washing machine* with *warm water* and a standard *laundry detergent*, but no fabric softener or bleach, and then tumble in a *dryer*. If the garment calls for dry-cleaning, tell the cleaner you want a clear, distilled solvent rinse.

To preserve a shell's water resistance, you need to reapply a water-resistant coating occasionally, because multiple washings (or a single trip to the dry cleaner) will remove the shell's fine water-resistant layer. (When water no longer beads up on your garment's outer shell, that's a sign that you've lost it.) The actual Gore-Tex layer will be OK, but the outer shell will need a new application of its coating, called durable water repellent (DWR). Gore-Tex sells an easy-to-use *spray-on durable water repellent* called Revivex. Look for it at camping stores, hunting stores, or high-performance bicycle shops.

Graffiti

The trick to removing graffiti is to do it as soon as possible. Most graffiti is paint (or a similar coating), which is applied wet and has binders that solidify as the paint solvents evaporate. The solubility of paint, therefore, is reduced the longer it has a chance to harden. If you remove the paint right away, you will have a good chance of succeeding. You will also deny the graffiti artist the satisfaction of showing off his or her handiwork—which might deter the defacer from doing it a next time—and you'll reduce the chances that copycats will scrawl more graffiti.

To remove some markings, try a simple solution of **warm water** and **dishwashing liquid.** If the paint or marker used was water-soluble and you've caught it early enough, this might just work. Carefully scrub the graffiti with a **nylon- or natural-bristled brush.** Rinse with the **spray nozzle** on your **garden hose,** if possible. The low pressure might lift the stain without damaging the surface it's on.

To remove stubborn graffiti, which won't wash off with water, try a **chemical paint remover.** (Keep in mind, however, that if the graffiti is on a painted surface, these paint removers won't discriminate between paints, and you may end up having to repaint your entire wall.) Gels and pastes typically work well because they are easy to apply and don't drip. Avoid aerosol graffiti removers, which can dissolve paint and then run down the wall, staining a previously clean area.

An **alkaline paste** that contain a caustic, such as sodium hydroxide or potassium hydroxide, works well. These are harsh chemicals, though, and you should follow the manufacturer's safety and use recommendations carefully. With such a paste, you typically wipe it on, let it stand and loosen the paint for a few minutes, and then wipe it off. Then you rinse with **water** and neutralize with a **separate acid-based neutralizing agent** (usually made by the same company). The neutralizing agent keeps the caustics from staining stone and other surfaces.

If all else fails, considering blasting the graffiti off. You've got two options—pressure **washing** or sandblasting. Both can be extremely harmful to wood, old brick, and stone. And all but the finest-grade sandblasters will damage metal. You can rent a **pressure washer** at an equipment rental store. Follow all safety instructions and use extreme caution, since these machines can be dangerous and harmful to your house. One way to reduce your chances of damaging the surface is to begin with a low water pressure and gradually increase it as necessary. You should probably leave the sandblasting up to the pros. Look in the yellow pages under Sandblasting.

If you can't beat 'em, join 'em. If the surface was painted to begin with, paint over the graffiti with a fresh coat or two of your original wall paint.

To remove graffiti from glass, it's best to use a ***single-edge razor blade***. Put it in a ***flat scraper*** (available at hardware stores), hold the scraper at a 30-degree angle to the glass, and patiently scrape the paint. Paint strippers aren't as effective on glass, since they tend to smear the paint, making it hard to remove the vestiges. And once you apply the paint stripper, the razor blade is not as effective, because the paint is now thinner.

Granite

All granite is not alike. In fact, what you're calling granite may not even be granite. Some of the countertops and other architectural stone sold as granite may have only the appearance of granite. When it comes to cleaning, knowing whether the material is genuine granite is important, because some cleaners that are considered safe for granite may react negatively with your stone. The acid in vinegar, for instance, eats away at calcium, which is not usually present in granite but may be in your stone.

And then there are the different types of surface finishes to consider, from raw stone to highly polished stone to chemically sealed stone. That may sound complicated, but cleaning the stone should not be. The best approach is the simplest.

To care for granite, keep off sand and dirt, especially on flat surfaces, where it can be ground down by shoe soles or boots. The grit can scratch the stone. For walls, floors, and other such surfaces, use either a ***vacuum cleaner*** or a ***dry dust mop***. For countertops and tables, dust with a ***clean, dry rag***. Wipe up spills immediately to avoid staining.

To clean granite countertops in kitchens and bathrooms, first try using only ***warm water***, wiping with a ***soft cloth or sponge***. Let caked-on food soak a bit before wiping. You should be able to remove spills, crumbs, sauces, and other things this way. If not, then add a little ***dishwashing liquid*** to the water. Rinse well with lots of ***clean water***. Too much soap can leave a film or cause streaking. Avoid stronger cleaning products, such as tub and tile cleaners or scouring powders, as these can stain or scratch your stone.

To remove difficult stains, keep it simple and be patient. Most stains are solid residue jammed in between the crystals of the stone after the liquid that carried it has evaporated. The trick is to put the solid back into solution so it can be removed. First, determine whether your stain is water-based (for example, from spilled grape juice) or oil-based (salad dressing).

- If the stain is water-based, pour *hot water* (from the tap, not the teakettle) on the stain and let it stand for a few minutes. Wipe away the excess water. Then stack *1/4 inch of paper towels* on the stain and saturate with *hot water*. Cover with a piece of *plastic* (plastic wrap or a plastic drop cloth will do) and a *flat, heavy weight*, such as a cast-iron skillet or a book (careful not to ruin the book). Let it stand for about 10 hours. (Do it overnight, and you won't have to worry about anyone moving it.) Next, throw away the paper towels, and the stain should go with them. Let the spot dry and then observe. If some of the stain is still present, repeat the treatment.
- If the stain is oil-based, follow the same procedure, only instead of water, use *acetone* (but do not heat). After the 10 hours is up, throw away the paper towels and rinse the spot with clean water. If necessary, repeat. Acetone can be found on the paint thinner shelf in hardware and home stores.

Grease Stains

Grease stains get worse over time, as dust and dirt attach themselves to the sticky surface. The longer you wait to clean a grease stain, the harder it will be to do it properly. How you clean depends on what you're cleaning.

To remove grease from fabric, first remove excess grease with a *paper towel*, a *plastic spatula*, or the *dull edge of a knife*. If possible, have the fabric professionally dry-cleaned. If you can't have it dry-cleaned, follow these steps.
1. Lay the stain facedown on a *soft, white, absorbent cloth*.
2. Apply a *dry-cleaning solvent*, such as K2r or Carbona, to *another cloth*.
3. Blot from the inside of the garment, forcing the stain out and into the other cloth as the solvent dissolves it.

Always follow the directions on the solvent product label. Before using a dry-cleaning solvent on a fabric, always test it in an inconspicuous corner of the stained item.

To remove grease from carpets, follow the same steps as for stains in fabrics. When it comes to applying the solvent, make sure to moisten a cloth with the solvent and blot the stain. Don't pour the solvent onto the carpet, because it may soak into the padding beneath and trigger new stains.

As a good substitute for a dry-cleaning solvent, use an **acetone-based nail polish remover**. But do not use it on anything made of acetate, because the acetone will dissolve the fabric. It's always safest to test in an out-of-sight corner of the material first.

To remove grease from a concrete floor, sprinkle *dry cement* over the grease. Once it has absorbed the grease, sweep it up with a *broom* and a *dustpan*. No dry cement handy? Try *salt*. If that fails, wet the stained area of concrete with *water* and sprinkle it with *powdered dishwasher detergent*. Wait a few minutes and then pour *boiling water* on the area. Wearing *rubber gloves* to protect your hands, scrub with a *stiff-bristled brush* and rinse with *water*.

Greenhouses

Think of your greenhouse as a hospital—the cleaner it is, the healthier the plants housed there. Dust, debris, and clutter are magnets for insects, diseases, and harmful microorganisms. Dirty windows block the sun's rejuvenating light. But you don't have to go so far as to garden in sanitary scrubs. Just follow this regimen, and your plants will have a healthy environment in which to thrive.

Dust your plants to remove fungal spores (such as gray mold and powdery mildews) and mites (such as the omnivorous spider mite). Most people hose off their plants, which is fine but tends to unsettle and spread the dust. An easier—and more effective—method is to vacuum them. Use a *shop vacuum* with a *dusting attachment*. This works best on sturdy leaves that you can hold in your hand while you quickly whisk the brush over the surface. Once a year is enough to halt the growth of the plant predators mentioned above.

Cut down on clutter in your greenhouse. Piles of dead plants, stacks of dirty pots, and sacks spilling over with potting soil can all be places for insects and microorganisms to spend the winter. Remove all of these things—and any other clutter—regularly. Try not to pile them right next to the greenhouse. Either get rid of them or store them in a shed, garage, or basement. Dead plant material is the worst offender. Purge dead plants and routinely pick up dead leaves.

OOPS!

Keep your greenhouse weed-free to get rid of yet another source of food for insects and bacteria. Weeds also boost a greenhouse's humidity level, which will make conditions even riper for disease and pestilence. Keep a sack of **hydrated lime** on hand (but don't clutter up the greenhouse with it). Sprinkle it under benches and in corners to deter weed growth. It lasts for a long time and is nontoxic to humans. You can buy hydrated lime at your hardware store or the local feed and seed store. *Never* use herbicides in your greenhouse. (See the Oops sidebar.)

Wash the greenhouse windows at least once a year. Do it when you have the least amount of living plant material in your greenhouse—or before you bring in those new seeds or seedlings to get growing for spring transplanting. For most people, window-washing time is during the fall. Your goal is to keep the glass or polyurethane as clear as possible, as well as to kill any harmful microbial growth on the inner surface. Use a mild dishwashing liquid; it not only loosens dirt but also has ingredients that break up proteins and fats—and subsequently rupture the membranes of bacteria and fungi. Depending on the size of your greenhouse, either put the **dishwashing liquid** in a **hose end sprayer** or mix it with **water** in a **clean spray bottle**. Rinse by spraying with the **garden hose**.

Guns

If you care about gun performance and shooting accuracy—and what gun owner doesn't?—keeping your gun clean is a top priority. Here's the reason: There's a tiny twisting groove (called the rifling) cut along the inside of the barrel, or bore, of rifles and most handguns. That groove is what keeps the rounds you fire on a straight course. When gunpowder and lead or copper residue build up in these grooves, they don't work as well—which might cause you to miss that 12-point buck next season. Of course, cleaning guns properly will help them last a lifetime or longer. Considering what they cost, that alone is not a bad incentive to clean.

The best time to clean a firearm is right after you use it. Remove all shells from the chamber or magazine. Be absolutely sure it's not loaded. If immediate cleaning isn't possible, at least wipe down the outside using a **cloth** and some sort of **oil** or **spray lubricant**. The salts in your fingerprints can corrode the metal.

To protect parts while cleaning, spread a **cloth or old towel** over your work surface. When cleaning, don't disassemble your gun too far. You might accidentally put it back together wrong, which could lead to a dangerous misfire. As a rule of thumb, break it down only to the point needed to reach areas where powder residue and fouling accumulate. Depending on the type of gun, this usually includes the bore, chamber, and bolt. Check once again to make sure that the gun is not loaded. It's better to be safe than sorry.

Having the appropriate cleaning tools is especially important with guns. Buy a *gun cleaning kit*, which should include a *cleaning rod, cleaning solvent, oil, rod-end accessories, brushes,* and *cleaning patches*. If you have more than one firearm, make sure to get a *universal cleaning kit*.

Clean your gun from breech to muzzle—in the same direction that the bullet travels. Open the breech end of rifles or remove the bolt. With handguns, either open the cylinder or remove the action. With shotguns, you can usually open the breech or remove the barrel. With some shotguns, cleaning from the breech end is not possible, but because shotguns don't usually have the spiraling groove down the bore, it's not as important. Just try not to push debris into the action.

The first step in cleaning the barrel is to choose the *largest patch holder* that will easily fit into the barrel. Attach it to the end of the *cleaning rod* and insert a *cleaning patch* in it. Saturate the patch with *gun cleaning solvent* (included in the kit or available at gun stores; you can also use an *all-purpose penetrating solvent*, such as WD-40). Run the patch through the bore once and remove the soiled patch as it exits the front end of the bore before pulling the rod back out. (Pulling a dirty patch back through a barrel can redeposit fouling and draw debris into the action.) Let the solvent soak a few minutes to remove any lead or carbon buildup. Remove the patch-holder accessory from the end of the rod. Wipe the rod clean with a *solvent-moistened rag*.

The next step in cleaning the barrel is to attach the *appropriate-sized bore brush* (nylon is less damaging to the gun than a metal brush) and soak it with *solvent*. Work it back and forth in the bore half a dozen times. Remove it and reattach the *patch holder* to the rod with a *newly soaked patch*. Repeat step one—running a patch down the bore and removing it—until a patch emerges from the bore unsoiled. Attach a *new patch or the kit's cotton mop* to the rod and put a *few drops of oil* on it. Run it down the bore to lightly coat the inside with oil and prevent rusting. Too much oil will gum up the spiraling groove you just cleaned.

To clean the action, dip a *nylon brush* (if not included in the kit, a *toothbrush* will do) in *solvent* and gently scrub away all the unburned powder and debris. When the action is clean, wipe with a *clean, dry cloth*. Then lightly coat the action with rust-preventing *oil* on a *rag*.

Reassemble the gun, wiping down any parts that you have touched—stock included—with a *silicone-impregnated cloth*, available at gun stores. If you don't have the silicone cloth, buff fingerprints off with a *dry cloth*. Don't wipe down the exterior with oil, because it will attract dust.

Gutters and Downspouts

Water is your home's worst enemy, and along with your roof, your gutter system is your best line of defense. But gutters and downspouts must be clean to work properly and not succumb to water's attack themselves. In fact, a plugged gutter is worse than no gutter at all for several reasons: It forces water down along the side of your house; a sagging, water-and-trash-heavy gutter can damage the fascia boards under your roof; and in winter, collected water can freeze and crack downspouts and gutters. So as much as you might groan about it, cleaning gutters is a must-do chore. If planned well, you'll have to do it only once or twice a year.

Clean out your gutters any time they are backed up. Usually this is in the fall, after the leaves have fallen, and in the spring, after the heaviest pollen and catkins (those fuzzy, flowerlike things that grow on willows and other trees) have dropped. Wear *heavy work gloves* (as thorns and roofing nails end up in gutters). Use a *ladder* tall enough to reach the gutters safely. Have a buddy on hand to hold the ladder, and take your time, moving it each time you need to reach a new section of gutter. Begin at the downspout and work your way to the other end, scooping the leaves and twigs that have collected there.

To make your own gutter scoop, cut the bottom off an *empty plastic jug* that has a rectangular shape—the kind that motor oil comes in ◀. Or just use your gloved hand to remove the gunk. Don't scrape the inside of the gutters with any sharp tools—spades, putty knives, or the like—because you might damage the metal. If you feel the need to scrape, try scrubbing instead with a *nylon-bristled brush*.

Flush the gutters with a *garden hose* once you've removed all the debris. (Flushing before scooping is a no-no, because you'll probably clog the downspout.) If the downspout is clogged, push the hose down into it to clear the pileup. If that does not work, try pushing the hose into the pipe from the bottom end. Dismantle the gutter if you have to. As a last resort, you may need to fish a *plumber's snake* down the pipe. You can rent one at an equipment rental store.

Make a gutter bucket, too. A gutter bucket is a handy tool to help with cleaning gutters, and it's easy to make. Take a plastic bucket with an all-metal handle. Using wire cutters, make a cut in the middle of the handle. Bend each end of the handle into a hook shape, turn the hooks toward the same side of the bucket, and hang the bucket from the gutter. Dump the leaves and such from your gutter into the bucket, rather than dropping the mess into the shrubbery below or onto your spouse's head. When the bucket's full, climb down and empty it on your mulch pile. Soggy leaves make a great garden additive.

Clean the outside of the gutters with a cleaning solution. This is not important for the functioning of the gutters, but it will make them look crisp and new and help keep them in good shape.
- For removing dirt, mix *1/3 cup laundry detergent, 2/3 cup trisodium phosphate*, and *1 gallon of warm water*.
- For mildew and algae, mix *1/3 cup detergent, 2/3 cup trisodium phosphate*, and *1 quart bleach* with *3 quarts water*.

In either case, put on *rubber gloves*, wipe the solution on with a *rag*, and rinse with a *garden hose*.

Hairbrushes

Most of us don't clean our hairbrushes often enough. When we finally get around to it, we spend more time untangling that hair ball mess than we do on the cleaning job itself. Clean more often using the following tips, and you'll save time in the long run.

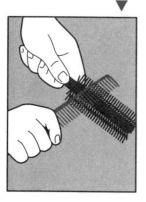

To clean a hairbrush, first pull out any loose hair from the bristles. Using a comb is often the easiest way ◄. Then make your own economical and effective cleaning solution by mixing *2 teaspoons of shampoo* and *1/4 cup of vinegar* in a **sink** filled with *warm water*. Soak the brush in the solution for several minutes. Pull a clean, *wide-toothed comb* down each row of bristles to remove any remaining hair.

By now, the solution should have loosened any buildup of oil, dirt, gel, and hair spray on the brush. Scrub the brush clean with a *nailbrush* (hold it down in the bathtub to contain the splatter) and rinse with *warm running water*. Let the brush air-dry.

To clean a makeup brush, avoid using commercial makeup brush cleaners, which often contain harsh chemicals. The chemicals aren't good for the sensitive skin of your face and can dry out a makeup brush, which can be quite expensive—especially the ones made of real animal hair (mink, yak, or squirrel). For a safe, nondrying alternative, mix *2 parts water* with *1 part gentle fabric wash*, such as Woolite. Dip the brush (tip only) into the solution. Don't dip the wooden or metal handle, because water can cause the bristles to fall out. Rinse in *clean water*. Repeat until the brush is clean (no more makeup color) and free of the wash solution. Dry the brush gently with a *towel*, being sure to move the towel "with the grain," or direction of the hair.

Hair Today, Gone Tomorrow >
Amby Longhofer, owner of a Beverly Hills salon, remembers a costly goof early in her career.

She used to clean her first collection of professional squirrel-hair makeup brushes with dishwashing detergent: "I would submerge the entire brush in water. The detergent dried the hair out. The moisture dissolved the glue that held the hair to the handle."

Hair Dryers

Modern dryers require minimal upkeep. But that little bit of maintenance is essential. A dryer with a debris-choked filter can overheat. It will perform poorly, possibly even damaging your hair. To keep that warm wind blowing properly, plan to clear its filter every three months if you use it daily.

What's the big hairy deal? It's all about airflow. Dryers work by fanning the surrounding air, directing it through the appliance's heating mechanism, and blowing it out through the nozzle as a stream of hot air. But the dryer pulls in dust and lint along with the air, and those particles lodge in a screen that filters the air before it hits the heating coils. Enough debris can accumulate in the filter to block air from flowing through. That's when things start to overheat. You may detect a warning odor like that (not surprisingly) of burning hair.

When a dryer overheats, its thermostat attempts to cool things down by tripping the heating coils off and on. You feel alternating hot and cold air blowing out, which won't provide the styling effects of consistently warm air. Extreme blockage may trigger the dryer's nonresettable shutdown device. Dryer demise.

▲

To clean your dryer filter, first unplug the dryer. Premium dryers have a filter cover that lifts off ▶, giving easy access for cleaning. Scrub the filter with a *dry, soft-bristled brush or toothbrush* to get out the lint, dust, and hair. Or use your *vacuum* with a *crevice attachment*. Pull out any stubborn bits with *tweezers*. If your dryer doesn't have a filter cover, you'll need to brush, vacuum, or tweeze the filter from the outside.

To clean the dryer body and accessories, just wipe with a *damp rag* (not a wet one, which could drip water into the heating element). Even the stickiest, slipperiest hair products are generally water soluble, so a damp cloth should remove them.

Hammocks

Hammocks are all about relaxing—which you wouldn't be able to do if you thought you were reclining in grime and mildew. Those backyard spoilsports mold and mildew thrive in moisture. Another threat to your hammock is rot, caused by strong sunlight and detergents that wear away at a hammock's natural-rope fibers.

To make your hammock last longer, you need to keep it not only dirt free but as dry as possible. So a good dose of prevention is called for.

- Before its maiden swing, spray your hammock with *fabric guard*, following the label instructions. Renew the treatment every three to five months.
- Don't hang the hammock in full sun, as the rays will fade synthetics and weaken cotton.
- Find a dry indoor spot to store the hammock in bad weather or whenever you won't be hanging out for a while.

A good universal hammock-cleaning approach is to mix *1 ounce of mild dishwashing detergent* with *2 gallons of water*. Spread the hammock out on a *large, debris-free, hard surface*, such as a deck. Keeping the wooden spreader bars dry, scrub one side of the hammock with a *soft cloth or sponge*, then flip it and clean

WATCH OUT

Skip sunbathing in your hammock. Sunscreens are like kryptonite for polyester and acrylic fibers, prematurely aging them. (Besides, that hammock's supposed to be in shade.) If you do spill sunscreen on a hammock, spot-clean it promptly with 1/2 teaspoon of dishwashing detergent in 1/4 cup of water. Scrub with a soft-bristled brush.

the other side. A **soft-bristled brush** will let you gently scrub dirty areas. Rinse well with **clear water** and hang the hammock to air-dry, preferably in a low-humidity breeze but not in direct sunlight. Quick drying keeps the fibers strong and discourages mold and mildew. The hammock should be fully dry in two days. Other cleaning approaches depend on the fabric and construction of your hammock.

To clean white cotton or cotton-polyester rope, just spot-clean dirt using **1 part gentle fabric wash**, such as Woolite, to **8 parts water**. If you see mold or mildew, draw the hammock a bath in your **tub** and soak it in a mild bleach solution (**1 capful of chlorine bleach** per **1 gallon of water**) for 30 minutes.

To clean synthetic fabrics such as polyester and acrylic, bind the hammock so that it won't tangle—if it is a model that has no spreader bars, such as a Mayan-style *hamaca*. Fold the hammock in half, bringing the two end rings together. Bind it with **twine** just below the rings, then at the fold, and finally in the middle of your bundle. This keeps the hardware out of the strings and saves the strings from becoming a tangled puzzle. Drop the bundle into a pillowcase and tie it closed. Put it in the **washing machine** on the **gentle cycle** and add **2 ounces of gentle fabric wash**. After washing, unbind and spread the hammock out to dry. Give it two days, and you'll be back in the swing of things!

You can also hand-wash it in a solution of **1 part gentle fabric wash** to **4 parts water**.

If the yarn is solution-dyed, meaning the dye was added when the synthetic was still liquid, you can rid it of mildew and stains by hand-washing it in a **bleach-and-water solution**. Don't go any stronger than a 50-50 mix. Use **rubber gloves** and test for color-fastness on an inconspicuous corner.

To clean colored rope, fabric, or quilted fabric hammocks, scrub using **1/4 cup of laundry detergent** in **5 gallons of warm water**. Test for colorfastness first. Hit mildewy areas with the **mild bleach solution** suggested above for cotton-rope hammocks. Spot-wash hammock pillows using your **mild dishwashing detergent solution** and a **soft-bristled brush**. Avoid soaking the batting inside.

If your hammock has wooden spreader bars, they will come covered with a protective coating such as marine varnish, which you can replenish every six months. You'll find **marine varnish** at hardware stores and marine supply stores. Follow the directions on the label. If your hammock is suspended on a wooden frame, touch up the frame with **linseed oil** every three to six months.

Handbags

Through the eons, pouches for fire-striking flint and trading shells evolved into handbags for car keys and ATM cards. Nowadays, a bag is an essential for many women and a few men. (Oh, sure, call it a European organizer.) So how do you keep your handbag from looking like that original cave dweller's pouch?

The general approach to cleaning a handbag is to first empty the bag of its contents. Brush away loose dirt—inside and outside the bag—with a *soft white cloth*, or *vacuum* it using an *upholstery attachment*. Next (with the exception of suede), wet a *soft cloth* in a *cleaning solution* appropriate for your bag's material. (See below.) Wring the cloth nearly dry and rub the bag inside and out, taking care to avoid dampening it any more than it takes to clean it.

Beyond visible dirt, you'll wipe away skin oils, hand lotion, makeup, and perspiration. A bag's handle, clasp, and straps are typically high-grime spots on the exterior. Inside, wipe the liner—especially the bottom—and interior hardware, such as zippers.

To clean a leather bag, use *saddle soap* or a *cream leather cleaner/conditioner*, available at shoe repair shops. Follow the label instructions. Always follow saddle soap with a *solvent-free leather conditioner*, such as Lexol, to avoid drying out the leather. Then buff with a *soft cloth*.

To clean a fabric bag, use *1/2 teaspoon of a gentle fabric wash*, such as Woolite, in *1/4 cup of lukewarm water* for all-over cleaning of sturdier fabrics. Use it full strength for spots. For more delicate fabrics, use barely damp *baby wipes*.

To clean patent leather, use a *cream cleaner/conditioner* if it's real patent leather. Be gentle—patent leather scratches easily. If it is imitation patent leather, use *mild dishwashing detergent* or a *car interior vinyl and plastic cleaner*, such as Meguiar's, available at auto supply stores.

To clean plastic, vinyl, or polyurethane, try a *plastic cleaner*, such as Novus (sold at marine and auto supply stores, as well as by suppliers of restoration products), if the handbag is made of a hard plastic such as Lucite. Wipe softer synthetics with a solution of *dishwashing detergent or a gentle fabric wash* and *water*. Alternatives: Use *baby wipes* or a *car interior vinyl and plastic cleaner*. To restore the shine to shiny plastics, spritz them with *silicone wax spray* after cleaning ▶. Then buff.

OOPS!

Dye-Hard Duo >

Never stack a leather handbag on top of or directly under a plastic one. The dye from the leather bag will leach and be absorbed by the plastic. Then you'll be holding a bag of a different color!

▲

To clean a straw bag, use *1 part liquid hand soap* to *3 parts water*.

To clean a suede bag, brush the nap with a *natural-bristle shoe brush*, which will remove surface dirt. Otherwise, have it professionally dry-cleaned. Use protectant sprays sparingly on suede, since some attract dirt.

Hard-Water Deposits

If you're in a hard-water area, you'll know it: Surfaces that get wet frequently will have colorful stains, whitish spots, or crusty deposits. The dreaded blighter lime scale may build up enough to interfere with the function of fixtures like showerheads and faucets. Soaps will seem to leave a residue, and it will take more detergent to get things clean than it has in other places you've lived. The effects of hard water include dull, sticky hair; dingy, scratchy clothes; and spotted dishes.

The culprits? Minerals in your water, mostly calcium and magnesium. For you chemistry majors, moderately hard water has concentrations of at least 61 milligrams of these minerals per liter, or 3.5 grains per gallon, and really hard water has double that amount.

To prevent mineral deposits, keep hard water away from the surfaces that it typically damages. Hard water does its mischief by evaporating and leaving behind mineral deposits. So to beat it, keep wet surfaces from air-drying in the following ways:
- Dab faucets dry.
- Keep lawn sprinklers away from windows.
- Fix leaks and drips.
- Rinse sinks, tubs, and shower stalls after use and then wipe or squeegee them dry.

It also helps to keep on hand a spray solution containing a non-precipitating water conditioner. (Calgon, White Rain, Blue Raindrops, and Spring Rain are examples.) Mix *1/2 teaspoon of water conditioner* in *1 quart of water* in a *spray bottle* and spray it on wet surfaces to capture the mineral particles along with the water as you wipe things dry.

To remove mineral deposits, a number of cleaners attack hard-water deposits with special chemicals. These compounds include
- sequestrants, which capture (or sequester) minerals so they don't leave a deposit (the phosphates in automatic dishwasher detergent are sequestrants);

simple SOLUTIONS

Give Your Showerhead a Bath >

Is your showerhead clogged with lime scale? If possible, unscrew the showerhead and soak it overnight in a bowl of white vinegar. In the morning, remove the deposits with a brush with moderately stiff bristles.

If you can't unscrew the showerhead, don't worry. Just pour the vinegar into a plastic bag and pull the bag up around the showerhead (see Showers).

HANDBAGS

- surfactants (short for *surface acting agents*), which loosen soil by reducing surface tension, allowing the water to wet things faster (the main ingredient in laundry detergent is a surfactant);
- acids, which help break down mineral deposits;
- alkalis (present in some cleaners), which help suspend soil so it can be rinsed away.

Consult the chart below to select the best cleaner for curing your hard-water blues.

Navigating Hard Water

Those pesky hard-water deposits can collect on a bewildering array of surfaces in your home. Here is a primer on which cleaners to use where. Read product labels to make sure you've got the right kind of cleaner, and test surfaces before doing an all-out cleanup. A word to the wise: Never mix chlorine bleach with ammonia-based or acidic products.

Brass (*unlacquered*)
• Mildly abrasive brass cleaner, such as Brasso.

Ceramic tile
• Acid-based kitchen-bathroom cleaner formulated for mineral deposits and soap scum, such as Scrub Free Soap Scum Remover. Avoid bleach.
• Nonabrasive all-purpose cleaner, such as Formula 409.
• 1 part white vinegar to 4 parts water.
• Lime-scale remover, such as CLR Calcium Lime Rust Remover.

Chrome
• Nonabrasive ammonia-based chrome cleaner, such as Windex.
• Kitchen-bathroom cleaner labeled suitable for chrome, such as CLR Bathroom & Kitchen Cleaner.

Faucet bases
• Paste of nonprecipitating water conditioner, such as Calgon, and water on a damp sponge.

Fiberglass
• 1 part white vinegar to 4 parts water.
• Nonabrasive all-purpose cleaner, such as Formula 409.
• Acid-based kitchen-bathroom cleaner labeled safe for fiberglass, such as Scrub Free Soap Scum Remover.
• Spray solution of 1/2 teaspoon nonprecipitating water conditioner, such as Calgon, per 1 quart of water.

Glass (*windows and shower doors*)
• Extra dishwasher detergent. Use up to double for tough hard-water film.
• Kitchen-bathroom cleaner formulated for mineral deposits and soap scum, such as CLR Bathroom & Kitchen Cleaner.

Glassware (*permanent etching or iridescent discoloration is not removable*)
• Undiluted white vinegar. Soak for 15 minutes, rinse, and dry.
• Dishwashing rinsing agent, such as Jet-Dry. Add to dishwasher.

Plastic laminate (*such as Formica*)
• Baking soda. Dip rag into bowl of warm water, then into bowl of baking soda, and rub. Wipe clean with a dry cloth.

Porcelain enamel
• Kitchen-bathroom cleaner formulated for mineral deposits and soap scum, such as CLR Bathroom & Kitchen Cleaner. Some toilet-bowl cleaners contain stronger acids—don't leave on surface long.
• Nonabrasive all-purpose cleaner, such as Formula 409.
• Lime-scale remover, such as CLR Calcium Lime Rust Remover.
• Rust remover, such as CLR.

Stainless steel
• Nonabrasive all-purpose cleaner, such as Formula 409.
• Spray solution of 1/2 teaspoon nonprecipitating water conditioner, such as Calgon, per 1 quart of water.
• Lime-scale remover labeled suitable for stainless steel, such as CLR Bathroom & Kitchen Cleaner. Rinse well.

Vitreous china fixtures
• Lime-scale remover, such as CLR Calcium Lime Rust Remover.

To get rid of hard water entirely, consider installing a water-softening system. These systems typically treat the water with sodium, which trades places with the calcium and magnesium particles in the water. But to properly address *all* of the minerals in the water—including manganese (brown-black stains) and iron (reddish-brown stains)—your water-softening system has to be customized to fit the water in your area.

What's the State of *Your Water?*

New England, the southern Atlantic Coast–Gulf Coast region, the Pacific Northwest, and Hawaii generally have the softest water in the United States. Many of the rivers in Tennessee, the Pacific Northwest, Alaska, and the Great Lakes region have moderately hard water. Just about every region of the United States has some streams with hard or very hard water. The hardest water in the United States, with more than 1,000 milligrams of minerals per liter, is found in some streams in Texas, New Mexico, Kansas, Arizona, and southern California.

Hats

Hats aren't just pieces of clothing that happen to sit atop your head. They're made from a wide variety of materials, and the methods you use to clean your T-shirts don't apply.

▲

To keep a fur, felt, velour, or beaver hat clean, regularly brush the dust and dirt from the surface with a *nylon or horsehair brush*. It's important for a hat to be dust free because if the hat gets wet, the dust will be harder to eliminate. With fur and felt hats, always brush with the nap (in the direction of the material) and use separate brushes for light and dark hats. You can often refresh a tired felt hat by holding it over steaming water for a second or two and brushing with the nap ◄. To deal with more extensive stains or soiling, take your hat to a professional for cleaning and shaping. It's a job specific to the hat and is based on fabric and soil—variables only a professional is equipped to handle. Avoid the temptation to use stain removal products. There's a good chance you'll damage your hat further and create stain rings.

If you spill something on your hat, blot it immediately with a *soft, absorbent cloth* to prevent it from seeping into the hat. If your hat gets spotted with mud, let it dry first. Then lightly brush it off with a *nylon or horsehair brush*.

To clean a baseball cap, place it in a *plastic cap frame* device, such as the Ball Cap Buddy, which will prevent it from losing its shape or shrinking during washing. Then run the whole thing through a *regular wash cycle* in the *washing machine*—or even the *dishwasher*. Check the cap for any laundering instructions. (You don't want to wash the cap if its colors will bleed.)

To clean a straw hat, brush it with a *brush or dry cloth* to remove dust and loose dirt. Past that, these hats are not really cleanable, even by a professional. With time, straw hats naturally turn yellow, and there's nothing you can do about it.

To clean a wool hat, use a *sticky fabric roller* designed to remove hairs and lint from clothing, or use a *whisk broom*. Brushes that are firmer are too rough to use on wool hats.

If a hat has faded in spots and you're ready to hang it up for good, here's how to get a little more life out of it:
- For a white hat, apply *talcum powder* using a *dry sponge*. (A makeup sponge works great.)
- For colored hats, grind down a *crayon* that matches the color, mix with the talcum powder, and apply.

Hearing Aids

Hearing aids open a new world to some people, but they must get daily attention to remain in top working order. Wax and moisture are common causes of hearing aid malfunction—wax on hearing aids that fit inside the ear, and moisture from perspiration on hearing aids worn outside the ear.

To clean an in-the-ear hearing aid, start by washing your hands to avoid contaminating the device. Then, using a *brush* (either one that your hearing care provider gave you or a clean toothbrush), remove any wax on the exterior of the hearing aid. Do this daily if you get a lot of wax, or every other day if you don't. Another option: Wipe the surface with a *dry cotton cloth* (an old T-shirt works well) or a cloth *lightly* dampened with *alcohol*. If you're using alcohol, wipe only the shell of the unit, not over the microphone or receiver, which can be damaged by moisture.
Cleaning a behind-the-ear hearing aid is a two-part operation. To clean the ear mold that fits inside the ear, use *water* and *soap* (Ivory, for instance) or a *germicidal soap* (such as Purell liquid). Put the soap on a cotton cloth dampened with lukewarm water. Wipe the ear mold clean, giving it a good rub. Rinse with lukewarm water and dry with a *towel*. To clean the hearing aid itself,

expert advice

Take the Inside Out >

If the satin lining of your hat is removable, you can wash it, says George Kapottos, owner of Mike the Hatter in Cleveland, Ohio. Fill a sink with cold water and add a couple of drops of dishwashing liquid. Place the satin lining in the water and rub it with a stiff scrub brush. To rinse, hold it under cold running water. Let it air-dry. If you want to remove wrinkles, expose it to the steam from your steam iron—without actually touching the iron to the lining.

WATCH OUT

- If you wear a behind-the-ear hearing aid, apply hair spray before you put on your hearing aid. The spray could damage the microphone.
- Don't wear your hearing aid when you're working in the yard or garden. Perspiration, hose water, dirt, and grass clippings could damage it.

simple SOLUTIONS

Put It in Dry Dock >

Keep your hearing aid working longer by storing it at night in a moisture-absorbing dry aid kit, also called a dehumidifier kit. You can purchase one from a hearing aid dealer.

To make your own, get a jar that has a good seal and a desiccant bag. Put the bag and your hearing aid in the jar and close it up. A desiccant bag will last for six months. Desiccant bags can be bought wherever you buy hearing aid equipment.

use just a **brush**. A toothbrush is fine—if you promise not to use it for anything else.

Every three months, take the hearing aid to your hearing care specialist for a thorough cleaning. He or she should have the appropriate tools for cleaning more deeply into the interior of your hearing aid.

The special tools and accessories that you use with your hearing aid need cleaning, too. In-the-ear hearing aids have wax guards, also called wax scepters, that protect the receiver from getting clogged with wax. Clean them with a brush. Behind-the-ear hearing aids can be fitted with a sleeve jacket that covers the component behind the ear and protects it from moisture. Wipe the sleeve clean with a **cloth**.

Like a computer, a hearing aid has an electronic chip in it. Water is its enemy, so watch the amount of liquid you use when cleaning. It's also a good idea to keep your hearing aid in a dry place when you're not using it—for example, in the bedroom while you're taking a shower, instead of in the bathroom.

Heat Pumps

The hallmark of a heat pump is its efficiency. Because a heat pump moves heat out of the outside air or the ground rather than converting it from a fuel, it can deliver 1.5 to 3 times more heat energy to a home than the electricity it consumes to operate. That said, your heat pump's performance will deteriorate without regular maintenance and service. The difference between the energy consumption of a well-maintained heat pump and a severely neglected one ranges from 10 to 25 percent, according to the U.S. Department of Energy.

Your heat pump is an investment. You can do some routine maintenance yourself, such as changing the filter and cleaning the outside unit. Other service should be left to the professionals. The following tips—except for the outside duties—apply to both air-source heat pumps, which draw heat from the outside air, and geothermal heat pumps, which draw heat from the ground. The outside unit of a geothermal heat pump is underground and not accessible.

Replace disposable filters once a month during the heating months. Prices of filters range from $1 to $50. The higher quality may be worth it if you have allergies or breathing problems.

Electronic filters are cleanable. Follow the manufacturer's instructions. If you don't clean an electronic filter, which charges air particles, you may eventually cause damage to the heat exchanger and filter.

Outdoor coils usually need to be cleaned annually—more often, if there's noticeable dirt on the coils. This chore isn't difficult, but it starts with safety.

1. Turn off power to the unit. The switch is located in a fuse box next to the unit.
2. Remove the top of the unit—you may need another person to help you—being careful not to pull, dislodge, or loosen the wires underneath.
3. Now, get out the *garden hose*. If you need to use soap, a *spray canister* that attaches to the end of the garden hose (about $5 at any hardware store) will make it easy. Put in 3 or 4 drops of *dishwashing detergent*, fill the rest of the way with *water*, and screw the hose onto the canister.
4. Spraying from the inside out, spray the three sides of the unit where the coil's fins are and leave the side with the compressor alone. (Don't use tools to try to remove stuck dirt or debris—you could cause a leak.) Then remove the soap holder and rinse until all the soapsuds are gone.
5. You can replace the cover immediately, but wait to turn on the power, because, chances are, there will be a lot of water around, your hands will probably be wet, and you don't want to electrocute yourself.

Have a professional technician service your heat pump every year. A qualified technician can inspect ducts, filters, blower, and the indoor coil for dirt and other obstructions; clean and tighten the electrical connections; check for leaks; check for proper operation; and more.

See also **Furnaces**.

simple SOLUTIONS

Attack of the Killer Grass >

To keep your heat pump running smoothly, remove plant life and debris from around it. If weeds build up, you can use a weed killer on them, but be careful not to get any of the spray on the coils. Rinse off any chemicals that do get on the unit.

Holiday Decorations

Holiday decorations do more than make your house pleasing to the eye; they evoke family traditions, memories, and sentiment. The lowliest decoration may occupy the most exalted position on your tree, mantle, or centerpiece. To ensure many happy holidays to come, proper cleaning and storage of your decorations are essential. New decorations often come with instructions. Make sure you read them before cleaning.

To clean painted ornaments, separate them so you can pick them up one at a time by the hanger. Lightly dust each ornament with a *feather duster*. Try not to handle the ornaments, since the oils in your hands can damage the paint. If you need to touch the ornament, wear **latex gloves.** (This is a must if your ornament is old and fragile.)

To clean glass ornaments, spray regular **glass cleaner** onto a *soft cloth* and wipe gently. (Clean Plexiglas with an **acrylic** or **Plexiglas cleaner**, such as Brillianize Plexi Cleaner, available at some hardware stores and from plastic and glass specialists.)

To clean porcelain or crystal ornaments, use a *feather duster*, brushing across the surface in a downward motion. Don't handle crystal decorations unless you wear **gloves**. A buffing *jewelry cloth* is also great to use on crystal. Simply wipe over the surface with the cloth.

To clean resin and wood ornaments, a *soft cotton cloth* works well. Again, just wipe across the surface.

Sterling silver and gold-plated ornaments come clean when wiped with a polishing *jewelry cloth*. Apply the cloth in circular motions to remove dust and fingerprints.

Cleaning glittered ornaments is a tricky business. Try using a *feather duster* on one area. If a lot of glitter comes off, it may be best to leave the decoration alone.

Storing your clean ornaments properly will ensure they will be sparkling, dust free, and ready to hang the next year. Here are some tips:

● Store ornaments in a **large box or rubber storage container** (about 24 inches by 36 inches or smaller) or, if you still have it, in their **original box**.

A Holiday Recipe

You can whip up an inexpensive solution for cleaning ornaments in seconds, says John Wood, operations manager of Extreme Cleaning in Arvada, Colorado, which offers holiday cleaning. The solution works magic on glass, plastic, and wood decorations.

Mix 2 teaspoons of vinegar in a cup of water and apply it to the decorations with a 100 percent cotton rag. Dip one corner of the cloth in the solution and then squeeze the rag. Put the rag over your index finger and gently wipe your finger over the ornament surface. By using one finger, you'll have more control and can pay attention to cleaning the details on the ornament.

Always test a small, inconspicuous area first. Be very careful with hand-painted or old painted decorations, because the dyes may not hold up as well. Lead or acid-based older paints will come off if cleaned with anything, so test, let the surface dry, and check for discoloration.

HOLIDAY DECORATIONS

- Place a thick layer of **crunched-up tissue paper** (use only nonacidic paper) in the bottom of the container.
- Lay a full layer of ornaments on top of the crunched-up tissue paper on the bottom.
- Put the more sturdy ornaments on the bottom and the delicate ones on top. Don't use more than two layers. Try to offset the upper layer so that the ornaments don't sit directly on top of the ornaments below. Don't pack the ornaments tightly, because they might break.
- Wrap each ornament individually using just **one layer of tissue paper** for the ornament.
- Lay **one or two layers of flat tissue paper** on top of the first layer of ornaments.
- Place the second layer of wrapped ornaments on top of the tissue paper over the previous layer of ornaments.
- Store your container of ornaments in a cool, dry, out-of-the-way place.

Hoses

Thankfully, hoses are almost—but not totally—maintenance free.

Always start cleaning garden hoses with the least abrasive method and work your way up. They probably require little cleaning other than removing dirt by spraying **water** *from* the hose *onto* the

Give Your Garden Hose a Long and Happy Life

To increase your hose's life expectancy, here are some more things you can do:

• Sure, hoses have UV retardants in them. Nevertheless, it helps to remove your hose from adverse conditions, such as sunlight and freezing temperatures. Over time, sunlight can break down the material so that it becomes brittle.

• While your hose isn't in use, store it on a reel to prevent it from forming kinks or knots. Place the reel out of sight (they're not that attractive, anyway) and out of the sun or on the east side of the house (so it only gets the morning sun).

• For winter storage, drain the hose and store it indoors. To drain it, first detach the hose from the tap. Starting at the end of the hose, pick it up so that the water runs through the hose ahead of you. Make large loops with the hose over your shoulder as you go. When you reach the end of the hose, all the water will have run out. If you have a long hose that's too heavy to loop over your shoulder, make loops around a bench or make your loops on a raised patch of ground.

• Place the hose out in the sun for two days to thoroughly dry it.

• Store the hose flat in large relaxed loops. If you hang your hose, you'll get bends that may freeze and damage the material.

• Never walk on or drive over a hose. Hoses aren't designed to withstand that much external pressure.

hose. If you need some extra cleaning muscle, dampen a rag in *warm water* and add to it some ***biodegradable soap*** (available at camping stores). Rub it over the hose and use ***clean water*** from the hose to rinse. Still have some dirt stuck on the hose? Use a ***vinyl cleaner*** on vinyl hoses or rubber hoses coated with vinyl. Follow the manufacturer's instructions.

If your hose is stopped up and you have no kinks in it, you could have a buildup of calcium deposits from minerals in the water. Bend the hose back and forth along the entire length of the hose to break up the buildup. If there's a nozzle on the business end of the hose, remove it and then turn on the water to flush out the loosened deposits.

Hot Tubs

How often should you clean your hot tub? Depends on how often you use it.

- If two people use it three nights a week, clean it thoroughly and drain it every three months.
- If you have a lot of kids, and the family uses it up to six nights a week, step up your cleaning to every two months.
- If your hot tub is more for decoration than relaxation, clean it as needed. You'll still have to test the chemical levels weekly.
- If you aren't keeping track of your use, here's a good rule of thumb: Don't keep the water in longer than three months—six months maximum. You won't need a calendar to know when you've waited too long. The water will be cloudy or foamy, or it'll smell like a science experiment.

Cleaning your hot tub's filter is important because a dirty, worn-out filter will fail to trap spa contaminants and will put undue strain on your spa's pump motor and heater. Remove your filter ◀ and rinse it weekly with ***water*** to get rid of coarse dirt and debris. Take a ***garden hose***, apply the stream at a 45 degree angle, and give it a pressure washing inside and out. Allow the filter to dry. Next, remove any fine particles of dirt carefully with a brush or by applying a stream of ***compressed air*** (from an air compressor or from an aerosol can, available at supermarkets as well as camera, computer, and discount stores) to the filter's outer surface.

If algae, suntan oil, or body oils still leave a coating, soak the filter overnight in a ***degreaser cleaning solution***, such as Filter Fresh or Leisure Time Filter Clean (available from your hot tub dealer). Some experts recommend that you soak the filter monthly in a degreaser. If clogging persists, check your water chemistry and adjust, drain, and clean the tub, or buy a new *filter cartridge*. Replace the filter annually.

Every three months, drain the water and clean the acrylic shell inside and out with a *nonsoap-based cleaner* such as Spray Away, a spa and nautical product that cuts grease easily. Spray it on the tub, let it sit for a minute, and then wipe off any scum or stains, or rub with a *sponge*. Refill the spa right away—or wax it after cleaning with an *aerosol wax*, such as Highlight Spa Brite spray wax, or Novus 1 Plastic Clean & Shine. You'll find that *old, clean cotton T-shirts* make great buffers. Be sure not to spray the cleaning solution and wax into the jets.

If you're still getting cloudy water, or your jets aren't working properly, or gunk is appearing on the water, you may have clogged pipes, and you'll have to use a *spa cleaning agent*, such as Swirl Away Plumbing Cleaner.

To clean hot-tub covers, use a *cover cleaning product* designed for the task, such as Leisure Time's Kover Kare & Konditioner or 303 Aerospace Protectant. Other *vinyl cleaners* or Spray Away will also do the job. Applying a *paste wax* to your hot tub cover is a good idea, because it creates a barrier between the cover and the sun, slowing down the sun's fading action.

When the cleaning is done, you're ready to refill the spa with *cold water*. It will take about an hour. Then do your water tests and add the amount of *chemicals* and *sanitizers* recommended by your hot tub's manufacturer. Start the spa. It will take six to 12 hours for the water to reheat. Until the next water change and cleaning, your chemicals and filtering will keep the 102° F water clear and fresh.

Houseplants

Your plants need more than regular watering. To maintain your plants' ability to grow, you need to clean them.

Remove dust and dirt from your houseplants the same way that you remove dust and dirt from yourself—with a shower. This is important to do, because grime is the enemy of photosynthesis, the process in which leaves absorb sunlight and carbon dioxide to make food for the plant. The shower will also help remove any insects.

First, prepare the plant's pot. Put the pot in a **plastic bag** and tie the bag tightly around the base of the plant without injuring it. You want to be sure the plant doesn't get overwatered in the shower. If your plant has multiple stems, lay **extra plastic bags** between the stems. Put the plant in the **shower** and set the water temperature to tepid—neither hot nor cold. Let the shower sprinkle the plant for a few minutes.

Sometimes minerals in the shower water will build up on the plant's leaves, making them look dull. To clean the minerals off hard-surfaced (not hairy) leaves, wipe with a **dry, clean rag**. Support each leaf with your free hand as you wipe. Another method: Gently scrape the minerals off with your thumb.

Cleaning plants with hairy leaves is a little trickier. First give them a gentle dusting with a **feather duster** and then hit the shower, as above.

After the plants have had their shower, allow them to dry thoroughly right in the shower stall or set them on **paper towels or old newspapers** until they're not dripping anymore. If you return them to direct sunlight while they're still wet, the light could burn the leaves.

Now check each plant's surroundings. Be sure the window you set your plant in is clean so that the plant will get optimal sunlight. White mineral deposits can be toxic to your plants, so gently scrape them from the soil surface and the inner rim of the pot. If you have an extreme case of mineral buildup, put the pot in a sink, where it can drain freely, and run a lot of water through the soil to remove the minerals. (Don't do this during times of low light or dormancy, however. Plants should be actively growing; otherwise they may develop root rot.)

Cleaning a cactus requires a gentle touch—not only to prevent skewering yourself, but also to protect the waxy coating that helps the plant conserve moisture in desert climates. Stick to misting your cactus with a **spray bottle** filled with **water**, and even then only clean the areas of the plant that are showing dirt or dust. Make the cleaning quick and gentle, and let the cactus dry before putting it back into direct sunlight. An alternative: Use long **tweezers** to carefully pick off any dust particles.

To clean succulents with fuzzy leaves, use a **soft paintbrush or feather duster** to remove dust. The fuzziness protects the plant in arid conditions, and washing can be hazardous to the leaves.

HOUSEPLANTS

Humidifiers

A humidifier is a blessing if you suffer from winter dryness of your nose, throat, lips, or skin. The air it dampens will also alleviate nuisances such as static electricity, peeling wallpaper, and cracks in paint and furniture. But humidifiers can encourage the growth of organisms such as dust mites and mold, which means proper care and cleaning are essential. If you use a humidifier, plan on a routine of daily cleaning, a more thorough cleaning every three days, and regular disinfecting. If this seems like a lot, remember that mold begins to grow after 48 hours.

To clean a portable humidifier, first turn it off. Empty the reservoir (the tank where the water sits) every day and wash it out with *hot, soapy water*, using a *brush* or other *scrubber* to remove mineral deposits or film. Rinse well under *running water*, taking care that no water gets into the motor. Wipe all surfaces dry with a *clean cloth*, and fill the reservoir. The use of *distilled water* is preferable because you'll avoid the buildup of mineral deposits, but *tap water* will suffice.

Every three days, clean your humidifier more thoroughly. Begin as you would the daily cleaning. After rinsing, wipe the reservoir with *white vinegar* (diluted with *water*, if you wish) to break up mineral deposits. Wipe off the mineral deposits, rinse again, wipe dry, and refill the reservoir.

Disinfecting your humidifier will reduce spore growth. Mix a solution of *1/2 cup household bleach*, such as Clorox, with *1 gallon of water* and add it to the humidifier's reservoir. Run the humidifier until it starts to mist or steam. (Be sure to do this outside or in a well-ventilated area and don't stand near the steamed bleach—it can injure your lungs.) Turn off the humidifier and let the bleach sit for a couple of minutes. Empty the reservoir into a sink and rinse the reservoir with *running water*. Fill it again with *fresh water*, run the system for two to three minutes, and then turn it off. Empty the reservoir and rinse again. Repeat the cycle until you no longer smell the bleach.

Note: If the manufacturer's instructions don't recommend bleach, don't use it. They may recommend instead a *3 percent solution of hydrogen peroxide*, which is fine but does not work as well as bleach.

If your humidifier has a filter, check it every third day. If it's gray, replace it. The filter can't be cleaned.

At the end of the humidifying season, clean the humidifier following the bleach method described previously. Make sure all parts are dry, and store the unit in a dry location. When it's time to use the humidifier again, clean the unit again and wipe up any dust on the outside with a damp cloth.

Humidifiers that are part of a central heating system need to be cleaned regularly. Otherwise, they may become breeding grounds for mold. The designs of such units vary widely, but typically a tube carries water from the water heater to a rectangular box mounted on the air supply duct that goes from the furnace to the rest of the house. The water flows across a disposable water panel or, in the case of older models, a rotating drum. The water evaporates into the air being fed throughout the house, thus raising the humidity. A drain removes the excess water.

If you have a newer system (no older than mid–1990s), replace the water panel every year. Do it more often if you have hard water, which builds up on the panel and makes it less effective. Clean the water distribution tray at the same time. To do this, open the access panel on the box and unsnap and discard the water panel. Unsnap the water distribution tray, take it to a *sink*, and give it a quick cleaning in *warm water* and *dishwashing detergent*. Wipe the drain (it's not removable) with a *soapy rag* and rinse with a *wet rag*. Reassemble the unit with a *new water panel*.

Cleaning the inner workings of an older system is not very different. Once a year, open the unit and replace the *filter* that wraps around the rotating drum. Remove the water tray and wash it in the sink. Two or three times a year, check the filter for mold or mineral deposits. If it needs cleaning, soak it for several hours in a solution of *1 part vinegar* to *2 parts water*. Rinse the filter thoroughly with *fresh water* and return it to the drum.

Ink Stains

If the sight of ink on your carpeting or clothing throws you into a panic, stop, take a deep breath, and reach for the alcohol—rubbing alcohol, that is. It's the best remedy for removing any kind of ink from leather, carpeting, upholstery, and clothing (as long as the stain isn't permanent ink, made by felt-tip pens, such as Magic Marker; India ink; or painting ink, for instance). Always clean an ink stain immediately, and always use cool water when you do it. (Heat will set the stain.) Before using a cleaner on any fabric or surface, test an inconspicuous spot for colorfastness. Various fabrics and surfaces react differently to ink stains, but the following are good general guidelines.

To remove ink from leather, vinyl, and most fabrics, moisten a section of a *clean white terry cloth towel* with *rubbing alcohol* and dab the alcohol on the ink stain. Let the alcohol sit for 30 minutes to give it time to dissolve the ink. Then use a *fresh white cloth* to blot up the stain. Move to a new spot on the cleaning cloth each time you blot, to avoid spreading the stain. Reapply the alcohol if necessary. Finally, rinse with a solution of *1/4 cup white vinegar* per *1 quart water* and then rinse again with *plain water*. (Yes, alcohol usually evaporates, but the rinsing ensures that the material won't be damaged by any lingering traces.)

If the ink resists removal with rubbing alcohol, ask your pharmacist for *denatured alcohol* or use *foam shaving cream*. (Gel shaving cream does not work.) Shaving cream contains two or three kinds of alcohol that can remove ink and many stubborn food stains. Apply the denatured alcohol or foam, wait 10 to 15 minutes, and then rinse as above.

When removing ink from fabrics, here are some other tips to keep in mind:

- Blot—never rub—the alcohol on. Rubbing the fabric will break down the fibers and weaken the material.
- To prevent large stains from spreading, work from the outside of the stain toward the center.
- Remember to protect your working surface when removing a stain from clothing. Place a piece of *plastic* on the work surface, with a *clean white terry towel* on top of that. Do the same between layers of clothing.
- Launder clothing or washable fabric after removing the stain and air-dry. Professionally dry-clean silk, wool, and linen that specifies dry cleaning. If the garment is hand-washable, allow

the alcohol to set only five minutes and rinse with **cool water**. Reapply if needed.

● Polyester reacts differently to ink stains than cotton and other fabrics do. If alcohol and denatured alcohol don't completely remove the ink, rinse the fabric with **cool water**, apply **3 percent hydrogen peroxide**, then rinse again. The hydrogen peroxide will bleach what is left of the ink so that it won't be noticeable. Peroxide is safe for colored clothing, but test an inconspicuous area first. Don't use peroxide on a wool, silk, or Persian carpet.

To treat ink stains with hydrogen peroxide instead of alcohol, mix equal parts **20 percent hydrogen peroxide** and **water** and proceed as above.

To remove ink from carpeting, moisten a section of a **clean white terry cloth towel** with **rubbing alcohol** and gently blot the spot. Wait 30 minutes for the alcohol to dissolve the ink, then press the knuckle of your index finger into the barely damp rag. Work your knuckle forward and backward over the stain. Change to a clean spot on the towel and repeat, this time working your knuckle left to right. Replenish alcohol if needed. To finish removing the stain, again press your knuckle into the damp towel, but this time twist your wrist in a clockwise direction. Carpet fibers are twisted clockwise. This motion will help remove stains from between the fibers without causing the carpet to fuzz. Rinse with a solution of **1/4 cup white vinegar** per **1 quart water** and then rinse again with **plain water**, applied using a **fresh towel** and the same knuckle technique.

To remove a surface ink mark on wood, apply a small amount of **rubbing alcohol** to the mark with a **cotton swab** and wait five minutes. Then blot the stain with a **clean white towel**. If ink remains, apply alcohol again. Wait 24 hours for the wood to completely dry and then polish it. If ink remains after two alcohol applications, use an **orange-based cleaner** to remove the mark.

Iron

Wrought iron, as defined metallurgically and by the process used in working the metal, is not produced anymore except for restorations. (Real wrought iron is worked white hot, hammered, and twisted into shape.) Today the term is often used, incorrectly, to include decorative iron, "mild steel," or cast iron.

Indoor iron pieces—such as bed frames, lamps, and chandeliers—are dust magnets. If your piece has a black-satin finish,

you might as well be shining a spotlight on the dust—everyone will see it. The easiest and quickest way to clean indoor pieces is with **compressed air**. It just blows the dust away and is especially good for all the edges, corners, and crevices of detailed iron, which defy the reach of a conventional cleaning rag. An alternative: Dust that intricate ornamentation with an **unused, soft-bristled paintbrush**.

To clean a smooth piece of wrought iron, wipe first with a **soft cotton rag**, to remove dust, and then wipe with any **furniture polish** sprayed onto a clean section of the rag. If there's dirt stuck to the wrought iron, the furniture polish may help lubricate and remove it. Water isn't recommended. It will collect in areas that can't be reached by a drying cloth, leading to rust. Furniture polish, on the other hand, provides a protective coating that repels water and resists dust.

To clean outdoor furniture that has a rust look or patina, let your item reach the desired rusty brown before you clean. Wipe off loose rust, dust, or dirt with a **rag**. Then coat the piece with a clear **lacquer paint** (available at hardware stores) to protect it from the elements and to prevent further rusting.

Seasoning: Old-Timey 'Teflon'

When you buy a new piece of cast-iron cookware, you need to season it. We're not talking about paprika here. Seasoning is a process that will protect your new pot from rust and give it a natural nonstick surface.

There are a number of methods for seasoning a new iron pot, but when Ronald V. O'Kelly tells you how, you know it's tried-and-true. After all, he's the owner of Frontier America Trading in Seattle, a merchandiser devoted to the kind of equipment Americans used in the 18th and 19th centuries. Here's his technique:

First, clean the new pot with dishwashing detergent and warm water to remove oils and debris from the manufacturing process. Fill the pot about two-thirds full with water. Add 1/3 cup white vinegar per 1 gallon water and boil the mixture for one hour. Let it cool and then dump the vinegar water. If the pot is rough, scour the inside with fine-grit wet/dry sandpaper or steel wool.

Wash the pot inside and out with plain water. Apply a light coating of vegetable oil or lard on the inside and outside surfaces. (Using a spray cooking oil is fine.) Heat the pot in a 250° to 350° F oven for an hour and then turn off the oven and let the cookware cool with the oven door closed. When the item has cooled, wipe off any excess oil. The seasoning is complete.

Now raise your right hand and take this oath: "From now on, no soap will touch the inside of this cast-iron pot." If you fail in this, you'll have to reseason it. Store it dry, with a very light coating of oil. Too much oil will leave a sticky mess.

The more you cook, the better the seasoning gets. With proper care, your pot should not rust. But if it does, repeat the seasoning process.

IRON

Outdoor furniture that isn't supposed to rust needs to be cleaned only when it looks dirty or has mud or grime caked on it. Remove dirt by spraying with a *garden hose*. Periodically check the piece for rust, which may start around areas such as bolts. If you see minor oxidation, gently apply a dry *wire brush* to remove the rust. Wipe off any dust particles you create. Before applying *touch-up paint* to the surface, wipe the area clean with *acetone* or *paint thinner* on a *cotton cloth*. This will make the paint adhere better by removing oils that got on the iron from your hands. It also will dissolve any remaining paint in the rusty area. Let the paint thinner dry before painting. Wear *gloves* and *goggles*, as acetone and paint thinner can be quite harsh to the skin and eyes.

Note: If your wrought iron has a lot of rust on it, you may have to take it to a professional for sandblasting.

To clean cast iron, the stuff poured into a mold at a foundry, use the same cleaning methods used on wrought iron. Cast-iron items typically include doorknobs, mailboxes, railings, and fences. *Hose* down such an item and then inspect it for rust. If you find rust, clean it with a *wire brush*. Then wipe away any dust your cleaning produced. A *rust-preventive paint*, such as Rust-Oleum, comes in many colors and is great for small touch-ups—indoors and outdoors—to protect the object from further rusting. Spray- and paint-on versions are available.

Cleaning well-seasoned iron cookware requires very little effort. Generally, all that's required is a little *boiling water*, light scraping with a *wooden spoon*, and a quick wipe with a *clean cloth*. Dry thoroughly and lightly oil again. For badly burned-on food, use a *copper wool scouring pad*. For extreme cases of burned-on food and grease, use any *common oven cleaner* according to the package directions. Rinse well. Then, unfortunately, you'll have to season the item as if it were a new piece. (See box, previous page.)

Store pots with the lids off to prevent condensation. Keep your cookware clean, dry, and oiled. Soak badly rusted pots overnight in *kerosene*, then scour. A *wire brush* is the best tool for removing rust. Really bad cases of rust may require *sandpaper or commercial rust removers*.

Irons

You've made the classic ironing boo-boo, and you have synthetic fibers stuck to the soleplate—your iron's flat undersurface.

To remove fibers such as nylon and polyester, heat the iron until the fibers liquefy. Then, on nonstick and aluminum or chrome soleplates, use a ***wooden spatula*** or ***flat stick*** (for instance, a Popsicle stick) to scrape off the fibers. Never scrape with plastic, metal, or anything abrasive. Run the iron over a ***terry cloth towel*** or some other rough material that the remaining fibers can stick to.

If you don't know what's stuck on your soleplate and the mark doesn't liquefy when you heat the iron, use any ***hot iron cleaner***, available at fabric shops and hardware stores.

If the stain still remains on an aluminum or chrome soleplate, your next option is to make a paste of ***baking soda*** and ***water*** in the consistency of toothpaste. Rub it on a cool iron with a ***soft cloth***, then wipe it off with ***another damp cloth***. Don't use this method on nonstick soleplates.

On Teflon or metallic coating nonstick surfaces, a ***damp cloth*** should wipe off any water marks, and a wooden spatula should remove any fiber stains. Should marks still remain, rub a ***nylon scouring pad*** on the iron's soleplate when it's *cool*.

Here's how to clean specific substances from your iron:

- To clean sticky, oil-based residue from an aluminum or chrome soleplate, use an ***all-purpose cleaner*** on a cold iron. Spray the cleaner onto the soleplate and rub with a ***soft cloth***. Remove the cleaner by rubbing with a ***wet cloth***. (Never rinse the electrical appliance in water.) Before using the iron again, heat it and rub the soleplate on a ***terry cloth rag*** to remove any traces of the cleaner and residue.
- To clean acetate or nylon that has melted and hardened on the soleplate, use ***acetone*** on a ***cloth*** and rub the affected area of the cold soleplate until the melted residue is gone. Don't get the acetone on the plastic shell of the iron, because the acetone will melt it.
- To clean a waxy stain (from a crayon, for instance), heat your iron as hot as possible and iron ***newspaper*** until the wax is gone. Don't worry. The print won't come off on your iron.
- To remove small bits of burned lint, use your iron's "burst of steam" feature as directed.
- To prevent stains from forming on the soleplate (so you can avoid having to clean as above), use a ***press cloth***, a lightweight pure cotton cloth, which will act as a barrier between the iron and your clothing. A press cloth will prevent synthetic fibers or starch from attaching to the iron.

To clean the iron's steam chamber, check the manufacturer's guidelines about the type of water to use, *distilled* or *tap water*. Generally, newer models use tap water—the minerals actually help in the steaming process. With the cord unplugged, fill the iron with water. Then plug in the iron and, depending on your model, either turn the iron to its cleaning mode function (most manufacturers recommend using the self-cleaning feature once a year) or to the steaming feature. Hold the steaming iron over a *sink*, the soleplate facedown, until the steam stops. Unplug the iron and leave it in the sink for another half hour to fully dry. An alternative: Place the iron facedown on a *heatproof cooking rack* while it steams. The steam will remove lint, dirt, dust, and mineral deposits that have built up in the steam vents. Finish by wiping with a *dry cloth*.

If you haven't steamed your iron for a while, you may find that the water or steam looks rusty. This is actually burned lint, which can stain your clothes. So it's important to clean your steam chamber and vents every couple of months.

Another way to clean the steam chamber: If the steam-cleaning technique described above doesn't remove the mineral deposits from the steam chamber, try using vinegar if your manufacturer's instructions allow it. Pour *white vinegar* into the steam chamber and steam it through the vents. Rinse out the vinegar and refill the chamber with *water*. Let the water steam through the iron to remove all the vinegar. If you're not careful about removing the vinegar, it may stain your clothes the next time you use the iron. The acidic nature of the vinegar may also etch and damage the interior of the iron if left inside the steam chamber. Besides, you don't want to walk around smelling like a salad.

In case the steam vents on the soleplate become clogged, unbend a *paper clip* and push it into the holes to reopen the vents ◀ before steaming the iron.

Cleaning the iron's outer shell is simple. Just wipe it with a damp rag. Always dry and cool your iron before putting it away, and store it in an upright position on the heel rest.

Ivory and Bone

Treat ivory and bone with care. Whether you're cleaning a figurine or a beaded necklace, it's important to assess the condition of the item, because that will determine your approach.

Does your ivory piece come from the tusk of an elephant or mammoth? If so, you have true ivory. Today, however, the tusks of other mammals, such as those of walruses and certain whales, and some synthetics are considered ivory as well. Ivory is chemically similar to bone and antler, but there are differences. Ivory has no blood vessels, whereas bone does. Bone is fragile and porous, whereas ivory is dense. Ivory and bone are similar in this respect: They're sensitive to heat, light, and moisture.

If your ivory item is fragile, take it to a conservator to be cleaned. Because ivory readily absorbs oils and stains, wear ***white cotton gloves*** while working with ivory, or, at the very least, wash your hands with ***soap and water*** to remove oils and dirt.

If your ivory or bone is sturdy and stable, clean off the surface dust or dirt with a ***barely damp cotton cloth or cotton swabs***. To dampen, use a solution of ***mild dishwashing detergent*** and ***water*** or use just water. If you use too much moisture, surface fractures may appear on the ivory. Now wipe the surface of your item with a ***dry cloth*** and apply a ***second cloth or cotton swab*** dampened with ***mineral spirits*** to remove any soap residue. Wipe with a ***dry cloth***.

   Never rub the surface of ivory and bone. You don't want to remove the original surface coats, pigments, or patinas.

To remove wax or oil from ivory, use a ***cloth*** or ***cotton swab*** barely dampened with ***mineral spirits***. If your ivory or bone has scrimshaw (engravings or decorations) on it, test an inconspicuous part of the scrimshaw to see whether it will withstand the cleaning technique. If it doesn't react well to the test, don't clean the scrimshaw yourself.

If your ivory or bone is stained (a yellowing stain is typical), you'll have to call a conservator. These stains are usually due to oxidation that comes with age or may be caused by the oils on your hands. Sometimes, placing the ivory or bone in sunlight bleaches it and helps it regain its warm white color. Keeping ivory or bone in the dark accelerates the yellowing associated with aging. But do not expose ivory or bone to long periods of intense sunlight or heat, because that will dry it out and cause it to crack.

Store ivory and bone in a carefully controlled environment, ideally 45 percent to 55 percent relative humidity and about 70° F, in low light. Conditions should be kept constant. The most severe damage to ivory and bone is caused by fluctuations in relative humidity and temperature. Low humidity will dry ivory out, causing shrinkage and cracking. High humidity and changes in temperature can cause your ivory to expand and contract.

WATCH OUT

All of these factors could damage your ivory or bone:
• Display areas exposed to sunlight or a spotlight
• A closed display case with light bulbs inside, heating the interior
• Nearby ventilation or heating ducts, the tops of appliances, or other sources of heat or cold
• Sulfur in rubber-based storage materials, adhesives, and paint (because sulfur in rubber can discolor ivory)

Kitchen Cabinets

You may not have a secretary of state or defense, but your kitchen cabinets contain many of the essentials of your household administration. So they should be handsome and clean.

To routinely clean the cabinet exteriors, dust with a *clean cloth* regularly and wipe with a *damp cloth* periodically. (In terms of frequency, the meaning of *regularly* and *periodically* will depend on your specific cabinets and frequency of use of the cabinets.) Never use abrasive cleaners or scourers on kitchen cabinets. Also avoid using your dishcloth, because it may contain grease or detergents that can add streaks and smears.

To wipe away the stains around handles on cabinet doors and drawers, bring on the heavy artillery, because those stains will probably be the most troublesome, being a mixture of skin oils, food smears, and softened finish. On cabinets made of plastic laminate, metal, or glass, try a strong *all-purpose household cleaner*, such as those you find in supermarkets. Spray it onto a *cloth or sponge* and apply to the dirty areas. Let the cleaner sit for a few minutes and then wipe it off with a *rinsed-out cloth or sponge*. Wipe with a *dry cloth*.

To clean wood cabinets, first try a little *dishwashing detergent* applied directly to a *cloth or sponge*. Rub into the dirty areas around the hardware. Then wash the entire cabinet with an *oil soap solution*. Use *1/4 cup of oil soap* (such as Murphy Oil Soap) to *1 gallon of water*. Apply with a *cloth* dipped in the solution and wrung out. Then go over the cabinets with a *cloth* dampened in *plain water*, followed by a *dry cloth*.

To protect the surface of the cabinets, apply a wax suitable for your cabinets' material. *Car wax or other paste waxes* work well on wood. Once a year, apply thinly to a clean surface with a *clean cloth* and then buff.

To clean cabinets that have windows, wash the glass with a cloth or *paper towel* sprayed with a little *glass cleaner*. Don't spray cleaner, or even plain water, directly onto the glass—it can drip down and damage the surrounding wood.

To clean the shelves, use the same methods as for the exterior surfaces. Shelves need cleaning only once or twice a year—assuming you clean up any spills as soon as they happen. To remove an old spill, sprinkle with *baking soda* and wipe with a *damp cloth*.

Knickknacks

Dust more, wash less. Or dust less, wash more. Take your pick. If you swoosh away the dust from your glass menagerie or curios often, it won't have a chance to turn to greasy grime that will require a more intrusive cleaning job.

To dust a whole rack of knickknacks, use a *hair dryer* or *feather duster* every couple of days—if you're of the swooshing school. Or wipe them, one at a time, with a clean *microfiber cloth* once a week. Either way, you'll probably rarely need to wash them.

To wash your knickknacks, mix a little *dishwashing liquid* in *warm water* in a *plastic bowl* and immerse the knickknacks, assuming they're made of china, glass, plastic, or metal. Use a *clean, thick cotton sock*, worn over your hand, as a cleaning mitt. That will get into most crevices. Use an *old toothbrush* on places that your hand can't get to. Rinse the items well with *fresh water* and dry with a *clean cloth*.

For an even speedier wash, run your knickknacks through the *dishwasher* on the gentlest setting.

To clean cloth items, try the *vacuum cleaner* first, using the *brush or crevice attachment*. If that isn't enough, put the articles in a *paper bag*, add a *couple of tablespoons of baking soda*, shake, and then shake some more. Remove the items from the bag and *brush* or vacuum off the baking soda.

Knives

Do you want a bright and shiny knife at all times? That would be stainless steel. The downside is that when it loses its edge, it doesn't take well to sharpening. Or would you prefer a really sharp knife, one that you can easily sharpen? That would be carbon steel. The downside is that it's difficult to keep bright and shiny.

To clean knives of either type, wash immediately after use in a little *dishwashing soap* and *hot water* with a *cloth or sponge*. Rinse with *hot water* and wipe with a *dry cloth*.

To remove stains from a carbon steel blade, try a paste made of *salt* and *vinegar*. Rub it on the blade with a cloth. Or dip a *slice of lemon* into *salt* and rub that on the blade. Some stains will respond to a *nylon scrubber* or *steel wool*.

To shine the blade, use *silver polish*, or even better, *Simichrome*, a German all-metal polish available at some auto supply stores. Or find it on the Internet by using a search engine and entering the name *Simichrome* in the search window.

To protect the edges of knives, store them in a *rack* or, if in a drawer, cover the blades with *cardboard sleeves*. You can make a sleeve by cutting a piece of *cardboard* (from a cereal box, for example) the length of the blade and twice as wide. Fold the cardboard in half lengthwise. Use *tape* to seal the side and one end. Insert the knife in the open end.

To clean a pocketknife, open all the blades—and in a Swiss Army–type knife, all those other gizmos, too. Wash them in *hot, soapy water*. Remove dirt from the little slots with a *toothbrush*. Rinse in *hot water*, dry with a *clean cloth*, and leave the knife open for a while to allow the slots to dry thoroughly. Lubricate the hinges periodically with a little *gun oil* or *sewing machine oil*, available at gun shops or fabric stores, respectively.

To clean a hunting knife, use the same method as for a pocketknife. After using your knife in the field, rinse it off in a *stream*, if possible, or wipe it clean with *leaves or grass*.

Life on the Edge

A sharp carbon steel knife edge has lots of practically invisible "teeth," which get bent out of line during use. Keep them as straight as possible by using a honing steel before each use.

1. Hold the steel in your left hand (if you're right-handed).
2. Place the knife against the steel at a 20- to 25-degree angle.
3. Draw the knife across, heel to tip, so that the entire blade passes over the top of the steel.
4. Repeat with the other side of the knife on the bottom of the steel. Continue for about a dozen strokes.

Eventually, the blade will get so dull that honing will no longer be effective. Then it's time for sharpening, a process that removes some metal and leaves a new edge. Many hardware, kitchen, or department stores offer sharpening service.

Lace

What does a prizewinning sheep have in common with lace? They both like to be washed with the same soap, one developed by Procter & Gamble for use on animals but now also used on delicate textiles.

Some precautions first. Lace is delicate material, so you shouldn't be surprised that there's a list of don'ts about cleaning it:

- Don't use the washing machine, dryer, your usual detergents or soaps, chlorine bleach, lemon juice, or salt.
- Don't rub lace or lift it by itself while it's wet.
- Don't send it to a dry cleaner, except for recently made lace that specifies dry cleaning on the care label.
- Don't clean fragile, old, or valuable lace yourself. Turn the job over to a professional conservator. You should wash only sturdy lace—for example, a tablecloth of no great value.

To clean lace, place a ***clean white towel*** in the bottom of the ***sink or bathtub*** you'll be using. Lay the lace cloth on the towel. Mix ***1 teaspoon of Orvus WA Paste*** per ***1 gallon of warm water***. (Orvus, the animal-cleaning soap mentioned above, is available at quilt shops, museum shops, tack shops, and farm supply stores and from that friendly sheep next door.) Make enough of the solution to cover the cloth. Soak for 15 minutes and then agitate by gently lifting and lowering the towel.

To rinse lace, use ***room–temperature distilled water***. Keep changing the ***water*** until it is totally clear. Drain. Use the towel as a sling to lift the lace.

To dry lace, first blot up as much water as possible with ***dry towels*** and then lay the lace flat on a ***clean, dry towel*** to dry completely.

To restore the shape of lace that has to fit a dress collar, for example, trace its shape on a piece of paper before washing it. Place the tracing on a corkboard and put a sheet of clear plastic over it. After washing the lace, place it over the plastic and gently shape it to fit the tracing. Then use stainless pins to hold the lace in place while it dries ▶.

▲

Lacquer

Lacquer is eye-catching because of its mirrorlike finish and also because that finish often belongs to furniture, such as a dining table or piano, that is the focal point of a room.

To dust a lacquered surface, use a *large, folded piece of cheesecloth* slightly moistened with *water*. Don't wipe in a circular motion—that could leave "whirlpools" on the finish. Wipe in only one direction, the one in which the piece was originally polished, if you can determine that.

To clean when dusting isn't enough, mix a little *dishwashing detergent* in *tepid water*, dip in a *soft cloth*, and wring it out. Wipe the surface down. Wipe again with a rinsed-out damp cloth, then again with a *dry cloth*.

To polish a dulled surface, use a *nonsilicone paste wax*. Silicone will cause problems if the piece ever needs to be refinished. Apply the wax with a *soft cloth* in one direction and buff the same way. Don't overdo the buffing, because rubbing creates static electricity, which will attract dust particles.

Lamps

Cleaning your lamps won't lead to fame and fortune as it did for Aladdin, but it will save you money, and it's guaranteed to brighten your surroundings.

To remove dust from a lamp, use a *microfiber cloth* regularly. The *vacuum cleaner* with its *brush attachment* may work better on some materials, such as unglazed pottery or wood. The more often you dust, the less often you'll have to do more intensive cleaning of your lamp.

Include the light bulb in your routine—that's where the money-saving comes in. Dust buildup reduces bulb efficiency, wastes energy, and raises your electricity bill.

To remove dirt, first unplug the lamp and remove the shade and the bulb. Start with a *clean cloth* or *sponge* dampened with plain *water*. Wipe all parts of the lamp, starting with the base and working up. Don't wet the socket or the plug.

To avoid dulling the finish, buff the lamp immediately with a *clean, dry cloth*. To attack more stubborn dirt, try about *1/2 teaspoon of dishwashing detergent* applied directly to a *cloth or sponge*. Wipe the dirty areas, scrubbing gently if necessary. Rinse the cloth or sponge in *clear water* and go over the surface to remove the detergent. Follow with the dry cloth. Polish the lamp occasionally with a *polish* suitable for the material the lamp is made of.

To wash glass globes or chimneys, clean them with a *cloth or sponge* and a solution of *hot water* and a little *dishwashing deter-*

gent. It's OK to immerse those parts as long as they don't have electrical connectors. Rinse with a solution of *hot water* and a *dash of ammonia* and wipe dry with a *clean cloth*.

Lamp Shades

A lamp shade can sometimes be a life-of-the-party hat, but more often it sets the mood in a room by directing and softening light. It does this best when it's clean.

To remove dust before it turns to grime, go over the surface— inside and out—with

- a *vacuum cleaner* with the *small brush attachment* for sturdy cloth shades;
- a *microfiber cloth* for glass, plastic, paper, or metal shades;
- a *soft-bristled horsehair paintbrush* for silk, acetate, and pleated shades ▶.

▲

Regular dusting will help you avoid higher-impact cleaning, which can be messy for you and dangerous for your lamp shade. Water can dissolve glue, for example, and this can cause the shade to fall apart.

To remove serious dirt, the safest cleaning method after dusting is to use a special sponge that's intended to be used dry. Ask for a *dry-cleaning sponge* at a hardware or home improvement store. Use it like an eraser to rub away dirt. Try it on any shade, but be sure to use it instead of water on paper shades and any other shade with glue.

To clean fabric shades that are stitched rather than glued, wash them in the *bathtub*. And while you're going to the trouble of doing one, it makes sense to do all your shades that need it. Metal and plastic shades can also be cleaned in the tub at the same time. To wash the shades, begin by drawing a *couple of inches of tepid water* into the tub. Add *1 tablespoon of dishwashing detergent* and swish it around. Lay the shade on its side in the tub and gently roll it in the water. Metal and plastic shades can stand a little more vigorous cleaning, with a *cloth or sponge*. Change the *water* when it becomes dirty and wash again.

To rinse, drain the wash water and draw *clear water*. Again, roll the shade in the water and change the *water* when it turns gray. Metal and plastic shades can be rinsed under *running water* and wiped dry with a *cloth*.

To dry a cloth shade, use a *towel* to press out as much water as you can. Finish with a *hair dryer*, tipping the shade upside down

frequently so that no water settles in the bottom of the shade, where it could leave a water stain. Drying quickly is important, because the metal parts of the shade can rust and stain the fabric.

To clean a glass shade, fill a *sink* with *warm water* and add *1 or 2 teaspoons of ammonia*. Immerse the shade in the water and wash it with a *cloth*. Use a *toothbrush* to get into crevices. Rinse and dry with a *clean cloth*.

Lattices

Lattices make attractive additions to a lawn or garden, but all those cracks and crevices! They create so many places for dirt and grime to hide.

To clean lattices with no plants attached, use a *hose* with a nozzle that sends the *water* out in a tightly focused stream. Use a *stiff-bristled nylon or fiber brush* to scrub dirty spots. If the lattices are wood, use the brush sparingly; you can use a freer hand on lattices of plastic, fiberglass, or metal. You may also use a *power washer*, available at tool-rental shops.

To attack that green moldy-mossy stuff that grows in shady spots, mix a solution of *1 gallon of water* and *1 1/2 cups of chlorine bleach* in a *bucket*. Scrub the solution on with a *brush*. Rinse with *plain water*.

simple SOLUTIONS

Plants in Your Way? >

To clean lattices that are supporting plants, wash them in the early spring. Prune the plants back to about 6 inches—most vines can easily take it—and remove the rest of the plant material from the lattices.

Lawn Mowers

Take good care of your power mower, and it will take good care of your lawn. Good care means keeping the mower clean and maintaining it regularly.

To clean the underside, make sure the engine is off and can't accidentally start. Remove the spark plug wire (or in the case of an electric mower, make sure it is unplugged). Prop up one side of the mower on a *block*—don't turn it completely over. Use a *garden hose* to wash off loose grass and dirt. Then remove the remainder with a *putty knife*, followed by a *stiff-bristled brush*. If you do this every time you use the mower, you'll never get that caked, cruddy grass buildup.

On the mower's exterior, keep the engine free of dead grass, leaves, and grease (fire hazard). To keep the mower running well, brush off the air-intake screen and the cooling fins on the engine with a *stiff brush* to keep them free of debris.

Attend to the mower's air filter after every 25 hours of use. Replace a *disposable paper filter* (available where lawn mowers are sold). A foam–type filter has a removable sponge that should be soaked in *warm water* and then dried. Follow by putting a *few drops of clean engine oil* into the sponge and squeezing it to distribute the oil. Then reinstall the sponge.

An annual professional tune-up for your lawn mower will save you a lot of trouble. It should include a carburetor adjustment and a cleaning of belts, cables, and switches. It also can include sharpening the blade and changing the oil, spark plug, and air filter if you prefer not to do those things yourself.

simple SOLUTIONS

A Kitchen Solution to a Yard Problem >

To prevent grass and dirt buildup under the deck of your lawn mower, use spray-on vegetable cooking oil. Clean the underside and then apply the oil on the metal after it dries. This will make it easy to clean the mower after each use.

Leaded Glass and Stained Glass

The lead in leaded glass does not refer to the glass or to lead crystal. It refers to the material used in the *cames*, which are the grooved metal rods that hold the panes of glass together. Some cames are made of copper or zinc, but it's still called leaded glass because lead got there first, historically speaking.

Stained glass is associated mostly with churches, but leaded and stained glass windows were stylish in homes, institutions, and transom windows in commercial buildings from about 1895 to 1925. Of course, there are also recent examples, and craftspeople make a wide variety of ornaments out of leaded and stained glass. The following directions for windows can also be applied to less hefty objects, such as lamp shades, boxes, light (or sun) catchers, and more.

WATCH OUT

If the glass has painting on it, don't clean it at all. Even water might damage or remove fragile paint. Painted parts of a window are usually recognizable as something like a bird or a face applied onto the glass, rather than an integral part of it. House numbers are also sometimes painted on.

Taking the *Long View*

Leaded and stained glass windows can last for centuries, as countless European churches show. But over time, they are subject to such ills as
• broken or cracked glass,
• loosened lead around the glass,
• broken or missing lead or solder joints,
• deterioration of putty, glass paint, or the frame that holds the window.

If you have a window that is more than 50 years old, it's a good idea to have a condition study done. Julie L. Sloan, a stained glass conservation consultant in North Adams, Massachusetts, says such a study will identify any problems and can be the focus of a restoration plan.

If you belong to a church with stained glass windows and want to participate in their preservation, you might organize a group to commission such a study. To find a consultant, seek advice from museums or large churches that have used such services. The next step would probably be to raise money, because window restoration is a time-consuming and expensive project demanding professional help.

To clean leaded or stained glass, use plain, *warm water*. Wash each pane individually with a *clean cloth* dampened in the water. If necessary, use a *cotton swab* to get into corners ◀. Don't use a spray bottle, because the water will drool into the cames. Wipe dry with a *clean, soft cloth or chamois cloth*. Never apply much force when washing such windows, because you can actually bend them, especially if the cames are lead, which is a very soft metal. Use only the damp cloth for cleaning the cames.

For more cleaning power, use *1 teaspoon of rubbing alcohol* in *1 quart of warm water* and follow the same procedure outlined above. If dirt or some kind of old finish remains, leave it alone. Never use common household glass cleaners, vinegar, lemon, ammonia, or any kind of abrasive cleaner.

Leather

Leather means any skin or hide that has been tanned, but after that the similarities end and the differences begin. Two main categories of leather require different cleaning techniques.

- Natural leather has little surface protection and is highly susceptible to staining. It is not dyed with pigments, has no finish coat of polyurethane, and is recognizable by its rustic, natural appearance. Even water or treatments suitable for other kinds of leather, such as saddle soap, may mar its surface.
- Coated leather has a pigment-dyed surface treated with a polyurethane coating. Most—but not all—leather garments, upholstery, purses, and shoes are coated leather.

A few guidelines apply to both kinds:

- If you have directions from the manufacturer, follow them.
- Test any cleaning method on an inconspicuous area before using it generally.
- For any valuable leather article or serious cleaning problem, consult a professional, such as a dry cleaner who specializes in cleaning leather.
- Avoid harsh cleaners and even excessive water, which can leave stains and remove dye and lubricants.
- Never dry wet leather near a heat source.

To clean natural leather, rely on frequent dusting with a *soft cloth*. You could try removing dirt with an *art gum eraser*, available at stationery and art supply stores, but even that might leave a smudge. There is little more you can do without making a problem worse. (See also *Suede*.)

LEADED GLASS AND STAINED GLASS

To clean coated leathers, dust regularly with a *cloth*, occasionally with a *dampened cloth*. Wash every six months or so with saddle soap, which is available at tack shops, sporting goods stores, some shoe stores, and hardware stores. Here's how:

1. Remove loose dirt with a *stiff brush or damp cloth*.
2. Rub a *damp cloth* on *saddle soap* and work up a lather.
3. Rub the soapy cloth on the leather using a circular motion. Wipe away the excess with *another damp cloth*. Let air-dry.
4. Buff with a *clean, soft cloth*.
5. Finish with a *protective leather cream* recommended by the manufacturer or a general-purpose one sold by leather retailers.

To treat spots on coated leathers, try these methods—but don't forget to test first:

- Apply *cornstarch* to greasy spots and let it absorb the grease. Wipe off with a *cloth*.
- Rub with a *cotton swab* dipped in *rubbing alcohol*.
- Make a paste of *equal parts lemon juice* and *cream of tartar*, work it into the spot (including scuff marks) with a *cloth*, let it sit for an hour or so, and wipe clean.
- Treat those ugly white stains on shoes and boots caused by water and road salt with a *50–50 mixture* of *water* and *white vinegar*. Dip a *cloth* into the solution and blot.
- On mildew, use a *50–50 solution* of *rubbing alcohol* and *water* on a *cloth*. *Saddle soap* also may work.

See also **Shoes**.

Light Fixtures

How do they manage it, those bugs? How do they sneak into a ceiling light fixture that has no visible gaps? Whatever their secret, now and then you will want to remove their dried-out little bodies—and clean the fixture too.

To clean a wall or ceiling fixture, first turn off the switch and plant a sturdy *stepladder* nearby. Remove any grilles, shades, shields, globes, light bulbs, or light tubes. This would be a good time to be one of those many-armed gods, as you may have to hold onto a globe while you remove screws and balance yourself to keep from falling.

To wash the removable parts, fill the *sink* with *hot water* and add a little *dishwashing detergent*. Lay a *towel or rubber mat* on the bottom of the sink to prevent damage. Immerse the pieces— except for the light bulbs or tubes—and clean with a *soft cloth* *or sponge*. Rinse and dry well with a **soft cloth**. Wipe the light bulbs or light tubes with a **damp cloth**, avoiding the ends that go into the sockets.

To wash the fixed parts, use a **cloth or sponge** dipped into the same **cleaning solution** and squeezed until it's barely damp. Wipe the fixture, being careful not to get any moisture in the socket or on the wiring. Rinse the sponge or cloth in **clean water** and wipe the fixture with it again. Wipe everything dry with **another cloth**, reassemble the fixture, and stand by with the flyswatter.

Litter Boxes

How, and how often, you clean Kitty's litter box depends on the litter and the box—and, especially, on Kitty, who's the boss.

Here are the basics for keeping the "boss" happy:
- To clean a litter box tray, remove solids daily—and don't slack off, or Kitty may find another spot to use.
- For a clumping litter, remove the poop and the urine clumps with a **slotted scoop** available at pet and discount stores. Clumping litter should be dumped and the box washed about every two weeks—sooner if your nose or eyes say it's time.
- For nonclumping litter, remove the solids daily with a **scoop**, and change the litter and wash the box once a week or more often if needed.
- To clean the self-cleaning boxes, which can include motors and other moving parts, follow the manufacturer's directions.

To wash the box, use a little **dishwashing detergent** and **water** and scrub with a **stiff brush**. Avoid using any cleaner with a strong smell, such as scented detergents or ammonia, which could turn up a sensitive feline nose. But do disinfect with a solution of **1 part chlorine bleach** to **10 parts water**. Rinse thoroughly with **plain water**—Kitty's nose, again—and if possible dry in the **sunshine**, a natural disinfectant. Otherwise, wipe dry with a **clean cloth** before adding fresh litter.

To stop the footprints emanating from the box area, put a piece of **carpet** or a **rubber mat** where Kitty leaves the box. This will collect some of the granules. More effective (and more expensive) is the special **Litter Welcome Mat**, which is a removable grid over a collecting tray. It's available for about $15 at some pet stores and many Internet sites. Maybe you can even teach Kitty to wipe its feet. (Fat chance!)

**OOPS!**

Whatever Kitty Wants, Kitty Gets >

You had the best intentions in the world in buying the scented litter, thinking your cat would appreciate the scent as much as you do. But alas, cats' noses are extremely sensitive—and unpredictable. Some cats take offense at even such a mild, inoffensive substance as baking soda.

If Kitty suddenly stops using its litter box and has substituted something else—such as the dining room rug—scent may be the problem. Switch to an unscented litter and see if that helps. If not, buy a new box. A lingering, if faint, urine smell embedded in the plastic could also be the cause of Kitty's litter issues.

Locks

You may never have given a thought to cleaning a lock. But when turning the key becomes difficult or impossible, dirt may be the problem.

To clean the lock exterior, wipe with a *damp cloth or sponge*. For more power, use a little *dishwashing detergent* applied to the cloth. Rinse the cloth before rinsing the lock parts. Wipe dry with a *clean cloth* and buff.

To achieve more shine, apply a polish appropriate to the metal, or use *Simichrome*, an all-metal polish available at some auto supply stores and Internet sites.

To clean the inside of a door lock, give it a good dousing with a *penetrating lubricant* such as WD-40. Take the *tiny tube* that comes with the lubricant and fit it over the spray nozzle. Poke the other end of the tube into the keyhole and spray for 10 seconds while holding a *paper towel* underneath to catch excess lubricant. This will flush out any grime and will not attract dirt. Don't use conventional oil inside a lock, as dust will stick to it and gum up the mechanism.

To clean a lock that no longer works, first take it apart. Wash the inside parts with a *degreaser*, following the label directions. Then lubricate the parts with a *multipurpose lubricant*. Both are available at hardware and auto supply stores.

simple SOLUTIONS

That Hard-to-Turn Lock >

To loosen a dead bolt that resists turning, insert graphite shavings in the keyhole. The graphite comes in a tube at hardware stores.

Louvers

Louver lovers like the look and the breeziness, but they dread the cleaning. Frequent dusting will postpone the day you have to tackle any heavy dirt buildup.

To dust louvers, you have several options. Use these tools separately or in combination:
- The *brush attachment* of a *vacuum cleaner*
- A soft *paintbrush* ▶
- A *clean, white cloth* wrapped around a *ruler or putty knife* or other flat object
- A *lamb's wool duster*

Dust from top to bottom, using a gentle wiping action, not a flicking one that will send dust back into the air. Shake the duster outside, not in the house.

To clean dirt from painted louvers—or louvers that have been coated with varnish or polyurethane—wipe with a *damp cloth*. For any grime you can't remove that way, rub with a little *dishwashing detergent* applied directly to the cloth. Rinse the cloth in *plain water* and wipe again. Some alternatives:

- Scrub with a *clean, handled paint pad*, which should fit between all but the most tightly spaced louvers.
- Dampen a *cotton glove* in *water*, squirt some *dishwashing liquid* on it, put the glove on, and slide each finger between a different slat. With this method, you can clean several louvers at the same time. Rinse with *another damp glove* or a *damp cloth*.

To clean wood that has an oil finish, wipe with a *cloth* dampened with *boiled linseed oil, mineral spirits*, or *turpentine*, all available at hardware and paint stores.

To clean jalousie windows, the glass version of louvers:

1. Mix a solution of *1 cup of vinegar* in *1 gallon of water*.
2. Open the window to its fullest extent so the slats are perpendicular to the window frame.
3. Take a *thick white cotton sock* and dip it into the solution; wring it out.
4. Put the sock over your hand like a mitten and clean the slats on both sides, one at a time, starting at the top.
5. Use another *clean, dry sock* to dry the slats in the same manner.

Luggage

Space-age technology has improved the materials used in today's luggage, making everything from flight bags to briefcases more durable and easier to clean.

To clean soft-sided luggage, use a mild, all-purpose cleaner mixed with water. One recommended cleaner is Simple Green, sold at supermarkets, hardware stores, drugstores, and auto stores. Mix *1 part all-purpose cleaner* to *7 parts water* and use a *brush, cleaning cloth, or sponge* to scrub dirt or spots with a circular motion, working your way outward. Most soft-sided luggage is made of tough nylon materials backed with plastic to repel water, and it is easily cleaned.

To clean hard-sided luggage, use a little *dishwashing detergent* in *warm water*. Wipe with a *sponge or cloth* that's been dipped into the solution and wrung out. Then rinse and dry. You can brighten the piece by waxing with a *silicone-based auto or furniture polish*, available at hardware stores. Follow the directions on the package. Don't use a combination cleaner-polish.

To clean leather luggage and briefcases, determine whether the leather has a natural or coated finish and follow the directions in the *Leather* entry.

To clean aluminum pieces, wash with a cloth dipped in the *dishwashing detergent solution* mentioned above. Never use ammonia-based cleaners, as they will darken the metal. For a nice shine and protection, polish with the all-metal cleaner *Simichrome*, available at some auto supply stores and on the Internet.

Lunch Boxes

With all the foodborne illnesses floating around, don't let any float into your environment via a crumby lunch box.

To clean metal or hard plastic lunch boxes, wash with a *sponge or cloth* in *hot water* and a little *dishwashing detergent*. Rinse and dry. Do this after each day's use.

To clean soft-sided lunch boxes and bags, wipe the inside with a *damp sponge or cloth*. For spills, use a sponge dampened in *hot, soapy water*. Allow to air-dry.

To clean a grimy old lunch box, begin by removing any loose dust or dirt with the *brush attachment* of your *vacuum cleaner*. You'll want as little scratchy stuff as possible on the lithograph design when you clean and polish it.

Wash the box using *hot water* with a little *dishwashing detergent*. Mix it in a separate container—not in the lunch box itself. Wash with a *sponge or soft cloth*, never with anything abrasive, and rinse the sponge under *running water* frequently. Scrub tough grime gently with a *toothbrush*, which is also useful for cleaning the handles. Rinse in *clear, warm water* and dry with a *soft cloth*. Leave the box open for an hour to let it dry thoroughly. Any wet areas are susceptible to rust.

To protect and polish the surface, apply a *nonabrasive auto polish* with a *soft cloth*, followed by a buffing with *another clean, soft cloth*. Use a *chrome polish* on the metal hardware, being careful not to get it on the lithograph. Auto and chrome polishes are available at hardware and auto supply stores.

Marble

Here's a stone-cold fact to keep in mind when cleaning marble: Although marble is a heavy stone that may seem indestructible, it is actually porous and far from impervious to harsh treatment.

In general, clean marble with a ***gentle liquid soap*** that does not have a grease remover. The safest course is to take it easy. Mix about ***2 tablespoons of mild liquid soap***, Ivory, for instance, in ***1/2 gallon of water***. Using a ***soft sponge***, or a ***sponge mop*** if you're cleaning a marble floor, wipe the marble clean. Follow with ***two to three water rinses***, depending on how soapy the cleaning mixture is. Then dry with a ***soft cloth***.

Clean marble floors regularly, before dirt and grit have a chance to scratch the surface. Wipe up spills immediately. As with a wood surface, avoid putting beverage glasses directly on marble, which can cause water rings. Water should bead on the marble. If the marble appears to be absorbing liquid, it's not sealed properly.

Reseal your marble floor annually at least—it's as easy as waxing a floor. Buy a ***stone sealer*** in a home improvement store. Take a ***sponge, sponge mop***, or ***rag*** and cover the entire marble surface, including corners and the backsplash. There's no need to strip the floor before you seal.

To clean surface stains, use a ***marble polishing powder***, such as tin oxide, which is available at home improvement stores. Follow the product's directions to the letter. If the marble item you're cleaning is stained but not of great value, you can try removing stains with a thick paste made of ***baking soda*** and ***water***. Apply the paste to the stain. Cover the paste with a ***sheet of plastic*** to keep the paste damp, and let it sit for 10 to 15 minutes before wiping it off. Rinse with ***warm water*** and dry. Repeat the procedure if the first application doesn't fully remove the stain. If stains still remain, it's time to call a professional marble restorer.

Mattresses and Box Springs

If you never give a thought to cleaning your mattress, here's a wake-up call: Dust mites are almost certainly feasting on dander in your neglected bed, and mold spores may also be multiplying.

Dust mites, tiny organisms that feed on the microscopic flakes of dead skin we all shed, can cause allergic reactions in some people, particularly those with asthma. Washing your sheets with

WATCH OUT

Never use lemon, vinegar, or any other acidic ingredient on marble. Acids will eat through the protective finish and damage the stone. Avoid ammonia as well. Abrasive cleaners like powdered Comet should not be used either, since the grit can scratch and dull the marble finish.

hot water and occasionally vacuuming the mattress will help keep mites under control.

Periodic care and cleaning of a mattress will prolong its life even if you don't have allergies. Here's how:

● Every six months, rotate your mattress end to end and *vacuum* the exposed surface. Run the *brush attachment* over the entire mattress, including the sides. This will remove not only dust mites, but also mold spores. Empty the vacuum cleaner bag outdoors after cleaning or, if the bag is disposable, throw it away.

● Once a year, flip the mattress over and *vacuum* it again. Remove the mattress and vacuum the box springs with the *brush attachment* as well. If you have the type of box springs with exposed springs, use a *bottle brush* to reach in there and lift away dust.

Removing stains from your mattress can be tricky, because moisture is a mattress's enemy. Clean with *upholstery shampoo*, following the package direction. Or you can lift the stains out using *dry suds*, which are made by whipping a grease-cutting *dishwashing liquid* or *clothes detergent* in water. Keep mixing until you have lots of suds.

Using a *clean cloth, soft brush, or sponge* dampened with *warm water*, apply the suds in a circular motion to the stain ▶. Then draw out the moisture with a *clean, dry towel*. Repeat the procedure if necessary, then wipe the area with a *clean cloth* dampened with *clear water*. Again, press a *dry towel* against the spot to draw out the moisture. The key is to leave as little water on the mattress as possible, because moisture in the mattress filling can lead to mold growth.

To speed drying, blow an *electric fan* toward the mattress, or haul the mattress outside and let the *sun* do the job. If you've cleaned the entire mattress (one small section at a time), you may want to use a *dehumidifier* in the bedroom to draw out even more moisture.

simple SOLUTIONS

Accidents Will Happen >

If bed-wetting is a problem in your house, invest in a waterproof mattress cover. But don't totally enclose your mattress in plastic. It needs to breathe. Get a cover with cloth sides and an open bottom.

Urine smells and stains are difficult to remove from a mattress. Sprinkle dry borax on the wet spot. Rub it in, let it dry, and vacuum.

▼

Medicine Cabinets

Family safety is the watchword when it comes to cleaning your medicine cabinet. Experts recommend an annual review of the contents of medicine cabinets and urge consumers to get rid of expired prescriptions, leftover antibiotics, cough syrup that has separated, and sterile gauze in broken packages.

Begin your review of medicines by examining the expiration date on each bottle or package and inspecting the contents for signs of deterioration. Pour expired liquids down the drain and flush expired pills down the toilet to keep them out of the mouths of children and pets. If you can't find an expiration date, it probably means the product was manufactured before the United States expiration date law went into effect in the 1980s. Which means it's old enough to retire. At the least, expired medications are ineffective. At worst, formulations that have degraded over time can create new problems when ingested. So when in doubt, throw it out.

Developing an annual clean-out habit works best if it's tied to some other event, such as spring cleaning.

Cleaning the medicine cabinet itself is simple. Use a *sponge* and mixture of *mild dishwashing liquid* in *warm water* to clean the interior and shelves. Or remove the shelves and put them in the top rack of your *dishwasher*.

*See also **Mirrors**.*

Microwave Ovens

Microwave ovens have revolutionized everyday cooking, and fast preparation isn't their only virtue. Compared to conventional ovens, microwaves are remarkably easy to clean.

To clean fresh food splatters before they have had time to dry, simply wipe down the microwave's interior with a *sponge or paper towel* dipped in a mixture of *dishwashing liquid* and *water*. Follow with a *clean water* rinse. Use the same method for washing removable trays or turntables in the sink.

To remove dried-on food, heat a *bowl* of *water* inside the microwave before cleaning. Heat *2 cups of water* for three to five minutes on high power. The resulting steam will soften the dried food. Then wipe down the interior with a *sponge or soft cloth*.

To get rid of odors in your microwave, wipe the interior with a solution of *1 cup of warm water* and *1 tablespoon of baking soda*. Rinse with *warm water*. Or combine *1 cup of water* with *1/2 cup of lemon juice* in a *measuring cup or bowl* and heat it on high for three to five minutes ◀. Let it stand in the microwave for five to ten minutes before removing.

MEDICINE CABINETS

To remove stains from the microwave's ceramic floor or turntable, make a paste of *baking soda* and *water* and apply it to the stain. Let it sit until the stain disappears, then wipe it off and rinse with a *wet sponge or cloth*.

Clean the microwave door with *paper towels* and *glass cleaner*.

Mildew

It's a home invasion, all right. Mildew is an intruder that can destroy fabric and upholstery, eat through wallboard, disintegrate wallpaper, and trigger allergies. But with some simple tools and know-how, you can defend your home against this micromenace.

Mildew occurs when moisture combines with mold, which is always present in the air. Mildew flourishes in damp, warm, dark places. Moisture can come from dripping pipes, a leaky roof, or simply high humidity. When conditions are right, mildew begins to grow within 24 to 48 hours and will continue unabated until you address the problem.

To prevent mildew, dry out water-damaged areas as soon as you notice them. Keeping your house clean, dry, and well-ventilated will prevent most mildew problems. Cleaning with *soap* and *water* will often take care of mildew stains, but actually killing mildew requires the power of *bleach*. Don't use straight bleach, though—it's too powerful and can create toxic fumes.

To remove mildew from the bathroom—one of the most common areas of infestation—mix *1 part bleach* with *11 parts water*. Wear *rubber gloves* and use a *sponge, cloth, or soft-bristled brush* to apply the solution. Rinse with a *damp sponge* and then wipe down the area with a *squeegee*. Turning on a *vent fan* before showering cuts down on moisture retention in the bathroom.

To remove musty odors in the basement—another mildew breeding ground—sprinkle *chlorinated lime* (also known as *bleaching powder*) over the floor. Let it soak up the odor for a day and then sweep or vacuum it up. If you use a *vacuum*, dispose of the bag afterward. If you sweep with a *broom*, collect the residue in a dustpan and dispose of it outdoors. You can also get rid of musty mildew smells by spraying with a *beach solution* (see *Odors*).

To remove mildew stains from fabric or upholstery, take the item outside. Begin by knocking off the surface mildew with a *stiff brush* and then air out the piece in the *sun*. If spots remain, wash

simple SOLUTIONS

Your Clout with Grout >

To remove mildew from tile grout, pour 1 ounce of bleach into a 32-ounce spray bottle and fill it the rest of the way with water. Spray the tile walls, and the mildew will fade away. For severe cases of mildew, try adding just a tad more bleach to the mixture.

the item according to the manufacturer's instructions. Use *hot water* and *laundry bleach* if the fabric can tolerate it.

To remove mildew from leather, use a solution of alcohol and water. Combine *1 cup of rubbing alcohol* with *1 cup of water*. Dip a *clean cloth* in the solution, wring it out, and wipe the affected area. Follow with a *cloth* dampened only with *water* and then dry the item in an airy place.

Mirrors

A variety of low-cost cleaning methods will produce sparkling mirrors that reflect a streak-free image.

To spiff up a mirror with glass cleaner, make sure you spray the *glass cleaner* on a *lint-free cotton cloth* or *rag* rather than directly on the mirror's surface. Not only do you use less cleaner, but you also prevent excess cleaner from running down the mirror's edges, where it can cause the mirror's silver backing to oxidize, turn black and brittle, and eventually flake.

Old newspapers do an excellent job of cleaning glass. Wear *rubber gloves* if you choose this method, to keep the printer's ink off your hands. Begin by mixing equal amounts of *vinegar* and *water* in a *bowl*. Crumple the *newspaper* into a ball, dip it into the mixture, and thoroughly wipe the mirror. Follow by rubbing with a *dry newspaper or cotton cloth*, to eliminate streaking. For extra shine after the mirror is dry, wipe it with a *clean blackboard eraser*.

To remove caked-on hair spray, wipe it off with a little *rubbing alcohol* on a soft cloth.

Motorcycles and Motor Scooters

Motorcycle mania isn't just for Harley-riding bad boys anymore. People who choose to travel on these lithe, lean machines ride a little taller when the bike gleams. So get out the garden hose and get ready to shine.

To keep water out of cables and controls, cover the handlebars with *plastic* before washing the bike. The plastic sleeves that newspapers are delivered in cover handlebars well. Put a piece of *plastic tape* over the ignition keyhole, too, to keep water out of the lock.

Before washing, spray the bike with a *garden hose*. If the bike is badly caked with mud and road grease, you'll probably want to use *high-pressure water*. But take care to not let the pressurized water hit the instruments, ignition keyhole, carburetor, or brakes. They could be damaged if water were to get inside.

Motorcycle stores sell a variety of *wash sprays* that remove oil and road grime, such as S100 cycle care products. Use such a spray on the engine and wheels, wipe with a *clean cloth*, and immediately rinse.

Next, wash the bike's painted areas. You'll find that *car wash solutions* work well, and a *terry cloth cotton mitt* will allow you to get into tight spots without cutting your fingers. Don't use laundry or dishwashing detergents—they're much too harsh and can take off the wax and leave streaks. Rinse the bike well with *fresh hose water* before any solution-coated areas have time to dry.

Dry the bike to prevent water spots. *Cotton towels* will work, but a *synthetic chamois* is best because it sheds less. It's a good idea to ride the bike within an hour of washing it, to get rid of any water drops that have collected in the engine, handlebars, and controls. Taking your bike for a spin also completely dries the brakes, which can be damaged by corrosion.

When your bike's finish starts to look dull, give the painted surfaces a coat of *wax*, applying it with a *dampened sponge*. *Cleaner waxes* and *polishes* are fine for older bikes. But on newer bikes, use *Carnauba Wax*, a natural wax that doesn't contain cleaners. Cleaners can literally take off the top layer of paint on a bike that is less than six months old.

Musical Instruments

A clean instrument produces a clearer sound, and periodic cleaning extends an instrument's life. You can cut down on cleanup with a little preventive maintenance: Habits as simple as washing your hands before playing and returning the instrument to its case whenever it's not being used go a long way. Here are notes (ha-ha!) on keeping the most common musical instruments as fit as a fiddle.

Clean a brass instrument regularly after using it. If you don't, the sound quality will slide. All that blowing pushes saliva down into the horn's bore, where it reacts with zinc in the metal to produce

WATCH OUT

When washing a motorcycle:
• Remove all rings and bracelets that could scratch the bike.
• Wait about an hour after riding before cleaning it. Never clean a hot engine, because the exhaust pipes can burn through skin if they haven't had time to cool.
• Make sure you that clean the bike on level ground; otherwise the side stand could slip and cause the bike to fall on you.

lime deposits. The gradual buildup of lime will cause the bore of the horn to get smaller and smaller, which in time will affect the quality of the sound. After each use, you'll need to perform routine maintenance.

Empty water from the horn. Then open each water key and blow through the instrument. Work the valves at the same time so excess water will be blown out. Wipe the outside with a *clean, soft cloth*, paying special attention to the area your hands have touched. Use a *mouthpiece brush* to clean the rim of the mouthpiece. Always store the instrument in its case, but make sure it's completely dry before putting it away.

Clean a brass instrument thoroughly every month or so, depending on how frequently you play. The process takes about an hour. Start by taking the instrument apart. If the valve caps or slides are stuck, don't try to force them. Instead, forget the home cleaning and take the instrument to a repair person. (To find the name of a good repair person, consult your music store or ask an instructor who plays your instrument.)

But if you're able to disassemble the instrument easily, put the valves, caps, and slides aside, keeping the valves in their proper order. (Each valve is numbered, with number 1 corresponding to your index finger.) Fill a *sink or bathtub*—depending on whether you're cleaning a trumpet or a tuba—with *lukewarm water* (hot water can damage the finish) mixed with a *squirt of dishwashing liquid*. Submerge the body of the instrument and the slides and swish the water around. If you have a *cleaning snake*, run it through each part. Rinse all the pieces in *clean, warm water* and dry them with a *cotton towel*. Place the parts on a *clean, dry towel* so the insides can dry. Clean the valves and caps by rinsing them with *warm water*, being careful not to get the felt at the top of each valve wet. Wipe them dry and let them air with the other parts.

When all the parts are dry, *lightly lubricate* each slide with *slide grease* and reinsert it. Use *valve oil* to lubricate the valves and then reinstall them and the valve caps in their proper order.

To clean your drums, use a *soft, damp cloth* to snare any dust that has collected. Wipe off the head and outside of the drum.

You'll need to do a thorough cleaning of your drums once a year. Remove the heads and hardware. Mix *1 teaspoon* of *mild dishwashing liquid* in a *couple of cups of water*. Dampen *a soft cloth* in the solution and wipe down the drums, heads, and hardware—taking care to keep the springs from getting wet. The tension rods may need extra attention. If they're black and coated with

expert advice

Of Temperature and Tempo >

Extreme temperature shifts in a short time pose a hazard to drum shells and their finishes, says Los Angeles drummer Dan Grody. As humidity and temperature change, the changing moisture content can cause the shells to expand, contract, warp, or even crack. Drums are safest when stored in a temperate climate—the same kind that feels comfortable to you.

old grease and grime, give them a quick bath using grease-cutting **dishwashing liquid**. Use **old rags** to wash and dry the rods, because the stains left behind on the cloth are tough to remove. Rinse by wiping all parts with a **cloth** dampened only with **water**. Then dry each piece individually with a **clean cloth**.

As for cymbals, it's best to simply dust them with a **dry cloth** and leave more rigorous cleaning to the pros. Cymbals are usually coated with a lacquer designed to prevent tarnishing. Cleaning solvents can eat through the coating.

Clean a stringed instrument regularly, and you'll never have to fret. Each time after you play the instrument, wipe the fingerboard and strings with a **clean, dry cloth or chamois**.

Every month or so, clean the instrument's body, which will increase the life span of the finish. Use a **soft cloth** dampened lightly with a **suitable cleaner**—which will vary depending on whether you're cleaning a guitar, violin, or cello—and apply evenly, following the grain of the wood. It's very important not to flood the instrument or allow cleaner to soak into seams or peg holes. After a good rubdown, go over it again with a dry cloth.

When you replace strings, that's a great time to clean the fret board. Usually, the built-up gunk—perspiration from fingers or rosin from a bow—can be removed with a **soft cloth**. But if necessary, give it a very light brushing of **steel wool (000 or 0000)**.

The metal tuning mechanisms will corrode over time and should be polished when they start looking dirty. Consult a music shop with a repair department for product recommendations. As a preventive measure, you can occasionally lubricate the gears on the tuning keys with a little **penetrating lubricant** such as WD-40 ▶.

Older, valuable instruments should be professionally cleaned once a year, since the varnishes are tricky and can be ruined by inexperienced hands.

Maintaining a woodwind instrument is important, although a thorough cleaning should be left to a professional—an amateur would just blow it. Serious players should have their instrument cleaned professionally every year. Every other year will suffice for casual players.

For regular maintenance, take these steps every time you play:
● Remove the reed (unless you have a flute or piccolo, of course), which will warp if left on the instrument. Dry it with a **soft cloth** and return it to its reed case.
● Swab inside each section of the instrument with a **cotton handkerchief** after each use. For flutes, you'll need to buy a

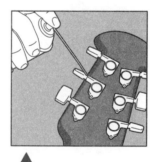

▲

cleaning rod, which is available at music stores (or you may still have the one that came with the instrument when it was new). To use a cleaning rod, thread a corner of a *cotton cloth* through the eye of the rod, wrap the cloth around the rod, and insert it in the flute body, rotating it to soak up moisture. Then withdraw the rod.

- Take special care with the pads that cover the tone holes on a flute and other woodwind instruments. They're usually made of a felt covered with a very thin, treated animal skin. When wet, they're easily torn. You can maintain the life of the pads by drying them after each use. Fold a *clean, absorbent paper towel*, place it between the keys and the body, close the keys, and let the paper absorb the moisture. Don't pull the paper towel out while the key is closed, which can tear the skin. Instead, open the key and remove the paper.
- Wipe the body of the instrument with a *soft, clean cloth* to remove all fingerprints.

Clean the mouthpiece weekly, either with a *mouthpiece brush* or, on larger instruments, by pulling a *handkerchief* through the mouthpiece.

Every month or so, take an *artist's sable brush* and brush out any dirt that's built up in the ribs (the body of the instrument where the keys are attached). You want to prevent dirt and grease from getting into the pads and mechanisms. Stay away from polishes, which can remove the top layer of metal on an instrument.

Make sure the instrument is completely dry before putting it back in its case.

See also **Pianos**.

MUSICAL INSTRUMENTS

Needlework

Cleaning needlework isn't as simple as it may sound. Techniques will vary according to the age of the piece and the fabric on which it's embroidered. If you are unsure of a piece's age or fabric, consult a pro with proven needle wisdom, particularly if the item is a family heirloom with sentimental value.

To clean needlework less than 15 years old that's embroidered on cotton or wool, follow these steps:

1. Use care in taking the item apart, whether it's cross-stitch in a frame or needlepoint on a pillow. If the piece has cut edges that might unravel, zigzag the edges on a *sewing machine* before cleaning. Measure the piece so you'll be able to return it to its original size.

2. Fill a *clean sink* with slightly *warm water* and a *squirt of gentle dishwashing liquid* that doesn't have a grease-cutting formula. (If you're unsure whether the threads are colorfast, use cold water. Red threads in particular are notorious for bleeding when warm water is used.)

3. Gently work the soapy water through the fabric, squeezing and agitating the piece. For stains, use a *spot remover* made for cotton or wool, or presoak the piece for at least 30 minutes in the dishwashing liquid–water solution.

4. Rinse the item several times in *clear, cold water*, making sure you get all the detergent out so that it doesn't turn the whites yellow.

5. After you've thoroughly rinsed the piece, place it on a *cotton towel*, roll up the towel to remove excess water, and unroll.

6. Using a *blocking board*, pin the piece facedown at its original measurements so that it will return to square as it dries. (Check your work with a T-square.) Blocking boards are scarce, but you can make one by using a cork board or the kind of foam core board used for matting artwork. Cover it with muslin, and secure the muslin with staples.

WATCH OUT

Dry cleaning isn't the best choice for cleaning needlework, because dry-cleaning fluids contain chemicals that could damage the piece. This is especially true if you're unsure of the type of fabric you're cleaning. In addition, the steam machines used by dry cleaners will take the sizing out of the piece, making it extremely difficult to block again.

When in doubt, turn to the pros, who are usually listed in the Yellow Pages under Needlework.

O

Odors

Did you know that certain odors—ammonia for instance—can cause physical pain? The majority of smells—pet urine, refrigerator odors, the lingering stench of cooked fish—simply cause mental anguish, which in some ways is worse. But trying to remove odors can really addle the brain, because you're trying to clean something you can't see. Masking the smell with perfumes and air fresheners is only a temporary solution. To truly quell a smell, you must remove what causes the smell—and do it promptly and completely. The key is patience.

If you have a culinary disaster in the oven and the kitchen fills with smoke, exchange the sooty, smelly air with fresh air. Turn off the oven. If the stove has an exhaust fan, turn it on high. Open windows to create cross-ventilation. (Windows on opposite sides of the room are ideal.) If possible, close doors leading to other parts of the house to confine the smoke.

To remove lingering cooking smells in your kitchen, be they from culinary catastrophes or masterpieces, use a *clean sponge or cloth* to wipe down kitchen surfaces (other than those that come into contact with your food) with a *degreaser*, such as Simple Green. You're trying to remove the particles and grease carried by smoke, steam, and splatter, so clean the walls and other surfaces close to the stove. Because heat rises and is drawn to cool areas, wipe down windows and window trim, light fixtures, and upper cabinets. Launder kitchen curtains and exposed dish towels in your *washer* and *dryer*.

Reduce garbage can smells by regularly cleaning your garbage can. Take it outside and *hose* it out, if weather permits. Scrub the inside with a *nylon-bristled brush* and a solution of water and bleach *(4 to 8 ounces of bleach per 1 gallon of warm water)* plus a *couple of squirts of dishwashing liquid*. Air-dry completely. Once the can is dry, sprinkle *borax* in the bottom of it to prevent the growth of odor-causing molds and bacteria.

To deodorize your sink's garbage disposer, grind *lemon or orange peels* every so often. If that does not work, the rubber gasket might be harboring odor-causing crud. Because it stays moist, it could be staying smelly. Turn off the disposer. Either remove the gasket for cleaning or lift up the flaps and clean underneath. Scrub it with a *nylon-bristled brush* and *dishwashing liquid*. (See also *Garbage Disposers*.)

To cut down on refrigerator odors, maintain a constant vigil against spoiled foods. Periodically purge your fridge of old luncheon meats, rotting veggies, and moldy leftovers. Wipe the inside surfaces with a *sponge* and *plain water*. Be sure to clean the rubber gasket that seals the door, because it's likely to hold odors. Keep an open *box of baking soda* on a shelf (and another in the freezer) to absorb odors. Replace the boxes several times a year.

To absorb stronger refrigerator odors, spread several ounces of *fine, activated charcoal*, available at stores that sell aquarium supplies, in a *shallow pan* and put the pan on a refrigerator or freezer shelf. (The pan of charcoal will not harm food.) After about eight hours, put the pan in a 350° F *oven* for 20 minutes to reactivate the charcoal. By reactivating the charcoal, you can reuse it many times. Put the charcoal back into the fridge until the smell is gone. In a pinch, use *kitty litter* in a pan to absorb smells. (No need to put it in the oven.) *Ground coffee* (unused) will do the same.

To remove musty smells in your basement or other parts of the house, first ventilate. The musty smell comes from mold and mildew, which thrive in dank, dark environments where the air is stale. Open windows and doors, use *fans* to circulate the air, and run a *dehumidifier* to reduce the air's humidity. Then kill the odor-producing growth, using one of these methods:

- Mix up a solution of *1 to 2 ounces of bleach* per *1 quart of water*. Pour it into a *spray bottle*. Spray any surfaces that won't be harmed by the bleach, such as cinderblock walls and concrete floors. (Test any colored materials first by applying the solution to an inconspicuous corner.) Scrub with a *nylon-bristled brush*.
- Sprinkle *chlorinated lime* (bleaching powder) on the basement floor. (See *Mildew*.)

Wash any washable fabrics that may have mildew growing on them in the *washing machine*.

To remove pet accident odors, completely remove the urine or poop as soon as possible using *newspapers, paper towels*, or a *heavy-duty vacuum cleaner*. For a full discussion, see *Pet Cleanup*.

Ovens

Oven spatters and spills are a class-A cleaning challenge. First, there's the grease. Even worse, though, are the melted cheeses, the bubbling, sugary pie fillings, and other foods that get fired to the hardness of pottery glaze on an oven's walls and bottom.

simple SOLUTIONS

Three Odor-Conquering Strategies >

- A quick fix for cutting cooking odors: Boil 1/4 cup vinegar per 1 quart of water. The rising heat will carry the odor-neutralizing vinegar particles to the same surfaces on which the smoke and grease landed.
- To reduce an onion smell on your hands, rub them before and after you cut onions with the sliced end of a celery stalk. A little vinegar rubbed on your hands before or after cutting onions has the same neutralizing effect.
- A short-term solution to a smelly basement is to cut an onion in half and leave it on a plate in the basement. The onion absorbs musty odors.

"Why bother?" you might say. "No one ever looks in there." The reason: Because proper cleaning improves your oven's efficiency, extends its life, and, most important, reduces the risk of fire. Read on for ways to remove oven deposits that don't involve jackhammers or hours of backbreaking scrubbing. Even if you have a self-cleaning or continuous-cleaning oven, neither of which is entirely self-sufficient, some of the tips that follow will help you clean it right.

simple SOLUTIONS

Grease Guard for Your Oven >

No matter what kind of oven you have, you can retard grease buildup by periodically wiping the interior of the oven with a vinegar-soaked cloth.

Wipe the exterior surfaces of your oven to remove food spills every time you wipe down your countertops. All you need is a *moist sponge*. Make it a habit, and you'll save time in the end, because even the exterior surfaces get warm enough to bake food on fast. Besides, this is the part of your oven people do see.

To clean the interior, start by removing all oven racks and broiler pans. Wash them by hand in a *sink or dishpan*, regardless of the type of oven you have. Use a solution of *warm water* and *dishwashing liquid*. Scrub with a *nylon-bristled brush or other gentle, nonmetal scrubber*. Anything abrasive, such as steel wool, will scratch the metal's finish, which can lead to rusting and will make food stick even more the next time.

To loosen baked-on deposits in a conventional oven, fill a *glass bowl* with *1/2 cup of full-strength ammonia*. After making sure the oven has cooled, put the bowl of ammonia in the oven, close the door, and let it stand overnight. The fumes will release the bond between the crusty food and the oven interior. The next day, open the door and let the fumes dissipate. Then remove the bowl and wipe away the loosened food with a *cloth or sponge*.

▲

To remove stubborn food that did not come off after the ammonia treatment in your conventional oven, try scouring with a *nonabrasive scrubber* dipped in a solution of *warm water* and *dishwashing liquid*. As with the racks and broiler pans, avoid scratching the oven's finish. On a flat surface, such as the door glass or the oven bottom, try scraping with a *plastic ice scraper*— the kind you use on your car windshield ◀.

As a last-ditch effort when cleaning a conventional oven, try a *commercial oven cleaner*. Follow the directions carefully and wear *protective rubber gloves* when applying. These products are strong and harmful to humans. Never spray a commercial oven cleaner on a hot oven, electric elements, or oven lights. Heat can make the cleaner even more caustic.

Help your self-cleaning oven by doing a little prep work. Self-cleaning simply means disintegrating food spills with temperatures as high as 900° F. But the high heat doesn't reach all parts of the oven, and in areas such as the frame around the oven opening and the edge of the door outside the gasket, the self-cleaning cycle can actually bake food on even more. So clean those parts first with a *nonabrasive scrubber* dipped in a sudsy solution of *hot water* and *dishwashing liquid*. Rinse well using a *sponge* and a *bucket of clean water*.

Once the self-cleaning cycle is complete and the oven has cooled down, wipe out the ashy residue with a *damp sponge*.

Give your continuous-cleaning oven that human touch. The interior of this type of oven is coated with a chemical mixture that lowers the temperature at which heat will dissolve foods. So whenever you bake or roast at a temperature above 350° F, you're disintegrating food that has splattered on the walls or bottom. But major spills, especially those involving sugar, can cancel out the effect. Therefore, clean up major spills as soon as possible. Occasionally wipe out the entire oven using a *nonabrasive scrubbing pad* and *warm water*. Then run the oven empty for an hour or two at 475° F to disintegrate any grease or food that the oven's normal cooking/cleaning cycle didn't take care of. Never use abrasive cleaners or cleaning tools in a continuous-cleaning oven.

WATCH OUT

• Never use commercial oven cleaners in a self-cleaning oven. When heated to those high temperatures, the chemical residue grows dangerously caustic.

• Never use commercial oven cleaners, cleaning powders, or metal scrubbers to clean a continuous-cleaning oven. These products may ruin the chemical mixture that allows the oven to clean itself.

Painted Surfaces

Paint is not only decorative—it's also a protective coating. But even though paint is made to stand up to considerable wear and tear, you must take care when cleaning it. Strong chemical cleaners or too much scrubbing to remove greasy fingerprints can dull the paint's finish in spots or, worse, remove it altogether. Since touch-up painting, even with a color match, tends to look splotchy, a cleaning mistake could lead to a complete repainting. Ugh.

Dust painted surfaces regularly, when possible, to keep dirt and grime from staining the surface when smeared or moistened. For painted furniture, shelves, door and window trim, or knickknacks that are coated in a semigloss or glossy paint, use a *clean dust cloth*, either dry or slightly dampened with *water*. Dusting—especially wet dusting—entire walls is not feasible, since many walls are covered with flat water-based paint, which wet dusting could actually remove.

To remove stubborn stains from semigloss or glossy paint, first try wiping gently with a cloth dampened with a sudsy solution of *warm water* and *dishwashing liquid*. If that doesn't work, try an *all-purpose cleaner*, but only after testing the cleaner on an inconspicuous corner of your painted surface. Clean from the bottom up so that your cleaning solution won't drip down, pick up grime, and leave dirty streaks.

Rinse with a *clean, moist cloth or sponge*. Dry well with *clean towels* to prevent water from damaging the paint or what's beneath it.

To remove marks from surfaces, such as walls, that are coated with flat paint, first try rubbing the area with a *white vinyl eraser*, the kind you'd find at an office supply store for erasing pencil marks. If that doesn't do the trick, try gently wiping the marks with a *water-moistened cloth*. Blot dry soon afterward with a *clean towel*. But be forewarned: Water can stain or even remove flat paint.

Painting Equipment

The best painters will tell you that a good cleanup at the end of the day is essential. Not only does it keep their tools in tip-top shape, which means easier application and cleaner lines, but it also prolongs the life of their rollers, pans, and brushes. On the other hand, the pros will also be the first to tell you that there are times when you *don't* have to completely clean your gear, and in these special cases (see below) that will save you valuable time and energy. If you dread dealing with the messy aftermath—the paint-smeared rags, the cloudy water or paint thinner, the matted paintbrushes or rollers—read on to discover a simple, environmentally friendly cleanup technique.

Start by putting the excess paint back into the paint container. Squeeze as much paint as you can from your brushes (wrap them in *newspaper* and press with your hands), empty your roller pans, and scrape paint off your rollers with the curved scraper on a *5-in-1 painter's tool*, available at paint and hardware stores. Then wipe off as much of the remaining paint as possible using something disposable, such as an *old rag, newspaper, or piece of cardboard*. Let the rag or paper dry and then stuff it in the garbage.

Use a two-bucket system to keep things tidy. Whether you're using water-based or oil-based paint, use *two large buckets* (plastic 5-gallon buckets work well) to contain your mess: one for washing and one for rinsing. The system is economical (because you can reuse solvents), it's friendly to the environment (you reserve rather than throw out paint or used solvent), and it's neat.

Use one bucket for washing. If you're cleaning up after using water-based paint, mix *warm water* with a *squirt of dishwashing liquid* in the bucket. If you've been using oil-based paint, put a small amount of *paint thinner or turpentine* into the bucket—

simple
SOLUTIONS

The Painter's Secret >

To renew an old, stiff paintbrush, place it in hot vinegar (acetic acid) for 15 minutes, wash the brush in dishwashing liquid and warm water, rinse, and air-dry.

The *Pro Painter's Cleanup:* *Four Easy Steps*

1. Squeeze, pour, and scrape excess paint from brushes, pans, and rollers back into the paint can. Wipe off what's left on an old rag, newspaper, or cardboard and dispose of it.

2. Use one 5-gallon bucket for washing. For water-based paint, use warm water with a squirt of dishwashing liquid. For oil-based paint, put 2 or 3 inches of paint thinner or turpentine into the bucket. Leave the dirty water or solvent in the bucket, cover the bucket, and let it stand.

3. Use another 5-gallon bucket for rinsing. Again, for water-based paint, use clean water. For oil-based paint, use fresh thinner. As with the wash bucket, leave the water or solvent in the bucket and cover it.

4. Let the paint solids settle to the bottom of the buckets overnight. The next day, pour the water off the top of the solids. Or pour the clean solvent off the top into the solvent's original container for reuse. Scrape the paint from the bottom of the buckets onto newspaper and discard.

2 or 3 inches in the bottom should be enough. Immerse the brushes, and use your fingers to gently work the paint out of them. Use a **brush comb** or an **old fork** to clean between the bristles. To remove paint from the metal band on the handle, scrub gently with a **wire brush**. Use a **roller spinner**, available at paint stores, to remove paint from the rollers, either spinning it in the wash bucket or, better yet, in a third, empty bucket ◀. (The paint really flies.) Wash the roller pans over the wash bucket using a **soft-bristled brush**. Leave the dirty water or solvent in the bucket, cover the bucket with **cardboard or newpaper** to prevent evaporation, and let it stand.

Use the second bucket for rinsing, after you've removed the bulk of the paint from your brushes or rollers. For water-based paint cleanup, use **clean water**; for oil-based cleanup, use **fresh thinner**. When the water or solvent squeezed from the brushes or rollers comes out clear, you'll know you're finished. As with the wash bucket, cover the rinse bucket containing water or solvent with **cardboard or newspaper** and let it stand.

Let the paint solids settle to the bottom of the wash and rinse buckets overnight. The next day, carefully pour the water off the top of the solids. Using a **putty knife or paint stirrer**, scrape the paint off the bottom of the buckets onto **newspaper** and discard it. As for paint thinner or turpentine, you can reuse it. Carefully pour the relatively pure liquid on top back into its original container. (Never store solvents in plastic, because solvents will damage plastic containers.) Again, scrape the solids up and discard.

If you'll be using oil paint again the next day, you don't need to thoroughly clean your brushes and rollers. Just give your oil brushes and rollers a cursory cleaning (squeeze and scrape off the excess paint) and then wrap them tightly in **aluminum foil or plastic wrap**. This will keep them from drying out—and will save you the hassle of cleaning up twice. You can save the thorough two-bucket cleanup routine for the end of the project.

If a water-based brush or roller just won't come clean, it may be because many of today's water-based paints contain resins, similar to those used in oil-based paints, to improve adhesion, gloss, and durability. After cleaning and rinsing the brush or roller in water, try a second rinse in **paint thinner or turpentine** to completely clean it. Afterward, wash with **clean, soapy water** to remove the thinner.

simple SOLUTIONS

For Supple Bristles >

To keep the bristles on a clean oil brush soft, rub a little petroleum jelly into them. Before using the brush, rinse it in paint thinner or turpentine. Never rinse out an oil brush in water. Water tends to make bristles turn dry and brittle.

Paneling

Paneling comes in two main varieties: real wood and simulated wood, also known as hardboard. Real wood paneling, made of walnut, oak, maple, or other kinds of woods, is hardly different in quality from the fine wood furniture in your home. It is usually either sealed with a hard surface coat, such as varnish or polyurethane, or it contains a penetrating stain or oil finish. Hardboard is a manufactured product made to look like real wood, and it is often coated in plastic. Understanding these differences is crucial when deciding how to clean your paneling.

To remove dust from raised molding, carving, or other features on either type of paneling, vacuum regularly using your *vacuum cleaner's brush attachment*, or wipe with a *cloth*. For hardboard, you can use a *moistened dust cloth*, but avoid using water on real wood. Moisture can damage wood.

To clean real wood paneling with a surface coat, such as polyurethane, you may have to use *water*, but begin by trying a *spray-on furniture polish*, such as Behold or Pledge. These products actually remove dirt and dust while adding a hard wax finish. For heavier cleaning, try a *cloth* lightly dampened with a *neutral cleaner*, such as Murphy Oil Soap.

To clean real wood paneling with a penetrating finish, such as oil, use a *cloth* dampened with *mineral spirits*, which is a type of solvent. Wipe gently back and forth in the direction of the wood grain. Mineral spirits will lift dirt and grime but will also remove the oil finish, so when you've finished cleaning, you may need to touch up—or reapply—the paneling's oil or stain finish.

Clean simulated wood paneling the same way you would a glossy painted surface. Its plastic coating, while not impermeable, means you can wipe it down with a *cloth* using a solution of *warm water* and a *squirt of dishwashing liquid*. If you need something stronger, try an *all-purpose cleaner*, but only after testing the cleaner on an inconspicuous corner of the hardboard. Clean from the bottom up, so your cleaning solution doesn't drip down, pick up grime, and leave dirty streaks.

Rinse the hardboard paneling with a *clean, moist cloth or sponge*. Once the surface is clean, dry well with *clean towels* so that the water won't damage the glue in the compressed wood beneath the coating.

Patios

The bad news is that patios are outside: They wind up stained by grease drippings from the barbecue grill, rusty metal furniture, and leaf tannins. The good news is also that they are outside: You can have at those stains with heavy-duty cleaners—and, if worst comes to worst, a high-pressure power washer. If only you could do the same with dirty bathroom grout.

To reduce staining, sweep the leaves and other debris off your patio regularly. Use an **outdoor-quality straw broom**, a **push broom,** or a **gas-powered leaf blower**.

Give your patio a more thorough cleaning at least once a year using a solution of **1 gallon of warm water** and **1 cup of trisodium phosphate** (TSP), a relatively mild cleaner available at hardware stores. Use a **stiff-bristled brush** (a long-handled one will be easier on your back and knees) to scrub the patio. Rinse with a **hose**. TSP runoff will not harm surrounding foliage. Use the TSP solution to spot-remove grill grease, tannins, and other stains.

To deep-clean a stone, brick, or concrete patio, use a **pressure washer**. Take care not to etch your patio material or injure yourself: Never use pressure rated at higher than 3,000 psi (pounds per square inch), never use a pinpoint nozzle (instead, use a 15- or 25-degree fan nozzle), and never hold the jet too close to the patio surface. If you rent a power washer, be sure to ask for detailed safety instructions.

Patio Furniture

WATCH OUT

To avoid stripping away the protective coatings often found on vinyl and other materials used in patio furniture, don't scrub with abrasive brushes or pads and don't clean with bleach, bleach-based cleaning products, or solvents.

Cleaning patio furniture—which is usually made of aluminum or a painted metal, vinyl, or plastic—is a lot like washing the car. Pick a warm day, don your shorts and sandals, turn on the garden hose, and have fun. It doesn't have to be a big deal—once in the spring and once in the fall should be often enough.

Before you wet anything, begin by brushing off any large matter, such as leaves, sticks, and bird droppings. Put on a **glove** and use your hand or use a **nylon-bristled brush**. Doing this while the furniture is dry is easier and leaves less chance for staining. Now you can play with the hose.

To remove dirt, pollen, tree sap, and other grime, use a **hose** to spray down your outdoor furniture and then scrub it with a **nylon-bristled brush** dipped in a **bucket of warm water** with a **squirt**

or three of dishwashing liquid. Use an *old toothbrush* for cleaning out small crevices. Rinse by spraying with the hose.

What about mildew? Mildew grows only on organic material, which means that if you have mildew-covered vinyl seat cushions, the mildew has probably sprouted on pollen and other organic droppings that have accumulated. It also means that you don't need bleach to kill it. Just scrub off the organic matter, and the mildew will be gone too.

To protect your patio furniture's frames, polish them with a *car wax*. Following the manufacturer's directions, lightly wax the frames' arms, legs, and other exposed areas ▶. Two thin coats are better than one thick coat. Use it on painted metal, aluminum, and plastic. Car wax gives the furniture a nice shine and protects it from rain, dust, tree droppings, and other harmful substances. Be careful, however, not to get the wax on the vinyl. It can stain vinyl and get gunked in the vinyl mesh that commonly covers patio seat cushions. And since vinyl, like leather, needs to breathe to stay pliant and strong, the wax is bad for it because it clogs its pores.

To restore aluminum furniture's shine, wipe it down with a *cloth* soaked in a *1-to-1 solution of vinegar* and *water*. Aluminum does not rust, but it can tarnish when exposed to airborne pollutants. The vinegar solution helps, as does coating the frame with car wax. Don't clean aluminum with alkaline cleaners, such as ammonia, baking soda, or trisodium phosphate, which will discolor it.

For patio umbrellas, see **Umbrellas**.

▲

The Vinyl Color Code >
Some vinyl colors stain more easily than others. When they took the lead out of vinyl, says Joe Griffin, of Contract Furnishings, Inc., browns and beiges began to stain worse. Other easy stainers: peach, rose, mauve, red, burgundy, and orange. Yellows, greens, blues, and whites don't stain as easily.

Pearls

Unlike hard, crystalline gemstones, pearls are as sensitive as they are beautiful. Perfume, cosmetics, and hair spray can stain them. The acids in your perspiration can eat away at their fine coating, called the nacre. And since a pearl's value is largely determined by its color, luster, and thickness of nacre, cleaning your pearls is essential for maintaining value. Fortunately, cleaning is also easy and harmless to the pearl, as long as you stick to the following simple regimen.

Wipe off your pearls after each wearing. Use a barely damp, very *soft cloth*. (Chamois is best.) This removes harmful substances such as perspiration, perfume, and makeup that can penetrate the pearls' porous surface. As a preventive measure, always apply perfume, makeup, and hair spray *before* you put on your pearls.

Occasionally clean your pearls more thoroughly to restore their natural finish and luster. Use a *mild bar soap*, such as Ivory, and *lukewarm water* to create light suds. Dip a *soft cloth* in the suds and gently wipe the pearls. Rinse with *clean water* and dry with *another soft cloth*. Never soak your pearls because that will get the string too wet.

When drying pearls, here are some things to keep to in mind:
● To make sure the pearls and string are dry, lay them on a *slightly damp cloth*. When the cloth is dry, the pearls will be too.
● If you wear pearls when their string is wet, the string might stretch and attract hard-to-remove dirt.
● Never hang pearls to dry, since that might also stretch the string.

To remove stubborn lumps of dirt, use your fingernail, which has a hardness of 2.5 or less on the Mohs' scale (a scale of mineral hardness on which 1 represents the hardness of talc). Pearls have a hardness of 2.5 to 4.5, which means your fingernail probably won't scratch them.

Pencil Marks

If you have children, it is inevitable: Pencil marks will find their way onto their clothes and your walls. While pencil marks can be tricky to clean, they are not as difficult as some inks.

If it's pencil, reach for an eraser. Try removing pencil from walls and fabric using a *soft eraser*, preferably a white vinyl eraser that will not leave marks of its own.

To remove pencil marks from washable fabrics (if the eraser does not work), put a *few drops of ammonia* on the mark. Rinse with *water*. Put a little bit of *laundry detergent* on the stain. Rinse. Repeat until the stain is gone.

To remove pencil marks from walls (again, if the eraser didn't work), try rubbing with a *slice of fresh rye bread*.

Pests

Removing pests is not as simple as blasting the buggers with some pesticide. For one thing, today we know more than ever about these chemicals' harmful side effects on humans. For another thing, this single-minded approach does not necessarily work. To really rid your home of pests, you've got to devise a strategy that includes killing *and* prevention, removing pests *and* blocking their entry. Sometimes it may not involve harsh chemicals at all.

For general pest prevention, tighten up the house. Fill gaps in basement floors and walls with ***caulk*** and ***grout***. Make sure baseboard molding forms a tight fit between the wall and floor. (If you have gaps, fill them with a paintable caulk or cover with quarter-round trim.) Inspect things like boxes and firewood for hitchhikers—roaches, ants, and spiders, for instance—before bringing them into your house. Cockroaches, for one, will eat nearly anything that is organic, including cardboard.

Next, cut off the pests' food and water supplies. Caulk around sinks and tubs to stop water from leaking behind fixtures. Repair leaky pipes. Don't let water stand in appliance drip pans or houseplant dishes. Keep food in tightly sealed containers. Wipe down countertops. Remove food that spills on the sides of and behind the stove.

Also attack pest breeding and living areas by filling holes in walls and floors, removing piles of cardboard and paper bags inside or around the house, and eliminating general clutter.

Rid your home of cockroaches. Kill existing roaches with ***powdered boric acid***, available at supermarkets and hardware stores. Boric acid kills roaches but does not harm humans when used correctly. Wearing ***gloves*** and a ***dust mask***, sprinkle it under and behind kitchen cabinets and appliances and in basements, bathrooms, and anywhere else they might live. Use a ***dust applicator***, available at feed and seed stores and through gardening catalogs, to make the job easier and to get to hard-to-reach spots.

To keep your abode flea free, here are some tips for controlling fleas (besides the light setup suggested in the Simple Solutions sidebar, which makes a decent trap). Even though your pet probably attracted the fleas, it's vital to keep your home clean, because 90 percent of a flea's life cycle is spent off the pet and in the bedding or rugs in its egg, larva, and pupa stages. Designate a pet sleeping area, such as a tiled mudroom, that is easy to clean, and clean it regularly—more often than the rest of the house if necessary. Cover your pet's bed with a ***washable blanket***. Then all you have to wash is the blanket, not the bed. When you pick the blanket up, carefully lift all four corners, so flea eggs won't roll off. If you have fleas, ***vacuum*** rugs and upholstered furniture, then seal

simple SOLUTIONS

A Deadly Pool for Fleas >

If you think you have fleas but aren't sure, turn on a gooseneck or folding arm lamp about 6 inches above a shallow pan of water containing a dash of dishwashing liquid. If you do have fleas, at night they will spring for the light and drop into the soapy water and drown.

the flea-contaminated vacuum bags in *plastic bags* and discard them immediately. *Steam cleaning* carpets is even more effective.

To kill adult fleas and their eggs, bathe pets with a *pyrethrin flea shampoo*. (Careful: Pyrethrin is toxic for some cats, so checking with your vet is a good idea.) Treat infected areas with an *insect growth regulator (IGR)*, such as methoprene (found in Precor and other products). IGRs have not been found harmful to pets and humans. Although IGRs don't kill adult fleas, they prevent fleas from reproducing.

Trap pesky fruit flies. Even though they were part of our high school genetics lessons, fruit flies are still a major annoyance, hovering over countertop fruit bowls like vultures over fresh road kill. Before you waste any more energy trying to swat them away, try this trick: Put *banana slices* in a *mason jar* and sprinkle them with *yeast*. Make a *paper funnel* and slip it into the top of the jar. When the jar fills up with flies—and their larvae—fill it with *very hot tap water* and slap the cap on it to kill both. Empty and then insert a new funnel and fresh bait.

Eliminate clothing moths. Thoroughly clean clothes before storing them in closets or drawers. These moths are attracted to the food, perspiration, and urine on soiled fabrics rather than to the wool or cotton itself. Once clean, seasonal clothes (except leather, which needs to breathe) should be stored in *airtight bags or plastic containers*. Commercial moth repellents usually contain paradichlorobenzene or naphthalene, which are harmful to humans, according to the Environmental Protection Agency. Instead of using such toxic chemicals, kill and deter moths with *essential oils*—cedar, eucalyptus, pennyroyal, lavender, and tansy—available at health food stores.

Make mice vanish for good. Did you know that in six months, two mice can eat 4 pounds of food and leave behind some 18,000 fecal pellets? Scary. Even more reason to keep your house free of these pests. While plenty of people have tried, it's hard to invent a better mousetrap than the standard snap-back trap. Poisons can be dangerous to your pets and can leave dead mice out of reach—where they can become a food source for other household pests.

For acute rodent problems, use lots of the *traps*, baited with *peanut butter, oatmeal, or cheese*, and spread them strategically around the house. Put them perpendicular to walls that mice scamper along ◀. Mice are renowned for their powerful noses, so wear **gloves** when baiting the traps to avoid leaving your scent. You don't like the mess of baiting traps with food? Use **cotton balls**, which greedy mice will try to grab when building nests.

Pet Cleanup

Pets, even the best-trained ones, make a mess. There's no getting around it. Until we can teach pets to clean up after themselves, we are responsible for scooping poop, wiping up pee and pet vomit, and removing pet hair from carpets and furniture. You owe it to your pet. Besides, proper pet hygiene keeps the house looking good and reduces odors, both of which make owning a pet more pleasurable.

To remove pet hair from furniture cushions, start with the **vacuum cleaner**. Buy a **lint-brush attachment** for your vacuum if you don't already have one. This gadget first pries up and then sucks up short, wiry hairs that have imbedded themselves in your upholstery. If you can't get your hands on a lint-brush attachment, wear a **damp rubber glove** and rub your hand across the sofa cushion. The hair will clump together for easy removal.

Vacuum your pet. If Fido sheds, try giving him the once-over with a **vacuum** every week using a **dusting or brush attachment**. As long as you are careful—and as long as your pet does not mind the sucking action and noise—this is a good way to make a preemptive strike against hair that is bound to fall out. You might find that your dog, or even your cat, loves the attention. It's like a pet massage. Then again, if the mere sound of the vacuum cleaner sends your pet scrambling under the bed, combing or brushing will do.

simple SOLUTIONS

Be a Pet Detective >

To locate old pet urine stains in a room, make like a crime scene investigator: Turn off the lights and scan the room with a black-light bulb, which makes otherwise invisible stains visible. It's important to clean up these old stains, because these are what keep a cat or dog, with its keen sense of smell, coming back. Outline the spots with pieces of string or by lightly tracing with chalk. Then follow the directions for removing urine stains.

Cleaning Up *After a Crasher*

Star Burr was in her Virginia home one evening when she heard a loud crash and glass breaking. She rushed to her living room to find her plate glass window shattered. In the far corner stood a deer—frightened, huffing, and bleeding all over the carpet. Burr called 911. Before the authorities arrived, however, the deer left the same way it had entered—but not before smashing the glass-top coffee table, kicking a hole in the bathroom door, gouging the wood floors, urinating on the carpet, and smearing blood on the couch and white dining room walls. The bad news: Burr's insurance didn't cover interior deer damage. (That required a separate rider.) The good news: Burr is in the cleaning business. She manages the local Merry Maids franchise.

To clean up pet vomit, start with the chunks. Remove them with a *paper towel or spatula*. If the vomit is on a hard surface, such as a vinyl or wood floor, simply wipe up the liquid with *moist paper towels* and then *mop* the spot.

If the vomit is on fabric, a carpet or rug, or upholstered furniture, blot up as much of the liquid as possible using *paper towels*. Next, apply an *enzymatic cleaner*. The enzymes in these special cleaning products, available at pet stores, actually digest the proteins found in the vomit. But they usually take a while. Let the cleaner stand for as long as the product's directions suggest. Then, for clothing, wash and rinse or dry-clean according to label instructions. For carpeting or furniture, blot with *clean, cool water* to rinse (but avoid using too much water, especially if there is a pad under the carpet or stuffing in the upholstered furniture). Then remove excess liquids by either repeatedly blotting with *fresh, dry paper towels* or using a *wet vac* or *extraction machine*, available at equipment rental stores. As with any pet accident, the key is to clean the vomit immediately.

To clean up pet feces, begin by removing any solids with *tissue paper*. Flush down the *toilet*. If there is little or no residue (as with firm feces on a hard floor), clean with *soapy water and paper towels*. Then rinse with *clean water* and *paper towels*. If there is residue (as with loose feces on a carpet), follow the steps listed for cleaning up vomit: Blot up as much of the liquid as possible using *paper towels* and apply an *enzymatic cleaner*. Wash and rinse according to the material.

To remove a fresh puddle of pee, wipe it up using *paper towels or newspaper*. Another efficient way to remove pet urine is to suck it up with a *heavy-duty vacuum cleaner* capable of picking up liquid, such as a *Shop-Vac* or a *wet vac*. The sooner you clean up your pet's indiscretion, the more likely it'll be that you'll stop the odor and keep your furry friend from revisiting the spot for a reprise. Urine is by far the worst pet odor in a home. Once it has soaked in and dried, it can be tough to remove.

If the urine is in a carpet, soak up as much of it as possible with *paper towels*. Then cover the spot with a *thick layer of dry paper towels*, with *newspaper* on top of that. (Make sure the newsprint doesn't rub off on the carpet.) Stand on the padding for a minute or so. Then remove the soaked padding and take it to your pet's bathroom area—the cat's litter box or the dog's designated outdoor area—to lure your pet there the next time. Repeat the process. Apply an *enzymatic cleaner*, available at pet stores, to digest proteins, which will help remove the urine smell.

Then rinse the accident zone by blotting with a *cloth soaked in clean water*. Remove excess water by blotting with *paper towels* (as above) or with a *wet vac or an extractor*. (As noted earlier, an extractor can also be rented from an equipment rental store.) Avoid using fragrant chemical cleaners, vinegar, or ammonia on a urine spot. As with the urine smell, these odors could draw the pet back to the scene of the crime.

Pet Equipment

You keep your children's things clean: their bedding and bowls, toys and sweaters. Do the same for your pet. It's a way of saying "I love you." Moreover, cleaning prolongs the life of the equipment, keeps your pet healthy, and reduces pet odors. If your pet could talk, it would say, "Thanks. I love you, too."

Wash food and water bowls daily to avoid the growth of bacteria. Put them in the *dishwasher*, if they are dishwasher safe. You can include them with your own dishes—the high dishwasher temperatures will sanitize everything. Or hand-wash using *hot, soapy water*. (Do this separately.) Keep two sets of dishes for your pet, and rotate them. Stainless steel bowls come clean easiest.

Clean leashes periodically to remove dirt and salt, which can corrode the metal parts. Soak nonleather leashes in a *sink* full of *warm water* with a *squirt of dishwashing liquid* and a *dash of liquid fabric softener* (to keep the leash soft, not stiff). Rub clean with a *sponge*. Rinse in a *sink* full of *clean, warm water*. Don't wash leashes in your clothes washer, because they could get tangled and the metal clasps could dent your machine. Hang to dry. (See also *Leather*.)

Hand-wash doggie sweaters using the same care you'd use on your own sweaters—unless the care instructions say otherwise. Most dog sweaters are made from the same materials as people sweaters—wool or acrylic. Fill a *basin* with *lukewarm water* and add a *gentle fabric wash*, such as Woolite, or a *squirt of mild dishwashing liquid*. Soak and then gently rub out any stains. Rinse thoroughly in *clear, lukewarm water*. Gently wring the sweater out. Wrap it in a *clean towel* to remove moisture. Lay the towel out on a *flat surface* and work the sweater into shape with your hands. Let it dry.

Or, if Snookums is worth it, have the sweater dry-cleaned.

Wash pet toys regularly to keep them clean and bacteria free. Wash rubber and plastic toys in a *sink* full of *hot, soapy water*

OOPS!

Rover in Clover >

Amy Goldman, president of CoverKnits, a maker of high-end pet sweaters, is befuddled by some pet owners' cleaning choices. There's the woman who bought one of Goodman's hand-knit, 100 percent wool dog sweaters at a posh Manhattan pet shop. "She ran the sweater in the washer and dryer and totally ruined it," says Goldman of the $120 item. "Then she had the nerve to try to return it." The woman had clearly not heeded the care tag on the sweater that warned against machine-washing.

Then there's the man who throws out his dog's sweater as soon as it gets dirty and buys a new one. If his dog is like most poop-wallowing, garden-digging canines, that could mean a lot of sweaters.

with a *dash of bleach* thrown in. Scrub with a *nylon-bristled brush*. Stuffed toys and rope toys can go in the *washing machine* and the *dryer*. When they fray, or the stuffing starts to escape, toss them and get a new toy.

To wipe nasty slobber off that Frisbee (or rubber ball) you've been throwing for Spot, use a *wet wipe*. Take along a portable travel carton of wipes when you play fetch in the park with Spot—or any other time you're away from your garden hose. All those fellow dog owners you meet and greet (with a handshake) will thank you.

*See also **Doghouses and Kennels** and **Pests**.*

Pewter

Did you know that pewter is the fourth most precious metal, behind platinum, gold, and silver? A tin alloy, pewter has long been prized for its lasting value. It does not rust and tarnishes only slightly or not at all (depending on the alloy's metal content). Antique pewter, which is usually high in lead, can look dark and dull, but that patina is part of its appeal and value as an antique. Before cleaning pewter, first determine whether your pewter piece is an antique or of more recent vintage.

To remove dirt and grime from antique or newer pewter, wash it in a sudsy solution of *warm water* and *dishwashing liquid*. Gently wipe the surface with a *sponge or soft cloth*. Rinse with *clean water* and then drip dry in a *dish rack* or on a *folded towel*. Never put pewter in the dishwasher. If your piece is an antique, stop here. Because of its metal content, polishing it won't necessarily make it shine—but it may decrease its value.

To make bright, modern pewter shine, use a *silver or brass polish* or a mildly abrasive *scouring powder*, such as Ajax, and a *soft cloth*. For severe corrosion, try applying the metal polish with *ultra-fine steel wool*. Use *grade 0000* only. Any coarser steel wool will scratch the finish. Buff with a *soft cloth* after using the steel wool.

Photographs, Slides, and Negatives

Photographs, slides, and negatives are easily damaged, and your options for cleaning them are quite limited. So keeping them out of harm's way is the name of the game. How much you're willing to do for a photograph probably depends on whether it's a

PET EQUIPMENT

family heirloom or just one out of a mountain of snapshots from last year's vacation.

The ultimate protection for a photograph is a *glass covering* and a *frame*. This way, the only thing that gets dirty is a hard surface that's easy to wipe clean. A frame will enhance the photograph's value and help it last longer. But don't set the photograph directly against the glass—use acid-free matting between the photo and the glass. And don't hang the photo where direct sunlight will reach it.

To clean the framed photo, take it off the wall and lay it flat. Spray some *glass cleaner* onto a *soft, clean cloth* and wipe off the dust. Never spray directly onto the glass—the cleaner could drip behind the frame and damage the photo.

For valuable unframed photos, *acid-free paper, plastic envelopes,* and *acid-free storage boxes* offer good protection. Another good storage option are *albums* made of high-quality materials.

Remember that high temperatures, high humidity, and direct sunlight will damage photographic materials.

Handle photographic materials very carefully. The salts and oils from your skin can damage them easily, so never touch the image area directly. Ideally, handle photographic material while wearing *white cotton gloves*. If you must use bare hands, handle your photos, slides, and negatives by the edges only.

If your photograph has dirt on the surface, see if it will come off with the gentle swipe of a *soft brush*. If not, stop there—anything more will put the photo at risk. You'll have to take it to a professional lab to be washed.

If your photo has finger marks around the edges or on an unimportant part of the image, you may be able to wipe it away. Dip a *cotton swab* in *distilled water* and wipe at the mark very gently. Don't go over the mark again and again, because you'll soften the emulsion and damage it. Let the photo dry before you store it.

To clean dust from slides and negatives, pick up a can of *compressed air* at a supermarket or at a camera, computer, or discount store. Test the can by spraying your skin first. If the can has been exposed to high temperatures or has been shaken, you might get some water spraying out with the compressed air, which you don't want to get on your photographic materials. Wearing *white cotton gloves*, hold your slide or negative by the edges and position the nozzle to the side, 3 inches from the film surface. Spray in several quick bursts to remove any dust.

RULES
OF THE GAME

To Protect Photos >

1. Handle photos, slides, and negatives only by the edges, preferably using white cotton gloves. Never touch the image area.
2. Frame important photos under glass, using acid-free matting.
3. For removal of serious dirt, take your photographic materials to a professional lab.
4. Limit exposure to heat, humidity, and sunlight.
5. Use acid-free storage materials (envelopes, sheathes, album pages, boxes, and such).

An antistatic cloth can remove dust from slides and negatives—provided you use a light touch. Buy an *antistatic cloth* at a photo shop. Hold the slide or negative by the edges in one hand. With the other hand, fold the cloth around the film so that it touches both sides. With as little pressure as possible, draw the cloth down the surface, moving only in one direction. The more pressure you apply, the more likely that you'll drag the dust across the surface and scratch it.

To protect your negatives from dirt and dust, slip them into the sleeves of *8 1/2-by-11-inch clear plastic sheets* that are sold in photography stores. Do this the moment you get the negatives home from the photo lab. These sheets fit into *ring binders* and are an excellent way to mark and catalog your negatives.

Pianos

Restraint is the name of the game when it comes to cleaning a piano. It's no small task, and most professionals recommend that do-it-yourselfers limit their input to the basics. A thorough cleaning is needed every three to five years and, thank goodness, a professional will come to your house to save you the trouble of transporting such a large instrument. The smaller jobs you can tackle yourself include polishing the exterior, vacuuming the keyboard, cleaning the keys, and dusting the soundboard.

If your piano's casework is covered with a high-gloss, black lacquer finish, it needs only dusting with a *soft, dry cloth*. Give it some extra elbow grease if you're buffing away fingerprints. (See *Lacquer* for more details on caring for this finish.) To brighten mahogany pianos, wipe with nonsilicone *furniture polish*. Put the polish on a *soft cloth* very sparingly—just enough to remove that last bit of dust clinging to the wood.

To clean the piano's keyboard, go over it with a *vacuum*, using the *brush attachment*. To clean plastic or ivory key tops, mix a solution of *mild dishwashing liquid* and *water*. Dip a *cleaning cloth* into the solution and wring it out thoroughly. Clean each key individually ◀ and dry it immediately. As you clean, make sure that no liquid drips down the sides of keys. Both plastic and ivory key tops can warp and pop off when wet. Rinse with a *barely damp cloth* and dry off with a *clean towel*.

Ivory keys, which yellow with age, can be cleaned with a *cloth* dampened with *rubbing alcohol*—but remember the yellowing of ivory is natural and can't be completely whitened. An alternative:

Dab some *regular (nongel) toothpaste* on a *damp cloth* and rub the keys. Wipe the toothpaste off and buff with a *dry cloth*. *Sunlight* also helps whiten real ivory keys, so try to position your piano so that it gets some sun (but not direct sunlight) and leave the cover open. (Sunlight has the reverse effect on plastic keys—it yellows them—so for plastic, leave the cover closed.) To protect your tuning, don't place your piano against a poorly insulated outside wall.

Cleaning the soundboard is the trickiest task in cleaning a piano. Grand pianos, with their open lids, collect a lot of dust. Use the *bare hose* of your *vacuum cleaner*, held just above the soundboard but not actually touching it, to suck away dust and dirt. You can cut down on dust by shutting the lid when the piano isn't being used or by placing *decorator felt* (available in piano stores) over the soundboard.

On an upright piano, cleaning the soundboard requires removing the bottom panel, which is heavy and therefore requires extra care. A spring that releases the panel is usually found beneath the key bed. Before vacuuming, look for small parts that may have fallen out of the piano or into the piano cabinet—a broken hammer, for instance. Again, the vacuum hose should hover above the soundboard and strings, never coming into direct contact.

Pillows

Attention, allergy sufferers: Pillows can be a big source of sneezes. Dust, body oil, perspiration, and dead skin particles gather on (and inside!) pillows. That combination is bad enough, but pillows also harbor dust mites, microscopic organisms that many people are allergic to. And if you have goose down, dust and dirt act as abrasives and shorten the life of the down. So at least twice a year, give your pillows—which are usually stuffed with either a synthetic fiber, goose down, or feathers—a good cleaning.

Most fiber-filled pillows can just be stuck in the *washing machine*. While you should always follow the instructions on the pillow's care tag, generally you can use the *cold-water cycle* for fiber-filled pillows and tumble them in the *dryer* on *low heat*. Or you can dry on a *clothesline*: Hang the pillow in the sun by one corner. Make sure it is completely dry before using.

Down and feather pillows should be machine-washed or dry-cleaned depending on the manufacturer's suggestion. Some recommend dry-cleaning only, claiming that machine-washing

WATCH OUT

Never polish the top of a piano bench—the polish will combine with skin oil and perspiration and soak deep into the wood, making it virtually impossible to get out.

down and feathers reduces their natural resilience. If you do decide to dry-clean your pillows, take them to a cleaner with experience cleaning down. If there are any lingering dry-cleaning solvent fumes, air the pillows until they are all gone.

If you machine-wash down pillows, consider using a ***special down detergent***, such as Down Wash, available at most camping stores (for use on down-filled sleeping bags). Or use a ***gentle cleanser***, such as Woolite. Don't wash more than two pillows at once. ***Tumble dry*** down pillows on ***low-to-medium heat.*** Toss in a couple of ***clean tennis balls*** to help fluff the feathers. Be prepared to wait—it might take four or more hours to completely dry them. To line dry, hang the pillow in the shade by one corner (not in the sun, as you would fiber-filled pillows, discussed above). Direct sun can make the feathers sweat, which creates an odor. Follow up a line drying by fluffing in a ***dryer*** on ***low heat***.

See also **Down**.

Plastic Containers

Plastic is the miracle product—tough, resilient, easy to clean. That is, until certain foods, most notably tomato-based sauces, etch their way into its pores and cause what seem to be permanent stains. But don't give up hope. Where there is a cleaning will, there is a way.

Nearly all plastic food containers are ***dishwasher*** safe. This includes the Tupperware and Ziploc brands. You also can hand-wash them in ***hot, soapy water***, using a ***sponge or nylon-bristled brush*** to scrub away stuck-on food.

To remove stubborn stains, such as the ones left by tomato sauce, try a ***plastic-cleaning dishwasher additive***, such as Cascade Plastic Booster, available at supermarkets and discount stores. Following the manufacturer's directions, add the proper amount to your dishwasher before running the machine.

To remove other stains, mix a paste of ***baking soda*** and ***warm water*** and scrub with a ***nylon-bristled brush*** if the stain is light. For heavier stains, try one of the following techniques:
- Scrub with a solution of ***1/4 cup dishwasher detergent*** mixed with ***1 cup warm water***. (Rinse well.)
- Soak in a solution of ***1/4 cup bleach*** mixed with ***1 quart warm water***. (Wash in ***soapy water*** afterward and rinse well.)
- Let the container stand in ***direct sunlight*** for a day or two.

simple SOLUTIONS

For Fluffy Pillows >

A quick way to freshen pillows is to tumble dry them on low heat for 10 minutes. It's much easier than a complete washing, and it removes some dust and dander. Do it twice a year, in between washings, to keep your pillows clean and nonallergenic.

To clean large plastic storage containers not meant for food, wipe out with a *moist cloth*. For stubborn stains, scrub with a *sponge or nylon-bristled brush* in a solution of *warm water* with a *squirt of mild dishwashing liquid*.

Playground Equipment

Because it was built to be outside, in the elements, playground equipment is durable and easy to clean. Don't worry about sanitizing it. You can't—and you don't need to. Just keep it safe—free from slippery mud and mildew—and respectable looking. Here's how.

Spray down playground equipment with a *garden hose* once every couple of weeks, inside and out ▶. This will remove sticks and leaves and muddy footprints. Depending on traffic, every so often scrub down parts with a solution of *dishwashing liquid* and *warm water*. Scrub swing seats, slides, platforms, vinyl tarps, and other areas with a *soft-bristled brush* to loosen stubborn bird poop and other grime. Rinse by spraying everything down with your *hose*. Don't use bleach or cleaning products containing chlorine on playground equipment. These chemicals can eat away at rubber material and destroy glue. Soapy water and a garden hose should be sufficient.

To clean plastic bubbles and windows, use the *same soapy solution* and a *soft cloth*. Don't scrub with a brush, since you may scratch these surfaces. If the surface is extremely dirty, let the soapy solution loosen the dirt, or loosen it with a jet from the *garden hose*, and then rub gently with the cloth, turning and rinsing the cloth often. Remove oil or tar by daubing with *naptha solvent*, available at paint and hardware stores, or *kerosene*, and then washing immediately with the soapy solution. Don't use solvents (such as acetone, gasoline, or thinners) or scouring powders on clear plastic.

Plexiglas

When it comes to cleaning sheet plastic or acrylic, better known by the brand name Plexiglas, one caution is worth stating right up front: Don't use commercial window cleaners. It may seem logical to reach for the Windex, but most window cleaners contain ammonia, which will eat into acrylic. So whether you're cleaning Plexiglas storm windows, furniture, or napkin holders, follow this advice.

To clean acrylic plastic, use a solution of *dishwashing liquid* and *lukewarm water* and apply it with a *soft cloth*. Avoid dry dusting, which can grind dirt into the acrylic's surface. If the surface is extremely dirty, let the soapy solution loosen the dirt and then rub gently with the cloth, turning it and rinsing it often. Remove oil or tar by daubing with *naptha solvent* or *kerosene* and then washing immediately with the soapy solution. Don't use solvents (such as acetone, gasoline or thinners) or scouring powders on sheet plastic.

Pool Tables

Despite their bulky size, pool tables are precision instruments, with finely balanced slate tops and baby-bottom-smooth felt coverings. You don't want to damage your table, even when armed with the good intention of cleaning it. Fortunately, there's not much you need to do to keep a pool table clean.

Dust the wooden legs and rails as you would fine furniture. Follow the pool table manufacturer's recommendations for the type of finish that's on the wood. When in doubt, use a *dry dusting cloth* or a *feather duster*.

Brush the felt top after each use. Use a *soft horsehair- or nylon-bristled brush* specifically designed for billiard felt. They're available at billiard supply stores. Brush in one direction only—the direction in which you usually break. This keeps the nap of the felt in good condition.

Dust the felt top periodically using your *vacuum cleaner* and a *brush attachment*. This picks up chalk and other dust from beneath the cloth, which can abrade the felt fibers over time. But be very careful not to use a nozzle that will pull the cloth away from the bed.

Porcelain

Porcelain is one of the most fragile of all ceramics. Fired at very high temperatures, it is glasslike, so clean with care. How you clean depends on which finish your porcelain has—a bisque, or unglazed, finish or a glossy glazed finish.

To wash porcelain, use a *rubber dishpan* or a *sink lined with a towel or rubber mat* to protect against breakage.

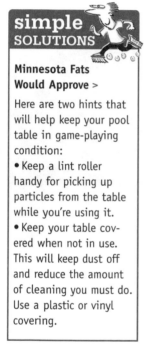

simple
SOLUTIONS

Minnesota Fats Would Approve >

Here are two hints that will help keep your pool table in game-playing condition:

• Keep a lint roller handy for picking up particles from the table while you're using it.

• Keep your table covered when not in use. This will keep dust off and reduce the amount of cleaning you must do. Use a plastic or vinyl covering.

PLEXIGLAS

To remove dirt and grime from either glazed or unglazed porcelain, first try a mild solution of *warm water* and *dishwashing liquid*. Wipe with a *cloth* or scrub gently with a *soft, nylon-bristled brush*. A *toothbrush* is great for nooks and crannies. Rinse well using *clean water*.

If that doesn't remove all the stains, try something stronger, such as an *all-purpose cleaner* such as Formula 409. Always rinse immediately and completely. These cleaning compounds can stain or etch porcelain. Air-dry in a *dish rack* or on a *folded towel* on the countertop.

To remove coffee or tea stains from the inside of porcelain cups or a porcelain teapot, scrub gently with a *cloth or soft-bristled brush* and a paste made from *baking soda* and *water*.

To remove dirt from hard-to-reach crannies, such as inside porcelain flowers or in the folded hands of a figurine, use a *spray-on bleach-based product*, such as Tilex. (You should have to do this only on bisque porcelain. On glazed porcelain, scrubbing the same crannies with a toothbrush and soapy water should be sufficient.) Spray the product on, wait a few minutes, and then rinse it well with *fresh water*. Always clean before trying the bleach spray. Otherwise the bleach may set the stain. (See Oops sidebar.)

For really stubborn stains on bisque porcelain, soak the piece (or the stained part of the piece) in a container filled with *hydrogen peroxide*. Leave it until the stain is gone, which could take 15 minutes or 72 hours. To rinse the piece, soak it in *clean water* (distilled water is best for really fine pieces) for as long as you soaked it in the hydrogen peroxide.

Pots and Pans

The good news: It's OK to put *some* cookware in the *dishwasher*. This goes for stainless steel and aluminum (as long as they have all-metal handles) as well as glass cookware. But to be safe, check the manufacturer's directions first.

Cast iron and copper should not go in the dishwasher, and manufacturers of nonstick cookware often advise against putting any of those pots or pans in the dishwasher as well. The environment in a dishwasher—with hot water spouts and spray rinses—is much harsher than soapy water and gentle care in the sink. Besides, dishwasher detergents generally rely on alkaline-heavy cleaners to cut grease, and extremely alkaline cleaners can mar cookware just as badly as acidic cleaners can.

Set in Stoneware >

Early in her career, professional restorer Andrea Daley, founder of the Association of Restorers, learned the hard way how not to clean smoke-damaged porcelain. Hired to restore a highly collectible Dorothy Doughty bird, at the time worth about $1,000, she skipped her normal cleaning steps. "It was so dirty from the smoke," she says, "I thought I'd cut to the chase and go straight for the bleach." She did, but something about the chemical mix of smoke and bleach set the stain permanently. Nothing would remove it. "I had to paint over the entire thing," she laments.

Hand-wash pots and pans that can't be put in the dishwasher much as you would dishes. Scrape out any food residue with a **wooden spoon or rubber spatula**. Fill the sink with moderately **hot water** and add a **squirt of dishwashing liquid**. As soon as the pot has cooled sufficiently, slide it into the soapy water and let it sit for a minute. Then gently scrub in a circular motion, using a **sponge, brush,** or **dishcloth**. Many nonstick surfaces—especially older ones—are easily scratched, so pay attention to the manufacturer's directions for cleaning. Clean the pot inside and out, sides and bottom. You'll know it's come clean when it's smooth to the touch. Rinse in **clean, hot water** and dry with a **kitchen towel**.

Removing burned-on food from your pots and pans can be done without working up a sweat—but you do need lots of patience, lots of **hot water**, and **dishwashing detergent**. Squirt some dishwashing detergent in the pot or pan, fill it with hot water, and leave the kitchen. Nothing removes burned-on food like a good two-hour soak in hot, soapy water.

If you have built up layers of baked-on food on cookware that is neither aluminum nor nonstick, mix **1/2 cup of ammonia** with **2 quarts of hot water** in your pot and let it sit for a couple of hours. (Don't mix ammonia or even vinegar with household cleaners, or you'll wind up sniffing noxious fumes.)

See also **Copper, Dishes,** *and* **Iron**.

When Germs Float in Uninvited

When the dirty pots and pans pile up, you probably fantasize about a massive flood swooshing through the kitchen and cleaning it all in seconds. Of course, it doesn't work that way, notes Hugh Rushing, executive director of the Cookware Manufacturers Association in Mountain Brook, Alabama. As any homeowner who's been in a real flood knows, a lot of silt and mud get left behind. Germs, too.

"We frequently get a lot of calls from people whose cookware has been in a flood," he says. All you can do, he advises, is mix hot water with soap and start scrubbing. If you're concerned that elbow grease won't get all of the germs, Rushing says, bake the offended cookware in a 250° F oven for one hour. This is even OK for cookware with plastic handles. "Most plastic handles won't stand over 350 degrees, but they'll be fine for an hour in 250."

POTS AND PANS

Pottery

There's pottery, such as pitchers, plates, flower vases, and garden containers. And then there's pottery that belongs in an art gallery or museum. One is utilitarian; the other is precious and requires a light touch—possibly a professional's care.

In the former category, there are two types of pottery: glazed and unglazed. Rule of thumb: *The thicker the glaze, the easier to clean.* You can get tougher on glazed pottery.

To clean glazed pottery—such household items as plates, mugs, serving trays and flower vases—proceed much as you would with your dishes. This stuff has been fired at 2,000° F, meaning it can stand up to any heat your **dishwasher** can dish out. Hand-wash fragile or expensive pieces in the **sink** with **warm water** and **dishwashing liquid**, so they won't run the risk of getting chipped in the dishwasher. A **scrubber sponge** will do nicely for most hand-washing, but the glaze will even stand up to the abrasion of a **steel wool pad** such as Brillo.

To remove heavy dirt and grease, first dampen a **cloth** in **rubbing alcohol**, wipe it over the glazed pottery, and then wash as usual in the dishwasher or sink.

To clean unglazed pottery—such as terra cotta flowerpots—just wash them in the **sink** with **warm water** and **dishwashing liquid**. Unglazed pottery is porous, meaning it will soak up water. It may take a day or two for the pot to dry out, but the water won't hurt it.

Fine antique or museum-quality pottery should be cleaned delicately if at all. If nothing is flaking loose on the surface, you can dust with a **soft brush**. If more cleaning is required, wipe gently with a **damp cloth** or a damp cloth with a little **dishwashing liquid** added. Inspect the piece first, however: If the pottery has been repaired in the past, such cleaning could damage the repair job. For more extensive cleaning, consult a professional conservator.

WATCH OUT

Some pottery is painted with acrylic, followed by a spray-on glaze that is not kiln-fired. This kind of glaze will not stand up to washing in water. To clean it, wipe with a damp cloth.

Power Tools

If you don't clean your power tools periodically, they'll get you back—by going into permanent retirement. Dust, sawdust, and rust can seep into the motor and accumulate, eventually bringing the tool to a standstill.

For Sticky Situations >

Glue this here, drill that there ... and before you know it, your power tools are smeared with adhesive. No problem, says Glen Kaszubski, technical director for Liquid Nails brand construction adhesives. Just apply a dab of petroleum jelly and rub the glue with a dry cloth until the goo is gone.

How frequently you clean your power tools depends on how often you use them and how carefully you store them. In general, give them a good cleaning any time you notice a buildup of residue such as saw dust, oil, or grease. To keep everything running smoothly, don't store your tools where weather can affect them. And remember, if you don't clean them often enough, simple dust clogs can render built-in safety features useless.

To clean your power tools, first disconnect the juice. Unplug them or, if they run on batteries, remove the batteries and wipe out the battery compartment with a *soft, dry cloth*.

Do not, under any circumstances, spray anything liquid into the motor of any tool you're cleaning. Instead, get out the professional gadgeteer's favorite cleaner—a *can of compressed air*. Make sure you hold the can level before you point the extension straw and hit the spray button. If you don't hold the can perfectly level, you might wind up spraying liquid into the motor, and that would be disastrous. Spray a blast of air into the air vents. If you see a cloud of dust puff out of the motor, you know you've waited too long to clean your tools.

If you're picky about your tools' appearance, don't use abrasive cleaners. Simply squirt some *glass cleaner* onto a *paper towel* and wipe away the ugly stuff.

Pressure Cookers

Pressure cookers are tricky. Food particles can get trapped in the pressure gauge (that thing that rattles when the cooker is doing its job), and so the gauge should be cleaned after every use to keep food particles from turning into bacterial debris.

For cleaning out the pressure gauge, the best tool is a large *safety pin*. (Even though a toothpick would do quite nicely, it could break off in the little hole and, oops, no more pressure cooking.) Go at the little hole from both sides. You'll be amazed at the gunk that you can force out.

▲

Also give regular attention to the gasket, that rubber ring that seals the deal between the cooker and the lid. If you don't keep it clean, food buildup can result in bacterial buildup, and that's not part of any recipe. Remove the gasket ◀, pour a little *dishwashing detergent* into your hands, hold them under the *tap* until you have suds, and then massage the gasket until you're confident you've removed anything that might breed bacteria. Be careful not to stretch the gasket unnecessarily.

With repeated washing, the gasket can stretch and lose its shape. And a gasket that doesn't fit properly is as good as no gasket at all. It can also get crunchy with wear, so after you wash and dry it, rub the gasket with some *oil—olive, canola, or vegetable*—anything but corn oil, which can get sticky and actually attract debris.

It's a good idea to keep an extra gasket on hand. (If you have trouble finding one for your cooker, order one from the store where you bought it or call the manufacturer for a list of places that sell the kind that fits your model.)

To clean the inside of the pot, nothing works better than good ol' garden variety *dishwashing detergent, hot water*, a *plastic scrubbing sponge*, and a little muscle power.

Printers

First, remove any paper from the paper tray and, if the tray comes off, remove it. Using a *dry cloth*, wipe off the tray. You don't want water anywhere near the printer innards.

Clean the paper rollers to prevent paper from sticking to them. Clean plastic rollers with *cotton swabs* dipped in *denatured alcohol*. For rubber rollers, use *latex paint remover*—notably, the Goof Off brand, available at hardware stores. It smells yucky, but it will do wonders to revive rubber rollers. Avoid getting the remover on plastic parts. Don't touch the printing mechanism.

Cleaning the printer's insides shouldn't be necessary, unless you have the bad habit of leaving the top open. If you think you'll feel better giving the inside a go, use a *keyboard vacuum cleaner*. But whatever you do, don't put your fingers inside, except to change the ink cartridges. This is also a situation where zapping an electronic gizmo with compressed air isn't a good idea.

If you spot a toner spill in a laser printer, wipe it up carefully with *paper towels* or use a special *toner vacuum with a microtoner filter.* (3M makes one kind.) Toner can be toxic; don't inhale it. Avoid getting toner on your hands or clothes; it's hard to remove.

Cleaning the outer casing is a simpler matter. You can get rid of any mysterious blob that won't budge with a little *rubbing alcohol* on a *gauze pad*. Or, if you have them, you can rip open one of those little *alcohol prep pads* the nurse wipes your arm with before you get a shot. A brisk swipe or two, and the goo goes away. Remember: This is only for the exterior.

*See also **Computers**.*

Quilts

If you buy a quilt in a department store these days, it's almost always washable. Just check the care label and follow instructions. But often quilts are old and handmade, requiring special care. Those that have been handed down or found in flea markets or vintage stores have character that comes from having been cherished. Unfortunately, that character often appears in the form of water rings, dye bleeds, stains of unknown origin, and tears—all of which will dictate how you wash it.

Even with meticulous care, you shouldn't expect your hand-me-down or heirloom quilt to look like new. Instead, embrace the flaws, the water rings, the color bleeds, the rips, and the mystery stains.

After you've tested for bleeds and deterioration (see "Test First, Wash Later"), it's time to wash. The more colorfast your quilt is, the warmer the *water* you can use, but don't go much warmer than tepid. If the quilt has weak spots in the seams or fabric, put it in a *mesh laundry bag* and keep the *washer* on the *lowest agitation level*.

If you're leery of a machine wash, fill your *bathtub* with enough *water* to cover the quilt with 3 to 4 inches to spare. (Don't put the quilt in yet!) Add *laundry detergent, 1 ounce of detergent* per *1 gallon of water.* To get rid of general soil and yellow rings, you can add *1 or 2 tablespoons of color-safe bleach* (nonchlorine). Swirl the water to mix. Then lay the quilt in the water, spreading it as much as possible. Plant yourself by the tub for 10 minutes, swishing, smoothing, and squeezing as you go to release the soil. If you detect a bleed, drain the tub immediately and rinse the quilt with cold water. But if all goes well, you can leave the quilt in for up to an hour.

When it's time to rinse, drain the tub and push the quilt to the end away from the drain. Bunch it up in the end until all the water has drained from the tub. Then squeeze the quilt to force out the excess water. Pick it up and cradle it like a baby until you've refilled the tub with *tepid water*. Rinse by agitating the quilt just as you did in the washing step. If the rinse water becomes discolored, repeat the drain-and-rinse process. If you used bleach, rinse it twice. Squeeze the quilt again.

To dry the quilt, try tumbling it in the *dryer* with cool air, if you think the quilt can stand it. If not, hang it on a *clothesline* to dry.

Test First, *Wash Later*

When you're dealing with a vintage or heirloom quilt, there are many uncertainties. How was it stored? Was it ever dry-cleaned? Are the fabrics colorfast? Depending on the quilt's history, there may be stains, tears, and deterioration that require special care. To avoid catastrophe, Steve Boorstein, author of *The Ultimate Guide to Shopping & Caring for Clothing*, recommends the following steps before washing:

• Test the fabric strength. Some fabrics are so fragile that they tear like tissue paper. Depending on the quilt's age and how much it was cherished or neglected, some pieces of the fabric can deteriorate by being touched. If you have such a weak patch, baste the area with needle and thread or consider replacing the patch altogether.

• Test dyes. You could have cotton, velvet, acetate, or silk, all in one patchwork quilt. Each piece of fabric and each dye need to be tested for colorfastness.

To test, mix 1 tablespoon each of ammonia and liquid laundry detergent per 3 tablespoons of water. You might have to fiddle with the proportions, depending on how hard or soft your water is. You'll want just enough soap to eliminate friction and not enough to generate lots of suds, says Boorstein.

Dampen a white towel or cloth diaper with the solution. Be sure not to wet the testing cloth too much, or you could do exactly the damage to the quilt that you're seeking to avoid. Touch—don't press— the damp cloth or towel to an obscure corner of the quilt. Leave it on for 30 seconds. Then lightly blot the spot with a dry part of the cloth. Did any of the fabric color bleed onto the cloth? If not, go for stage two, which is a slightly more aggressive version of what you just did.

Go to another part of the quilt, a colorful one that you suspect might bleed. Find a dry spot on the white cloth and dampen it in the solution. This time, press harder on the damp cloth and wait a whole minute before blotting. "Patience is very important," Boorstein warns. On the second go-round, you might see some dye or soil come off on the blot cloth. If you see any hint of dye, you'll know there will be a little bleeding when you wash. But if you just see dirt, your quilt is probably colorfast. To make sure, take a third run at it. Go to another part of the quilt, press harder with the damp cloth so that the quilt actually absorbs a little of the cleaning solution, and lightly rub. If your white cloth is still white or has picked up no more than a trace of the color from the test spot, you're good to wash.

Radiators

A dusty radiator can be worse than ugly—it can be costly. Layers of dust can actually compromise the ability of your radiator to do its job. A weekly dusting with a feather duster or a dust cloth will keep accumulation down. Twice a year is often enough to do a major radiator cleaning, unless you live in an environment that is particularly dusty.

Don't try to clean a hot radiator. The best times to do it are in the spring or summer, when you're no longer using it, and in the fall, before you turn it on again. That way, there's no danger of burning yourself or igniting anything flammable.

To clean a cast-iron steam radiator, first, remove as much of the surface dirt as possible using a *hand vacuum* or the *brush attachment* of your vacuum cleaner. The brush can actually go some way toward getting in between the tubes. But the thin *nozzle attachment* goes farther. You won't get everything out with a vacuum, and you'll find that there are more effective ways to clean inside the crevices.

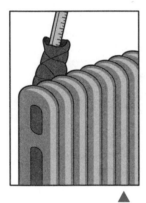

To reach the dust trapped between tubes, use a couple of common kitchen items. Wrap a *paper towel* around the broad end of a *kitchen spatula* and secure it with a *rubber band*. Then slide the spatula up and down both sides of each tube of the radiator. For resistant substances (sticky spills, especially), spray some *all-purpose cleaner*, such as Formula 409, on the paper-swathed spatula and have another go at it. If the radiator is tall, you might need to use a *rag* on a *yardstick* instead ◀.

Take care of rust spots as soon as you see them. You can get the larger chips off with a *wire kitchen brush*, followed by some *medium-* and then *fine-grade sandpaper*. Be sure to get rid of all the rust so the corrosion will stop after painting. Once you've smoothed the surface and there is no visible rust residue, spray the spot with a *rust-resistant paint*, such as Rust-Oleum, which comes in many colors.

Vacuum baseboard radiators to prevent dust from building up between the thin metal fins that distribute the heat. If you have an access panel, open it and vacuum inside the casing with the *brush attachment*. Be careful not to bend the delicate metal fins.

To clean a portable electric radiator, make sure you unplug it before you begin and then follow the directions given above for cleaning traditional steam radiators. (You won't need the derusting and painting steps.) When you put your electric radiator away for the summer, store it in a plastic trash bag to keep dust accumulation down.

Range Hoods

Because they're set over the stove, range hoods collect a lot of fat residue. The spatters from whatever you're cooking go up with the steam, and tiny filaments of dust attach to the fat, further gunking up the hood, inside and out. Ick.

To clean the outside of the hood, mix *1 teaspoon of dishwashing detergent* with *4 cups of warm water* to cut the grease. Soak a *sponge* in the solution and, to keep it from dripping, squeeze it thoroughly before attacking the hood. If your hood isn't painted, wipe the sponge with the grain of the stainless steel so you won't leave swirly marks.

If a stubborn food splatter is stuck to the hood, use a *plastic dish scrubber* or your fingernail to dislodge it. If that doesn't work, squirt the spot with an *all-purpose cleaner* such as Formula 409, let it sit for five minutes, and then scrub with a *sponge*. Don't use anything abrasive, because it will scratch the surface and take some paint off.

To clean the underside of the hood, lay a *towel* on top of the stove to catch falling dirt. (You checked that the burners are off and cool, right?) If you have a gas stove, lay a *couple of pans* across the stovetop first to create some separation between the towel and the pilot lights. In a *spritzer bottle*, mix a solution of *1 part dishwashing soap* to *2 parts warm water*. Spray underneath the hood and let the solution sit for 15 minutes. While the solution breaks down the accumulation of grease, you can remove the fan filter. Some newer range hood filters can go right into the *dishwasher*. But if your model doesn't allow for dishwasher cleaning, soak the filter in a solution of *1/2 cup of warm white vinegar, 1 teaspoon of dishwashing soap*, and *warm water* until you see the greasy debris loosening. Rinse the filter first with *warm water* to get rid of any remaining sticky stuff and then with *cool water*. Once the underside of the hood has been soaking for 15 minutes, wipe up the grease with *paper towels*. (You'll ruin cloths.) If grease remains, give it another spray and wipe.

expert advice

The Only Way to Fry >

It's your party, and you'll fry if you want to. And when you do, use only canola oil, recommends Sharyl Heavin, family consumer scientist for DCS, a maker and distributor of high-end appliances based in Huntington Beach, California. Corn oil tends to leave a much filmier, stickier residue that's harder to clean.

Records

Some of us still listen to music on plastic platters called records. Most of us neglect the albums, but a little regular cleaning will make them last longer and sound better.

Velvet record brushes (the Stanton VC-1 cleaning system, for instance) are the favorite of many who do clean their records. They have a handle for gripping and a velvet-grained fabric on the bottom. They come with a liquid, which is mostly water with a dash of mild soap. Harsher chemicals will damage record vinyl.

Put *a few drops of the liquid* on the **brush**. Place the record on the turntable (if you're too young to know what a turntable is, you're reading the wrong entry) and turn it on. Hold the brush lightly on the surface of the record as it spins. This will get rid of any dust that might interrupt a pleasurable listening experience with skips.

If you don't have a velvet record brush, you can use a *very soft cloth* with a fine weave to clean your records. A *cloth diaper* is ideal. Don't use anything that creates lint—that's what you're trying to get rid of. Make a mixture of *99 percent water* and *1 percent baby shampoo*. Barely dampen the cloth—make sure it isn't wet—and hold it lightly on the record as it spins. Be careful not to touch the record with a fingernail.

If you have heavier, sticky grime on a record, go at it again with the *baby shampoo mixture* and a little more pressure on the *diaper*. If that doesn't get rid of the goo, take the record off the turntable, holding it only by the edges. Rest an edge against your body and hold the other edge in one hand. With your free hand, wipe the record with the damp diaper, moving back and forth in the direction of the grooves.

Refrigerators and Freezers

Keeping your refrigerator and freezer clean is not only important to the appearance (and smell) of your home, it's also crucial to the sanitation of your food and thus to the health of your family. There are three major aspects of keeping refrigerators and freezers clean: removing dirt, killing germs, and deodorizing the interior.

Cleaning the fridge is only a half-hour job, so there's no need to haul out the cooler to keep your refrigerated goods cold. Instead, empty one shelf at a time, so food on the other shelves can stay chilled. Remove the first shelf and spray it liberally with a **disin-fecting all-purpose cleaner**, such as Lysol, to vanquish the inevitable sticky spills. (Glass cleaner probably isn't going to do the job.) Or sanitize it with a squirt of good ol' **white vinegar** in a **spray bottle**. Wipe the shelf dry with a **paper towel** and reinsert it in the refrigerator. Repeat the procedure with each shelf.

To clean the drawers, pull them out of the fridge one at a time, place them in the sink, and fill them with **warm water** and a healthy **squirt of dishwashing detergent**. Let the water sit in them for 10 minutes. Then pour the water out, rinse with **fresh water**, and wipe dry with a **towel.**

Keeping your fridge germ free is a priority. Meat and poultry juices dripping on refrigerator surfaces are not only unsightly; they are potentially harmful vehicles for the spread of salmonella and *E. coli*. Even though a refrigerator's temperature is low, it doesn't stop the growth of all bacteria. Some bacteria can grow even in refrigerated temperatures. And, while some are harmless, some can make you really sick. For instance, when you're thawing meat or poultry in the fridge, if those juices drip down or contaminate a shelf, it could lead to serious health problems. So as you remove each shelf, spray the inside of the refrigerator with a **disinfecting all-purpose cleaner**. Remember, just because it looks clean doesn't mean that it is clean.

Cleaning the freezer isn't quite the ordeal that cleaning the fridge is. Most freezers aren't so big that they take more than 20 minutes to clean, and it takes frozen food hours to thaw, so you probably won't need to enlist a friend's freezer or even your

A *Crack Cleaning* Technique

Those crafty little egg cups in the door of your refrigerator are a bane and a blessing. They're pretty good at keeping eggs from bumping into each other. But somehow, the occasional egg cracks, despite the efficient design, and then you've got trouble.

Eggs are a popular breeding place for salmonella, so that egg ooze drying right under your nose could be quite a hazard, warns Lysol microbiologist Joe Rubino. Take these steps to remedy the situation:
• First, remove as much of the substance as you can with a paper towel.
• If it has begun to harden, try scraping it out with a spoon.
• If the broken egg has had a while to harden, there may be some stubborn residue left. An all-purpose disinfecting degreaser is just about the only thing that will cut that mess, says Rubino. Spray the cleaner on and let it sit for several minutes while you clean the rest of the fridge. By then, you should be able to lift the rest of the egg goop out with a paper towel. Rinse thoroughly.

trusty cooler. Just put the food in the sink. If you pile frozen items on top of each other, they'll keep each other cold.

Soak a *sponge* in *warm water* and squeeze out enough water that you won't create trickles that will add to your work. Wipe each rack in the freezer, top and bottom. If you have a thick, frozen spill, scrape it first with a *stiff plastic spatula* that has a thin edge (no metal), and then spot clean it with a *soapy sponge*.

Regularly sanitizing the door handles is perhaps the most important aspect of fridge cleaning. When you're preparing food it's best to wash your hands each and every time you handle raw meat. That's easy to forget in the midst of creating an elegant entrée, however, and when you transfer that contamination to the door handles, another family member who uses the refrigerator could pick up the germs. The solution: Keep a *box or tube of all-purpose wipes* (Clorox makes good ones) near the refrigerator and make it a habit to wipe off the handle frequently.

Vacuuming the coils under a frost-free fridge (or on the back of a cycle defrost unit) should be a part of your regular kitchen cleanup about once a month—especially if you have a shedding pet. Unplug the refrigerator and push the *crevice tool* as far under the unit as you can ◄. Be careful not to bend the tubing or the fins.

▲

expert advice

Removing Those Christmas "Decorations" >

At Tricolor Tree Transplanting and Nursery in West Chester, Pennsylvania, where their cash crop is Christmas trees, Ruth Constable is an expert at removing gluey tree resins from work clothes. She dabs on Lestoil, a heavy-duty cleaner, and lets it dry. Then she soaks the garment in Lestoil and warm water. "Get the worst out before you throw it in the washer," she advises.

Resins

Resin is the sticky stuff, commonly known as pine sap, that can make a gooey mess on clothing, carpeting, and skin. A hot water wash won't do the trick—resin needs a more aggressive approach. When removing tree tar from clothing and carpeting, these methods should resin-ate with you.

If you're confronted with gobs of goo, first scrape off what you can with a *dull knife or tongue depressor*. Then apply *turpentine, rubbing alcohol, cleaning solvent*, or a *prewash stain remover*, such as Shout, testing a hidden part of the garment or carpet beforehand to make sure it's colorfast.

To treat a garment, place it facedown on a *clean, absorbent rag*. Sponge or spray *solvent* (see above) full strength on the front and back of the sticky stuff to saturate it. Allow it to dry. (If you use rubbing alcohol, dilute it, using *1 part alcohol* to *2 parts water*, just to be safe.) The resin should dissolve and seep into the rag underneath. If it doesn't, repeat.

REFRIGERATORS AND FREEZERS

For small resin spots, saturate a *cotton pad* or *swab* in *full-strength alcohol* and dab on the spot, blotting all the while. Then launder the garment separately, using *liquid laundry detergent* and the *hottest water* the fabric can take. If the stain persists, mix *equal parts liquid laundry detergent* and *ammonia* and soak. Then launder again as above.

For carpets, always apply the *solvent of your choice* to a *clean rag* and then apply the rag to the sappy mess and blot.

To remove resin from skin, dab *full-strength rubbing alcohol* on the stain with a *cotton pad or swab*. Wash with *soap* and the *hottest water* you can stand.

Roofing

Moss, algae, and mildew adore your roof. They feast on shingles and burrow below, causing shingles to blacken and lose layers.

Embark cautiously on do-it-yourself roof cleaning. When you combine a steep pitch with the use of ladders and cleaners that make the roof slippery, you have a recipe for potential disaster hanging over your head.

To clean asphalt roofs as well as cedar and other shake-shingled roofs, first go to your home improvement store and pick up a *cleaner for treated-wood decks*—one that contains oxygen bleach. (Don't use chlorine bleach.) On a cloudy day, when the roof is cool, mix the cleaner according to the package directions and squirt it on the roof with a *garden sprayer*. (High-pressure sprayers will damage the roof.) Let the cleaner sit for half an hour. Then give it a scrubbing with a *broom* or *brush*. Rinse thoroughly with a *garden hose*.

Tile roofs can attract moss and other growth, too, but cleaning them yourself is not recommended because wet tiles are delicate and extremely slippery. Let a professional do the job.

To create an inhospitable environment for growth on your roof, apply *zinc strips* close to the top (or comb) of the roof. Rainwater reacts with the zinc and drips down the roof, discouraging growth. To get the strips, visit a roofing supply company.

Several kinds of metal roofing, including painted steel and copper, need little maintenance. Costly to install, such roofs nonetheless last many years.

expert advice

Paint on a Cool Tin Roof >

The biggest problem with maintaining a tin roof is keeping it painted, according to Galen Smoker, who owns Diversified Exteriors, a roofing, siding, and gutter company in Parkesburg, Pennsylvania. Paint often sheds from tin roofs in sheets. Then you've got big problems, mostly with rust.

Choose a sunny but cool day to paint a tin roof. Wash it first, using a soapy solution in your garden sprayer. Rinse well. Allow it to dry. Then paint with a rust-proof, oil-based paint.

Rugs

The best way to keep a rug looking fresh is to keep it from getting dirty in the first place. Remove your outdoor shoes when entering the house and you'll cut down on 80 percent of the dirt tracked in. Keep a basket of clean socks and fresh slippers by the door for guests.

Give rugs a good, regular shake outside. *Vacuum* them often, front *and* back, against the nap to pick up ground-in dirt. Rugs in high-traffic areas need a more thorough cleaning at least once a year; those in out-of-the-way places, less often.

To shampoo a small rug, follow these steps:

1. *Vacuum* the rug.
2. Mix *1/2 cup mild dishwashing liquid* or *rug shampoo* with *1/2 gallon of cool water* in a *clean bucket*. (Don't use harsh detergents, sudsy ammonia, or regular ammonia on your rugs.) Aerosol *rug sprays* (Resolve, for instance) also work well on smaller rugs or small areas of carpeting. Test the cleaner you're using on a hidden spot to make sure the rug is colorfast.
3. With a *long-bristled, soft brush* or a *firm, nonshedding sponge*, brush the solution on the pile in the direction of the nap. Don't scrub. Wet thoroughly.
4. Wash the rug's fringe, if any. If the floor is wood or otherwise easily damaged by water, place a *plastic or rubber drop cloth or sheet* under the fringe. Then put a *clean white towel* on top of that (still beneath the fringe). Using a *brush or sponge* moistened (not sopping) with the cleaning solution, brush the fringe from the knots out to the end. To rinse, replace the first towel under the fringe with a *dry towel* and blot the fringe with yet *another towel* dampened with *warm water*. Allow the fringe to dry on a *third dry towel.*
5. To rinse the main part of the rug, wet *clean rags* with *warm water* and press them against the rug.
6. Squeeze out excess. (A *window squeegee* works great.) Squeegee the pile in the direction of the nap until no more water comes out. Use more towels to mop up any excess.
7. If you have plastic underneath the rug and it's now wet, replace it with *dry plastic*. Lay down *dry towels* and lay the rug flat on the towels to dry thoroughly on one side. Then flip it over to dry the other, replacing the *towels again* if need be. Another technique: Dry the rug atop a *picnic table* in the shade outside.
8. If the pile feels stiff, vacuum or brush it gently.

To remove a rug stain, several rules of thumb apply. Attack problems in this order:

- Blot stains, using *clean rags or absorbent white towels*.
- Scrape up whatever solids you can, using a *kitchen knife, spatula, or putty knife*.
- Work from the stain's outer edges to its center, rather than from the inside out, which could spread the stain.
- If the stain has penetrated the entire rug, place a *clean rag* underneath the rug to absorb what seeped through.
- Dilute the stain by blotting with a *cloth* dampened with *water or plain club soda* (no flavors).
- Try a dab of *rug cleaner,* such as Resolve, according to package directions. (Test first on a hidden area.)
- If this doesn't work, mix *1 teaspoon of mild dishwashing liquid* with *1 cup of warm water*. Blot with a *white towel* dampened with *clear water*. Don't saturate.
- Shaving cream can also work wonders. Moisten the spot with *water*, work in the *shaving cream*, and rinse with a *clean rag* dampened with *cool water*.
- Mix *1 tablespoon of household ammonia* with *1/2 cup of water*. Dab the solution on with a *clean rag*. Then mix *1/2 cup of vinegar* and *1 cup of water*. Blot this mix on to curb the ammonia action. Rinse with a *clean rag* dampened with *cool water*.
- Mix enough *powdered enzyme laundry detergent* with *water* to make a paste. Be sure the detergent has no bluing or whitening agents. Let the paste sit 10 minutes and then remove any residue with a *wooden spoon*. Blot with a *clean towel* and rinse with *another towel* wrung out in *warm water*.

See also **Carpeting**.

Rust

Rust is unsightly and destructive. When metal reacts with air, rust proliferates—affecting iron, steel, chrome, bathtubs, toilets, sinks, concrete, garden tools, metal outdoor furniture, carpeting, and fabric, among other things.

Steel yourself for this flurry of cleaning tips:

To banish rust from iron and steel, first remove the rust and then repaint. Use *fine sandpaper or steel wool* for the removal job. If more drastic measures are needed, dip your abrasive in *kerosene*.

Remove rust from metal baking dishes and other cookware by sprinkling *powdered dishwasher or laundry detergent* onto the spot and scouring with the cut edge of a *raw potato half*. Another method: Pour *cola* on the rust and let it work its magic overnight. Then wash off the cookware in the morning.

For rust on bathtubs, toilets, and sinks, rub with *automotive rubbing compound* on a *clean rag*. If the rust is really thick, use a *pumice stone* to penetrate the rust, along with more rubbing compound. Rubbing compound and pumice are readily available at most hardware and home improvement stores.

If your stainless steel sink gets rusty, rub it with *lighter fluid*. Be careful, though. As you might have guessed, this stuff is highly flammable.

To tackle rust stains on concrete, sprinkle *dry cement powder* on the rust and use a *small piece of flagstone* (what patios are often made of) to rub out the stain. The combination of powder and stone acts like pumice and will often eradicate the rust.

To remove rust stains from patio stones, here's a technique you wouldn't expect. Wet the area with a *hose* and cover it with *powdered lemonade mix*. Cover that with a *piece of plastic* (to prevent the moisture from evaporating) and hold it down with *something heavy*. Let it stand for 10 minutes or so. Scrub with a *stiff-bristled brush* and rinse with the hose. Repeat if necessary.

If the lemonade mix does not work, first rinse the area with *water* and then apply a solution of *1 part muriatic acid* to no

Beware the Water

Sometimes municipalities or water companies (depending on where you live) flush the lines of their water systems. Rust from inside those pipes can wind up in your water, sullying your clothes. If you unwittingly wash clothes during "the flush," your laundry may become rust-stained or yellowed. (Often, municipalities or water companies warn residents that they're about to do "the flush," so heed those warnings and refrain from washing clothes until the dirty work is done.) Should your clothes get stained in this manner, don't ever dry them in the dryer—this only sets the stains. Don't use bleach either. Chlorine makes a temporary rust stain permanent.

Here are your choices:
• Wash the clothes immediately in clear water using heavy-duty detergent.
• Wash the clothes with 1 cup nonprecipitating water conditioner (such as Spring Rain or Calgon)—no detergent! (Sometimes water conditioner, working in concert with detergent, can set a rust stain.)
• For white clothing, fill a large soup pot with water and boil with 1 cup of cream of tartar. Dip the garment for a few minutes, then rinse.
• Launder with a commercial rust remover, following package directions. Common brands are RoVer, Rit Rust Remover, Iron Out laundry products (Rust Out and Yellow Out), and Whink.

RUST

fewer than **5 parts water**. Let the solution stand for a few minutes and then rinse with **water**. Wear **rubber gloves** and **eye protection** when using muriatic acid.

When metal deck and porch furniture is badly rusted, wrap the rusted part in a **kerosene-soaked cloth** for a few days. Then sand with medium-grit **sandpaper** ▶. Wash, rinse, and dry thoroughly and then paint with a **rustproof paint**.

If your carpet or rug has rust stains, try this: Mix **water** with **baking soda** into a paste. Apply the paste to the stain, allow it to sit three or four hours, and then use a **commercial carpet shampoo** according to the package directions.

For rust stains on clothing, apply a paste of **lemon juice** and **baking soda** to a hidden spot on the garment to make sure the color holds. If all is well, apply the paste to the rust stains. Let it sit an hour before hanging the clothing outside to dry, then launder the garment as usual.

For rust on white clothes, try this alternative remedy: Mix **cream of tartar** with **lemon juice** and apply it to the stain. Allow the garment to dry and then rinse thoroughly before washing as usual.

S

Saddles and Tack

How often you clean saddles and tack depends on how often you use them. At a minimum, saddle up to clean and condition them at least twice a year—more often, if you're caught in the rain or live in a cold climate, which can leach natural oils from leather and cause dry rot to take over.

To clean a saddle, use **saddle soap**, a **sponge**, and **warm water** to work up a foamy lather. Stirrups, stirrup leathers, and fenders attract the most dirt, so pay particular attention to those, wiping them on both sides. If dirt is really ingrained, let the foamy saddle soap sit to soften it. Rinse off the soap—and be sure to do it thoroughly. (If you leave soap residue on the leather, it will attract rather than repel dirt.) Use **toothpicks** to lift out dirt on deeply tooled leather.

Allow the saddle to air-dry overnight, but not in the sun, where it could dry out too much. Then condition the leather lightly: On Western saddles, use either **pure neat's-foot oil** (a light yellow oil made from cattle shinbones and feet) or a **leather conditioner**, such as Lexol. Remember that neat's foot (or any other oil, for that matter) will darken the leather. On English saddles, use a **leather dressing**, such as Skidmore's Leather Cream, applied with a **soft cloth**. Don't miss the underside of the seat, fenders, and (on Western saddles) jockeys, the pieces of leather underneath the seat of the saddle. Then buff with a clean, **soft cloth** to bring out the leather's natural shine.

To clean your tack, use the same general technique as with saddles, but be sure to take it apart first. Bits must be taken off the headstall and reins, for instance. Brush off any loose dirt with a **rag** or **soft brush**.

Storing your saddle and tack is also important.
- Store a saddle on a **rack** with air circulating freely.
- To preserve that characteristic twist in the leather strap that connects Western-style stirrups to the saddle, turn the stirrups in the correct direction and then insert a **wooden dowel** through one stirrup, under the saddle, and through the other stirrup.
- Hang bridles and halters on a **rack shaped like a horse's head**. (Nails or hooks can cause leather to bend and weaken.)
- Finally, leave dirt in the dust by shrouding your saddle with a **dust cover**.

expert advice

Want a Fungus on Your Saddle? Neigh! >

For saddles and tack in humid climates, use saddle oil boosted with a fungicide. Otherwise, leather can get moldy and mildewy, says Bob Brenner, a custom saddle maker in Black Forest, Colorado. He recommends using a fungicide-impregnated saddle oil such as #1 Saddle Oil with fungicides, from Bee Natural Leathercare products, to keep mold and mildew at bay.

Satin

Cleaning satin is tricky because this shiny fabric picks up and shows grease and other stains so easily.

If you get a greasy stain on satin of any kind—be it on blanket binding, satin sheets, pillows, holiday decorations, or other items—try blotting (don't rub!) the stain first with a *clean white rag*. Then cover the stain with *flour* or *cornmeal*. Let it sit for an hour. The milled grain should absorb most of the stain. Gently brush the fabric with a *soft-bristled brush* and launder a washable item according to the instructions on the fabric care label. If a blanket is washable, its binding is too. Treat stains first with a *prewash stain remover*. If an item is not washable, take it to a *dry cleaner*.

Satin sheets are a little trickier to care for because there are several types.

- If you have woven acetate sheets or silk satin sheets, dry-clean them, or hand-wash them in a *laundry tub* or *bathtub* in *room temperature water* and a *gentle fabric wash* such as Woolite. Hand-wring gently, wrapping up the sheet in an *absorbent white towel*, and hang to dry.
- Polyester and nylon satin sheets are more durable. You may machine-wash them, but hand-washing will keep pilling to a minimum. If you are putting them in a *washing machine*, use *warm* or *cool water* and *very little detergent*. Never use bleach. Put in the *dryer* on the *lowest setting*. Never line dry nylon sheets in the sun.

To clean satin pillows and holiday decorations, *vacuum* them using the *soft brush attachment*. Give greasy stains the *flour* or *cornmeal* treatment described above. If stains persist, launder a satin pillow only if its cover comes off. It's best to dry-clean satin holiday decorations, as well as satin curtains, bedspreads, and comforters. Differences in their linings may cause the fabrics to dry differently.

WATCH OUT

- Shield sheets made of silk and nylon from the sun. Never line dry nylon satin sheets, for sun is nylon's public enemy No. 1. If your bedroom is sunny, choose acetate or polyester satin.
- Never dry woven acetate sheets in a dryer.
- Be especially careful when wringing silk satin sheets—silk is usually thin and tears easily.

Scissors

To keep scissors on the cutting edge, it's important to clean them. Buy different kinds of scissors for different tasks: a pair for cutting paper and for craft projects, another pair for working with fabric, scissors for snipping hair, and so on.

To keep your scissors cutting smoothly, wipe the blades after each use with a *soft rag*. This prevents lint and other stuff from getting caught in the blade pivot area, where it can interfere with the performance of your scissors.

Oil scissors occasionally at the pivot area (around the screw head and between the blades) using a *penetrating lubricant*, such as WD-40. Never use vegetable oil or any other oil that attracts dirt and gets gummy. Gently work the blades a few times to force the lubricant into the joint.

If your scissors get dirty, wash them in *dishwashing liquid* and *water*, removing any sticky stuff with lighter fluid. Dry scissors thoroughly with a *soft cloth* before storing them.

If your scissors get rusty, soak them first in *white vinegar*. Then use *fine sandpaper* on the handles and blades, being careful to avoid the cutting edges. Store scissors in a dry, cool, clean place.

To keep those blades sharp, some scissors makers recommend using sharpeners. Most experts, however, suggest that you take them to a professional.

To clean haircutting scissors, try these steps for shear delight:

- Wipe the blades clean after each use with *a clean, soft cloth*. Or use a *silicone cloth*, available anywhere you buy hunting gear, which leaves a welcome (and protective) film.
- Spray scissors occasionally with an *antibacterial solution* (Barbicide, for instance, or see *Combs* for a home recipe). Dry completely.
- Oil the pivot with *light shear oil or clipper oil*, available at beauty or barber supply stores. An acceptable substitute is *light gun oil*. When it's time to stash your shears, close the blades and store the scissors somewhere dry.

Screens

Window screens can get absolutely filthy. Not surprising when you consider that their job is to keep dust, pollen, bugs, and other airborne detritus on the outside looking in. Clean screens at least once a year, preferably when the weather first turns balmy and it's time to put them up.

To clean window screens, move them to a flat surface, being careful not to place them where underlying objects can damage them. If you lay them in your yard, remove rocks or other sharp objects underneath. Placing them atop a *large drop cloth* or *old shower curtain* is a good idea, or just lay them on a *paved driveway*.

simple SOLUTIONS

Watch How You Use Pinking Shears >

Prolong the life of pinking shears by being sure there is always fabric between the blades when you cut. Never open or close the blades without fabric in between.

expert advice

Getting Screens in the Right Windows >

Number your screens, so you'll be able to tell which goes where. Put a number on each window frame, in a hidden spot, and then write or scratch the corresponding number on its screen frame.

In a *large bucket*, mix *3 parts warm water* with *1 part ammonia* and *2 tablespoons each of liquid dishwashing soap* and *borax*. (Or purchase an *all-purpose cleaner* at the hardware store.) Wearing *rubber gloves*, pour the mixture into a *trigger spray bottle*. Wet the screens thoroughly with a *garden hose*. Spray the cleaner onto the screens, front and back, being careful not to miss those grimy corners. Allow the cleaning solution to sit on the screens at least five minutes, to better penetrate the mesh and do the dirty work for you. The less scrubbing you do on screens the better, for they get brittle and often loosen with age.

Scrub both sides—gently—with a *soft-bristled brush*, using an *old toothbrush* to get into grimy corners ▶. Rinse the brushes as you toil so that you won't smear around more grime than you remove. Rinse the screens thoroughly with the hose and then air-dry them in the sun, propped up against the house or bushes.

▲

Sewing Machines

Isaac Merrit Singer, whose name was once synonymous with the sewing machine, would be spinning in his grave if he knew you had a dirty sewing machine. Take care of that machine. It will last longer, you'll sew better, and the old boy will rest in peace. The instructions below apply primarily to traditional mechanical sewing machines operated by an electric motor. To clean the more fragile computerized machines, follow the directions in your owner's manual.

For a mechanical sewing machine, be sure you use the right oil to keep it humming. Use *sewing machine oil* (available at fabric stores and sewing machine shops). Other common lubricants, such as 3-in-One oil and WD-40, dry too fast and will eventually cause the machine to seize and stop. Put no more than one or two drops of sewing machine oil in each of the 30-odd holes that pockmark your machine.

Floss your machine to banish the fuzzies and keep it running smoothly. Slide the edges of a thin piece of *muslin* between the tension disks (those metal pieces the thread passes through). Be sure the presser foot is up to slacken the tension springs. (If you have no muslin, gently slide a *credit card* between the disks to loosen dust and dirt caught between them.) Remove the machine's cover. Using a *can of compressed air* or a *hair dryer*, hit movable parts with a stream of air, from back to front, to remove any loose threads, lint, and fuzzies.

WATCH OUT

Never oil a computerized sewing machine or use any kind of liquid anywhere near it. (Oil and liquids can irreparably damage circuit boards.) Use a hair dryer to blow away lint. If you're unsure about cleaning your computerized sewing machine, take it to a sewing machine repair shop.

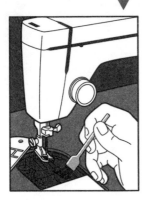

Take off the throat plate (sometimes called the needle plate), paying close attention to how it is removed and replaced. On some models, it screws in. On others, it's spring-loaded. Same thing goes for the bobbin, bobbin case (also called the shuttle), and hook race—watch what you're taking apart, or you may not get it together again. Use compressed air, the hair dryer, or a small **stiff-bristled nylon brush** to clean these parts ◄. In a pinch, a **pipe cleaner** will extract small fibers from moving parts. So will a **dental pick**. Don't use toothpicks—they're too flimsy and could break.

Dust the outside with a **clean cloth**. (Microfiber cloth works well.) A **mild household cleaner** such as Formula 409 or Windex does the job on grimy fingerprints. Spray first on a **cloth** and then wipe. If the case is metal, **sewing machine oil or WD-40**, sprayed first on a **rag**, will shine it up.

Keep your machine clean by covering it when you're not using it. Ready-made **plastic covers** are sold at notions and sewing machine shops. Or make one yourself from an **old pillowcase**. Keep the machine away from heat, light, and open windows.

Shades

expert advice

Catch Those Dust Bunnies >

A microfiber dust cloth works wonders on shades of all types, advises Deborah Weiner, an interior designer in Silver Spring, Maryland, and owner of Designing Solutions. Once a week, lightly run the dust cloth, which typically has more than 90,000 fibers per square inch, over the front and back of your shades to keep those dust bunnies from multiplying.

To keep window shades from looking shady, dust them each week with one of those ticklish **feather dusters** or the **soft brush attachment** on your **vacuum cleaner**. If you have vinyl shades, wash them twice a year with a **sponge or soft cloth**, using a solution of **1/4 cup of white vinegar** and **1 quart of warm water**.

Many fabric shades can be washed—carefully—and dried. Take a close look at the care instructions for your shade before attempting the following method:

1. Take down the shade and immerse it for no more than a minute in a **bathtub** full of **warm water** to which you've added **1/4 cup of mild dishwashing liquid**.
2. Use a **soft brush** to scrub both sides.
3. Rinse with **fresh water** and hang to air-dry.

If your shades can't be washed, scour them with **cornmeal** or **flour**, applied with a **flannel rag**. Or use an **art gum** or other **soft eraser** to remove spots and stains. You can also have them professionally **dry-cleaned**.

If you have parchment shades, keep them clean by applying a **thin coat of paste wax** (what you'd use on wood floors), buffing to a shine with a **soft cloth**.

If a shade gets a small tear, seal it with *clear nail polish*. This also works with vinyl-backed shades.

Shells

Even the most beautiful live seashells can stink to high heaven if you don't remove decaying matter stuck inside. Seashells come in myriad sizes and varieties, but they're mainly characterized as either dead or alive. Dead seashells have no animal tissue inside. Shells with animal tissue inside are called live even if the critter inside isn't.

To clean dead seashells, soak them in a *50-50 solution* of *bleach* and *water*. How long you do this depends on what shells you're cleaning, as well as how many you do at once. Soak first for 30 minutes, longer if you want shells bleached white or if they feel really grimy. Before you remove them from the solution, make sure that the periostracum—the leatherlike, flaky covering on some shells—is gone. Rinse thoroughly with *fresh, warm water*.

- If barnacles and other clingy stuff persist, use a *dental pick or ice pick* to remove them.
- If the lip of a seashell gets chipped, use a *rotary grinder* or *file* to smooth out rough edges.
- If you like your shells to shine, coat them with a light layer of *mineral oil or baby oil*.

To clean live seashells, you have this choice of methods for getting rid of the flesh:
- Bury the shells 18 inches deep in your *yard* for a month or two. Insects, bacteria, worms, larvae, and other tiny organisms will eat everything that you want to get out of the shell.
- Give them the deep freeze treatment. Place the shells in a *waterproof bag*, add enough water to the bag to cover the shells, and stick them in the *freezer* for a few days. Then let them thaw to room temperature. You should be able to grab the tissue inside and pull it out.
- Boil *water* in a *large pot* and submerge the shells for five minutes. Using *tongs* and being careful not to burn yourself, remove one shell at a time and, grasping it with *gloves* or a *towel*, pull out the tissue inside.
- A smelly but no less effective way to clean shells: "Cook" them in the *microwave*. (Time will vary depending on the oven's power and the strength of the shell.) Start with 30 sec-

onds and increase the time in 10-second increments. Use *tongs* and special care as you remove the shells and grab whatever animal tissue remains.

Should tiny pieces of living tissue remain, put the shell outdoors and allow flies, bugs, and ants to feast on what's left. Once all the flesh is gone, treat the shells as described above for dead shells. Give them a bleach bath and rinse completely.

Shoes

A wise man once observed that you can tell a lot about a person by seeing whether his or her shoes are polished. Only trouble is, much of the footwear men, women, and children wear today is not leather. Still, taking care of your shoes means you'll extend their useful life, even if that spit-shine first impression isn't as relevant as it once was.

To protect new leather shoes, spray or rub them with a *water and stain repellent* such as Scotchgard before wearing them. Be sure to use a repellent made especially for leather. Then polish them before stepping out. Leather shoes are usually malnourished and dry when they come out of the box, and the extra layer of polish will protect them.

To give leather shoes and boots a shine—without the spit—follow these steps:
1. Remove laces.
2. Brush off loose dirt with a *stiff brush* or *cloth*.
3. If the shoes are especially dirty, clean them with *saddle soap*, following package directions.
4. Rub a *clean cotton cloth* in *polish* and then onto the shoes. Let the polish dry 10 minutes.
5. Buff with a clean cloth or old panty hose.

▲

To clean patent leather shoes, first remove any scuff marks with a garden-variety *eraser*. Then shine them with *baby oil*, *furniture polish*, *petroleum jelly*, or *cream leather cleaner/conditioner*, available at shoe repair shops ◄. Buff with a *paper towel* or *clean cloth*. Be gentle—patent leather scratches easily. In a pinch, rub leather or patent shoes with *hand cream* and then buff. On imitation patent leather, use *mild dishwashing detergent* or a *car interior vinyl and plastic cleaner*, such as Meguiar's, available at auto supply stores.

To remove salt stains from leather shoes, rub with *equal parts* of *water* and *vinegar*, applied with a *cotton pad*.

To clean white shoes, give them a swipe with a *cloth* dabbed in *ammonia*. (This works well on canvas, too.) Remove scuff marks with a *dab of white toothpaste*. Then buff.

To protect suede shoes, apply a *stain repellent* designed for suede or nubuck. Use a *rubber-tipped* or *plastic brush* to brush the nap and remove dirt. If you get a stain, remove it pronto with a *solvent* made for either material. An *oil-absorbent block*, made especially for suede shoes and available at shoe stores, will also wick away the stain when held against it. Or you can blot an oily stain with *baby powder* or *chalk dust* (which you can pulverize in a resealable plastic bag using a small hammer or rolling pin). Allow the powder to sit overnight. Then brush it off.

To erase scuff marks on smooth leather shoes, rub the marks with the cut edge of a *raw potato* and then buff.

See also **Sneakers**.

simple SOLUTIONS

When You Don't Have Time to Polish >

For an instant shine, use baby wipes. This technique will dry out the leather over time, so follow up with polish later on.

Showers

How can the shower—the place where you clean yourself—get so dirty? Nowhere, save for the kitchen sink, does a home show grime more than in the shower. Soap, shampoo, and dirt from the shower's temporary denizens combine to make an unsightly mess.

To keep your shower sparkling, try these:
- Next time you shower, clean the shower, too. The steam from your shower will help loosen any grime and make the job easier.
- For tiled shower walls and floor, use dishwasher detergent (either powder or liquid will do). Mix *1/4 cup dishwasher detergent* with *warm water* in a *small pump spray bottle* and shake to dissolve the detergent. Spritz liberally on walls, let it sit two or three hours, and then scrub with a *sponge*. Use a *sponge mop* to scrub high spots and the floor.
- To clean tile grout, make a paste of *baking soda* and *bleach* (add bleach to the powder until it's a thick goo). Smear the paste on with a *spatula*. Air-dry for an hour and then scrub with a *toothbrush* and *water*. (Never use ammonia nearby, since ammonia and bleach don't mix.)
- To prevent water spots, rub the shower walls and doors with a *squeegee* right after you have taken your shower. If you have no squeegee, an old *wiper blade* will do. Or try one of the *daily shower cleaners*. Mist surfaces right after you shower,

while the walls are still warm and wet. The cleaner will prevent deposits from forming and will wash down the drain the next time you shower.

If your shower sprouts mold, try this trick: Wipe down the walls with a solution of *1 teaspoon water softener*, *1 tablespoon ammonia*, and *1 tablespoon vinegar* in *3/4 cup warm water*. Rinse with *fresh water*. Buff dry.

To clean your shower doors, follow these pointers:
● Wash them with *white vinegar* to banish soap scum.
● Or take that leftover *white wine* that's rapidly turning to vinegar, empty it into a *trigger spray bottle*, and squirt it on your shower doors. Rinse well with *water* and dry with a *soft cloth*.
● Wipe down the doors with *fabric softener* on a *damp cloth*. Buff with a *clean*, *dry cloth*.
● Another way to keep soap scum away: Wipe down the shower doors with *lemon oil*. *Baby oil* works too, as does *furniture polish*, buffed with a soft cloth. (This also works on tiled showers, but don't put these slippery substances on a shower floor.)
● Scrub shower door runners with *white toothpaste* and an *old toothbrush*. Brush with *vinegar* to rinse. Or dip a *stiff-bristled paintbrush* in vinegar and scrub.
● To keep runners from growing a bumper crop of mildew, run the head of a *small sponge paintbrush* along the bottom runner channels when you've finished showering.

To remove soap film on a plastic shower curtain, place it in the washer with *two or three large bath towels*. Add *1/2 cup of vinegar* and wash, removing it before the spin cycle. Hang it up pronto to dry. If mildew is out of control, use *3/4 cup of chlorine bleach* instead. To avoid that soapy buildup on the bottom of the shower curtain, rub it with *baby oil*. Always keep a shower curtain unfurled to give the fuzzy stuff a less inviting place to grow.

To clean the showerhead, remove it and soak it in a *container* with a *50–50 mix* of *hot water* and *vinegar*.

If you don't want to take the showerhead off, pour *3 inches of vinegar* into a *plastic sandwich bag* and then pull the bag up over the entire head. Secure the bag with *duct tape* and it leave overnight ◀.

*See also **Bathtubs** and **Tiles**.*

Shutters

It's one of those curious little ironies of life that shutters—hung to gussy up the inside or outside of your house—often become more unsightly than decorative as the dust and grime accumulate.

Regular maintenance will keep your indoor shutter-cleaning chores to a minimum. Dust every month on both sides with the *soft brush attachment* of your *vacuum*. In between sessions with your vacuum, touch up the shutters with a *microfiber cloth or feather duster*.

To clean indoor shutters, remove the shutters from their hinges and put them somewhere level—a *workbench* topped with a *white towel*, for instance. Spray the shutters with a gentle *all-purpose cleaner*, such as Fantastik or Formula 409, taking special care to penetrate the cracks and crevices. Allow the cleaner to sit on the shutters five minutes before rolling up your sleeves. Pull on some *rubber gloves* and start cleaning at the top of shutters and work toward the bottom. Clean the slats with a *terry cloth towel*, your rubber-gloved fingers, or a *small soft-bristled brush* for nooks and crannies. Use a *trigger spray bottle* filled with *warm water* to spray away dirt and other grime from the slats. Using a *dry cloth*, dry the slats one at a time. You can reach hard-to-dry areas with a rag wrapped around the handle of a *wooden spoon*.

Cleaning outdoor shutters is basically the same operation—with a few refinements. Remove the shutters from the outside walls and lay them flat or prop them against a *sawhorse* or other secure support. Wet down the shutters with an *all-purpose cleaner* or a *spray bottle* of *water* with a *squirt of dishwashing liquid* added. Leave the cleaner on for a few minutes. Then use a *screwdriver*, wrapped in a *towel*, to attack hard-to-reach spots. Rinse with a *garden hose*, using as much water pressure as your hose can muster. Dry the slats with a *towel*. Let them finish drying in the *sun*.

See also **Louvers**.

Siding

Like window screens, siding attracts all sorts of gunk—everything from tree sheddings, dust, and mildew (especially in shady spots) to pollution, pollen, and rain. Sometimes torrential rain cleans your siding. Other times, it just makes matters worse. Here's how to clean any kind of siding—aluminum, vinyl, or wood.

To remove dust and grime on your windows, just dampen a *cloth*, sprinkle on a little *baking soda*, and wipe the dirt away.

If your siding needs only light cleaning, try this once a year: Squirt with the *garden hose* and scrub the siding one section at a time, using a *soft-bristled, long-handled brush*. A *long car-wash brush attachment* on your hose ◀ is a good tool to use, letting you get to hard-to-reach areas. Don't miss the underside of the siding slats, where dirt loves to accumulate. Hose again to rinse.

▼

If your siding is really soiled, use a *siding and deck cleaner*, such as Jomax House Cleaner and Mildew Killer. This concentrate contains mildew retardants and detergent and can be combined with *bleach* (see package directions) for extra cleaning power. Mix, spray the cleaner onto the siding, and rinse. A *pressure washer* hooked up to your garden hose is also an effective way to blast away the dirt on your siding.

*See also **Aluminum** and **Vinyl**.*

Silk

WATCH OUT

When cleaning silk, always keep these precautions in mind:
• Never use chlorine bleach; it can irreparably damage the fabric.
• Never dry silk in sunlight; it will fade.
• Never wash silk ties; both the silk and its lining are prone to shrinkage. (The lining will usually shrivel first.) Instead, take them to a dry cleaner.
• When you're dressing, apply hair spray, make-up, and other beauty and grooming aids before donning anything made of silk. The alcohol in them could cause dyes to bleed.

When cleaning silk, you don't want to turn a silk purse into a sow's ear by using the wrong technique. Many silk garments are washable if you are careful. Check the fabric care label.

Treat stains from spills and such before you wash silk clothing. (See below for special ways to treat perspiration and deodorant stains.) On a hidden spot, apply a paste of *powdered laundry starch* and *cold water* to make sure the silk is colorfast. If it is, apply the paste to the stain, let it dry, and brush it away.

To wash a silk garment, you can either do it by hand or use the *delicate cycle* and *cool or warm water* in your *washing machine*. A *mild detergent*, such as Woolite, works best. Carefully roll the garment in an *absorbent white towel* to blot up excess moisture. Then either lay it flat to dry or hang it on a *padded hanger*.

To iron silk, use a *low setting* and iron on the inside of the garment only.

Perspiration and deodorant stains can discolor and weaken silk. (The salt in perspiration, and aluminum chloride and other chemicals in deodorants and antiperspirants, can stain silk.) Dry-clean or wash perspiration-stained garments as soon as possible.

To treat perspiration or deodorant stains on washable silk garments, try one of these remedies, but first test it on a hidden spot to see whether the fabric dye holds:

- Soak the perspiration stain in *warm water* and a paste of *table salt* and *white vinegar.*
- Make a paste of *cream of tartar* and *warm water* and apply it to the stain. Allow the paste to dry, brush it off, and launder.
- Apply a mixture of *warm water* and *water softener* to the stained area and then rub with a *bar of laundry soap.* Brush it off and then wash.
- Dissolve *2 aspirins* in *1/2 cup of warm water* and apply it to the stain. Let it dry for hours, brush it off, and launder.

To avoid persperation stains in the first place, apply deodorant and then use your hair dryer to dry your underarms before you dress.

See also **Satin**.

Silver Jewelry

Air and light are the two biggest foes of silver jewelry. So how you store your silver jewelry makes a big difference in how much it tarnishes.

Always store clean silver jewelry in a cool, dry place, wrapped separately in a *soft cloth* and then enclosed in a *resealable plastic bag* to prevent it from getting jostled about and scratched.

Clean your silver jewelry once a month if you wear it frequently. The best cleaner? A good old-fashioned *silver paste* or *liquid polish.* Apply with a *soft cloth* as directed and then buff with *another cloth.* Rinse gently in *warm water* if needed.

Another method: Rub with a *soft cloth* dipped in *baking soda,* using a *frayed toothbrush* for hard-to-reach areas. Rinse well in *warm water* and buff dry with *another cloth.*

Still another trick: Line a *small bowl* with *aluminum foil,* shiny side toward you. Fill the bowl with *hot water* and mix in *1 tablespoon of bleach-free powdered laundry detergent* (not liquid), such as Tide. Put the jewelry in the solution and let it soak one minute. Rinse completely and air-dry.

To clean badly tarnished or dirty silver jewelry, fill a *small plastic bowl* with *warm water* and add a *few drops of liquid dishwashing detergent.* Soak the jewelry in the solution overnight. Should the dirt persist after the overnight soak, clean the piece with an *old toothbrush* ▶. Then rinse and dry carefully with a *soft cloth.*

▲

Specially treated *antitarnish cloths*, available at most grocery and hardware stores, may also be used to touch up silver jewelry.

Silver Serving Pieces

Silver serving pieces, whether plated or sterling, benefit from frequent use. Rotate your pieces so that they will age uniformly.

Clean your silver twice a year following this tried-and-true method: Use a *high-quality silver polish* with antitarnish ability (3M's Tarni-Shield Silver Polish is one), a *soft cloth* to apply the polish in a circular motion, and *warm water* to rinse.

If you have candle wax on your silver, don't scrape it off—you could scratch the surface. Instead, soften the wax in a *warm oven* or with a *hair dryer* on low ◀, then peel it off. Or dribble on a little *turpentine*, *mineral spirits*, or *denatured alcohol* to dislodge the wax.

To clean ornate silver pieces, sprinkle on *baking soda* and rub gently with a *soft cloth*.

To wash silver, do it by hand in *mild dishwashing detergent* and *warm water* and dry immediately with a *soft cloth*. Water left on silver can pit and corrode it. Be especially careful with silver candlesticks, candelabra, and knife handles filled with paste or wax: If you rub too hard or rinse in hot water, they could soften and bend.

As a general rule, don't wash silver in the dishwasher; it's simply too soft to withstand the jostling and abrasion. If you must wash silver in the dishwasher, keep it away from metals such as copper and stainless steel. They will mark each other if they touch.

To restore silver's shine between cleanings, use *polishing gloves* and *cloths* or a *jeweler's rouge cloth* (flannel treated with a red polishing powder). These items are sold at hardware stores and many department stores.

To store a silver serving piece, slip it into an *antitarnish bag* or *cloth*. *Nonbuffered tissue paper*, an acid-free product sold at craft stores, also works. Then place that in a *plastic bag*. (Don't use newspaper, because its carbon can eat into silver.) *Silica gel packets* placed inside will inhibit moisture. Don't use rubber bands to close the bag—they contain sulfur, which damages silver. Store silver servers away from sunlight.

Sinks

With all the soap and water that flow through your sink, you'd think it would be clean all the time. But the likes of soapy deposits, food stains, rust, and water spots have a way of accumulating quickly.

For general cleaning of any sink, get out the liquid dishwashing detergent, liquid laundry detergent, or all-purpose cleaners (such as Formula 409 and Dow Bathroom Cleaner). Using a *dime-size amount of detergent* and a *couple of drops of water*, scrub the sink with a *soft sponge*. Rinse away residue. Don't use an abrasive cleaning agent or applicator. A *nonabrasive cleaner*, such as Spic and Span, Mr. Clean, or Bon Ami, is good for very bad stains.

For a lightly stained porcelain sink, try one of these treatments:
- Rub a *freshly cut lemon* around the sink to cut through the grease. Rinse with *running water*.
- Use *baking soda* or *trisodium phosphate* (available at home improvement stores) in *warm water*. Sprinkle a little baking soda around the sink and then rub it with a *damp sponge*. Rinse with *vinegar or lemon juice* to help neutralize the alkaline cleaner and then rinse with *running water*.
- Make a *paste* the consistency of toothpaste with *baking soda* and *water* and gently rub the sink with a *sponge or soft nylon brush*. Polish with a *paper towel or soft cloth*.

Never use scouring powders or steel wool on porcelain sinks, because they will scratch.

To remove heavy stains, even rust, rub the sink with a paste consisting of *8 ounces of powdered borax* (available in the laundry section of supermarkets) and *2 ounces of lemon juice*. Dab a *cloth* or *sponge* in the paste, rub around the sink, and then rinse with *running water*.

To remove rust from stainless steel or iron sinks, wipe *WD-40* on the rust mark with a *cloth* and rinse thoroughly.

To remove water spots from any sink, use a *cloth* dampened with *rubbing alcohol* or *vinegar*.

For a sparkling white sink, place *paper towels* across the bottom and saturate them with *household bleach*. Let it sit for 30 minutes and rinse with *running water*. Note: Do not use bleach in colored porcelain sinks, because it will fade the color. Clean these sinks with mild liquid detergents, vinegar, or baking soda.

simple SOLUTIONS

Neutralize That Acid >
You can cut your cleaning chores by not leaving acidic foods—citrus fruits, cranberries, vinegar, salad dressings, tea, or coffee—on your sink's surface for a long time. Either wash the dishes right away or put them in a dishwasher, advises Mary Findley, owner of Mary Moppins Cleaning System in Eugene, Oregon. Dry the sink immediately after use to prevent water spotting.

expert advice

The Faucet Fix >

The white mineral deposits that settle on faucet spouts and handles succumb to white wine vinegar. Carol Houlik, product director for kitchens at American Standard, likes to soak a paper towel in the vinegar, squeeze out the excess, and wrap the towel around the chrome fixture. After 10 minutes, she takes off the wet towel and buffs the chrome with a dry one. Voilà—clean chrome! She has this word of caution: Do not use this method on brass or colored fixtures, as these finishes might react or discolor.

Houlik offers an additional tip: "While you have the vinegar out, it also works to unclog sink drains mucked up with soap residue. And it's safer than chemical drain openers."

To maintain your sink's luster, apply *Gel-Gloss*, an automobile cleaner and wax, with a *soft cotton towel*. Wipe the cleaner on, let it dry for five to ten minutes, and then wipe it off. Do this every three months.

Stains in Corian-type sinks can be removed with *toothpaste* or a paste of *baking soda* and *water*. Gently scrub the paste on with a *white scrubbing pad*, available at home improvement stores. Your last resort is scrubbing *very* gently with *800 grit wet-or-dry sandpaper*. Scrubbing too hard could wear a groove in the material. Polish the cleaned spot with a *special polish* made for Corian surfaces sold at home improvement centers.

Water spots that have etched themselves into a sink's porcelain are extremely difficult to remove. Buff such spots out with a polishing compound as soon as you notice the spots. Use *jeweler's rouge* with porcelain sinks, or go to a lapidary store and ask for *cerium oxide*. Pink cerium oxide is used for polishing gold and silver. Make a paste according to the package directions and then scrub.

To cover a chip or scratch on a white porcelain surface—including sinks, tubs, and appliances—pick up a container of *white enamel paint* at your hardware or paint store. Following the package directions, paint over the mar with a *small artist's brush*, let it dry, rub with *fine sandpaper*, and paint again. Repeat the process until the painted area is even with the surrounding surface. If you want to get fancier, buy a *porcelain repair kit*, which will include filler, hardener, cleaning spray, sandpaper, and more.

Skylights

What better way to let natural light into your home—while maintaining your privacy—than with skylights. To keep from looking into a dirty sky, do some simple maintenance to preserve your view. The materials depend on whether you have glass or acrylic skylights.

To clean the exterior of your glass skylights, either climb to the roof and clean while standing securely on a *ladder*, or reach the skylight with a *telescopic pole* and attachments—a *squeegee* and a sponge mop end. (If you feel safer, climb onto the roof and squat next to the window.) You can use a detergent-and-water solution (*1 ounce of dishwashing detergent* to *20 ounces of water*), any *alcohol-based cleaner* (such as Spray Away), or a *50-50 solution* of *vinegar* and *water*.

To remove loose and caked on dirt, wet the window with a *hose*, dip the sponge mop into your cleaning solution (or spray it onto the mop head until it's damp), and wipe over the window. Rinse out the mop and wipe again with *water*, then dry it with the squeegee. Clean the frames around your skylights at the same time that you clean the glass, watching for any sharp edges. A twice-a-year cleaning of your skylights and frames is sufficient because you don't want to wear down the silicone seal around the skylight and cause leaks.

The interior of your glass skylights is cleaned much the same way. Remove loose dirt and dust with a *barely dampened mop*, rinse out the mop or change it, and then clean with one of the solutions mentioned above. (Don't forget to protect your carpet or floor.) Do this monthly—or perhaps just twice a year if the skylight is difficult to reach. Wooden frames can be cleaned with a *furniture polish* if reachable. They'll also need to be finished, painted, or stained every three years to protect the wood against damage from ultraviolet rays.

If your skylight is made of acrylic, strong cleaning solvents can easily scratch and damage the acrylic. Even using glass cleaner on acrylic can be a problem. To clean the inside and outside of your acrylic window, mix *1 tablespoon of dishwashing liquid* in *1 gallon of warm water*. Dip a *soft cloth* into the solution, wipe over the window, and rinse well. If stubborn stains remain, use any *plastic cleaner*, such as Permatex Plastic Cleaner, also referred to as 403D cleaner. Spray the cleaner on a *cloth* and wipe over the acrylic pane. Also use the plastic cleaner to remove marks on vinyl frames.

If you find that roof tar or pinesap has stuck to the exterior of the acrylic window, use a *citrus-based cleaner*, such as Orange Glo. If it doesn't work, try a little *kerosene* dabbed on a *cloth* and wiped over the marks. Don't forget to wear *gloves*. Rinse thoroughly with a *garden hose* or a *bucket of clear water*. Don't use a power washer; it could damage the insulation around the window, cause leaks, and loosen roof shingles.

If your skylight has a screen, you'll need to remove it to clean the inside of the window. If this is too difficult, open the window and clean the inside at the same time that you clean the outside. To clean the screen, *vacuum* it using the *brush attachment*. If the screen is really dirty and you can remove it, wash it with a *soft brush* dipped in a solution of *dishwashing liquid* and *warm water*. Then rinse thoroughly.

Slate

Whether you have slate flooring, a slate mantel, or a slate kitchen counter, light cleaning is simple.

To remove dust on slate, just *vacuum* or wipe it with a *damp cloth* or a *damp mop*.

To remove floor dirt, mix *1/2 cup of ammonia* in *1/2 bucket of water* (1.5 gallons). Apply the cleaning solution with a *sponge mop*. (You can use other cleaners, such as Mr. Clean, Comet Cleanser, or warm water with a squirt of *dishwashing liquid*. However, the advantage of ammonia is that it requires no rinsing.) If you dust weekly, you can do a thorough cleaning with ammonia once a month or every other month.

To protect slate floors from staining, apply a *stone sealer*—either gloss or satin—after it's installed. Slate is especially susceptible to oil stains (from salad oils, for instance). So sealing a slate floor in a kitchen or eating area may be a good idea. If you wish, follow the sealer with a *wax finish* that can protect the sealer and make it last longer. The sealer and the wax work together to make slate easier to clean.

To clean a slate countertop, scour the surface using a *cleaner* such as Comet Cleanser and a *damp sponge*. Do not use abrasive pads, because they might remove some of the stone and change its appearance.

To clean up oil stains on a slate countertop, sprinkle a *liberal amount of cornstarch* on the surface and let it sit for 10 minutes. Then scrub the surface with a *grease-cutting cleaner*, such as Fantastik or Formula 409, or use *warm water* with a *squirt of dishwashing liquid*.

To protect a slate kitchen counter, oil it with a *50–50 mixture of boiled linseed oil and turpentine*. Wipe the solution on the slate with a *cloth* and then buff the slate with a *soft cloth*, *terry cloth rag*, *or old bath towel* until it's dry. Oil will darken the slate and give it a satin finish while creating a protective barrier. Oil your kitchen counter once or twice a year. Oil other nonfloor surfaces—mantels or hearths, for instance—every two years.

Sleeping Bags

Sleeping bags come with one of three types of insulation: natural (down or down and feather), synthetic fibers, or fiber-pile (fleece). But whatever type of sleeping bag you have, if you use it only a couple of times a year and treat it well, you might be able to go 10 years without giving it a thorough cleaning.

To keep a sleeping bag in good shape, here are some guidelines:
- Use a liner or wear pants and a T-shirt when you're using the sleeping bag.
- Spot clean after a trip with a *sponge* and *soapy water*.
- After a camping trip, air your sleeping bag for a couple of hours or place it in the *dryer* for 10 to 15 minutes to get rid of any moisture.
- Store your bag in a large breathable storage sack, not in the stuff sack or in a plastic bag.

To hand-wash a sleeping bag—the most careful way to do it—fill a *bathtub* with *warm water* and just a little soap. For down bags, select a *down liquid soap* (available from either a store specializing in down comforters or a camping supplies store). You can also safely use a *mild laundry detergent*, such as Woolite or Ivory Snow. Don't use any detergent containing bleach on a down bag (but it's OK for synthetic-fiber bags). Check the package directions to determine the amount of detergent to use. Remember that using too much will mean more rinsing later on. Gently knead the bag to help the soapy water penetrate the material.

If your sleeping bag has a waterproof outer shell, turn the entire bag inside out before you immerse it so the soapy water will be able to penetrate.

Rinse your bag twice—several times if necessary—with *clear water*. Don't cut corners on this step, particularly if you're working with a down bag. It's very important to remove all the soap before the down has dried. Do not wring water from your sleeping bag. Instead, squeeze out the water by rolling up the bag tightly and carefully.

To machine-wash a sleeping bag, your best bet is to visit a *self-service laundry*. Using a *front-loading machine* to wash down or synthetic-fiber sleeping bags is a good idea, because top-loading agitator machines can damage them. You can machine-wash just about any sleeping bag if you use *warm water* and a *gentle cycle*, but it's best to check the manufacturer's label. The last spin cycle should remove a lot of the water, but be sure the bag is evenly distributed in the machine. This will save dryer time.

Drying is the key to preserving your sleeping bag. If your bag is not dried thoroughly before you store it away, the matted lumps that formed when it was wet will stay that way. The bag will lose

simple SOLUTIONS

The Squeeze Play >

When hand-washing a sleeping bag, try this simple trick to prevent the compartments formed by baffles (those stitched partitions that keep the fill evenly distributed) from inflating and floating to the surface: Keep the bag in its stuff sack and immerse both bag and sack in the tub of water. You've already forced the air out of the bag when you put it in the stuff sack. Once both are immersed, you can remove the sleeping bag from the sack and work the soapy water into the bag.

its loft, will no longer offer optimum insulation, and will probably mildew. For these reasons, it's better to dry your bag at a *self-service laundry*, where you can use a *large dryer*. In a home dryer, the sleeping bag will take up so much room that it won't tumble well. Consequently, the clumps of down or synthetic fibers will not be broken up during drying.

If you decide to wash your sleeping bag at home and then dry it at a self-service laundry, put it in a *plastic bag* for the trip to the laundry. Use the largest dryer set to *high heat*. Melting the nylon shell is not a danger because the bag has room to tumble, but if you're in doubt, use a lower setting. Once the nylon shell is dry, set the dryer on *medium heat* so that the interior feathers can dry. Toss in a couple of *clean tennis balls* to help break up clumps of down. Remove the bag as soon as it's finished tumbling.

A note of caution: Even if your bag feels dry, the down insulation may not be. Check for lumps—a sign the down is still wet.

After drying a sleeping bag with fiber-pile insulation, gently fluff up the fleece with a *comb* or *brush*.

Slide Projectors and Screens

Cleaning electronic gadgetry is not rocket science. It merely requires know-how (supplied by this book) and patience (supplied by you). If you get into a rush, you may damage your projector.

To clean a slide projector, start with the outside of the unit (but only if it is completely cool). Separate and set aside the optical assemblies—the lens, which is easily removable from its track, and the lamp, which slides out the back of the projector. Use an *aerosol can of deionized compressed air* to blow any dust or loose dirt off the projector casing. (If it's really dirty, walk outside to spray it, so that you won't have another mess to clean up inside.) Spray any openings inside the casing to loosen dust. With a *clean, 1-inch bristle paintbrush* (preferably new), dust all the nooks and crannies, making sure to clean around the gate area, which catches the dropping slides, and the exhaust grill, where dirt tends to collect. Once again, blow compressed air on the case to remove any remaining dust. Spray a *surface cleaner* (either a product such as Windex or a lens cleaner from a camera store) on a *clean, lint-free cloth* and wipe the exterior surfaces of the projector to remove fingerprints and grime.

To clean the projector's optics—which you removed and set aside—be extra careful not to scratch the lenses. Use the *com-*

WATCH OUT

Dry cleaning is not recommended for down or synthetic sleeping bags. It can strip the natural oils in the down and take the silicone coating off the synthetic-filled bags. You probably can dry-clean a fiber-pile sleeping bag, but check the manufacturer's recommendations first.

pressed air to first dust the projection lens. Place a couple of drops of *surface cleaner* on both the front and rear of the lens and, with the *lens tissue*, rub gently in a circular motion to remove dust or water condensation marks. No matter how tempted you may be—and this goes for AV geeks as well as the rest of us—*don't try to clean the internal lens.* The optics are very sensitive parts. Among other things, unskilled fingers can disturb the finely calibrated focusing mechanism. (Every five years or so, have the slide projector serviced by a professional, who can clean and lubricate the internal systems.)

To clean the projector's lamp, set the cleaned projection lens aside and locate the lamp, which is typically next to the exhaust fan and tends to get really dirty. Again, remove dust with the *compressed air*, loosen dirt with the *paintbrush*, and give the lamp a final canned-air "rinse." Using the *lens tissue* and *surface cleaner*, gently wipe the mirror that accompanies the lamp. There should be a clear condenser lens bracketed in front of the lamp. Unscrew the bracket, gently remove the lens (holding it on the edges only), and clean it as you did the other lenses. Reattach it to the lamp assembly. If the condenser lens is tinted green (as it often is on models made more than a decade ago), take even more care when handling it. Don't touch the lens with bare fingers (handle it with a clean cloth or tissue), and if you must set it down, do so on a cloth. This time, don't use the cleaning solution; wipe it very gently with the *lens tissue*.

After reassembling the projector, turn it on. You may smell a strange odor, generated by the dust disturbed during the cleaning. The smell will stop after the dust has settled. If the unit still smells after 30 minutes, something is probably wrong. Call a service center for advice—or a friend who spent his or her youth tinkering with AV equipment.

Cleaning the projection screen is the easy part. Although there are different screen materials, the cleaning techniques are the same for nearly all. Make a solution of *mild dishwashing liquid* and *warm water*. Gently wipe away dust and dirt with a *sponge* dipped in the solution. Rinse by wiping with a *clean, wet sponge*. Blot dry using a *clean cloth*. That's it. Never use solvents, such as acetone or paint thinner, and never use abrasive cleaners.

If you have a glass bead screen or a screen with a delicate surface, don't clean it with water and soap. Instead, simply brush away dust using a *soft-bristled brush* or *a clean, lint-free cloth*. Happy viewing.

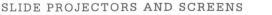

Sliding Doors

That sliding glass door to your patio or deck provides a nice view but also collects a lot of sand, dust, and debris in its tracks. How you clean the door depends on its frame—wood, aluminum or, more common in newer construction, vinyl.

Vacuuming the sill tracks is the first step in cleaning any sliding door. Run the *vacuum* over the tracks at least once in the spring and fall—or weekly if you use the door frequently (at a beach house, for instance). Timesaving tip: Regularly sweep or vacuum the area just outside the sliding door to help reduce the amount of dirt that gets dragged into the tracks.

To keep your door sliding smoothly, spray *silicone* on a *soft*, *dry cloth* and wipe it onto the track. Don't allow the silicone to come into contact with wood surfaces or the weather strip. Lubricate rollers with *light oil* (3-in-One, for instance).

To clean the outside of a vinyl frame, use a mild *dishwashing detergent.* Add a *couple of squirts of detergent* to *1 gallon of hot or warm water* and apply the soapy solution with a *soft sponge or cloth*. Rinse with *clear water*. Make sure you clean the frame before you wash the window so that you won't get your sparkling window wet and smeary again. Start at the top of the frame and work down.

To clean the inside of a vinyl frame, wipe with a *damp cloth* at the time that you clean the window. Don't use abrasive cleaners, abrasive scouring pads, or sandpaper in an attempt to buff or shine the vinyl frame or to remove marks.

To clean wood-framed sliding doors, fill a *misting bottle* with *warm water* and a *squirt of mild dishwashing liquid*. Spray the sliding door frames and wipe off any dirt with a soft cloth. Finish by gently drying with *another soft cloth*. Never use a hose or any high-pressure washer on the door. Likewise, if your wooden door frame is painted, never use abrasive cleaners, as they can soften latex paint. A few will even soften oil-based paint. If the residue won't come off with water or a mild detergent, consider lightly sanding it and then refinishing.

It's important to make a thorough inspection of your wooden door frame at least once a year—monthly in coastal or harsh climates. That's because wood is highly susceptible to attacks by fungi and other deterioration.

WATCH OUT

Do not clean the aluminum frames in direct sunlight or very hot or cold temperatures, because the cleaning solution may dry too quickly and streak the surface. If that happens, it would be difficult to restore the aluminum to its original appearance.

To clean aluminum-clad sliding doors, again your best bet is *mild dishwashing detergent* and *water* applied with a *sponge* or *soft brush* from top to bottom. Rinse immediately. Air-dry or wipe with a soft, dry *cloth*. For a protective coating, apply *car wax* to the aluminum. You should plan an annual cleaning for all exterior aluminum frames.

Next, clean the glass, inside and out. (See *Windows* for cleaning solutions and techniques.) Any *window cleaner* will be fine for this job, but avoid getting the cleaner on the window frames, because ingredients in some glass cleaners will damage the frame materials.

Finally, clean the screen door, if you have one, by gently vacuuming it with a *brush attachment* that will not harm the mesh. Vacuum both sides.

Slipcovers

Your cleaning schedule for slipcovers will depend on your lifestyle. How often do you use the furniture with the slipcovers on? How many children do you have? Do you have pets? On average, slipcovers should be cleaned three or four times a year— more often if they look or get grubby sooner. Care for your slipcovers as you would any of your upholstered furniture.

To remove dust and debris, give the slipcovers a going-over while they're still on the furniture with your *vacuum cleaner*, using the *upholstery attachment*. On pillowcases, use the *vacuum nozzle* without any attachments.

To clean slipcovers, remove them and give them a good shake outdoors. You'll either be able to wash the slipcovers (follow the fabric care instructions), or you'll need to take them to the dry cleaner. Most slipcovers can be washed, with the exception of rayon, which often requires dry-cleaning. Either way, clean all matching slipcovers at the same time so that the color will stay even, since they may fade with washing. For example, on a sofa, wash all the slipcovers and pillowcases at the same time, using exactly the same amount of detergent and the same water temperature. Wash the curtains, too, if they're made of the same fabric.

Pretreat any stains after removing the slipcovers and before washing. Use a method appropriate to the stain. (See *Stains*.) Place the slipcovers in the *washing machine* on a *soak cycle* to

expert advice

On the Rack >

Darby Jacobs has learned a few things over the years in his Veradale, Washington, upholstery shop, and one is how to get the best fit for slipcovers. Jacobs says the trick is to put the covers on the frame or cushions before they're completely dry—somewhere in between being damp and almost dry. This way they'll stretch around the object nicely (especially true of fitted slipcovers). This method will help the wrinkles out, too. You can speed the drying process by using nature—open the window in good weather—or an electric fan near the window or furniture. If you use this technique, don't use the furniture until the slipcovers are completely dry.

remove extra soil before the wash cycle begins. Don't leave the slipcovers in the wash cycle for long, as this could loosen their stitching. Wash in **warm water** with any laundry detergent and use a **cold rinse**. Slipcovers will sometimes shrink the first time they're laundered, but it shouldn't be very much. While your slipcovers are washing, vacuum the upholstery of the furniture while it's uncovered.

Before drying the slipcovers, check to see whether the stains have been removed. If the stains are still there, drying will set them. You'll need to treat the stains once more and rinse or launder again. And if you do that, you should launder every other item a second time, too, to keep the color even.

To dry your slipcovers, check the care label and either hang the slipcovers over a **drying rack** or put them in a **dryer**. Some people feel that machine-drying is too harsh and recommend laying the slipcovers flat. If you use a dryer, dry on **low heat** and avoid overdrying. If you air-dry, don't dry on a clothesline, because the weight of the slipcover might pull the fabric out of shape.

Once the slipcovers are dry, put them back on the furniture, smooth them, and pull all the seams and cording into place. Pinch any pleats into sharp creases and smooth any ruffles. If you like, iron the pleats before refitting to the furniture.

Smoke

"Smoke Gets in Your Eyes" sounds almost benign, even romantic, in the famous song. But in reality, there's nothing appealing about the stale smell of smoke in your house or on your clothes.

To remove smoke odor from clothing, whether it's from a fire or cigarettes, hang the clothes outside in the sun. **Sunlight** breaks down smoke molecules, and **fresh air** is great for the fabric. You may want to attach a **fan** to an **extension cord** and allow the fan to force air across the clothes. Check the clothing every two hours and leave it outside until the smell dissipates. You'll have more effective results in the wash—your next step.

To launder smoky clothes, first presoak the garment in a sink filled with **3/4 cup of baking soda** and **5 gallons of water**. Then place the garment directly into the washing machine, using a **detergent with oxygen bleach**, such as Surf or Tide. These detergents remove the odor, not merely mask it with a perfume. Wash contaminated clothing separately from your general family laundry.

After washing, hang the clothes to dry. Using a dryer is not recommended, because the heat can set the smoke odor into any fabric from which it hasn't been completely removed. Neutralize any residual smoke odor with a **deodorizer** such as Febreze.

If the clothing label says "Dry clean only," that's what you should do—and be sure the **dry cleaner** specializes in smoke removal. Don't forget to air the clothing first. Your dry cleaner will appreciate the gesture.

Removing protein-generated smoke—from cooking ham or chicken, for instance—can be more difficult because these items produce heavy, greasy smoke that fabric readily absorbs. (Wood smoke tends to be flaky and easier to clean.) Air clothing affected by protein smoke on a hanger. Then, before washing, you'll probably need to treat the clothing with a **"thermo fog" machine** (the Thermo-Gen Fogger, for instance), which puffs out a cloud of odor-destroying particles. You can rent such machines from a commercial cleaning supply house.

To remove just a little smoke from a small area in your home, such as a chest of drawers, use **baking soda**, **cedar blocks**, or even a **bowl of sliced apples** to absorb the odor. Close up or seal off the area first.

If smoke has penetrated a large part of your home, understand that you have an extensive cleanup job on your hands involving a variety of materials that require different cleaning techniques. Your safest bet is to contact your insurance company and professional cleaners.

To clean smoke from walls and ceilings, first **vacuum** up any visible residue. Wipe down the walls with a **chemical sponge** (available at drugstores, janitorial supply stores, conservation suppliers, and online). Then dilute a **special smoke-removal cleaner** such as Smoke-Solv Liquid Wall Wash (available at janitorial supply stores and conservation suppliers) according to the package directions. Fill a **spray bottle** with the cleaner. Spray and wipe one section of the wall or ceiling at a time, using a **clean cloth**. For walls, start from the bottom and work your way up to avoid streaking. You may have to repeat the process several times. Oil-based paint will hold up well to washing. Latex paint can wear off if you scrub aggressively or wash too many times.

See also **Soot**.

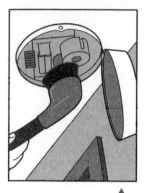

Smoke Alarms

You already know to change the batteries in your smoke alarms yearly. But did you know that you should also clean them every other month? Cobwebs, dust, and even spiders can cause your smoke alarm to misbehave.

Clean the outside and inside of the alarm using a *vacuum cleaner* and a *brush attachment* ◀. Flip open or unscrew the casing to get inside. If you can't reach the alarm with your vacuum's *extension tubes*, stand on a *ladder*. A can of *compressed air* can also be sprayed on the casing and inside the alarm to clean it.

Test your alarm, once you've cleaned it, to see that it's working properly. Stand by the alarm, light a *candle*, and then blow it out. The smoke should activate the alarm. Or, if your system's activated by light (it should say so on the box), shine a *flashlight* into the alarm to set it off. Simply pressing the button on the alarm casing is not a test. That only indicates the horn is working, not the detection mechanism.

Cover the alarm anytime you're doing work in the house that could send dust into the air. Don't forget to remove this covering promptly after you've finished. You should also protect the alarm if you're painting around it—never paint the alarm casing.

Sneakers

To wash or not to wash in a washing machine? That's the main question about cleaning sneakers. And the answer is (drumroll, please): It depends.

Most shoe manufacturers discourage machine-washing because detergents and the machine's agitation don't agree with many leathers and adhesives and can ruin their shape. But some simple canvas or all-synthetic shoes can safely take a spin in the washer.

Before cleaning any type of sneaker, check the care label. Manufacturers include detailed instructions for each style they make. You may want to purchase a sneaker care kit designed for athletic shoes, particularly if you have leather shoes.

For leather sneakers, it's best to use a regular *leather cleaner* and *conditioner*. Just don't use saddle soap. It may be great for saddles, but it can damage other kinds of leather.

To clean canvas or synthetic sneakers in a *washing machine*, spray them first with a *stain removal spray*, especially if the sneakers are grass stained. Wipe the spray around the shoe, let it sit for a couple of minutes, and then put the shoes in the wash. Include *light-colored towels* in the wash. The rubbing action of the towels will not only help clean the sneakers, but will also keep them from bouncing around. If you have items in the same wash load that you want to protect, put the sneakers in an *old pillowcase* ▶.

To clean canvas and synthetic sneakers by hand, *rinse* the shoes in *clear water* and then use a *soft brush* to scrub the shoes with a *neutral cleaner,* such as Tide Liquid detergent. For scuff marks, scour with a *white, nylon-backed scrub pad.* Rinse as long as necessary to remove all traces of detergent and then air-dry. Stuff the shoes with *white paper* to retain their shape.

An alternative for canvas sneakers: Squirt on some *foam shaving cream,* let it sit for half an hour, and brush off what remains. Then wipe your sneakers with a *clean, damp cloth.*

For faster drying of your cleaned sneakers, place them below the *refrigerator door* so the warm air blowing out hits them. It's not as hot as a hair dryer and will speed up the drying process. Avoid direct sunlight, as it might fade the sneakers. And don't stuff your shoes with newspaper—the ink might transfer to the fabric. Make sure your shoes are completely dry before you wear them.

To give your sneakers a fresh smell, place a sheet of *fabric softener* in them overnight. Or make a baking soda sachet: Place a *couple of teaspoons of baking soda* in the center of a *cotton cloth.* Close the cloth around the baking soda and secure it with a string or rubber band. Put one sachet in each shoe overnight. You can reuse the sachets in any kind of shoe.

If you want to waterproof sneakers and they're made of materials other than leather, use a waterproofing product specifically designed for sneakers.

Washing by the Dozen >
Goodwill Industries of Denver, Colorado, cleans all donated sneakers en masse in commercial washing machines. John Farnam, vice president of marketing, says the group has very few problems with machine-washing. First, the exterior of the sneaker is brushed free of soil. Then the sneakers are put into the wash on a cold cycle with regular household detergent. Laces are kept in but not tied. After washing, the laces are tied to help maintain the sneakers' shape while they air-dry on a shoe rack.

Snowblowers

Snowblowers save time, your back, and perhaps your life—considering how many people have fatal heart attacks while shoveling snow. No matter what your unit's size or whether it's self-propelled or mounted on a tractor, you need to know your instruction manual before you clean it.

To clean your snowblower, sponge *dishwashing detergent* and *warm water* over the machine and rinse it with *clear water.* Stay away from harsh cleaners that might affect the paint. Keep an eye out for rust during your cleaning. If your machine is heavily caked with dirt and deposits of salt from the last season, you could take it to a *car wash* and use the *power hose*.

In good weather, leave the machine in the sun to dry or wipe it down with a *rag or old towel*. Apply a *car wax* with a *soft cloth* in a circular motion to help prevent the buildup of snow.

If you spot rust on any exposed metal part, treat the area. Use *emery paper*, *emery cloth*, *or steel wool* and apply in circular motions to remove the rust and smooth the surface. Then apply *high gloss machinery enamel* for outdoor use. The high gloss will also curb the buildup of snow by providing a smooth and lubricated surface. For a little more money, *epoxy paint* works well. It dries very hard and forms an abrasive-resistant surface. Give yourself time to spot and fix trouble. Epoxy paint takes 7 to 14 days to cure properly. Follow directions and apply only in a well-ventilated area.

After each use of your snowblower, wipe down the exterior and interior of all surfaces on the machine with a *dry rag or old towel*. Check for rust and deal with it immediately. Always make sure the machine is left dry so water from snowmelt won't freeze on it, leading to rust or clogging the chute.

Safety should be your top priority. Before cleaning or removing blockages or plugs in the chute or auger, shut off the machine. Get into the habit of removing the spark plug wire on machines with gas engines. That way, if you're vigorously cleaning and causing the blades to rotate, you won't cause the engine to fire and start. Remove the power cord from the electrical socket on electrically powered units.

Snowmobiles

Approach cleaning your snowmobile just as you would your car. Definitely clean it at the beginning and end of each season—more often if you use it regularly. But the first rule of cleaning your snowmobile is to refer to the owner's manual for recommendations on cleaning, waxing, lubricating, and greasing. Once a year, have the snowmobile inspected and the gear casing checked to make sure it is safe.

To remove loose dirt, spray the snowmobile with *water* from a *garden hose or power hose*. Choose a part of the yard where the run-off water will be harmless if it freezes. Take care around the engine if you're using a power hose. You don't want to force

water through the air intake, clutches, seals, and bearings. As an extra precaution, cover the air intake box with a **rag or plastic bag**. Also watch out for decals on the hood that could be removed by a power hose.

Use any mild car cleaner or a cleaner like Simple Green. (Use the latter full strength.) Apply the **soapy water or cleaner** to the exterior with a **sponge or rag**. Where dirt has built up, use a **soft-bristled brush**. On hard-to-reach areas, an old **toothbrush** will get where your hand can't. Let the cleaning solution sit for three to five minutes and then rinse it off with **fresh water**. Follow with a light **car polish** for the painted parts, spread on with a **terry cloth or other rag**. Apply a **chrome polish** such as Simichrome Polish on chrome and aluminum. Wipe the polish off. There's no need for buffing.

To clean the seat and protect it from the elements, spray on a **cleaner** such as Armor All and then wipe it off. If your seat has a manufacturer's logo on it, don't use degreasing soap products (car wash soap) at full strength, because they will in time remove or mess up the logo.

To clean the windshield, use either a **glass cleaner** or Simple Green again.

Here are some special considerations for cleaning snowmobiles:
- If your engine is incredibly dirty and greasy, spray it with a **degreaser**, such as Simple Green. This method is not recommended for the clutch. Wait until the cleaner starts to break up the grease before you remove it.

- To clean exhaust residue from the belly pan, use a **combustion chamber cleaner** such as Yamaha Combustion Chamber Cleaner. Spray it on the sides of the belly pan and wipe it off quickly. It shouldn't be left sitting, so do one side at a time. You can also try using a **degreaser** to remove the residue, but you may have to scrub a little harder. If you use the combustion chamber cleaner, do this cleaning before your overall snowmobile wash, because the cleaner will need to be washed off with **soap** and **water**. If you use a degreaser, do the general cleaning first to remove some of the grease and dirt before specifically tackling the engine and belly pan.
- Use a **plastic cleaner** for windshields, as you would on a motorbike helmet. Apply and wipe until the windshield comes clean.
- To protect against corrosion, apply **silicone spray** and multi-purpose grease to all metal parts. For suspension pivot shaft

lubrication, use a greaser formulated for cold temperatures. A *special low-temperature grease* such as Amsoil Heavy Duty Synthetic Grease should be sprayed on the steering and suspension pivot joints, following your user's manual directions. These lubricants are available from snowmobile dealers.

- After each use, wash your snowmobile and wipe it dry to prevent a buildup of dirt. Keep it covered when not in use to prevent fading and corrosion.

Soot

The oily black film known as soot is nasty to clean. A byproduct of smoke, this combination of oil, carbon, and tar can settle into microscopic cracks of the myriad objects in your home. Run your finger across a wall with soot on it, and the oils in your finger, combined with the soot, will permanently mark the surface. Even after you clean the wall, that soot mark will remain.

So what should you do?

Before you start, assess how widespread the soot contamination is to see whether you need to call a professional. Test in two or three rooms in an inconspicuous, high area. Take a *paper towel* folded into a pad, dampen it with *water*, and wipe across the surface. If the paper towel turns gray, you've got dust. If it turns black, you've got soot. If there's a *lot* of the black stuff, call a pro.

In general, you can treat light surface soot if it isn't widespread. Widespread surface soot may need professional attention, because if soot isn't totally cleaned, it can recirculate in the house through the heating system. Call a professional anytime you have greasy soot.

To eradicate soot, systematically plan your cleaning. The general rule is to work from the top to the bottom of an area—except when using the wet method described below. Then you'll need to work from the bottom up. First remove as much soot as you can through a dry method. Wear *old clothes*, *rubber gloves*, *a baseball cap*, *a disposable paper dust mask*, and *safety goggles*, especially when removing loose particles.

To use the dry method of cleaning, follow these steps:

- Vacuum, sweep, or feather dust the surfaces involved. Use a quick, flicking motion with a *broom* or *duster* or keep the *vacuum head* about 1/4 inch from the surface to avoid scratching. Don't rub—unless you want a huge smear to clean! Place *newspapers* under affected surfaces to catch soot for easy removal.

- **Vacuum** upholstery. If this doesn't work, call a professional fire and smoke restorer or dry cleaner specializing in soot removal.
- On lamp shades and on sturdy but small objects, try **compressed air** to blow the soot off the object. Take it outside to do this.
- Use a **special soot sponge or chemical sponge** (available at drugstores, janitorial supply stores, conservation suppliers, and online) on walls and ceilings or on unfinished wood. Apply the sponge to the surface in methodical lines so you can keep track of where you have cleaned. To apply to ceilings or walls, attach the sponge to a **pole**. When the sponge is filthy on all sides, shave off the dirty layer with a **razor** or wash it alone in the **washing machine**. Don't wring it, or you will ruin the chemical treatment.

Next, use the wet cleaning method, following these steps:
- The wet method is the last resort after you've removed as much of the soot as possible by vacuuming (or dusting or brushing) and using the soot sponge. Put down a **plastic drop cloth** and wash the surfaces with a solution of **warm water** and **a couple of drops of degreaser**. Apply liberally to the surface with a **sponge**, **rag**, or **hard-bristled scrub brush**. Rinse with water and wipe dry. If necessary, repeat this procedure.
- If a small stain remains after repeated washing, apply **mineral spirits** carefully with **cotton swabs** made by tightly rolling **cotton balls** around the end of a **wooden skewer**. These are preferable to commercially available cotton swabs, because solvents can dissolve the plastic stalks. Lightly moisten the swab with the mineral spirits and gently roll it across the object. Don't rub or wipe, since this might ingrain the soot and carbon in the surface of the object. Never fully immerse an object in solvent. Work slowly and methodically. Test this method on an inconspicuous part of the object first.

Here are some tips for specific soot-removal jobs:
- On objects with a glossy finish, such as coffee tables, vacuum first. Dampen a **cloth** with **cleaner** such as Formula 409, Fantastik, or Windex and wipe over the surface after testing on an inconspicuous area.
- For vinyl surfaces, including wallpaper, **vacuum** and then use the wet method straight away. A soot sponge will not absorb the soot on glossy surfaces, and it will leave smeary marks.
- To clean ceilings, try **vacuuming** and then using the **soot sponge** for a flat painted ceiling. Then use the wet method.
- To use the wet method on walls, clean from the bottom up. Start in small sections, wipe the **wet sponge** onto the wall in

circular motions, and then wipe dry with an **old towel** or **rag**. It's very important to wipe any soot drips immediately.

- Clean floors first *and* last. Before attacking any other part of the room, **vacuum** thoroughly to get up any loose material so it won't be ground into the flooring. Then protect the floor with **drop cloths** while you clean the rest of the room. Return to the floors again for a thorough cleaning at the end. Try **water and a degreaser** first on wood and tile, and for carpeting use a regular **carpet shampoo** applied either with a **carpet-cleaning machine** or a **wet vac**. If a wood floor won't come clean, you'll have to refinish it. If small soot stains remain on the carpet, apply **mineral spirits**, scrub, and then shampoo the carpet again. Seek professional help if this doesn't work.

- If sooty marks remain on walls, ceilings, or cabinets despite your best efforts, painting is the last option. First, seal the mark using a **stain-resistant primer-sealer** such as Bin or Kilz, available at paint stores, and then paint with the color of your choice.

*See also **Smoke**.*

Spills

As long as there is gravity, there will be spills. So it makes sense to prepare yourself for the next jostled cup of juice or puddle of sloshed soda pop. To win out over spills, you have to keep your cool, work fast, and, above all, know what you're doing so that you won't make matters worse.

To tackle spills on hard surfaces, such as vinyl or wood floors, simply soak up the excess liquid as soon as possible with **paper towels**, **a cloth**, or some other clean, **absorbent material**. Once the liquid is up, rinse by wiping with paper towels or a cloth moistened with **clear water**. Dry with paper towels or a cloth.

For spills on textiles, such as carpeting, upholstery, or clothing, begin by blotting up as much of the excess liquid as possible. For washable fabrics, soak in **cold water** (hot water can set some stains, such as those that are protein-based). Don't rub or brush, because you might damage the textile's texture. For big spills, work from the outer edge of the spill to the center to contain it. Your next step depends on what spilled. Follow the specific guidelines in **Stains**.

Sports Equipment

Luckily, most sports equipment is made of tough materials and can stand getting dirty and scuffed. In fact, overcleaning can be as much of a problem as undercleaning, since rackets, balls, skis, and other sporting goods often contain finely calibrated, high-tech materials. The trick is in knowing how and how often to clean sports gear.

To keep your archery gear clean, wipe off your bow and the shafts of arrows after each use with a *clean, moist cloth*. To remove stubborn dirt, wipe them with a mild solution of *dishwashing liquid* and *warm water*. Rinse with a *water-soaked cloth*. Dry with a *clean towel*. Don't use solvents on your bow or bowstring.

To keep your string from drying out and breaking, wax it monthly using *string wax*. Most compound bow pulley systems are self-lubricating, so there is no need to lubricate wheels and cams. Wipe off the metal limb bolts (which hold the compound parts together) with a *silicone-soaked rag*, available at stores that sell hunting and fishing gear. Periodically spray arrow feathers with an *arrow waterproofing spray*.

To clean a baseball glove, first brush away dirt with a *stiff-bristled leather-care brush*, available at shoe stores. If the mitt gets muddy, let the mud dry and then brush it off. Don't use water on your leather mitt. If your glove gets rained on, let it dry naturally in a warm, well-ventilated place. Don't put it on or near a radiator or fireplace. After all, you've probably spent a lot of time getting the leather soft and supple, and heat does just the opposite: causes leather to stiffen and crack. After the mitt has dried, use *lanolin* or a *lanolin-based shaving cream* to soften the leather.

To clean an outdoor basketball, which is typically made of rubber, use a *cloth* and a solution of *water* and *dishwashing liquid*. Rinse with *clean water* and air-dry. Indoor basketballs are either made of leather (the really high-end balls) or synthetic leather. When cared for properly and kept indoors, neither should need much cleaning.

To keep darts clean, there's not much you have to do as long as you keep your darts out of your beer. Keep the points free of burrs by turning them gently in the concave part of a round *sharpening stone* (available where darts are sold). Every so often, remove the number ring from your dart board and rotate it, so that the wear is distributed evenly.

To care for a football, which is usually made of synthetic leather, keep it dry. If your football gets dirty, wipe it with a *moist rag*. If it gets wet, air-dry it. Don't use a heat source such as a hair dryer or a radiator to dry a football.

To keep golf clubs clean, wipe the dirt and mud off them after each day of golfing. Use a *cloth* and *plain water* or a very mild solution of *dishwashing liquid* and *water*. Rinse by wiping with a *wet cloth*. Dry well with a *dry cloth*. Try not to get the leather grips wet. Large deposits of dirt can hurt your game, so keep a *moist cloth* handy while playing to spot-clean after digging up divots.

To clean a synthetic golf bag, wipe it with *plain water* or the same *mild*, *soapy solution* recommended for clubs. *Vacuum* out the bottom and the pockets occasionally. To clean a leather golf bag, follow the instructions for coated leather in the *Leather* entry.

To keep hockey gear in good working order, the most important thing is to allow it to dry properly—which means letting gear dry naturally, not with the help of an additional heat source. Proper care also means taking gear out of the car trunk and stick bag ASAP. After each game, dry and store pads (hanging them, if possible) in an upright position. The same goes for the stick. Dry skates and blades with a *cloth* after each use to avoid rusting. Wipe visors clean with a *moist cloth* after each use.

Hush-Hush Laundry

There's a nondescript little cleaning business in a small town outside Boston. It's the kind of place you'd pass by without a second look, which is exactly how the managers want it. We were sworn to secrecy, so we can't even reveal the business's name. You see, this media-shy company cleans equipment—helmets, pads, uniforms—for the New England Patriots, the Boston Bruins, the Boston Red Sox, and other professional sports teams. With the high prices paid these days for sports memorabilia, not to mention the extremes some pro sports fans go to for sweat-soaked souvenirs, keeping a low profile is as important to the laundry's business as is making football jerseys sparkle for the cameras on Sunday afternoons.

"We don't advertise what we do," said a longtime sales representative who wished to remain nameless. In fact, the company does just the opposite: It keeps its core business strictly confidential. "That's why these teams feel safe having us clean their uniforms," the sales rep explained. The gear goes in, gets shuttled through the cleaning process by a company overseer, and goes back out within 24 hours. "Unless someone knew the inner workings of our shop, they'd have a hard time taking anything."

Employees are screened before they are hired and are bound by an honor code forbidding them to tuck so much as a smelly sock into their lunch boxes. "If something did go missing," said the sales rep, "we'd lose that account."

To get the most out of your in-line skates, rotate the wheels as soon as you notice that they are wearing down. Switch the most worn with the least worn. Switch from one skate to the other. Since wheels wear faster on the inside edge, turn the less worn side inward. If the bearings get wet, remove them from the wheels and wipe them dry as soon as possible, using a *clean, lint-free cloth*. Don't lubricate the outside of the bearing—that will attract dirt.

Clean bearings that have removable outer shields. You'll know they need cleaning when they spin slowly or make a noise while spinning (the sound of dirt inside). After following the manufacturer's instructions for removing the shields, clean the bearings by inserting a *stick*, *pen*, or *pencil* through their doughnut-shaped casing. Dip them in a *container of mineral spirits* and spin them in the liquid until the dirt is gone. Lay the bearings on a *paper towel* to dry, or blow them dry with a *can of compressed air*. Finish up by lubricating them with *bearing lubricant*, available at skate supply stores.

To maintain a skateboard, keep in mind that most skateboards are made of laminated wood and shouldn't get wet. Dry them if they do. To clean dirty decks, scrub the grip tape with a soft-bristled brush dipped in *clean water*. Rinse by wiping with a *wet cloth or sponge*. Dry well with a *clean cloth* as soon as you've finished rinsing.

As with in-line skate wheels, skateboard wheels should be rotated when you notice they are wearing down. Switch the most worn with the least worn. If the bearings get wet, remove them from the wheels and wipe them dry as soon as possible using a *clean, lint-free cloth*. Don't lubricate the outside of the bearing, because that will attract dirt.

If your bearings have removable outer shields, you can clean and lubricate them. Follow the instructions described above for cleaning and lubricating in-line skate bearings.

To clean skis and poles, wipe them down with a *moist rag* and then dry with a *dry rag*, or use a sudsy solution of *warm water* and *dishwashing liquid*. Rinse and dry them well. Wax your skis every few times you use them. Each time you wax them, clean the bases either by using a *spray-on/wipe-off base cleaner* (available at ski shops) or by putting on *hot wax* with an *old iron* and scraping it off with a plastic scraper before it has dried. (Scrapers are available at ski shops, or in a pinch you can use a plastic windshield scraper. Once you've used an iron for waxing, never use it on clothes.) After you ski, always dry your skis and poles with a *cloth* to keep them from rusting.

To clean ski boots, wipe them off with a *damp cloth*—if they are the hard-plastic variety—and remove the inner boot after each use so that both will dry properly. Wipe leather boots with a *damp cloth*, but avoid getting them very wet. Let them air-dry, but never near heat, which will dry out and crack leather. If your leather ski boots do get wet, remove the insoles and stuff *single sheets of newspaper* in them. Keep leather boots coated with a *leather waterproofing product*, available at sporting goods and shoe stores.

To clean a snowboard, follow the instructions for cleaning and waxing skis described above. Every time you snowboard, dry your board afterward with a *cloth* to keep it from rusting.

To clean a soccer ball, which is typically made of easy-to-clean synthetic leather, just wipe it off with a *moist cloth*. But a soccer ball should rarely need cleaning.

To clean your tennis racket—or your racquetball, squash, or badminton racket—wipe it with a *damp cloth*. Don't get the strings wet, because moisture can ruin them. Try not to wet the leather grip either, as moisture can take away the grip's tackiness and make it slippery. Instead, wipe perspiration off with a *dry cloth*. If your overgrip (the material you can wrap around or slip over the grip) gets dirty, replace it.

When washing outfits for any sport, promptness is key. Don't let sweaty outfits remain in lockers or balled up in gym bags. Wash them in your *washing machine* without delay. Shrinkage is another big issue. You can't play well if your pants and jersey are too small. To avoid shrinkage, stick to *cold-water wash cycles* and *air-drying* instead of using the dryer. Hot dryers can also make the screen-printed numbers and team names on uniforms crack.

If you need to clean pads and protectors for sports such as hockey and football, surface clean them with a *cloth* and *plain water* or a very mild solution of *dishwashing liquid* and *water*. Rinse by wiping with a *wet cloth*. Don't submerge pads or protectors— the water might remain in the padding and lead to bacteria growth and odors. Spray pads with a *fabric waterproofing product*, such as Scotchgard, to help keep them clean and less susceptible to moisture.

SPORTS EQUIPMENT

Sprinklers

Your lawn sprinkler system will let you know when it needs cleaning by spraying in an oddball pattern—or not at all—when it gets jammed by sediment or mineral deposits. Clean it once at the beginning of the watering season and once at the end, and you can reduce the misfiring.

Remove sprinkler spray heads (if possible) and rinse in a *bucket* of *water*. Look for any sediment that may be clogging the nozzles. Scrub lightly with a *toothbrush*. Use your *hose* to force high-pressured water back through the holes. Since most sprinklers these days are made of plastic parts, don't use soaps, oils, or solvents, which can create a buildup or degrade the plastic. If all else fails, try to loosen the sediment by gently pushing a *wire* into the nozzle as water flows out. If you have a mineral buildup, wipe with or soak in a solution of *1 part vinegar* to *3 parts water*.

Take valves apart and clean them the same way you would the spray heads, first using *water* and a *toothbrush* and then, if that doesn't work, *vinegar* and *water*. Rinse any clogged screens in *clean water*.

simple SOLUTIONS

Clogged Sprinkler? >

If you are drawing the water for watering your lawn from a well or pond, it's more likely to contain sprinkler-clogging sediment than water from a municipal system. To reduce the sediment, install an in-line filter, which you can buy at hardware stores and home improvement stores.

Stainless Steel

Yes, it's stainless, but that doesn't mean you don't have to clean and care for stainless steel. It will dull over time and pick up oily fingerprints as well as mineral spots from hard water. The big issue with stainless steel is scratching. Scratch it and you remove the hard, thin oxide coating that makes it stainless. Then it will rust like any old steel.

Wash stainless steel flatware and pots in *hot*, *soapy water* or in your *dishwasher*. Scrub off stubborn food with a *cloth*, *sponge*, or *nylon-bristled brush*, but avoid abrasives. If you're washing it in the dishwasher, be careful not to spill powdered dishwasher detergent on stainless steel—the strong powder will cause dark spots. To remove baked-on food, scrub with a paste of *baking soda* and *water*.

Polish stainless steel with a *clean*, *dry cloth* to remove hard-water spots. For stubborn spots, wipe with a *cloth* soaked in *straight vinegar*. Or use a *stainless steel polishing product*, such as Stainless Steel Magic, Revere Copper and Stainless Steel Cleaner, or Wenol All-Purpose Metal Polish. Follow the label directions.

WATCH OUT

• To avoid corroding stainless steel, rinse acidic, salty, or milk-based foods off stainless steel utensils that won't be washed right away.
• Never use abrasive scrubbers, such as steel wool, on stainless steel. They will dull the finish and may even cause it to rust.

Clean stainless steel sinks and appliances with a solution of *warm water* and a *squirt of dishwashing liquid*, using a *soft cloth or sponge*. Always scrub in the direction of the stainless steel grain. Rinse with a *cloth or sponge* and *clear water*. Polish dry to avoid spotting, using *paper towels or a cloth*. For more cleaning power, use a solution of *1 cup white vinegar* and *3 cups water*, or scrub with a paste made of *baking soda* and *hot water*.

Stains

Stains happen. It's a fact of life. It might be a grass stain on your son's pants, red wine on the wall-to-wall, or hot coffee on a clean shirt. (Talk about a morning eye-opener!) But stains don't have to be permanent, which means you don't have to toss out that shirt or live with that splotchy red carpet.

You see, stains aren't as mysterious as some people think. Most stains fall into one of four main stain categories: protein, oil-based, tannin, and dye. The rest are usually some combination of those stain categories. By understanding what is in a stain, textile scientists can determine what will remove it. Armed with this stain-removal know-how, you too can beat most stains before they beat you—with a few exceptions, of course.

Before moving on to stain-removal specifics, be sure to read the general guidelines in the box opposite. Also be sure to use the appropriate technique for the material that is stained.

There are three main categories of textiles that can be stained: washable fabrics (clothing, linens, towels), carpets, and upholstered furniture. Below are the general steps to follow when attempting to remove stains from these three textile categories.

With washable fabrics, one of the advantages you have (apart from the fact that you *can* machine-wash it) is that you have access to both sides of the stain. Pretreatment often consists of pushing the stain out from the back side of the fabric.

1. Remove as much of the stain-causing material as possible by blotting with *paper towels* or scraping with a *dull knife*.
2. Pretreat the stain by soaking or applying a *cleaning solution*. It helps to lightly agitate the fabric being soaked or to gently rub together the stained fabric with your hands.
3. Launder in your *washing machine* according to the instructions on the fabric's care label.
4. If necessary, repeat the preceding steps, possibly using a stronger cleaning solution.

With carpeting, you typically have access to the top side only for stain removal. But you should never soak carpet stains, because most carpets and rugs have pads under them. Getting cleaning solutions into those pads can actually attract dirt and lead to other problems, such as mildew and glue deterioration. Try these methods instead:

1. Remove as much of the stain-causing material as you can by blotting with *paper towels* or scraping with a *dull knife*. When blotting up a large stain, always blot from the edge of the stain to the center to contain it.
2. Avoid rubbing or pushing the stain deeper into the pile. Avoid using a circular motion, which can destroy a carpet's texture.
3. Because you should never soak a carpet, *spray bottles* are good for applying a light amount of water-based cleaning solution and rinse water.
4. To dry patches of carpet that have been rinsed with water, lay a *pad of paper towels* on the spot and place a *weight*, such as a brick, on the pad. To prevent transferring color from the brick to the carpet, put the brick in a *plastic bag* or wrap it in *foil*. When the carpet is dry, remove the paper towels. *Brush* the carpet pile to restore a consistent texture.

Some *General Guidelines* for Removing Stains

• Follow the instructions on care labels. These days, most fabric items, including clothes, rugs, linens, and upholstery, have care labels. Because fabrics differ in so many ways—type of material, type of weave, color, style—use those instructions as your baseline.

• Remove spills before they become stains. Blot up spilled liquids, scrape away solids, and begin your step-by-step stain removal as soon as possible. Factors such as heat and evaporation make stains that are older than about 24 hours much harder to remove.

• To remove stains from dry clean-only fabrics, first remove as much of the stain residue as possible and then have the item dry-cleaned as soon as you can (within a day or two).

• Be patient. As effective as stain-removal know-how can be, it is often a multistep approach, from mildest to harshest treatment. Try one tactic, and if that doesn't work, move on to a stronger cleaning solution. If you lose patience and try to jump ahead, you may make things worse.

• Test cleaning solutions on an inconspicuous part of an item, such as an inside seam or hidden corner. That way, if the fabric or fabric colors react poorly to the cleaning solution, you haven't ruined the whole thing. To test a chlorine bleach solution, mix 1 tablespoon of bleach with 1/4 cup of water. Use an eyedropper or cotton swab to apply a drop of the solution to the fabric. Let the garment stand for two minutes and then blot dry with a clean cloth.

• If a stain persists, don't put it in the dryer, because its heat could set the stain permanently. Because your first approach may not remove the stain, always check for persistent stains on items after they've gone through the wash. If your washer cycle didn't remove a stain, pull that item and let it air-dry. Likewise, don't iron or press something if a stain is still in it.

With upholstery, you face the same problem you have with carpeting: You rarely have a chance to get at both sides of the stain. Even if you can remove the upholstery material, most upholstery manufacturers warn against washing cushion covers separately from the cushions because of possible shrinking and other problems. The trick, as with carpeting and pads, is to remove the stain from the top side without soaking the cushion beneath. So follow the steps for removing carpet stains, listed above, to deal with your upholstery stains.

> PROTEIN-BASED STAINS are caused by such substances as *baby food and formula, cream- or cheese-based foods, eggs, feces, and urine.*

For fresh protein stains, *cold water* is sometimes all you'll need to remove them. Don't use hot water, because it can cook the proteins, causing the stain to coagulate between the fibers in the fabric. (Think blue-jean omelets.) For washable fabrics, soak in *cold water* for half an hour, put the stain under *running cold water*, and gently rub the fabric against itself to loosen the stain. Launder in the *washing machine* in *warm water*.

For an old or dried protein stain, you may have to take your stain-removal tactics to the next level. Soak washable fabrics for half an hour in a solution of *1 teaspoon of liquid detergent* (preferably one containing enzymes—the label will say whether it has them) per *1/2 gallon of cold water*. Follow this soaking by laundering the fabric in your *washing machine* in *warm water*. Inspect the item before drying. If the stain is still there, soak the fabric an additional half hour and then launder again. If the stain remains after that, your only option may be to add the recommended amount of *bleach* to the next wash cycle, especially if the stain was caused by colored ice cream or baby food.

For a fresh protein stain in carpeting or upholstery, spray with *cold water* and blot, repeating until clean.

For a dried protein stain in carpeting or upholstery, lightly apply a solution of *1/4 teaspoon mild dishwashing liquid* (one that doesn't contain lanolin or bleach) in *1 quart cold water*. Apply the solution to a *cloth*, and use a blotting motion to work the solution into the affected area. Blot with a *clean paper towel* to remove the solution. Rinse by lightly spraying the stain with *water* and then blotting. Do this until all the suds are gone. Then spray again lightly with *water*. Don't blot this time. Instead, lay a *pad of paper towels* over the spot, put a *weight* on it, and let it dry. (See step 4 of removing stains from carpeting, page 339.)

If the stain persists, repeat the procedure with a stronger solution: *1/2 teaspoon of liquid detergent* (preferably one containing enzymes) per *1 quart of cold water*.

If that still doesn't completely remove the stain, moisten the stained tufts with *3 percent hydrogen peroxide*. Let it stand for one hour. Blot and repeat until the carpet or upholstery is stain free. No rinsing is necessary following this procedure, because light will cause the peroxide to change to water. To dry, use the method mentioned previously involving a *pad of paper towels* and a *weight*. But be careful: Hydrogen peroxide is bleach and can whiten colors.

> OIL-BASED STAINS include those from *auto grease or motor oil, hair oil and mousse, hand lotion, kitchen grease, lard, butter, bacon, oils, ointments, salad dressing,* and *suntan lotion*. Oil-based stains aren't as difficult to get rid of as most people think. Many prewash stain-removal products, such as Spray 'n Wash and Shout, contain special solvents for removing oil and grease.

For oil-based stains in washable fabrics, pretreat new and old stains with a *commercial prewash stain remover*. If you don't have one of those products, apply *liquid laundry detergent* (or a paste made from *granular detergent* mixed with *water*) directly to the stain. Work the detergent into the stain. Immediately after pretreatment, launder the item in the *washing machine* in *hot water* (if that is safe for the fabric and colors). Before drying the fabric, inspect it. If the stain is still evident, repeat the process until it is gone. For heavy stains, lay the stain facedown on a *clean white towel* (or *stack of paper towels*) and press a *dry-cleaning solvent*, such as K2r or Carbona, on the stain, forcing it out and into the towels. Repeat and then launder.

For oil-based stains in carpets and upholstery, apply *isopropyl (rubbing) alcohol* to a *clean white cloth or white paper towel* and blot the stain. Discard the dirty towels and repeat using *fresh paper towels* and alcohol until the stain is gone. Don't let the alcohol penetrate the carpet backing, as it can destroy the latex lining. If that treatment doesn't remove the stain, try the method recommended above for removing dried protein stains from carpeting and upholstery.

> TANNIN STAINS include those from *alcoholic drinks, coffee or tea without milk, fruits and juices, soft drinks,* and *wine*. Most *jellies* also contain tannins, but cherry and blueberry jellies should be treated as dye stains. (See page 343.)

For tannin stains in washable fabric, soak for half an hour in a solution of *1 teaspoon liquid detergent* (preferably one containing

A Bottle of Red, a Bottle of White >

A butler who wishes to remain anonymous (discretion being part of a butler's code of conduct) was employed by an American family in England. One day, he was horrified to find a large red stain on the family's cream-colored carpet. He contacted a carpet-cleaning company, which agreed to come immediately. Before the cleaners arrived, however, the butler surprised two of the family's children, ages 11 and 14, sneaking across the hallway with a half-empty bottle of *very* expensive white wine from their father's cellar. The children's friends had told them that they could remove a red wine stain with white wine. Naturally, they had tested the theory. "All I will say," adds the butler, "is that the red wine/white wine stain theory cost them a very large amount of their allowance over the coming months."

enzymes) per *1/2 gallon of warm water*. Then launder in the *washing machine* in the *hottest water* that is safe for the fabric, using laundry detergent and not soap. Natural soaps—including soap flakes, bar soap, and detergent containing soap—make tannin stains harder to remove. To remove stubborn tannin stains, you may need to wash with bleach. If all the sugars from one of these stains aren't removed, they could turn brown when put into the dryer, as the sugar will caramelize.

For tannin stains in carpeting or upholstery, lightly apply a solution of *1/4 teaspoon mild dishwashing liquid* and *1 quart water*. Use a blotting motion to work the solution into the affected area. Blot with a *clean paper towel* to remove the solution. Rinse by lightly spraying with *water* and blotting to remove excess water. Do this until all the suds are gone. Then spray lightly with water again, but don't blot. Instead, lay a *pad of paper towels* down, *weight* it, and let it dry. If the blemish persists, repeat the procedure using a solution of *1/2 teaspoon liquid detergent* (preferably one containing enzymes) per *1 quart of water*. If that doesn't completely remove the stain, moisten the tufts in the stained area with *3 percent hydrogen peroxide*. Let stand for one hour. Blot and repeat until the stain has disappeared. No rinsing is necessary following this procedure. To dry, lay down the weighted pad of paper towels mentioned above.

Tracking Down Mystery Stains

You don't always have the luxury of knowing what caused a stain, as anyone who has children can attest. So how do you handle a mystery stain? Like a detective, of course.

Start by using your senses to pick up clues: how the stain smells, what color it is, and where it is on a garment. For example:
• You typically find food stains on the front of clothes.
• Black grease, the kind you find on cars and other heavy machinery, often turns up on pants and skirts at the level of your car door latch.
• Colors can be misleading. For instance, old dried blood can be black, not red.

If you can't figure a stain out, use trial and error to remove the stain. First off, avoid washing unknown stains in hot water, which will set protein-based stains, such as egg or blood. Try the mildest method first, then escalate:
• Soak in cold water, which just might remove a protein-based stain.
• If that doesn't work, pretreat by rubbing with liquid laundry detergent and then wash with warm or hot water.
• If that doesn't work, try spraying with a pretreatment product or blotting with dry-cleaning solvent.
• Still no luck? Time for the bleaches, beginning with oxygen (all-fabric) bleach. Use a diluted chlorine bleach soak as a last resort.

STAINS

> **DYE STAINS** include those from *blueberries, cherries, grass,* and *mustard.* Dye stains can be doozies. After all, dyes are usually meant to stick. They're what color our clothes.

For dye stains in washable fabrics, pretreat with a commercial prewash stain remover. Or apply liquid laundry detergent directly to the stain, work the detergent into the stain, and rinse well. Next, soak the fabric in a diluted solution of ***oxygen bleach*** (identified as "all-fabric" or "perborate" on the label), following the directions on the packaging. Launder. Inspect the item to see whether the stain is still there. If so, try soaking the entire garment in a solution of ***chlorine bleach*** and water. (Again, follow the directions on the bleach container.) But be careful: Bleach can drastically alter colors and weaken fabric.

For dye stains in carpet or upholstery, good luck. You may have to call a professional cleaner or, in the case of a solid-colored carpet, cut the stained part out and patch it with clean carpet. But before you go that far, try the procedure described above for tannin stains on carpet or upholstery.

> **COMBINATION STAINS** contain both oils or waxes and dyes. They are commonly divided into two categories:

- Group A combination stains include those from *lipstick, eye makeup (mascara, pencil, liner, eye shadow), furniture polish,* and *shoe polish.*
- Group B combination stains include *chocolate, gravy, hair spray, face makeup (foundation, powder, rouge), peanut butter,* and *tomato-based foods.*

To remove these stains, you first must remove the oily or waxy portion, and then you can try to remove the dye. As with any tough stain, your success is not guaranteed. But by following the steps below, you do stand a chance, especially if you get to the stain while it's fresh.

For washable fabrics with stains in Group A, begin by applying a ***dry-cleaning solvent***, such as K2r or Carbona. Next, rub with a ***liquid detergent*** and scrub in hot water. This should remove the oily or waxy part. Then launder, using a ***laundry detergent*** and an ***oxygen*** or ***all-fabric bleach***. Inspect before drying. If the stain persists, try washing with ***chlorine bleach***.

For washable fabrics with stains in Group B, skip the dry-cleaning solvent. Rub the stain with a ***liquid laundry detergent*** and launder in the ***washing machine*** in the ***hottest water*** possible for the fabric. If that doesn't work, try first the ***oxygen bleach*** and then, if that fails, the ***chlorine bleach***.

**Last-Minute Leaf
Cleaning >**

In preparation for a holiday party, a butler working for a family in San Francisco had just finished refreshing all the foliage in his employer's house. "The day of the party, I was doing a walk-through to inspect the house," recalls the butler, "when I noticed that all of the plants—orchids, palms, fresh flowers—had a sticky whitish substance covering them. Half the orchids had wilted. I had a mini heart attack!" Rallying his domestic troops, the butler and his crew cleaned every leaf and replaced every orchid in time for the evening's party. The mystery was solved when the butler learned that the family's children, ages 9 and 11, had decided to help by filling their Aveda hair spray bottles with water and watering every plant in the house. The problem was that they didn't empty out the hair spray first.

STAINS

343

For combination stains in carpets and upholstery, also begin by removing the oily or waxy part first. Apply *isopropyl (rubbing) alcohol* to a *clean white cloth or white paper towel* and blot the stain. Discard the dirty towels and repeat using *fresh paper towels* and alcohol until the stain is gone. Don't let the alcohol penetrate the carpet backing, as it could destroy the latex lining.

If the alcohol treatment doesn't work, try the next step:

Lightly apply a solution of *1/4 teaspoon of mild dishwashing liquid* (one that doesn't contain lanolin or bleach) and *1 quart of water*. Use a blotting motion to work the solution into the affected area. Blot with a *clean paper towel* to remove the solution. Rinse by lightly spraying with *water* and blotting. Do this until all the suds are gone. Then spray again lightly with *water*. But instead of blotting this time, lay a *pad of paper towels* down, put a *weight* on it, and let it dry.

Finally, if that doesn't completely remove the stain, moisten the stained tufts with *3 percent hydrogen peroxide* and let stand for one hour. Blot and repeat until the stain is gone. No rinsing is necessary following this procedure. To dry, use a pad of paper towels and weight.

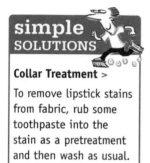

simple SOLUTIONS

Collar Treatment >

To remove lipstick stains from fabric, rub some toothpaste into the stain as a pretreatment and then wash as usual.

> OTHER STAINS not in the categories already mentioned include stains produced by *perspiration, glue, paint, mud,* and *nail polish.*

Treat deodorant and perspiration stains as you would dye stains. The aluminum or zinc salt buildup from deodorants can make them particularly stubborn.

To remove glue, begin by scraping off whatever you can with a *dull knife* (rubbing *ice* on it first to harden it). If the glue is white school glue, such as Elmer's, treat it as you would a protein-based stain, which means no hot water—the hot water could cook the proteins. If it is model-airplane glue, treat it as an oil-based stain. If the glue won't come out, place the stain facedown on *absorbent paper towels*. To force the stain out, blot the back of the fabric with a *cloth* moistened with *dry-cleaning solvent*.

Treat latex paint while it is wet. Soak the fabric in *cold water* and then wash it in *cold water* with *laundry detergent*. If the paint has dried, even for as little as six hours, treat it as you would a Group A combination stain.

Remove oil-based paint when it is wet, too. Spot treat with *paint thinner* or *turpentine* and a *sponge or cloth* until the paint is loosened and as much is removed as possible. Then, before it can dry, wash in *hot water* and *detergent*.

STAINS

Handle mud as you would a protein-based stain, with one exception: It's best to wait until mud has dried before cleaning it. Once it has dried, scrape off the excess solids. Then follow the protein-stain procedures.

If a rust stain remains after removing the mud, treat it with a **commercial rust remover**, available at supermarkets. Since rust removers can be toxic, follow the directions on the container carefully. A solution of **lemon juice** and **salt** sometimes removes rust. Sprinkle salt on the stain, squeeze lemon juice on it, and put the item in the **sun** to dry. Be sure to test the lemon juice first, since it can bleach some fabrics. And be forewarned: Chlorine bleach makes rust stains permanent.

To remove nail polish, blot with a **clean cloth** moistened with **acetone or nail polish remover** until the stain is gone. If possible, lay the stain facedown on white paper towels and blot from the back side to force the stain out the way it came in. Don't use acetone or nail polish remover on acetate, triacetate, or modacrylic fabrics. It will dissolve these fabrics.

Yellowing of a fabric can occur for several reasons: not enough detergent in a wash cycle, too much detergent, insufficient wash temperatures, color transfer from other items while washing, or a fabric's loss of artificial whiteners. Your best bet for restoring brightness and whiteness is to launder with the proper amount of **detergent** and **bleach**. First, try **oxygen bleach**. If that doesn't work, try a cycle with **chlorine bleach**.

Stairs and Steps

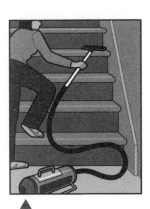

You're vacuuming away, knocking out room after room, and then you hit the stairs, which can be a cleaning roadblock, especially if they are carpeted. Such an awkward upward procession of small surfaces, so many dust-filled corners! And then there's the danger factor—tripping over the cord while both hands are busy juggling the vacuum cleaner and its wand. What to do?

Use vacuum cleaner savvy. If you don't have one already, buy an **extension tube** for your **vacuum cleaner**. Often 12 feet in length, an extension tube usually comes in an attachment kit that costs about $30. There are extenders for upright and canister vacs. Added to your existing 6 or 7 feet of hose, these extenders will allow you to leave the heavy vacuum cleaner on the ground floor while cleaning entire flights ▶. Good-bye roadblock.

For carpet-covered stairs, buy a *turbo tool*, which is also a relatively inexpensive (and well worth the money) add-on for your vacuum cleaner. Powered by the incoming airflow (hence the name *turbo*), these attachments act like small beater bars to help loosen and pull up hairs, lint, and dirt from carpet pile. But because they don't need a power cord to rotate, they can be attached to extension hoses. Or, better yet, buy one of the new, reasonably priced *compact vacuum cleaners* made especially for stairs. These are handheld and have long cords that are made to reach up a flight of steps.

Clean stairs from bottom to top. That way, you don't grind dirt into the carpet or spread it around on hardwood floors. After cleaning the broad stair treads, use a *vacuum crevice tool* to get into the cracks along the wall and where the vertical riser meets the tread. Periodically, vacuum the carpeted risers.

Stereo Equipment

Cleaning electronic equipment, such as stereo components, usually makes people shudder. It's so complicated, they think. But it's not really—and it is important to keep your stereo clean, because dust and lint can damage the fine electronic parts. The following is a step-by-step cleaning approach that is easy and doesn't involve getting into the guts of the machinery.

Clean the front panels with a *soft cotton cloth* and *glass cleaner*. (First, make sure all components are off.) Don't spray the glass cleaner directly on the equipment. Instead, spray it on the cloth and gently wipe the cloth on the panel. For sensitive areas, such as around the panel controls and buttons, dust with a *small, dry paintbrush*. Don't apply cleaner to these areas, since it could seep into the controls. The paintbrush is also a good hedge against accidentally changing your control settings.

To clean the component's chassis—that is, the sides and top—use a *soft cloth* that is either dry or lightly misted with *glass cleaner*. Don't wet the cloth, since any residue left on the chassis could collect dust and lead to corrosion. Never spray anything directly onto the chassis. Wipe away from, not toward, the vent holes to avoid pushing dust into the innards.

Dust the back of the unit, where the cable jacks are, with a *dry paintbrush*. Don't use cleaner around this sensitive area. If you must remove cables to access the rear, label the cables before-

STAIRS AND STEPS

hand with **masking tape** or **preprinted stereo component labels**, which are sold at audio stores. But be forewarned: Many components store data for user settings, clocks, and timers, and this memory can be lost when the component is unplugged from the electrical outlet.

Wipe cables down with a **cloth** misted with the same **cleaner** you used on the panels. Be careful not to pull any cables out.

See also **Cassette Players**, **CD Players and CDs**, *and* **DVD Players**.

Stickers

These days gummy, hard-to-remove stickers and price tags are plastered on almost every new product, from toys to toilets to individual Granny Smith apples. It's enough to make you want to stop shopping. Well, nothing could really do that—but stickers *can* be frustrating.

For stickers with water-soluble glue, the kind that must be dampened before applying, soak the sticker in a **basin of warm water** until the glue dissolves and the sticker comes off. If you can't soak it in water, soak a **towel** in water and apply that to the sticker.

To remove pressure-sensitive adhesive labels (those that are peeled from a backing and then pressed into place, such as the stickers that come on glassware and the "My name is Bob" nametags you get at high school reunions), start by peeling as much of the label off as possible. Then rub the remaining adhesive off with your fingers the way you would "thumb-roll" rubber cement into small pellets. Coax up difficult adhesive with your **fingernail or a dull knife**.

If the adhesive is old or dried out, you may have to try a different method. Depending on the type of material the sticker is stuck to, try removing it with **warm, soapy water** or a **50–50 solution** of **vinegar** and **warm water**. You might also try **salad oil, WD-40, or acetone** (or an **acetone-based fingernail polish remover**—that's the kind that smells like bananas).

If these tactics don't work, move up to solvents, such as **lacquer thinner** or **rubber cement thinner**, always being careful not to damage the surface.

If the pressure-sensitive adhesive label is on wood, blot with **rubbing alcohol** or heat with a **hair dryer** to remove.

Stone

Stone is one of the most durable materials on earth. Most of it has been here for thousands—even millions—of years. But durable is one thing; clean and scratch-free is another. Even tough stone can be scratched by everyday grit and damaged by some of the most common household substances, including that old cleaning friend, vinegar. Take care of your stone, and it will surely outlast you.

Sweep or dust stone often to remove sand and dirt from flat surfaces, where particles can be ground down by shoe soles, furniture, or pots and pans. The grit can scratch the stone. Dust using either a *vacuum cleaner or dry dust mop* (for floors) or a *clean, dry rag* (countertops and tables). Wipe up spills immediately to avoid staining.

To clean a stone countertop, first try using only *warm water.* Wipe it off with a *soft cloth or sponge.* Let caked-on food soak a bit before wiping. You should be able to remove spills, crumbs, sauces, and other substances this way. If not, add a little *dishwashing liquid* to the water. Rinse well with *clean water,* because leftover soap can leave a film or cause streaking. Avoid stronger cleaning products, such as tub and tile cleaners and scouring powders. These can stain or scratch your stone. Never use vinegar, lemon juice, or other acidic cleaners on marble, travertine, or limestone. The acid will eat away at the calcium in the stone.

To remove stains, keep it simple and be patient. Most stone stains are solid residue jammed in between the crystals of the stone after the liquid that carried it has evaporated. The trick is to put the solid back into solution so it can be removed. First, determine whether your stain is water-based (for example, from spilled grape juice) or oil-based (salad dressing).

- If it is water-based, pour *hot water* (from the tap, not the teakettle) onto the stain and let it stand for a few minutes. Wipe away the excess water. Stack *1/4 inch of paper towels* on the stain and saturate with *hot water.* Cover with a *piece of plastic* and a *flat, heavy weight,* such as a cast-iron skillet or a book (careful not to ruin the book). Let stand for about 10 hours. (Do it overnight and you won't have to worry about anyone's moving it.) Next, throw away the paper towels, and the stain should go with them.
- If the stain is oil-based, follow the same procedure, only instead of water, use *acetone* (but don't heat). After the 10 hours is up,

throw away the paper towels and wash the stain. In both cases, let the spot dry and then observe. If some of the stain is still present, repeat with *hot water or more acetone*.

Sweep patio stone regularly to remove leaves and sticks, which can stain and hold mold-growing moisture. Once a year, give your patio stone a more thorough cleaning using a solution of *1 gallon of warm water* and *1 cup of trisodium phosphate (TSP)*, a relatively mild cleaner available at hardware stores. Use a *stiff-bristled brush* (a long-handled one will be easier on your back and knees) to scrub the patio. Rinse the stones with a *garden hose*. TSP runoff won't harm surrounding foliage. Use the TSP solution to spot-remove grill grease, tannins, and other stains from stone.

See also **Countertops** and **Patios**.

Stoves

As with ovens, there's a very practical and important reason to keep your stove clean: It reduces the risk of fire from oil, grease, and other food spills. The trick is to stay on top of the food spills and splatters—not let them build up and harden into something that will make you groan with cleaning dread.

Wipe off your stove after you cook, every time. That may sound like something only *The Odd Couple*'s Felix Unger would do, but those few minutes of prevention will save time in the long run. Use a clean, *moist sponge or cloth* to remove crumbs and oil. Wipe the control panel. Do it while the oven is still warm, and the job will be even easier. For more stubborn spatters and spills, use a solution of *dishwashing liquid* and *warm water* or a *50–50 solution* of *vinegar* and *warm water*. Never use abrasive scrubbers, such as steel wool.

Periodically give the parts a more extensive cleaning. Wash burner drip plates and other removable accessories (but not electric burner coils) either by hand in the sink or by running them with your next *dishwasher* load (if the owner's manual for your stove says they are dishwasher safe). Carefully remove control panel knobs (usually by pulling straight out) and clean around the knobs' bases. Wash the knobs in *hot, soapy water*, rinse, and dry before replacing them.

If your stove doesn't have a sealed cooktop, periodically lift up the cooktop (like lifting the hood of a car) and clean beneath it.

This is an important, often overlooked way to cut down on potential cooking fires. Follow the owner's manual instructions for lifting the top without damaging it. Then clean the grease buildup with a *sponge* and *soapy water* or a *50-50 solution* of *vinegar* and *warm water*. Rinse with *clean water* and a *sponge*.

For electric stoves, periodically wipe spilled food from the coils once they have cooled. Remove the coils to make the job easier. Use a *damp rag* and *soapy water* or a *vinegar solution* for more stubborn food.

For gas stoves, periodically remove and clean burner caps (also called burner heads) and grates. Wait until they have cooled. Use a *damp rag* and *soapy water* or a *vinegar solution* for stubborn food. For stuck-on food, put the burner caps (if they are removable), grates, and drip plates in a *plastic bag* with a *small bowl* of *ammonia*. Seal it and let it stand overnight. The ammonia fumes will loosen the food and grease. Follow up by cleaning with *soapy water*, rinsing with *fresh water*, and air-drying.

▲

   If the burner caps aren't removable and get clogged with food, clear them with a *sewing needle* ◀. If the flame pattern remains jumpy, let the cap cool and clean again with the needle. Repeat until the flame pattern is consistent.

For ceramic or glass cooktops, clean often but with great care. These can be the easiest stovetops to keep clean, but they are also quite sensitive. Never use anything abrasive, including plastic brushes or scrubbing pads, unless recommended by the manufacturer. Don't use harsh cleaning chemicals. Wipe with *water or soapy water*. Use a *ceramic polish*, such as Cerama Bryte, available at appliance stores and home improvement centers. Typically, a drop or two will do. Spread it over the top and then polish dry with a *dry cloth or paper towel*.

For the tough, cooked-on, yellow-brown deposits that build up on porcelain enamel stovetops, try these tips:

● Moisten a *paper towel*, add a *squirt of dishwashing liquid*, and squeeze the towel to distribute the detergent. Lay the towel over the deposit and leave it for 10 minutes. Then gently remove the softened gunk with your *fingernail* or a *nylon scrubber* (nothing more abrasive), being careful not the scratch the surface. If needed, follow up with a *squirt of a degreaser*, such as Formula 409, or an *orange oil cleaner*, such as Right Stuff Citrus Cleaner.

● Attack the deposit with a *special cleaner* designed specifically for stovetops, such as CookTop Magic or Cerama Bryte.

STOVES

Stuffed Toy Animals

Stuffed animals tend to spend a lot of time on floors mingling with dust bunnies or snuggling with loving children, who unintentionally rub whatever food and grime they have on their hands into the fake fur. Because of the variety of stuffing materials and accessories, such as clothing and ribbons, cleaning them can be trickier than simply tossing them in the washing machine.

Periodically dust your stuffed animal toys to keep them fresh, allergen free, and looking their best. Use your *vacuum cleaner's brush attachment* to remove dust. Be sure not to suck up any loose buttons or clothing accessories. Preen the fake hair with a *clean hairbrush* and then vacuum again to lift whatever the brush loosened. (So that you won't get dirt and hair-product residue on the animals, buy a brush that you use only for this purpose.) To remove pet hair and lint, use a *lint roller*.

To remove light dirt, just lightly clean the surface. Wipe with a *damp cloth*, trying not to get moisture into the stuffing. Follow up by preening with a *hairbrush*.

To remove juice and other spills on stuffed animals, do what a live animal would do if you doused it with liquid: Shake. Shake the toy, outside or in a bathtub, to keep the liquid from splashing onto anything else. This will remove some of the liquid without smearing it into the fur—or worse, the stuffing. Blot up as much remaining liquid as you can with *paper towels*. Never rub. Wet with a *cloth or sponge*. Blot again. Rinse the cloth or sponge. Repeat until the spill is gone.

For deeper cleaning, start by reading the care tag sewn into the seam. Machine-washing is OK for some stuffed animals, such as those filled with most synthetic fibers, but it can ruin others, such as those filled with Styrofoam or that have cardboard stiffeners. The same goes for drying: For some stuffed toys, a dryer is fine, but other toys are stuffed so tightly that they will mildew or will never dry out.

If your toy isn't machine washable, surface-clean using a solution of *warm water* and *mild dishwashing liquid*. Rub gently with a *cloth or sponge* dampened in the solution, being sure not to soak the filling. Rinse by wiping with a *cloth or sponge* dampened with *clear water*. To maintain a consistent look to the surface, clean the whole animal and not just one spot. Air-dry and then preen with a *hairbrush*.

simple SOLUTIONS

Take Eeyore for a Spin >

For a quick and easy way to dust and freshen plush toys, toss them into a dryer and tumble on the fluff setting for 10 minutes. To remove odors from your favorite stuffed animals, add a scented dryer sheet when you tumble them in the dryer.

If the tag says it's OK to wash, tie the stuffed toy up in a *cloth bag*, such as a laundry bag or pillowcase (but not a mesh bag), to protect the fur. It's OK to put several toy animals in the bag, as long as they fit loosely and aren't too big for the *washing machine*. Wash in *cold water* using a *mild detergent* on a *gentle cycle*. Don't use bleach or fabric softeners. Put the whole bag in the *dryer* and tumble on the machine's *gentlest setting*.

Suede

Suede, leather with a soft-napped finish, is one of the trickiest materials to clean. It can be one of the most expensive materials as well. As tough as suede seems, it is easy to ruin. If you must get suede dirty—and since you're reading this entry, you probably already have—then there are a few tricks to cleaning it. Above all, be careful and patient.

WATCH OUT

Don't get perfume, hair spray, or any other cosmetic products containing alcohol on your suede. They can make the colors run. For the same reason, never use a liquid or solvent-based spot remover on suede. Your blue suede shoes might wind up blotchy. Elvis would never forgive you.

Brush your suede regularly to remove dirt and restore the nap. When you are going to put it away for a while, brush the item with a *suede brush*, available at stores that sell leather goods or shoes. Do it gently and in a slow, circular motion. No suede brush? Use a *clean, dry kitchen sponge*.

If you stain your suede, the best thing to do is blot up as much of the stain as possible and then take the item to a professional cleaner who has experience cleaning leather and suede. Here are a couple of exceptions:

● For grease or oil stains, cover the stain with a *small pile of corn starch or talcum powder*. Let it stand overnight. The powder might absorb the stain.

● Remove dried water marks by brushing lightly with a *suede brush or clean, dry sponge*.

Swimming Pools

No pool is maintenance-free. These days, many pool owners use advanced pool-cleaning systems, such as automatic underwater vacuums, pumps, and filters. But as experts in the swimming pool business like to say, these automated systems are meant to keep a clean pool clean. Let the algae and pool grime really build up, and you'll end up spending hours scrubbing by hand. So the trick to keeping pool cleaning to a minimum is to stay on top of it, even if you have an automated system.

Spend at least five minutes every day with your pool. Walk around it, picking up debris near the edge and making sure the water is clear and not cloudy—a sign of improper pH levels. Any time you see more than five or six leaves or sticks, use a *long pole and net* to scoop them up. Although an automatic vacuum system will pick up the occasional leaf or twig, its main job is cleaning dirt. Too many leaves can clog the system.

Keep up the chemical regimen. Maintain your pool with the manufacturer's recommended dosage of *chlorine*, which kills bacteria and germs. Use an *algicide*—not chlorine—to reduce algae. After rains, watch for algae blooms, especially mustard algae, which are present in the air. If you have a Gunite pool, be careful about using a copper-based algicide, which can stain the Gunite. Read the label—algicides containing suspended copper are typically OK to use on Gunite.

Clean skimmers and filters regularly. Do it at least once a week, and more often if needed. (See Expert Advice sidebar.)

Periodically "sweep" the surface. Walk around the pool's edge, scooping up debris with the *pole and net* as you go. Empty the net occasionally to keep leaves from falling back into the pool. When you've finished the edges, net the middle by stretching the net out, letting it fall upside down in the water, and dragging it back toward you. Repeat this while making your way around the pool. Do this once a week or as needed.

Clean the sides using a *long-handled pool brush*. Starting at the top of the pool wall, make one smooth motion downward with the brush. When you reach the bottom, bring it back to the top and do it again, moved over one brush width. Continue until you've circled the pool once. Do this once a week or as needed.

Once a week, scrub the tile using a *pool tile cleaner* and a *tile brush*, available at pool supply stores. Use as little cleaner as possible to keep the product from filling your pool with suds.

Vacuum the pool floor—once you have brushed the sides and cleaned the tile—to remove dirt and debris. (Make sure all sediment has settled.) Begin by netting up large debris. Then attach your *vacuum head and hose* to your *extended pole*. Work your way around the pool, vacuuming toward the main drain. To fill your vacuum hose with water (which you must do before vacuuming), hold the end up to your pool's return water jet until it is full. This way, you won't have to laboriously dip and raise the hose to fill it.

expert advice

Yikes! What's That in My Skimmer? >

It's the job of the pool skimmer, those little round baskets along the sides of pools, to catch debris. Sometimes that debris is less than savory and can be downright dangerous. "I'm not real wild about sticking my hand into a leaf-filled skimmer basket that I can't see," says Mary Robertson of Blue Haven Pools in Tyler, Texas. Robertson warns of scummy leaves, dead insects, even drowned rodents. "The other day, a woman called me to say she found a baby copperhead snake in her skimmer." Robertson's technique for getting around this, er, touchy problem? She lifts skimmer baskets using a hook made from an old wire coat hanger.

Table Linens

Because of the food stains they so easily accumulate, most table-cloths and cloth napkins are, thankfully, machine washable. But simply tossing dirty or stained table linens into the washer may not be enough to keep them looking crisp and fresh under your fine china, crystal, and silver. A few tricks of the trade will help.

Wash table linens before stains set. After spills or big, messy dinner parties, wash them in a *washing machine* as soon as possible, following the manufacturer's recommendations on the care label. Pretreat stains with a *commercial spot remover*. For best results, don't let the pretreatment dry before washing.

When ironing tablecloths, cut down on the creasing by placing a *table* next to your *ironing board*. Let the tablecloth hang over the table but don't let it drag on the floor.

If your table linens have lace, make sure the lace is machine washable. Some lace is not and might shrink considerably when washed in water.
- If the lace is not washable, have it *dry-cleaned*.
- If it is washable—and luckily, most table linen lace is—wash it gently. The safest technique is to hand-wash it in *warm water* with a *squirt or two of dishwashing liquid*.
- If it is *machine washable*, wash it in a *mesh bag* tied at the top. This prevents the lace from snagging.
- To keep the lace from wrinkling, which it will do in a machine dryer, air-dry it, laying it as flat as possible.
- When ironing, make small, gentle circular motions with your *iron* to avoid stretching the lace.

Tapestries

Tapestries are like fine rugs hung on walls, except that, fortunately, they are not subject to the abuse that rugs get. But tapestries still need regular care and cleaning. Antique tapestries can be extremely valuable—and fragile, since age deteriorates textile fibers. If you have an antique tapestry that needs cleaning, play it safe and take it to a professional—a textile restorer or a dealer in antique tapestries or oriental rugs who has cleaning experience.

Periodically dust your tapestry using your *vacuum cleaner* with its *upholstery attachment*. If possible, leave the tapestry hanging and carefully, gently vacuum it in place. This will save the time and hassle of having to take it down and rehang it. Depending on the conditions in your home (how much dust you have), do it once or twice a year.

If you need to spot-clean a tapestry, make a suds shampoo by mixing *1/2 teaspoon liquid dishwashing detergent* in *1 quart of warm water*. Squeeze a *sponge* in the solution to whip up a head of suds. Test for colorfastness by rubbing a *cotton swab* dipped in the suds on an inconspicuous corner of the tapestry. If the color holds, continue. Using as little water as possible, scoop the suds off the top, applying them sparingly with a sponge to the tapestry surface. Rub gently. Before the suds dry, lightly rinse each area as you go with a *clean, damp sponge*. Be sure to remove all the suds, or the residue will cause the textile to soil faster.

For a deeper cleaning, have the tapestry *dry-cleaned* by a professional. Make sure the dry cleaner has experience cleaning the type of tapestry you own.

To remove wrinkles or creases, iron the back of your tapestry with a *steam iron* on a *medium setting*. If you must iron the front, lay a *thin towel* on the tapestry to protect the fibers.

Tar

There's a reason all those prehistoric animals died in California's La Brea Tar Pits. They couldn't get out of the sticky mess. While tar on your car's upholstery or rug won't kill you, it can frustrate you half to death. But before it reaches that point, try these cleaning steps.

First, remove as much tar as possible by scraping with a *spoon or dull knife*. Remove further residue by blotting with a *clean, dry paper towel*.

Next, blot off the remaining tar with *rubbing alcohol* on a *paper towel*. Repeat several times, using *clean paper towels* with *more freshly applied alcohol*.

If the tar stain still remains, next try a sudsy solution of *warm water* and *a squirt of dishwashing liquid*. Put a small amount on the stain and work it in by blotting with a *paper towel*. Rinse by spraying lightly with *clean water*. Dry by stacking *paper towels* on the stain and weighting them down with a *flat, heavy weight*, such as a brick.

WATCH OUT

If you are using alcohol to remove tar on an upholstered cushion or carpet, try not to let the alcohol soak into the stuffing or backing material. It can destroy the bonds of certain synthetic materials.

Tarpaulins

We throw up tarps to protect our lawn mowers, boats, lumber, and other things from the elements. As a result, tarps take a beating, catching bird droppings, diesel smoke, sap, and dust. Cleaning your tarp can help it do its job longer.

There are two main types of tarps:

- The heavy-duty vinyl tarps you see covering boats and party tents.
- The garden variety lightweight polyethylene tarps, which come in blues and greens and browns and appear to be woven.

To clean heavy-duty vinyl tarps, scrub with a *nylon-bristled brush*, a solution of *dishwashing liquid* and *water*, and lots of elbow grease. Lay the tarp out on a *freshly hosed off driveway or clean parking lot*. To make the job easier on your back, scrub with a *long-handled industrial push broom*. For stubborn stains, add vinegar (*1 cup of white vinegar* per *gallon of water*) to the soapy water.

Clean polyethylene tarps the same way, but expect to clean them less often. Because of their chemical makeup, polyethylene tarps don't attract dirt as readily as vinyl.

Taxidermy

You're proud of your trophy. That's why you had it preserved. So you want to keep it looking as noble as the day it came home from the taxidermist. And not like something from the Addams Family house.

Don't pet the animals. A taxidermic specimen isn't made for manhandling. Often it contains insecticides to prevent moths, larvae, and other organisms from setting up house and feasting on it. So inspect it regularly for signs of damage from these pests. But avoid touching it. Besides leaving damaging skin oils on the piece, you might expose yourself to insecticides or even to toxic heavy metals such as arsenic and mercury, which may have been used in preserving it.

Dust is another sneaky enemy of your stuffed wonder. It can find its way into fur and feathers and be a stubborn tenant that fails to respond to eviction notices. But leaking toxins can migrate into a dust cloth or become airborne as you dust. Besides stirring up heavy metals, you could send asbestos flying, if the modeling compound used to construct parts such as facial features contains asbestos, as some do.

For a thorough cleaning, call a professional. Unless you know that your taxidermic treasure was preserved without dangerous toxins—perhaps because you requested it be done without them—realize that even minimal cleaning involves risks. Experts recommend that specimens be cleaned by a professional every 10 years or so. That's the lowest-risk way to get the job done.

If you know your specimen is free of these toxins, or you have decided to give it a quick once-over regardless, gingerly dust fur-bearing trophies with a *barely damp soft cloth*, following the natural direction of the fur. Wipe only the fur: Even slightly dampened skin will begin to stretch, and fats in the wet skin can begin to turn rancid. For birds, use a *feather duster* (of course!), working from the bill or beak back, following the natural direction of the feather pattern.

To keep those eyes bright, apply *glass cleaner* or a mix of *1 part white vinegar* to *4 parts water* to a small patch of *clean cloth* and wipe onto the glass eyes. *Baby oil*, applied similarly, will bring back the luster of horns and tusks. In either case, keep the cleaner away from fur, feathers, and skin. Avoid getting any solvents on specimens, particularly on preserved fish—they'll dissolve the fish's lacquer finish.

Telephones

You use it every day. So do the other members of your household. And guests. And repair people calling their offices to get final approvals on how much to charge you this time. With all the people who reach out and touch your telephone receiver, you can bet it needs an occasional cleaning. And disinfecting.

But simply spraying it with disinfectant won't do. Your phone is an electronic instrument with intricate wiring and receiver and speaker holes that you don't want to gum up. Follow the iron-clad electronics-cleaning rule: Apply cleaner (or sanitizer) to a cloth and use the dampened cloth to wipe it clean.

To simultaneously clean and disinfect a phone, use *isopropyl (rubbing) alcohol*. Pour a little onto a *cleaning cloth* and wipe the entire phone, paying particular attention to the receiver and receiver bed. Wait a few minutes and then buff with a *dry cloth*.

You also can give your phone the one-two punch of a cleaner followed by a disinfectant. Pick an *all-purpose cleaner* that's labeled safe for plastics. (You won't want a cleaner that contains strong solvents like those used to clean petroleum or tar—

they'll damage the phone.) For a natural, plastics-friendly cleaner, use *1 tablespoon of borax* in *3 cups of water*.

Follow the cleanser with a *sanitizer* such as Lysol, dabbed onto a *rag or cotton pad*. Leave the sanitizer on the phone surface for 5 to 10 minutes. Then buff with a *dry cloth*.

An alternative disinfectant: Use a *strong, germ-killing mouth-wash*, such as Listerine. (What's good for the mouth is good for the mouthpiece.)

Perhaps the easiest option for cleaning and disinfecting your telephone is the *premoistened towelette* made specifically for telephones and sold in office supply stores. Towelettes are the more expensive way to go but are certainly effective and easy—just wipe and toss.

Televisions

In fourth grade, you and your classmates happily shocked one another with static electricity. Now, somewhat older and presumably somewhat more mature, you are shocked to discover that the same static electricity is a dust magnet that covers your television screen with minute gray fuzz. Unless you have a toddler or you've been tossing chips and dip at the screen whenever a ref makes a bad call, dust is likely to be your biggest TV-cleaning challenge.

First things first: Unplug the television before you clean it, particularly if you need to use a wet cleaner.

To clean a TV screen, first identify the type of screen you have. Only standard tubes and plasma screens can be wiped with a wet cleaner as described below for the TV's case. Liquid crystal display screens, which include not only LCD TVs but also projection TVs with digital light processing (DLP) screens, should be wiped clean with a *dry, clean cotton cloth*. Consult your owner's manual (you kept it, right?) for what the manufacturer suggests. If the TV came with a *cleaning kit*, use its cleaner and cloths.

To clean a TV's case—or to clean a tube or plasma screen that allows liquid cleaner—slightly dampen a *soft cotton cloth* with your chosen cleaner. (Pick a nonraveling fabric to avoid having ragged ends catch in the ventilation slits.) *Glass cleaner, denatured alcohol, or rubbing alcohol* make good cleaners because they will evaporate quickly. Or use a solution of *1 part liquid fabric softener* to *4 parts water* as your cleaner. Wring out the cloth so it's just barely damp, never dripping, and wipe down the tele-

RULES

OF THE GAME

Tube Tactics >

The primary, nonnegotiable rules for cleaning TVs are these:

1. Pull the plug before you clean.

2. Identify the type of screen you have. Some don't take well to liquid cleaners.

3. Never spray any liquid directly onto the television or its screen. Spray cleaner onto a cloth to slightly dampen it and then use the cloth to wipe it.

vision. Never apply liquid cleaner directly to your screen or casing—the drips could damage the electronics. Buff the screen afterward with a *dry cloth*.

Some other ways to clean your TV:
- Simply wipe the screen with an *electrostatic dust cloth*.
- Dust the body of the box with a *dry cloth*, or clean it with a solution of *1 part neutral-pH cleaner* (such as liquid hand soap) to *3 parts water*.

Tents

Think how dirty you are when you return from a camping trip, and then consider your tent, which lies on the ground so you don't have to. Today's high-performance tents are not cheap. Keeping them clean is a wise choice. By doing so, you'll keep zippers working longer and prolong the life of your tent's waterproof coating, among other things.

After every camping trip, shake out loose dirt and wipe the floor and fly. Use a *soft sponge* and *warm tap water*. Let the tent dry completely before storing. Not only is dirt unsightly, but grit and sand can also wear down the inside of the zipper slider (the metal part you slide to zip and unzip the tent), causing it to quit working properly. (If the slider fails, allowing the zipper to open behind the slider, carefully work the slider back to the beginning. Then use a small *pair of pliers* to gently pinch one rear corner of the slider and then the other, so that the slider's upper and lower parts grip the zipper track better.)

Keep zippers lubricated. Use a specialty *zipper-lubricating product*, such as McNett Zip Care, a cleaner and lubricant sold at camping and sporting goods stores. *Paraffin wax* or *candle wax* will also help. Some campers even use *lip balm*. Don't, however, use petroleum-based products.

Occasionally clean your tent more thoroughly. Set it up outside and lightly spray it with a *garden hose*. Mix up a mild solution of *water* and a *gentle fabric cleaner* such as Woolite or—even better—use a *tent soap* (sold at camping stores). Use a *sponge or soft cloth* to gently wipe the tent clean. Rinse well, but don't saturate the tent material. Let the tent dry in *indirect sunlight*.

To clean mildew from a tent, wash the tent with *soapy water* (as detailed above) and then wipe it out with a solution of *1 cup salt, 1 cup concentrated lemon juice*, and *1 gallon hot water*. Don't

WATCH OUT

After washing a tent, make sure that the seams, which stay damp the longest, are dry before storing it. Moisture can cause mildew and mold to grow. Mildew can work its way in between the waterproof coating and the tent fabric, loosening and separating the coating from the fabric as it spreads.

rinse. Air-dry. To help prevent mildew, always store your tent in a cool, dry place. Instead of cramming it into a stuff sack, store it loosely in a large **cotton bag or box**, so that air can circulate.

If the waterproof coating starts to peel because of mildew or any other cause, reapply a waterproofing compound. Look for the appropriate **waterproofing product** at your local camping store.

To remove sap or tar from your tent, try cleaning it off with **mineral oil** and a **clean cloth**. If that does not work, try a small amount of **kerosene**. Be sure to test first on an inconspicuous part of the tent.

Thermos Bottles

Thermos bottles are not new, but they're just as amazing as the day they were invented, for they keep your coffee hot and your vichyssoise cold. Thermos bottles are less exciting when it comes to cleaning. Some you're not supposed to submerge; many have necks too narrow to access with brushes. So how do you clean them?

Clean thermos bottles after each use with **hot, soapy water**. Scrub them with a **bottle brush**, if possible. Rinse well and air-dry. Try not to get water between the outer casing and the inner insulating flask.

For stubborn or hard-to-reach stains, fill the thermos with **hot water**, drop in **two denture-cleaning tablets**, and let stand overnight. In the morning, rinse with **clean water** and air-dry.

If your thermos has taken on a funky odor that regular washing does not overcome, pour in **a few tablespoons of vinegar or baking soda**. Fill the thermos the rest of the way with **hot water** and let it sit for half an hour. Then pour the solution out and rinse.

Ties

Per square inch, ties are certainly the most valuable garment in a man's wardrobe, especially for men who like a nice tie. It's easy to ruin a tie, though—easy for you and easy for a dry cleaner who is not very experienced in cleaning ties.

Have a silk tie professionally cleaned once or twice a year, depending on how often you wear it. Clean a visibly dirty or stained tie immediately. Look for a dry cleaner who's experienced in cleaning silk ties. Ask how they "finish" the tie after cleaning it. Ties should not be pressed—they should be rolled and reshaped with steam. If you are trying a new dry cleaner, don't give it your best ties first.

To refresh a tired-looking silk tie, you can try a little steam. You can hang the tie in a steamy bathroom. Or wrap a damp cloth over the soleplate of your iron and pass the steaming iron over the tie without actually touching it ▶.

If you spill something on your tie, blot away the excess using a *clean white cloth or napkin* and then take the tie to a dry cleaner as soon as possible. Stains, especially food stains, tend to set after 24 or 48 hours. Never try to rub the stain out. You might rub the color from the fabric, especially if it's silk.

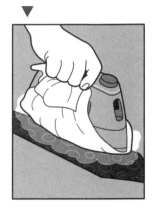

Tiles

While they are two dramatically different materials, ceramic and vinyl tile are relatively low-maintenance, easy-to-clean surfaces. Both can scratch, however, so it's important to keep them dirt-free.

For regular cleaning of floor tiles—both ceramic and vinyl— sweep with a *broom* or *vacuum*. Trapped dirt and sand are highly abrasive and can cause lasting damage to matte and glossy finishes. If you vacuum, avoid using the machine's beater bar, which can permanently damage tile finishes.

Once a week, clean floor tiles by going over them with a *damp mop*. Again, this goes for both ceramic and vinyl tile. Damp mopping removes stubborn, smeared-on dirt. Never use excessive amounts of water with vinyl tile, since the water can seep

Grimy Grout? Hit the Bleach

For really grimy grout that stubbornly resists standard cleaning methods, try a solution of chlorine bleach and water. Make sure the area you're working in is well ventilated, and wear rubber gloves. Then mix together a cup of bleach and a half-gallon of water in a bucket. Using a toothbrush or nylon scrub brush, scrub the dirty areas, then let the solution soak for 10 to 20 minutes before rinsing with clean water. Rinse a second time—again with clean water, not the water you used in the first rinse—and wipe the area dry with a clean cloth.

After the grout dries thoroughly, apply a silicone sealer (available at home improvement stores) to reduce future maintenance. Grout manufacturers generally recommend resealing grout joints twice a year to prevent staining. You can skip this step if the joint is filled with epoxy grout.

under the tile and damage the glue. Avoid soapy or oily cleaners, as they can leave a dull film. If anything, add a *splash of vinegar* to the *mop water*. An alkaline-based *all-purpose cleaner*, such as Spic and Span or Mr. Clean, is also effective. Or use a specialty *tile floor cleaner*, such as Armstrong's Once 'n Done, sold at flooring stores and home improvement stores. Follow directions on the package.

For ceramic wall tiles, wipe them regularly with a *damp sponge*. As with floor tiles, avoid soapy or oily cleaners. Add a *splash of vinegar* to the *water*, or use a commercial *tub-and-tile cleaner*. Another alternative: Add *1 capful of rubbing alcohol* to *1 gallon of water* in a *bucket* and wipe down the tiles using a *sponge or clean, soft cloth*. Never use abrasive scrubbers or cleaning products, such as scouring powders. These can scratch glazed tile, dulling the finish and making it more susceptible to dirt.

To keep grout clean, it's best to do it regularly so that the scum and mildew don't have a chance to get a foothold in the porous surface. Indeed, it's a good idea to clean grout after you shower, while it's still steamy moist and the soil has been loosened. Mix together *1/4 cup of vinegar* with *1 gallon of water* and scrub the grout with a *toothbrush or nylon scrub pad* ◀. For more cleaning power, go over it once with a degreaser, such as Simple Green, which will loosen the germ-harboring soap scum, and then with a *disinfectant*, such as Mr. Clean or Top Job, to kill the germs themselves. Let your cleaning products do the work for you. Too much scrubbing grinds the grime in deeper. Spray or wipe each product on and let it stand for several seconds. Wipe it down with a *clean, wet sponge* to rinse off the cleaning solution. If you must scrub, use a *long-bristled brush* that is not too stiff (you don't want to wear down the grout) or use an *old toothbrush*. Steel wool is too abrasive. If the grout is really grungy, see the box on the previous page.

See also **Floors**.

Tin

Tin, silvery white with a brilliant luster, is used as a decorative plating and to protect metals from rusting. You see it often on Mexican crafts and inexpensive kitchenware. Be careful not to scratch it when cleaning. If you do, you'll invite rust.

Dust decorative items regularly. Use a *feather duster* for pieces with lots of detail. Or wipe with a *dry or slightly damp rag*.

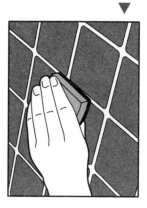

Wash tin in a solution of *mild dishwashing liquid* and *warm water* and a *soft cloth*. Don't use abrasive scrubbers or cleaners, because they may scratch through the tin plating.

To remove rust on tin, rub it *with superfine (0000) steel wool*. Once the rust is gone, wash the tin in the *sudsy solution*. Rinse well and dry completely. To prevent rust from returning, apply a *thin coat of paste wax*—an auto wax, for instance.

Toaster Ovens

Toaster ovens typically need a more thorough cleaning than toasters, since many people do more than just toast bread in their toaster ovens. They make drippy cheese toast, heat oozing fruit pies, and even broil small grease-spattering hens. Until there is such a thing as a self-cleaning toaster oven, it's up to you to manually get the gunk out.

Keep the outside of the toaster oven clean by regularly wiping it with a *damp cloth*. Add a *splash of vinegar* or a *squirt of dishwashing liquid* to the *wash water* for added cleaning power. The control buttons may pull off to make cleaning the control panel easier. Check your owner's manual.

Every week or two, depending on use, empty the crumb tray, which, in most toaster ovens, is removable. Some even have doors underneath for removing the crumbs that fall past the tray. If you'll be opening this trapdoor, unplug the unit first. Wash the removable tray. Most trays are thin aluminum and may not be dishwasher safe. Read your owner's manual to find out. If you're unsure, hand-wash the tray in *warm, soapy water*.

Clean the oven soon after messy toaster-oven cooking sessions. Let the oven cool, unplug it, and then remove any cooking trays or racks. Clean trays and racks in *hot, soapy water*. Wipe the inside of the oven with a damp cloth. If you're lucky, your toaster has a nonstick surface on the inside, and baked-on food will come right off. Carefully lift up the heating element (if possible) and clean under it.

For stuck-on food, try a moist *plastic or nylon scrubber*. Never use anything abrasive, such as steel wool. You'll scratch the smooth surface, which will make food stick worse next time. If the plastic scrubber fails, put a *small bowl of full-strength ammonia* inside the unplugged oven with the door closed. Leave overnight and then remove the ammonia. The fumes will loosen the food. Wipe the inside again and let the oven air out before using.

Toasters

Turn bread into toast and you're bound to get crumbs. When those crumbs fall into the toaster, you've got to get them out. Fortunately, most toaster makers are aware of this and design their appliances for easy cleanup.

Empty the crumbs out of your toaster once every week or so, depending on how much you use it. Some toasters have slide-out crumb trays; others have hinged doors that allow you to empty the crumbs. No matter what kind of toaster you have or what sort of mechanism it has for crumb removal, always unplug the toaster before cleaning it.

If you can't get them all out, try disintegrating them with heat. Run the toaster empty on the hottest setting two or three times. This is also the principle behind self-cleaning ovens.

For hard-to-remove crumbs, use a *clean, dry toothbrush* (not that dirty one you use to scrub grout—a new one) or an *old, clean paintbrush* ◀. Again, be sure the toaster is unplugged. Loosen crumbs with the brush and then dump them out. Turn the toaster upside down and shake. Do it gently, being careful not to damage the heating element.

Wipe down the outside of the toaster with a *damp cloth.* Wipe around the control knobs. Add a *dash of vinegar or squirt of dishwashing liquid* to the *cleaning water* for more cleaning power. For stainless steel toasters, polish with a *stainless steel polish,* available at supermarkets and home improvement stores.

Toilets

We all have them. We all have to clean them. There's no getting around that. But most people are not very efficient at cleaning their toilets. And many are stumped by those stubborn rings left around the bowl. (See Simple Solutions sidebar opposite.)

To clean a toilet, work from the top down. Start with the tank, move to the seat, clean inside the bowl, and then clean the base. Doing it this way will help you focus. Moreover, the dirtiest part of the toilet—and hence the last place you want your rag to touch—is the base, where the dust bunnies mingle with the urine dribbles.

For everything but the bowl, use a **dry cloth** (**diapers** work well) and a **spray-on bathroom cleaner**, preferably one that contains **ammonia**. Spray the cleaner on the toilet surface and wipe it off with the diaper. Keeping the cloth dry makes it easier to wipe everything up. Wet it, and you'll be chasing that moisture around, wringing and rewringing the rag. Change rags when one becomes soaked with cleaner. Avoid sponges, which work OK but can absorb—and transfer—microorganisms. (You wash your rags after each use, but do you wash your sponges? See Disinfecting Your Kitchen Sponges, on page 431.)

Clean the bowl with a **rounded bowl brush** and **cleaner**. Avoid brushes with metal wire, since the metal can scratch the toilet bowl.

To clean around the hardware that holds the seat to the toilet and the toilet to the floor, use a **grout brush** or an **old toothbrush**.

Tools

In the old days, toolmakers dated their tools—carving the year into the wooden block of a plane, for example—in the expectation that the tools would last for generations. Back then, a tool would last a long time if its owner took care of it. The same is true today. In this disposable world we live in, a well-built tool is one of the few goods meant to last. Luckily, most don't need much in the way of cleaning.

The most basic goal with hand tools, especially those made of wood and metal, is to keep them dry. If a tool gets wet, wipe it dry. If it gets sweaty or dusty, clean it with **a damp cloth** and then wipe it dry with **another cloth**. Water can rust a saw blade and warp a wooden level.

Keep retractable measuring tapes free of dirt, sand, drywall dust, and other debris. These foreign objects can scratch the Mylar coating. Once it is scratched, the metal tape will rust. Frequently wipe the tape clean with a **dry cloth**. Don't use a wet cloth—and don't let your tape get wet. Moisture will find its way into the spring mechanism and will rust it. To remove tar and glue from the tape, use **alcohol or mineral spirits**. Avoid solvents, which can melt the protective coating.

*See also **Power Tools** and **Yard Tools**.*

simple SOLUTIONS

Ring Around the Bowl >

For stubborn rings around the toilet bowl, use a pumice stone, available at drugstores and bath-product stores. (Pumice stones are the same product you use to rub corns off your feet.) Keeping the stone wet, rub it on the ring until it's gone. This works for old rings as well. It will not scratch white vitreous china, which is what most toilets are made of, but it will scratch fiberglass, enamel, plastic, and other materials.

WATCH OUT

Avoid oiling most tools (garden tools are the exception), since the oil could get on the handle, causing the tool to slip. Tools that slip are dangerous.

Toys

Chances are your children don't know the meaning of cleaning. Sure, they may pitch in by putting clothes in their hampers and straightening their rooms. But until they reach adulthood—really, until they have children of their own—they will never fully understand what goes into keeping a home and the things in it clean. For that reason, they'll continue to wipe dirty hands on their clothes, spill juice with abandon, and run their toys through the mud. Fortunately, most toys these days are made of easy-to-clean plastics. The main issue in cleaning toys is to never use anything toxic. Even if your son or daughter no longer chews on toys, hands will wind up in mouths, since few children fully understand germs either.

Wash toys regularly to keep them clean and bacteria-free. Wash rubber and plastic toys with *warm water* combined with a *squirt of dishwashing liquid*. Wipe clean with a *soft cloth or sponge*. Be careful of painted-on features, such as faces, numbers, or other designs. These could rub off. Dry with a *cloth* or air-dry. For bigger plastic toys, such as plastic wagons and plastic playhouses, use a *hose*, a *bucket* of *soapy water*, and a *soft-bristled scrub brush*.

Wipe down metal toys, such as tractors and cars, using a *damp cloth*. Water leads to rust, so avoid soap (since suds require rinsing) and don't submerge such toys. If a metal toy or a toy with metal parts gets wet, dry it quickly with a *hair dryer* to avoid rust. If there are batteries, beeping sounds, or blinking lights, don't wet the toy. Water will ruin the circuitry.

Clean wooden toys with a mild solution of a *neutral cleaner*, such as Murphy Oil Soap, and *water*. (Follow the manufacturer's directions for amounts.) Use a *cloth or soft-bristled brush*. Don't soak or submerge the wooden toy. Instead, dip the cloth or brush in the soapy water and wipe the toy clean. Rinse with a *clean cloth* and *plain water*. Dry with a *clean, dry towel*. If the toy is scratched, splintered, or chipped, or if the water has raised the grain (making the wood feel rough), lightly sand it with *fine sandpaper* once the toy has dried.

If a wooden toy has a natural, oil-based finish, reapply oil to keep the wood conditioned. Since toys often wind up in children's mouths (wooden baby chew toys are expressly meant for this purpose), use a *food-grade vegetable or mineral oil*. Allow oil to penetrate for about an hour and then wipe off the excess.

It is especially important not to clean wooden toys with harsh chemicals, because wood absorbs and harbors such chemicals.

Clean Barbies and similar dolls by wiping with a *cloth* and *water* mixed with a little *dishwashing liquid*. Wash hair with *baby shampoo*. (A *drop of hair conditioner* will soften the hair.) Don't use any heat source, such as a hair dryer, to dry the hair, as that will turn it frizzy. Instead, comb the hair out gently, starting from the bottom and working up to remove tangles. Let the doll air-dry. For more doll-cleaning advice, see *Dolls*.

See also *Stuffed Animal Toys*.

Trash Compactors

Like vacuum cleaners and dishwashers, the trash compactor is your cleaning ally. It squeezes garbage into manageable blocks so you don't have to empty the trash so often. But you've got to take care of your compactor if you want to keep it on your cleaning team—and if you want to prevent odors.

Regularly wipe the outside of your compactor with a *sponge or cloth* and *warm water* with a *squirt of dishwashing liquid*. Rinse with a *damp cloth*. Dry with a *cloth*. Wipe up spills right away.

When needed, clean inside the drawer. First, follow the manufacturer's instructions for disabling your compactor. (Whirlpool compactors, for instance, have a key switch for turning them off.) Then remove the bag. Tilt down the drawer front, if possible. (Read your owner's manual for how to access the drawer.) Wearing *sturdy work gloves* to protect your hands against any broken glass, wipe down the inside of the drawer with a *sponge* dipped in the *sudsy water*. Use a *nonabrasive plastic or nylon scrubber* to remove stuck-on soil. Rinse by wiping with a *damp sponge*. Either air-dry or dry with a *cloth*.

Occasionally remove the drawer and clean out the cabinet. Most compactors allow you to remove the drawer for cleaning and service. (Read your owner's manual to find out how.) Typically, the drawers are on slides or runners, like cabinet drawers. Again, wear sturdy *gloves*. Start by cleaning up any liquid spills with *paper towels*. Then *vacuum* crumbs, bits of glass, and other debris out of the cabinet. Wipe down the inside of the cabinet with *soapy water*, rinse, and dry.

Wipe off the ram cover. This is the part that presses the trash. Be careful of glass bits. Wipe off food with a **cloth** and **warm, sudsy water**. Scrub with a **nylon brush**, if necessary. Rinse and dry.

Typewriters

Raise your hand if you still have a typewriter. Yeah, we knew there would be a lot of you. It's nearly impossible to get rid of this precursor of computer word processing. And for good reason—a typewriter is dependable and still useful for personal letters, applications, labels, and other needs. But does anyone remember how to clean one? We do.

Dust your typewriter regularly to keep the lint bunnies from burrowing into the keys. You can use a **vacuum cleaner** with an **upholstery attachment** to suck the dust out, or the reverse—a **can of compressed air**, available at office supply stores—to blow it out. Or you can brush between the keys with a **small, dry paintbrush**.

Wipe the case and body of the typewriter with a **clean, lint-free cloth** lightly moistened with a **commercial window cleaner**—emphasis on *lightly* moistened. You don't want to risk letting liquid drip into the body of the typewriter, especially if it is an electric typewriter. Wipe the key tops, buttons, and bars. Fight the urge to use paper towels, since they might tear and leave little pieces stuck in the mechanism.

To clean beneath the keys, wrap the **same cloth** around the end of a **letter opener** and gently work it between the keys.

Wipe the black roller, known as the platen, with the **same cloth**. It is likely to have ink on it (especially if you have children who like to press the keys without paper in the machine). The ink may or may not come completely off. Don't worry. A little leftover ink is better than trying to remove it with an ink stain remover that contains alcohol, which will dry the platen out and make it brittle. You want it to remain soft and slightly pliable. The ammonia in the glass cleaner will help condition the platen.

Have your typewriter professionally lubricated every so often. Don't try to do it yourself. You might do more harm than good.

Umbrellas

Umbrellas don't get very dirty, which is fortunate, because they've got to be among the most awkward things in the world to clean—like trying to bathe a stork. But what about large patio umbrellas, which stand outside rain or shine and catch tree pollen, wet leaves, and bird droppings?

Here are some tips for both types:

To clean your regular umbrella, just let the rain do the job the next time it showers. To prevent mold and mildew, open the umbrella and let it dry thoroughly before you put it away. If you must clean it more thoroughly, open it up, spray it with a *hose*, and scrub gently with a *sponge* dipped in *warm water* with a *squirt of dishwashing liquid*. Rinse and, again, dry thoroughly.

To remove dirt, pollen, and bird poop from a patio umbrella—which is usually made of either vinyl or a coarse fabric—spray it with a *garden hose*. Then scrub it with a *nylon-bristled brush* dipped in a *bucket* containing a sudsy solution of *warm water* and *dishwashing liquid*. Rinse by spraying the umbrella with the hose.

Protect a patio umbrella's metal rods by polishing them with *car wax*. Wax also makes the metal easier to clean in the future. Following the manufacturer's directions, lightly wax the metal. Take care not to get the wax on the umbrella covering, as it can stain fabric and gunk up vinyl mesh.

WATCH OUT

To avoid stripping away the protective coating often found on vinyl patio umbrellas, don't scrub yours with abrasive brushes or pads, and don't clean with bleach, bleach-based cleaning products, or solvents. This coating protects the material from the sun's deteriorating UV rays. Removing the coating can cut the life span of vinyl in half, making it prematurely weak and brittle.

Upholstery

Upholstery poses a cleaning challenge, since it almost always covers some sort of padding—be it cotton batting or foam rubber—and since it's often not removable. Even when upholstery material can be removed from the padding, as in the case of zip-up sofa cushions, the experts warn against removing and washing it. If the upholstery shrinks, it may not fit back on the cushion. The most basic tenet in most upholstery cleaning, therefore, is to clean without soaking the padding beneath.

Vacuum upholstery regularly to remove dust and the dust mites it harbors. Use an *upholstery attachment* with a gentle brush end, so you don't damage the upholstery material. Use a *crevice tool attachment* for nooks and crannies. If your upholstered piece is stuffed with feathers, do not vacuum it unless it is lined with a downproof ticking. You might suck the feathers out. If you have no vacuum-cleaner attachments, brush the dust away with a **soft-bristled brush** at least once a month. Dust, when moistened or ground in, can stain upholstery.

For more thorough cleaning, or to remove stains, your upholstery will need washing. First, check the upholstery manufacturer's suggestions, usually tagged to new upholstery fabric sold after 1970. This tag will tell you whether you should use a water-based shampoo, a dry-cleaning solvent, or neither of the two. Next, pick an inconspicuous spot on the upholstery and pretest whatever cleaning technique is recommended. If there is shrinking, bleeding, or running colors, contact a professional cleaner. If not, proceed to clean it.

If shampooing is allowable, use as little moisture as possible. You don't want to wet the upholstery's stuffing, because it dries very slowly and can attract dust mites and mold. Clean using suds only. The easiest method is to use a foaming **commercial shampoo in an aerosol can**. Follow directions on the can, which typically will tell you to allow the foam to stand until dry and then to **vacuum** it off ◀.

To make your own upholstery shampoo, mix **1/2 teaspoon of dishwashing liquid** per **1 quart of warm water**. Make suds by squeezing a **sponge** in the solution. Scoop the suds off the top, applying them sparingly with the sponge to the upholstery. Rub gently in the direction of the fabric's grain. Rather than letting the suds

Upholstery *Stain-Removal* Basics

To find out what specific solution you should use to remove a particular stain—what takes out chocolate or grease, for example—see Stains. Meanwhile, here are some general tips for removing stains from upholstery:

1. Remove as much stain-causing material as you can by blotting with paper towels or scraping with a dull knife. When blotting up a large stain, always blot from the edge of the stain to the center to contain it.

2. Avoid rubbing or pushing the stain deeper into the upholstery.

3. Since you never want to soak an upholstered cushion or piece of furniture, spray bottles are good for lightly applying water-based cleaning solutions and rinse water.

4. To dry upholstery that has been rinsed with water, lay a pad of paper towels on the spot and place a weight, such as a brick, on the pad. (Put the brick in a plastic bag or on a piece of foil to prevent color transfer from the brick to the upholstery.) Let the upholstery dry and then remove the towels.

dry as you would a commercial shampoo, work on a small area at a time, lightly rinsing each area as you go with a ***clean, damp sponge***. Again, avoid soaking the fabric. Be sure to remove all the suds, or the residue will cause the fabric to soil faster.

If the fabric calls for dry cleaning only and the upholstery is portable, have it professionally cleaned. If, however, you are cleaning a stain—or if the upholstery is part of a large piece of furniture—you can do it yourself, using a ***commercial dry-cleaning solvent***, such as K2r or Carbona. Don't pour the solvent on the stain. Instead, moisten a ***clean, white cloth*** with the solvent and use the cloth to draw the stain out. Blot repeatedly—never rub. Rubbing can stretch or damage the texture of the fabric. Always use solvents sparingly and in a ***well-ventilated area***. And don't use them on upholstery filled with latex foam rubber padding, because the solvent can dissolve the padding.

V

Dirty vases not only look bad, but they also reduce the longevity of the cut flowers you keep in them. The residue in vases, including growth such as algae, plugs up the stems of the water-drinking flowers and causes the flowers to dry up more quickly.

The easiest way to clean vases is to scrub them with *hot, soapy water* and a *bottle brush*. Rinse well and let them dry completely before storing.

To remove white mineral deposit stains from the inside of vases, swirl a mixture of *rock salt* and *vinegar* around inside the vase. The salt will gently scour the surface while the vinegar breaks down the deposits.

VCRs and Videotapes

As with any electronic gear, the cleaner you keep your VCR, the better all those little parts will work—and the longer the piece of equipment will last. That said, it usually doesn't pay to open up your VCR for interior cleaning. You can cause more harm than good. Luckily, the innards rarely need cleaning if you keep the outside clean. The only interior part you need to clean is the playback head—but that you can do with a head-cleaning tape.

Clean the front panel with a *soft cotton cloth* and *glass cleaner*. (First, turn off the VCR.) No paper towels: They can tear and shed lint. Don't spray the glass cleaner directly on the unit. Instead, spray it on the cloth and gently wipe the cloth on the panel. For sensitive areas, such as around the panel control knobs and buttons, dust with a *small, dry paintbrush*. Don't apply cleaner to these areas, since it could seep into the controls. This way, you won't accidentally change your control settings, either.

To clean the chassis of the VCR—that is, the sides and top—use a *soft cloth* either dry or lightly misted with *glass cleaner*. Don't wet the cloth, since any residue left on the chassis could collect dust and lead to corrosion. Never spray anything directly on the chassis. Wipe away from vent holes (not toward them) to avoid pushing dust into the workings of the VCR.

Dust the back of the unit, where the cable jacks are, with a *dry paintbrush*. Don't use cleaner around this sensitive area. If you must remove the cables to access the back, be forewarned: Many units store information for user settings, clock, and timers, and

simple SOLUTIONS

Oh, Those Narrow-Neck Vases >

If you can't get to the inside of a vase with a bottle brush, fill the vase with hot water and add a couple of denture-cleaning tablets— Efferdent, for instance— and let it stand overnight. Rinse well and dry.

WATCH OUT

Avoid videocassette-cleaning machines. Because these devices sometimes involve rewinding machines, they often damage the tape by stretching it.

this memory can be lost when the unit is unplugged from the electrical outlet.

Wipe cables down with a *cloth* misted with the *same cleaner* you used on the panels. Be careful not to pull cables out.

Clean the playback head periodically—once every few months, depending on use, or when the playback quality indicates a problem. If you rent a lot of videotapes, you may need to clean more often, since rental tapes bring with them dirt and debris picked up from all the other VCRs they've been played in.

Use a good-quality *dry head-cleaning cassette*—"dry" because the liquid that sometimes comes with head-cleaning cassettes may not evaporate completely before another tape is inserted, which can worsen the situation by attracting grime from the tape to the playback head. And that could lead to a pricey service call. Be sure to read your owner's manual. If your VCR incorporates an automatic head-cleaning system, the manufacturer may recommend that you not use any kind of head-cleaning tape.

If you need to clean a videotape's case, carefully wipe it with a *damp cloth*. Make sure you don't wet the tape itself or the tape path. Remove any labels or adhesives that are coming off. Labels that fall off are one of the biggest causes of tape jams.

Velcro

When Velcro gets "dirty"—meaning the two sides get clogged up with lint and fuzz balls—it stops working. When that Velcro is attached to a pair of sandals or a handbag, you might be tempted to get rid of the sandals or handbag. Don't. It's easy to freshen Velcro up so that it works the way it did when it was new.

To remove lint from the bristly side of Velcro, use a *fine-toothed comb*. Gently comb out the lint and hair and stray threads. If possible, submerge the Velcro in *water* while combing.

To remove lint from the soft side of Velcro, use the sticky side of *duct tape* the way you would use a lint roller.

To keep Velcro fresh, seal the two parts together when it's not in use or while machine-washing. If you need to, buy extra Velcro tape from a fabric or craft store and use that to seal the Velcro.

If worst comes to worst, instead of throwing away that shoe or handbag, replace the Velcro. Cobblers and tailors will often do the job for a few dollars.

RULES
OF THE GAME

Step-by-Step VCR Cleaning >

1. Turn off the VCR.
2. Spray glass cleaner on a soft cloth and gently wipe the front panel.
3. Dust control knobs and buttons with a small, dry paintbrush.
4. Clean the sides and top with a soft cloth (dry or lightly misted with glass cleaner).
5. Dust the rear with a dry paintbrush. Wipe cables with a cloth misted with cleaner.
6. Clean the playback head with a good-quality dry head-cleaning cassette. First, check your owner's manual.

Ventilation Systems

Air quality is in the news a lot these days. Every scary new story about allergic reactions and illnesses caused by household dust and mold makes it easier for duct-cleaning companies to sell their services. It's not surprising that some of these companies are fly-by-night—or, as they are known in the trade, "blow-and-go," for the shoddy jobs they do. The U.S. Environmental Protection Agency (EPA) has done studies on the issue, and its advice is simple: Relax. Few, if any, homeowners need to clean their ventilation systems on an annual basis, as some contractors suggest. Having the ductwork cleaned might actually make matters worse by dislodging dust and mold that might otherwise not have circulated through the house.

The most important thing you can do is prevent dust and moisture from building up. And if you do determine that your ducts need cleaning, you should hire a reputable service provider. (See "Choosing an Air Duct Cleaning Service" box below.)

Keep your system clean by using *high-quality filters* and changing them at least twice a year, in the spring and fall. If they become clogged, change them more often. Not only does that excess dust fill the air, but it also makes your air handler work harder, raising power bills and shortening the life of the motor.

Choosing an *Air Duct* Cleaning Service

There are plenty of opportunists out there making big bucks off the fear stirred up by stories about mold illness and allergy. These conning contractors may charge up to $1,000 for a duct-cleaning job that is both shoddy and unnecessary. What's worse, they may leave your home's air quality worse than it was before they began tinkering with your ducts.

If you have determined that you really do need your ducts cleaned (see Simple Solutions sidebar), take these steps to ensure that you get your money's worth for a job well done:

1. Contact the Washington, D.C.-based National Air Duct Cleaners Association (www.nadca.com) for a contractor recommendation in your area.
2. Talk to at least three contractors. Get written estimates. Compare their services. Check references. If they make any claims about mold or dust as a reason your ducts need cleaning, ask them to show you the evidence. Ask how they will protect you and your pets from contamination while cleaning. Check any licenses or certifications they say they have.

3. Beware the cleaner who makes broad claims about duct cleaning's being good for your health. Those claims have not been proved. Certainly steer clear of any cleaner who recommends duct cleaning as a regular part of maintaining your heating and cooling system.
4. Check with your county or city office of consumer affairs or local Better Business Bureau to find out whether complaints have been filed against any of the duct-cleaning services you are thinking of using.

To make changing filters more convenient (and cheaper), buy the filters in bulk and store them in the basement.

Vacuum your house often and use a *high-efficiency HEPA-filtered vacuum cleaner*. The more often you vacuum, the less potential dust there will be to get into your ventilation system. The HEPA system keeps the machine from sucking up dust and blowing it back into the air. As a part of your vacuuming routine, be sure to vacuum your ventilation system's vents. (See *Vents* below.)

Control moisture—the essential ingredient for biological growth—by repairing any leaks or water damage in your system. Make sure the ducts are properly sealed and insulated in non-air-conditioned spaces, such as attics and crawl spaces. This will prevent moisture from condensing inside the system.

If your ductwork does need cleaning, hire a reputable professional. This is one of those jobs that is impossible without the right equipment and know-how. The pros typically hook the entire duct system up to a high-powered vacuum and then use special tools to snake around the ducts loosening dust and debris. It can be expensive, so take your time in choosing the right contractor.

Vents

An important part of your home's ventilation system are the vents—registers, returns—at the end of the ductwork. Located in floors, walls, and ceilings, vents typically have angled louvers to keep large debris from getting into the system. These louvers, however, also collect lint and dust. Fortunately, they are easy to access. In fact, vents are the only part of household ventilation systems that most homeowners are able to—and should—clean on a regular basis.

Vacuum the outside of the vent often. Make it part of your regular vacuuming routine, and you'll cut down on dust and lint buildup considerably. Use a *brush attachment*, which helps loosen dust.

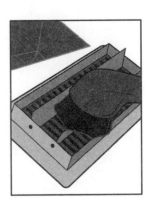

At least twice a year, remove registers and returns and clean both sides of them ▶. Try cleaning them with the *vacuum*. If that does not completely remove the dust, wipe them with a *moist dust cloth*. If you replace filters behind your returns more often than twice a year, clean the return vents every time you remove them.

▲

Vinyl

"Vinyl is final," the saying goes, meaning no more painting for a vinyl-sided house. But painting is only part of maintenance, and siding is just one of thousands of uses of vinyl.

To wash vinyl siding, use a *garden hose* attached to a *long-handled car brush attachment* (the Deluxe Car Wash Brush by Parts Master, for instance) and *water*. Such brushes are available at hardware, discount, and auto supply stores. If the siding is especially dirty, use the car brush to apply a cleaner consisting of *1/2 cup of powdered laundry detergent, 2/3 cup of trisodium phosphate* (available at hardware and paint stores), and *1 gallon of water*. If mildew is a problem, substitute *1 quart of chlorine bleach* for 1 quart of the water. Strain the cleaner through an *old sock* to remove any lumps.

Apply the cleaner with the brush (you can detach it from the hose for this part, if you want), working from the bottom up. Allow the cleaner to sit for a few minutes. Rinse with *clear water* from the top down before the detergent solution dries (unless you like the streaky look on your siding). Vinyl siding should be washed every 12 to 18 months, depending on the climate and presence of air pollutants.

To clean siding more thoroughly, use a *pressure washer* rated at about 2,500 pounds per square inch (psi). Cover any electrical outlets and wear *safety goggles*. Move methodically from side to side from the bottom up, reversing direction for the rinse cycle.

To clean aluminum siding, see *Aluminum*.

To clean articles made of vinyl, here are several cleaners to try:
- A little *liquid dishwashing detergent* in *warm water*
- A solution of *1 gallon of water* and *2 tablespoons of borax*, available in the detergent section of supermarkets
- Mild cleaners such as *Murphy Oil Soap* or *Simple Green*
- For mold and mildew, a solution of *1 part white vinegar* to *2 parts water*

To keep vinyl soft and pliable, rub a little *petroleum jelly* into the surface and then buff with a *soft cloth*. Or use a *vinyl cleaner/conditioner*, which you can buy at hardware and auto supply stores.

WATCH OUT

When cleaning vinyl, avoid harsh solvents and cleaners. They may cause the vinyl to become brittle.

Vomit

Cleaning up vomit is a job no one relishes, but few can avoid the task forever. Certainly not parents and pet owners.

On a floor or other hard surface, dump *clean kitty litter* onto fresh vomit. It will absorb most of it and can then be swept up. Follow by wiping with a *damp sponge or cloth*. If you don't have any litter, use *baking soda* or *cornstarch*.

If the vomit is old on a hard surface, scrape off as much as possible with a *putty knife, kitchen knife, or spatula*. Wash the surface with a little *undiluted dishwashing liquid* applied to a *sponge or cloth*. Then rinse and dry. If the vomit's acid ate away wax or an underlying finish, renew it with a spot application.

To clean vomit from a carpet or upholstery, lift off any solids with *paper towels* and then *sponge* with *cool water*. Follow by saturating the spot with plenty of *baking soda*, which will absorb the liquid, neutralize the acid, and wipe out the odor. Allow the soda to dry. Then *vacuum*. *Sponge* the stain with a solution of *1 teaspoon of dishwashing liquid* in *1 cup of cool water*. Rinse and blot dry.

To clean clothing, bedding, or table linens, flush fresh messes with *cold water*. Hold the item under the faucet with the soiled side down. Don't use hot water—it will cook the protein and make it harder to remove. For dried vomit, scrape off any solids and then soak in *cold water*, using an *enzyme presoak*, for several hours. For both new and old stains, follow by rubbing a little *undiluted liquid laundry detergent* into the stain and washing in *warm water* with *detergent*. If any stain remains, soak again in the enzyme, or use *chlorine bleach* on white fabrics or *oxygen bleach* on colored ones. If possible, dry on a *clothesline* rather than in a dryer.

See also **Pet Cleanup**.

Wading Pools

Because kids (and perhaps a dog or two) are the main users, wading pools can get dirty fast.

After each day's use, empty the pool and *hose* it out to prevent it from becoming a germ or mosquito incubator. Store it under cover, upside down, or propped on its side.

To remove scum from the sides, clean with a *sponge or cloth* dipped in a solution of *1/4 cup of baking soda* in *1 gallon of warm water*. Or wash with a solution of *1 tablespoon of dishwashing liquid* in *1 gallon of water*. Rinse with a *hose*.

When Someone Poops in the Pool

Sooner or later it will probably happen, despite your best efforts at prevention. If it does, immediately remove all children from the pool. Wash them all over with soap and water. Chlorine in the water from your tap dissipates quickly, so a wading pool can become a rich medium for the growth and spread of germs, says Michael Beach, an epidemiologist at the Centers for Disease Control and Prevention in Atlanta. Even small amounts of fecal matter can easily sicken kids if the germs get into their mouths.

As for the pool, here's what to do in case of an accident:
1. Pour the contents into a bucket and flush it down the toilet.
2. Wash the pool with a solution of 1 part chlorine bleach to 99 parts water (about 1 cup for every 6 gallons).
3. Allow to air-dry.

Take these precautionary steps to minimize the risk of transmitting illness:

• Don't let children use the pool if they have diarrhea, open sores, or rashes or if they haven't been toilet trained.
• Have children go to the bathroom before using the pool.
• Make the kids take frequent bathroom breaks.

Wading pools at day care centers are subject to state regulations, which differ from state to state.

Waffle Irons

Most waffle irons these days have a nonstick surface, but some people still prefer uncoated surfaces because of their better heating qualities.

To clean a waffle iron with a nonstick surface, wipe with a *damp cloth* while the iron is still warm (but not while it's hot). Use a *brush,* such as a pastry brush, to remove bits of food and crumbs from the crevices.

A waffle iron without a nonstick surface needs to be seasoned before you can use it the first time and will need reseasoning whenever it doesn't release waffles easily. To season a waffle iron, follow these steps:

1. Brush a generous amount of *fat*, such as unsalted butter or corn oil, on the grids.
2. Heat the iron until the grids start to smoke.
3. To absorb the fat, cook a waffle and throw it away (unless you like fat-logged waffles).

To clean a seasoned waffle iron, wipe with a *damp cloth.* If that doesn't do the job, try one of these solutions:

● If the iron has removable plates, take them out and wash them in *dishwashing liquid* and *hot water.* Scrub with a *nylon scouring pad* if necessary.

● If the plates are not removable, use a *toothbrush* dipped in the *dishwashing detergent solution* to clean the grids, and rinse with a *damp cloth.*

 Repeat the seasoning process anytime you scrub the grids.

To clean the outside of a waffle iron, wipe it with a *damp cloth.* If you need extra cleaning power, add a *few drops of dishwashing liquid* to the cloth. Don't use an abrasive cleaner or scrubber. Never immerse the iron in water, unless the directions for your machine specify that immersion is OK.

Wall Coverings

The most common wall covering is washable wallpaper, which is treated with vinyl for easier cleaning. But many other coverings exist, including delicate papers; fabrics, such as cotton, linen, silk, rayon, burlap, and velvet; and coverings made from grass, reeds, hemp, cork, or leather. They generally are not washable, although some gentle cleaning methods won't hurt them.

To determine whether wallpaper is washable, wet an inconspicuous area with a solution of a little *dishwashing liquid* and *water.* If the paper absorbs water or darkens, or if the colors run, it's not washable, because the cleaning solution will damage it.

To clean washable wallpaper, use one of the three cleaning solutions recommended in the *Walls* entry, which follows. Follow the directions in that entry, with these precautions:

● Don't flood the surface with water, overwet the seams or edges, or leave water on for more than a minute.

● Don't scrub unless the manufacturer says the covering is scrubbable.

● Don't use harsh, abrasive cleaners.

expert advice

Cooking for a Crowd >

The Waffle House chain has served 420 million waffles since 1955. They use irons without non-stick coatings; they distribute heat better and last longer. Waffle House cooks spray oil on the waffle-iron plates and clean them after every shift. Then, every seven days, the plates are soaked for 30 minutes in a product specially made for commercial waffle irons and scrubbed with a wire brush. Then they're rinsed, dried, reseasoned with butter and waffle batter, and put back into use.

simple SOLUTIONS

Smudged Wallpaper? >

● To remove fingerprints and smudges, try an art gum eraser, available at office supply stores.

● To remove greasy spots, make a paste of cornstarch and water. Apply to the spot, let it dry, and vacuum.

● To remove wax, heavy crayon, or grease, hold a double thickness of paper towels on the spot and go over it with a warm iron.

To clean other wall coverings, *vacuum* regularly, using the *small brush attachment.* Another acceptable cleaner is *wallpaper dough,* available at hardware, home improvement, paint, and wallpaper stores. Roll the dough into a ball and then roll it on the dirty area. When the dough ball gets dirty, knead the dirty part back into the middle, make a new ball, and continue. You can use *white bread* in the same way.

Walls

There are two major sources of the dirt that gets on walls: stuff that comes off people's hands and stuff that comes out of thin air. How often your walls need washing will depend largely on the hands and air that touch them. If you have a smoker or a wood-burning stove or fireplace in the house, your walls will show it. If you have children, your walls will reflect their handiwork.

To dust walls, a *lamb's wool duster* works well. Or wrap a *microfiber dust cloth* or clean *white cloth* around a *broom* and dust with that ◀. It's especially useful on the highest places and for the ceiling.

To remove spots, rub gently with an *art gum eraser,* available at arts and crafts and office supply stores, or with a paste of *baking soda* and *water.* Use *mineral spirits* on grease and *WD-40* (both available at hardware stores) on crayon marks. Use *rubbing alcohol* on ink or marker. (Apply cleaners to the cloth, not the wall, and test on an inconspicuous area first.)

Three cleaning solutions for washing walls that are painted or covered with vinyl paper include the following:

- *One cup of borax* (sold in the detergent section of supermarkets) and *2 tablespoons of dishwashing liquid* in *1 gallon of warm water*.
- *One cup of ammonia*, *1 teaspoon of dishwashing liquid*, and *1 gallon of water*.
- If you're washing before applying new paint, a good cleaner to use is *trisodium phosphate*, also called TSP, available at hardware and paint stores.

  Keep the cleaning solution in *one bucket* and *plain water* for rinsing in *another bucket.* To protect the floor, use a *drop cloth.*

To keep water from running down your arms when they're raised, use this trick: wrap **rags** around your wrists and hold them on with *rubber bands.*

RULES
OF THE GAME

Work Your Way Up >

Don't start at the top and work down when you wash walls. Dirty water running down a dirty wall leaves worse streaks than dirty water running down a clean wall.
1. Apply cleaning solution over a small area at the bottom.
2. Wash, using circular strokes.
3. Rinse with plain water.
4. Dry with a towel.
5. Move up.

To clean the walls, wash with one of the solutions mentioned above using a *natural sponge,* available at hardware or home improvement stores, or a *white cloth.* Follow the guidelines in the Rules of the Game sidebar for applying the cleaning solution. Reach the high points by standing on a *sturdy stepladder* tall enough that you won't need to stand on the upper two steps.

See also Painted Surfaces and Wall Coverings.

Washers and Dryers

Every now and then you have to give back. That is, clean the washers and dryers that do so much cleaning for you. Fortunately, it's easy to do—and these machines even help to clean *themselves* occasionally.

To clean the exteriors of your washer or dryer, you don't have to do a lot. The most common spots are blotches of spilled laundry detergent, fabric softener, or bleach. They're all designed to respond best to warm water, right? So wipe them up with a *cloth* dipped in a solution of *warm water* and *mild dishwashing liquid,* which will vanquish dirt and dust, too.

To clean a washer's interior, open the washer and wipe down the inside of the door using the same solution of *warm water* and *mild dishwashing liquid* on the *cloth* that you used on the exterior. Use an *old toothbrush* to clean the crevices of the molded frame around the door. If you have a removable bleach dispenser cup, take it out to clean it. If it's built in, clean it as thoroughly as you can, using a *pipe cleaner,* if necessary. The rest of the interior of your washer gets a pretty good cleaning every time you use it.

If your washer develops a musty odor, you can easily cure it by running the machine through a *wash cycle* without any clothes in it. Use the *hottest temperature setting* available and a *medium or high water level.* While the washer is filling, pour in *2 cups of bleach.* As a preventive measure, follow this routine once a year.

When cleaning a dryer, task No. 1 is to clean the filter. Dryers work by heating air, drawing it across your wet clothes to sop up the moisture, and pushing the soggy air outside through a vent. So the name of the game is air traffic control. If that airway gets clogged up, your dryer won't be able to do its job, and your power bill will skyrocket needlessly. So clean the filter before or after every load of clothes.

simple SOLUTIONS

Keep Your Dryer's Duct Clean >

If you keep your dryer's filter clean but it still isn't as efficient as it used to be, the duct ushering the air outside may be blocked. Detach the duct from the back of your dryer and clean it out. (Do this once a year as a matter of habit.) Make sure the vent cover on the outside of your house is clean and in place. (Replacements are available at home improvement stores.) This should prevent rodents and birds from taking up residence in your vent and *really* slowing down the airflow.

Cleaning a dryer filter is very straightforward. Most dryers have a removable filter made of metal or plastic. Pull the filter out of the dryer, hold it over a **trash can,** and scrape the little blanket of lint off the filter with your hand. If some of the lint won't come free, take the filter to a sink and clean it with **warm water** and a **mild dishwashing liquid.**

If you discover crayon marks inside your dryer, run the dryer empty for five minutes to heat it up and soften up the marks. Then wipe them away with a **cloth** dipped in a **solution of water and dishwashing liquid.**

Wastebaskets

The details of cleaning wastebaskets vary according to the materials they're made of, but the beginning is always the same: Take the waste out of the basket.

To clean a wastebasket made of a natural material—such as cardboard, paper, wicker, straw, or wood—use a **vacuum cleaner** with the **small brush attachment.** If the basket becomes soiled, wipe it with a **damp cloth** or **sponge.** Don't use harsh cleaners.

To clean a plastic or metal wastebasket, wash it with a solution of **1/4 cup of baking soda or borax** (available in the detergent section of supermarkets) in **1 gallon of warm water.** Use a **cloth,** a **sponge,** or, for more challenging dirt, a **stiff brush.** Rinse and dry with a **soft cloth.**

To clean the kitchen wastebasket at the same time you're mopping the kitchen floor, just mix up your cleaner-and-water solution right in the wastebasket instead of in a bucket. During the 10 or 15 minutes it takes to mop the floor, the dirt in the wastebasket will be loosening. When you pour out the mop water, give the interior of the wastebasket a once-over with a **stiff brush,** rinse with **running water,** and dry with a **cloth.**

Watches

Salt water is one of your watch's biggest enemies, and your watch is exposed to it even if you never set foot on a beach. It comes from your sweat, of course. Other contaminants include skin oils, dirt, and substances such as lotions and insect repellents. Clean only the band and the outside of the watch, leaving the inner workings for a pro.

For daily cleaning, wipe the band and watch with a *damp cloth,* then with a *clean, dry cloth.*

For more extensive cleaning, remove the band by releasing the pins on both sides of the watch.
- Clean a leather band with *saddle soap,* followed by buffing with a *dry cloth.*
- Wash a cloth band with a little *dishwashing detergent* and *water,* rinse in *clean water,* and lay flat to dry.
- Clean a metal band by soaking it in a solution of *dishwashing detergent* and *water.* Use an *old toothbrush* to scrub. Rinse in *clean water* and dry with a *soft cloth.*

Check the crystal and have it replaced immediately if you notice any damage to it or to the face of the watch, which indicates moisture has entered. A jeweler can also buff out scratches in a plastic crystal.

To store your watch, keep it in an individual compartment in a *jewelry box* or wrap it in a *piece of soft cloth.*

To clean the inner workings, take the watch to a professional. Mechanical watches (the kind you wind) need an overhaul about every two years, and analog quartz watches (with hands and batteries) need one every three to five years, just about when you need to replace the battery anyway. Digital watches, which have no mechanical works, don't need an internal cleaning, although you will eventually need to replace the battery.

Water Beds

Water beds are easy to keep clean, especially if you use a mattress cover that can be removed and laundered.

To wash the mattress itself, wipe it off with a *damp cloth or sponge.* You should not have to do that very often.

To clean the water inside the mattress, use a *special conditioner* made for water beds and sold at water bed stores. The conditioner keeps bacteria, algae, and other slimy undesirables from growing inside. It also bursts noisy bubbles and conditions the vinyl of the mattress. Follow the directions provided by the bed maker, but a general recommendation is to add conditioner every year. There is no need to change the water for the sake of cleanliness, but you *will* have to empty it to move the bed.

Water Heaters

All water has some sediment in it, and one of its purposes in life is to create problems for water heaters. If you live in a hard-water area, you're already familiar with the floating stuff in the bottom of a glass in which the ice has melted, or with minerals in the teakettle. The cause, in both cases, is calcium and magnesium salts, which precipitate out of water when it is frozen or heated.

To counteract mineral buildup, you have several choices:
- Have a plumber flush the heater or install a water softener.
- Buy a "self-cleaning" water heater.
- Buy a "tankless" water heater. It's more expensive, but it's also more energy efficient.
- Flush the heater yourself.

If you decide to do the job, here's how:
1. Turn off the heater and the cold water that runs into it.
2. Hook a *garden hose* to the drain valve (the one near the bottom of the tank). Make sure there are no kinks in the hose. Put the other end of it where you want the hot water from the tank to go.
3. Open the drain valve.
4. Disconnect the cold water inlet pipe on the top of the water heater to let air into the water heater so it will drain. After all the water has drained, close the drain valve.
5. Pour *1 gallon of a food-grade delimer* (available at plumbing supply stores and some hardware stores) into the cold water inlet pipe. Pour only one cup at a time and pause between cups. Let it work for several hours.
6. Drain the cleaner.
7. Reconnect the cold water inlet pipe, open the valve, and let water run through the heater for several minutes, flushing out the cleaner and dissolved sediment.
8. Close the drain valve and open the hot water faucet nearest to the water heater. Let the water heater fill up.
9. When water comes out of the open faucet, reopen the drain valve and let the water heater rinse until the water running out appears clear.
10. Close the drain valve and open all the hot water faucets to remove the air from the heater and pipes.
11. Turn the water heater back on and remove the garden hose from the drain valve.

simple SOLUTIONS

Check for the Hard Stuff >

To determine whether your water is hard, look in the teakettle. If there's white, scaly stuff inside, that's just a little of what you have in your water heater. The precipitate will:
• Cut the efficiency of the heater.
• Cost you more money in electricity or gas bills.
• Reduce the water-holding capacity of the tank.
• Cause the heating element in an electric heater to eventually burn out.
• Cause an alarming rumbling sound in a gas heater, which means your heater is inefficient but doesn't mean it's about to blow up.

Water Stains

It seems a little ironic that the most abundant cleaner, water, is itself capable of leaving one of the toughest stains to remove.

To treat furniture with a white water stain, remedies abound. If one of the solutions below doesn't work, another one probably will. In all cases, unless otherwise noted, rub with a *cloth* dipped in the cleaner, going with the grain of the wood ▶. Follow this up by buffing with a **clean cloth** and applying your *regular furniture polish.*

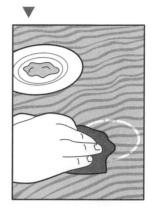

- A **50-50 mix** of **baking soda** with **white toothpaste** (not colored or gel)
- **Mayonnaise**—let sit for an hour
- **Petroleum jelly**—let sit for a day
- A solution of a little **hot water** with a **few drops of clear ammonia** added.
- A solution of equal parts of **vinegar, boiled linseed oil,** and **turpentine,** the latter two available at hardware and paint stores.
- **Paste wax** applied with **superfine (0000) steel wool,** both available at hardware and home stores

If none of the above solutions works, refinishing may be the only cure.

To treat furniture with a black water stain, there's only one remedy: Strip off the finish and bleach the wood. Chances are, if the wood has such a stain, the finish is already next to nonexistent,

No Watertight Answers *for Cloth*

Water stains on washable cloth are water soluble to some extent, especially when recent, according to textile conservator Deborah Bede, owner of Stillwater Textile Conservation Studio in Bradford, New Hampshire. But detergent isn't much help, because the water stain isn't dirt; it's caused by a change in the fibers. Bleach helps, but caution is in order. Chlorine bleach can damage fibers and leave a residue.

Don't use it on items that you care about.
- To treat stains on washable cloth, use a color-safe bleach, which is not chlorine-based. Treat the whole item, not just the spot. Use 1/4 cup per quart of water, and rinse several times.
- For fragile antique items, Bede recommends washing in a solution of 1 teaspoon of Orvus WA Paste per gallon of distilled water. Look for Orvus

at quilt shops, museum supply stores, tack shops, or farm supply stores. Rinse in distilled water until the water runs clear. For especially valuable or precious items, consult a professional conservator.
- For unwashable items, such as those made of wool or silk, you're probably stuck with the stain. Because it's caused by water, dry-cleaning won't help.

so removing it shouldn't be too difficult. Use a **paint and varnish remover,** available at hardware and paint stores. Let the piece dry; then treat it with **oxalic acid bleach,** available at hardware stores. Follow the directions on the labels of these products.

To treat water stains on painted walls or ceilings, dab with a mixture of **1/4 cup of chlorine bleach** in **1 quart of warm water.** If several applications don't work, you'll need to repaint. But first apply a **sealant** so the stain won't bleed through. Zinsser BIN Primer Sealer, available at hardware stores, is a good one.

To treat water stains on a carpet or upholstery, try a **50–50 solution** of **water** and **white vinegar.** Wet a **cloth** with the solution and gently blot the surface. If this doesn't work, your best bet is to call a professional.

Wax

simple SOLUTIONS

No-Wax Mahogany >

The birthday party ended with your aged aunt blowing out all the candles—and wax all over your beautiful mahogany table. Thank goodness there were only 85 candles, not 100!
Take heart—wax comes off fairly easily from wood surfaces.
1. If you get at the wax while it is still warm, wipe up all you can with a clean cloth.
2. If the wax has hardened, soften it with a hair dryer set on medium and then wipe.
3. Remove the last bits with a cloth dampened with mineral spirits.

If you burn candles, inevitably some wax will spill. One way to minimize damage in advance is to burn only white candles. The dye in colored candles—especially red ones—compounds the problem.

To remove white wax from carpeting or upholstery, use the fire-and-ice approach:
1. Put some **ice cubes** into a **plastic bag** and place it on the wax for a few minutes to make the wax more brittle.
2. Scrape off the wax with the dull side of a **table knife.**
3. Use a **hair dryer** on *high* to soften the remaining wax.
4. Scrape again.
5. Put a layer of **paper towels or white rags** over the wax and pass a **warm iron** over the area. Keep moving a clean area of the towels or rags onto the spot.
6. Test some **dry-cleaning solvent** on an inconspicuous area, and if it does no damage, blot a little into the remaining wax stain. The solvent is available at hardware stores.

To remove white wax from table linens or clothing, use the above methods, with these changes:
● Put the item in a **plastic bag** and then into the **freezer** for a half hour before scraping.
● On washable items, saturate the final stain with a solution of **1 part rubbing alcohol** to **2 parts water** and let it sit for a half hour. Rinse and then launder in the **washing machine.** Send nonwashable items to the dry cleaner.

WATER STAINS

For colored wax, skip the ironing. The heat will only help set the dye. Instead, try this:

1. After freezing and scraping, use **mineral spirits,** available at hardware and paint stores, on the rest of the wax. Test first and work on only tiny areas at a time, blotting with a rag. Only you can judge whether the treatment is worse than the disease, because mineral spirits may damage some materials. Some dyes may not be removable.
2. Treat washable colorfast fabrics with **bleach,** following directions on the package. Then launder.
3. For fine rugs or upholstery, consult a professional.

To remove wax from dishes and glass, heat with a **hair dryer** and wipe with a **cloth.** Then keep wiping and polishing with **used fabric softener sheets.**

Wheelchairs

Regular cleaning and maintenance will repay the effort with better performance and longer life for your wheelchair.

To clean a wheelchair, wash the frame, wheels, tires, seat, and back with **warm water** and a little **dishwashing detergent.** Apply with a **clean cloth or sponge,** rinse with **plain water,** and dry with a **clean cloth.** Don't get water in the wheel or caster bearings. This kind of cleaning should be done about once a month. For daily cleaning, wiping with a **damp cloth** is usually sufficient.

To clean the caster axle bolts, remove the bolt, wipe crud away with a **cleaning cloth,** and put back the bolt. This spot tends to collect hair, string, and other debris that will make the chair harder to propel.

To clean the axles, remove the wheels and wipe the axles with a **clean cloth** containing a **few drops of oil** (whatever oil is recommended by your owner's manual). This area, which can accumulate mud and dirt quickly, should be cleaned once a month or more.

To clean between users, disinfect the chair with a **disinfectant.** One product that is used by hospitals is HB Quat Disinfectant Cleaner. It is made by 3M and is available at medical supply stores and on the Internet.

Whirlpools

Whirlpools have two dimensions that require cleaning: the seen and the unseen.

To clean the tub surfaces, wipe with a *cloth* after each use. Clean periodically with a solution of *hot water* and *dishwashing detergent* and rinse. Don't use abrasive scrubbers or cleaners, which will harm the glossy finish.

To clean the circulation system, follow the instructions that came with your unit. Or do this:

1. Adjust the jets so they are not drawing air.
2. Leave the water in the whirlpool after using.
3. Add *2 gallons of white vinegar.* Or add *2 teaspoons of powdered dishwasher detergent* and *2 cups of chlorine bleach.*
4. Run the whirlpool system, following the operating instructions, for 5 to 10 minutes.
5. Drain and refill with *cold water.* Circulate for five minutes.
6. Drain and wipe dry with a *clean cloth.*

How often you clean the circulation system depends on the recommendation of the manufacturer and how often you use the whirlpool. Recommendations vary from once every three months to twice a month or more.

Wicker, Rattan, and Bamboo

Wicker is not a single material. It's a term for something made of any of several natural materials that are bent and woven together. The most common are rattan (a solid-cored vine of a climbing palm), cane (the skin or bark of large rattans), reed (swamp grasses or rattan core), bamboo (a large grass with a hollow core), willow, and twisted paper fiber. Wicker comes in many finishes, ranging from natural to oil, varnish, shellac, or paint. There are also synthetic versions of wicker made from resin, plastic, or fiberglass. And when it comes to cleaning, the materials aren't all created equal.

When cleaning synthetic wicker, you can be aggressive. This is the only wicker that should be allowed to remain outdoors. Clean it with a *garden hose* and *plain water,* using a *cloth or sponge,* or scrub with a *stiff brush* and a solution of a little *dishwashing detergent* in *water.* Rinse with the hose and dry with a *clean cloth.*

To clean natural-fiber wicker, keep pieces free of dirt with a *vacuum cleaner,* using the *brush attachment.* Other useful tools are a *toothbrush,* a *stiff paintbrush,* and a *pencil-sized dowel* sharpened in a pencil sharpener. Wipe the wicker with a *damp cloth or sponge,* but undertake more extensive wet cleaning cautiously. Consult an expert before doing any major cleaning or refinishing of antique pieces. To find an expert, check with antiques dealers or on the Internet.

To wash most natural-fiber wicker, use a solution of a little *mild soap*—dishwashing detergent or Murphy Oil Soap, for example—in *warm water.* Wipe with a *cloth or sponge* wrung out in the solution. Rinse with a *garden hose* and dry quickly—in the *sun* or with a *hair dryer or fan.* Don't sit on the furniture for two or three days, because you could stretch the fibers and cause them to sag.

Some exceptions: Don't hose down bamboo or twisted paper wicker. Clean these with a *sponge* dampened with *soapy water,* followed by a *sponge* dampened with *clear water.* Wipe dry.

To treat for dryness and cracking, use *1 part turpentine* to *2 parts boiled linseed oil* on natural-fiber wicker, except for bamboo. Apply with a *paintbrush,* using as much as the wicker will absorb. Wipe off any excess with a *cloth* and let it dry for three or four days. For bamboo, you should apply a *thin coat of liquid or paste wax* periodically.

Wigs

Wigs are made of synthetic materials, human hair, or a combination of the two. Synthetic wigs are easier to care for but not as versatile in accepting styling. For example, heat, such as in a curling iron, can ruin them. Human hair wigs can be colored, permed, and curled with a curling iron or heated rollers.

To wash a wig, follow these steps:
1. Gently straighten the hair with a *comb.*
2. Draw *water—cool to lukewarm,* not hot—into a *pan* large enough to immerse the wig.
3. Dissolve about *1 tablespoon each* of *shampoo* and *baking soda* in the water.
4. Swish the wig around in the solution.
5. Rinse well in *cool water.*
6. Dissolve *1 tablespoon of conditioner* in a *pan* of *fresh water.* Swish the wig in the solution. Then rinse.

simple SOLUTIONS

Canned Air for Hair >

Yet another use for canned air—from the maker of Dust-Off: Between washings, use it to blow away loose dirt from your wig. Set the wig on its stand and hold the can upright so it doesn't spew out propellant. Separate the layers of hair and have a blast!

7. Lay the wig on a *towel* and roll it up to remove as much water as you can. Don't wring!
8. Remove the wig from the towel and gently shake it out. Use your fingers to loosen the fibers, but don't try to remove tangles with a comb or brush while the wig is wet.
9. Set the wig on a *bottle* or some other tall item to dry.

To clean makeup from the front of the cap or hair area, make a paste of *baking soda* and *shampoo.* Apply it during the shampooing process with an *old toothbrush* and scrub gently.

Windows

So much has been printed about the fastest and best way to clean windows that you'd think it was an Olympic event. Well, let's just relax. The truth is, lots of things work.

Here are a few simple hints that apply to most windows:
- Clean the windowsills and frames before the glass. *Vacuum* to remove loose dirt before wiping with a *damp cloth.*
- Start at the top and work down to avoid dripping onto clean windows.
- Don't clean windows in direct sunlight. The cleaner will dry before you can wipe it off, creating streaks.
- Make your drying strokes go up and down on one side of the window and back and forth on the other. That way you can tell which side streaks are on.

Double the Fun for Double-Hung

Many double-hung windows—that's the most common type of window—are now made so they can be tilted inward for cleaning. But if you don't have that kind, you can still clean both sides from inside the house—provided both upper and lower windows move fully, as they're supposed to. Here are instructions for reaching the outside of both windows—you can figure out the inside for yourself.

1. Pull the top window all the way down. (It will be on the outside.)
2. Reach through the opening to clean the top part of the outside. Wash, then wipe.
3. Raise both windows all the way to the top.
4. Reach through the opening to clean the bottom part of the outside.
5. Lower the inside window enough to reach the outside window and push it all the way to the bottom.
6. Reach through the opening to clean the top part of the inside window.
7. Raise the outside window all the way to the top and lower the inside window as much as possible while leaving room for your arm to pass through the opening.
8. Reach through the opening to clean the bottom part of the inside window.

- Your drying technique and materials affect the final appearance more than the kind of cleaner.

Now let's move on to the contentious part.

The cheapest way to clean a window is to use *plain water* and *newspaper.* Apply the water with a *sponge or window wand,* available at hardware stores. Dip the wand into a *bucket* of water, picking up just enough to wet the window without drenching it. Then wad up the newspaper a little and rub the window until it's dry.

This method, besides being inexpensive, is environmentally friendly. The disadvantage is that the ink from the newsprint will get on your hands (you can wear *rubber gloves*) and can soil the nonglass window parts. *Paper towels* also work but are expensive and wasteful. A *chamois cloth* works as well.

Using a squeegee to clean windows is the method preferred by many people, including most professional window cleaners. If it's your choice, buy a good *squeegee with a removable rubber blade* so that it can be replaced as it wears. The main disadvantage of a squeegee is that it's impractical on small panes of glass. When using a squeegee, technique is important:

1. First, wet the squeegee.
2. Draw it across the top of the pane *(A)* ▶.

(A)

3. Start the squeegee at the bottom edge of that swath and draw it down one side of the glass to about 2 inches from the bottom *(B)* ▶.
4. Repeat this step, overlapping each stroke as you work your way across the window *(C)* ▶.
5. Draw the squeegee across the bottom of the pane. Wipe the squeegee on a *cloth* between strokes.
6. Use a *clean cloth* to wipe the window edges, if necessary.
7. On very large windows, wash and dry the top half, then the bottom half.

(B)

For added cleaning power on dirty glass, here are some formulas to try:

- For grease or hard-water deposits, use *1 cup of white vinegar* in *1 gallon of water*, plus a *squirt of dishwashing liquid*.
- For grime, grease, or smoke, use *1/2 cup of clear ammonia* in *2 quarts of water*.
- For tough jobs, use *2 cups of rubbing alcohol* and *2 tablespoons each* of *clear ammonia* and *dishwashing detergent*. This formula requires rinsing.

(C)

- For the toughest jobs, use *automotive rubbing compound*, available at hardware and auto supply stores, following the directions on the can. It takes a lot of time, so you aren't likely to use this for general-purpose cleaning.

See also **Glass**.

Woks

A well-seasoned wok has the equivalent of a nonstick surface and needs only light cleaning.

To clean a new wok made of carbon steel (the authentic kind), begin by removing the temporary protective coating applied by the manufacturer. Scrub the wok inside and out with *dishwashing detergent* and *steel wool* and rinse with *hot water.* If some coating remains, fill the wok with *water* and boil it until the coating dissolves. Empty the water and scrub again with steel wool and soap.

To season a new wok, after washing it as described above, follow these steps:
1. Set the wok on a *burner* and heat it until a *few drops of water* sprinkled into the wok do a mad dance. As it heats, the wok will change color.
2. When it turns black, dip some *wadded-up paper towels* into *sesame oil.* Hold the wad in a *pair of tongs* and wipe the oil over the inside of the wok.
3. Turn the heat down to low and let the wok sit on it for 15 minutes. If the surface looks dry, wipe with another thin coat of oil.
4. Turn the heat off and let the wok cool.
5. Repeat the oiling and heating process once more before using the wok for cooking.

To clean a wok after cooking, wipe it out with a *paper towel or damp cloth.* Scrubbing a seasoned wok or using a detergent will ruin the carefully cultivated patina, but if you do need to scrub or wash with detergent, the good news is that the wok can be reseasoned as described above. Similarly, if a wok gets rusty, just follow the steps for cleaning and seasoning a new wok.

To clean an electric wok, follow the manufacturer's directions, which will vary depending on what kind of surface the wok has and whether it is immersible in water.

Wood Stoves

Keeping your wood stove clean isn't only a matter of cleanliness. It's also a vital matter of safety. Every year wood stoves are responsible for fires that destroy homes and kill people. One common cause is improper disposal of ashes.

To dispose of ashes safely, remove them with a metal *ash shovel* and place them in a *tightly covered metal bucket.* No plastic shovels, no paper bags, no cardboard boxes—no substitutions! Then take the bucket outside and let it sit for a couple of days to ensure that the harmless-looking ashes aren't harboring any embers. For final disposal, add to garden soil or sprinkle on the lawn to use the potassium and other minerals. This is the cleaning chore that needs to be done most often during the heating season, whenever the ashes are 3 or 4 inches deep.

To clean a stovepipe, another chore you may have to perform several times during a season, disconnect it from the chimney and from the stove when the fire is out. Take the stovepipe outside and shake it into a *metal bucket* to remove the soot and creosote. If there are stubborn clumps of residue, use a *stiff-bristled brush.*

To ensure the cleanest operation of your stove, burn hardwood (maple, ash, oak, beech, birch, and hickory, for example) that has been seasoned for a year. Burn a *hot* fire for at least half an hour every week during the heating season. If you are an inexperienced wood burner, you can buy a *stovepipe thermometer* from a hearth shop or wood stove dealer to tell you the meaning of *hot* in this context.

To clean the outside of the stove, *vacuum* when there is no fire, using the *small brush attachment.* For dirt that vacuuming won't remove, wipe the surface of enameled stoves with a *damp sponge.* Use *stove polish,* available at hardware stores and hearth shops, on stoves made of cast iron, plate steel, sheet metal, or a combination of these materials. Balled-up *waxed paper,* used on a warm stove, also shines those finishes. Rust or other heavy dirt may be cleaned from a cold stove with *fine steel wool* and *WD-40,* available in hardware stores.

To clean glass doors, follow the directions in your owner's manual. A mixture of *water* and a little *ammonia* works well to remove smoke, but check your manual first to make sure the glass doesn't have a special protective coating, which might be harmed by the ammonia.

OOPS!

No Easy Way Out > Don't rely on chemical cleaners, such as cleaning logs, to clean your stove and chimney. According to Mark McSweeney, executive director of the Chimney Safety Institute of America (CSIA), it's OK to use those cleaners. They might reduce some of the soot and creosote, causing it to flake and fall. However they won't get rid of it. "They can give a false sense of security," McSweeney says.

The only way to get rid of soot and creosote is by mechanically brushing and scraping. Have an annual inspection and cleaning if necessary by a CSIA-certified chimney sweep. To find one, visit www.csia.org or call (800) 536-0118.

Other stove parts that need periodic cleaning are baffles, smoke shelves, and catalytic combustors. These gizmos increase the efficiency of your stove and reduce pollution. They're often located near the spot where the stovepipe meets the stove. Your owner's manual will tell you if your stove has one or more of these parts and will explain how to clean them.

Woodwork

Woodwork usually gets dirty faster than walls because it's the edging around doors and windows that most often comes into contact with little hands and dirty fingers. Woodwork will probably need cleaning more often than walls, but fortunately it takes up a lot less area.

For routine cleaning, vacuum baseboards, chair rails (the waist-level molding on walls that prevents chairs from marking the walls), wainscoting, and casings (the framework around doors and windows) with the *small brush attachment.* Dust the top surfaces of this woodwork periodically with a *microfiber cloth.*

To wash woodwork, use a solution of a little *dishwashing liquid* in *warm water.* Apply with a *wrung-out sponge or rag* and then rinse with *plain water.* If the gloss has been dulled, follow by rubbing with a *cloth* that has a *tiny amount of furniture polish* on it. This works on both painted and urethane surfaces.

To clean heavily soiled areas, apply a little *undiluted dishwashing liquid* directly to the *sponge or cloth.* Rub the dirty area and rinse with *plain water.*

To prepare the surface for new paint, wash with a solution of *1 cup of trisodium phosphate* in *1 gallon of water.* Wear *rubber gloves* and rinse afterward.

To clean woodwork with a varnish or shellac finish, use a *solvent-based* (not water-based) *wood cleaner,* available at home improvement stores and hardware stores. It is both a cleaner and wax in one product. Apply it with a cloth and buff afterward.

Yard Tools

The tools we use in our yards range from caveman-type implements to high-tech motorized devices with computer-controlled innards. In the former category are axes, shovels, rakes, manual edgers, hand clippers, pruning saws, wheelbarrows, and carts, to name a few. The more modern gizmos, powered by gas or electricity, include trimmers, clippers, blowers, power edgers, and chain saws.

To help your tools last longer and work better, follow these general cleaning guidelines:

● To ensure safe, sound operation, especially of power tools, read and keep your owner's manuals. Refer to them often and follow their instructions!

● To keep dirt from becoming caked on, clean tools after each use. Remove grass, leaves, and dirt with a **brush** of appropriate size and stiffness, and wipe with a **dry or damp cloth.**

● To keep tools from rusting, don't leave them outdoors. Put them away after each use and store them under cover. Organize a special place to hang them so they're easy to find and easy to put away.

● To stay on the cutting edge, sharpen cutting tools regularly. Sharp tools not only work better but are also safer. Dull tools are more likely to miss the mark, break, or kick back, not to mention frustrate the user. Most hand tools can be sharpened with a **file,** which you can buy at a hardware store.

● For power tools such as chain saws and hedge trimmers, consult your owner's manual for sharpening instructions or take them to service centers that do the job.

● Pay attention to handles, especially of power tools. Make sure they are dry and free of oils and grease. A slip of your grip could result in a serious accident.

● Inspect screws and nuts periodically to be sure they're tight.

Before putting tools away for the season, follow a thorough cleaning and maintenance routine to ensure long life and trouble-free operation. Here are some tips for such routines:

● To care for hand tools, wipe wooden handles with a mixture of **equal parts vinegar, boiled linseed oil,** and **turpentine.** The latter two items are available at hardware and paint stores. This treatment will help keep the handles from becoming brittle and breaking off. Wipe the metal parts with a **rag** dampened with **kerosene or old motor oil.** To make tools such as shovels and saws really glide, polish them with **car wax.**

- To prepare gas-powered tools for storage, empty the fuel from the tank and run the tool until it stops. That will use up the fuel in the carburetor. Take the fuel to a recycling center—don't save it for future use. Wipe all metal parts with a *damp cloth* followed by an *oil-dampened cloth.* Follow any other instructions in your owner's manual, such as for cleaning air filters, spark plugs, and mufflers.

- To prepare electrical tools for storage, unplug. In fact, unplug them anytime they're not in use and especially when you're working on the tool. Follow any other directions in your owner's manual.

- To clean plastic parts, wipe with a *damp cloth* or use one dipped in a solution of a little *dishwashing detergent* and *water.* Do not use strong detergents, household cleaners, or solvents, such as kerosene or turpentine.

- To remove rust from tools, scrub them with *steel wool* dipped in *kerosene or turpentine.*

- To care for carts and wheelbarrows, wash them regularly during the season with a *garden hose.* Before putting them away, scrub with a *stiff brush* if they need it and wipe them with *oil* on a *rag.* Repaint as necessary. Lubricate wheels with a little *general purpose oil.*

Zippers

Yes, there are times when you should clean a zipper independently of the item it fastens. For example, the zippers in tents, sleeping bags, luggage, wet suits, fishing gear, jackets, and boots may need separate attention now and then.

To clean zippers in washable items, wash the item with *water* and *detergent* that is suitable for the fabric. Close the zipper before putting the article into the *washing machine.* When ironing, protect the zipper by closing it and covering it with a *cloth.* Excessive heat from the iron can damage or destroy nylon, plastic, and polyester zippers.

To make the slider work more smoothly, rub a *candle* along the zipper teeth and move the slider up and down several times to work in the wax ▶. A white candle works best, so you don't smear dye around. Wipe off any excess. This treatment will counteract the damage done by detergents and bleach to the factory-applied coating that keeps zippers slippery.

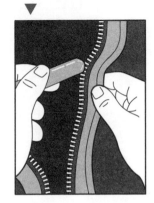

To clean the zippers on large articles—such as tents, backpacks, wet suits, suitcases, and boots—first unzip the zipper. Remove any loose dirt from the teeth with—what else?—a toothbrush. To wash the zipper, dip the *toothbrush* in a solution of a little *dishwashing liquid* and *warm water.* Rinse with *plain water* and leave the zipper open until it has dried. Lubricate the teeth with a *candle.* A *special zipper cleaner* available at outdoors stores, Zip Care, comes with its own brush, works on nylon and metal zippers, and is both a cleaner and a lubricant.

Yikes!

(A Guide to Household Cleaning Crises)

Chewing gum in your hair,

fleas in the carpet,

a pen springing a leak in your pocket—

life's just chockfull of surprises!

Here's a quick-look-up guide

to household disasters.

Part Three

Cleaning Crises

and Special Situations

Animal pee, poop, or vomit
on floor or carpet

Remove the pee, poop, or vomit as soon as possible. Stash a crisis kit containing the following items in your broom closet or utility room: ***paper towels, plastic grocery bags*** (for disposing of solids and used paper towels), a ***sponge,*** and an ***enzyme-based cleaner*** (available at pet stores). Start by removing any solids. Next, blot up as much of the liquid content as possible. Soak the accident site in the enzyme cleaner. Rinse residue with ***plain water*** to avoid leaving any fragrant clues that might draw the pet back to use the same spot.

Baby pee, poop, or upchuck
on clothes or upholstery

First try cold water, which may be all you'll need to remove any of these protein stains if they're fresh. Don't use hot water, since hot water can cook the proteins, causing the stain to coagulate between the fibers in the fabric. Soak washables in ***cold water*** for half an hour, run the stain under ***cold tap water,*** and gently rub the fabric against itself to loosen the stain. Then launder in your ***washer in warm water.*** For carpeting or upholstery, spray with ***cold water*** and blot with a ***clean cloth or paper towels.*** Repeat until the stain is gone. If residue remains, soak the accident site in ***enzyme cleaner.*** Wash and rinse according to product directions.

Berry stains
on clothing or kitchen towels

Berry stains are considered dye stains, and they're tough. For washable clothes and towels, pretreat the stain with a ***commercial stain remover.*** Or apply ***liquid laundry detergent*** directly to the stain. Work the detergent in well. Next, soak the fabric in a diluted solution of ***oxygen bleach*** (identified as "all-fabric" or "perborate" on the label—follow directions on the packaging). Launder in your ***washer.*** For dry-clean-only clothes, blot a ***dry-cleaning solution,*** such as Carbona, on the stain with a ***clean white towel.***

Big party mess
to clean up

Gather cups, bottles, and glasses first. As you do so, look for spills and address them right away. Empty the cups, bottles, and glasses in the kitchen sink, tossing trash into a ***garbage bag*** and setting the glasses on the counter. Fill your ***dishwasher*** and start the first load. Next, gather up the rest of the party garbage, starting in the outer rooms and working your way toward the kitchen. The goal: to centralize the clutter. Dust and ***vacuum,*** again working your way toward the kitchen. Clean the kitchen last. Take the garbage out as soon as bags are filled and tied (to prevent accidental leaks and odors).

Blood
on fabric or carpet

If it's fresh, cold water should be all you'll need to remove this protein stain. Don't use hot water, since hot water can cook the proteins, causing the stain to coagulate between the fibers in the fabric. Soak washables in *cold water* for half an hour, run the stain under *cold tap water,* and gently rub the fabric against itself to loosen the stain. Launder in *warm water.* For carpeting or upholstery, spray with *cold water* and blot with a *clean white towel* (white, so there's no chance of dye transfer), repeating until clean.

Candle wax
on fabric or carpet

If the wax is still soft, blot up the excess with a *paper towel.* If it is hard, gently scrape the excess with a *dull knife.* Next, lay a *plain brown bag or white paper towel* (no dyes or printing inks) over the wax and run a *hot iron* over the paper. The heat will melt the wax, and the paper will absorb it. Continue by moving the bag or paper towel around to unsaturated sections until all the wax is absorbed. Remove residue by blotting with a *dry-cleaning solvent,* such as Carbona. Be sure to test the solvent first on an inconspicuous spot.

Chewing gum
on upholstery, carpet, or hair

Use *ice* to remove chewing gum from a variety of places: clothing, upholstery, carpeting, and hard surfaces. Simply rub the ice on the gum until it freezes and hardens. To avoid water drips, put the ice in a *plastic bag* before rubbing it on the gum. Scrape away the hardened gum with a *dull knife.* If residue remains, remove it by blotting with a *dry-cleaning solvent,* such as Carbona. Be sure to test the solvent first on an inconspicuous spot. For gum in your hair, apply a *few drops of mineral oil, cooking oil,* or *peanut butter* to the gum and knead the gum until it's soft. Keep pulling away bits of gum until it's gone, then *shampoo.*

Coffee
on clothes

For washable fabrics, soak for a half hour in a solution of *1 teaspoon liquid laundry detergent* (preferably one containing enzymes) per *1/2 gallon warm water.* Then launder in the *washing machine* with the *hottest water* that is safe for the fabric, using *laundry detergent,* not soap. Natural soap—including soap flakes, bar soap, and detergent containing soap—makes tannin stains harder to remove. To remove stubborn tannin stains, you may need to wash with *bleach.* If all the sugars from one of these stains are not removed, they could turn brown in your dryer, as the sugar is caramelized by the heat.

Cooking odor *permeating the house*

Open the windows and turn on a fan to get fresh air circulating. Next, wipe surfaces with a *degreaser,* such as Simple Green, to remove the particles and grease deposited by the smoke. Clean walls and other surfaces close to the stove. Because heat rises and is drawn to cool areas, concentrate on wiping windows and window trim, light fixtures, and upper cabinets.

A quick fix for cutting cooking odors: Mix *1/4 cup vinegar* in *1 quart water* and boil on the *stove.* The rising warm air will carry the odor-neutralizing vinegar particles to the surfaces on which the smoke and grease settled.

Cooking oil splatters *on stove, counters, or clothes*

First, the stove and counters: Wipe oil from counters and the stove with *paper towels.* Then wipe surfaces with a *moist sponge* and a solution of *dishwashing liquid* and *warm water* or a *50-50 solution* of *vinegar* and *warm water.* Check beneath the cooktop (if it's not sealed—follow owner's manual instructions) and wipe up oil there to prevent a cooking fire.

For oil on clothes you must dry-clean, blot the grease with a *paper towel* dampened with *acetone-based nail polish remover.*

(Do not use it on acetate, however—acetone will dissolve the fabric.) For washable clothes, use a *commercial prewash stain remover* or a *liquid laundry detergent.* Work the detergent into the stain. Immediately after pretreatment, launder the item in hot water (if that is safe for the fabric and colors).

Felt-tip marker *on fridge, counter, or furniture*

First, try wiping the marks off with a *paper towel or dry cloth.* Depending on the surface and whether the marker ink is still wet, you may be able to remove the mark. If not, you can try wiping with a *clean cloth* moistened with *rubbing alcohol.* If that doesn't work, try *mineral spirits or kerosene.* But be careful: These solvents are all flammable. Test them first in an inconspicuous corner of the material.

Fleas *in carpeting*

Vacuum the carpeting, concentrating on areas frequented by your pet and under seats and sofas. Also vacuum upholstered furniture in the vicinity. Wash any removable throw rugs or pet bedding. Using a *spray bottle,* apply an *insect growth regulator,* which is nontoxic to humans but stops fleas from reproducing. Once the carpet has dried, vacuum again. Vacuum often for the next two weeks. Don't leave the vacuum bag in the machine when you've finished. Remove it and tie it up tightly in a *plastic bag,* so that the fleas will not spread.

Furnace malfunction *spreading soot*

Turn the furnace off or cut power. If you need to keep the system running, remove the register and return covers, lay *two layers of cheesecloth,* sprayed lightly with *WD-40,* over the vents, and loosely screw the covers back on. Turn off computers, stereos, and any other electronics, because the soot can be sucked in by motor fans and can damage the circuitry. Soot is oily and acidic, and the particles are extremely fine. Vacuum only if you have a *vacuum cleaner* that has a *HEPA filter* (with a minimum of 2 micron entrapment); use *brush attachments* so that you won't grind soot into materials. Don't touch anything: Oils from your skin can set soot stains on surfaces. Wipe metals—doorknobs, hinges, faucets—with an *alkaline degreaser,* such as Simple Green. If the problem is severe, hire a professional restoration company that is familiar with furnace soot. Otherwise, you risk making the soot stains worse.

Garbage bag spill *on carpeting*

Quickly pick up large solids and put them in a *new bag or garbage can.* Clean up any small solids, such as coffee grounds or dirt, with a *vacuum.* Blot up liquids with *paper towels.* If there are stains remaining, figure out what they are and address each using the appropriate stain-removal technique. (See *Stains* on page 338.) For big spills, work from the outer edge of the spill to the center to contain the spill.

Glass
broken in crowded room

Leave someone near the spot to warn others. Go get a *small cardboard box* (or a *bucket*), a pair of *work gloves,* and a *broom and dustpan* (for hard floors) or a *vacuum cleaner* (for carpets). Donning gloves, pick up the big pieces and put them in the box or bucket. On a hard floor, inspect in a wide circle around the crash site for pieces that may have skittered hither and yon. Check your guests' pants cuffs. Next, sweep or vacuum. Vacuum the carpet several times to make sure you have removed all tiny shards. Empty the vacuum bag when finished. Transfer the glass from the bucket to a box. Seal the box and put it in the trash. The box will protect your hands and those of the garbage collector.

Glue
spilled on furniture, sofa

Start by scraping up whatever you can using a *dull knife.* If the glue is white school glue, such as Elmer's, treat it as you would a protein-based stain (page 340), which means no hot water— the hot water can cook the proteins. Instead, spray the spot with *cold water* and blot with a *clean cloth,* repeating until clean. If it is airplane model glue, blot it with a *cloth* moistened with *dry-cleaning solvent or rubbing alcohol.*

Lipstick
on clothing

Lipstick contains both an oily/waxy base and dyes. You must first remove the oily/waxy part and then you can try to remove the dye. For washable fabrics, begin by applying a *dry-cleaning solvent,* such as K2r or Carbona. Next, rub with a *liquid laundry detergent* and scrub in *hot water.* This should remove the oily/waxy part. Then launder in your *washer* using a *laundry detergent* and an *oxygen or all-fabric bleach.*

Mud or salt
tracked in on rug

Mud wreaks havoc on a rug. Don't despair: Let the mud dry first, and you'll have a better chance of getting it out. If the mud is ground in, *brush* it to the surface, then get up as much as you can with a *dull knife.* After that, *vacuum.* If you still see muddy paw- or footprints, mix *1/4 teaspoon dishwashing liquid* with *1 cup warm water* and blot the solution onto the rug with a *clean white towel.* Use *another damp towel* to rinse and remove soap.

For salt stains tracked in on wet shoes and boots in snowy weather, mix equal parts *vinegar* and *water* and dab the mixture on with a *towel.* Blot with *cool water* and dry.

Mustard is a dye stain. For washable clothes and towels, pretreat with a *commercial stain remover.* Or apply *liquid laundry detergent* directly on the stain. Work the detergent in well. Next, soak the fabric in a diluted solution of *oxygen bleach* (identified as "all-fabric" or "perborate" on the label—follow directions on the packaging). Launder in your *washer.* For dry-clean-only clothes, blot with a *dry-cleaning solution,* such as Carbona, on a *clean white towel.*

Mustard
on clothing

Blot up excess with a *paper towel.* Then blot with a *cloth* moistened with *acetone-based nail polish remover.* Don't let the nail polish remover seep into a carpet's latex backing. To remove the nail polish remover, mix a solution of *1 squirt mild dishwashing liquid* (containing no bleach or lanolin) with *1 quart water.* Wipe the wood or work the solution into the textile with a *clean towel.* Draw the solution back out by blotting with a *dry paper towel.* Rinse by lightly spraying with *clean water* and then blot the water up with *fresh paper towels.*

Nail polish
on furniture, floor, or carpet

Blot up as much as you can with a *paper towel* or carefully scrape solids up with a *dull knife.* For clothes that can only be dry-cleaned, blot the grease with a *paper towel* dampened with *acetone-based nail polish remover.* (Don't use acetone on acetate, because it will dissolve the fabric.) For washable clothes, spray with a *commercial prewash stain remover* or use a *liquid laundry detergent.* Work the detergent into the stain. Immediately after pretreatment, launder the item in your *washer* using *hot water* (if that is safe for the fabric and colors).

Oil and grease
on clothes

Start by blotting up as much dripped paint as possible using *paper towels.* If it is latex paint, spray with *clean water* and blot. Repeat until you've removed as much paint as possible. If it is oil-based paint, blot with a *clean cloth or paper towel* moistened with *paint thinner or turpentine,* refreshing *cloths or paper towels* repeatedly. If vestiges of the paint remain on the carpet, moisten the tufts with *3 percent hydrogen peroxide* and let that stand for an hour. Blot with a *clean paper towel.*

Paint drippings
on floor or carpeting

Pen ink
on your
pocket

Remove the pen and put it in the garbage. Remove the item of clothing, making sure not to smear the ink stain on anything else. Place the stain facedown on **white paper towels.** (Put **plastic** beneath, to keep the ink from bleeding through and staining the surface you're working on.) Blot with a **cloth** moistened with **rubbing alcohol,** forcing the stain into the paper towels. If that does not work, try **mineral spirits or kerosene.** Be careful, because these solvents are flammable. Also test them first in an inconspicuous corner of the material. Rinse with **water** and launder in your **washer.**

Rotten smell
from
unknown
source

Follow your nose. First, try to isolate the odor. Is it in a particular room? Is it wafting up from the basement? Is it a dead critter smell, a pet accident smell, a musty mold smell, a cooking odor? Use deductive reasoning: If it's in the kitchen and smells like rotten food, check the refrigerator and the garbage disposal. Look under cabinets or appliances for dropped food. If it's a musty odor, such as mold or mildew, check the sink drain or refrigerator drip pan. Look in the basement for mildew. Look for dead rodents. Here's how to handle a few common odor problems:

● For a kitchen with lingering cooking smells, wipe down all hard surfaces near the stove with a **degreaser** such as Simple Green, including windows, light fixtures, and cabinets. Wash curtains and dish towels.

● To deodorize your garbage disposal, grind up some **lemon or orange peels** in it.

● To deodorize your refrigerator, toss any old food, wipe down the interior with a **damp sponge,** and place an open **box of baking soda** inside.

Scorch
on fabric

Bad scorch stains cannot be removed. Try laundering the fabric in your **washer** using **bleach,** if that is safe for the fabric. If not, soak in **all-fabric bleach** and **hot water** and then launder.

First, avoid using any toilets, sinks, tubs, or showers in the house until the backup is corrected. And avoid direct contact with the contamination. (You may need rubber gloves and boots.) If you are part of a municipal sewage system, contact the city. It should send someone to diagnose the problem—and clean it up if it was the city's fault. If it's your fault, call a plumber or correct the backup using a *plumber's snake* to clear the blockage. Clean up the mess using a *wet vac* and *mop* to remove the spillage. Mop the floors and wipe the walls with a *heavy-duty cleaner/disinfectant.* Then clean plumbing fixtures. Finally, call a professional to steam clean your carpets and rugs (the easiest and most effective approach), or do it yourself by renting or buying a steam cleaner (also known as a hot water extraction machine) and following the directions that come with the machine.

Sewage *backing up through drains*

When smoke from the fireplace comes into the house, first make sure there is no chimney fire. Check for a loud roaring or sparks in the chimney. If it's a chimney fire, call the fire department. If it's not, then chances are your chimney is not drawing well. Open a door or window on the windward side of the house to help the chimney draw. To clear out existing smoke, open more windows and doors on the windward side and use *fans* to circulate the air. If the smoke smell lingers, wash the drapes and clean the upholstery. (Rugs should be OK, as smoke rises.) Wipe all exposed metal in the room with a *degreaser,* since smoke seeks out cool surfaces. (The acidic soot can etch metal.)

Smoke *from fireplace*

First, turn off the oven or stove. Contain the smoke by closing the doors to other rooms. Open the windows and turn on *fans* to circulate air. Next, wipe surfaces with a *degreaser,* such as Simple Green, to remove the particles and grease deposited by the smoke. Clean the walls and other surfaces close to the stove. Wipe the windows and window trim, light fixtures, and upper cabinets. Later, wash the kitchen curtains and exposed dish towels.

Smoke *filling kitchen*

To get rid of the smoke odor quickly, combine *1/4 cup vinegar* with *1 quart water* and boil on the *stove.* The rising hot air will carry odor-neutralizing vinegar particles to the surfaces on which the smoke and grease settled.

Suntan lotion
on clothing

Blot excess lotion with a *paper towel* or carefully scrape up the excess with a *dull knife.* On washable clothes, spray the stained area with a *commercial prewash stain remover.* If you do not have that product, apply *liquid laundry detergent* directly to the stain and work it in. Immediately after pretreatment, launder the item in your *washer* in *hot water* (if that is safe for the fabric and colors). With dry-clean-only clothes, blot with a *paper towel* dampened with *acetone-based nail polish remover.* (Acetone will dissolve acetate, however, so don't use on that fabric.)

Tar
on shoes

Remove as much of the tar as possible by gently scraping with an *old spoon.* Remove further residue by blotting with a *clean, dry paper towel.* Next, apply *rubbing alcohol* to a *paper towel* and blot or gently rub. Repeat several times using *clean paper towels* with *freshly applied alcohol.* If any tar remains, try wiping with a sudsy solution of *warm water* and a *squirt of dishwashing liquid.* Put a small amount on a **cloth** and gently blot or rub. Rinse by spraying lightly with *clean water* and wiping dry.

Washer, toilet, tub, or sink
overflowing onto floor

This—along with bathing the dog—is why you keep those old towels around. First, turn off the water source and open any drains. Then grab as many *old towels* as needed and toss them onto the pooling water to soak it up. With another towel or several smaller rags, contain the water by soaking it up from the outside toward the center. *Mop* or use a *wet vac* and then let dry, using *fans* and *dehumidifiers,* if necessary.

Water or alcohol stain
on furniture

If it's a fresh stain, soak up any excess water or alcohol with a *paper towel* and then rub the spot vigorously in the direction of the grain with the *palm of your hand* or a *cloth dipped in furniture polish.* If it's an old, dry stain, you'll need an abrasive/lubricant combination: Use a few drops of *mineral oil with rottenstone* (a fine abrasive available at hardware stores) sprinkled on top or apply a *paste wax* with a *very fine grade of steel wool* (such as 0000). In a pinch, you can even use *cigarette ashes and mayonnaise.* No matter what combination you use, rub gently with the grain using a *clean, dry cloth.*

Blot up what you can with *paper towels.* For large spills, work from the outside in to contain the spill. Next, lightly apply a solution of *1/4 teaspoon mild dishwashing liquid* and *1 quart water.* Work the solution into the affected area. Blot with *clean paper towels* to remove. Rinse by lightly spraying with *water.* Blot to remove excess water. Do this until all suds are gone. Then spray lightly with *water* and don't blot. Instead, lay a *pad of paper towels* down, put a *weight* on the pad, and let the towels dry. If the stain persists, moisten the tufts with *3 percent hydrogen peroxide.* Let that stand for an hour. Blot with *clean paper towels.*

Wine
on carpet

Regardless of the type of wine, if the fabric is washable, soak it for half an hour in a solution of *1 teaspoon liquid laundry detergent* (preferably one containing *enzymes*) per *1/2 gallon warm water.* Then launder in your *washer* using the *hottest water* that's safe for the fabric and *laundry detergent,* not soap. Natural soap—including soap flakes, bar soap, and detergent containing soap—makes tannin stains harder to remove. To remove stubborn tannin stains, you may need to wash with *bleach.* If all the sugars from one of these stains are not removed, they could turn brown in the dryer, as the sugar is caramelized.

Wine
on table linen

Abrasive cleaners

Baking soda

Car polishes

Dusters

Enzyme digesters

Floor care products

Garbage bags

Hydrogen peroxide

Mops

Oven cleaners

Paper towels

Rubber gloves

Squeegees

Toilet cleaners

Vacuum cleaners

Part Four

Tools

of the Cleaning Trade

Abrasive Cleaners

Using abrasive cleaners is a mechanical process. Abrasive cleaners are made of particles, usually minerals, that scratch off the offending grime with friction created when you rub. The finer the particle, the less abrasive the cleaner; the coarser the particle, the more abrasive the cleaner. Many abrasive cleaners, which come in powdered and liquid forms, also contain cleaning chemicals such as detergent or bleach.

USE A FULL-STRENGTH ABRASIVE CLEANER—a scouring powder, such as Ajax or Comet—to wear off dirt, stains, tarnish, and hard-water deposits. Rub across the surface of the item with a sponge or brush and then rinse.

USE A MILD ABRASIVE CLEANER, such as Soft Scrub, for cleaning sinks, tiles, showers, tubs, toilets, and countertops. Follow the package instructions. Be careful not to rub too hard. Even mildly abrasive cleaners can scratch and damage hard, smooth surfaces, making them rough and difficult to clean in the future.

A PUMICE STONE, the same kind of abrasive block you use to file away corns on your feet, will help remove a particularly stubborn toilet bowl stain.

SCRUBBING PADS, ranging from nylon mesh to steel wool soap pads, also work by abrasion.

SOME COMMON HOUSEHOLD COMPOUNDS can be used instead of commercially prepared abrasives:

● Baking soda is a mild abrasive. Sprinkle it on the item to be cleaned or make a paste by adding water to baking soda until it's a little thicker than toothpaste. Baking soda can be used to scour pots and pans, ovens, and drip pans.

● Toothpaste can remove water marks in sinks and clean tarnish on silver. Coat the silver with toothpaste, run it under warm water, work it into a foam, and rinse it off.

● Salt is abrasive. Reach for the saltshaker if you have a spill in your oven. With the oven still warm, wet the spill lightly and sprinkle on salt. When the oven cools, scrape away the spill and wash the area clean.

ABRASIVES CAN BE FOUND in supermarkets, home improvement stores, and hardware stores. They include all common scouring powders.

Absorbents

Absorbents do their cleaning by sucking up liquids or gases. They're particularly handy for wet, messy situations such as food spills, oil spills, pet accidents, vomit, and blood. Absorbents include such household products as baking soda, baby powder, cornstarch, kitty litter, and table salt as well as commercial products. Not all absorbent products are granular, pour-on materials, of course. Paper towels and cloths do their mess-fixing magic by absorption, too.

Common absorbents and their uses include these:

PAPER TOWELS are the old standby for removing spills, especially from the floor.

WASHABLE COTTON CLOTHS (old cotton T-shirts and diapers, for example) are also great for spills and are more economical.

MICROFIBER CLEANING CLOTHS, which can absorb several times their own weight, are great for general cleaning.

BAKING SODA, in the box, tucked in a corner of your refrigerator, is a good absorber of food odors. Out of the box, baking soda is good for absorbing grease around a stove or spills in an oven— even for cleaning vomit. Just add soda until the liquid solidifies. Then scrape off.

DON'T OVERLOOK THESE HANDY ABSORBENTS:

● Salt absorbs grease spots on carpet. Immediately pour salt on the grease to absorb it and prevent staining. Vacuum off.

● Kitty litter works well on outdoor oil spills. In addition, it can be used to solidify very small quantities of paint and other liquids.

● Sand or soil also works well for oil spills outside or in a garage.

COMMERCIAL GRANULAR ABSORBENT PRODUCTS, such as Super-Sorb, D-Vour, and ZGoop, are the favorite solution of school janitors when breakfast or lunch fails to stay in a student's tummy.

ABSORBENT PRODUCTS ARE AVAILABLE at supermarkets, home improvement stores, drugstores, and janitorial supply outlets.

Acidic Cleaners

Acid is the opposite of alkali (or basic) on the pH scale,

NOTE: For laundry products, see Chapter 5, Laundry—Loads of Advice, p.26.

with 0 indicating extreme acidity, 7 neutrality, and 14 extreme alkalinity. Each point that you move away from neutral pH 7 is ten times more alkaline or acidic. So you don't need to go far from pH 7 to get a strong cleaner. Some common acids include lemon juice (citric acid), vinegar (acetic acid), hydrochloric acid, and phosphoric acid.

COMMON USES FOR ACIDIC CLEANERS include removing rust stains, mineral deposits, stains on concrete, and stains on grout, as well as unclogging pipes. Read product labels and use extreme caution when using acidic cleaners. Otherwise, you risk damaging finishes and injuring yourself. A rundown of acidic cleaners at various pH levels follows:

HYDROCHLORIC ACID (pH 0) is the strongest acid and is used in extreme cases of hard-water deposits, lime, and rust, most often in the toilet bowl. A cleaner with 9 percent hydrochloric acid has a significant amount of acid in it and could etch surfaces and burn skin. Wear gloves and eye protection and follow directions. If the label says the product merely "contains" hydrochloric acid, it's likely to be fairly diluted and mild.

PHOSPHORIC ACID (pH 2 to 4) is milder than hydrochloric and can be used on bathtubs, sinks, and tile to dissolve mineral deposits, rust stains, and mildew. Cleaning agents with phosphoric acid are fairly gentle on metal trims of shower doors and on faucets if you rinse thoroughly after cleaning. Be aware that phosphoric acid doesn't really "clean." It etches surfaces, and if you use it too

frequently, you could dissolve the grout around your tile.

VINEGAR AND CITRIC ACID (pH 2 to 4) and other acids in this category work well for frequent cleaning. They're commonly used on glassware, coffeepots, and other common kitchen items.

For washing clothes, add 1 cup of white vinegar to the final rinse to eliminate soap residue. Vinegar breaks down uric acid, so it's especially good for babies' clothes. To get wool and cotton blankets fluffy, add 2 cups of white vinegar to the rinse.

Lemon juice is a good acid for removing stains in clothing, such as berry stains. It acts like bleach, which also makes it good for cleaning cutting boards and countertops. To remove a stain on a counter, squeeze on fresh lemon juice, let it sit for 45 minutes, sprinkle on baking soda, and rub with a sponge or soft cloth. Then rinse out the sponge or cloth and wipe again.

TAKE PRECAUTIONS when using acidic cleaners:

● Don't use vinegar if you add chlorine bleach to your rinse water. The mixture will produce harmful vapors.

● Don't use vinegar on wooden floors.

● Don't let acidic cleaners sit too long on metal fixtures, or they'll damage the chrome.

● Don't use acid on stone (including granite and marble) or concrete—both materials are alkaline and will dissolve with acid.

BUY ACIDIC CLEANERS at local supermarkets, home improvement stores, and janitorial supply outlets.

Air Cleaners

The air in a home can be improved in a number of ways, but all approaches to doing it fall into these two broad categories:

● Chemical products that attack the sources of odors or mask odors

● Air-cleaning devices and filters that pull irritants out of the air

DISINFECTING CLEANERS don't clean the air directly, but they do eliminate the source of odors. To destroy mold or bacteria that generate a bad odor, just spray the surface where the offending microbes are growing with a traditional disinfecting cleaner such as Lysol. New sprays that have recently hit the market (Oust, for instance) claim to kill odor-causing bacteria actually in the air and to neutralize other malodorous particles.

AIR FRESHENERS don't really eliminate odors—they just cover up the smell. They come in spray and time-release forms.

A spray, such as Glade, can mask an unpleasant odor by simply using it in the area with the offending odor. A time-release air freshener—a wick, solid cake, or saturated wood block—has a longer freshening effect. Air fresheners of either kind are commonly used in restrooms and kitchens.

THE FURNACE FILTER that's part of the typical forced-air heating and cooling system does the crucial job of removing irritants from the air in your home. Everyday filters should be changed once a month during prime heating and cooling seasons. These disposable filters, which cost $2 to $3, remove less than 10 percent of the particles in the air. If you upgrade, a medium-efficiency filter for your forced-air system will run you $5 to $20 and will snag 20 to 50 percent of the particles in the air.

A STAND-ALONE AIR-FILTERING APPLIANCE should be considered for heavy-duty air cleaning. Such units filter air in a variety of ways, but for all-around removal of airborne particles, high-efficiency particulate air (HEPA) filters are a great choice, particularly for people with allergies. They trap particles in fine, disposable filters and are rated at 60 to 95 percent efficiency. Electrostatic precipitators also do a good job of trapping particles, and their filters are reusable. A good room unit air filter costs from $170 to $500. Whole-house air-filtering units are available for about $500, plus installation.

BUY CHEMICAL AIR FRESHENERS at supermarkets, discount stores, drugstores, and home improvement stores. Air-filtering systems are available at department stores, home improvement stores, hardware stores, discount stores, allergy supply stores, drugstores, and medical supply companies.

Alcohol

Alcohol is an effective solvent for cleaning and eliminating stains, and it kills germs, too. Lysol disinfectant spray, for instance, is 79 percent ethyl alcohol.

ALCOHOL COMES IN SEVERAL FORMS. Alcohol is an organic compound consisting of hydrocarbons. It's a colorless liquid, has a mild odor, and is highly flammable. Common

forms are isopropyl alcohol (often called rubbing alcohol, used for massages, as an antiseptic, and as a cleaning solvent) and ethyl alcohol, or ethanol (the stuff in alcoholic drinks and a common ingredient in cleaning products, mouthwash, and hairsprays). Denatured alcohol is ethanol that contains a small amount of poisonous methanol, or wood alcohol, making it unfit for consumption. It's commonly used to thin or remove paint and varnish, and to remove greasy smudges from surfaces.

USE ALCOHOL-BASED CLEANERS when you need a solvent that evaporates quickly. They are especially suited to cleaning glass because they clean and quickly vanish without leaving streaks. They are also useful for cleaning telephones and the keyboards of computers, calculators, and such. Apply alcohol to electronic items with a cotton swab.

Alcohol is also a handy solvent for eliminating oil-based stains in carpeting and upholstery, for removing hair spray from mirrors, and for dissolving ink, lipstick, crayon, and other stains.

BE CAREFUL with alcohol on some finishes. Alcohol can soften plastic and paint, so don't let alcohol-based cleaners remain on such surfaces for too long.

A WORD OF WARNING: Denatured alcohol is undrinkable. Rubbing alcohol is toxic, too. Drinking even an ounce or two of these alcohols can blind you, put you in a coma, or even kill you. Keep this stuff out of the reach of children.

WHERE YOU BUY ALCOHOL CLEANING PRODUCTS depends on what type they are. Alcohol-based cleaners and disinfectants are available in grocery stores, janitorial supply stores, home improvement stores, discount stores, and drugstores. Isopropyl alcohol is available in drugstores. Denatured alcohol can be found on the paint thinner shelf in hardware and home improvement stores.

Alkali Cleaners

Alkali cleaners are at the opposite end of the pH scale from acidic cleaners. (See pages 412–413.) Any cleaner above pH 7 (neutral) is considered an alkali. Most multipurpose cleaners have an alkali base because alkali cleaners neutralize acid, and most spills and stains are acidic.

COMMON USES FOR ALKALI CLEANERS include degreasing and removing heavy soil. They're also good for washing windows and dealing with coffee and tea stains. Alkali cleaners include dishwashing liquid, mild detergents such as Woolite, all-purpose cleaners such as Formula 409 and Fantastik, and glass cleaners such as Windex. The more aggressive degreasers, oven cleaners, lye drain openers, and wax strippers are also alkali-based products.

Here's a rundown of various alkali cleaners. The higher the pH number, the more caustic the cleaner is:

THE MILDEST ALKALI CLEANERS (pH 8 and pH 9) include dishwashing liquid and baking soda, the Swiss Army knife of the cleaning world. In a solution with water (2 tablespoons of baking soda per 1 quart of warm water), baking soda cleans hard surfaces such as glass, tile, porcelain, stainless steel, chrome, and fiberglass. For heavier soil, sprinkle baking soda on a damp sponge and rub.

MODERATE ALKALIS (pH 9 to pH 11) include all-purpose degreasers, such as Formula 409; borax (which boosts the cleaning power of laundry detergent); trisodium phosphate (for cleaning painted surfaces, porcelain, and tile); ammonia (a general cleaner, grease cutter, and wax stripper); soaps; scouring powders; and window cleaners.

THE STRONGEST ALKALIS (pH 12 to pH 14) include lye (used in drain openers and oven cleaners), garage floor degreasers, carpet shampoos, and washing soda (for extra cleaning power in the laundry room).

SOME CAUTIONARY NOTES about alkali cleaners:

- Strong alkalis can damage skin and fabrics. They also corrode and darken aluminum. Wear hand and eye protection when handling the stronger alkalis.
- Most alkalis, except baking soda, are toxic if swallowed.
- To remove an alkali residue from a surface you have cleaned, rinse with a solution of 2 tablespoons of vinegar in a quart of water. Then wipe dry.

ALKALI CLEANERS CAN BE FOUND in grocery stores, janitorial supply stores, cleaning supply stores, home improvement stores, and drugstores.

All-Purpose Cleaners

All-purpose cleaners are just what their name implies—they do a wide variety of cleaning jobs. Most of them are moderately alkaline, meaning they're superb grease cutters.

THE BIG ADVANTAGE OF ALL-PURPOSE CLEANERS is that you don't have to keep a lot of specialty cleaners around the house. Don't assume, however, that your all-purpose cleaner disinfects. Check the label if you're hoping to give some germs a hard time.

YOU CAN USE ALL-PURPOSE CLEANERS safely on most surfaces and fabrics—counters, cabinets, walls, floors, and patio furniture. They will even remove fingerprints. It's best to test an all-purpose cleaner on an inconspicuous part of the item you're cleaning before you squirt it over the entire object. Because many all-purpose cleaners have a relatively high pH, they may cause colors to run. They can also damage wood.

CITRUS-BASED CLEANERS, such as Fantastik Orange Action and Formula 409 Orange Power, are increasing in popularity. Use them on clothes, carpets, grout, shower curtains, trash cans, decks, toilets, the kitchen, and stains. They will remove gum, tar, and grease. And they smell nice.

ALL-PURPOSE CLEANERS CAN BE BOUGHT almost anywhere—supermarkets, home improvement stores, janitorial supply stores, drugstores, discount stores. They're more economical if you buy them in concentrate form, because you're not paying for the water.

Ammonia

Ammonia is made up of nitrogen and hydrogen—yup, it's a gas, one that's suspended in water. Ammonia is an alkali booster (by itself, it's not a cleaner) that helps detergents with degreasing, stripping wax, and removing soil.

MANY COMMON CLEANERS use solutions that are 5 to 7 percent ammonia. If you have a container of household ammonia, it's actually mostly water, and the ammonia content is 5 to 10 percent. Sudsy ammonia has a detergent added.

SUDSY AMMONIA works well on stove rings, boiler pans, floors, ceramic tiles, and stainless steel. A bowl of ammonia left in the oven overnight will loosen burned-on grease and grime—just wipe it off in the morning. Ammonia is also a star ingredient in commercial window cleaners.

TAKE EXTRA CARE when working with ammonia:

- Keep the area well ventilated. Evaporating ammonia fumes will curl your toes—if it doesn't make you sick.
- Never mix ammonia with chlorine bleach, which creates poisonous chlorine gas.
- Ammonia can darken aluminum and discolor some fabrics, so proceed carefully.

Ammonia can be bought at grocery stores, home improvement stores, janitorial supply stores, drugstores, and discount stores.

Baking Soda

It can't sing and dance, but this venerable white powder is still the most versatile substance around. Baking soda is known by various names, including sodium bicarbonate, bicarbonate of soda, and—for those of you who stayed awake during chemistry class—$NaHCO_3$. These nontoxic crystals act as a chemical cleaner, double as a scouring powder, neutralize odors, keep your drains clog-free, and are handy for putting out grease or electrical fires. (Sprinkle it on dry.) Oh, yeah—baking soda has a starring role in baking, too.

THE CLEANING USES OF BAKING SODA are myriad. Entire books have been written about them. Here's just a sampling:

- For regular cleaning on hard surfaces, pour a little baking soda on a damp sponge or cleaning cloth and wipe. Follow up with another clean, damp sponge or cloth.

- To remove surface stains in the kitchen or bath, pour out enough baking soda to cover the stain and add just enough water to make a paste. Let the paste stay on the stain for several minutes, then scrub with a sponge and wipe it away.

- To help remove oil and grease stains from clothing, add 1/2 cup of baking soda to the wash.

- To keep your kitchen sink clog-free, pour 1/2 cup of baking soda down the drain each night, followed by warm water. Do the same thing for other drains in your house once a week.

THE ODOR-KILLING POWERS OF BAKING SODA are equally famous. There's a good chance you have an open box in the back of your refrigerator right now. Here are a few more dry applications:

- Sprinkle baking soda on carpeting, rugs, and even car mats. Let it stand for 15 minutes and then vacuum.

- When you're changing the cat litter, sprinkle some in the bottom of the cat box and then a little on top of the new litter (unless your cat litter already includes baking soda).

- Pour baking soda into ashtrays to control the stench of tamped-out butts.

BAKING SODA ALSO SOPS UP ODORS when it's dissolved in water. Pour 4 tablespoons of baking soda into 1 quart of warm water. Use the solution to:

- Rinse your mouth to get rid of garlic breath.

- Deodorize a stinky plastic container. Fill it with the solution and let it sit overnight.

- Soak a diaper that smells like ammonia because of urine.

BAKING SODA IS READILY AVAILABLE at supermarkets and discount retailers.

Bathroom Cleaners

Bathroom cleaners are designed to eliminate soap scum and mildew on tubs, tiles, showers, and grout. It's a good idea to use bathroom cleaners that disinfect—that is, kill germs. Not all bathroom cleaners are disinfectants, so be sure to check the label. In general, these are tough cleaners for a tough job, so wearing rubber gloves is usually a good idea.

ALL-PURPOSE CLEANERS, such as Lysol Basin, Tub & Tile Cleaner, are the best choice for cleaning the whole bathroom. Look for a product that will attack germs and soap scum at the same time.

ACIDIC BATHROOM CLEANERS, such as Lime-A-Way, handle everyday cases of soap scum

nicely. Soft Scrub also works, but it is slightly abrasive and could scratch surfaces, especially stainless steel. First just try white vinegar mixed in equal parts with water. If you need to pull out the big guns, pick up phosphoric acid in a 20 percent concentration at a janitorial supply store. For the worst cases of buildup, use it full strength. Otherwise, dilute it to 2 parts water and 1 part phosphoric acid. Apply the solution with a damp sponge or cloth and rinse thoroughly.

COMMERCIAL BOWL CLEANING PRODUCTS, such as Lysol Disinfectant Toilet Bowl Cleaner, are numerous and widely available. But you may not even need a special cleaner, because baking soda or nonchlorine scouring powder will often do the job. Put the baking soda or cleaner on a sponge or on the surface you want to clean, scrub, and rinse. To remove stains from toilet bowls, pour in 1/4 cup of borax and let it sit for at least 30 minutes—overnight is better. Scrub the bowl well and flush.

BATHROOM CLEANERS CAN BE PURCHASED almost anywhere: supermarkets, home improvement stores, discount retailers, and janitorial supply stores.

Brooms

Yes, vacuum cleaners swept into homes in recent decades and wrested away many of the cleaning duties once performed by brooms. But there are still plenty of times when a broom will do a superior job. Besides, they're easier to haul out than a vacuum cleaner and, of course, they don't require electricity.

BROOMS COME in two basic styles:
- Push brooms, with a head measuring 18 to 48 inches wide. These are good for sweeping garages, patios, sidewalks, and such.
- Traditional household kitchen brooms, with the narrower head. These are better for interior use on hard floors.

WHAT A BROOM IS MADE OF is important. While most brooms today have synthetic bristles, there are still plenty available with natural bristles, including corn, straw, horsehair, and hog hair. Flagged bristles are split at the ends to make the bristles thinner and better able to pick up dirt. Nonflagged bristles are thicker and better for sweeping up larger refuse (pebbles and such). Some brooms have both types of bristles—flagged bristles on the outside and nonflagged bristles on the inner row. These brooms can tackle pebbles and fine dust at the same time. For interior use, softer nylon bristles are a good bet, because they won't scratch the floor.

IF YOU STORE YOUR BROOM by standing it on its bristles, the bristles may curl, giving you less-than-perfect sweeping or brushing action. Therefore, it's better to hang up your broom. Many models come with a loop on the handle for just this purpose. If necessary, drill a hole in the handle and make a loop for it, or use the hole to hang the broom on a nail. There are also broom and mop holders you can attach to a wall.

THE BEST PLACE TO PURCHASE A BROOM is in a janitorial supply store, which usually carries a large selection. Supermarkets, hardware stores, discount

stores, and home improvement stores also carry brooms.

Brushes

There's a special brush out there for just about anything you'd ever want to give the brush-off—everything from dirt to mildew, barbecue grime to counter crumbs. They can be used dry (to remove surface dirt from irregularly shaped objects) or wet (to work in conjunction with cleaners).

Make sure the brush you're using won't damage the object you're trying to clean. Brush bristles can be made of soft hair, synthetics, natural fibers, or metal (often stainless steel or brass).

Brushes fall into the following main categories:

KITCHEN BRUSHES include these:
- Oven brushes for cleaning the racks and the sides of the oven. (Best on stainless steel ovens; painted enamel and chrome ovens will scratch.)
- Scouring brushes for use on pots and pans
- Scrub brushes for use on floors and grout
- Counter brushes, which originally were used in stores to sweep crumbs from the counter. Now they're typically sold as a set with a dustpan.
- Bottle brushes, for scrubbing inside tight spaces

FLOOR BRUSHES include these:
- Handheld brushes that have stiff bristles
- Deck brushes (similar to the handheld brushes, but with poles in them)
- Carpet-spotting brushes (pole-mounted brushes for removing spots on carpets)

SPECIALTY BRUSHES include:
- Automotive brushes
- Tile brushes, which are small-headed brushes with fine bristles for cleaning tile and grout
- Window brushes
- Wire brushes for tough jobs, such as cleaning barbecue grills
- Radiator brushes, for getting into narrow spaces
- Vacuum cleaner brush attachments, for a gentle touch when you're suctioning up dirt
- Paintbrushes, which can be adapted to cleaning purposes. For instance, they're great for dusting between the pleats of a lamp shade

PERSONAL HYGIENE AND GROOMING BRUSHES include:
- Old, used toothbrushes and nail brushes that you've recruited for other purposes—cleaning around faucets, for instance
- Whisk brushes used for removing lint, dirt, and dust from clothing

BRUSHES CAN BE BOUGHT from supermarkets, hardware stores, home improvement stores, and discount retailers.

Buckets

You've known what a bucket was ever since you were introduced to those water-haulers Jack and Jill. But are you sure you know how to use one?

THE PROBLEM WITH BUCKETS is that they can redistribute dirt and germs on the floor that you're trying to clean. For example, let's say you're mopping the bathroom. You mop up the grunge, and when you put the mop back into the bucket, the dirt and germs get spread throughout the water. Then you mop another section of the floor, spreading that nasty stuff all around.

THE SOLUTION is to purchase a bucket with two chambers for holding liquid, plus a wringer for squeezing your mop. Rinse water goes in one side of the bucket, and cleaning solution in the other. After the first round of mopping, place the mop in the rinse water and then squeeze it through the wringer to remove the dirt. Then dip the mop back into the cleaning solution and mop some more.

TWO-COMPARTMENT BUCKETS typically come on rollers, which help if you hate all that lifting (a gallon of water weighs 8 pounds, you know). When purchasing a bucket, make sure it's wide enough for your mop to fit inside, and get one with measurement marks on the inside so you can tell how much water you've poured in.

YOU CAN BUY BUCKETS at supermarkets and discount retailers, but for one with two compartments you may have to visit a home improvement store or a janitorial supply store.

Caddies

When it's time to clean, you don't want to waste time tracking down supplies. A sturdy cleaning caddy will hold and organize your cleaning products and cloths, and as is spelled out in Chapter 6 of Part One, it is an essential part of an organized cleaning system. For tips on what supplies to put in your caddy, see page 44.

THE DESIGN OF A CADDY IS SOME-THING that you need to pay attention to. Look for one with dividers, so you can separate smaller items from large ones. The individual slots also enable you to separate items you use less frequently, so they will be less likely to fall out when you reach for the most-used cleaners. Caddies with higher side walls also prevent your cleaners from going AWOL.

Make sure your caddy has a handle mounted in the center, and arrange your products so the caddy is well balanced. Spend an extra dollar or two on a caddy with a rubber-coated handle, which is easier to tote when fully loaded.

THE MATERIAL A CADDY IS MADE FROM is also important. Avoid wooden caddies, since wet wood will warp and is an excellent breeding ground for mildew. Rubber, vinyl-coated wire, or plastic caddies are better alternatives, but avoid cheap, flimsy plastic that will crack.

CADDIES CAN BE BOUGHT at home improvement stores, larger supermarkets, and discount retailers.

Carpet Deep-Cleaners

Not too long ago, buying your own deep-cleaning carpet machine was an iffy proposition. It was easy to overwet your carpet with them, running a risk of encouraging mildew, and some models didn't heat the water well enough to do a good cleaning job. Some new models have overcome those problems, but you still would be wise to weigh the alternatives before deciding to park another vacuum-cleaner-sized appliance in your closet.

A PROFESSIONAL CLEANER is still likely to do a better job of cleaning your carpet than you can do by yourself with a home unit. Then again, you could pay for a home unit with the money you'd shell out to a pro for just a visit or two.

RENTING A DEEP-CLEANING UNIT is economical (about $20 a day), but hauling the gear from the store to your house and back again is a hassle, and it's hard to know what condition your rental unit will be in.

IF YOU DECIDE TO BUY A UNIT, you can expect to pay $250 to $350 for a full-sized rig. The higher-end home machines include such features as dials that automatically adjust the amount of cleaner dispensed based on whether you're cleaning a low- or high-traffic area; an on-board heater that gets the water about 25 degrees hotter than your hot tap water; a self-propelled feature (if you have a self-propelled lawn mower or vacuum cleaner, you'll appreciate this); and a powered hand tool attachment made especially for cleaning small spaces such as stairwells and around toilets.

DEEP CLEANERS WORK by forcing a heated cleaning mixture into the carpet, then sucking about 90 percent of the liquid back out—and with it grime and embedded dirt. (They are sometimes called steam cleaners, but they actually use hot water, not steam.) Even the best vacuum cleaners can't reach the dirt at the base of a carpet, so periodic deep cleaning is important. Every 6 to 18 months ought to do it. Most deep cleaners are now upright models instead of those squat canisters with a hose.

CONSIDER STORAGE AND MANEU-VERABILITY when shopping for a deep cleaner. The units can weigh up to 23 pounds and have nozzle widths up to 14 inches for full-sized models.

DRYING TIME varies from about four to six hours, depending on the thickness of the carpet and pad.

CARPET DEEP-CLEANERS ARE AVAILABLE at discount retailers, department stores, and home improvement stores.

Car Polishes

There's a big difference between polishing a car and waxing one. Polishing adds brilliance. Wax provides protection. And if you polish your car at least once a month, you'll probably eliminate the need to wax.

BEFORE YOU POLISH, though, the car must be clean, or you'll rub tiny particles of dirt into the finish and create noticeable scratches. Clean the exterior with car wash solution rather than dishwashing detergent—detergents draw oil out of the car's paint, which accelerates oxidation and makes the paint look cloudy.

After the car is clean and free of bonded contaminants like tree sap and bug residue, it's time to polish. The role of polish is to condition and nourish the paint and give it a deep, wet-look shine.

Done properly, polishing adds brilliance and makes a car as smooth as glass before you wax. The paint is rejuvenated, and unlike the wax buildup you can get from overwaxing, polishing only improves the paint finish with each use.

THE KEY TO PROPER POLISHING is using clean cloths. Have several cloths (100 percent cotton or microfiber) on hand and constantly rotate the area of cloth you use so you're not pushing the residue you've already removed right back into the paint. When there are no more totally unused areas on the cloth, switch to a clean one.

Another benefit of polish is that if you've just had your car painted and you have been instructed not to wax it for three months, you can still polish, since polish doesn't inhibit the curing process.

SPRAY-ON POLISHES are the easiest to apply, but there are trade-offs: They aren't as good at rejuvenating an oxidized finish, and their shine does not tend to last as long.

LIQUID AND PASTE POLISHES require more elbow grease, but the effect is more durable. And a warning: If the label of a polish tells you to keep the product away from the rubber and plastic trim on your car, take heed. Such polishes will leave permanent, unsightly streaks on the trim.

CAR POLISHES ARE WIDELY AVAILABLE, but you'll find the best selection at automotive stores. Even high-end polishes made by industry leaders such as Meguiar's and Mothers are relatively inexpensive—$5 to $6 for a 16-ounce bottle.

Cleaning Cloths

Cleaning cloths were once a simple proposition: Pull out some clean, 100 percent cotton rags and get to work. But newer products are augmenting the traditional standby, and they

score considerable points for effectiveness and ease of use.

MICROFIBER CLOTHS are taking off in the cleaning world, due to interwoven fibers that are ten times finer than silk. They grab and trap dust and pull it off the surface you're cleaning, without scratching. They're all the rage for cleaning computers, CDs, and TV screens—any surface that's especially vulnerable to scratching.

USE MICROFIBER CLOTHS for dusting and polishing household surfaces, or you can combine them with cleansers, polishes, or water for an unlimited number of household tasks. Because they absorb several times their weight in fluids, they're particularly adept at streak-free cleaning.

CLEANING MICROFIBER CLOTHS is easy, too. Shake them out when they're filled with dry dust and machine-wash them when they look especially dirty. Also available in mitts, the cloths can be used and washed up to 500 times (lasting about two years under normal use) before losing effectiveness. When washing microfiber cloths, though, avoid using fabric softener or bleach, including softener sheets in the dryer. Also avoid drying them with towels, since lint from the towels will stick to the microfibers. Some microfibers are treated with cleaning solutions and should not be washed, such as microfiber jewelry cleaning cloths that remove tarnish and polish precious metals.

COTTON CLOTHS still make great cleaning aids. Old T-shirts are a top choice. Old socks are also handy, because you can wear them like mittens and just use your hands to dust. If you don't want to give up your cotton cloths, just make sure you wash them between uses.

YOU CAN BUY MICROFIBER CLOTHS in home improvement stores and automotive stores. They are more expensive and less widely available than cotton cloths. They cost about $6 for a 15 in. x 15 in. square—but compared to one-use disposable wipes, they're downright economical.

Dishwashers

When shopping for a dishwasher, the first order of business is finding a model that cleans thoroughly and fits your budget. And since the whole point of a dishwasher is to ease the burden of manual washing, it makes sense to find a model that doesn't require a lot of rinsing of dishes before you load them in.

WATER AND ENERGY USE are major considerations when you shop for a dishwasher. Look for features that will reduce water use, such as booster heaters and smart controls. Ask the sales staff how many gallons of water the dishwasher uses during different cycles. Dishwashers that use the least amount of water will cost the least to operate.

With rising water and energy costs, consumers should also consider the dishwasher's energy factor (EF). The EF number represents the number of complete cycles that a dishwasher will run through while using one kilowatt-hour of electricity. It is part of the Energy Star program, which was created by the U.S.

Department of Energy and the U.S. Environmental Protection Agency to help shoppers identify the most energy-efficient appliances. Products that carry the government's Energy Star rating are the most efficient of all, typically exceeding federal efficiency standards by 13 percent to 20 percent.

THE COST OF A DISHWASHER varies enormously, from about $300 for a basic unit to $1,700 or more for a sleek, deluxe model that makes no more noise than a pot of boiling water and has adjustable heat settings that can handle everything from fine crystal to the grungiest pots and pans.

CHECK A MACHINE'S NOISE LEVEL. Today's open architecture, in which kitchens are connected to dens and entertainment areas, increase the importance of finding a model that isn't noisy. Ask the sales rep to explain the decibel level of the unit you're considering. High-end models have a decibel level in the low 40s (about as loud as quiet conversation), while less expensive units are in the middle to high 50s (comparable to the noise in an average office).

WHAT ELSE DO YOU GET WITH A HIGH-END MODEL? One of the Cadillacs of dishwashers is made by Miele Inc., a German company founded in 1900, with prices ranging from $800 to $1,700. Each model features three spray arms, which provide more thorough cleaning compared to the one spray arm in lower-end dishwashers. Miele also doesn't have an exposed heating element. This internal heating, as it's called, is more energy efficient and adds to the appliance's longevity

(20 years compared to 8 to 10 years for lower cost units). Internal heating provides a greater range of heating temperatures, from a low of about 115° F for china and crystal to 170° F for pots and pans. The internal heating feature also prevents the melting of plastic parts that fall to the bottom of the dishwasher.

Design and craftsmanship are other considerations. You'll pay more for a stainless steel model with a cutting edge design and the latest technology.

DISHWASHERS ARE SOLD at appliance stores, home improvement stores, discount merchandisers, and some department stores.

Dishwashing Detergents

You have two choices when it's time to do the dishes: Load them into the dishwasher or wash them by hand.

Let's look first at the easier method. Newer dishwasher models (those manufactured in the last five years) tend to work fine even if you don't rinse the food off first. And rinsing agents can eliminate the water spots and film that used to make it necessary to rewash some glasses by hand before using.

Automatic dishwashing detergents come in three forms: powdered, gel, and tablet. All of them are effective, so let personal preference be your guide.

POWDERED FORMULAS have been around the longest and are still generally the least expensive to use. The newer products—gels and tablets—offer some added benefits in certain situations, though. Powders can turn to grit if your dishwater doesn't get hot enough (140° F) to dissolve all the powder.

DISHWASHING GELS dissolve more quickly than powders or tablets and so begin cleaning dishes faster. Gels are also a good choice if you live in a humid climate, where powders have a tendency to cake.

TABLETS offer the convenience of eliminating the need to measure, since each tablet is formulated to clean one load.

RINSE PRODUCTS prevent spotting and filming by lowering the surface tension of the water, causing it to sheet off dishes. They also enable dishes to dry faster when left to air-dry or when you use the energy-saving function on your dishwasher. Rinse agents come in liquid and solid forms. Liquids may be used only in dishwashers with a built-in rinse reservoir. Solid forms are made to attach to the upper dishwasher rack, where they dissolve slowly during the various cycles.

TWO OTHER SPECIALTY PRODUCTS can be helpful in getting the most from your dishwasher.

- Cleaning boosters for plastic, such as Cascade Plastic Booster, remove tough stains from plastic ware.
- Film removers are powdered alkaline products containing chlorine. They remove hard-water film and cloudiness on dishes and can be combined with dishwasher detergent.

In general, though, if you have a good dishwasher, soft water, and water that heats to at least 140° F, just about any automatic dishwashing detergent will get the job done. In that case, use the least expensive product.

HAND DISHWASHING PRODUCTS are among the gentlest detergents available and can also be used to wash everything from delicate clothing to the family dog. Dishwashing liquids work by loosening grime and suspending it until it can be rinsed away. When the suds disappear, so does the cleaning action, so you'll need to add more detergent. If you buy a cheap brand that gives out quickly, you'll just have to use more—and then it's not really a bargain.

DISHWASHING LIQUID INNOVATIONS include hand care ingredients such as vitamin E, aloe vera, and aromatherapy-inspired scents added to the liquid. There's also an alternative to soaking your dishes in the sink to loosen dried-on food: You can spray a dishwashing pretreatment, such as Dawn Power Dissolver, on food stains and leave the dishes on the counter until you clean (after about 15 minutes).

NEVER USE HAND DISHWASHING LIQUID in your dishwasher, because the suds and foam it produces can inhibit the cleaning process in the machine. Always use automatic dishwashing detergents, which are specially formulated for dishwashers and produce little or no suds.

DISHWASHING DETERGENTS ARE AVAILABLE at supermarkets and discount retailers.

Disinfectants

Disinfectants are designed to kill germs on surfaces, including bacteria and viruses that spoil food, create unpleasant odors, and cause illness. Some products clean as they disinfect, so read the label if you're looking for a dual-purpose disinfectant. A product that does both will tout that benefit.

DISINFECTANTS CONTAIN microbe killers, which show up on the label as pine oil, quaternary ammonium compounds, or phenols. Disinfecting cleaners also contain surfactants (surface-active agents) to remove soils.

WHEN CHOOSING A DISINFECTANT, checking the label is especially important. Depending on the formulation and active ingredients, disinfectants may be designed to kill:

- Bacteria that cause intestinal illnesses, such as *E. coli* and salmonella
- Staphylococcus, kinds of bacteria that cause skin infections
- Fungi that cause athlete's foot
- Viruses, such as rhinovirus, which is the primary cause of the common cold.

The Environmental Protection Agency requires that products labeled as disinfectants meet established guidelines. The products must be registered with the EPA and have an EPA registration number on the label.

FOR DISINFECTANTS TO WORK, follow the package directions to the letter. That usually means letting the disinfectant sit on the soiled surface for at least ten minutes to kill bacteria. Many people use diluted household chlorine bleach as a disinfectant and stain remover. Make sure you follow label directions and dilute accordingly.

The Soap and Detergent Association, in Washington, D.C., recommends daily cleaning and disinfecting of areas where you prepare food. Moist surfaces such as sinks and toilets are also germ breeding grounds and should be cleaned daily if someone in the family is sick or especially vulnerable to infection.

BE CAREFUL NOT TO REINFECT AN AREA you've just cleaned by using a dirty cloth or sponge. If you clean a surface with disinfectant but then wipe with a contaminated cloth, you're simply redepositing germs on the clean surface. Some people prefer using paper towels after disinfecting, since you throw away the contaminants. Paper towels are a more expensive way to clean, though. Cloths and sponges work as well, if not better, as long as you launder them with chlorine bleach and let them dry thoroughly between uses.

DISINFECTANTS ARE AVAILABLE from such sources as supermarkets, home improvement stores, and discount stores.

Disposable Wipes

Disposable wipes have taken the cleaning world by storm in the last several years, generating the most growth in the household cleaning marketplace. American consumers spent $872 million on the products in 2002, according to Packages Facts, a consulting company.

THE APPEAL OF DISPOSABLE WIPES is understandable. In terms of convenience, it's hard to beat a pretreated product that you toss after a single use. The popularity of wipes is driven by what's known as the three E's of consumer product value—they're effective, efficient, and expedient.

SOME OF THE LATEST WIPE PRODUCTS include these:

● Disposable cloths treated with dishwashing liquid—you simply add water for a sudsy cleaning cloth.
● Heat-activated microwave wipes to clean baked-on foods from a microwave's interior.
● Specialty wipes for disinfecting surfaces such as toilets, sinks, and countertops. (In such cases, disposing of germs along with the cleaning cloth is an especially attractive feature.)
● Furniture wipes to clean and shine wood.
● Both dry and premoistened floor wipes, which are attached to floor sweepers and specially designed mops.

DRY DISPOSABLE WIPES rely on an electrostatic charge to attract dust. Disposable mitts, also electrostatically charged, make quick work of dusting surfaces like wood, ceramic, and vinyl. The dust sticks to the mitt instead of becoming airborne.

DISPOSABLE WIPES ARE WIDELY AVAILABLE from such sources as supermarkets, home improvement stores, and discount stores. Obviously, it's more expensive to use a disposable wipe that lasts for only one use. But if you're a convenience-driven consumer, you'll pay the price.

Drain Cleaners

Drain cleaners come in four varieties—acids, alkalis, oxidizers, and enzymatics—and their job is to get rid of blockages in drains, most commonly in kitchens and bathrooms.

Compared to mechanical drain cleaners, chemical and enzymatic cleaners are easy to use, but chemical cleaners also have the potential to harm the user if instructions aren't followed exactly. Enzymatic cleaners have a slower, biological reaction and therefore are more benign.

ACIDS AND ALKALIS are the most popular of the drain cleaners for removing blockages of hair, grease, soap, and other wastes. Some of these drain cleaners, particularly the faster-acting ones, cause bubbling that can splash harmful chemicals back out of the drain. So stand back once you've poured the drain opener in. Never use muriatic acid (a dilute form of hydrochloric acid) to clear drain blocks. It's highly dangerous.

OXIDIZERS are effective on organic blockages. These chemicals react with and combine with the blocking material, breaking it up and disintegrating it (rather than dissolving it).

The majority of commercial cleaners, such as Red Devil, Liquid-Plumr, and Drano, are a combination of caustic (alkaline) and oxidizing components, meaning the cleaners work in two ways.

ENZYMATIC DRAIN CLEANERS are slower-acting as they consume or digest waste blockages, but they're easier on your pipes than acids, caustics, and oxidizers (which is more of a concern with old plumbing). They're also thought to do less harm to septic systems.

PREVENT DRAIN CLOG UPS in your kitchen sink with this once-a-month treatment using household products: Pour 1 cup of baking soda around the kitchen sink drain opening. Rinse the baking soda into the drain with 1 cup of hydrogen peroxide. The bubbling and fizzing action helps to clear away the residue clinging to your pipes.

DRAIN CLEANERS CAN BE PURCHASED at a variety of stores-supermarkets, discount stores, hardware stores, home improvement stores, and plumbing supply stores.

Dusters

Feather dusters and lamb's wool dusters have taken a backseat these days to microfiber dusters, which can get into cracks and crevices, attracting soil and speeding your dusting chores.

MICROFIBER DUSTERS are the cutting edge in technology. Their interwoven fibers are ten times finer than silk, making them good at snagging dust without scratching. For dusting, washing, or spot cleaning, microfiber dusters are easy to use and their heads can be removed and tossed in the washing machine when you're done. (Don't use bleach or fabric softener on them.)

FEATHER DUSTERS, on the other hand, may still have their place in your broom closet. While feather dusters have a reputation of just spreading dust around the room, they are great for dusting in hard-to-reach areas, such as inside a lamp, in the pleats of a lamp shade, and in the corners of ceilings where cobwebs collect. Feather dusters blow the dust off the object you're

cleaning, allowing you to then vacuum or wipe the dust up.

LAMB'S WOOL creates a lot of static, which attracts dust. These dusters are typically good on baseboards, ceilings, ceiling fans, and blinds. Lamb's wool is not a good choice for objects that are heavily blanketed with dust.

DUSTERS ARE WIDELY AVAILABLE at home improvement stores, discount retailers, and janitorial supply stores.

Dustpans

The marrying of dustpan and brush is a match that goes back 100 years, and it's still popular. Dustpans are useful little household tools consisting of a flat pan with a tapered edge and a handle. You use a counter brush to sweep dust and debris into the pan.

GET A PLASTIC DUSTPAN. Originally constructed of heavy metal, dustpans came with a brush about 12 inches long with 2- to 3-inch natural bristles. Today's dustpans are usually plastic or rubber vinyl with plastic handles and acrylic brushes. Rubbermaid, for example, makes popular soft plastic dustpans that won't break, so if you drop them no damage is done—to the pan or the floor. If you drop a metal pan, it can scratch your floor's finish, and the pan's edges may bend or curl. Plastic dustpans won't rust, either.

A TIGHT PAN-TO-FLOOR SEAL is important. Dustpans often have a rubber, tapered edge to create a tight seal with the floor so dust won't go underneath the pan when you brush dirt into it. Some other styles

have a plastic edge. Both types work well, but the rubber edge may not last as long as the plastic.

Even with a good pan-to-floor seal, it's doubtful you'll be able to collect all floor dirt with a single sweep. Even if no dirt escapes under the dustpan's edge, the finest dirt often collects in a line along the edge. This is easily remedied by sweeping, moving your dustpan back a couple of inches, and sweeping again.

USE DUSTPANS INDOORS AND OUT, although you might want to have one for each area. You wouldn't want to set a dirty outdoor dustpan down on a clean indoor floor. Dustpans for outdoor use are larger, with pans available in metal and plastic.

YOU CAN BUY DUSTPANS in supermarkets, pharmacies, hardware stores, convenience stores, and home improvement stores. If you prefer to have a dustpan on a long handle, known to janitors as a lobby pan, try a janitorial supply store. Dustpans often come with a brush, but if yours doesn't, make sure the brush you buy is shorter than the width of the dustpan, so you won't be sweeping dust around the sides of the pan instead of into it.

Enzyme Digesters

Enzyme digesters are chemicals, created by microorganisms, that eat away organic matter. So they're effective on organic stains—in other words, such unpleasant things as urine, vomit, fecal matter, protein stains, and the odors associated with them.

USE ENZYMES around the toilet and flooring to keep your bathroom smelling fresh by digesting soil, spills, bodily oils, and bacteria. You'll also find enzymes in drain openers and in carpet, upholstery, and laundry products. Enzymes are safe for septic systems and can also be used in garbage disposal drains. Enzymes are temperature sensitive, so don't use them with hot water. Disinfectants will also render them ineffective. Once you open an enzyme digester, it has a short shelf life.

ENZYME DIGESTERS COME as a powder that you activate with warm water, triggering their eating frenzy on organic matter. If you've ever cleaned spilled milk from a carpet, only to have the odor return days later, you need to use an enzyme product. Most cleaners mask the odor but don't remove the organic source.

WHEN TREATING A CARPET STAIN with an enzyme cleaner, first soak up as much of the stain as possible with old bath towels. (Use a wet vac if there's a lot of volume.) Apply the enzyme according to the package directions. Pour it over the stain and make sure the enzyme penetrates to the padding. If it doesn't, you're wasting your time—the stain and odor will remain. Keep the carpet wet the entire time the enzyme is "eating" the cause of the odor. It's a good idea to cover the area with plastic and place weights on the edges until the recommended time is up. Then rinse with 1/2 cup of distilled white vinegar per 1 gallon of water. Rinse a second time with plain water.

ENZYME DIGESTERS MAKE A GREAT LAUNDRY PRESOAK that eats away at organic stains before you run garments through the wash. Use warm water in the soak, according to the package directions (the exception being blood, which requires cold water). Careful: Enzymes will eat away at animal fibers, including silk and wool.

TO PURCHASE ENZYME PRODUCTS, pet stores are your best bet. You can select proteolytic enzymes for protein stains such as meat juice, egg, blood, and milk, or amylolytic enzymes for starch and carbohydrate stains. Since enzymes are costly, and starches and carbohydrates generally do not leave stains, you're probably better off buying proteolytic enzymes.

Floor Care Products

Floor cleaners, polishes, and finishes are not interchangeable. Floor cleaners, as the term implies, remove dirt. Floor polishes remove scratches because they're slightly abrasive. And, yes, floor finishes finish the job—they seal and protect the cleaned surface. While some people call the finishing stage "waxing," real wax isn't used anymore on the most popular kinds of modern flooring. Various polymers have replaced it.

WHAT DOES YOUR FLOOR'S MANUFACTURER RECOMMEND? Each manufacturer has recommendations for cleaning and protecting its products, so try to check the manufacturer's directions and follow them. As a general rule, you want to remove all dirt from your

floor before you apply the appropriate protective finish. Otherwise, you'll end up with a shiny, dirty floor. If you don't have the cleaning instructions from your floor's manufacturer, here is a general rundown of the products you'll need. Be sure to read any product's label to make sure it's OK for the floor you're working on.

FOR VINYL FLOORS, start by cleaning with a mild detergent or all-purpose cleaner such as Spic and Span. After rinsing, apply a water-based floor polish and finish, such as Future, according to the package directions. You can find one-step clean-and-polish products, but you probably won't be as happy with the results. This same approach works for asphalt and rubber flooring. Solvent-based paste wax will also shine vinyl flooring (it requires buffing) but shouldn't be used on asphalt or rubber.

FOR WOOD FLOORS, a commercial product such as Minwax Hardwood Floor Cleaner will do nicely on a modern polyurethane finish. Floors with an old-time lacquer, varnish, or shellac finish need the protection of wax. Some waxes, such as Lite 'n' Natural and Dark 'n' Rich, clean and wax floors of a particular hardwood color.

FOR CERAMIC TILE FLOORS, a general household cleaner such as Mr. Clean will do a good job. Specialized tile-cleaning products also are available. Avoid abrasive cleaners. Grout is easier to clean when it has been treated with a silicone sealer.

FLOOR CARE PRODUCTS CAN BE BOUGHT at supermarkets, home

improvement stores, discount retailers, hardware stores, or janitorial supply stores.

Furniture Waxes and Polishes

When you apply a wax or polish to your wood furniture, you're not beautifying the wood itself—you're beautifying the finish on the wood. Use either polish or wax—not both. If you put polish on wax, it will just puddle. Polishes don't offer as much protection as wax—they're meant to be a quick way to put sparkle in a dull-looking finish.

FURNITURE WAXES—be they paste or liquid—are made from combinations of synthetic and natural waxes. The synthetic element is paraffin, distilled from petroleum and other sources. The natural elements include beeswax and carnauba, a vegetable extract. Avoid waxes that contain toluene, a solvent that carries un unwelcome paint-thinner smell.

THE WAY WAX WORKS is to provide a barrier against moisture seeping into the wood of your furniture. This barrier also speeds your cleaning because you'll be able to remove marks and dust more easily. Before you wax, check the manufacturer's instructions. Generally, gloss or semigloss furniture can be waxed. If your furniture has a satin or flat finish, wax may give it a random, messy-looking sheen.

TO APPLY WAX, rub it on thinly with a clean, cotton cloth. Then let it sit for several minutes (check the label for precise timing) and buff it with another clean cloth.

WHEN YOU CHOOSE A WAX, consider your furniture's color. If you have light furniture, pick a neutral tone; for mahogany, use clear or a red/brown wax for more richness; for cherry, use walnut or brown; for oak, use a chocolate brown to a yellow. For pine furniture that doesn't have much of a finish, beeswax on its own is a good choice; after buffing, it produces a unique soft glow.

FURNITURE POLISHES often contain mineral oil, mineral spirits (paint thinner), perfume (scents such as lemon or orange oil), and dye (to give them the color of lemon or orange). Not all polishes use mineral spirits, which thins the mineral oil to make the polish easier to use.

COMMON MINERAL OIL-BASED POLISHES, such as Old English, Orange Glo, and Scott's Liquid Gold, are sold in bottles or aerosol cans and are easy to apply. However, some experts frown on polishes, saying they collect dust and create a dirt-and-oil mix on the furniture.

POLISHES THAT ACT AS REVIVERS, such as Guardsman Furniture Polish, contain fine abrasive pumice in the polish formula and don't contain mineral oil. They clean and protect the surface and are really more like a wax.

POLISHES THAT CONTAIN SILICONE produce a nice shine but can make refinishing the furniture more difficult in the future. Look for products that say they're silicone-free (Guardsman, for instance).

WAXES AND POLISHES CAN BE BOUGHT wherever cleaning products are sold—supermarkets, discount stores, hardware stores, and home improvement stores.

Garbage Bags

Stock splits you can handle. Garbage bag splits are another story altogether. These polyethylene sacks for trash are not exactly complex equipment. Still, there are a number of features to consider.

PAY ATTENTION TO THICKNESS if you want a bag that won't split under a heavy load. Thickness is measured in millimeters. Heavy-lifting bags are 2 1/2 to 3 millimeters thick. The plastic bags you haul your groceries home in, by comparison, are about 1/2 to 1 millimeter thick.

THINK COLOR. Garbage bags advertised for kitchen use are usually white and are 1/2 millimeter or less in thickness. White bags make a statement of cleanliness and freshness. Dark-colored bags, 1 1/2 to 3 millimeters thick, are designed for outdoor or commercial use. For cost-saving reasons, trash bags used in commercial settings are generally reused (after their contents are poured into a master trash barrel) until they start to smell or stains become noticeable.

THE BAGS' TYING METHOD is also something to consider. Some bags have built-in drawstring ties. These bags cost a little more but make a neat, quick fastener. Other bags have plastic, notched wrap fasteners or twist ties like those that secure bread bags. These bags often come on a roll and are torn off along a perforated line. Still other bags have a handle cut tend to cost the least have no tie at all; you have to secure them by making a knot with the top edge of the bag.

IF YOU HAVE TO TIE YOUR OWN GARBAGE BAG, make simple overlapping knots, as commercial cleaners do. Pull the trash bag from the can and shake the contents so they settle to the bottom. Next, take one corner with the left hand and the opposite one with the right hand, pull the corners to the center, and tie a tight square knot across the top of the garbage. Then take the other two opposing corners and tie a second square knot. These right-over-left and left-over-right knots allow you to pick up the bag and carry it without spilling the contents.

GARBAGE BAGS ARE READILY AVAILABLE in supermarkets and discount stores. Thick garbage bags can be purchased at home improvement stores, janitorial supply stores, and hardware stores.

Glass Cleaners

Commercial glass cleaners contain either ammonia or alcohol. They clean dirt, smears, and grease and can be used on surfaces other than glass, such as Formica and laminate—but not on Corian or marble.

THE COMPOSITION OF A GLASS CLEANER, such as Windex, is a mix of ingredients: detergents or surfactants to dissolve dirt and grime; fragrances; ammonia, an alkaline cleaner; coloring; alcohol, to remove filmy residues and prevent streaks; and solvents, to dissolve oily films.

CHOOSE A GLASS CLEANER that does not contain phosphorus, which has a tendency to smear glass. Those popular citrus cleaners may not be the best choice for your home's windows either, since they often contain a solvent called limonene, which can damage wood and vinyl frames. Some glass cleaners are formulated specifically to prevent dripping.

HOMEMADE GLASS CLEANERS are not only cheap and effective but are also easy to put together. Here are two:

- For general cleaning, in a bucket mix 2 squirts of a mild dishwashing detergent (preferably one that does not contain phosphorus), 1/2 cup of rubbing alcohol, and 1 gallon of warm water.
- For cleaning up smeary glass, in a 32-ounce spray bottle mix 1/3 cup of distilled white vinegar, 1/4 cup of rubbing alcohol, and distilled water to fill the bottle.

WHEN YOU'RE USING GLASS CLEANERS to actually clean glass, do it in the morning or early evening—not during the day, when the sun's rays will be heating the glass. Hot glass causes whatever window cleaner you're using to dry quickly, and you're likely to have a problem with streaks.

GLASS CLEANERS CAN BE BOUGHT in supermarkets, discount stores, hardware stores, and home improvement stores. Home improvement stores also sell money-saving concentrates.

Hydrogen Peroxide

Hydrogen peroxide is an oxidizing agent, similar to bleach, that removes color and sanitizes surfaces. Many products that promise to brighten or whiten clothes contain hydrogen peroxide. Use it with care. Peroxide is made of two parts hydrogen and two parts oxygen, and it's the extra oxygen molecule that turns plain water into a potent oxidizer. You can purchase hydrogen peroxide in concentrations ranging from 3 percent to 50 percent.

PEROXIDE IS A GERM KILLER as well as a substitute for bleach. It's a potent enemy of salmonella and *E. coli* bacteria. To kill these germs, spray 3 percent hydrogen peroxide on a counter or cutting board, for example, followed by a spritz of white distilled vinegar. Then rinse with fresh water.

Other uses for hydrogen peroxide abound. Here are a few examples:

FOR REMOVING CARPET STAINS, 3 percent hydrogen peroxide is a good choice. Pour the peroxide on the spot, wait 30 minutes, and blot it up with paper towels. Rinse with 1/4 cup of white vinegar mixed with 1 quart of water, blot, rinse again with plain water, and blot once more. Test on an inconspicuous spot first.

TO FIGHT MOLD IN BATHROOMS, 30 or 35 percent peroxide, mixed 50-50 with water, is effective. Spray it on, wait an hour, and spray again. No rinsing necessary. If mold remains, spray again in two days. Don't use hydrogen peroxide on colored grout.

BRIGHTEN YOUR DINGY LAUNDRY WHITES by adding 1/2 cup of 30 percent peroxide, 2 cups of 3 percent peroxide, or 1 cup of 6 percent peroxide to your wash.

TO REMOVE YELLOW UNDER-ARM STAINS, pour 3 percent peroxide directly on the stain, let it sit for several hours, and then rinse.

REMOVE RED DYE STAINS caused by Popsicles, punch, or Kool-Aid with 3 percent peroxide poured directly on the spot. Wait 30 minutes and rinse.

YOU CAN BUY 3 percent hydrogen peroxide in supermarkets and drugstores. Beauty salons carry 6 percent peroxide, medical supply stores sell 30 percent, and health food stores carry both 35 percent and 50 percent, which is considered food grade.

Metal Polishes

Commercial metal polishes remove tarnish (oxidation) and create a burnish, or shine, when you apply some elbow grease. Read labels to find a polish suited to the specific metal you want to clean up. (You won't be as happy with a general-purpose metal polish.) Metal polishes typically do their job through mild abrasion combined with chemical cleaners.

METAL POLISHES COME in liquids and creams. Convenient polishing cloths that are lightly saturated with polish also are available.

HOW OFTEN YOU POLISH an item depends on how often the item is handled. Every time you handle a metal piece, you transfer acid from your hands to the item, which translates into oxidation.

TO APPLY POLISH, use a cotton T-shirt or lint-free cotton cloth. Then use a terry cloth towel to remove any excess and a microfiber cloth to buff the polish on the metal. Be sure to remove as much of the residue of the polish as possible afterward, as the chemicals can damage metals over time. To reach nooks and crannies, use an old toothbrush. Some metal polishes contain strong chemicals, so be sure to wear rubber gloves and work in a well-ventilated area.

METAL POLISHES ARE AVAILABLE in hardware stores, supermarkets, home improvement stores, and janitorial supply outlets.

Mops

Back in simpler times, mops came in two varieties—string or sponge. Now the choices include sponge, cotton string, terry cloth towel, disposable towelettes (electrostatic or premoistened), and microfiber.

MOPS ARE USED to clean floors in two ways—dry-mopping or wet-mopping. To dry-mop, microfiber mops and the disposables (Swiffer, for instance) are good choices because they easily snag dirt and dust. If you have heavier or coarser dirt near entrances, you may need to do a quick sweep first with a broom and dustpan. To remove dried-on grime from a surface, wet-mopping is the way to go.

Here's a rundown on the five types of mops:

CELLULOSE SPONGE MOPS are made of open-cell foam and are good at cleaning vinyl. To use, dip the mop in a bucket of cleaner and warm water, wring out the excess moisture, and mop. A sponge mop is also good for stripping and waxing a vinyl floor, but not for use on hardwood or marble flooring. The head of your sponge mop will need to be replaced—how often depends on use.

STRING MOPS are usually 100 percent cotton (although some contain polyester), with strings 12 to 18 inches long. Mops have been around quite a while. In 1893, Thomas Stewart patented a string mop with a clamping mechanism worked by a lever to wring out water. Today's string mops can be used indoors or outdoors. They're good for cleaning garage floors and decks, tile and linoleum floors, and uneven surfaces of granite flooring. But string mops are not the ideal choice for hardwood or marble floors, because they can hold a lot of moisture, which can damage those surfaces. You can extend the life of the mop by machine-washing and drying the cotton head.

TOWEL MOPS use ordinary terry cloth towels secured with a holding device. Towel mops can be used wet on all floors, you can replace the towels easily when they become soiled, and you can wash and dry them. Among the many terry towels on the market, the heavy-duty hand towels will give you the best results. In addition to floor cleaning, you can use towel mops to dust cobwebs and clean ceilings.

DISPOSABLE TOWELETTE MOPS are a recent arrival on the market. They're available dry or with premoistened disposable pads or wipes. Just place them on the swivel head and start mopping. When the towelette is soiled, replace it with a fresh one. One model comes with a spray bottle that holds cleaning fluid. You simply pull a trigger on the handle and the cleaner is sprayed on the floor in front of the mop. These mops are convenient and easy to use, but the replacement towels can be expensive.

MICROFIBER MOPS are another relatively new thing. They are made of microscopic synthetic fibers that act as hooks to latch on to dust, dirt, and grime. They can hold several times their weight in water. The fibers are lint free and nonabrasive. The lightweight mops can be used on all floor types. To use the mop, dip the microfiber head into the cleaning solution and wring it by hand, leaving it damp. Wipe the floor, but don't put the mop back in the bucket. Change the mop head after mopping each room.

A study by the University of California Davis Medical Center found that microfiber mops use far less water and cleaning solution than conventional mops because the mop head is changed frequently. The study found 1 gallon of cleaner-and-water solution cleaned 22 rooms. Although microfiber mop heads cost more and have to be laundered separately from other rags, they last for years and prove cost-effective over time.

WHEN BUYING A MOP, you can pick up a sponge, string, or disposable towelette model from most supermarkets, drugstores, discount retailers, hardware stores, and home improvement stores. Terry towel mops can be purchased at department stores, discount retailers, home improvement stores, and linen specialty stores. Microfiber mops are available at janitorial supply stores and are gradually being introduced into mass-market stores.

Oils

Oils used on natural wood surfaces or leather make them look healthy. Most oils for wood or leather are extracted naturally from animals, seeds, or the peel of citrus fruits. Oils should never be used on stone, which is porous and will absorb the oil, producing dark spots in the stone. When you're thinking of using oil on wood or leather, always test it first on an inconspicuous spot. Some commonly used oils are listed below.

CITRUS OIL (ORANGE, LEMON, AND GRAPEFRUIT), such as Pledge with Orange Oil, will help restore the finish on wood that has been neglected or has faded. Citrus oil penetrates to moisturize and condition wood. They are often combined with a chemical cleaner. Apply lightly, putting the oil on a cloth and then wiping onto the furniture or woodwork. Oil has a tendency to streak if you apply too much. Count on 30 minutes for the oil to dry.

PINE OIL is a general cleaner and disinfectant for floors, counters, and bathrooms. It comes from the turpentine family and has a distinct aroma. To use, dilute it in a spray bottle or in mop water according to the package directions.

TUNG OIL AND LINSEED OIL are good for natural wood, table-tops, wood paneling, and wooden floors. Some brands have dyes in them, so they act like a stain. Linseed oil is also good for protecting outdoor furniture. Both tung oil and linseed oil can combust spontaneously, so be very careful not to leave oil-soaked rags lying around the house or in a garbage bag. Hang such rags outside to dry thoroughly before you dispose of them in an outdoor garbage can. Or dispose of them in a sealed metal container outside in the shade.

NEAT'S-FOOT OIL, which is a light yellow, is obtained from the feet and shinbones of cattle. (So to a cow, it's not so neat.) It's a great conditioner for leather (boots, saddles, and such), keeping the leather soft.

TO USE AN OIL, apply it with a cloth, let it soak in for about five to ten minutes, and buff or polish it dry, using circular motions. Cotton towels, diapers, or old T-shirts are great for this.

YOU CAN BUY citrus oil and pine oil anywhere home supplies are sold—supermarkets, hardware stores, home improvement stores, and discount retailers. Tung oil and linseed oil are available from janitorial supply stores and hardware stores. Neat's-foot oil can be purchased at stores that sell leather goods or at shoe repair shops.

Oven Cleaners

These are among the strongest—and most toxic—cleaners available to homeowners. Most contain a strong cleaning alkali, usually sodium hydroxide or potassium hydroxide. This caustic soda, or lye, converts fats to soapy, water-soluble compounds that wipe away easily.

OVEN CLEANERS COME in aerosol sprays, liquids, pastes, and powders and are usually thick so that they can stick on the vertical walls of an oven. They are toxic and can cause deep burns and blindness if they come into contact with skin or eyes. If swallowed, oven cleaners can be fatal. Don't use oven cleaners on self-cleaning ovens, which break down fats and other food with high heat instead of chemicals.

BE CAREFUL WITH ALL OVEN CLEANERS. Wear rubber gloves and protective goggles and work in a well-ventilated area. Never spray commercial oven cleaner on a hot oven, electric elements, or oven lights—heat can make it even more caustic.

PURCHASE OVEN CLEANERS at supermarkets and discount retailers.

Paper Towels

Professional cleaners use paper only for quick cleanups, such as emergency spills. It would be a major waste of trees to go through an entire roll of paper towels cleaning, say, a bathroom. And since paper towels are major lint producers, they leave behind a paper trail on mirrors, on windows, and anytime you attempt any serious scrubbing with them.

FOR EMERGENCY OR MESSY WIPE-UPS, paper towels are a great convenience, but they've got to be within arm's reach to be truly convenient. Keep paper towels around for juice spills, pet accidents, and wiping up anything (such as wet paint or cooking grease) that might ruin a rag or ruin anything in the same wash load with it. Keep a roll in the kitchen, another in the garage or shop (they're great for wiping oil and grease off hands), and another in the laundry room for bleach and liquid detergent spills.

PAPER TOWELS CAN BE PURCHASED at supermarkets and discount retailers. As long as you've got the room to store them, buy in bulk to save money. They won't go bad, and you'll eventually use them. And skip the decorative prints, since the printing inks can occasionally bleed. Isn't white more elegant anyway?

Rubber Gloves

When it comes to household cleaning, safety is essential. Gloves are important for protecting your hands when using harsh cleaning chemicals or working with hot water. In addition to protecting your hands from injury, gloves keep them soft and smooth.

WHEN SELECTING PROTECTIVE GLOVES, you can get ones made of either rubber or soft plastic polymers. The level of protection depends on how permeable they are, which typically depends on thickness. The thicker the glove, the more protection it provides.

- For general household use, standard latex dish gloves are fine. (Choose a latex substitute if you are allergic to latex.)
- For using paint strippers and solvents, you'll need a thicker glove. The thicker the glove, however, the bulkier and clumsier it will be.

REPLACE GLOVES before they wear out and can't protect you. Signs that suggest your gloves need replacing include staining or color change; softening, swelling or bubbling; stiffening or cracking; and of course, leaking.

DISPOSABLE GLOVES are available in bulk containers. If you reuse your disposable gloves, be sure to wash them well with warm, soapy water. Let the outside dry and then reverse them, letting the inside dry. When the inside is dry, turn them right side out again and sprinkle talcum powder inside them.

PURCHASE RUBBER GLOVES at supermarkets, discount stores, hardware stores, and home improvement stores.

Sealants

Grime is toughest to remove when it gets a foothold in our materials. When lodged in the fibers of a sofa cushion, the grains of wood in a deck, or the pores of ceramic tile grout, things like food spills and mildew can remain there permanently. To prevent grime from taking up longtime residence, scientists have devised sealants—for textiles, grout, wood, brick, and concrete—to block pores, making surfaces less susceptible to staining and easier to wipe clean.

FABRIC SEALANTS come in two varieties—fluorochemical sealants, such as Scotchgard and Teflon, and silicone sealants. Silicone sealants work only against water-based spills, such as juices; any spill containing oil can penetrate the sealant. Silicone sealants can even trap oily stains, making them harder to remove. Some upholstery comes presealed. If the sealant wears off, reapply it or have a professional reapply it. Before reapplying a fabric sealant, be sure to clean the fabric well and remove all cleaning residue. Otherwise the sealant will not bond well.

BRICK AND CONCRETE FLOOR SEALANTS, like fabric sealants, add a protective layer to floors, making cleaning easier. Always clean and prepare a floor surface well before applying a sealer. Reapply when signs of wear appear.

WOOD SEALANTS also protect against scratching and water damage. They come in the following varieties:

- Penetrating sealers seep into the grain of the wood and keep dust and dirt from doing the same.
- Surface coating sealers—polyurethanes, shellacs, and varnishes—form a protective layer over the wood surface. The most popular surface sealant is polyurethane, which is durable and relatively easy to use. Polyurethane sealers are either oil- or water-based, and they come in a variety of finishes, from matte to high gloss.

GROUT SEALANTS combat what has traditionally been one of the toughest things in the house to clean. This sealant, available at home and hardware stores and easily applied with a sponge paintbrush, prevents oil, dirt, and mildew from staining grout lines.

YOU CAN PURCHASE fabric sealants at supermarkets, discount stores, and stores that sell carpets and upholstered furniture, as well as through professional cleaning companies. Sealants for hard surfaces typically are available at hardware, paint, and home improvement stores.

Soap

Apart from plain water, soap may be *Homo sapiens'* oldest cleaner. During the excavation of ancient Babylon, archaeologists found a soaplike material in clay cylinders dating back to 2900 B.C. According to ancient Roman legend, soap got its name from Mount Sapo, a place of animal sacrifice. Rain mixed the melted animal fat with wood ashes and washed it down to the clay soil along the Tiber River, where women washed clothes. The women found that the mixture removed the soil from clothes far better and more easily than plain water.

HOW SOAP IS MADE has not changed: Animal or vegetable fats are still treated with a strong alkali, such as sodium or potassium. Soap differs from detergent, which is a synthetic product first made in Germany in 1916 in response to a shortage of soap-making fats. Both contain "surface-active" agents, or surfactants, which reduce the surface tension of water and soil, in effect loosening the soil, dispersing it in water, and holding it in suspension until it can be rinsed away.

SOAP IS USED these days almost solely for personal skin and body care. In most other cleaning endeavors, synthetic detergents have almost completely re-placed natural soaps, especially for machine-washing dishes and clothes. In hard water, soap is not as effective as detergent, and it forms a curd or soap scum that can ruin clothes and stain tubs and sinks.

DON'T USE SOAP ON TANNIN STAINS, such as ones produced by coffee, fruit, or jelly if you can avoid it. Soap makes the stain harder to remove.

SOAP IS WIDELY AVAILABLE in supermarkets, drugstores, department stores, and discount stores.

Solvents

Water is the universal solvent, since it can be used to dissolve many different substances, from dirt to blood to certain paints. In cleaning terminology, however, solvent refers to liquids other than water that are used to dissolve things water can't dissolve. Water can't dissolve grease, for instance. Working on the principle that "like dissolves like," you'd need a nonwater-based solvent, such as mineral spirits, to dissolve grease.

COMMON CLEANING SOLVENTS include acetone (found in many nail polish removers), denatured alcohol, and turpentine, as well as petroleum-based chemicals, such as mineral spirits, naphtha, kerosene, and dry-cleaning fluids.

CLEANING USES FOR SOLVENTS typically include removing greasy or oily substances, cleaning materials that can be harmed by water (for instance, spot-cleaning dry-clean-only fabrics), and removing decals, wood finishes, oil-based paint, and waxes.

SOLVENTS ARE A LAST RESORT, to be used for the few things that water and detergent won't clean. Solvents tend to be strong, aggressive cleaners. Although they can be dangerous to breathe and dangerous when they contact your skin and eyes, they vary in their degree of toxicity.

ALWAYS TAKE SAFETY PRECAU-
TIONS when using solvents.

- Solvents are highly flammable. Never use them near open flames, including pilot lights and sparks.
- Always ventilate the area in which you are working.
- Wear the proper gear, including chemical-resistant gloves, long-sleeved shirts and long pants, protective eyewear, and, depending on the solvent, a ventilator.

SOLVENTS ARE TYPICALLY AVAIL-
ABLE in hardware and home improvement stores.

Sponges

Household cleaning sponges, typically made of cellulose, are great at absorbing liquids, and they hold lots of cleaning solution. For that reason, sponges are fast and efficient cleaning tools. But they are also a breeding ground for bacteria. The key to using sponges is to understand their limitations and, specifically, to avoid cross-contamination.

PLAIN CELLULOSE SPONGES
are well suited to bathrooms, where being able to wipe moisture off walls, counter-tops, sinks, tubs, and showers is handy. But keep them in the bathroom. Don't use the bath-room sponge in the kitchen, where germs can spread. Don't use a toilet sponge on the countertop where you store your toothbrush. Let a sponge dry between each use. Throw sponges away after a few weeks.

ABRASIVE KITCHEN SPONGES are designed for dishwashing. These might be wrapped in a lightly abrasive mesh or backed by more heavily abrasive scrubbing pads. Use common sense when cleaning

with sponge abrasives. They will scratch Teflon-coated pots and pans, stainless steel sinks, countertops, and the like. And kitchen sponges are just as apt to grow bacteria. Keep them as clean as possible and throw them out after a few weeks of use. Even if you don't use sponges on a regular basis, keep them around for spills.

NATURAL SPONGES—the brown, irregularly round ones—have been used for thousands of years for bathing and household cleaning. Although synthetic sponges, introduced in the 1940s, now have the lion's share of the market, natural sponges are still used for bathing, clean-ing, and a number of industrial applications ranging from print-ing to surgery.

A natural sponge is actually the skeleton of a sea animal. There are more than 2,000 species of sponge in the ocean, but these three are mainly used commercially:

- Sheepswool or sea wool sponge: the softest, longest lasting, and most absorbent
- Yellow sponge: a slightly stiffer variety
- Grass sponge: finer pores and more delicate

Natural sponges are consid-ered a renewable resource. They can regenerate them-selves from fragments. When divers harvest them off the seafloor, they're careful to leave the root so they will regrow.

DISINFECTING YOUR KITCHEN
SPONGES regularly is important. Moist sponges are notorious for harboring bacteria. You may think you're cleaning, but you're really slathering a layer of germs all over your sink, countertops, appliances, and

kitchen table with that infect-ed sponge. Here are three ways to disinfect those squishy wiper-uppers. First, rinse your sponges completely to remove any food particles. Then do one of the following:

- Toss them into the top rack of your dishwasher.
- Put them in a microwave oven for 30 seconds. (Careful—they get hot.)
- Pour 1 gallon of water into the kitchen sink, add 3/4 cup of chlorine bleach, and soak your sponges for ten minutes.

SPONGES ARE WIDELY AVAILABLE
at supermarkets, discount stores, and home improvement stores—the cellulose variety, that is. For natural sponges, try at paint, hardware, home improvement, and bath and beauty stores.

Spot Removers

The grocery shelves are lined with spot and stain removers. While the number of different ingredients in spot removers is mind-boggling, these products do fall into two main cate-gories—wet and dry.

WET SPOT REMOVERS, such as Spray 'n Wash, are water solu-ble. These typically contain a concentrated laundry deter-gent and work best on food stains, such as drink spills and ketchup. But some wet spot removers also contain second-ary solvents, such as alcohol and mineral spirits, to boost their stain-removal power and make them more effective on greasy stains.

DRY SPOT REMOVERS, such as K2r, contain chemical solvents, including some that dry clean-ers use. (Liquid is still involved. The "dry" means water isn't used.) These are best for dry-clean-only fabrics as well as greasy or oily stains.

CARPET AND UPHOLSTERY SPOT REMOVERS, such as Spot Shot and Perky, are specially designed for use on those materials. They are sometimes foamy, since low-moisture vacuumable foams are typically better for textiles with pads or cushions beneath.

A WORD OF CAUTION: Be sure to use the right spot removal product for the right job. To make sure the material you're cleaning is colorfast, pretest the product in an inconspicuous corner or seam. Always follow the manufacturer's directions carefully.

SPOT REMOVERS ARE WIDELY AVAILABLE at supermarkets and discount stores.

Spray Bottles

Spray bottles can be time- and money-savers. Not only do they allow you to mix your own cleaning solutions—or buy bulk jugs of your favorite commercial cleaners—but they also make applying cleaning solutions much easier and more exact than simply pouring them on. Even when you're just using water—for instance, if you need to lightly wet a carpet stain—spray bottles do a great job.

TO FIND GOOD SPRAY BOTTLES—ones that are more durable and have a larger capacity—drop by a janitorial supply store. These professional-grade squirters will have more pumping power, making your work easier.

WHEN USING SPRAY BOTTLES, the most important rule is to label them. Some bottles come with white rectangles on the side intended for labeling with a permanent marker. Some spray bottles also have handy check-off boxes that you can use to list the ingredients inside. Don't pour in your bleach solution thinking you'll label it later. Do it right away to avoid future confusion—and possible safety issues. And to avoid contaminating nearby surfaces, use the appropriate nozzle setting for the job you're doing. Use a tighter stream for smaller areas, such as toilet seats, and a wider mist for larger areas, such as large bathroom mirrors.

A WARNING: If you're using a harmful cleaning chemical, such as bleach, in a spray bottle, avoid making the mist too fine. It will aerosolize the chemical, making it easier to inhale or get in your eyes.

SPRAY BOTTLES ARE AVAILABLE at home improvement stores, dollar stores, and janitorial supply stores.

Squeegees

Cleaning pros rely on squeegees. Anyone faced with cleaning smooth surfaces—such as windows, mirrors, and tile—should too. They are quicker and more effective at removing cleaning solutions and the dirt those solutions loosen. They don't streak. They don't leave behind lint, as paper towels do, and they're not as messy as newspapers.

A 9- to 12-inch-wide squeegee is the most suitable size for glass cleaning. Any bigger, and it will be unwieldy.

Any smaller, and it won't cover enough surface area. (Sure, you can have a smaller, secondary squeegee for smaller, divided windowpanes.)

BUY A GOOD-QUALITY MODEL that will work well and last. Get one with a high-quality (pliable and flexible) wiping blade. Cheaper squeegees have hard-rubber blades. When they get nicked, they leave a line of water behind, meaning you have to work twice as hard or buy a new one.

WHEN USING A SQUEEGEE, keep a dry towel in your other hand, and wipe the squeegee on the towel after each swipe. For how to clean a window with a squeegee, see *Windows,* page 391.

SMALL BATHROOM SQUEEGEES are available for wiping down wet shower walls, thus preventing soap scum buildup.

SQUEEGEES CAN BE BOUGHT at hardware, discount, and home improvement stores.

Steel Wool

Steel wool is a specialty cleaning product and should never be used for general cleaning purposes. Even the finest steel wool is abrasive and can scratch (and ruin) many surfaces. That said, steel wool can be extremely useful for removing the most stubborn grime and for doing it without harsh chemicals.

STEEL WOOL COMES in grades that range from superfine (grade 0000) to extra coarse (grade 4). Traditionally, it has been used to remove baked-on food from pots and pans. Some brands have soap already embedded in the pads for convenience. But with the ubiquity of nonstick cooking surfaces, it is less important to keep those woolly balls under the kitchen sink these days. Besides making surfaces look bad, when steel wool scratches something, it creates a surface that attracts stains and rust. Use steel wool as a last resort or on surfaces that you don't mind scratching.

STEEL WOOL IS AVAILABLE in supermarkets, hardware stores, discount stores, and home improvement stores.

Toilet Cleaners

Commercial toilet cleaners tend to be strong and acid-based. Often they contain hydrochloric acid for eating away at stubborn stains and mineral deposits—those rings that seem cemented to the toilet bowl. Often they are of a thick consistency, which helps them stick to the wall of the toilet long enough to do their job.

FOR REGULAR TOILET CLEANING, hydrochloric acid is probably overkill. The less you use it, the safer you are and the less chance you have of damaging some nearby surface with an accidental spill or drip. Try a mild detergent or tub-and-tile cleaner or look for a product with a milder acid, such as phosphoric acid.

IF A TOILET BOWL IS GRUNGY— you haven't cleaned it in a while or your household water is hard or contains excess iron—you may need the stronger product. Or, for an entirely chemical-free approach, use a pumice stone (the same product you use to rub corns off your feet).

Keeping the stone wet, rub it on the ring until it's gone. This works for old rings as well as recent ones. Pumice will not scratch white vitreous china, which is what most toilets are made of, but it will scratch fiberglass, enamel, plastic, and other materials.

HERE'S A TIP: Apply your toilet bowl cleaner and then go clean the bathtub or the sink. Come back to the toilet five minutes later, when the cleaner has had plenty of time to loosen the grime.

Toilet bowl cleaners are widely available at supermarkets, discount stores, and home improvement stores. Pumice stones are available at drugstores and bath-product stores.

Vacuum Cleaners

Page through this book and count the number of times a vacuum cleaner is called for in a particular cleaning job, and you'll quickly get tired of counting. A good vacuum cleaner is a key cleaning ally for any homeowner, both for routine dust and dirt removal and for emergency situations, such as broken glass and upturned potted plants.

CHOOSING A VACUUM CLEANER is more confusing than ever, since the differences between canister and upright vacs have been blurred. What used to be a matter of floor type— upright for carpets, canister for bare floors—is now almost a Coke/Pepsi-style personal preference. The good news is that the similarities, and overall improvements in quality, make it hard to go wrong when buying a vacuum cleaner.

In addition to uprights and canisters, there are also

wet/dry vacuum cleaners (sometimes known as shop vacs) and handheld vacuum cleaners, each with its own functions and features. Generally speaking, some features are marketing gimmicks, whereas others are genuinely useful.

FEATURES TO CONSIDER when buying a vacuum include the following:

● The onboard tools, such as crevice and upholstery tools, extension wands, and nozzles with rotating bars, are essential for nonfloor cleaning duties (drapes and upholstered furniture, for instance).

● Manual pile adjustment is important not only for better dirt retrieval when you're vacuuming carpets, but also for better carpet protection, since the "standard" setting on many beater bars can destroy a carpet's fibers and wear down the vacuum's motor.

● A gauge alerting users when the bag is full improves efficiency. (Full bags don't draw as well, making you work harder to pick up the dirt.)

FILTRATION SYSTEMS are among the best features to find their way onto vacuum cleaners in recent years. These systems improve air quality by capturing tiny particles that otherwise would be blown back into your home in the machine's exhaust. The machines with the best filters, known as high efficiency particulate air (HEPA) filters, are expensive to buy and to replace—but for people with asthma or allergies, they are extremely beneficial. Some manufacturers claim their machines have "microfiltration" systems. Although these might not be true HEPA filters, they may be an improvement over the standard, filterless vacuum cleaner. If you want to buy a filtering machine, it's worth doing your homework. Check the results of tests done by organizations such as Consumers Union, the nonprofit organization that publishes *Consumer Reports* magazine.

MORE GIMMICKY FEATURES include dirt sensors, which alert you to how much dirt is passing through your vacuum cleaner, not how much dirt is left in a rug. These devices are unnecessary and can be misleading. Vac makers these days also like to brag about power, usually in the form of number of amps or suction amps. Amps measure electric current, not a machine's ability to clean. More important is how one machine stacks up to another in real tests, those you read about in consumer magazines and those you experience while "test-driving" a vacuum cleaner in the store, which is something you should do before spending hundreds of dollars on a machine.

Here's a look at the various styles available:

UPRIGHT VACUUMS were once the clear choice for homes with lots of carpets because of their powerful rotating "beater bars." No longer. Yet while canister vacs these days also come with beater bar attachments, uprights are still easier to operate on carpets and easier to store when you're done. They are taller and often self-propelled, reducing the amount of stooping and pushing required to vacuum a carpeted room. And because they often come with a hose and assorted attachments, they are versatile.

If your house is filled with carpeting, an upright will be faster and more efficient. If your house has a mix of carpet and bare floors, it's a toss-up.

CANISTER VACUUMS are usually the better choice if your house has mostly bare floors or if you have lots of draperies, upholstery, and window blinds to vacuum. These models have a built-in hose, plus attachments, usually including a powered nozzle with a beater bar. Canister machines are easier to carry around the house and up the stairs. But they are typically more awkward to store, since they take up more floor space than uprights. One nice convenience when it's time to put away your canister vac: Most come with button-operated retractable cords instead of cords you have to manually wrap around and around for storage.

WET/DRY VACUUMS tend to be powerful, less expensive workhorses. Also known as shop vacs, these special canister machines are notable for being able to safely pick up water—unlike other vacuums. They are most at home in garages and basements, where they're useful for sucking up everything from sawdust to smelly water leaks. Generally speaking, the more you spend, the more reliable the machine will be and the more extras it will include.

HANDHELD VACUUMS are portable battery-operated machines. Ever since the introduction, years ago, of the DustBuster, handheld vacs have been hugely popular. Most are powerful and surprisingly inexpensive. But since they

have limited battery power—often less than ten minutes at a shot—they are useful only for quick jobs, such as spills and cleaning up toddler crumb trails. Today, they come with more and more features and attachments, including better filtration systems (which may or may not be necessary for the kinds of jobs they tackle). As with full-size machines, don't get tempted by useless extras. When buying, stick to the basics—brand reliability, warranties, and battery power.

IF YOU HAVE STAIRS TO CLEAN, instead of buying a separate, smaller vacuum cleaner made for stair-cleaning, outfit your existing machine with the appropriate extras. First, buy an extension tube (usually 12 feet long), which will allow you to leave your machine on the ground floor while you clean the entire flight of steps. You can buy extension tubes for both uprights and canister vacs.

For carpet-covered stairs, buy a turbo tool. Powered by the incoming airflow (hence the name turbo), these attachments act like small beater bars to help loosen and pull up hairs, lint, and dirt from carpet pile. But because they do not need a power cord to rotate, they can be attached to extension hoses. They are much lighter than motor-driven beater-bar nozzles.

VACUUM CLEANERS ARE SOLD at department stores, discount stores, and home improvement stores.

Index

Baby oil (cont'd)
  in furniture polish, 197
  for patent leather, 308
  for scratched plastic, 116
  for seashells, 307
  for showers, 310
  for taxidermy, 357
Baby powder, 89, 309
Baby shampoo, 294
Baby wipes, 217, 309. See also
  Disposable wipes
Backpacks, 69–70
Badminton rackets, 336
Baking powder, as cleaner, 145
Baking soda, as cleaner, 412, 414–416
  for air filters, 173
  for baby equipment, 69
  for bathtubs, 75
  for beadwork, 76
  for brass, 91
  for burn marks, 97
  for carpeting, 111
  for china, 155
  for chrome, 128
  for combs, 133
  for cookware, 167
  for coolers (ice chests), 139
  for countertops, 142
  for decanters, 150
  as deodorizer, 263, 295, 327, 406
  for doghouses and kennels, 156
  for drains, 160–161, 423
  for drawers, 162
  for garbage disposers, 200
  for grout, 309
  for hard water deposits, 219
  harmful effects of, 272
  for iron soleplates, 235
  for kitchen cabinets, 238
  for knickknacks, 239
  for marble, 252
  for microwaves, 254–255
  for plastic containers, 282
  for porcelain, 285
  for silver, 313, 314
  for sinks, 315, 316
  for smoke odors, 324, 325
  for stainless steel, 337
  for stain removal, 144, 301, 385
  for thermos bottles, 360
  for toilets, 416
  for vomit, 377
  for wading pools, 378
  for walls, 380
  for wastebaskets, 382
  for wigs, 389–390
  for windows, 312
Ball Cap Buddy, 221
Bamboo, 388–389
Bananas, for pest control, 274
Banisters, 70. See also Stairs and steps
Banners, 179–180
Barbecue grills, 70–72
Barbicide, homemade, 132
Bar Keepers Friend, 140

Baseball caps, 221
Baseball gloves, 333
Baseboard radiators, 292
Baseboards, 72–73, 273. See also
  Woodwork
Basements, 73–74, 255, 263, 273
Basketballs, 333
Baskets, 74–75
Bathrooms. See also specific fixtures
  cleaning agents for, 416
  cleaning guidelines for, 44, 46–47
  countertops in, 141–143, 207–208
  decorating choices in, 17
  fiberglass in, 172–173
  hard water deposits in, 219
  mold or mildew in, 255, 426
Bathtubs, 74–76, 300
Beadwork, 76
Beams, exposed, 76–77
Bearing lubricants, 335
Bedding. See also Mattresses
  bedspreads, 77–78, 303
  blankets, 83–85
  bloodstains on, 87–88
  comforters, 133–134, 303
  quilts, 290–291
  satin sheets, 303
  vomit on, 377
Bedrooms, 46–47
Bedspreads, 77–78, 303
Belts, 78–79
Berry stains, 341, 343, 400
Bicycles, 79–81. See also Stationary
  bicycles
Binoculars, 81
Birdbaths, 82–83
Bird feeders, 83
Birdhouses, 83
Bisque porcelain, 285
Blankets, 83–85
Bleach
  for aquariums, 61–62
  for baby equipment, 69
  for berry stains, 400
  for birdbaths, 82
  for bird feeders, 83
  for butcher blocks, 98
  for candle wax stains, 386
  for china, 155
  for coffee stains, 401
  for combs, 133
  for coolers (ice chests), 139
  for cutting boards, 149
  for decks, 151
  for dish drainers, 154
  for elastic, 165
  for exercise equipment, 169
  for flowerpots, 185
  for food grinders, 189
  for fountains, 190–192
  for garbage cans, 199, 262
  for garden ornaments, 200
  for grout, 183, 309
  for gutters and downspouts, 213

for hammocks, 216
harmful effects of, 153, 270, 272, 312
for humidifiers, 229
for lipstick stains, 404
for litter boxes, 248
for mildew, 67, 74, 255, 263
for mustard stains, 405
for plastic containers, 282
for playground equipment, 283
for porcelain, 285
for quilts, 290
for scorched fabric, 406
for seashells, 307
for sinks, 315
for smoky clothes, 324
for stain removal, 340, 342, 343, 345
types of, 31
for vinyl siding, 376
for vomit, 377
for washing machines, 381
for water stains, 385, 386
for whirlpools, 388
for wine stains, 409
Bleaching powder, 255
Blended households, clutter in, 25
Blinds, 85–86, 162
Blocking boards, 261
Bloodstains, 86–88, 401
Blow dryers. See Hair dryers
Bluing, 31–32
Boat cleaners, for fiberglass, 173
Boats, 88
Bone, 99, 236–237
Book bags, 69–70
Books, 89
Boots, 89–90. See also Shoes
Borax, 415
  for bathtubs, 75
  for crystal, 145
  for garbage cans, 199, 262
  for sinks, 315
  for telephones, 358
  for tile floors, 183
  for toilets, 416
  for vinyl, 184, 376
  for walls, 380
  for wastebaskets, 382
  for window screens, 305
Boric acid, 273
Bottle brushes, 145, 417. See also spe-
  cific cleaning jobs
Bottles, 90–91
Box springs, 252–253
Brass, 91–92, 219
Brass musical instruments, 257–258
Brass polish, 278
Bread, as cleaner, 141, 272, 380
Brick, 92–93
Brick sealers, 430
Bridal gowns, 92–94
Briefcases, 94
Brocade, 94–95
Bronze, 95–96

Brooms, 416–417
Brushes, 417. *See also specific brushes or cleaning jobs*
Buckets, 417–418
Bulb syringes, 102
Burns, 96–97
Butcher blocks, 97–98
Buttons, 98–99

C

Cabinets, kitchen, 238–239
Cactus, 228
Calculators, 100
Camcorders, 100–101
Cameos, 101
Cameras, 102–103
Camping gear, 318–320, 359–360
Candelabra, 104–105
Candlesticks, 104–105
Candle wax
    on candlesticks, 104–105
    on carpeting, 110, 401
    on doormats, 158
    on fabric, 401
    for flowerpots, 185
    on furniture, 197
    as lubricant, 359, 397
    removal guidelines, 386–387
    on silver serving pieces, 314
Candlewick bedspreads, 78
Caning, 105
Canning, 289
Canola oil, 289, 293
Can openers, 104
Canopies, 66–67
Carbon, for aquariums, 61
Carbona Color Run Remover, 180
Care labels, 14–15, 39, 339
Car interior cleaners, 217, 308
Car mats, 114–115, 416
Carpet cleaning machines, 418–419
Carpeting. *See also* Rugs
    automotive, 115
    bloodstains on, 87, 401
    candle wax on, 110, 386, 401
    chewing gum on, 124–125, 401
    cleaning methods for, 107–108
    crayon marks on, 144
    effect of alcohol on, 355
    fiber content of, 106
    fleas in, 403
    garbage bag spills on, 403
    grease stains on, 208–209
    ink stains on, 232
    nail polish on, 405
    odors in, 111, 416
    paint on, 405
    pet accidents on, 111, 276, 400
    rust stains on, 301
    sap on, 297
    soot in, 332
    spill or stain treatment for, 12, 107, 109–111, 332, 338–345, 424, 426

vacuuming, 105–107
water stains on, 386
wine on, 409
Carpet shampoo, 301, 332, 415
Carpet spot removers, 432
Car polishes, 419
    for cars, 113, 118
    for luggage, 251
    for lunch boxes, 251
    for snowmobiles, 329
Cars
    cleaning chrome, 128
    cleaning interior, 114–117
    polishing, 113, 118
    removing asphalt from, 65
    washing, 111–113, 115, 117–118, 119
    waxing, 113–114, 118–119
Car washes, as cleaning tool, 71, 328, 388
Cashmere, 36–37
Cassette players, 119–120
Cast iron, 233, 234, 285
Cast iron radiators, 292
Cat boxes, 248, 416. *See also* Kitty litter, as absorbent
CD players, 120–121
CDs, 121
Cedar, as deodorizer, 324
Ceiling fans, 172
Ceilings, 121–122, 325, 331, 386
Celery, as deodorizer, 263
Cement, as cleaner, 137, 209, 300
Ceramic cooktops, 350. *See also* Stoves
Ceramic polish, 350
Ceramics, 122–123
Ceramic tile
    floors, 183, 332, 361–362, 424
    grout, 183, 255, 361, 362
    hard water deposits on, 219
    showers, 309
    walls, 362
Cerium oxide, 316
Chairs, kitchen, 19
Chalk, as cleaner, 93, 309
Chandeliers, 123–124, 162
Changing tables, 69
Cheese-based food stains, 340–341
Chemical sponges, 331
Cherry stains, 341, 343
Chewing gum, removing, 124–125, 158, 401
Children, teaching to clean, 10, 11
Chimneys, 125–127
Chimney Safety Institute of America, 126
Chimney sweeps, 126
China, 127–128, 154–156
Chlorinated lime, 255, 263
Chlorine bleach. *See* Bleach
Chrome, 128–129, 219, 413

Chrome polish, 251, 329
Cigarette ashes, as cleaner, 97, 408
Citrus-based cleaners, 415. *See also* Orange oil cleaners
Citrus oil, 428
Cleaning
    philosophy of, 10–11
    professional help with, 42
    routines and strategies for, 11, 13–15, 16–21, 41–49
    types of, 9
Cleaning agents and products. *See also* specific cleaning job, agents or products
    basic, 44
    safety with, 15, 75, 219, 286, 413, 415, 422, 429
    testing, 75, 339
    using, 13–15, 19
Cleaning caddies, 14, 44, 418
Cleaning cloths, 419–420
Cleaning methods, 13, 14
Cleaning putty, for blinds, 85
Cleaning services. *See* Professional cleaners
Cleaning tools, 19–20, 44–45, 65. *See also* specific tools
"Clean your clock," 129
Clipper oil, 304
Clocks, 129–130
Clothing. *See also* Laundry; specific items
    antique, 57–58
    athletic, 334, 336
    burns in, 96
    care labels for, 39
    chewing gum on, 124–125
    as clutter, 24
    sap on, 296–297
    smoke odors in, 324–325
    spills or stains on, 12, 27–28, 33, 35, 332, 338–345 (*See also* specific stains)
    stain resistant, 35
Club soda, as cleaner, 87, 93, 95, 109, 299
Clutter control, 22–25, 41–42, 161–162, 209, 273
Cockroaches, 273
Coffee, as deodorizer, 263
Coffee grinders, 130
Coffee makers, 130–131
Coffee stains, 285, 341–342, 401
Coffee tables, 331
Coins, 131–132
Cola, for rust, 300
Colorfastness tests, 291, 355
Combination stains, 343–344
Combs, 132–133
Combustion chamber cleaner, 329
Comforters, 133–134, 303
Compressed air
    for electric shavers, 167

Compressed air *(cont'd)*
  for electronics, 102–103, 135, 136, 164
  for hot tub filters, 226
  for in-line skates, 335
  for power tools, 288
  for sewing machines, 305
  for slide projectors, 320–321
  for slides and negatives, 279
  for smoke alarms, 326
  for soot, 331
  for typewriters, 368
  for wigs, 389
  for wrought iron, 233
Computer peripherals, 136, 289
Computers, 14, 134–136
Concrete, 74, 136–137, 209, 300
Concrete sealers, 18, 74, 430
Contact lenses, 137–138
Cooking, preventive measures, 18
Cooking odors, 262, 263, 402, 406
Cooking oil. *See* Vegetable oil
Cooking spray, 72, 245, 328
Cookware
  cast iron, 233, 234
  cleaning agents for, 412
  cleaning guidelines for, 285–286
  copper, 140
  enameled, 167–168
  rust on, 299–300
  seasoning, 233, 379, 392
  stainless steel, 337
  woks, 392
Coolers (ice chests), 139
Copper, 139–140, 285
Corian, 142, 316
Cork, 140–141, 178
Cornmeal, as cleaner, 87, 303, 306
Cornstarch, as cleaner
  for bloodstains, 87
  for carpeting, 110
  for leather, 247
  for slate, 318
  for suede, 352
  for vomit, 377
  for wallpaper, 379
Cosmetics, 93, 312, 352, 390, 404
Cotton, 37, 84–85, 179–180, 216, 261
Cotton swabs
  for banisters, 70
  for baskets, 74
  for copper, 140
  for curling irons, 146
  effect of solvents on, 331
  for electronics, 100, 119, 120, 135, 136, 289
  for fishing rods, 177
  for fountain pens, 192
  testing products with, 67
Countertop grills, 165–166
Countertops
  acidic cleaners for, 413
  choices in, 17
  cleaning guidelines for, 141–143
  felt-tip marker on, 402

granite, 207–208
  oil splatters on, 401
  preventive measures for, 18, 318
  slate, 318
  stone, 348–349
Crayon marks, 143–144, 235, 379, 380
Crayons, as dye, 221
Cream-based food stains, 340–341
Cream of tartar
  for bathtubs, 75
  for chrome, 128
  for coffeemakers, 131
  for countertops, 142
  for leather, 247
  for pressure cookers, 289
  for rust stains, 300, 301
  for silk, 313
Credit cards, as cleaner, 305
Cribs, 69
Crystal, 144–145, 224
Curlers, 145–146
Curling irons, 146
Curtains, 146–147, 303
Cushions, 147–148, 187, 355
Cutting boards, 149

D

Darts, 333
Dead bolts, 249
Decalcifiers, 131
Decanters, 150
Dechlorinating products, 60, 62
Decks, 151–152
Deep-heating rub, as cleaner, 125
Deer, 275
Degreasers, 415
  as basic supply, 44
  for bicycles, 79
  for cooking odors, 262, 402, 406
  hot tubs, 226–227
  for lava rocks, 72
  for locks, 249
  for smoke, 407
  for snowmobiles, 329
  for soot, 331, 332, 403
  for stoves, 350
Dehumidifier kits, for hearing aids, 222
Dehumidifiers, 152, 263, 408
Denatured alcohol
  for candle wax, 314
  for computers, 135, 136
  for crystal, 145
  for glassware, 203
  for ink stains, 231
  for printers, 289
  for televisions, 358
Dental picks, as cleaners, 306, 307
Denture-cleaning tablets
  for bottles, 90
  for coffeemakers, 131
  for crystal, 145
  for decanters, 150

for dentures, 153
  for thermos bottles, 360
  for vases, 372
Dentures, 152–153
Deodorant stains, 312–313, 344
Detergent boosters, 32
Detergents. *See* Laundry detergent; *specific cleaning jobs*
Diaper pails, 69
Diapers, 294, 412, 416
Dining areas, 47–49
Dirt prevention. *See* Preventive measures
Dish drainers, 153–154
Dishes, 154–156, 277, 387
Dishwashers
  baby bottles in, 68
  buying, 420
  caps in, 221
  china in, 127, 155–156
  food graters in, 189
  food processors in, 190
  glassware in, 203
  plastic containers in, 282
  range hood filters in, 293
  silver in, 314
  using, 154
Dishwashing detergents, 420–421. *See also specific cleaning jobs*
Dishwashing liquid, 421. *See also specific cleaning jobs*
Disinfectants, 421–422
  after sewage backups, 407
  for combs, 133
  for grout, 362
  for odors, 413
  for telephones, 358
  for wheelchairs, 387
Disposable wipes, 422
  for combs, 133
  for guitar strings, 259
  for handbags, 217
  for pet equipment, 278
  for printers, 289
  for shoes, 309
  for telephones, 358
Doggie sweaters, 277
Doghouses, 156
Dolls, 157–158, 367
Doormats, 16–17, 44, 158
Doors
  aluminum frames on, 56
  cleaning guidelines for, 158–159
  painted trim on, 266
  as preventive tool, 19, 20
  sliding, 322–323
Double-hung windows, 390
Down, 159–160, 281–282, 318–320
Downspouts, 212–213
Drain openers, 92, 161, 316, 422–423
Drains, 160–161, 407
Drapes. *See* Curtains
Drawers, 20, 161–162

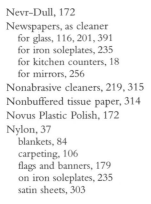

Nevr-Dull, 172
Newspapers, as cleaner
   for glass, 116, 201, 391
   for iron soleplates, 235
   for kitchen counters, 18
   for mirrors, 256
Nonabrasive cleaners, 219, 315
Nonbuffered tissue paper, 314
Novus Plastic Polish, 172
Nylon, 37
   blankets, 84
   carpeting, 106
   flags and banners, 179
   on iron soleplates, 235
   satin sheets, 303

O

Odors. *See also* Urine stains and
    odors
   cleaning agents for, 413, 416
   cooking, 262, 263, 402, 406
   in garbage cans, 199, 262
   in garbage disposers, 262, 406
   in microwaves, 254
   musty, 89, 111, 250, 255, 263, 381
   pet accident, 263
   in refrigerators, 263, 406
   smoke, 324–325
   in trash compactors, 367–368
Oil-absorbent block, 309
Oil-based spills or stains. *See also*
    Grease stains
   on asphalt, 64–65
   on carpeting, 110
   cleaning agents for, 412
   cleaning guidelines for, 341
   on clothing, 28, 405
   on slate, 318
Oil (cleaning), 428. *See also* Vegetable
    oil; *specific oils*
Oil (lubricating)
   for clocks, 129
   for knives, 240
   for scissors, 304
   for sliding doors, 322
   for tools, 365, 396
   for wheelchairs, 387
Olefin carpeting, 106
Olive oil, 101, 132, 162, 197, 289
Onion, odors and, 263
Orange oil cleaners, 65, 75, 232, 317,
   350
Orange peels, for garbage disposers,
   200, 262, 406
Organic cleaners, 156
Orvus WA Paste, 241
Outdoor furniture, 233–234,
   270–271, 301
Oven cleaners, 428–429
   for barbecue grills, 71
   for brick, 92
   for cast iron cookware, 234
   for grout, 310
   for ovens, 264, 265

Ovens
   for candle wax removal, 314
   cleaning agents for, 412, 415
   cleaning guidelines for, 18, 263–265
   drying coins in, 132
   odors from, 262
Over-the-counter drugs, 253–254
Oxygen bleach. *See* Bleach
Ozone machines, 325

P

Paint
   for artificial or dried flowers, 186
   for baskets, 74
   for cast iron, 234
   for chipped porcelain, 316
   choices in, 18
   for fireplace tools, 176
   for outdoor furniture, 301
   smoke alarms and, 326
   for snowblowers, 328
   on tin roofs, 297
Paintbrushes, as cleaning tool
   for artwork, 63, 64
   for blinds, 85
   for cameras, 102–103
   for caning, 105
   for exhaust fans, 170
   for flowers, 185
   for lamp shades, 162, 243
   for louvers, 249
   for shower doors, 310
   for slide projectors, 320–321
   for stereos, 346
   for toasters, 364
   for typewriters, 368
   for VCRs, 372–373
   for wrought iron, 233
Paintbrushes, cleaning, 266–268
Painted surfaces, 266
Painting equipment, 266–268
Paintings, 63, 64
Paint removers, 206, 289
Paint stains, 173, 197, 344, 405
Paint thinner, 173, 234, 267–268,
   344, 405
Paneling, 269
Pantyhose, 27, 61, 104, 133
Paper, as clutter, 23–24
Paper bags, for protecting counter-
   tops, 18
Paper clips, for cleaning irons, 236
Paper towels, 412, 429. *See also specific*
   cleaning jobs
Party messes, 400
Pastry brushes, 116, 130
Patent leather, 217, 308
Patio furniture, 233–234, 270–271,
   301
Patios, 270, 300, 349
Patio umbrellas, 369
Peanut butter, as cleaner, 125, 197, 401
Peanut oil, as cleaner, 125

Pearls, 271–272
Pee. *See* Urine stains and odors
Pencil marks, 272
Perspiration stains, 312–313, 344, 427
Pest control, 272–275
Pesticides, 272–273
Pet dander, 53
Petroleum jelly, as cleaner
   for alabaster, 56
   for fishing rods, 177
   for paintbrushes, 268
   for patent leather, 308
   for power tools, 288
   for vinyl, 376
   for water stains, 385
Pets
   accident cleanup, 111, 275, 276–277,
    400
   equipment for, 277–278
   flea control, 273–274
   hair cleanup, 21, 43, 115, 275
   litter boxes, 248, 416
   odors from, 263
   preventive measures for, 18, 20–21,
    53, 275
Pewter, 180, 278
Phosphoric acid, 413
Photographs, 278–280
Pianos, 280–281
Pilling, of clothing, 40
Pillows, 187, 281–282, 303
Pine oil, 428
Pine sap, removing, 296–297, 317,
   360
Pinking shears, 304
Pipe cleaners, for sewing machines,
   306
Plants, 53, 209, 227–228, 244
Plastic cleaners, 217, 317, 329
Plastic containers, 282–283, 416
Plastic handbags, 217
Plastic wrap, 159, 268
Playground equipment, 283
Plexiglas cleaners, 224, 283–284, 317
Plumbing crises, 407, 408
Plumbing fixtures. *See* Bathrooms;
   specific fixtures
Pocketknives, 240
Polishing gloves, 314
Polyester, 37
   flags and banners, 179
   hammocks, 215, 216
   ink stains on, 232
   satin sheets, 303
Polyethylene tarps, 356
Polyurethane handbags, 217
Pool tables, 284
Poop. *See* Feces
Porcelain, 224, 284–285
Porcelain enamel, 219, 315, 350
Porcelain repair kit, 316

About the Author

The author wishes to thank Lisa Bacon, Judy Capar, Mary Beausoleil, Deborah Kelly, Sarah Moran, Alice Perry, and Logan Ward for their valuable and notable contributions to the text. Many thanks are also due to Alexandra Benwell for research and to the more than 370 cleaning experts who generously answered questions and offered advice on every aspect of household cleaning.

Jeff Bredenberg has been writing and editing home and health advice for newspapers, books, and websites for more than 25 years. Among the many books he has edited or written are *Clean It Fast, Clean It Right; Beat the System; Make it Last; Home Remedies from the Country Doctor;* and *Food Smart.* In his newspaper days, Jeff worked for the *Chicago Sun-Times,* the *Rocky Mountain News* in Denver, and *The News-Journal* in Wilmington, Delaware, among others. Along the way, Jeff has published three novels and several short stories, and served as vice president for content at the website InteliHealth.

With his wife and two sons, he lives in the Philadelphia suburbs, where he teaches Sunday school and is an active Boy Scout and Cub Scout volunteer.